Gallipoli
1915

A Personal Diary

Sir Roger Keyes, Vice-Admiral de Robeck, Sir Ian Hamilton, General Braithwaite

Gallipoli
1915

A Personal Diary

By Sir Ian Hamilton

Legacy Books Press
Military Classics

Published by Legacy Books Press
RPO Princess, Box 21031
445 Princess Street
Kingston, Ontario, K7L 5P5
Canada

www.legacybookspress.com

The scanning, uploading, and/or distribution of this book via the Internet or any other means without the permission of the publisher is illegal and punishable by law.

This edition first published in 2024 by Legacy Books Press
1

This edition © 2024 Legacy Books Press, all rights reserved.

ISBN: 978-1-927537-88-6

First published in two volumes as *Gallipoli Diary,* by Edward Arnold in 1905.

Printed and bound in the United States of America and the United Kingdom.

This book is typeset in a Times New Roman 11-point font.

Table of Contents

Publisher's Note 3

Preface 5

Letter from General D'Amade to the Author 9

Chapter I – The Start. 13

Chapter II – The Straits. 26

Chapter III – Egypt 49

Chapter IV – Clearing for Action 74

Chapter V – The Landing 101

Chapter VI – Making Good 124

Chapter VII – Shells 151

Chapter VIII – Two Corps or an Ally? 167

Chapter IX – Submarines 184

Chapter X – A Decision and the Plan 212

Chapter XI – Bombs and Journalists 236

Chapter XII – A Victory and After 257

Chapter XIII – K.'s Advice and the P.M.'s Envoy 289

Chapter XIV – The Force — Real and Imaginary 308

Chapter XV – Sari Bair and Suvla 328

Table of Contents

Chapter XVI – Kavak Tepe Attack Collapses 355

Chapter XVII – The Last Battle 377

Chapter XVIII – Misunderstandings.................... 393

Chapter XIX – The French Plan....................... 407

Chapter XX – Loos and Salonika...................... 430

Chapter XXI – The Beginning of the End 456

Appendix I – Statement on Artillery.................... 487

Appendix II – Dardanelles Expedition Notes............. 500

Appendix III – General Instructions.................... 506

Appendix IV – Instructions to Major-General H. de Lisle, C.B., D.S.O................................... 547

Maps 551

Index 556

About the Author 571

Publisher's Note

The original edition of this book contained a number of untranslated phrases and passages in languages such as French German, and Latin. Where it would aid understanding, translations have been provided in the footnotes and as part of the text. These translations were created with the assistance of DeepL Pro translation software.

Some paragraphs have been reformatted for ease of reading.

Additionally, due to the time in which it was first published, this book contains words or phrases that some may find offensive. Reader discretion is advised.

Preface

On the heels of the South African War came the sleuth-hounds pursuing the criminals, I mean the customary Royal Commissions. Ten thousand words of mine stand embedded in their Blue Books, cold and dead as so many mammoths in glaciers. But my long spun-out intercourse with the Royal Commissioners did have living issue— my Manchurian and Gallipoli notes. Only constant observation of civilian Judges and soldier witnesses could have shown me how fallible is the unaided military memory or have led me by three steps to a War Diary:

(1) There is nothing certain about war except that one side won't win.
(2) The winner is asked no questions— the loser has to answer for everything.
(3) Soldiers think of nothing so little as failure and yet, to the extent of fixing intentions, orders, facts, dates firmly in their own minds, they ought to be prepared.

Conclusion: In war, keep your own counsel, preferably in a note-book.

The first test of the new resolve was the Manchurian Campaign, 1904-5; and it was a hard test. Once that Manchurian Campaign was over I never put pen to paper— in the diary sense[*] — until I was under orders for Constantinople. Then I bought a note-book as well as a Colt's automatic (in fact, these were the only two items of special outfit I did buy), and here are the contents— not of the auto but of the book. Also, from the moment I took up the command, I kept cables, letters and copies (actions quite foreign to my natural disposition), having been taught in my youth by Lord Roberts that nothing written to a Commander-in-Chief, or his Military Secretary, can be private if it has a bearing on operations. A letter which may influence the Chief Command of an Army and, therefore, the life of a nation, may be "Secret" for reasons of State; it cannot possibly be "Private" for personal reasons.[†]

At the time, I am sure my diary was a help to me in my work. The crossings to and from the Peninsula gave me many chances of reckoning up the day's business, sometimes in clear, sometimes in a queer cipher of my own. Ink stands with me for an emblem of futurity, and the act of writing seemed to set back the crisis of the moment into a calmer perspective. Later on, the diary helped me again, for although the Dardanelles Commission did not avail themselves of my formal offer to submit what I had written to their scrutiny, there the records were. Whenever an event, a date and a place were duly entered in their actual coincidence, no argument to the contrary could prevent them from falling into the picture: an advocate might just as well waste eloquence in disputing the right of a piece to its own place in a jig-saw puzzle. Where, on the other hand, incidents were not entered, anything might happen and did happen; *vide*, for instance, the curious misapprehension set forth in the footnotes to pages 59, 60, Vol. II.

So much for the past. Whether these entries have not served their turn is now the question. They were written red-hot amidst

---

[*] Except in a small way at some foreign manœuvres.

[†] The letters, cables, etc., published here have either: (*a*) been submitted to the Dardanelles Commission; or, (*b*) have been printed by permission.— *Ian H.*

tumult, but faintly now, and as in some far echo, sounds the battle-cry that once stopped the beating of thousands of human hearts as it was borne out upon the night wind to the ships. Those dread shapes we saw through our periscopes are dust: "the pestilence that walketh in darkness" and "the destruction that wasteth at noonday" are already images of speech: only the vastness of the stakes; the intensity of the effort and the grandeur of the sacrifice still stand out clearly when we, in dreams, behold the Dardanelles. Why not leave that shining impression as a martial cloak to cover the errors and vicissitudes of all the poor mortals who, in the words of Thucydides, "dared beyond their strength, hazarded against their judgment, and in extremities were of an excellent hope?"

Why not? The tendency of every diary is towards self-justification and complaint; yet, to-day, personally, I have "no complaints." Would it not be wiser, then, as well as more dignified, to let the Dardanelles R.I.P.? The public will not be starved. A Dardanelles library exists— - nothing less— from which three luminous works by Masefield, Nevinson and Callwell stand out; works each written by a man who had the right to write; each as distinct from its fellow as one primary colour from another, each essentially true. On the top of these comes the Report of the Dardanelles Commission and the Life of Lord Kitchener, where his side of the story is so admirably set forth by his intimate friend, Sir George Arthur. The tale has been told and retold. Every morsel of the wreckage of our Armada seems to have been brought to the surface. There are fifty reasons against publishing, reasons which I know by heart. On the other side there are only three things to be said:

(1) Though the bodies recovered from the tragedy have been stripped and laid out in the Morgue, no hand has yet dared remove the masks from their faces.
(2 I cannot destroy this diary. Before his death Cranmer thrust his own hand into the flames: "his heart was found entire amidst the ashes."
(3) I will not leave my diary to be flung at posterity from behind the cover of my coffin. In case anyone wishes to challenge anything I have said, I must be above ground to give him satisfaction.

Therefore, I will publish and at once.

A man has only one life on earth. The rest is silence. Whether God will approve of my actions at a moment when the destinies of hundreds of millions of human beings hung upon them, God alone knows. But before I go I want to have the verdict of my comrades of all ranks at the Dardanelles, and until they know the truth, as it appeared to me at the time, how can they give that verdict?

IAN HAMILTON.
LULLENDEN FARM, DORMANSLAND
April 25, 1920.

Letter from General D'Amade to the Author

MON GÉNÉRAL,

Dans la guerre Sud Africaine, ensuite en Angleterre, j'avais en spectateur vécu avec votre armée. Avec elle je souhaitais revivre en frère d'armes, combattant pour la même cause. Les Dardanelles ont réalisé mon rêve. Mais le lecteur ne doit pas s'attarder avec moi. Lire le récit de celui même qui a commandé: quel avantage! L'Histoire, comme un fleuve, se charge d'impuretés en s'éloignent de ses sources. En en remontant le cours, dans votre Journal, j'ai découvert les causes de certains effets demeuré, pour moi des énigmes.

Au début je n'avais pas cru à la possibilité de forcer les Dardanelles sans l'intervention de l'armée. C'est pour cela que, si la décision m'eût appartenus et avant d'avoir été placé sous vos ordres, j'avais songé à débarquer à Adramit, dans les eaux calmes de Mithylène, à courir ensuite à Brousse et Constantinople, pour y saisir les clefs du détroit.

En présence de l'opiniâtre confiance de l'amiral de Robecq j'abaissai mon pavillion de terrien et l'inclinai devant son autorité de marin Anglais. Nous fûmes conquis par cette confiance.

Notre théâtre de guerre de Gallipoli était très borné sur le terrain. Ce front restreint a permis à chacun de vos soldats de vous connaître. Autant qu'avec leurs armes, ils combattaient avec votre ardeur de grand chef et votre inflexible volonté.

Dans le passé ce théâtre qui était la Troade, venait se souder aux éternels récommencements de l'Histoire.

Dans l'avenir son domaine était aussi vaste. "Si nos navires avaient pu franchir les détroits, a dit le Premier Ministre Loyd Georges le 18 décembre 1919 aux Communes, la guerre aurait été raccourcie de 2 ou 3 ans."

Il y a pire qu'une guerre, c'est une guerre qui se prolonge. Car les dévastations s'accumulent. Le vaincu qui a eu l'habileté de les éviter à son pays, se donnera, sur les ruines, des manières de vainqueur. Le premier but de guerre n'est il pas d'infliger à l'adversaire plus de mal qu'il ne vous en fait?

Si nous avions atteint Constantinople dans l'été 1915 c'était alors terminer la guerre, éviter la tourmente russe et tous les obstacles dressés par ce cataclysme devant le rétablissement de la paix du monde. C'était épargner à nos Patries des milliards de dépenses et des centaines de milliers de deuils.

Que nous n'ayons pas atteint ce but ne saurait établir qu'il n'ait été juste et sage de le poursuivre.

Voilà pour quelle cause sont tombés les soldats des Dardanelles. "Honneur à vous, soldats de France et soldats du Roi! ainsi que vous les adjuriez en les lançant à l'attaque.

"Morts héroïques! il n'a rien manqué à votre gloire, pas même une apparence d'oubli. Des triomphes des autres vous n'avez recueilli que les rayons extrêmes: ceux qui ont franchi la cime des arcs de triomphe pour aller au loin, coups égarés de la grande gerbe, éclairer vos tombés.

"Mais 'Ne jugez pas avant le temps.' Le crépuscule éteint, laissez encore passer la nuit. Vous aurez pour vous le soleil Levant."

Vous, Mon Général, vous aurez été l'ouvrier de cette grande idée, et l'annonciateur de cette aurore.

GÉN A D'AMADE.
Fronsac, Gironde, France. 22 décembre, 1919.

Letter from General D'Amade to the Author

My dear General,

In the South African war, then in England, I had lived with your army as a spectator. With it I wished to live again as a brother in arms, fighting for the same cause. The Dardanelles made my dream come true. But the reader need not linger with me. What an advantage to read the account of the man who actually commanded! History, like a river, takes on impurities as it flows away from its source. By tracing its course in your Diary, I discovered the reasons for certain events that had remained enigmas for me.

At first, I didn't believe in the possibility of forcing the Dardanelles without the intervention of the army. That's why, if the decision had been mine and before being placed under your command, I had thought of landing at Adramit, in the calm waters of Mithylene, and then running to Brousse and Constantinople, to seize the keys to the strait.

In the presence of Admiral de Robecq's stubborn confidence, I lowered my landlubber's flag and bowed to his authority as an English sailor. We were won over by this confidence.

Our Gallipoli theater of war was very limited in size. This limited front allowed each of your soldiers to get to know you. As much as with their weapons, they fought with your ardour as a great leader and your indomitable will.

In the past, this theater, which was the land of Troy, was part of the eternal memory of history.

In the future, its reach was just as vast. "If our ships had been able to cross the straits," Prime Minister Lloyd Georges told the Commons on December 18, 1919, "the war would have been shortened by two or three years."

Worse than a war is a war that drags on. For the devastation is mounting. A vanquished warrior who has been clever enough to avoid devastation for his country, will look like a victor on the ruins. Isn't the first aim of war to inflict more harm on your enemy than he does on you?

If we had reached Constantinople in the summer of 1915, it would have meant ending the war, avoiding the Russian turmoil and all the obstacles that this cataclysm had put in the way of restoring world peace. It would have spared our homelands billions in expenses and hundreds of thousands in mourning.

The fact that we did not achieve this goal does not mean that it was not right and wise to pursue it.

This is the cause for which the soldiers of the Dardanelles fell. "Honor to you, soldiers of France and soldiers of the King!" as you enjoined them when you launched them into the attack.

"Heroic dead! your glory has not been forgotten. From the victories of others you have gathered only the most distant light: that which has crossed the summit of the triumphal arches to shine on your graves, the stray light of the great wreath.

"But 'Judge not before the proper time.' Twilight extinguished, let the night slip by. The rising sun will be yours."

You, my dear General, will have been the worker of this grand design, and the harbinger of this dawn.

Gén A d'Amade.
Fronsac, Gironde, France. December 22, 1919.

Chapter I – The Start

*I*n *the train between Paris and Marseilles, 14th March, 1915.*
Neither the Asquith banquet, nor the talk at the Admiralty that midnight had persuaded me I was going to do what I am actually doing at this moment. K. had made no sign nor waved his magic baton. So I just kept as cool as I could and had a sound sleep.

Next morning, that is the 12th instant, I was working at the Horse Guards when, about 10 a.m., K. sent for me. I wondered! Opening the door I bade him good morning and walked up to his desk where he went on writing like a graven image. After a moment, he looked up and said in a matter-of-fact tone, "We are sending a military force to support the Fleet now at the Dardanelles, and you are to have Command."

Something in voice or words touched a chord in my memory. We were once more standing, K. and I, in our workroom at Pretoria, having just finished reading the night's crop of sixty or seventy wires. K. was saying to me, "You had better go out to the Western Transvaal." I asked no question, packed up my kit, ordered my train, started that night. Not another syllable was said on the subject. Uninstructed and unaccredited I left that night for the front; my outfit one A.D.C., two horses, two mules and a buggy. Whether I inspected the columns and came back and reported to K. in my capacity as his Chief Staff Officer; or, whether, making use of my rank to assume command in the field, I beat up de la Rey in his den— all this rested entirely with me.

So I made my choice and fought my fight at Roodewal, last strange battle in the West. That is K.'s way. The envoy goes forth; does his best with whatever forces he can muster and, if he loses;— well, unless he had liked the job he should not have taken it on.

At that moment K. wished me to bow, leave the room and make a start as I did some thirteen years ago. But the conditions were no longer the same. In those old Pretoria days I had known the Transvaal by heart; the number, value and disposition of the British forces; the characters of the Boer leaders; the nature of the country. But my knowledge of the Dardanelles was nil; of the Turk nil; of the strength of our own forces next to nil. Although I have met K. almost every day during the past six months, and although he has twice hinted I might be sent to Salonika; never once, to the best of my recollection, had he mentioned the word Dardanelles.

I had plenty of time for these reflections as K., after his one tremendous remark had resumed his writing at the desk. At last, he looked up and inquired, "Well?"

"We have done this sort of thing before, Lord K." I said; "we have run this sort of show before and you know without saying I am most deeply grateful and you know without saying I will do my best and that you can trust my loyalty— but I must say something— I must ask you some questions." Then I began.

K. frowned; shrugged his shoulders; I thought he was going to be impatient, but although he gave curt answers at first he slowly broadened out, until, at the end, no one else could get a word in edgeways.*

My troops were to be Australians and New Zealanders under Birdwood (a friend); strength, say, about 30,000. (A year ago I inspected them in their own Antipodes and no finer material exists); the 29th Division, strength, say 19,000 under Hunter-Weston — a slashing man of action; an acute theorist; the Royal Naval Division, 11,000 strong (an excellent type of Officer and

---

* I.e. after the others had come in.— *Ian H., 1920.*

The Start

man, under a solid Commander — Paris); a French contingent, strength at present uncertain, say, about a Division, under my old war comrade the chivalrous d'Amade, now at Tunis.

Say then grand total about 80,000 — probably panning out at some 50,000 rifles in the firing line. Of these the 29th Division are extras — *division de luxe.**

K. went on; he was now fairly under weigh and got up and walked about the room as he spoke. I knew, he said, his (K.'s) feelings as to the political and strategic value of the Near East where one clever tactical thrust delivered on the spot and at the spot might rally the wavering Balkans. Rifle for rifle, *at that moment*, we could nowhere make as good use of the 29th Division as by sending it to the Dardanelles, where each of its 13,000 rifles might attract a hundred more to our side of the war. Employed in France or Flanders the 29th would at best help to push back the German line a few miles; at the Dardanelles the stakes were enormous. He spoke, so it struck me, as if he was defending himself in argument: he asked if I agreed. I said, "Yes."

"Well," he rejoined, "You may just as well realize at once that G.H.Q. in France do not agree. They think they have only to drive the Germans back fifty miles nearer to their base to win the war. Those are the same fellows who used to write me saying they wanted no New Army; that they would be amply content if only the old Old Army and the Territorials could be kept up to strength. Now they've been down to Aldershot and seen the New Army they are changing their tune, but I am by no means sure, *now*, that I'll give it to them. French and his Staff believe firmly that the British Imperial Armies can pitch their camp down in one corner of Europe and there fight a world war to a finish. The thing is absurd but French, plus France, are a strong combine and they are fighting tooth and nail for the 29th Division. It must clearly be understood then:

(1) That the 29th Division are only to be a loan and are to be returned the moment they can be spared.

---

* "Luxury division."

(2) That all things ear-marked for the East are looked on by powerful interests both at home and in France as having been stolen from the West."

Did I take this in? I said, "I take it from you." Did I myself, speaking as actual Commander of the Central Striking Force and executively responsible for the land defence of England, think the 29th Division could be spared at all? "Yes," I said, "and four more Territorial Divisions as well."

K. used two or three very bad words and added, with his usual affability, that I would find myself walking about in civilian costume instead of going to Constantinople if he found me making any wild statements of that sort to the politicians. I laughed and reminded him of my testimony before the Committee of Imperial Defence about my Malta amphibious manœuvres; about the Malta Submarines and the way they had destroyed the battleships conveying my landing forces. If there was any politician, I said, who cared a hang about my opinions he knew quite well already my views on an invasion of England; namely, that it would be like trying to hurt a monkey by throwing nuts at him. I didn't want to steal what French wanted, but now that the rifles had come and the troops had finished their musketry, there was no need to squabble over a Division. Why not let French have two of my Central Force Territorial Division at once, — they were jolly good and were wasting their time over here. That would sweeten French and he and Joffre would make no more trouble about the 29th.

K. glared at me. I don't know what he was going to say when Callwell came into the room with some papers.

We moved to the map in the window and Callwell took us through a plan of attack upon the Forts at the Dardanelles, worked out by the Greek General Staff. The Greeks had meant to employ (as far as I can remember) 150,000 men. Their landing was to have taken place on the North-west coast of the Southern part of the Peninsula, opposite Kilid Bahr. "But," said K., "half that number of men will do you handsomely; the Turks are busy elsewhere; I hope you will not have to land at all; if you *do* have to land, why then the powerful Fleet at your back will be the prime factor in your choice of time and place."

I asked K. if he would not move the Admiralty to work a submarine or two up the Straits at once so as to prevent reinforcements and supplies coming down by sea from Constantinople. By now the Turks must be on the alert and it was commonsense to suppose they would be sending some sort of help to their Forts. However things might pan out we could not be going wrong if we made the Marmora unhealthy for the Turkish ships. Lord K. thereupon made the remark that if we could get one submarine into the Marmora the defences of the Dardanelles would collapse. "Supposing," he said, "one submarine pops up opposite the town of Gallipoli and waves a Union Jack three times, the whole Turkish garrison on the Peninsula will take to their heels and make a bee line for Bulair."

In reply to a question about Staff, Lord K., in the gruff voice he puts on when he wants no argument, told me I could not take my own Chief of Staff, Ellison, and that Braithwaite would go with me in his place. Ellison and I have worked hand in glove for several years; our qualities usefully complement one another; there was no earthly reason I could think of why Ellison should *not* have come with me, but; I like Braithwaite; he had been on my General Staff for a time in the Southern Command; he is cheery, popular and competent.

Wolfe Murray, the Chief of the Imperial General Staff, was then called in, also Archie Murray, Inspector of Home Forces, and Braithwaite. This was the first (apparently) either of the Murrays had heard of the project!!! Both seemed to be quite taken aback, and I do not remember that either of them made a remark.

Braithwaite was very nice and took a chance to whisper his hopes he would not give me too much cause to regret Ellison. He only said onething to K. and that produced an explosion. He said it was vital that we should have a better air service than the Turks in case it came to fighting over a small area like the Gallipoli Peninsula: he begged, therefore, that whatever else we got, or did not get, we might be fitted out with a contingent of up-to-date aeroplanes, pilots and observers. K. turned on him with flashing spectacles and rent him with the words,*"Not one!"*

15th March, 1915. H.M.S. "Phaeton." Toulon Harbour. Embarked at Marseilles last night at 6 p.m. and slept on board. Owing to some mistake no oil fuel had been taken aboard so we have had to come round here this morning to get it. Have just breakfasted with the Captain, Cameron by name, and have let the Staff go ashore to see the town. We do not sail till 2 p.m.: after special trains and everything a clean chuck-away of 20 hours.

I left off in the S. of S.'s room at the War Office. After the bursting of the aeroplane bomb K. did most of the talking. I find it hard to remember all he said: here are the outstanding points:

(1) We soldiers are to understand we are string Number 2. The sailors are sure they can force the Dardanelles on their own and the whole enterprise has been framed on that basis: we are to lie low and to bear in mind the Cabinet does not want to hear anything of the Army till it sails through the Straits. But if the Admiral fails, then we will have to go in.

(2) If the Army has to be used, whether on the Bosphorus or at the Dardanelles, I am to bear in mind his order that no serious operation is to take place until the whole of my force is complete; ready; concentrated and on the spot. No piecemeal attack is to be made.

(3) If we do start fighting, once we *have* started we are to burn our boats. Once landed the Government are resolved to see the enterprise through.

(4) Asia is out of bounds. K. laid special stress on this. Our sea command and the restricted area of Gallipoli would enable us to undertake a landing on the Peninsula with clearly limited liabilities. Once we began marching about continents, situations calling for heavy reinforcements would probably be created. Although I, Hamilton, seemed ready to run risks in the defence of London, he, K., was not, and as he had already explained, big demands would make his position difficult with France; difficult everywhere; and might end by putting him (K.) in the cart. Besika Bay and Alexandretta were, therefore, taboo — not to be touched! Even after we force the Narrows no troops

The Start

are to be landed along the Asian coastline. Nor are we to garrison any part of the Gallipoli Peninsula excepting only the Bulair Lines which had best be permanently held, K. thinks, by the Naval Division.

When we get into the Marmora I shall be faced by a series of big problems. What would I do? From what quarter could I attack Constantinople? How would I hold it when I had taken it? K. asked me the questions.

With the mud of prosaic Whitehall drying upon my boots these remarks of K.'s sounded to me odd. But, knowing Constantinople, and — what was more to the point at the moment — knowing K.'s hatred of hesitation, I managed to pull myself together so far as to suggest that if the city was weakly held and if, as he had said, (I forgot to enter that) the bulk of the Thracian troops were dispersed throughout the Provinces, or else moving to re-occupy Adrianople, why then, possibly, by a *coup de main*, we might pounce upon the Chatalja Lines from the South before the Turks could climb back into them from the North. Lord K. made a grimace; he thought this too chancy. The best would be if we did not land a man until the Turks had come to terms. Once the Fleet got through the Dardanelles, Constantinople could not hold out. Modern Constantinople could not last a week if blockaded by sea and land. That was a sure thing; a thing whereon he could speak with full confidence. The Fleet could lie off out of sight and range of the Turks and with their guns would dominate the railways and, if necessary, burn the place to ashes. The bulk of the people were not Osmanli or even Mahomedan and there would be a revolution at the mere sight of the smoke from the funnels of our warships. But if, for some cause at present non-apparent, we were forced to put troops ashore against organized Turkish opposition, then he advocated a landing on the Asiatic side of the Bosphorus to hold out a hand to the Russians, who would simultaneously land there from the Black Sea. He only made the suggestion, for the man on the spot must be the best judge. Several of the audience left us here, at Lord K.'s suggestion, to get on with their work. K. went on:

The moment the holding of Constantinople comes along the French and the Russians will be very jealous and prickly. Luckily we British have an easy part to play as the more we efface ourselves at that stage, the better he, K., will be pleased. The Army in France have means of making their views work in high places and pressure is sure to be put on by them and by their friends for the return of the 29th and Naval Divisions the moment we bring Turkey to book. Therefore, it will be best in any case to "let the French and Russians garrison Constantinople and sing their hymns in S. Sophia," whilst my own troops hold the railway line and perhaps Adrianople. Thus they will be at a loose end and we shall be free to bring them back to the West; to land them at Odessa or to push them up the Danube, without weakening the Allied grip on the waterway linking the Mediterranean with the Black Sea.

This was the essence of our talk: as it lasted about an hour and a half, I can only have put down about one tenth of it.

At odd times I have been recipient of K.'s reveries but always, *always*, he has rejected with a sort of horror the idea of being War Minister or Commander-in-Chief. Now by an extreme exercise of its ironic spirit, Providence has made him both.

In pre-war days, when we met in Egypt and at Malta, K. made no bones about what he wanted. He wanted to be Viceroy of India or Ambassador at Constantinople.

I remember very well one conversation we had when I asked him why he wanted to hang on to great place, and whether he had not done enough already. He said he could not bear to see India being mismanaged by nincompoops or our influence in Turkey being chucked out of the window with both hands: I answered him, I remember, by saying there were only two things worth doing as Viceroy and they would not take very long. One was to put a huge import duty on aniline dyes and so bring back the lovely vegetable dyes of old India, the saffrons, indigoes, madders, etc.; the other was to build a black marble Taj at Agra opposite the white and join the two by a silver bridge. I expected to get a rise, but actually he took the ideas quite seriously and I am sure made a mental note of them. Anyway, as Viceroy, K. would have flung the whole vast weight of India into the scale of this war; he would have poured Army after Army from East to West. Under K. India could have

The Start

beaten Turkey single-handed; aye, and with one arm tied behind her back. With K. as Ambassador at Constantinople he would have prevented Turkey coming into the war. There is no doubt of it. Neither Enver Pasha nor Talaat would have dared to enrage K., and as for the idea of their deporting him, it is grotesque. They might have shot him in the back; they could never have faced him with a war declaration in their hands. As an impresser of Orientals he is a nonesuch. So we put him into the War Office in the ways of which he is something of an amateur, with a big prestige and a big power of drive. Yes, we remove the best experts from the War Office and pop in K. like a powerful engine from which we have removed all controls, regulators and safety valves. Yet see what wonders he has worked!

Still, he remains, in the War Office sense, an amateur. The Staff left by French at the W.O. may not have been von Moltke's, but they were K.'s only Councillors. An old War Office hand would have used them. But in no case, even had they been the best, could K. have had truck or parley with any system of decentralization of work — of semi-independent specialists each running a show of his own. As late (so-called) Chief of Staff to Lord K. in South Africa, I could have told them that whatever work K. fancies at the moment he must swipe at it, that very moment, off his own bat. The one-man show carried on royally in South Africa and all the narrow squeaks we had have been completely swallowed up in the final success; but how will his no-system system work now? Perhaps he may pull it through; anyway he is starting with a beautifully cleaned slate. He has surpassed himself, in fact, for I confess even with past experience to guide me, I did not imagine our machinery could have been so thoroughly smashed in so short a time. Ten long years of General Staff; Lyttelton, Nicholson, French, Douglas; where are your well-thought-out schemes for an amphibious attack on Constantinople? Not a sign! Braithwaite set to work in the Intelligence Branch at once. But beyond the ordinary text books those pigeon holes were drawn blank. The Dardanelles and Bosphorus might be in the moon for all the military information I have got to go upon. One text book and one book of travellers' tales don't take long to master and I have not been so free from work or preoccupation since the war started.

There is no use trying to make plans unless there is some sort of material, political, naval, military or geographical to work upon.

Winston had been in a fever to get us off and had ordered a special train for that very afternoon. My new Staff were doubtful if they could get fixed up so quickly and K. settled the matter by saying there was no need to hustle. For myself, I was very keen to get away. The best plan to save slips between cup and lip is to swallow the liquor. But K. thought it wisest to wait, so I 'phoned over to Eddie to let Winston know we should not want his train that day.

Next morning, the 13th, I handed over the Central Force Command to Rundle and then, at 10.30 went in with Braithwaite to say good-bye. K. was standing by his desk splashing about with his pen at three different drafts of instructions. One of them had been drafted by Fitz — I suppose under somebody's guidance; the other was by young Buckley; the third K. was working on himself. Braithwaite, Fitz and I were in the room; no one else except Callwell who popped in and out. The instructions went over most of the ground of yesterday's debate and were too vague. When I asked the crucial question: the enemy's strength? K. thought I had better be prepared for 40,000. How many guns? No one knows. Who was in command? Djavad Pasha, it is believed. But, K. says, I may take it that the Kilid Bahr Plateau has been entrenched and is sufficiently held. South of Kilid Bahr to the point at Cape Helles, I may take it that the Peninsula is open to a landing on very easy terms. The cross fire from the Fleet lying part in the Aegean and part in the mouth of the Straits must sweep that flat and open stretch of country so as to render it untenable by the enemy. Lord K. demonstrated this cross fire upon the map. He toiled over the wording of his instructions. They were headed "Constantinople Expeditionary Force." I begged him to alter this to avert Fate's evil eye. He consented and both this corrected draft and the copy as finally approved are now in Braithwaite's despatch box more modestly headed "Mediterranean Expeditionary Force." None of the drafts help us with facts about the enemy; the politics; the country and our allies, the Russians. In sober fact these "instructions" leave me to my own devices in the East, almost as much as K.'s laconic order "git" left me to myself when I quitted Pretoria for the West thirteen years ago.

So I said good-bye to old K. as casually as if we were to meet together at dinner. Actually my heart went out to my old Chief. He was giving me the best thing in his gift and I hated to leave him amongst people who were frightened of him. But there was no use saying a word. He did not even wish me luck and I did not expect him to, but he did say, rather unexpectedly, *after* I had said goodbye and just as I was taking up my cap from the table, "If the Fleet gets through, Constantinople will fall of itself and you will have won, not a battle, but the war."

At 5 o'clock that afternoon we bade adieu to London. Winston was disappointed we didn't dash away yesterday but we have not really let much grass grow under our feet. He and some friends came down to Charing Cross to see us off. I told Winston Lord K. would not think me loyal if I wrote to another Secretary of State. He understood and said that if I wanted him to be aware of some special request all I had to say was, "You will agree perhaps that the First Lord should see." Then the S. of S. for War would be bound to show him the letter: which proves that with all his cleverness Winston has yet some points to learn about his K. of K.!

My Staff still bear the bewildered look of men who have hurriedly been snatched from desks to do some extraordinary turn on some unheard of theatre. One or two of them put on uniform for the first time in their lives an hour ago. Leggings awry, spurs upside down, belts over shoulder straps! I haven't a notion of who they all are: nine-tenths of my few hours of warning has been taken up in winding up the affairs of the Central Force.

At Dover embarked on H.M.S. *Foresight*, — a misnomer, for we ran into a fog and had to lie-to for a devil of a time. Heard far-off guns on French front, — which was cheering.

At 10.30 p.m. we left Calais for Marseilles and during the next day the French authorities caused me to be met by Officers of their Railway Mobilization Section. Had my first breathing space wherein to talk over matters with Braithwaite, and he and I tried to piece together the various scraps of views we had picked up at the War Office into a pattern which should serve us for a doctrine. But we haven't got very much to go upon. A diagram he had drawn up with half the spaces unfilled showing the General Staff. Another diagram with its blank spaces only showed that our Q. branch was not in being. Three queried names, Woodward for A.G., Winter for

Q.M.G. and Williams for Cipher Officer. The first two had been left behind, the third was with us. The following hurried jottings by Braithwaite: "Only 1600 rounds for the 4.5 Howitzers!!! High Explosive essential. Who is to be C.R.E.? Engineer Stores? French are to remain at Tunis until the day comes that they are required. Egyptian troops also remain in Egypt till last moment. Everything we want by 30th (it is hoped). Await arrival of 29th Division before undertaking anything big. If Carden wants military help it is for Sir Ian's consideration whether to give or to withhold it."

These rough notes; the text book on the Turkish Army, and two small guide books: not a very luminous outfit. Braithwaite tells me our force are not to take with them the usual 10 per cent. extra margin of reserves to fill casualties. Wish I had realised this earlier. He had not time to tell me he says. The General Staff thought we ought certainly to have these and he and Wolfe Murray went in and made a personal appeal to the A.G. But he was obdurate. This seems hard luck. Why should we not have our losses quickly replaced — supposing we do lose men? I doubt though, if I should have been able to do very much even if I had known. To press K. would have been difficult. Like insisting on an extra half-crown when you've just been given Fortunatus' purse. Still, fair play's a jewel, and surely if formations destined for the French front cross the Channel with 10 per cent. extra, over and above their establishment, troops bound for Constantinople ought to have a 25 per cent. margin over establishment?

17th March, 1915. H.M.S. "Phaeton." At sea. Last night we raced past Corfu — my birthplace — at thirty knots an hour. My first baby breath was drawn from these thyme scented breezes. This crimson in the Eastern sky, these waves of liquid opal are natal, vital.

Thirty miles an hour through Paradise! Since the 16th January, 1853, we have learnt to go the pace and as a result the world shrinks; the horizons close in upon us; the spacious days are gone!

Thoughts of my Mother, who died when I was but three. Thoughts of her refusal as she lay dying — gasping in mortal pain — her refusal to touch an opiate, because the Minister, Norman

Macleod, had told her she so might dim the clearness of her spiritual insight — of her thoughts ascending heavenwards. What pluck — what grit — what faith — what an example to a soldier.

Exquisite, exquisite air; sea like an undulating carpet of blue velvet outspread for Aphrodite. Have been in the Aegean since dawn. At noon passed a cruiser taking back Admiral Carden invalided to Malta. One week ago the thunder of his guns shook the firm foundations of the world. Now a sheer hulk lies poor old Carden. *Vanitas vanitatum.*[*]

Have got into touch with my staff. They are all General Staff: no Administrative Staff. The Adjutant-General-to-be (I don't know him) and the Chief Medico (I don't know who he is to be) could not get ready in time to come off with us, and the Q.M.G., too, was undecided when I left. There are nine of the General Staff. I like the looks of them. Quite characteristic of K., though, that barring Braithwaite, not one of the associates he has told off to work hand in glove with me in this enterprise should ever have served with me before.

Only two sorts of Commanders-in-Chief could possibly find time to scribble like this on their way to take up an enterprise in many ways unprecedented — a German and a Britisher. The first, because every possible contingency would have been worked out for him beforehand; the second, because he has nothing — literally nothing — in his portfolio except a blank cheque signed with those grand yet simple words — John Bull. The German General is the product of an organising nation. The British General is the product of an improvising nation. Each army would be better commanded by the other army's General. Sounds fantastic but is true.[†]

---

[*] "Vanity of vanities."

[†] More than four years after this was written a member of a British Commission sent out to collect facts at the Dardanelles was speaking to the Turkish Commander-in-Chief, Djavad Pasha. In the course of the conversation His Excellency said, "I prefer the British to the Germans for they resemble us so closely — the Germans do not. The Germans are good organisers but they do not love fighting for itself as we do — and as you do. Then again, although the Turks and British are so fond of fighting they are never ready for it: in that respect also the resemblance between our nations is extraordinary." — Ian H., 1920.

Chapter II – The Straits

Cast anchor at Tenedos at 3 p.m., 17th March, 1915, having entered the harbour at the very same instant as le général d'Amade.

Hurried over at once to a meeting aboard that lovely sea monster, H.M.S. *Queen Elizabeth*.

Present:
    Admiral de Robeck,
    Commodore Roger Keyes,
    Admiral Guépratte, cmdg. French Fleet,
    General d'Amade,
    General Braithwaite,
    Admiral Wemyss,
    Captain Pollen,
    Myself.

De Robeck greeted me in the friendliest fashion. He is a fine looking man with great charm of manner. After a word or two to d'Amade and being introduced to Wemyss, Guépratte and Keyes, we sat down round a table and the Admiral began. His chief worry lies in the clever way the enemy are now handling their mobile artillery. He can silence the big fortress ordnance, but the howitzers and field guns fire from concealed positions and make the clearing of the minefields something of a V.C. sort of job for the smaller craft. Even when the Fleet gets through, these moveable guns will make it very nasty for store ships or transports which follow. The mine-sweepers are slow and bad with worn out engines. Some of the civilian masters and crews of the trawlers have to consider wives and kids as well as V.C.s. The problem of getting the Fleet through or of getting submarines through is a problem of clearing away the mines. With a more powerfully engined type of mine-sweeper and regular naval commanders and crews to man them, the business would be easy. But as things actually stand there is real cause for anxiety as to mines.

The Peninsula itself is being fortified and many Turks work every night on trenches, redoubts and entanglements. Not one single living soul has been seen, since the engagement of our Marines at the end of February, although each morning brings forth fresh evidences of nocturnal activity, in patches of freshly turned up soil. All landing places are now commanded by lines of trenches and are ranged by field guns and howitzers, which, thus far, cannot be located as our naval seaplanes are too heavy to rise out of rifle range. There has been a muddle about these seaplanes. Nominally they possess very powerful Sunbeam engines; actually the d —— d things can barely rise off the water. The naval guns do not seem able to knock the Turkish Infantry out of their deep trenches although they can silence their fire for awhile. This was proved at that last landing by Marines. The Turkish searchlights are both fixed and mobile. They are of the latest pattern and are run by skilled observers. He gave us, in fact, to understand that German thoroughness and forethought have gripped the old go-as-you-please Turk and are making him march to the *Parade-schritt*.[*]

The Admiral would prefer to force a passage on his own, and is sure he can do so. Setting Constantinople on one side for the moment, *if* the Fleet gets through and the Army *then* attacks at

---

[*] "Parade step."

Bulair, we would have the Turkish Army on the Peninsula in a regular trap. Therefore, whether from the local or the larger point of view, he has no wish to call us in until he has had a real good try. He means straightway to put the whole proposition to a practical test.

His views dovetail in to a hair's breadth with K.'s views. The Admiral's "real good try" leads up towards K.'s "after every effort has been exhausted."

That's a bit of luck for our kick-off, anyway. What we soldiers have to do now is to hammer away at our band-o-bast* whilst the Navy pushes as hard, as fast and as far as its horsepower, manpower and gunpower will carry it.

The Admiral asked to see my instructions and Braithwaite read them out. When he stopped, Roger Keyes, the Commodore, inquired, "Is that all?" And when Braithwaite confessed that it was, everyone looked a little blank.

Asked what I meant to do, I said I proposed to get ready for a landing, as, whether the Fleet forces the passage and disembarked us on the Bosphorus; or, whether the Fleet did not force the passage and we had to "go for" the Peninsula, the *band-o-bast* could be made to suit either case.

The Admiral asked if I meant to land at Bulair? I replied my mind was open on that point: that I was a believer in seeing things for myself and that I would not come to any decision on the map if it were possible to come to it on the ground. He then said he would send me up to look at the place through my own glasses in the Phaeton to-morrow; that it would not be possible to land large forces on the neck of Bulair itself as there were no beaches, but that I should reconnoitre the coast at the head of the Gulf as landing would be easier with every few miles we drew away towards the North. I told him it would be useless to land at any distance from my objective, for the simple reason that I had no transport, mechanical or horse, wheeled or pack, to enable me to support myself further than five or six miles from the Fleet and it would take many weeks and many ships to get it together;

---

* Arrangements. — *Ian H., 1920.*

however, I ended, I would to-morrow see for myself.

The air of the Aegean hardly differs so much from the North Sea haze as does the moral atmosphere of Tenedos differ from that of the War Office. This is always the way. Until the plunge is taken, the man in the arm chair clamps rose coloured spectacles on to his nose and the man on the spot is anxious; *but*, once the men on the spot jump off they become as jolly as sandboys, whilst the man in the arm chair sits searching for a set-back with a blue lens telescope.

Here, the Peninsula looks a tougher nut to crack than it did on Lord K.'s small and featureless map. I do not speak for myself for I have so far only examined the terrain through a field glass. I refer to the tone of the sailors, which strikes me as being graver and less irresponsible than the tone of the War Office.

The Admiral believes that, at the time of the first bombardment, 5000 men could have marched from Cape Helles right up to the Bulair lines. (Before leaving the ship I learnt that some of the sailors do not agree). Now that phase has passed. Many more troops have come down, German Staff Officers have grappled with the situation, and have got their troops scientifically disposed and heavily entrenched. This skilful siting of the Turkish trenches has been admired by all competent British observers; the number of field guns on the Peninsula is now many times greater than it was.

After this the discussion became informal. Referring again to my instructions, I laid stress on the point that I was a waiting man and that it was the Admiral's innings for so long as he could keep his wicket up. Braithwaite asked a question or two about the trenches and all of us deplored the lack of aeroplanes whereby we were blinded in our attack upon an enemy who espied every boat's crew moving over the water.

The more I revolve these matters in my mind, the more easy does it seem to accept K.'s order not to be in too great a hurry to bring the Army to the front. I devoutly hope indeed (and I think the fiercest of our fellows agree) that the Navy will pull us out the chestnuts from the fire.

At the close of the sitting I made these notes of what had happened and drafted a first cable to Lord K., giving him an epitome of the Admiral's opening statement about the enemy's clever use of field guns to hinder the clearing of the minefields; his good entrenchments and the nightly work thereon; our handicap in all these matters because the type of seaplanes sent us "are too heavy to rise out of effective rifle range" — (one has to put these things mildly). I add that the Admiral, "while not making light of dangers was evidently determined to exhaust every effort before calling upon the soldiers for their help on a large scale"; and I wind up by telling him Lemnos seems a bad base and that I am off tomorrow on an inspection of the coasts of the Peninsula. Having got these matters off my chest on to the chest of K., was then taken round the ship by the Flag Captain, G.P.W. Hope. By this time it was nearly 7 so I stayed and dined with the Admiral — a charming host. After dinner got back here.

18th March, 1915. H.M.S. "Phaeton." Cleared Tenedos Harbour at 4 a.m. and reached Lemnos at 6 a.m. I never saw so many ships collected together in my life; no, not even at Hong Kong, Bombay or New York. Filled up with oil fuel and at 7 a.m. d'Amade and Major-General Paris, commanding the Royal Naval Division, came on board with one or two Staff Officers. After consulting these Officers as well as McLagan, the Australian Brigadier, cabled Lord K. to say Alexandria *must* be our base as "the Naval Division transports have been loaded up as in peace time and they must be completely discharged and every ship reloaded," in war fashion. At Lemnos, where there are neither wharfs, piers, labour nor water, the thing could not be done. Therefore, "the closeness of Lemnos to the Dardanelles, as implying the rapid transport of troops, is illusory."

The moment I got this done, namely, at 8.30 a.m., we worked our way out of the long narrow neck of Mudros Harbour and sailed for the Gulf of Saros. Spent the first half of the sixty mile run to the Dardanelles in scribbling. Wrote my first epistle to K., using for the first time the formal "Dear Lord Kitchener." My letters to him will have to be formal, and dull also, as he may hand them around. I begin, "I have just sent you off a cable giving my first impressions of the situation, and am now steaming in company with Generals d'Amade and Paris to inspect the North-western coast of the Gallipoli Peninsula." I tell him that the real place "looks a much tougher nut to crack than it did over the map," — I say that his "impression that the ground between Cape Helles and Krithia was clear of the enemy," was mistaken. "Not a bit of it." I say, "The Admiral tells me that there is a large number of men tucked away in the folds of the ground there, not to speak of several field Batteries." Therefore, I conclude, "If it eventually becomes necessary to take the Gallipoli Peninsula by military force, we shall have to proceed bit by bit." This will vex him no doubt. He likes plans to move as fast as his own wishes and is apt to forget, or to pretend he has forgotten, that swiftness in war comes from slow preparations. It is fairer to tell K. this now, when the question has not yet arisen, than hereafter if it does then arise.

Passing the mouth of the Dardanelles we got a wonderful view of the stage whereon the Great Showman has caused so many of his amusing puppets to strut their tiny hour. For the purpose it stands matchless. No other panorama can touch it. There, Hero trimmed her little lamp; yonder the amorous breath of Leander changed to soft sea form. Far away to the Eastwards, painted in dim and lovely hues, lies Mount Ida. Just so, on the far horizon line she lay fair and still, when Hector fell and smoke from burning Troy blackened the mid-day sun. Against this enchanted background to deeds done by immortals and mortals as they struggled for ten long years five thousand years ago, — stands forth formidably the Peninsula. Glowing with bright, springtime colours it sweeps upwards from the sea like the glacis of a giant's fortress.

So we sailed on Northwards, giving a wide berth to the shore. When we got within a mile of the head of the Gulf of Saros, we turned, steering a South-westerly course, parallel to, and one to two miles distant from, the coastline. Then my first fears as to the outworks of the fortress were strengthened. The head of the Gulf is filled in with a horrible marsh. No landing there. Did we land far away to the Westward we must still march round the marsh, or else we must cross it on one single road whose long and easily destructible bridges we could see spanning the bog holes some three miles inland. Opposite the fortified lines we stood in to within easy field gun range, trusting that the Turks would not wish prematurely to disclose their artillery positions. So we managed a peep at close quarters, and were startled to see the ramifications and extent of the spider's web of deep, narrow trenches along the coast and on either front of the lines of Bulair. My Staff agree that they must have taken ten thousand men a month's hard work from dark to dawn. In advance of the trenches, Williams in the crow's nest reported that with his strong glasses he could pick out the glitter of wire over a wide expanse of ground. To the depth of a mile the whole Aegean slope of the neck of the Peninsula was scarred with spade work and it is clear to a tiro that to take these trenches would take from us a bigger toll of ammunition and life than we can afford: especially so seeing that we can only see one half of the theatre; the other half would have to be worked out of sight and support of our own ships and in view of the Turkish Fleet. Only one small dent in the rockbound coast offered a chance of landing but that was also heavily dug in. In a word, if Bulair had been the only way open to me and I had no alternative but to take it or wash my hands of the whole business, I should have to go right about turn and cable my master he had sent me on a fool's errand.

Between Bulair and Suvla Bay the coastline was precipitous; high cliffs and no sort of creeks or beaches — impracticable. Suvla Bay itself seems a fine harbour but too far North were the aim to combine a landing there together with an attack on the Southern end of the Peninsula. Were we, on the other hand, to try to work the whole force ashore from Suvla Bay, the country is too big; it is the broadest part of the Peninsula; also, we should be too far from its waist and from the Narrows we wish to dominate. Merely to hold our line of Communications we should need a couple of Divisions. All the coast between Suvla Bay and for a little way South of Gaba Tepe seems feasible for landing. I mean we could get ashore on a calm day if there was no enemy. Gaba Tepe itself would be ideal, but, alas, the Turks are not blind; it is a mass of trenches and wire. Further, it must be well under fire of guns from Kilid Bahr plateau, and is entirely commanded by the high ridge to the North of it. To land there would be to enter a defile without first crowning the heights.

The Straits

Between Gaba Tepe and Cape Helles, the point of the Peninsula, the coastline consists of cliffs from 100 to 300 feet high. But there are, in many places, sandy strips at their base. Opinions differ but I believe myself the cliffs are not unclimbable. I thoroughly believe also in going for at least one spot that *seems* impracticable.

Sailing Southwards we are becoming more and more conscious of the tremendous bombardment going on in the Straits. Now and then, too, we can see a huge shell hit the top of Achi Baba and turn it into the semblance of a volcano. Everyone excited and trying to look calm.

At 4 p.m., precisely, we rounded Cape Helles. I had promised de Robeck not to take his fastest cruiser, fragile as an egg, into the actual Straits, but the Captain and the Commander (Cameron and Rosomore), were frightfully keen to see the fight, and I thought it fair to allow one mile as being the *mouth* of the Straits and not *the* Straits. Before we had covered that mile we found ourselves on the outskirts of — dream of my life — a naval battle! Nor did the reality pan out short of my hopes. Here it was; we had only to keep on at thirty knots; in one minute we should be in the thick of it; and who would be brave enough to cry halt!

The world had gone mad; common sense was only moonshine after all; the elephant and the whale of Bismarckian parable were at it tooth and nail! Shells of all sizes flew hissing through the skies. Before my very eyes, the graves of those old Gods whom Christ had risen from the dead to destroy were shaking to the shock of Messrs. Armstrong's patent thunder bolts!

Ever since the far-away days of Afghanistan and Majuba Hill friends have been fond of asking me what soldiers feel when death draws close up beside them. Before he charged in at Edgehill, Astley (if my memory serves me) exclaimed, "O, God, I've been too busy fixing up this battle to think much about you, but, for Heaven's sake, don't you go and forget about me," or words to that effect.

The Yankee's prayer for fair play just as he joined issue with the grizzly bear gives another glimpse of these secrets between man and his Maker. As for myself, there are two moments; one when I think I would not miss the show for millions; another when

I think "what an ass I am to be here"; and between these two moments there *is* a border land when the mind runs all about Life's workshop and tries to do one last bit of stock-taking.

But the process can no more be fixed in the memory than the sequence of a dream when the dew is off the grass. All I remember is a sort of wonder: why these incredible pains to seek out an amphibious battle ground whereon two sets of people who have no cause of quarrel can blow one another to atoms? Why are these Straits the cockpit of the world? What is it all about? What on earth has happened to sanity when the whale and elephant are locked in mortal combat making between them a picture which might be painted by one of H.M.'s Commissioners in Lunacy to decorate an asylum for homicides.

Whizz — flop — bang — what an ass I am to be here. If we keep on another thirty seconds we are in for a visit to Davy Jones's Locker.

Now above the *Queen Elizabeth*, making slowly backwards and forwards up in the neck of the Narrows, were other men-o'-war spitting tons of hot metal at the Turks. The Forts made no reply — or none that we could make out, either with our ears or with glasses. Perhaps there was an attempt; if so, it must have been very half-hearted. The enemy's fixed defences were silenced but the concealed mobile guns from the Peninsula and from Asia were far too busy and were having it all their own way.

Close to us were steam trawlers and mine-sweepers steaming along with columns of spray spouting up close by them from falling field gun shells, with here and there a biggish fellow amongst them, probably a five or six inch field howitzer. One of them was in the act of catching a great mine as we drew up level with her. Some 250 yards from us was the *Inflexible* slowly coming out of the Straits, her wireless cut away and a number of shrapnel holes through her tops and crow's nest. Suddenly, so quickly did we turn that, going at speed, the decks were at an angle of 45° and several of us (d'Amade for one) narrowly escaped slipping down the railless decks into the sea. The *Inflexible* had signalled us she had struck a mine, and that we must stand by and see her home to Tenedos. We spun round like a top (escaping thereby a salvo of four from a field battery) and followed as close as we dared.

The Straits

My blood ran cold — for sheer deliberate awfulness this beat everything. We gazed spellbound: no one knew what moment the great ship might not dive into the depths. The pumps were going hard. We fixed our eyes on marks about the water line to see if the sea was gaining upon them or not. She was very much down by the bows, that was a sure thing. Crew and stokers were in a mass standing strictly at attention on the main deck. A whole bevy of destroyers crowded round the wounded warrior. In the sight of all those men standing still, silent, orderly in their ranks, facing the imminence of death, I got my answer to the hasty moralizings about war, drawn from me (really) by a regret that I would very soon be drowned. On the deck of that battleship staggering along at a stone's throw was a vindication of war in itself; of war, the state of being, quite apart from war motives or gains. Ten thousand years of peace would fail to produce a spectacle of so great virtue. Where, in peace, passengers have also shown high constancy, it is because war and martial discipline have lent them its standards. Once in a generation a mysterious wish for war passes through the people. Their instinct tells them that *there is no other way* of progress and of escape from habits that no longer fit them. Whole generations of statesmen will fumble over reforms for a lifetime which are put into full-blooded execution within a week of a declaration of war. There is *no other way*. Only by intense sufferings can the nations grow, just as the snake once a year must with anguish slough off the once beautiful coat which has now become a strait jacket.

How was it going to end? How touching the devotion of all these small satellites so anxiously forming escort? Onwards, at snail's pace, moved our cortege which might at any moment be transformed into a funeral affair, but slow as we went we yet went fast enough to give the go-by to the French battleship *Gaulois*, also creeping out towards Tenedos in a lamentable manner attended by another crowd of T.B.s and destroyers eager to stand to and save.

The *Inflexible* managed to crawl into Tenedos under her own steam but we stood by until we saw the *Gaulois* ground on some rocks called Rabbit Island, when I decided to clear right out so as not to be in the way of the Navy at a time of so much stress. After we had gone ten miles or so, the *Phaeton* intercepted a wireless from the *Queen Elizabeth*, ordering the *Ocean* to take the *Irresistible* in tow, from which it would appear that she (the *Irresistible*) has also met with some misfortune.

Thank God we were in time! That is my dominant feeling. We have seen a spectacle which would be purchased cheap by five years of life and, more vital yet, I have caught a glimpse of the forces of the enemy and of their Forts. What with my hurried scamper down the Aegean coast of the Peninsula and the battle in the Straits, I begin to form some first-hand notion of my problem. More by good luck than good guidance I have got into personal touch with the outer fringes of the thing we are up against and that is so much to the good. But oh, that we had been here earlier! Winston in his hurry to push me out has shown a more soldierly grip than those who said there was no hurry. It is up to me now to revolve to-day's doings in my mind; to digest them and to turn myself into the eyes and ears of the War Office whose own so far have certainly not proved themselves very acute. How much better would I be able to make them see and hear had I been out a week or two; did I know the outside of the Peninsula by heart; had I made friends with the Fleet! And why should I not have been?

Have added a P.S. to K.'s letter:

Between Tenedos and Lemnos. 6 p.m. — This has been a very bad day for us judging by what has come under my own personal observation. After going right up to Bulair and down again to the South-west point looking at the network of trenches the Turks have dug commanding all possible landing places, we turned into the Dardanelles themselves and went up about a mile. The scene was what I believe Naval writers describe as 'lively.'

(Then follows an account based on my Diary jottings). I end:

I have not had time to reflect over these matters, nor can I yet realise on my present slight information the extent of these losses. Certainly it looks at present as if the Fleet would not be able to carry on at this rate, and, if so, the soldiers will have to do the trick.

Later.

The *Irresistible*, the *Ocean* and the *Bouvet* are gone! The *Bouvet*, they say, just slithered down like a saucer slithers down in a bath. The *Inflexible* and the *Gaulois* are badly mauled.

19th March, 1915. H.M.S. "Franconia." — Last night I left H.M.S. *Phaeton* and went on board the *Franconia*. To-day, we have been busy fixing things up. The chance sailors, seen by the Staff, have been using highly coloured expletives about the mines. Sheer bad luck they swear; bad luck that would not happen once in a hundred tries. They had knocked out the Forts, they claim, and one, three-word order, "Full steam ahead," would have cut the Gordian Knot the diplomats have been fumbling at for over a hundred years by slicing their old Turkey in two. Then came the big delay owing to ships changing stations during which mines set loose from up above had time to float down the current, when, by the Devil's own fluke, they impinge upon our battleships, and blow de Robeck and his plans into the middle of next week — or later! These are ward-room yarns. De Robeck was working by stages and never meant, so far as we know, to run through to the Marmora yesterday.

Cabled to Lord K. telling him of yesterday's reconnaissance by me and the battle by de Robeck. Have said I have no official report to go upon but from what I saw with my own eyes "I am being most reluctantly driven to the conclusion that the Straits are not likely to be forced by battleships as at one time seemed probable and that, if my troops are to take part, it will not take the subsidiary form anticipated. The Army's part will be more than mere landings of parties to destroy Forts, it must be a deliberate and progressive military operation carried out at full strength so as to open a passage for the Navy."

To be able, if necessary, to act up to my own words I sent another message to the Admiral and told him, if he could spare the troops from the vicinity of the Straits, I would like to take them right off to Alexandria so as to shake them out there and reship them ready for anything. He has wirelessed back asking me, on political grounds, to delay removing the troops "until our attack is renewed in a few days' time."

Bravo, the Admiral! Still; if there are to be even a few days' delay I must land somewhere as mules and horses are dying. And, practically, Alexandria is the only port possible.

Wemyss has just sent me over the following letter. It confirms officially the loss of the three battleships:

Friday.

MY DEAR GENERAL,

The enclosed is a copy of a Signal I have received from de Robeck. I sincerely hope that the word disastrous is too hard. It depends upon what results we have achieved I think. I gather from intercepted signals that the *Ocean* also is sunk, but of this I am not quite certain. I am off in *Dublin* immediately she comes in and expect I may be back to-night. This of course depends a good deal upon what de Robeck wants. Captain Boyle brings this and will be at your disposal. He is the Senior Naval Officer here in my absence.

Believe me, Sir,
Yours sincerely,
(*Sd.*) R. Wemyss.

Copy of Telegram enclosed:

From V.A.E.M.S.
To S.N.O. Mudros.
Date, *18th March, 1915.*

Negative demonstration at Gaba Tepe, 19th. Will you come to Tenedos and see me to-morrow. We have had disastrous day owing either to floating mines or torpedoes from shore tubes fired at long range. H.M.S. *Irresistible* and *Bouvet* sunk. H.M.S. *Ocean* still afloat, but probably lost. H.M.S. *Inflexible* damaged by mine. *Gaulois* badly damaged by gunfire. Other ships all right, and we had much the best of the Ports.

20th March, 1915. H.M.S. "Franconia." Mudros Harbour. Stormy weather, and even here, inside Mudros harbour, touch with the shore is cut off.

After I was asleep last night, an answer came in from K., straight, strong and to the point. He says, "You know my view that the Dardanelles passage must be forced, and that if large military operations on the Gallipoli Peninsula by your troops are necessary to clear the way, those operations must be undertaken after careful consideration of the local defences and must be carried through." Very well: all hinges on the Admiral.

21st March, 1915. H.M.S. "Franconia." A talk with Admiral Wemyss and General d'Amade. Wemyss is clear that the Navy must not admit a check and must get to work again as quickly as they can. Wemyss is Senior Naval Officer at the Dardanelles and is much liked by everyone. He has put his seniority in his pocket and is under his junior — fighting first, rank afterwards!

A letter from de Robeck, dated "Q.E. the 19th," has only just come to hand:

> Our men were splendid and thank heaven our loss of life was quite small, though the French lost over 100 men when *Bouvet* struck a mine.
>
> How our ships struck mines in an area that was reported clear and swept the previous night I do not know, unless they were floating mines started from the Narrows!
>
> I was sad to lose ships and my heart aches when one thinks of it; one must do what one is told and take risks or otherwise we cannot win. We are all getting ready for another 'go' and not in the least beaten or downhearted. The big forts were silenced for a long time and everything was going well, until *Bouvet* struck a mine. It is hard to say what amount of damage we did, I don't know, there were big explosions in the Forts!

Little Birdie, now grown up into a grand General, turned up at 3 p.m. I was enchanted to see him. We had hundreds and thousands of things to talk over. Although the confidence of the sailors seems quite unshaken by the events of the 18th, Birdie seems to have made up his mind that the Navy have shot their bolt for the time being and that we have no time to lose in getting ready for a landing. But then he did not see the battle and cannot, therefore, gauge the extent to which the Turkish Forts were beaten.

22nd March, 1915. H.M.S. "Franconia." At 10 a.m. we had another Conference on board the *Queen Elizabeth.*

Present:
    Admiral de Robeck,
    Admiral Wemyss,
    General Birdwood,
    General Braithwaite,
    Captain Pollen,
    Myself.

The moment we sat down de Robeck told us *he was now quite clear he could not get through without the help of all my troops.*

Before ever we went aboard Braithwaite, Birdwood and I had agreed that, whatever we landsmen might think, we must leave the seamen to settle their own job, saying nothing for or against land operations or amphibious operations until the sailors themselves turned to us and said they had abandoned the idea of forcing the passage by naval operations alone.

They have done so. The fat (that is us) is fairly in the fire.

No doubt we had our views. Birdie and my own Staff disliked the idea of chancing mines with million pound ships. The hesitants who always make hay in foul weather had been extra active since the sinking of the three men-of-war. Suppose the Fleet *could* get through with the loss of another battleship or two — how the devil would our troopships be able to follow? And the store ships? And the colliers?

This had made me turn contrary. During the battle I had cabled that the chances of the Navy pushing through on their own were hardly fair fighting chances, but, since then, de Robeck, the man who should know, had said twice that he *did* think there was a fair fighting chance. Had he stuck to that opinion at the conference, then I was ready, as a soldier, to make light of military croaks about troopships. Constantinople must surrender, revolt or scuttle within a very few hours of our battleships entering the Marmora. Memories of one or two obsolete six inchers at Ladysmith helped me to feel as Constantinople would feel when her rail and sea communications were cut and a rain of shell fell upon the penned-in populace from de Robeck's terrific batteries. Given a good wind that nest of iniquity would go up like Sodom and Gomorrah in a winding sheet of flame.

But once the Admiral said his battleships could not fight through without help, there was no foothold left for the views of a landsman.

So there was no discussion. At once we turned our faces to the land scheme. Very sketchy; how could it be otherwise? On the German system plans for a landing on Gallipoli would have been in my pocket, up-to-date and worked out to a ball cartridge and a pail of water. By the British system (?) I have been obliged to concoct my own plans in a brace of shakes almost under fire. Strategically and tactically our method may have its merits, for though it piles everything on to one man, the Commander, yet he is the chap who has got to see it through. But, in matters of supply, transport, organisation and administration our way is the way of Colney Hatch.

Here am I still minus my Adjutant-General; my Quartermaster-General and my Medical Chief, charged with settling the basic question of whether the Army should push off from Lemnos or from Alexandria. Nothing in the world to guide me beyond my own experience and that of my Chief of the General Staff, whose sphere of work and experience lies quite outside these administrative matters. I can see that Lemnos is practically impossible; I fix on Alexandria in the light of Braithwaite's advice and my own hasty study of the map. Almost incredible really, we should have to decide so tremendous an administrative problem off the reel and without any Administrative Staff. But time presses, the responsibility cannot be shirked, and so I have cabled K. that Lemnos must be a wash-out and that I am sending my troops to get ship-shape at Alexandria although, thereby, I upset every previous arrangement. Then I have had to cable for Engineers, trench mortars, bombs, hand grenades, periscopes. Then again, seeing things are going less swimmingly than K. had thought they would, I have had to harden my heart against his horror of being asked for more men and have decided to cable for leave to bring over from Egypt a Brigade of Gurkhas to complete Birdwood's New Zealand Division. Last, and worst, I have had to risk the fury of the Q.M.G.

to the Forces by telling the War Office that their transports are so loaded (water carts in one ship; water cart horses in another; guns in one ship; limbers in another; entrenching tools anyhow) that they must be emptied and reloaded before we can land under fire.

These points were touched upon at the Conference. I told them too that my Intelligence folk fix the numbers of the enemy now at the Dardanelles as 40,000 on the Gallipoli Peninsula with a reserve of 30,000 behind Bulair: on the Asiatic side of the Straits there are at least a Division, but there *may* be several Divisions. The Admiral's information tallies and, so Birdie says, does that of the Army in Egypt. The War Office notion that the guns of the Fleet can sweep the enemy off the tongue of the Peninsula from Achi Baba Southwards is moonshine. My trump card turns out to be the Joker; best of all cards only it don't happen to be included in this particular pack!

As ideas for getting round this prickly problem were passing through my mind, two suggestions for dealing with it were put forward. The sailors say some lighters were being built, and probably by now are built, for the purpose of a landing in the North: they would carry five hundred men; had bullet-proof bulwarks and are to work under their own gas engines. If I can possibly get a petition for these through to Winston we would very likely be lent some and with their aid the landing under fire will be child's play to what it will be otherwise. But the cable must get to Winston: if it falls into the hands of Fisher it fails, as the sailors tell me he is obsessed by the other old plan and grudges us every rope's end or ha'porth of tar that finds its way out here.

Rotten luck to have cut myself off from wiring to Winston: still I see no way out of it: with K. jealous as a tiger — what can I do? Also, although the sailors want me to pull this particular chestnut out of the fire, it is just as well they should know I am not going to speak to their Boss even under the most tempting circs.: but they won't cable themselves: frightened of Fisher: so I then and there drafted this to K. from myself:

> Our first step of landing under fire will be the most critical as well as the most vital of the whole operations. If the Admiralty will improvise and send us out post haste 20 to 30 large lighters difficulty and

The Straits

duration of this phase will be cut down to at least one half. The lighters should each be capable of conveying 400 to 500 men or 30 to 40 horses. They should be protected by bullet-proof armour.

Everyone agreed but Birdwood pointed out that, by sending this message, we implied in so many words, that we would not land until the lighters came out from England. He assumed that we had definitely turned down any plan of scrambling ashore forthwith, as best we could? I said, "Yes," and that the Navy were with me in that view, a statement confirmed by de Robeck and Wemyss who nodded their heads. Birdwood said he only wanted to be quite clear about it, and there the matter dropped.

Actually I had thought a lot about that possibility. To a man of my temperament there was every temptation to have a go in and revenge the loss of the battleships forthwith. We might sup tomorrow night on Achi Baba. With luck we really might. Had I been here for ten days instead of five, and had I had any time to draft out any sort of scheme, I might have had a dart. But the operation of landing in face of an enemy is the most complicated and difficult in war. Under existing conditions the whole attempt would be partial, *décousu*,* happy-go-lucky to the last degree. There are no small craft to speak of. There is no provision for carrying water. There is no information *at all* about springs or wells ashore. There is no arrangement for getting off the wounded and my Principal Medical Officer and his Staff won't be here for a fortnight. My orders against piecemeal occupation are specific. But the 29th Division is our *pièce de résistance* and it won't be here, we reckon — not complete — for another three weeks.

All the same, I might chance it, for, by taking all these off chances we *might* pull off the main chance of stealing a march upon the Turks. What puts me off is not the chances of war but the certainties of commonsense. If I did so handle my troops on the spot as to sup on Achi Baba to-morrow night, I still could not counter the inevitable reaction of numbers, time and space. The Turks would have at least a fortnight to concentrate their whole

---

* "Disjointed."

force against my half force; to defeat them and then to defy the other half.

I must wait for the 29th Division. By the time they come I can get things straight for a smashing simultaneous blow and I am resolved that, so far as in me lies, the orders and preparations will then be so thoroughly worked out — so carefully rehearsed as to give every chance to my men.*

If the 29th Division were here — or near at hand — I could balance shortage against the obvious evils of giving the Turks time to reinforce and to dig. Could I hope for the 29th Division within a week it might be worth my while to fly in the face of K. by grasping the Peninsula firmly by her toe: or, — had my staff and self been here ten days ago, we could have already got well forward with our plans and orders, as well as with the laying of our hands upon the thousand odds and ends demanded by the invasion of a barren, trackless extremity of an Empire — odds and ends never thought of by anyone until the spur of reality brought them galloping to the front. Then the moment the Fleet cried off, we might have had a dash in, right away, with what we have here. The onslaught could have been supported from Egypt and the 29th Division might have been treated as a reserve.

But, taking things as they are:

(1) No detail thought out, much less worked out or practised, as to form or manner of landing;
(2) Absence of 29th Division;
(3) Lack of gear (naval and military) for any landing on a large scale or maintenance thereafter;
(4) Unsettled weather; my ground is not solid enough to support me were I to put it to K. that I had broken away from his explicit instructions.

The Navy, i.e., de Robeck, Wemyss and Keyes, entirely agree. They see as well as we do that the military force ought to have

---

* Since these early days, Birdwood has told me he does not think a scheme of an immediate landing could have been carried out. — *Ian H., 1920.*

been ready before the Navy began to attack. What we have to do now is to repair a first false step. The Admiral undertakes to keep pegging away at the Straits whilst we in Alexandria are putting on our war paint. He will see to it, he says, that they think more of battleships than of landings. He is greatly relieved to hear *I* have practically made up my mind to go for the South of the Peninsula and to keep in closest touch with the Fleet. The Commodore also seems well pleased: he told us he hoped to get his Fleet Sweeps so reorganised as to do away with the danger from mines by the 3rd or 4th of April; then, he says, with us to do the spotting for the naval guns, the battleships can smother the Forts and will alarm the Turkish Infantry as to that tenderest part of an Army — its rear. So I may say that all are in full agreement, — a blessing.

Have cabled home begging for more engineers, a lot of hand grenades, trench mortars, periscopes and tools. The barbed wire bothers me! Am specially keen about trench mortars; if it comes to close fighting on the Peninsula with its restricted area trench mortars may make up for our lack of artillery and especially of howitzers. Luckily, they can be turned out quickly.

23rd March, 1915. H.M.S. "Franconia." At 9 a.m. General d'Amade and his Staff came aboard. D'Amade had been kept yesterday by his own pressing business from attending the Conference. I have read him these notes and have shown him my cable of yesterday to Lord K. in which I say that "The French Commander is equally convinced that a move to Alexandria is a practical necessity, although a point of honour makes it impossible for him to suggest turning his back to the Turks to his own Government." But, I say, "he will be enchanted if they give him the order." D'Amade says I have not quite correctly represented his views. Not fantastic honour, he says, caused him to say we had better, for a while, hold on, but rather the sense of prestige. He thought the departure of the troops following so closely on the heels of the naval repulse would have a bad moral effect on the Balkans. But he agrees that, in practice, the move has now become imperative; the animals are dying; the men are overcrowded, whilst Mudros is impossible as a base. My cable, therefore, may stand.

At 10 o'clock he, Birdie and myself landed to inspect a Battalion of Australians (9th Battalion of the 3rd Brigade). I made them carry out a little attack on a row of windmills, and really, they did not show much more imagination over the business than did Don Quixote in a similar encounter. But the men are superb specimens.

Some of the troop transports left harbour for Egypt during the afternoon. Bad to see these transports sailing the wrong way. What a d——d pity! is what every soldier here feels — and says. But to look on the bright side, our fellows will be twice as well trained to boat work, and twice as well equipped by the time the 29th turn up, and by then the weather will be more settled. As d'Amade said too, it will be worth a great deal to us if the French troops get a chance of working a little over the ground together with their British comrades before they go shoulder to shoulder against the common enemy. All the same, if I had my men and guns handy, I'd rather get at the Turks quick than be sure of good weather and good *band-o-bast* and be sure also of a well-prepared enemy.

In the afternoon Braithwaite brought me a draft cable for Lord K. *re* yesterday's Conference. I have approved. In it I say, "on the thoroughness with which I can make the preliminary arrangements, of which the proper allocation of troops, etc., to transports is not the least important, the success of my plans will largely depend." Therefore, I am going to Alexandria, as a convenient place for this work and, "the Turks will be kept busy meanwhile by the Admiral."

24th March, 1915. H.M.S. "Franconia." D'Amade and Staff came aboard at 10 a.m. He has got leave to move and will sail to Alexandria forthwith. Roger Keyes from the Flagship came shortly afterward. He is sick as a she-bear robbed of her cubs that his pets: battleships, T.B.s, destroyers, submarines, etc., should have to wait for the Army. Well, we are not to blame! Keyes has been shown my cables to K. and is pleased with them. He accepts the fact, I think, that the Army must tackle the mobile artillery of the Turks before the Navy can expect to silence the light guns protecting the mine fields and then clear out the mines with the present type of mine sweeper. But the Admiral's going to fix up the mine sweeper question while we are away. Once he has done that, Keyes believes the Fleet can knock out the Forts; wipe out the protective batteries and sweep up the mines quite comfortably. He said one illuminating and encouraging thing to Braithwaite; viz., that he had never felt so possessed of the power of the Navy to force a passage through the Narrows as in the small hours of the 19th when he got back to the Flagship after trying in vain to salve the *Ocean* and the*Irresistible*.

Keyes brought me a first class letter from the Admiral — very much to the point:

H.M.S. *Q.E.*
24th March, 15.

MY DEAR GENERAL,

I hear the Authorities at 'Home' have been sending hastening telegrams to you. They most unfortunately did the same to us and probably if our work had been slower and more thorough it would have been better. If only they were on the *spot*, they would realise that to hurry would write failure. In my very humble opinion, good cooperation and organisation means everything for the future. A great triumph is much better than scraping through and poor results! We are entirely with you and can be relied on to give any assistance in our power. We will not be idle!

Believe me,
Yours sincerely,
(*Sd.*) "J.M. de Robeck.

11-15. Admiral Thursby (just arrived with the *Queen* and *Implacable*) came to make his salaams. We served together at Malta and both broke sinews in our calves playing lawn tennis — a bond of union.

Have cabled to Lord K. telling him I am just off to Alexandria. Have said that the ruling factor of my date of landing must be the arrival of the 29th Division "(see para. 2 of your formal instructions to me the foresight of which appeals to me with double force now we are at close quarters with the problem)."* I have pointed out that Birdwood's Australians are very weak in artillery; that the Naval Division has none at all and that the guns of the 29th Division make that body even more indispensable than he had probably realised. I would very much like to add that these are no times for infantry divisions minus artillery seeing that they ought to have three times the pre-war complement of guns, but Braithwaite's good advice has prevailed. As promised at the Conference I express a hope that I may be allowed "to complete Birdwood's New Zealand Division with a Brigade of Gurkhas who would work admirably in the terrain" of the Peninsula. In view of what we have gathered from Keyes, I wind up by saying, "The Admiral, whose confidence in the Navy seems to have been raised even higher by recent events, and who is a thruster if ever there was one, is in agreement with this telegram."

Actually Keyes will show him a copy; we will wait one hour before sending it off and, if we don't hear then, we may take it de Robeck will have endorsed the purport. Of course, if he does not agree the last sentence must come out, and he will have to put his own points to the Admiralty.

Later. — Have sent Doughty Wylie to Athens to do "Intelligence": the cable was approved by Navy; duly despatched; and now — up anchor!

---

* Para. 2. "Before any serious undertaking is carried out in the Gallipoli Peninsula all the British military forces detailed for the expedition should be assembled so that their full weight can be thrown in."

Chapter III – Egypt

25th March, 1915. H.M.S. "Franconia." At Sea. A fine smooth sea and a flowing tide. Have written to K. and Mr. Asquith. Number two has caused me *fikr*.* The P.M. lives in another plane from us soldiers. So it came quite easily to his lips to ask *me* to write to him, — a high honour, likewise an order. But K. is my soldier chief. As C.-in-C. in India he refused point blank to write letters to autocratic John Morley behind the back of the Viceroy, and Morley never forgave him. K. told me this himself and he told me also that he resented the correspondence which was, he knew, being carried on, behind his (K.'s) back, between the army in France and his (K.'s) own political Boss: that sort of action was, he considered, calculated to undermine authority.

I have had a long talk with Braithwaite *re* this quandary. He strongly holds that my first duty is to K. and that it is for us a question of K. and no one but K. Were the S. of S. only a civilian (instead of being a Field Marshal) the case *might* admit of argument; as things are, it does not. So have written the P.M. on

---

* An Indian word denoting anxious thought.

these lines and shall send K. the carbons of all my letters to him. To K. himself I have written backing up my cable and begging for a Brigade of Gurkhas. Really, it is like going up to a tiger and asking for a small slice of venison: I remember only too well his warning not to make his position impossible by pressing for troops, etc., but Egypt is not England; the Westerners don't want the Gurkhas who are too short to fit into their trenches and, last but not least, our landing is not going to be the simple, row-as-you-please he once pictured. The situation in fact, is not in the least what he supposed it to be when I started; therefore, I am justified, I think, in making this appeal:

> I am very anxious, if possible, to get a Brigade of Gurkhas, so as to complete the New Zealand Divisional organisation with a type of man who will, I am certain, be most valuable on the Gallipoli Peninsula. The scrubby hillsides on the South-west face of the plateau are just the sort of terrain where those little fellows are at their brilliant best. There is already a small Indian commissariat attached to the Mountain Batteries, so there would be no trouble on the score of supply.
>
> As you may imagine, I have no wish to ask for anything the giving of which would seriously weaken our hold on Egypt, but you will remember that four Mounted Brigades belonging to Birdwood's force are being left behind to look after the land of the Pharaohs, and a Mounted Brigade for a battalion seems a fair exchange. Egypt, in fact, so far as I can make out, seems stiff with troops, and each little Gurkha might be worth his full weight in gold at Gallipoli.

Wrote Fitz in much the same sense:

> We are desperately keen to extract a Gurkha Brigade out of Egypt and you might lend a hand, not only to us, but to all your own Sikh and Dogra Regiments, by making K. see that the Indian Army was never given a dog's chance in the mudholes. They were benumbed: *it was not their show.* Here, in the warm sun; pitted against the hereditary *dushman** who comes on shouting 'Allah!' they would gain much

---

* Enemy.

izzat.* Now mind, if you see any chance of an Indian contingent for Constantinople, do everyone a good turn by rubbing these ideas into K.

Braithwaite has already picked up a number of useful hints from Roger Keyes. His old friendship with the Commodore should be a help. Keyes is a fine fellow; radiating resolve to do and vigour to carry through — hereditary qualities. His Mother, of whom he is an ugly likeness, was as high-spirited, fascinating, clever a creature as ever I saw. Camel riding, hawking, dancing, making good *band-o-bast* for a picnic, she was always at the top of the hunt; the idol of the Punjab Frontier Force. His Father, Sir Charles, grim old Paladin of the Marshes, whose loss of several fingers from a sword cut earned him my special boyish veneration, was really the devil of a fellow. My first flutter out of the sheltered nest of safe England into the outer sphere of battle, murder and sudden death, took place under the auspices of that warrior so famouséd in fight when I was aged twenty. Riding together in the early morning from the mud fort of Dera Ismail Khan towards the Mountain of Sheikh Budin, we suddenly barged into a mob of wild Waziri tribesmen who jumped out of the ditch and held us up — hand on bridle. The old General spoke Pushtu fluently, and there was a parley, begun by him, ordinarily the most silent of mankind. Where were they going to? To buy camels at Dera Ghazi Khan. How far had they come? Three days' march; but they had no money. The General simulated amazement — "You have come all that distance to buy camels without money? Those are strange tales you tell me. I fear when you pass through Dera Ismail you will have to raise the wind by selling your nice pistols and knives: oh yes, I see them quite well; they are peeping at me from under your poshteens." The Waziris laughed and took their hands off our reins. Instantly, the General shouted to me, "Come on — gallop!" And in less than no time we were going hell for leather along the lonely frontier road towards our next relay of horses. "That was a narrow squeak," said the General, "but *you may take liberties with a Waziri if only you can make him laugh.*"

---

* Kudos.

Lafayette phot.
LIEUT.-GEN. THE RT. HON. SIR J. G. MAXWELL, G.C.B., K.C.M.G.

26th March, 1915. H.M.S. "Franconia." At Sea. Inspected troops on board. A keen, likely looking lot. All Naval Division; living monuments, these fellows, to Winston Churchill's contempt for convention.

Reached Port Said about 3.30 p.m. Nipped into a "Special" which seems to have become my "ordinary" vehicle and left for Cairo. Opened despatches from London. "Bullet-proof lighters cannot be provided." "I quite agree that the 29th Division with its artillery is necessary." Not a word about the Gurkhas. Arrived at 10 p.m., and was met by Maxwell.

27th March, 1915 Cairo. Working hard at Headquarters all day till 6.15 p.m., when I made my salaam to the Sultan at the Abdin Palace. A real Generals' dinner — what we used to call a *burra khana* — at Maxwell's hospitable board:

General Birdwood,
General Godley,
General Bridges,
General Douglas,
General Braithwaite,
Myself.

28th March, 1915. Cairo. Inspected East Lancashire Division and a Yeomanry Brigade (Westminster Dragoons and Herts). How I envied Maxwell these beautiful troops. They will only be eating their heads off here, with summer coming up and the desert getting as dry as a bone. The Lancashire men especially are eye-openers. How on earth have they managed to pick up the swank and devil-may-care airs of crack regulars? They *are* Regulars, only they are bigger, more effective specimens than Manchester mills or East Lancashire mines can spare us for the Regular Service in peace time. Anyway, no soldier need wish to see a finer lot. On them has descended the mantle of my old comrades[*] of Elandslaagte and Caesar's Camp, and worthily beyond doubt they will wear it.

The enthusiasm of the natives was a pleasing part of the show. During four years of Egyptian Inspections I recall no single

---

[*] The 1st Manchesters.

instance of any manifestation of friendliness to our troops, or even of interest in them, by Gyppies. But the Territorials seem, somehow, to have conquered their goodwill. As each stalwart company swung past there was a spontaneous effervescence of waving hands along the crowded street and murmurs of applause from Bedouins, Blacks and Fellaheen.

 Maxwell will have a fit if I ask for them! He will fall down in a fit, I am sure. Already he is vexed at my having cabled and written Lord K. for *his* (Maxwell's) Brigade of Gurkhas. To him I appear careless of his (Maxwell's) position and of the narrowness of his margin of safety. For the life of him K. can't help putting his Lieutenants into this particular cart. The same old story as the eight small columns in the Western Transvaal: co-equal and each thinking his own beat on the veldt the only critical spot in South Africa: and the funny thing is that Maxwell was then running the base at Vryberg and I was in command in the field! But *there* my word was law; *here* Maxwell is entirely independent of me, which is as much as to say, that the feet are not under control of the head; i.e., that the expedition must move like a drunken man. That is my fear: Maxwell will do what lies in him to help, but in action it is better to order than to ask.

 Grand lunch at the Abdin Palace with the Sultan. Most of the Cabinet present. The Sultan spoke French well and seems clever as well as most gracious and friendly. He assured me that the Turkish Forts at the Dardanelles were absolutely impregnable. The words "absolute" and "impregnable" don't impress me overmuch. They are only human opinions used to gloss over flaws in the human knowledge or will. Nothing is impregnable either — that's a sure thing. No reasons were given me by His Highness.

 Have just written home about these things: midnight.

29th March, 1915. 9.30 p.m. Palace Hotel, Alexandria. Early start to the Mena Camp to see the Australians. A devil of a blinding storm gave a foretaste of dust to dust. That was when they were marching past, but afterwards I inspected the Infantry at close quarters, taking a good look at each man and speaking to hundreds. Many had been at my inspections in their own country a year ago, but most were new hands who had never worn uniform till they 'listed for the war. The troops then marched back to Camp in mass of quarter columns — or rather swept by like a huge yellow cloud at the heart of which sparkled thousands of bayonets.

Next I reviewed the Artillery, Engineers and Cavalry; winding up with the overhaul of the supply and transport column. This took time, and I had to make the motor travel getting across twelve miles or so to inspect a mixed Division of Australians and New Zealanders at Heliopolis. Godley commanded. Great fun seeing him again. These fellows made a real good show; superb physique: numbers of old friends especially amongst the New Zealanders. Another scurry in the motor to catch the 4.15 for Alexandria. Tiring day if I had it in my mind to be tired, but this 30,000 crowd of Birdwood's would straighten up the back of a pacifist. There is a bravery in their air — a keenness upon their clean cut features — they are spoiling for a scrap! Where they have sprung from it is hard to say. Not in Brisbane, Adelaide, Sydney, Melbourne or Perth — no, nor in Dunedin, Christchurch, Wellington or Auckland, did I meet specimens like unto these. The spirit of War has breathed its fires into their hearts; the drill sergeant has taken thought and has added one cubit to their stature.

D'Amade has just been to make me known to a couple of Frenchmen about to join my Staff. They seem to be nice fellows. The French have been here some days and they are getting on well. Hunter-Weston landed this morning; his first batch of transports are in the harbour. I am to see the French troops in four days' time; Hunter-Weston's 29th Division on the fifth day. Neither Commander has yet worked out how long it will take before he has reloaded his transports. They declare it takes three times as long to repack a ship loaded at haphazard as it would have taken to have loaded her on a system in the first instance. Six days per ship is their notion of what they can do, but I trust to improve a bit on that.

Hunter-Weston had written me a letter from Malta (just to hand) putting it down in black and white that we have not a reasonable prospect of success. He seemed keen and sanguine when we met and made no reference to this letter: so it comes in now as rather a startler. But it is best to have the black points thrust upon one's notice beforehand — so long always as I keep it fixed in the back of my mind that there was never yet a great thought or a great deed which was not cried down as unreasonable before the fact by a number of reasonable people!

30th March, 1915. Alexandria. Have just dictated a long letter to Lord K. in the course of which I have forced myself to say something which may cause the great man annoyance. I feel it is up to me to risk that. One thing — he knows I am not one of those rotters who ask for more than they can possibly be given so that, if things go wrong, they may complain of their tools. I have promised K. to help him by keeping my demands down to bedrock necessities. I make no demand for ammunition on the France and Flanders scale but — we must have *some*! There must be a depot somewhere within hail. Here is the crucial para.:

> I realise how hard up you must be for ammunition, but I hope the M.G.O. will have by now put in hand the building up of some reserves at our base in Alexandria. If our batteries or battalions now serving in France run short, something, at a pinch, can always be scraped together in England and issued to them within 24 hours. Here it would be a question of almost as many days, and, if it were to turn out that we have a long and severe struggle, with no reserves nearer us than Woolwich — well — it would not be pleasant! Moreover the number of howitzers, guns and rifles in France is so enormous that it is morally impossible they should all be hotly engaged at the same time. Thus they automatically form their own reserves. In other words, a force possessing only ten howitzers ought to have at least twice the reserves of a force possessing a hundred howitzers. So at least it seems to me.

In the same letter I tell him about "Birdwood's crowd" and of their splendid physique; their growing sense of discipline, their exceeding great keenness, and wind up by saying that, given a fair chance, they will, for certain, "render a very good account of themselves."

Confabs with d'Amade and Hunter-Weston. Hunter-Weston's "appreciation" of the situation at the Dardanelles is to be treated as an *ad interim** paper; he wrote it, he says now, without the fuller knowledge he is daily acquiring — knowledge which is tending to make him more sanguine. His stay at Malta and his talks with Officers there had greatly impressed him with the hardness of the nut we have to try and crack; so much so that his paper suggests an indefinite putting off of the attempt to throw open the Straits. I asked him if he had laid his view before K. in London and he said, No; that he had not then come to it and that he had not definitely come to it now.

D'Amade's own inclinations would have led him to Asia. When he left France he did not know he was to be under me and he had made up his mind to land at Adramiti. But now he waives all preconceived ideas and is keen to throw himself heart and soul into Lord K.'s ideas and mine. He would rather I did not even refer to his former views as he sees they are expressly barred by the tenor of my instructions. The French are working to time in getting shipshape. The 29th Division are arriving up to date and about one-third of them have landed. We are fixing up our gear for floating and other piers and are trying to improvise ways and means of coping with the water problem — this ugly nightmare of a water problem. The question of the carriage and storage of water for thousands of men and horses over a roadless, mainly waterless track of country should have been tackled before we left England.

To solve these conundrums we have had to recreate for ourselves a special field service system of food, water and ammunition supply. As an instance we have had to re-organise baggage sections of trains and fit up store ships as substitutes for additional ammunition columns and parks. We are getting on fairly fast with our work of telling off troops to transports so that each boat load of men landed will be, so to say, on its own; victualled, watered and munitioned. But it takes some doing. Greatly handicapped by absence of any Administrative, or Q. Staff. The General Staff are working double shifts, at a task for which they have never been trained:

---

* "In the interim."

It's a way we have in the Aaarmy!
It's a way we have in the NAAAAvy!!
It's a way we have in the Eeeeeempire!!!
That nobody can deny!!!!

What would my friends on the Japanese General Staff say — or my quondam friends on the German General Staff — if they knew that a Commander-in-Chief had been for a fortnight in touch with his troops, engaged with them upon a huge administrative job, and that he had not one administrative Staff Officer to help him, but was willynilly using his General Staff for the work? They would say "mad Englishmen" and this time they would be right. The British public services are poisoned by two enormous fallacies: (*a*) if a man does well in one business, he will do equally well or better in another; (*b*) if a man does badly in one business he will do equally badly or worse in another. There is nothing beyond a vague, floating reputation or public opinion to enable a new Minister to know his subordinates. The Germans have tabulated the experiences and deficiencies of our leaders, active and potential, in peace and war — we have not! Every British General of any note is analysed, characterised and turned inside out in the bureau records of the great German General Staff in Berlin. We only attempt anything of that sort with burglars. My own portrait is in those archives and is very good if not very flattering; so a German who had read it has told me. This is organisation: this 66] is business; but official circles in England are so remote in their methods from these particular notions of business that I must turn to a big newspaper shop to let anyone even begin to understand what it is to run Q. business with a G.S. team.

Suppose Lord Northcliffe decided to embark upon a journalistic campaign in Canada and that his scheme turned upon time; that it was a question of Northcliffe catching time by the forelock or of time laying Northcliffe by the heels. Suppose, further, that he had no first-hand knowledge of Canada and had decided to place the conduct of the campaign in the hands of his brother who would spy out the land; choose the best site; buy a building; order the printing press; engage hands and start the paper. Well; what staff would he send with him? A couple of leader writers, a trio of special correspondents and half a dozen reporters? Probably; but would there not also be berths taken in the Cunarder for a manager trained in the business side of journalism? Quite a fair way of putting the present case, although, on the other side, it is also fair to add that British Officers have usually had to play so many parts in the charade of square pegs in round holes, that they can catch a hold anywhere, at any time, and carry on somehow.

31st March, 1915. Alexandria. — Quill driving and dictating. Have made several remonstrances lately at the way McMahon is permitting the Egyptian Press to betray our intentions, numbers, etc. It is almost incredible and Maxwell doesn't see his way clear to interfere. For the last day or two they have been telling the Turks openly where we are bound for. So I have written McMahon the following:

GENERAL HEADQUARTERS,
18 RUE EL CAID GOHAR,
ALEXANDRIA, 31/3/15.

DEAR HIGH COMMISSIONER,

I was somewhat startled a couple of mornings ago by an article in the *Egyptian Gazette* giving away the arrival of the French troops, and making open references to the Gallipoli Peninsula. The very frankness of such communications may of course mislead the Turk into thinking we mean thereby to take his mind off some other place which is our real objective, but I doubt it. He knows our usual methods too well.

Consequently as it is very important at least to throw him into some state of bewilderment as to our movements, I propose sending the following cable to Lord Kitchener:

'Whether of set purpose or through inadvertence articles have appeared in Egyptian Press openly discussing arrival of French and British troops and naming Gallipoli as their destination. Is there any political objection to my cautiously spreading rumour that our true objective is, say, Smyrna?'

Before I despatch the wire, however, I think I should like you to see it, in case you have any objections. I have all the facilities for spreading any rumour I like through my Intelligence Branch, which would be less suspected than information leaking out from political sources.

Could you kindly send me a wire on receipt of this?

Yours sincerely,(*Sd.*)

IAN HAMILTON.

I only propose to ask Lord K. in case there may be political reasons why I should not select any particular place about which to spread a rumour of our landing.

Forgot to note a step taken yesterday — to nowhere perhaps — perhaps to Constantinople. Yesterday the *Doris* brought me a copy of a long cable sent by Winston to de Robeck six days ago, together with a copy of the V.A.'s reply. The First Lord is clearly in favour of the Fleet going on knocking the Forts to pieces whilst the Army are getting on with their preparations; clearly also he thinks that, under rough handling from Q.E. & Co., the Turkish resistance might at any moment collapse. Then we should sail through as per Lord K.'s programme. Well; nothing would suit me so well. If we are to have an opposed landing better kill two birds with one stone and land bang upon the Bosphorus. The nearer to the heart I can strike my first blow, the more telling it will be. Cable 140 puts the case very well. Winston hits the nail on the head, so it seems to me, when he points out that the Navy is not tied to the apron strings of the Army but that it is the other way about: i.e., if the Fleet makes another big push whilst we are getting ready, they can still fall back on the combined show with us if they fail; whereas, if they succeed they will save us all the loss of life and energy implied by an opposed landing at the Dardanelles. Certainly Braithwaite and I had understood that de Robeck would work to that end; that this is what he was driving at when he said he would not be idle but would keep the Turks busy whilst we were getting ready. Nothing will induce me to volunteer opinions on Naval affairs. But de Robeck's reply to Winston might be read as if I *had* expressed an opinion, so I am bound to clear up that point — definitely.

Egypt

From GENERAL SIR IAN HAMILTON.
To VICE-ADMIRAL SIR JOHN DE ROBECK.

Copy of number 140 from Admiralty received AAA I had already communicated outline of our plan to Lord Kitchener and am pushing on preparations as fast as possible AAA War Office still seems to cherish hope that you may break through without landing troops AAA Therefore, as regards yourself I think wisest procedure will be to push on systematically though not recklessly in attack on Forts AAA It is always possible that opposition may crumple up AAA If you should succeed be sure to leave light cruisers enough to see me through my military attack in the event of that being after all necessary AAA If you do not succeed then I think we quite understand one another AAA

IAN HAMILTON.

1st April, 1915. Alexandria. The *Arcadian* has arrived bringing my A.G. and Q.M.G. with the second echelon of the Staff. God be praised for this immense relief! The General Staff can now turn to their legitimate business — the enemy, instead of struggling night and day with A.G. and Q.M.G. affairs; allocating troops and transports; preparing for water supply; tackling questions of procedure and discipline. We are all sorry for the Q. Staff who, through no fault of their own, have been late for the fair, *their* special fair, the preparation, and find the show is practically over. On paper at least, the Australians and New Zealanders and the 29th Division are properly fixed up. We should begin embarking these formations within the next three days. After that will come the Naval Division from Port Said and the French Division from here.

2nd April, 1915. Alexandria. Hard at it all day in office. Am leaving to-night by special train for Port Said to hurry things along.

A cable in from the Foreign Office telling me that the Russian part of my force consists of a complete Army Corps under General Istomine — evidently War and Foreign Offices still work in watertight compartments!

Left Alexandria last night at 11 and came into Port Said at

dawn. After breakfast mounted an Arab charger which seems to have emerged out of the desert to meet my wishes just as do special trains and banquets: as if I wore on my finger the magic ring of the Arabian fairy tale: so I do I suppose, in the command it has pleased K., Imperial Grand Vizier, to bestow upon this humble but lively speck of dust. Mounting we cantered through the heavy sand towards the parade ground near the docks. Here, like a wall, stood Winston's far-famed Naval Division drawn up in its battle array. General Paris received me backed by Olivant and Staff. After my inspection the Division marched past, and marched past very well indeed, much better than they did when I saw them some months ago in Kent, although the sand was against them, muffling the stamp of feet which binds a Company together and telling unevenly on different parts of the line. Admiral Pierce and his Flag Captain, Burmeister, honoured the occasion: they were on foot and so, not to elevate the stature of the Army above that of the Senior Service, I took the salute dismounted.

Next had a look round camp. Found things so, so. Saw Arthur Asquith and Rupert Brooke of the Howe Battalion, both sick, neither bad. Asked Brooke to join my personal Staff, not as a fire insurance (seeing what happened to Ronnie Brooke at Elandslaagte and to Ava at Waggon Hill) but still as enabling me to keep an eye on the most distinguished of the Georgians. Young Brooke replied, as a *preux chevalier*[*] would naturally reply, — he realised the privileges he was foregoing, but he felt bound to do the landing shoulder-to-shoulder with his comrades. He looked extraordinarily handsome, quite a knightly presence, stretched out there on the sand with the only world that counts at his feet.

Lunched on the *Franconia* and conversed with Lieutenant-Colonel Matthews and Major Mewes of the Plymouth Battalion; also with Major Palmer. To see with your eyes; to hear with your ears; to touch with your fingers enables you to bring the truth home to yourself. Five minutes of that personal touch tells a man more than five weeks of report reading. In five minutes I gained from these Officers five times more knowledge about Sedd-el-Bahr and

---

[*] "Noble knight."

Kum Kale than all their own bald despatches describing their own landings and cutting-out enterprises had given me. Paris' account had not helped me much either, the reason being that it was not first hand, — was only so many words that he had heard, — was not what he had *felt*. Now, I do really, at last and for the first time, realistically grasp the lie of the land and of the Turks. The prospect is not too rosy, but Wolfe, I daresay, saw blue as he gazed over the water at his problem, without map or General Staff plan to help him. There lay Quebec; within cannon shot; but that enemy was thrice his strength; entrenched in a fortress — there they lay confident — a landing was "impossible!" But all things are possible — to faith. He had faith in Pitt; faith in his own bright particular star; faith in the British Fleet standing resolute at his back: he launched his attack; he got badly beaten at the landing; he pulled himself together; he met a thousand and one mishaps and delays, and when, at the long last, he fell, he had the plum in his pocket.

The Turks lie close within a few yards of the water's edge on the Peninsula. Matthews smiled sarcastically at the War Office idea that no Turks can exist South of Achi Baba! At Sedd-el-Bahr, the first houses are empty, being open to the fire of the Fleet, but the best part of the other houses are defiladed by the ground and a month ago they were held. Glad I did not lose a minute after seeing the ground in asking Maxwell and Methuen to make me some trench mortars. Methuen says he can't help, but Maxwell's Ordnance people have already fixed up a sample or two — rough things, but better than nothing. We have too little shrapnel to be able to spare any for cutting entanglements. Trench mortars may help where the Fleet can't bring their guns to bear. The thought of all that barbed wire tucked away into the folds of the ground by the shore follows me about like my shadow.

Left Port Said for Kantara and got there in half an hour. General Cox, an old Indian friend of the days when I was A.D.C. to Sir Fred., met me at the station. He commands the Indian troops in Egypt. We nipped into a launch on the Canal, and crossed over to inspect the Companies of the Nelson, Drake, Howe and Anson Battalions in their Fort, whilst Cox hurried off to fix up a parade of his own.

The Indian Brigade were drawn up under Brigadier-General Mercer. After inspection, the troops marched past headed by the band of the 14th Sikhs. No one not a soldier can understand what it means to an old soldier who began fighting in the Afghan War under Roberts of Kandaharto be in touch once again with Sikhs and Gurkhas, those splendid knights-errant of India.

After about eighteen years' silence, I thought my Hindustani would fail me, but the words seemed to drop down from Heaven on to my tongue. Am able now to understand the astonishment of St. Paul when he found himself jabbering nineteen to the dozen in lingo, Greek to him till then. But he at least was exempt from my worst terror which was that at any moment I might burst into German!

After our little *durbar*, the men were dismissed to their lines and I walked back to the Fort. There I suddenly ordered the alarm to be sounded (I had not told anyone of my intention) so the swift yet smooth fall-in to danger posts was a feather in Cox's helmet.

Back to main camp and there saw troops not manning the Fort. There were the:

Queen Victoria's Own Sappers.	Captain Hogg, R.E.,
69th Punjabis.	Colonel Harding,
89th Punjabis.	Colonel Campbell,
14th K.G.O. Sikhs.	Colonel Palin,
1st Bn. 6th Gurkhas.	Colonel Bruce,
29th Mountain Battery and the Bikaner Camel Corps	Major Bruce.

Had a second good talk to the Native Officers, shaking hands all round. Much struck with the turn-out of the 29th Mountain Battery which is to come along with the Australian and New Zealand Army Corps to the Dardanelles.

From the platform of the Fort the lines of our defences and the way the Turks attacked them stood out very clearly to a pair of field glasses. Why, with so many mounted men some effort was not made to harry the enemy's retreat, Cox cannot tell me. There were no trenches and the desert had no limits.

Now (in the train on my way back to Alexandria) I must have one more try at K. about these Gurkhas! My official cable and letter asking for the Gurkha Brigade have fallen upon stony ground. No notice of any sort has been vouchsafed to my modest request. Has *any* action been taken upon them? Possibly the matter has been referred to Maxwell for opinion? If so, he has said nothing about it, which does not promise well. Cox has heard nothing from Cairo; only no end of camp rumours. Most likely K. is vexed with me for asking for these troops at all, and thinks I am already forgetting his warning not to put him in the cart by asking for too many things. France must not be made jealous and Egypt ditto, I suppose. I cannot possibly repeat my official cable and my demi-official letter. The whole is *most* disappointing. Here is Cox and here are his men, absolutely wasted and frightfully keen to come. There are the Dardanelles short-handed; there is the New Zealand Division short of a Brigade. If surplus and deficit had the same common denominator, say "K." or "G.S." they would wipe themselves out to the instant simplification of the problem. As it is, they are kept on separate sheets of paper:

too many troops	too few troops
Maxwell	Hamilton

Have just finished dictating a letter to K., giving him an account of my inspection of the Indian troops and of how "they made my mouth water, especially the 6th Gurkhas." I ask him if I could not anyway have *them* "as a sort of escort to the Mountain Battery," and go on to say, "The desert is drying up, Cox tells me; such water as there is is becoming more and more brackish and undrinkable; and no other serious raid, in his opinion, will be possible this summer." I might have added that once we open the ball at the Dardanelles the old Turks must dance to our tune, and draw in their troops for the defence of Constantinople but it does not do to be too instructive to one's Grandmother. So there it is: I have done the best I can.

4th April, 1915. Alexandria. Busy day in office. Things beginning to hum. A marvellous case of "two great minds." K. has proffered his advice upon the tactical problem, and how it should be dealt with, and, as I have just cabled in answer, "No need to send you my plan as you have got it in one, even down to details, only I have not shells enough to cut through barbed wire with my field guns or howitzers." I say also, "Ishould much like to have some hint as to my future supply of gun and rifle ammunition. The Naval Division has only 430 rounds per rifle and the 29th Division only 500 rounds which means running it fine."

What might seem, to a civilian, a marvellous case of coincidence or telepathy were he ever to compare my completed plan with K.'s cabled suggestion is really one more instance of the identity of procedure born of a common doctrine between two soldiers who have worked a great deal together. Given the same facts the odds are in favour of these facts being seen eye to eye by each.

Forgot to note that McMahon answered my letter of the 31st personally, on the telephone, saying he had no objection to my cabling K. or spreading any reports I liked through my Intelligence, but that he is not keeper of the *Egyptian Gazette* and must not quarrel with it as Egypt is not at war! No wonder he prefers the telephone to the telegram I begged him to send me if he makes these sort of answers. Egypt is in the war area and, if it were not, McMahon can do anything he likes. The *Gazette* continues to publish full details of our actions and my only hope is that the Turks will not be able to believe in folly so incredible.

5th April, 1915. Alexandria. Motored after early breakfast to French Headquarters at the Victoria College. Here I was met by d'Amade and anescort of Cuirassiers, and, getting on to my Australian horse, trotted off to parade.

REVIEW OF FRENCH TROOPS AT ALEXANDRIA

GENERAL D'AMADE is saying: "We swear that these colours—red, white and blue—shall be defended to the death. We swear looking at this red earth, this white city, and this blue sea, and in the presence of our Commander, GENERAL HAMILTON."

Coming on to the ground, the French trumpeters blew a lively fanfare which was followed by a roll of drums. Never was so picturesque a parade, the verdict of one who can let his mind rove back through the military pageants of India, Russia, Japan, Germany, Austria, Switzerland, China, Canada, U.S.A., Australia, and New Zealand. Yes, Alexandria has seen some pretty shows in its time; Cleopatra had an eye to effect and so, too, had the great Napoleon. But I doubt whether the townsfolk have ever seen anything to equal the *coup d'oeil* engineered by d'Amade. Under an Eastern sun the colours of the French uniforms, gaudy in themselves, ran riot, and the troops had surely been posted by one who was an artist in more than soldiering. Where the yellow sand was broken by a number of small conical knolls with here and there a group, and here and there a line, of waving palms, there, on the knolls, were clustered the Mountain Batteries and the Batteries of Mitrailleuses. The Horse, Foot and Guns were drawn up, Infantry in front, Cavalry in rear, and the Field Artillery — the famous 75s — at right angles.

Infantry of the Line in grey; Zouaves in blue and red; Senegalese wore dark blue and the Foreign Legion blue-grey. The Cavalry rode Arabs and barbs mostly white stallions; they wore pale blue tunics and bright scarlet breeches.

I rode down the lines of Infantry first and then galloped through the heavy sand to the right of the Cavalry and inspected them, by d'Amade'srequest, at a trot, winding up with the six Batteries of Artillery. On reaching the Saluting Base, I was introduced to the French Minister whilst d'Amade presented colours to two Regiments (175th Régiment de marche d'Afrique and the 4th Colonial Regiment) making a short and eloquent speech.

He then took command of the parade and marched past me at the head of his forces. Were all the Houris of Paradise waving lily hands on the one side, and were these French soldiers on the other side, I would give my cold shoulder to the Houris.

The Cavalry swung along at the trot to the cadence of the trumpets and to the clink-clank and glitter of steel. The beautiful, high-stepping barbs; the trembling of the earth beneath their hoofs; the banner streaming; the swordsmen of France sweeping past the saluting base; breaking into the gallop; sounding the charge; charging; *ventre à terre*; out into the desert where, in an instant, they were snatched from our sight and changed into a pillar of dust!

High, high soared our hopes. Jerusalem—Constantinople? No limit to what these soldiers may achieve. The thought passed through the massed spectators and set enthusiasm coursing through their veins. Loudly they cheered; hats off; and hurrah for the Infantry! Hurrah, hurrah for the Cavalry!! Hurrah, hurrah, hurrah for the 75s!!!

At the end I said a few farewell words to the French Minister and then galloped off with d'Amade. The bystanders gave us, too, the warmest greetings, the bulk of them (French and Greek) calling out "d'Amade!" and the Britishers also shouting all sorts of things at the pitch of their voices.

Almost lost my temper with Woodward, my new A.G., and this was the thusness thereof:

Time presses: K. prods us from the rear: the Admiral from the front. To their eyes we seem to be dallying amidst the fleshpots of Egypt whereas, really, we are struggling like drowning mariners in a sea of chaos; chaos in the offices; chaos on the ships; chaos in the camps; chaos along the wharves; chaos half seas over rolling down the Seven Sisters Road. The powers of Maxwell as C.-in-C., Egypt; of the Sultan and McMahon, High Commissioner of Egypt, and of myself, C.-in-C., M.E.F., not to speak of the powers of our police civil and military, have all to be defined and wheeled into line. We cannot go rushing off into space leaving Pandemonium behind us as our Base! I know these things from a very long experience. Braithwaite believes in the principle as a student and ex-teacher of students. And yet that call to the front!

We've *got* to tackle the landing scheme on the spot and quick. Luckily the problems at Alexandria are *all* non-tactical; pure A.G. and Q.M.G. Staff questions; whereas, at present, the problems awaiting me at the Dardanelles are mainly tactical; G.S. questions. So I am going to treat G.H.Q. as Solomon threatened to treat the baby; i.e., leave the Administrative Staff here until they knock their pidgin more or less into shape and send off the G.S. to pluck *their* pidgin at the Straits. The Q. people have still to commandeer offices for Woodward's men, three quarters of whom stay here permanently to do the casualty work; they have to formulate a local code of discipline; take up buildings for base hospitals and arrange for their personnel and equipment; outline their schemes for getting sick and wounded back from the front; finish up the loading of the ships, etc., etc., etc., *ad infinitum*. Whilst the Q. Staff are thus pulling their full weight, the G. Staff will sail off quickly and put their heads together with the Admiral and his Staff. As to myself, I'm off: I cannot afford to lose more time in getting into touch with the sailors, and the scene of action.

All was well until the Commander-in-Chief said he was going, but that moment arose the good old trouble — the trouble which muddled our start for the Relief of Chitral and ruined the Tirah Campaign. Everyone wants to rush off to the excitement of the firing line — (a spasm usually cured by the first hard fight), and to leave the hum-drum business of the Base and Line of Communication to shift for itself. Braithwaite, of all people, was good natured enough to plead for the Administration. He came to tell me that it might tend towards goodwill amongst the charmed circle of G.H.Q. if even now, at the eleventh hour, I would sweeten Woodward by bringing him along. I said, yes, if he, Braithwaite, would stand surety that he, Woodward, had fixed up his base hospitals and third echelon, but if not, no! Next came Woodward himself. With great pertinacity he represented that his subordinates could do all that had to be done at the base. He says he speaks for the Q.M.G., as well as for the Director General of Medical Services, and that they all want to accompany me on my reconnaissance of the coasts of the Peninsula. I was a little sharp with him. These heads of Departments think they must be sitting in the C.-in-C.'s pocket lest they lose caste. But I say the Departments must be where their work lies, or else the C.-in-C. will lose caste, and luckily he can still put his own Staff where he will. Finally, I agreed to take with me the Assistant to the Director of Medical Services to advise his own Chief as to the local bearings of his scheme for clearing out the sick and wounded; the others stay here until they get their several shows into working order, and with that my A.G. had fain to be content.

Egypt

D'Amade and two or three Frenchmen are dining with me tonight. Sir John Maxwell has just arrived.

6th April, 1915. Alexandria. Started out at 9.15 with d'Amade and Sir John to review the Mounted troops of the 29th Division. We first saw them march down the road in column of route. What a contrast between these solid looking men on their magnificent weight-carrying horses and our wiry little Allies on their barbs and Arabs. The R.H.A. were superb.

After seeing the troops I motored to Mex Camp and inspected the 86th and 87th Infantry Brigades. There was a strong wind blowing which tried to spoil the show, but could not — that Infantry was too superb! Alexander, Hannibal, Caesar, Napoleon; not one of them had the handling of legionaries like these. The Fusilier Brigade were the heavier. If we don't win, I won't be able to put it on the men.

Maxwell left at 4 p.m. for Cairo. I have pressed him hard about Cox's Indian Brigade and told him of my conversation with Cox himself and of how keen all ranks of the Brigade are to come. No use. He expects, so he says, a big attack on the Canal any moment; he has heard nothing from K.; the fact that K. has ignored my direct appeal to him shows he would not approve, etc., etc., etc. All this is just the line I myself would probably take — I admit it — if asked by another General to part with my troops. The arrangement whereby I have to sponge on Maxwell for men if I want them is a detestable arrangement. At the last he consented to cable K. direct on the point himself and then he is to let me know. Two things are quite certain; the Brigade are not wanted in Egypt. Old campaigners versed in Egyptian war lore tell me that the drying up of the wells must put the lid on to any move across the desert until the winter rains, and, apart from this, how in the name of the beard of their own false prophet can the Turks attack Egypt whilst we are at the gates of Constantinople?

But if the Brigade are not wanted on the Canal, we are bound to be the better for them at the Dardanelles, whatever course matters there maytake. Concentration is the cue! The German or Japanese General Staffs would tumble to these truths and act upon them presto. K. sees them too, but nothing can overcome his passion for playing off one Commander against another, whereby K. of K. keeps all reins in his hands and remains sole arbiter between them.

Birdwood has just turned up. We're off to-morrow evening.

'Phoned Maxwell last thing telling him to be sure not to forget to jog K.'s elbow about Cox and his Gurkhas.

7th April, 1915. S.S. "Arcadian." 10 p.m. D'Amade looked in to say good-bye.

On my way down to the harbour I overhauled the Assyrian Jewish Refugee Mule Corps at the Wardian Camp. Their Commander, author of that thrilling shocker, "The Man-killers of Tsavo," finds Assyrians and mules rather a mouthful and is going to tabloid bipeds and quadrupeds into "The Zion Corps." The mules look very fit; so do the Assyrians and, although I did not notice that their cohorts were gleaming with purple or gold, they may help us to those habiliments: they may, in fact, serve as ground bait to entice the big Jew journalists and bankers towards our cause; the former will lend us the colour, the latter the coin. Anyway, so far as I can, I mean to give the chosen people a chance.

Got aboard at 5.15, but owing to some hitch in the arrangements for filling up our tanks with fresh water, we are held up and won't get off until to-morrow morning.

If there drops a gnat into the ointment of the General, be sure there are ten thousand flies stinking the ointment of the troops.

8th April, 1915. S.S. "Arcadian." Sailing free to the Northwards. A fine day and a smooth sea. What would not Richard Cœur de Lion or Napoleon have given for the *Arcadian* to take them to St. Jean d'Acre and Jerusalem?

As we were clearing harbour a letter was brought out to us by a launch:

Union Club,
Alexandria.

Egypt

The following telephone received from General Maxwell, Cairo: Your message re Cox, I will do my best to meet your wishes. Will you in your turn assist me in getting the seaplanes arriving here in *Ganges*? I have wired to Admiral de Robeck, I want them badly, so please help me if you can.

Forwarded by ADMIRAL ROBINSON.

Cutlet for cutlet! I wish it had occurred to me sooner to do a deal with some aeroplanes. But, then I have none. No matter: I should have promised him de Robeck's! South Africa repeats itself! Egypt and Mudros are not one but two. Maxwell and I are co-equal allies; *not* a combine under a Boss!

Chapter IV – Clearing for Action

9th April, 1915. S.S. "Arcadian." Isles of the Aegean; one more lovely than the other; weather warm; wireless off; a great ship steaming fast towards a great adventure — why do I walk up and down the deck feeling a ton's weight of trouble weighing down upon my shoulders? Never till to-day has solicitude become painful. This is the fault of Birdwood, Hunter-Weston and Paris. I read their "appreciations of the situation" some days ago, but until to-day I have not had the unbroken hour needed to digest them. Birdwood begins by excusing himself in advance against any charge of vacillation. At our first meeting he said he was convinced our best plan would be to go for the South of the Gallipoli Peninsula. Now he has, in fact, very much shifted his ground under the influence of a new consideration, "(which I only learned after leaving Lemnos) that the Turks now have guns or howitzers on the Asiatic side which could actually command our transports should they anchor off Morto Bay." "As I told you," he says, "after thinking it out thoroughly, I was convinced our best plan would be to go for the South of the Gallipoli Peninsula," but now he continues, he finds his Staff "all seem to be keen on a landing somewhere between Saros Bay and Enos. For this I have no use, as though I think we should doubtless be able to effect a landing there pretty easily, yet I do not see that we shall be any 'forrarder' by doing so. We might put ourselves in front of the Bulair Lines, but there would be far less object in attacking them and working South-west with the Navy only partially able to help us, than by working up from the other end with the Navy on either flank."

Birdwood himself rather inclines towards a landing on the Asiatic side, for preference somewhere South of Tenedos. The attractive part of his idea is that if we did this the Turks must withdraw most of their mobile artillery from the Peninsula to meet us, which would give the Navy just the opportunity they require for mine-sweeping and so forcing the Narrows forthwith. They know they can give the superstition of old Forts being stronger than new ships its quietus if only they can clear a passage through the minefield. There are forts and forts, ships and ships, no doubt. But from what we have done already the sailors know that our ships here can knock out those forts here. But first they must tackle the light guns which protect the minefield from the sweepers. Birdwood seems to think we might dominate the Peninsula from the country round Chunuk. In his P.S. he suggests that anyway, if we are beaten off in our attempt to land on the Peninsula we may have this Asiatic scheme in our mind as a second string. Disembarkation plans already made would "probably be suitable *anywhere* with very slight modifications. We might perhaps even think of this — if we try the other first and can't pull it off?"

In my answer, I say I am still for taking the shortest, most direct route to my objective, the Narrows.

First, because "I have no roving commission to conquer Asia Minor." My instructions deny me the whole of that country when they lay down as a principle that "The occupation of the Asiatic side by military forces is to be strongly deprecated."

Secondly, because I agree that a landing between Saros Bay and Enos would leave us no "forrarder." There we should be attacked in front from Rodosto; in flank from Adrianople; in rear from Bulair; whilst, as we advanced, we would lose touch with the Fleet. But if our scheme is to be based on severance from the Fleet we must delay another month or six weeks to collect pack transport.

Thirdly, the Asiatic side *does not* dominate the Peninsula whereas the Kilid Bahr plateau *does* dominate the Asiatic narrows.

Fourthly, the whole point of our being here is to work hand-in-glove with the Fleet. We are here to help get the Fleet through the Dardanelles in the first instance and to help the Russians to take Constantinople in the second. The War Office, the Admiralty, the Vice-Admiral and the French Commander-in-Chief all agree now that the Peninsula is the best place for our first step towards these objects.

Hunter-Weston's appreciation, written on his way out at Malta, is a masterly piece of work. He understands clearly that our true objective is to let our warships through the Narrows to attack Constantinople. "The immediate object," he says, "of operations in the Dardanelles is to enable our warships, with the necessary colliers and other unarmoured supply ships — without which capital ships cannot maintain themselves — to pass through the Straits in order to attack Constantinople."

And again:

> It is evident that land operations at this stage must be directed entirely towards assisting the Fleet; and no operations should be commenced unless it is clear that their result will be to enable our warships, with their necessary colliers, etc., to have the use of the Straits.

The Fleet, he holds, cannot do this without our help because of:

(1) Improvement of the defences.
(2) The mobile howitzers.
(3) The Leon floating mines.

Things being so, he sets himself to consider how far the Army can help, in the light of the following premises:

> The Turkish Army having been warned by our early bombardments and by the landings carried out some time ago, has concentrated a large force in and near the Gallipoli Peninsula.
>
> It has converted the Peninsula into an entrenched camp, has, under

German direction, made several lines of entrenchments covering the landing places, with concealed machine gun emplacements and land mines on the beach; and has put in concealed positions guns and howitzers capable of covering the landing places and approaches with their fire.

The Turkish Army in the Peninsula is being supplied and reinforced from the Asiatic side and from the Sea of Marmora and is not dependent on the Isthmus of Bulair. The passage of the Isthmus of Bulair by troops and supplies at night cannot be denied by the guns of our Fleet.

After estimates of our forces and of the difficulties they may expect to encounter, Hunter-Weston comes to the conclusion that,

the only landing places worth serious consideration are:

(1) Those near Cape Suvla,
(2) Those near Cape Helles.

Of these two he advises Helles, because: "the Fleet can also surround this end of the Peninsula and bring a concentrated fire on any Turks holding it. We, therefore, should be able to make sure of securing the Achi Baba position." Also, because our force is too weak to hold the big country round Suvla Bay and at the same time operate against Kilid Bahr.

If this landing at Helles is successful, he considers the probable further course of the operations. Broadly, he thinks that we are so short of ammunition and particularly of high explosive shell that there is every prospect of our getting tied up on an extended line across the Peninsula in front of the Kilid Bahr trenches. Should the enemy submarines arrive we should be "up a tree."

The cards in the game of life are the characters of men. Staking on those cards I take my own opinions — always. But when we play the game of death, things are our counters — guns, rivers, shells, bread, roads, forests, ships — and in totting up the values of these my friend Hunter-Weston has very few equals in the Army.

Therefore, his conclusion depresses me very much, but not so much as it would have done had I not seen him. For certainly during his conference on the 30th March with d'Amade and myself he never said or implied in any way that under conditions as he found them and as they were then set before him, there was no reasonable prospect of success: quite the contrary. Here are the conclusions as written at Malta:

> Conclusion. The information available goes to show that if this Expedition had been carefully and secretly prepared in England, France and Egypt, and the Naval and Military details of organisation, equipment and disembarkation carefully worked out by the General Staff and the Naval War Staff, and if no bombardment or other warning had been given till the troops, landing gear, etc., were all ready and despatched, (the troops from England ostensibly for service in Egypt and those in Egypt ostensibly for service in France) the capture of the Gallipoli Peninsula and the forcing of the Dardanelles would have been successful.
>
> Von der Goltz is reported to have visited the Dardanelles on 11th February and before that date it appears that very little had been done.
>
> Now big guns have been brought from Chatalja, Adrianople and elsewhere, — roads have been made, — heavy movable armaments provided, — troops and machine guns have been poured into the Peninsula, — several lines of trenches have been dug, — every landing place has been trenched and mined, and all that clever German Officers under Von der Goltz can design, and hard working diggers like the Turks can carry out, has been done to make the Peninsula impregnable.
>
> The prizes of success in this Expedition are very great.
>
> It was indeed the most hopeful method of finishing the war.
>
> No loss would be too heavy and no risks too great if thereby success would be attained.
>
> But if the views expressed in this paper be sound, there is not in present circumstances a reasonable chance of success. (The views are founded on the information available to the writer at the time of leaving Malta, and may be modified by further information at first hand on arrival at Force Head Quarters.)
>
> The return of the Expedition when it has gone so far will cause discontent, much talk, and some laughter; will confirm Roumania and Greece in the wisdom of their neutrality, and will impair the power of our valuable friend M. Venezelos. It will be a heavy blow to all of us soldiers, and will need great strength and moral courage on the part of the Commander and Government.

But it will not do irreparable harm to our cause, whereas to attempt a landing and fail to secure a passage through the Dardanelles would be a disaster to the Empire.

The threat of invasion by the Allies is evidently having considerable effect on the Balkan States.

It is therefore advisable to continue our preparations; — to train our troops for landing, and to get our expedition properly equipped and organised for this difficult operation of war; so as to be ready to take advantage of any opportunity for successful action that may occur.

But I would repeat; no action should be taken unless it has been carefully thought out in all its possibilities and details and unless there is a reasonable *probability* of success.

A. HUNTER-WESTON, M.G.

Paris's appreciation gives no very clear lead. "The enemy is of strength unknown," he says, "but within striking distance there must be 250,000." He also lays stress on the point that the enemy are expecting us — "Surprise is now impossible — .... The difficulties are now increased a hundredfold.... To land would be difficult enough if surprise was possible but hazardous in the extreme under present conditions." He discusses Gaba Tepe as a landing place; also Smyrna, and Bulair. On the whole, he favours Sedd-el-Bahr as it "is the only place where transports could come in close and where the actual landing may be unopposed. It is open to question whether a landing could be effected elsewhere. With the aid of the Fleet it may be possible to land near Cape Helles almost unopposed and an advance of ten miles would enormously facilitate the landing of the remainder South of Gaba Tepe."

The truth is, every one of these fellows agrees in his heart with old Von der Goltz, the Berlin experts, and the Sultan of Egypt that the landing is impossible. Well, we shall see, D.V., we shall see!! One thing is certain: we must work up our preparations to the *n*th degree of perfection: the impossible can only be overborne by the unprecedented; i.e., by an original method or idea.

10th April, 1915. S.S. "Arcadian." Lemnos. Cast anchor at 7 a.m. After breakfast went on board the *Queen Elizabeth* where

Braithwaite and I worked for three hours with Admiral de Robeck, Admiral Wemyss and Commodore Roger Keyes.

Last time the Admiral made the running; to-day it was my turn for I had to unfold my scheme and go through it point by point with the sailors. But first I felt it my duty to read out the appreciations of Hunter-Weston, Birdwood and Paris. Then I gave them my own view that history had never offered any nation so clean cut a chance of bringing off an immeasurably big coup as she had done by putting our Fleet and Army precisely where it was at present on the map of the war world. Half that unique chance had already been muddled away by the lack of secrecy and swiftness in our methods. With check mate within our grasp we had given two moves to the enemy. Still, perhaps; nay, probably, there was time. Were we to prolong hesitation, or, were we, now that we had done the best we could with the means under our hands, to go boldly forward? Here was the great issue: there was no use discussing detail until the principle was settled. By God's mercy the Vice-Admiral, Wemyss and Keyes were all quite clear and quite determined. They rejected Bulair; they rejected Asia; most of all they spurned the thought of further delay or of hanging about hoping for something to turn up.

So I then told them my plan. The more, I said, I had pondered over the map and reflected upon the character, probable numbers and supposed positions of the enemy, the more convinced I had become that the first and foremost step towards a victorious landing was to upset the equilibrium of Liman von Sanders, the enemy Commander who has succeeded Djavad in the Command of the Fifth Army. I must try to move so that he should be unable to concentrate either his mind or his men against us. Here I was handicapped by having no knowledge of my opponent whereas the German General Staff is certain to have transferred the "life-like picture" Schröder told me they had of me to Constantinople. Still, sea power and the mobility it confers is a great help, and we ought to be able to rattle the enemy however imperturbable may be his nature and whatever he knows about us if we throw every man we can carry in our small craft in one simultaneous rush against selected points, whilst using all the balance in feints against other likely places. Prudence here is entirely out of place. There will be and can be no reconnaissance, no half measures, no tentatives. Several cautious proposals have been set before me but this is neither the time nor the place for paddling about the shore putting one foot on to the beaches with the idea of drawing it back again if it happens to alight upon a land mine. No; we've got to take a good run at the Peninsula and jump plump on — both feet together. At a given moment we must plunge and stake everything on the one hazard.

I would like to land my whole force in one, — like a hammer stroke — with the fullest violence of its mass effect — as close as I can to my objective, the Kilid Bahr plateau. But, apart from lack of small craft, the thing cannot be done; the beach space is so cramped that the men and their stores could not be put ashore. I have to separate my forces and the effect of momentum, which cannot be produced by cohesion, must be reproduced by the simultaneous nature of the movement. From the South, Achi Baba mountain is our first point of attack, and the direct move against it will start from the beaches at Cape Helles and Sedd-el-Bahr. As it is believed that the Turks are there in some force to oppose us, envelopment will be attempted by landing detachments in Morto Bay and opposite Krithia village. At the same time, also, the A. and N.Z. Corps will land between Gaba Tepe and Fisherman's Hut to try and seize the high backbone of the Peninsula and cut the line of retreat of the enemy on the Kilid Bahr plateau. In any case, the move is bound to interfere with the movements of Turkish reinforcements towards the toe of the Peninsula. While these real attacks are taking place upon the foot and at the waist of the Peninsula, the knife will be flourished at its neck. Transports containing troops which cannot be landed during the first two days must sail up to Bulair; make as much splash as they can with their small boats and try to provide matter for alarm wires to Constantinople and the enemy's Chief.

So much for Europe. Asia is forbidden but I hold myself free, as a measure of battle tactics, to take half a step Troywards. The French are to land a Brigade at Kum Kale (perhaps a Regiment may do) so as, first, to draw the fire of any enemy big guns which can range Morto Bay; secondly, to prevent Turkish troops being shipped across the Narrows.

With luck, then, within the space of an hour, the enemy Chief will be beset by a series of S.O.S. signals. Over an area of 100 miles, from five or six places; from Krithia and Morto Bay; from Gaba Tepe; from Bulair and from Kum Kale in Asia, as well as, if the French can manage it, from Besika Bay, the cables will pour in. I reckon Liman von Sanders will not dare concentrate and that he will fight with his local troops only for the first forty-eight hours. But what is the number of these local troops? Alas, there is the doubtful point. We think forty thousand rifles and a hundred guns, but, if my scheme comes off, not a tenth of them should be South of Achi Baba for the first two days. Hints have been thrown out that we are asking the French cat to pull the hottest chestnut out of the fire. Not at all. At Kum Kale, with their own ships at their back, and the deep Mendere River to their front, d'Amade's men should easily be able to hold their own for a day or two, — all that we ask of them.

The backbone of my enterprise is the 29th Division. At dawn I intend to land the covering force of that Division at Sedd-el-Bahr, Cape Helles and, D.V., in Morto Bay. I tack my D.V. on to Morto Bay because the transports will there be under fire from Asia unless the French succeed in silencing the guns about Troy or in diverting their aim. Whether then our transports can stick it or not is uncertain, like everything else in war, only more so. They must if they can and if they can they must; that is all that can be said at present.

As to the effort to be made to envelop the enemy's right flank along the coast between Helles and Krithia, I have not yet quite fixed on the exact spot, but I am personally bent upon having it done as even a small force so landed should threaten the line of retreat and tend to shake the confidence of any Turks resisting us at the Southernmost point. Some think these cliffs along that Northwest coast unclimbable, but I am sure our fellows will manage to scramble up, and I think their losses should be less in doing so than in making the more easy seeming lodgment at Sedd-el-Bahr or Helles. The more broken and precipitous the glacis, the more the ground leading up to the objective is dead. The guns of the Fleet can clear the crest of the cliffs and the strip of sand at their foot should then be as healthy as Brighton. If the Turks down at Helles are nervous, even a handful landing behind their first line (stretching from the old Castle Northwards to the coast) should make them begin to look over their shoulders.

As to the A. and N.Z. landing, that will be of the nature of a strong feint, which may, and we hope will, develop into the real thing. My General Staff have marked out on the maps a good circular holding position, starting from Fisherman's Hut in the North round along the Upper Spurs of the high ridges and following them down to where they reach the sea, a little way above Gaba Tepe. If only Birdwood can seize this line and fix himself there for a bit, he should in due course be able to push on forward to Kojah Dere whence he will be able to choke the Turks on the Southern part of the Peninsula with a closer grip and a more deadly than we could ever hope to exercise from far away Bulair.

We are bound to suffer serious loss from concealed guns, both on the sea and also during the first part of our landing before we can win ground for our guns. That is part of the hardness of the nut. The landings at Gaba Tepe and to the South will between them take up all our small craft and launches. So I am unable to throw the Naval Division into action at the first go off. They will man the transports that sail to make a show at Bulair.

This is the substance of my opening remarks at the meeting: discussion followed, and, at the end, the Navy signified full approval. Neither de Robeck, Wemyss nor Roger Keyes are men to buy pigs in pokes; they wanted to know all about it and to be quite sure they could play their part in the programme. Their agreement is all the more precious. They (the Admirals and the Commodore) are also, I fancy, happier in their minds now that they know for sure what we soldiers are after. Rumours had been busy in the Fleet that we were shaping our course for Bulair. Had that been the basis of my plan, we should have come to loggerheads, I think. As it is, the sailors seem eager to meet us in every possible way. So now we've got to get our orders out.

On maps and charts the scheme may look neat and simple. On land and water, the trouble will begin and only by the closest thought and prevision will we find ourselves in a position to cope with it. To throw so many men ashore in so short a time in the teeth of so rapid a current on to a few cramped beaches; to take the chances of finding drinking water and of a smooth sea; these elemental hazards alone would suffice to give a man grey hairs were we practising a manœuvre exercise on the peaceful Essex coast. So much thought; so much *band-o-bast*; so much dovetailing and welding together of naval and military methods, signals, technical words, etc., and the worst punishment should any link in the composite chain give way. And then — taking success for granted — on the top of all this — comes the Turk; "unspeakable" he used to be, "unknowable" now. But we shall give him a startler too. If only our plans come off the Turk won't have time to turn; much less to bring into play all the clever moves foreseen for him by some whose stomachs for the fight have been satisfied by their appreciation of its dangers.

Units of the 29th Division have been coming along in their transports all day. The bay is alive with ships.

11th April, 1915. S.S. "Arcadian." One of those exquisite days when the sunlight penetrates to the heart. Admiral Guépratte, commanding the French Fleet, called at 9.45 and in due course I returned his visit, when I was electrified to find at his cabin door no common sentry but a Beefeater armed with a large battleaxe, dating from about the period of Charlemagne. The Admiral lives quite in the old style and is a delightful personage; very gay and very eager for a chance to measure himself against the enemy. Guépratte, though he knows nothing officially, believes that his Government are holding up their sleeve a second French Division ear-marked Gallipoli! But why bottle up trumps; trumps worth a King's ransome, or a Kaiser's? He gives twice who gives quickly (in peace); he gives tenfold who gives quickly (in war). The devil of it is the French dare not cable home to ask questions, and as for myself, I have not been much encouraged — so far!

During the afternoon Admirals de Robeck and Wemyss came on board to work together with the General Staff on technical details. They too have heard these rumours about the second French Division, and Wemyss is in dismay at the thought of having to squeeze more ships into Mudros harbour. His anxiety has given me exactly the excuse I wanted, so I have dropped this fly just in front of K.'s nose, telling him that "There are persistent rumours here amongst the French that General d'Amade's Command is to be joined by another French Division. Just in case there is truth in the report you should know that Mudros harbour is as full as it will hold until our dash for the Peninsula has been made." We will see what he says. If the Division exists, then the Naval people will recommend Bizerta for their base; the ships can sail right up to the Peninsula from there and land right away until things on Lemnos and Tenedos have shaken themselves down.

Our first Taube: it passed over the harbour at a great height. One of our lumbering seaplanes went up after it like an owl in sunlight, but could rise no higher than the masts of the Fleet.

12th April, 1915. S.S. "Arcadian." Lemnos. The *Queen Elizabeth* has been having some trouble with her engines and in the battle of the 18th was only able to use one of her propellers. Now she has been overhauled and the Admiral has asked me to come on board for her steam trials. These are to take place along the coastline of the Peninsula and I have got leave to bring with me a party selected from Divisions and Brigades. So when I went aboard this morning at 8.30 there were about thirty-five Officers present. Starting at once, we steamed at great pace half way up the Gulf of Saros and about 1 o'clock turned to go back, slowing down and closing in to let me take a second good look at the coast. Our studies were enlivened by an amusing incident. Nearing Cape Helles, the *Queen Elizabeth* went astern, so as to test her reverse turbines. The enemy, who must have been watching us like a mouse does a cat, had the ill-luck to select just this moment to salute us with a couple of shells. As they had been allowing for our speed they were ludicrously out of it, the shot striking the water half a mile ahead. We then lay off Cape Helles whilst a very careful survey of the whole of that section was being made. The Turks, disgusted by their own bad aim, did not fire again. On our way back we passed three fakes, old liners painted up, funnelled and armed with dummy guns to take off the *Tiger,* the *Inflexible* and the *Indomitable.* Riding at anchor there, they had quite the man-o'-war air and if they draw the teeth of enemy submarines (their torpedoes), as they are meant to do, the artists should be given decorations. At 6 p.m. dropped anchor and I transhipped myself to the *Arcadian*. Birdwood and Hunter-Weston had turned up during the day; the latter dined and is now more sanguine than myself. He has been getting to know his new command better and he says that he did not appreciate the 29th Division when he wrote his appreciation!

13th April, 1915. S.S. "Arcadian." Heavy squalls of rain and wind last night. *Band-o-bast* badly upset; boats also bottoms upwards and at dawn — here in harbour — we found ourselves clean cut off from the shore. What a ticklish affair the great landing is going to be! How much at the mercy of the winds and waves! Aeolus and Neptune have hardly lost power since Greeks and Trojans made history out yonder!

Have sent K. an electrical pick-me-up saying that the height of the *Queen Elizabeth* fire control station had enabled me to see the lie of the land better than on my previous reconnaissance, and that, given good luck, we hope to get ashore without too great a loss.

In the afternoon the wind moderated and I spent an hour or two watching practice landings by Senegalese. Our delay is loss, but yet not clear loss; that's a sure thing. These niggy-wigs were as awkward as golly-wogs in the boats. Every extra hour's practice will save some lives by teaching them how to make short work of the ugliest bit of their job.

14th April, 1915. S.S. "Arcadian," Lemnos. A day so exquisitely lovely that it should be chronicled in deathless verse. But we gaze at the glassy sea and turn to the deep blue cloudless sky, victory our only thought.

Colonel Dick, King's Messenger, has arrived bringing letters up to 3rd instant. Or rather, he was supposed to have brought them, and it was hoped the abundance of his intelligence would have borne some relation to the cost of his journey, — about £80 it has been reckoned. As a matter of fact, apart from some rubbish, he brings *one* letter for me; none for any of the others. Not even a file of newspapers; not even a newspaper! In India many, many years ago, we used to call Dick *Burra dik hai*, Hindustani for, *it is a great worry*. So he is only playing up to his sobriquet. The little ewe lamb is an epistle from Fitz giving me a lively sketch of the rumpus at the War Office when its pontiffs grasped for the first time the true bearing of their own orders. There was a rush to saddle poor us with the delay as soon as the Cabinet began to show impatience. They seem to have expected the 29th Division to arrive at top speed in a united squadron to rush straightway ashore. They don't yet quite realise, I daresay, that not one of their lovely ships has yet put in an appearance. That the men who packed the transports and fixed their time tables should say we are too slow is hardly playing the game.

Never lose your hair: that is a good soldier's motto. My cable of last night, wherein I tried to calm their minds by telling them the sea was rough and that, even if every one had been here with gaiter buttons complete, I must have waited for a change in the weather, has answered Fitz's letter by anticipation.

Worked all day in my office like a nigger and by mid-day had got almost as black as my simile! We are coaling and life has grown dark and noisy. In the middle of it, Ashmead-Bartlett came aboard to see me. He has his quarters on the *Queen Elizabeth* as one of the Admiralty authorised Press Correspondents, or rather, as the only authorised correspondent. In Manchuria he was known and his writing was well liked. When he had gone, de Robeck and I put through a good lot of business very smoothly. A little later on, Captain Ivanoff, commanding H.I.M.S. *Askold*, (a Russian cruiser well-known to fame in Manchurian days), did me the honour to call.

After lunch went ashore and saw parties of Australians at embarking and disembarking drill. Colonel Paterson, the very man who bear-led me on tour during my Australian inspection, was keeping an eye on the "Boys." The work of the Australians and Senegalese gave us a good object lesson of the relative brain capacities of the two races. Next I went and inspected the Armoured Car Section of the Royal Naval Division under Lieutenant-Commander Wedgwood. He is a mighty queer chap. Took active part in the South African War. Afterwards became a pacifist M.P.; here he is again with war paint and tomahawk. Give me a Pacifist in peace and a Jingo in war. Too often it is the other way about.

All this took me on to 5.30 p.m. and when I came back on board, Hunter-Weston was here. He has been out since last night on H.M.S. *Dartmouth* to inspect the various landing places. His whole tone about the Expedition has been transformed. Now he has become the most sanguine of us all. He has great hopes that we shall have Achi Baba in our hands by sunset on the day of landing. If so he thinks we need have no fear for the future.

All is worked out now and I do not quite see how we could improve upon our scheme with the means at our disposal. If these "means" included a larger number of boats and steam launches, then certainly, by strengthening our forces on either flank, viz., at Morto Bay (where we are sending only one Battalion) and at a landing under the cliffs a mile West of Krithia (where we are sending one Battalion), we should greatly better our chances. Also, a battery of field guns attached to the Morto Bay column, and a couple of mountain guns added to the Krithia column would add to our prospects of making a real big scoop. But we cannot spare the sea transport except by too much weakening and delaying the landing at the point of the Peninsula; nor dare I leave myself without any reserve under my own hand. I am inclined, all the same, to squeeze one Marine Battalion out of the Naval Division to strengthen our threat to Krithia. Hunter-Weston will be in executive command of everything South of Achi Baba; Birdwood of everything to the North.

I went very closely with Hunter-Weston into the question of a day or night attack. My own leanings are in favour of the first boat-loads getting ashore before break of dawn, but Hunter-Weston is clear and strong for daylight. There is a very strong current running round the point; the exact lie of the beaches is unknown and he thinks the confusion inseparable from any landing will be so aggravated by attempting it in the dark that he had rather face the losses the men in boats must suffer from aimed fire. Executively he is responsible and he is backed by his naval associates.

Birdwood, on the other hand, is of one mind with me and is going to get his first boat-loads ashore before it is light enough to aim. He has no current to trouble him, it is true, but he is not landing on any surveyed beach and the opposition he will meet with is even more unknown than in the case of Helles and Sedd-el-Bahr.

When a sportsman goes shark fishing, he should beware lest he be mistaken for the bait. Gaily I cast my fly over K. and now he has snapped off my head. That story about a second French Division was false. K. merely quotes the number of my question and adds, "The rumour is baseless." Well, "*tant pis*,"[*] as Guépratte would say with a shrug of his shoulders. Our first step won't have the weight behind it we had permitted ourselves for some hours to hope. *Everywhere* the first is the step that counts but *nowhere* more so than in an Oriental War.

Now that the French Division has been snuffed out, how about the Grand Duke Nicholas, General Istomine and their Russian Divisions? Are they also to prove phantoms? Certainly, in some form or another, they ought to be brought into our scheme and, even if only at a distance, bring some pressure to bear upon the Turks at the time of our opening move. I think my best way of getting into touch will be by wireless from de Robeck to the Russian Admiral in the Black Sea.

Dick dines, also Birdwood.

15th April, 1915. S.S. "Arcadian." Lemnos. Boarded H.M.S. *Dublin* (Captain Kelly) at 9.30 this morning, where Admiral de Robeck met me. Sailed at once and dropped anchor off Tenedos at noon.

Landed and made a close inspection of the Aerodrome where we were taken round by two young friends of mine, Commander Samson and Captain Davies, Naval Air Service. By a queer fluke these are the very two men with whom I did my very first flight! On that never to be forgotten day Samson took up Winston and Davies took me. Like mallards we shot over the Medway and saw the battleships as if they were little children's playthings far away

---

[*] "Too bad."

down below us. Now the children are going to use their pretty toys and will make a nice noise with them in the world.

After lunch spent the best part of two hours in a small cottage with Samson and Keyes trying to digest the honey brought back by our busy aeroplane bees from their various flights over Gallipoli. The Admiral went off on some other naval quest.

Samson and Davies are fliers of the first water — and not only in the air. They carry the whole technique of their job at their finger tips. The result of K.'s washing his hands of the Air is that the Admiralty run that element entirely. Samson is Boss. He has brought with him two Maurice Farmans and three B.E.2s. The Maurice Farmans with 100 H.P. Renaults; the B.E.2s with 70 Renaults. These five machines are good although one of the B.E.2s is dead old.

Also, he brought eight Henri Farmans with 80 Gnome engines. He took them because they were new and there was nothing else new; but they are no use for war.

Two B.E.2C.s with 70 Renaults: these are absolutely useless as they won't take a passenger.

One Broguet 200 H.P. Canton engine; won't fly.

Two Sopwith Scouts: 80 Gnome engines; very old and can't be used owing to weakness of engine mounting.

One very old but still useful Maurice Farman with 140 Canton engine. That is the demnition total and it pans out at five serviceable aeroplanes for the Army. There are also some seaplanes with us but they are not under Samson, and are purely for naval purposes. Amongst those are two good "Shorts," but the others are no use, they say, being wrong type and underpowered.

The total nominal strength of Samson's Corps is eleven pilots and one hundred and twenty men. As everyone knows, no Corps or Service is ever up to its nominal strength; least of all an Air Corps. The dangerous shortage is that in two-seater aeroplanes as we want our Air Service now for spotting and reconnaissances. If, *after* that requirement had been met, we had only a bombing force at our disposal, the Gallipoli Peninsula, being a very limited space with only one road and two or three harbours on it, could probably be made untenable.

Commander Samson's estimate of a minimum force for this "stunt," as he calls our great enterprise, is 30 good two-seater machines; 24 fighters; 40 pilots and 400 men. So equipped he reckons he could take the Peninsula by himself and save us all a vast lot of trouble.

But, strange as it may seem, flying is not my "stunt." I dare not even mention the word "aeroplane" to K., and I have cut myself off from correspondence with Winston. I did this thing deliberately as Braithwaite reminds me every time I am tempted to sit down and unbosom myself to one who would sympathise and lend us a hand if he could: in truth, I am torn in two about this; but I still feel it is wiser and better so; not only from the K. point of view but also from de Robeck's. He (de Robeck) might be quite glad I should write once to Winston on one subject but he would never be sure afterwards I was not writing on others. On the way back I spoke to the Admiral, but I don't know whether he will write himself or not. Ventured also a little bit out of my own element in another direction, and begged him not to put off sending the submarine through the Straits until the day of our landing, but to let her go directly she was ready. He does not agree. He has an idea (I hope a premonition) that the submarine will catch Enver hurrying down to the scene of action if we wait till the day of the attack.

Even more than in the Fleet I find in the Air Service the profound conviction that, if they could only get into direct touch with Winston Churchill, all would be well. Their faith in the First Lord is, in every sense, *touching*. But they can't get the contact and they are thoroughly imbued with the idea that the Sea Lords are at the best half-hearted; at the worst, actively antagonistic to us and to the whole of our enterprise. The photographs, etc., I have studied make it only too clear that the Turks have not let the grass grow under their feet since the first bombardment; the Peninsula, in fact, is better defended than it was. *Per contra* the momentum, precision, swiftness and staying power of our actual attack will be at least twice as great now as it would have been at the end of March.

Returned to Lemnos about 7.30 p.m.

While we were away my Staff got aboard the destroyer *Colne* and steamed in her to the mouth of the Dardanelles. There the whole precious load of red tabs transshipped to H.M.S. *Triumph* (Captain Fitzmaurice), who forthwith took up her station opposite Morto Bay and began firing salvos with her 6-inch guns at the trenches on the face of the hill. At first the Staff watched the show with much enjoyment from the bridge, but when howitzers from the Asiatic side began to lob shell over the ship, the Captain hustled them all into the conning tower. The Turks seem to have shot pretty straight. The first three fell fifty yards short of the ship; the fourth shell about twenty yards over her. The next three got home. One cut plumb through the bridge (where all my brains had been playing about two minutes previously) and burst on the deck just outside the conning tower. Some cordite cartridges were lying outside of it and these went off with a great flare. Another struck the funnel and the third came in on the waterline. Fifteen more shells were then fired with just a little bit too much elevation and passed over. Only two men were wounded — fractured legs. Captain Fitzmaurice now decided that honour and dignity were satisfied and so fell back slowly towards Cape Helles to try the effect of his guns on the barbed wire entanglements. A good deal of ammunition was expended but only one hit on the entanglement was registered, and that did not seem to do any harm. The fire was described to me as inaccurate. The fact is, as was agreed between the two services at Malta, the whole principle of naval gunnery is different from the principles of garrison or field artillery shooting. Before they will be much good at landmarks, the sailors will have to take lessons in the art.

Passed a very interesting evening, every one excited, I with my aeroplane reports; the Staff with the powder they had smelt. 114]

Two of the Australian Commanding Officers dined and I showed them the aerial photographs of the enemy trenches, etc. The face of one of them grew very long; so long, in fact, that I feared he was afraid; for I own these photos are frightening. So I said, "You don't seem to like the look of that barbed wire, Colonel?" To which he replied, "I was worrying how and where I would feed and water the prisoners."

16th April, 1915. S.S. "Arcadian." Lemnos. Spent the forenoon in interviews beginning at 10 a.m. with de Robeck and Mr. Fitzmaurice, late dragoman at the Embassy at Constantinople. Mr. Fitzmaurice says the Turks will put up a great fight at the Dardanelles. They had believed in the British Navy, and, a month ago, they were shaking in their shoes. But they had not believed in the British Army or that a body so infinitely small would be so saucy as to attack them on their own chosen ground. Even now, he says, they can hardly credit their spies, or their eyes, and it ought to be easy enough to make them think all this is a blind, and that we are really going to Smyrna or Adramiti. They are fond of saying, "If the English are fools enough to enter our mouth we only have to close it." Enver especially brags he will make very short work with us if we set foot so near to the heart of his Empire, and gives it out that the whole of us will be marching through the streets of Constantinople, not as conquerors, but as prisoners, within a week from the date of our making the attempt. All the same, despite this bragging, the Turks realise that if we were to get the Fleet through the Narrows; or, if it were to force its own way through whilst we absorb the attention of their mobile guns, the game would be up. So they are straining every nerve to be ready for anything.

The moral of all these rather contradictory remarks is just what I have said time and again since South Africa. The fact that war has become a highly scientific business should not blind us to the other fact that its roots still draw their nutriment from primitive feelings and methods; the feelings and methods of boy scouts and Red Indians. It is a huge handicap to us here that our great men keep all their tricks for their political friends and have none to spare for their natural enemies. There has been very little attempt to disguise our aims in England, and Maxwell and McMahon in Egypt have allowed their Press to report every arrival of French and British troops, and to announce openly that we are about to attack at Gallipoli. I have protested and reported the matter to K. but nothing in the strategic sphere can be done now although, in the tactical sphere, we have several deceptions ready for them.

Colonel Napier, Military Attaché at Sofia, and Braithwaite came in after these pseudo-secrets had been discussed and joined in the conversation. I doubt whether either Fitzmaurice or Napier have solid information as to what is in front of us, and their yarns about Balkan politics are neither here nor there. John Bull is quite out of his depth in the defiles of the Balkans. With just so much pull over the bulk of my compatriots as has been given me by my having spent a little time with their Armies, I may say that the Balkan nations loathe and mistrust one another to so great a degree that it is sheer waste of time to think of roping them all in on our side, as Fitzmaurice and Napier seem to propose. We may get Greece to join us, and Russia may get Roumania to join her — *if we win here* — but then we make an enemy of Bulgaria, and *vice versa*. If they will unearth my 1909 report at the War Office they will see that, at that time, one Bulgarian Battalion of Infantry was worth two Battalions of Roumanian Infantry — which may be a help to them in making their choice. The Balkan problem is so intricate that it must be simply handled. The simple thing is to pay your money and pick the best card, knowing you can't have a full hand. So let us have no more beating about the bush and may we be inspired to make use of the big boom this Expedition has given to Great Britain in the Balkans to pick out a partner straightway.

Birdie came later and we took stock together of ways and means. We see eye to eye now on every point. Just before lunch we heard the transport *Manitou* had been attacked by a Turkish torpedo boat from Smyrna. The first wireless came in saying the enemy had made a bad shot and only a few men had been drowned lowering the boats. Admiral Rosy Wemyss and Hope, the Flag-Captain, of the Q.E. were my guests and naturally they were greatly perturbed. Late in the evening we heard that the Turkish T.B. had been chased by our destroyers and had run ashore on a GreekIsland where she was destroyed (international laws notwithstanding) by our landing parties.

At 7.30 p.m. Hunter-Weston came along and I had the best part of an hour with him.

17th April, 1915. S.S. "Arcadian." Lemnos. Hunter-Weston came over early to finish off business left undone last night. Admiral Wemyss also took part in our discussions over the landing. Picture puzzles are child's play compared with this game of working an unheard of number of craft to and fro, in and out, of little bits of beaches. At mid-day the *Manitou* steamed into harbour and Colonel Peel, Commander of the troops, came on board and reported fully to me about the attack by the Turkish torpedo boat. The Turks seem to have behaved quite decently giving our men time to get into their boats and steaming some distance off whilst they did so. During the interval the Turks must have got wind of British warships, for they rushed back in a great hurry and fired torpedoes at so short a range that they passed under the ship. Very exciting, we were told, watching them dart beneath the keel through the crystal clear water. I can well believe it.

Went ashore in the afternoon to watch the Australian Artillery embark. Spoke to a lot of the men, some of whom had met me during my tour through Australia last year.

General Paris came to see me this evening.

18th April, 1915. S.S. "Arcadian." Lemnos. Working all morning in office. In the afternoon inspected embarkation of some howitzers. D'Amade turned up later from the *Southland*. We went over the landing at Kum Kale. He is in full sympathy and understands. Winter, Woodward and their administrative Staffs also arrived in the *Southland* and have taken up their quarters on this ship. They report everything fixed up at Alexandria before they sailed. We are all together now and their coming will be a great relief to the General Staff.

Quite hot to-day. Sea dead smooth. The usual ebb and flow of visitors. Saw the three Corps Commanders and many Staff Officers. We are rather on wires now that the time is drawing near; Woodward, though he has only been here one night, is on barbed wires. His cabin is next the signallers and he could not get to sleep. He wants some medical detachments sent up post haste from Alexandria. I have agreed to cable for them and now he is more calm. A big pow-wow on the "Q.E." (d'Amade, Birdie, Hunter-Weston, Godley, Bridges, Guépratte, Thursby, Wemyss, Phillimore, Vyvian, Dent, Loring), whereat the 23rd was fixed for our attack and the naval landing orders were read and fully threshed out. I did not attend as the meeting was rather for the purpose of going point by point into orders already approved in principle than of starting any fresh hares. Staff Officers who have only had to do with land operations would be surprised, I am sure, at the amount of original thinking and improvisation demanded by a landing operation. The Naval and Military Beach Personnel is in itself a very big and intricate business whichhas no place in ordinary soldier tactics. The diagrams of the ships and transports; the lists of tows; the action of the Destroyers; tugs; lighters; signal arrangements for combined operations: these are unfamiliar subjects and need very careful fitting in. Braithwaite came back and reported all serene; everyone keen and cooperating very loyally. D'Amade has now received the formal letter I wrote him yesterday after my interview and sees his way clear about Kum Kale.

Went ashore in the afternoon and saw big landing by Australians, who took mules and donkeys with them and got them in and out of lighters. These Australians are shaping into Marines in double quick time and Cairo high jinks are wild oats sown and buried. Where everyone wants to do well and to do it in the same way, discipline goes down as slick as Mother's milk. Action is a discipline in itself.

The three Officers forming the French Mission to my Headquarters made salaams, viz., Captain Bertier de Sauvigny, Lieutenant Pelliot and Lieutenant de la Borde. The first is a man of the world, with manners suave and distinguished; the second is a savant and knows the habits of obscure and out of the way people. What de la Borde's points may be, I do not know: he is a frank, good looking young fellow and spoke perfect English.

20th April, 1915. S.S. "Arcadian." Lemnos. A big wind rose in the night.

A clerk from my central office at the Horse Guards developed small pox this morning. No doubt he has been in some rotten hole in Alexandria and this is the result, — a disgusting one to all of us as we have had to be vaccinated.

Ready now, but so long as the wind blows, we have to twiddle our thumbs.

Got the full text of d'Amades' orders for his Kum Kale landing as well as for the Besika Bay make-believe.

21st April, 1915. S.S. "Arcadian." Lemnos. Blowing big guns. The event with which old mother time is in labour is so big that her pains are prodigious and prolonged out of all nature. So near are we now to our opening that the storm means a twenty four hours' delay.

Have issued my orders to the troops. Yesterday our plans were but plans. To-day the irrevocable steps out on to the stage.

GENERAL HEADQUARTERS,
21st April, 1915.

Soldiers of France and of the King.

Before us lies an adventure unprecedented in modern war. Together with our comrades of the Fleet, we are about to force a landing upon an open beach in face of positions which have been vaunted by our enemies as impregnable.

The landing will be made good, by the help of God and the Navy; the positions will be stormed, and the War brought one step nearer to a glorious close.

"Remember," said Lord Kitchener when bidding adieu to your Commander, "Remember, once you set foot upon the Gallipoli Peninsula, you must fight the thing through to a finish."

The whole world will be watching your progress. Let us prove our selves worthy of the great feat of arms entrusted to us.

IAN HAMILTON, *General.*

22nd April, 1915. S.S. "Arcadian." Lemnos. Wind worse than ever, but weather brighter. Another twenty four hours' delay. Russian Military Attaché from Athens (Makalinsky) came to see me at 2.30 p.m. He cannot give me much idea of how the minds of the Athenians are working. He says our Russian troops are of the very best. Delay is the worst nerve-cracker.

Charley Burn, King's Messenger, came; with him a Captain

Coddan, to be liaison between me and Istomine's Russians. The King sends his blessing.

> SPECIAL ORDER.
> GENERAL HEADQUARTERS,
> *22nd April, 1915.*
>
> The following gracious message has been received to-day by the General Commanding:
>
> > The King wishes you and your Army every success, and you are constantly in His Majesty's thoughts and prayers."

23rd April, 1915. S.S. "Arcadian." Lemnos. A gorgeous day at last; fitting frame to the most brilliant and yet touching of pageants.

All afternoon transports were very, very slowly coming out of harbour winding their way in and out through the other painted ships lying thick on the wonderful blue of the bay. The troops wild with enthusiasm and tremendously cheering especially as they passed the warships of our Allies.

Nunc Dimittis,* O Lord of Hosts! Not a man but knows he is making for the jaws of death. They know, these men do, they are being asked to prove their enemies to have lied when they swore a landing on Gallipoli's shore could never make good. They know that lie must pass for truth until they have become targets to guns, machine guns and rifles — huddled together in boats, helpless, plain to the enemy's sight. And they are wild with joy; uplifted! Life spins superbly through their veins at the very moment they seek to sacrifice it for a cause. O death, where is thy sting? O grave, where is thy victory?

A shadow has been cast over the wonders of the day by a wireless to say that Rupert Brooke is very dangerously ill — from the wording we fear there can be no hope.

---

* "Now release."

Clearing for Action

Dent, principal Naval Transport Officer, left to-day to get ready. Wemyss said good-bye on going to take up command of his Squadron.

Have got d'Amade's revised orders for the landing at Kum Kale and also for the feint at Besika Bay. Very clear and good.

At 7.15 p.m. we got this message from K.:

Please communicate the following messages at a propitious moment to each of those concerned.

(1) My best wishes to you and all your force in carrying to a successful conclusion the operations you have before you, which will undoubtedly have a momentous effect on the war. The task they have to perform will need all the grit Britishers have never failed to show, and I am confident your troops will victoriously clear the way for the Fleet to advance on Constantinople.

(2) Convey to the Admiral my best wishes that all success may attend the Fleet. The Army knows they can rely on their energy and effective co-operation while dealing with the land forces of the enemy.

(3) Assure General d'Amade and the French troops of our entire confidence that their courage and skill will result in the triumph of their arms.

(End of message) — Personal:
All my thoughts will be with you when operations begin.

We, here, think of Lord K. too. May his shadow fall dark upon the Germans and strike the fear of death into their hearts.

Just got following from the Admiral:

H.M.S. *Queen Elizabeth,*
23rd April, 1915.

My dear General,

I have sent orders to all Admirals that operations are to proceed and they are to take the necessary measures to have their commands in their assigned positions by Sunday morning, April 25th!

I pray that the weather may be favourable and nothing will prevent our proceeding with the scheme. 'May heaven's light be our guide' and God give us the victory.

Think everything is ready and in some ways the delay has been

useful, as we have now a few more lighters and tugs available.
Yours sincerely,
(*Sd.*) "J. M. DE ROBECK."

I have sent a reply:

S.S. *Arcadian*,
23rd April, 1915.

My dear Admiral,
Your note just received gives expression to my own sentiments. The sooner we get to work now the better and may the best cause win.
Yours sincerely,
(*Sd.*) "IAN HAMILTON."

Rupert Brooke is dead. Straightaway he will be buried. The rest is silence.

Twice was "the sight" vouchsafed me: in London when I told Eddie I would bespeak the boy's services; at Port Said when I bespoke them.

Death on the eve of battle, death on a wedding day — nothing so tragic save that most black mishap, death in action after peace has been signed. Death grins at my elbow. I cannot get him out of my thoughts. He is fed up with the old and sick — only the flower of the flock will serve him now, for God has started a celestial spring cleaning, and our star is to be scrubbed bright with the blood of our bravest and our best.

Youth and poetry are the links binding the children of the world to come to the grandsires of the world that was. War will smash, pulverise, sweep into the dustbins of eternity the whole fabric of the old world: therefore, the firstborn in intellect must die. Is *that* the reading of the riddle?

Almighty God, Watchman of the Milky Way, Shepherd of the Golden Stars, have mercy upon us, smallest of the heavenly Shiners. Our star burns dim as a corpse light: the huge black chasm of space closes in: if only by blood ...? Thy Will be done. *En avant*[*] — at all costs — *en avant!*

---

[*] "Forward."

Chapter V – The Landing

24th April, 1915. H.M.S. "Queen Elizabeth." Tenedos. Boarded the Queen Lizzie at 1.30 p.m. Anchored off Tenedos just before 4 p.m. Lay outside the roadstead; close by us is the British Fleet with an Armada of transports, — all at anchor. As we were closing up to them we spotted a floating mine which must have been passed touch-and-go during the night by all those warships and troopships. A good omen surely that not one of them fell foul of the death that lurks in that ugly, horned devil — not dead itself, but very much alive, for it answered a shot from one of our three pounders with the dull roar and spitting of fire and smoke bred for our benefit by the kindly German Kultur.

I hope I may sleep to-night. I think so. If not, my wakefulness will wish the clock's hand forward.

25th April, 1915. H.M.S. "Queen Elizabeth." Our *Queen* chose the cold grey hour of 4 a.m. to make her war toilette. By 4.15 she had sunk the lady and put on the man of war. Gone were the gay companions; closed the tight compartments and stowed away under armour were all her furbelows and frills. In plain English, our mighty battleship was cleared for action, and — my mind — that also has now been cleared of its everyday lumber: and I am ready.

If this is a queer start for me, so it is also for de Robeck. In sea warfare, the Fleet lies in the grip of its Admiral like a platoon in the hands of a Subaltern. The Admiral sees; speaks the executive word and the whole Fleet moves; not, as with us, each Commander carrying out the order in his own way, but each Captain steaming, firing, retiring to the letter of the signal. In the Navy the man at the gun, the man at the helm, the man sending up shells in the hoist has no discretion unless indeed the gear goes wrong, and he has to use his wits to put it right again. With us the infantry scout, a boy in his teens perhaps, may have to decide whether to open fire, to lie low or to fall back; whether to bring on a battle or avoid it. But the Fleet to-day is working like an army; the ships are widely scattered each one on its own, except in so far as wireless may serve, and that is why I say de Robeck is working under conditions just as unusual to him as mine are to me.

My station is up in the conning tower with de Robeck. The conning tower is a circular metal chamber, like a big cooking pot. Here we are, all eyes, like potatoes in the cooking pot aforesaid, trying to peep through a slit where the lid is raised a few inches, *ad hoc*, as these blasted politicians like to say. My Staff are not with me in this holy of holies, but are stowed away in steel towers or jammed into 6-inch batteries.

So we kept moving along and at 4.30 a.m. were off Sedd-el-Bahr. All quiet and grey. Thence we steamed for Gaba Tepe and midway, about 5 o'clock, heard a very heavy fire from Helles behind us. The Turks are putting up some fight. Now we are off Gaba Tepe!

The day was just breaking over the jagged hills; the sea was glassy smooth; the landing of the lads from the South was in full swing; the shrapnel was bursting over the water; the patter of musketry came creeping out to sea; we are in for it now; the machine guns muttered as through chattering teeth — up to our necks in it now. But would we be out of it? No; not one of us; not for five hundred years stuffed full of dullness and routine.

By 5.35 the rattle of small arms quieted down; we heard that about 4,000 fighting men had been landed; we could see boat-loads making for the land; swarms trying to straighten themselves out along the shore; other groups digging and hacking down the brushwood. Even with our glasses they did not look much bigger than ants. God, one would think, cannot see them at all or He would put a stop to this sort of panorama altogether. And yet, it would be a pity if He missed it; for these fellows have been worth the making. They are not charging up into this Sari Bair range for money or by compulsion. They fight for love — all the way from the Southern Cross for love of the old country and of liberty. Wave after wave of the little ants press up and disappear. We lose sight of them the moment they lie down. Bravo! every man on our great ship longs to be with them. But the main battle called. The Admiral was keen to take me when and where the need might most arise. So we turned South and steamed slowly back along the coast to Cape Helles.

Opposite Krithia came another great moment. We have made good the landing — sure — it is a fact. I have to repeat the word to myself several times, "fact," "fact," "fact," so as to be sure I am awake and standing here looking at live men through a long telescope. The thing seems unreal; as though I were in a dream, instead of on a battleship. To see words working themselves out upon the ground; to watch thoughts move over the ground as fighting men....!

Both Battalions, the Plymouth and the K.O.S.B.s, had climbed the high cliff without loss; so it was signalled; there is no firing; the Turks have made themselves scarce; nothing to show danger or stress; only parties of our men struggling up the sandy precipice by zigzags, carrying munitions and large glittering kerosine tins of water. Through the telescope we can now make out a number of our fellows in groups along the crest of the cliff, quite peacefully reposing — probably smoking. This promises great results to our arms — not the repose or the smoking, for I hope that won't last long — but the enemy's surprise. In spite of Egypt and the *Egyptian Gazette*; in spite of the spy system of Constantinople, we have brought off our tactical *coup* and surprised the enemy Chief. The bulk of the Turks are not at Gaba Tepe; here, at "Y," there are none at all!

In a sense, and no mean sense either, I am as much relieved, and as sanguine too, at the *coup* we have brought off here as I was just now to see Birdie's four thousand driving the Turks before them into the mountains. The schemes are not on the same scale. If the Australians get through to Mal Tepe the whole Turkish Army on the Peninsula will be done in. If the "Y" Beach lot press their advantage they may cut off the enemy troops on the toe of the Peninsula. With any luck, the K.O.S.B.s and Plymouths at "Y" should get right on the line of retreat of the Turks who are now fighting to the South.

The point at issue as we sailed down to "X" Beach was whether that little force at "Y" should not be reinforced by the Naval Division who were making a feint against the Bulair Lines and had, by now, probably finished their work. Braithwaite has been speaking to me about it. The idea appealed to me very strongly because I have been all along most keen on the "Y" Beach plan which is my own special child; and this would be to make the most of it and press it for all it was worth. But, until the main battle develops more clearly at Gaba Tepe and at Sedd-el-Bahr I must not commit the only troops I have in hand as my Commander-in-Chief's reserve.

When we got to "X" Beach the foreshore and cliffs had been made good without much loss in the first instance, we were told, though there is a hot fight going on just south of it. But fresh troops will soon be landing: so far so good. Further round, at "W" Beach, another lodgment had been effected; very desperate and bloody, we are told by the Naval Beachmaster: and indeed we can see some of the dead, but the Lancashire Fusiliers hold the beach though we don't seem yet to have penetrated inland. By Sedd-el-Bahr, where we hove to about 6.45, the light was very baffling; land wrapped in haze, sun full in our eyes. Here we watched as best we could over the fight being put up by the Turks against our forlorn hope on the *River Clyde*. Very soon it became clear that we were being held. Through our glasses we could quite clearly watch the sea being whipped up all along the beach and about the *River Clyde* by a pelting storm of rifle bullets. We could see also how a number of our dare-devils were up to their necks in this tormented water trying to struggle on to land from the barges linking the River

Clyde to the shore. There was a line of men lying flat down under cover of a little sandbank in the centre of the beach. They were so held under by fire they dared not, evidently, stir.

S.S. "RIVER CLYDE" "Central News" phot.

Watching these gallant souls from the safety of a battleship gave me a hateful feeling: Roger Keyes said to me he simply could not bear it. Often a Commander may have to watch tragedies from a post of safety. That is all right. I have had my share of the hair's breadth business and now it becomes the turn of the youngsters. But, from the battleship, you are outside the frame of the picture. The thing becomes monstrous; too cold-blooded; like looking on at gladiators from the dress circle. The moment we became satisfied that none of our men had made their way further than a few feet above sea level, the *Queen* opened a heavy fire from her 6-inch batteries upon the Castle, the village and the high steep ground ringing round the beach in a semi-circle. The enemy lay very low somewhere underground. At times the *River Clyde* signalled that the worst fire came from the old Fort and Sedd-el-Bahr; at times that these bullets were pouring out from about the second highest rung of seats on the West of that amphitheatre in which we were striving to take our places. Ashore the machine guns and rifles never ceased — tic tac, tic tac, brrrr — tic tac, tic tac, brrrrrr...... Drowned every few seconds by our tremendous salvoes, this more nervous noise crept back insistently into our ears in the interval. As men fixed in the grip of nightmare, we were powerless — unable to do anything but wait.

When we saw our covering party fairly hung up under the fire from the Castle and its outworks, it became a question of issuing fresh orders to the main body who had not yet been committed to that attack. There was no use throwing them ashore to increase the number of targets on the beach. Roger Keyes started the notion that these troops might well be diverted to "Y" where they could land unopposed and whence they might be able to help their advance guard at "V" more effectively than by direct reinforcement if they threatened to cut the Turkish line of retreat from Sedd-el-Bahr. Braithwaite was rather dubious from the orthodox General Staff point of view as to whether it was sound for G.H.Q. to barge into Hunter-Weston's plans, seeing he was executive Commander of the whole of this southern invasion. But to me the idea seemed simple common sense. If it did not suit Hunter-Weston's book, he had only to say so. Certainly Hunter-Weston was in closer touch with all these landings than we were; it was not for me to force his hands: there was no question of that: so at 9.15 I wirelessed as follows:

G.O.C. in C. to G.O.C. *Euryalus.*

"Would you like to get some more men ashore on 'Y' beach? If so, trawlers are available."

Three quarters of an hour passed; the state of affairs at Sedd-el-Bahr was no better, and in an attack if you don't get better you get worse; the supports were not being landed; no answer had come to hand. So repeated my signal to Hunter-Weston, making it this time personal from me to him and ordering him to acknowledge receipt. (Lord Bobs' wrinkle):

General Hamilton to General Hunter-Weston, *Euryalus.*

Do you want any more men landed at 'Y'? There are trawlers available. Acknowledge the signal.

At 11 a.m. I got this answer:

From General Hunter-Weston to G.O.C. *Queen Elizabeth*.

Admiral Wemyss and Principal Naval Transport Officer state that to interfere with present arrangements and try to land men at 'Y' Beach would delay disembarkation.

There was some fuss about the *Cornwallis*. She ought to have been back from Morto Bay and lending a hand here, but she had not turned up. All sorts of surmises. Now we hear she has landed our right flank attack very dashingly and that we have stormed de Tott's Battery! I fear the South Wales Borderers are hardly strong enough alone to move across and threaten Sedd-el-Bahr from the North. But the news is fine. How I wish we had left "V" Beach severely alone. Big flanking attacks at "Y" and "S" might have converged on Sedd-el-Bahr and carried it from the rear when none of the garrison could have escaped. But then, until we tried, we were afraid fire from Asia might defeat the de Tott's Battery attack and that the "Y" party might not scale the cliffs. The Turks are stronger down here than at Gaba Tepe. Still, I should doubt if they are in any great force; quite clearly the bulk of them have been led astray by our feints, and false rumours. Otherwise, had they even a regiment in close reserve, they must have eaten up the S.W.B. as they stormed the Battery.

About noon, a Naval Officer (Lieutenant Smith), a fine fellow, came off to get some more small arm ammunition for the machine guns on the *River Clyde*. He said the state of things on and around that ship was "awful," a word which carried twentyfold weight owing to the fact that it was spoken by a youth never very emotional, I am sure, and now on his mettle to make his report 135] with indifference and calm. The whole landing place at "V" Beach is ringed round with fire. The shots from our naval guns, smashing as their impact appears, might as well be confetti for all the effect they have upon the Turkish trenches. The *River Clyde* is commanded and swept not only by rifles at 100 yards' range, but by pom-poms and field guns. Her own double battery of machine guns mounted in a sandbag revetment in her bows are to some extent forcing the enemy to keep their heads down and preventing them from actually rushing the little party of our men who are crouching behind the sand bank. But these same men of ours cannot raise head or hand one inch beyond that lucky ledge of sand by the water's brink. And the bay at Sedd-el-Bahr, so the last messengers have told us, had turned red. The *River Clyde* so far saves the situation. She was only ready two days before we plunged.

At 1.30 heard that d'Amade had taken Kum Kale. De Robeck had already heard independently by wireless that the French (the 6th Colonials under Nogués) had carried the village by a bayonet charge at 9.35 a.m. On the Asiatic side, then, things are going as we had hoped. The Russian *Askold* and the *Jeanne d'Arc* are supporting our Allies in their attack. Being so hung up at "V," I have told d'Amade that he will not be able to disembark there as arranged, but that he will have to take his troops round to "W" and march them across.

At two o'clock a large number of our wounded who had taken refuge under the base of the arches of the old Fort at Sedd-el-Bahr began to signal for help. The *Queen Elizabeth* sent away a picket boat which passed through the bullet storm and most gallantly brought off the best part of them.

Soon after 2 o'clock we were cheered by sighting our own brave fellows making a push from the direction of "W." We reckon they must be Worcesters and Essex men moving up to support the Royal Fusiliers and the Lancashire Fusiliers, who have been struggling unaided against the bulk of the Turkish troops. The new lot came along by rushes from the Westwards, across from "X" to "W" towards Sedd-el-Bahr, and we prayed God very fervently they might be able to press on so as to strike the right rear of the enemy troops encircling "V" Beach. At 3.10 the leading heroes — we were amazed at their daring — actually stood up in order the better to cut through a broad belt of wire entanglement. One by one the men passed through and fought their way to within a few yards of a redoubt dominating the hill between Beaches "W" and "V." This belt of wire ran perpendicularly, not parallel, to the coastline and had evidently been fixed up precisely to prevent what we were now about to attempt. To watch V.C.s being won by wire cutting; to see the very figure and attitude of the hero; to be safe oneself except from the off chance of a shell, — was like being stretched upon the rack! All day we hung *vis-à-vis* this inferno. With so great loss and with so desperate a situation the white flag would have gone up in the South African War but there was no idea of it to-day and I don't feel afraid of it even now, in the dark of a moonless night, where evil thoughts are given most power over the mind.

Nor does Hunter-Weston. We had a hurried dinner, de Robeck, Keyes, Braithwaite, Godfrey, Hope and I, in the signal office under the bridge. As we were finishing Hunter-Weston came on board. After he had told us his story, breathlessly and listened to with breathless interest, I asked him what about our troops at "Y"? He thought they were now in touch with our troops at "X" but that they had been through some hard fighting to get there. His last message had been that they were being hard pressed but as he had heard nothing more since then he assumed they were all right — ! Anyway, he was cheery, stout-hearted, quite a good tonic and — on the whole — his news is good.

To sum up the doings of the day; the French have dealt a brilliant stroke at Kum Kale; we have fixed a grip on the hills to the North of Gaba Tepe; also, we have broken through the enemy's defences at "X" and "W," two out of the three beaches at the South point of the Peninsula. The "hold-up" at the third, "V" (or Sedd-el-Bahr) causes me the keenest anxiety — it would never do if we were forced to re-embark at night as has been suggested — we must stick it until our advance from "X" and "W" opens that sally port from the sea. There is always in the background of my mind dread lest help should reach the enemy *before* we have done with Sedd-el-Bahr. The enveloping attacks on both enemy flanks have come off brilliantly, but have not cut the enemy's line of retreat, or so threatened it that they have to make haste to get back. At "S" (Eski Hissarlick or Morto Bay) the 2nd South Wales Borderers have landed in very dashing style though under fire from big fortress artillery as well as field guns and musketry. On shore they deployed and, helped by sailors from the *Cornwallis*, have carried the Turkish trenches in front of them at the bayonet's point. They are now dug in on a commanding spur but are anxious at finding themselves all alone and say they do not feel able, owing to their weakness, to manœuvre or to advance. From "Y," opposite Krithia, there is no further news. But two good battalions at large and on the war path some four or five miles in rear of the enemy should do something during the next few hours. I was right, so it seems, about getting ashore before the enemy could see to shoot out to sea. At Gaba Tepe; opposite Krithia and by Morto Bay we landed without too much loss. Where we waited to bombard, as at Helles and Sedd-el-Bahr, we have got it in the neck.

This "V" Beach business is the blot. Sedd-el-Bahr was supposed to be the softest landing of the lot, as it was the best harbour and seemed to lie specially at the mercy of the big guns of the Fleet. Would that we had left it severely alone and had landed a big force at Morto Bay whence we could have forced the Sedd-el-Bahr Turks to fall back.

One thing is sure. Whatever happens to us here we are bound to win glory. There are no other soldiers quite of the calibre of our chaps in the world; they have *esprit de corps*; they are *volunteers* every one of them; they are *for it*; our Officers — our rank and file — have been so *entered* to this attack that they will all die — that we will all die — sooner than give way before the Turk. The men are not fighting blindly as in South Africa: they are not fighting against forces with whose motives they half sympathise. They have been told, and told again, exactly what we are after. They understand. Their eyes are wide open: they *know* that the war can only be brought to an end by our joining hands quickly with the Russians: they *know* that the fate of the Empire depends on the courage they display. Should the Fates so decree, the whole brave Army may disappear during the night more dreadfully than that of Sennacherib; but assuredly they will not surrender: where so much is dark, where many are discouraged, in this knowledge I feel both light and joy.

Here I write — think — have my being. To-morrow night where shall we be? Well; what then; what of the worst? At least we shall have lived, acted, dared. We are half way through — we shall not look back.

As night began to settle down over the land, the *Queen Elizabeth* seemed to feel the time had come to give full vent to her wrath. An order from the bridge, and, in the twinkling of an eye, she shook from stem to stern with the recoil from her own efforts. The great ship was fighting all out, all in action. Every gun spouted flame and a roar went up fit to shiver the stars of Heaven. Ears stopped with wax; eyes half blinded by the scorching yellow blasts; still, in some chance seconds interval, we could hear the hive-like b rr rr rr rr rr r r r r of the small arms plying on the shore; still see, through some break in the acrid smoke, the profile of the castle and houses; nay, of the very earth itself and the rocky cliff; see them all, change, break, dissolve into dust; crumble as if by enchantment into strange new outlines, under the enormous explosions of our 15-in. lyddite shells. Buildings gutted: walls and trenches turned inside out and upside down: friend and foe surely must be wiped out together under such a fire: at least they are stupefied — must cease taking a hand with their puny rifles and machine guns? Not so. Amidst falling ruins; under smoke clouds of yellow, black, green and white; the beach, the cliffs and the ramparts of the Castle began, in the oncoming dusk, to sparkle all over with hundreds of tiny flecks of rifle fire.

Just before the shadows of night hid everything from sight, we could see that many of our men, who had been crouching all day under the sandy bank in the centre of the arena, were taking advantage of the pillars of smoke raised between them and their enemy to edge away to their right and scale the rampart leading to the Fort of Sedd-el-Bahr. Other small clusters lay still — they have made their last attack.

Now try to sleep. What of those men fighting for their lives in the darkness. I put them there. Might they not, all of them, be sailing back to safe England, but for me? And I sleep! To sleep whilst thousands are killing one another close by! Well, why not; I *must* sleep whilst I may. The legend whereby a Commander-in-Chief works wonders during a battle dies hard. He may still lose the battle in a moment by losing heart. He may still help to win the battle by putting a brave face upon the game when it seems to be up. By his character, he may still stop the rot and inspire his men to advance once more to the assault. The old Bible idea of the Commander: when his hands grew heavy Amalek advanced; when he raised them and willed victory Israel prevailed over the heathen! As regards directions, modifications, orders, counter-orders, — in precise proportion as his preparations and operation orders have been thoroughly conceived and carried out, so will the actual conflict find him leaving the actual handling of the troops to Hunter-Weston as I am bound to do. Old Oyama cooled his brain during the battle of the Shaho by shooting pigeons sitting on Chinese chimneys. King Richard before Bosworth saw ghosts. My own dark hours pass more easily as I make my cryptic jottings in pedlar's French. The detachment of the writer comes over me; calms down the tumult of the mind and paves a path towards the refuge of sleep. No order is to be issued until I get reports and requests. I can't think now of anything left undone that I ought to have done; I have no more troops to lay my hands on — Hunter-Weston has more than he can land to-night; I won't mend matters much by prowling up and down the gangways. Braithwaite calls me if he must. No word yet about the losses except that they have been heavy. If the Turks get hold of a lot of fresh men and throw them upon us during the night, — perhaps they may knock us off into the sea. No General knows his luck. That's the beauty of the business. But I feel sanguine in the spirit of the men; sanguine in my own spirit; sanguine in the soundness of my scheme. What with the landing at Gaba Tepe and at Kum Kale, and the feints at Bulair and Besika Bay, the Turkish troops here will get no help to-night. And our fellows are steadily pouring ashore.

26th April, 1915. H.M.S. "Queen Elizabeth." At 12.5 a.m. I was dragged out of a dead sleep by Braithwaite who kept shaking me by the shoulder and saying, "Sir Ian! Sir Ian!!" I had been having a good time for an hour far away somewhere, far from bloody turmoil, and before I quite knew where I was, my Chief of Staff repeated what he had, I think, said several times already, "Sir Ian, you've got to come right along — a question of life and death — you must settle it!" Braithwaite is a cool hand, but his tone made me wide awake in a second. I sprang from bed; flung on my "British Warm" and crossed to the Admiral's cabin — not his own cabin but the dining saloon — where I found de Robeck himself, Rear-Admiral Thursby (in charge of the landing of the Australian and New Zealand Army Corps), Roger Keyes, Braithwaite,

The Landing

Brigadier-General Carruthers (Deputy Adjutant and Quartermaster-General of the Australian and New Zealand Army Corps) and Brigadier-General Cunliffe Owen (Commanding Royal Artillery of the Australian and New Zealand Army Corps). A cold hand clutched my heart as I scanned their faces. Carruthers gave me a message from Birdwood written in Godley's writing. I read it aloud:

> Both my Divisional Generals and Brigadiers have represented to me that they fear their men are thoroughly demoralised by shrapnel fire to which they have been subjected all day after exhaustion and gallant work in morning. Numbers have dribbled back from firing line and cannot be collected in this difficult country. Even New Zealand Brigade which has been only recently engaged lost heavily and is to some extent demoralised. If troops are subjected to shell fire again tomorrow morning there is likely to be a fiasco as I have no fresh troops with which to replace those in firing line. I know my representation is most serious but if we are to re-embark it must be at once.
>
> (*Sd.*) "BIRDWOOD.

The faces round that table took on a look — when I close my eyes there they sit, — a look like nothing on earth unless it be the guests when their host flings salt upon the burning raisins. To gain time I asked one or two questions about the tactical position on shore, but Carruthers and Cunliffe Owen seemed unable to add any detail to Birdwood's general statement.

I turned to Thursby and said, "Admiral, what do you think?"

He said, "It will take the best part of three days to get that crowd off the beaches."

"And where are the Turks?" I asked.

"On the top of 'em!"

"Well, then," I persisted, "tell me, Admiral, what do *you* think?"

"What do I think: well, I think myself they will stick it out if only it is put to them that they must."

Without another word, all keeping silence, I wrote Birdwood as follows:

> Your news is indeed serious. But there is nothing for it but to dig

yourselves right in and stick it out. It would take at least two days to re-embark you as Admiral Thursby will explain to you. Meanwhile, the Australian submarine has got up through the Narrows and has torpedoed a gunboat at Chunuk. Hunter-Weston despite his heavy losses will be advancing to-morrow which should divert pressure from you. Make a personal appeal to your men and Godley's to make a supreme effort to hold their ground.

(*Sd.*) "IAN HAMILTON.

P.S. You have got through the difficult business, now you have only to dig, dig, dig, until you are safe. Ian H."

The men from Gaba Tepe made off with this letter; not the men who came down here at all, but new men carrying a clear order. Be the upshot what it may, I shall never repent that order. Better to die like heroes on the enemy's ground than be butchered like sheep on the beaches like the runaway Persians at Marathon.

De Robeck and Keyes were aghast; they pat me on the back; I hope they will go on doing so if things go horribly wrong. Midnight decisions take it out of one. Turned in and slept for three solid hours like a top till I was set spinning once more at 4 a.m.

At dawn we were off Gaba Tepe. Thank God the idea of retreat had already made itself scarce. The old *Queen* let fly her first shot at 5.30 a.m. Her shrapnel is a knockout. The explosion of the monstrous shell darkens the rising sun; the bullets cover an acre; the enemy seems stunned for a while after each discharge. One after the other she took on the Turkish guns along Sari Bair and swept the skyline with them.

A message of relief and thankfulness came out to us from the shore. Seeing how much they loved us — or rather our Long Toms — we hung around until about half-past eight smothering the enemy's guns whenever they dared show their snouts. By that hour our troops had regained their grip of themselves and also of the enemy, and the firing of the Turks was growing feeble. An organised counter-attack on the grand scale at dawn was the one thing I dreaded, and that has not come off; only a bit of a push over the downland by Gaba Tepe which was steadied by one of our enormous shrapnel. About this time we heard from Hunter-Weston that there was no material change in the situation at Helles and

Sedd-el-Bahr. I wirelessed, therefore, to d'Amade telling him he would not be able to land his men at "V" under Sedd-el-Bahr as arranged but that he should bring all the rest of the French troops up from Tenedos and disembark them at "W" by Cape Helles.

About this time, also, i.e., somewhere about 9 a.m., we picked up a wireless from the O.C. "Y" Beach which caused us some uneasiness. "We are holding the ridge," it said, "till the wounded are embarked."

Why "till"? So I told the Admiral that as Birdwood seemed fairly comfortable, I thought we ought to lose no time getting back to Sedd-el-Bahr, taking "Y" Beach on our way.

At once we steamed South and hove to off "Y" Beach at 9.30 a.m. There the *Sapphire*, *Dublin* and *Goliath* were lying close inshore and we could see a trickle of our men coming down the steep cliff and parties being ferried off to the *Goliath*: the wounded no doubt, but we did not see a single soul going *up* the cliff whereas there were many loose groups hanging about on the beach. I disliked and mistrusted the looks of these aimless dawdlers by the sea. There was no fighting; a rifle shot now and then from the crests where we saw our fellows clearly. The little crowd and the boats on the beach were right under them and no one paid any attention or seemed to be in a hurry. Our naval and military signallers were at sixes and sevens. The *Goliath* wouldn't answer; the *Dublin* said the force was coming off, and we could not get into touch with the soldiers at all. At about a quarter to ten the *Sapphire* asked us to fire over the cliffs into the country some hundreds of yards further in, and so the *Queen E.* gave Krithia and the South of it a taste of her metal. Not much use as the high crests hid the intervening hinterland from view, even from the crow's nests. 147] A couple of shrapnel were also fired at the crestline of the cliff about half a mile further North where there appeared to be some snipers.

But the trickling down the cliffs continued. No one liked the look of things ashore. Our chaps can hardly be making off in this deliberate way without orders; and yet, if they *are* making off "by order," Hunter-Weston ought to have consulted me first as Birdwood consulted me in the case of the Australians and New Zealanders last night. My inclination was to take a hand myself in this affair but the Staff are clear against interference when I have no knowledge of the facts — and I suppose they are right. To see a part of my scheme, from which I had hoped so much, go wrong before my eyes is maddening! I imagined it: I pressed it through: a second Battalion was added to it and then the South Wales Borderers' Company. Many sailors and soldiers, good men, had doubts as to whether the boats could get in, or whether, having done so, men armed and accoutred would be able to scale the yellow cliffs; or whether, having by some miracle climbed, they would not be knocked off into the sea with bayonets as they got to the top. I admitted every one of these possibilities but said, every time, that taken together, they destroyed one another. If the venture seemed so desperate even to ourselves, who are desperadoes, then the enemy Chief would be of the same opinion only more so; so that, supposing we *did* get up, at least we would not find resistance organised against us. Whether this was agreed to, or not, I cannot say. The logic of a C.-in-C. has a convincing way of its own. But in all our discussions one thing was taken for granted — no one doubted that once our troops had got ashore, scaled the heights and dug themselves in, they would be able to hold on: no one doubted that, with the British Fleet at their backs, they would at least maintain their bridge-head into the enemy's vitals until we could decide what to do with it.

At a quarter past ten we steamed, with anxious minds, for Cape Helles, and on the way there, Braithwaite and I finished off our first cable to K.:

> Thanks to God who calmed the seas and to the Royal Navy who rowed our fellows ashore as coolly as if at a regatta; thanks also to the dauntless spirit shown by all ranks of both Services, we have landed 29,000 upon six beaches in the face of desperate resistance from strong Turkish Infantry forces well backed by Artillery. Enemy are entrenched, line upon line, behind wire entanglements spread to catch us wherever we might try to concentrate for an advance. Worst danger zone, the open sea, now traversed, but on land not yet out of the wood. Our main covering detachment held up on water's edge, at foot of amphitheatre of low cliffs round the little bay West of Sedd-el-Bahr. At sunset last night a dashing attack was made by the 29th Division South-west along the heights from Tekke Burnu to set free

the Dublins, Munsters and Hants, but at the hour of writing they are still pinned down to the beach.

The Australians have done wonderfully at Gaba Tepe. They got 8,000 ashore to one beach between 3.30 a.m. and 8.30 a.m.: due to their courage; organisation; sea discipline and steady course of boat practice. Navy report not one word spoken or movement made by any of these thousands of untried troops either during the transit over the water in the darkness or nearing the land when the bullets took their toll. But, as the keel of the boats touched bottom, each boat-load dashed into the water and then into the enemy's fire. At first it seemed that nothing could stop them, but by degrees wire, scrub and cliffs; thirst, sheer exhaustion broke the back of their impetus. Then the enemy's howitzers and field guns had it all their own way, forcing attack to yield a lot of ground. Things looked anxious for a bit, but by this morning's dawn all are dug in, cool, confident.

But for the number and good shooting of Turkish field guns and howitzers, Birdwood would surely have carried the whole main ridge of Sari Bair. As it is, his troops are holding a long curve upon the crests of the lower ridges, identical, to a hundred yards, with the line planned by my General Staff in their instructions and pencilled by them upon the map.

The French have stormed Kum Kale and are attacking Yeni Shahr. Although you excluded Asia from my operations, have been forced by tactical needs to ask d'Amade to do this and so relieve us from Artillery fire from the Asiatic shore.

Deeply regret to report the death of Brigadier-General Napier and to say that our losses, though not yet estimated, are sure to be very heavy.

If only this night passes without misadventures, I propose to attack Achi Baba to-morrow with whatever Hunter-Weston can scrape together of the 29th Division. Such an attack should force the enemy to relax their grip on Sedd-el-Bahr. I can look now to the Australians to keep any enemy reinforcements from crossing the waist of the Peninsula.[*]

Relief about Gaba Tepe is almost swallowed up by the "Y" Beach fiasco — as we must, I suppose, take it to be. No word yet from Hunter-Weston.

---

[*] This was my original draft; it was slightly condensed for cyphering home. — *Ian H., 1920.*

At Helles things are much the same as last night; only, the South Wales Borderers are now well dug in on a spur above Morto Bay and are confident.

At 1.45 d'Amade came aboard in a torpedo boat to see me. He has been ashore at Kum Kale and reports violent fighting and, for the time being, victory. A very dashing landing, the village stormed; house to house struggles; failure to carry the cemetery; last evening defensive measures, loopholed walls, barbed wire fastened to corpses; at night savage counter attacks led by Germans; their repulse; a wall some hundred yards long and several feet high of Turkish corpses; our own losses also very heavy and some good Officers among them. All this partly from d'Amade to me; partly his Staff to my Staff. Nogués and his brave lads have done their bit indeed for the glory of the Army of France. Meanwhile, d'Amade is anxious to get his men off soon: he cannot well stay where he is unless he carries the village of Yeni Shahr. Yeni Shahr is perched on the height a mile to the South of him, but it has been reinforced from the Besika Bay direction and to take it would be a major operation needing a disembarkation of at least the whole of his Division. He is keen to clear out: I agreed, and at 12.5 he went to make his preparations.

Ten minutes later, when we were on our way back to Gaba Tepe, the Admiral and Braithwaite both tackled me, and urged that the French should be ordered to hold on for another twenty-four hours — even if for no longer. Had they only raised their point before d'Amade left the *Queen Elizabeth*! As it is, to change my mind and my orders would upset the French very much and — on the whole — I do not think we have enough to go upon to warrant me in doing so. The Admiral has always been keen on Kum Kale and I quite understand that Naval aspect of the case. But it is all I can do, as far as things have gone, to hang on by my eyelids to the Peninsula, and let alone K.'s strong, clear order, I can hardly consent, as a soldier, to entangle myself further in Asia, before I have made good Achi Baba. We dare not lose another moment in getting a firm footing on the Peninsula and that was why I had signalled d'Amade from Gaba Tepe to bring up all the rest of his troops from Tenedos and to disembark them at "W" (seeing we were still held up at "V") and why I cannot now perceive any other issue. We are not strong enough to attack on both sides of the Straits. Given one more Division we might try: as things are, my troops won't cover the mileage. On a small scale map, in an office, you may make mole-hills of mountains; on the ground there's no escaping from its features.

As soon as the French Commander took his leave, we steamed back for Gaba Tepe, passing Cape Helles at 12.20 p.m. Weather now much brighter and warmer. Passing "Y" Beach the re-embarkation of troops was still going on. All quiet, the *Goliath* says: the enemy was so roughly handled in an attack they made last night that they do not trouble our withdrawal — too pleased to see us go, it seems! So this part of our plan has gone clean off the rails. Keyes, Braithwaite, Aspinall, Dawnay, Godfrey are sick — but their disappointment is nothing to mine. De Robeck agrees that we don't know enough yet to warrant us in fault-finding or intervention. My orders ought to have been taken before a single unwounded Officer or man was ferried back aboard ship. Never, since modern battles were invented by the Devil, has a Commander-in-Chief been so accessible to a message or an appeal from any part of the force. Each theatre has its outfit of signallers, wireless, etc., and I can either answer within five minutes, or send help, or rush myself upon the scene at 25 miles an hour with the *Q.E.'s* fifteen inchers in my pocket. Here there is no question of emergency, or enemy pressure, or of haste; so much we see plain enough with our own eyes.

Whilst having a hurried meal, Jack Churchill rushed down from the crow's nest to say that he thought we had carried the Fort above Sedd-el-Bahr. He had seen through a powerful naval glass some figures standing erect and silhouetted against the sky on the parapet. Only, he argued, British soldiers would stand against the skyline during a general action. That is so, and we were encouraged to be hopeful.

On to Gaba Tepe just in time to see the opening, the climax and the end of the dreaded Turkish counter attack. The Turks have been fighting us off and on all the time, but this is — or rather I can happily now say "was" — an organised effort to burst in through our centre. Whether burglars or battles are in question, give me sunshine. What had been a terror when Braithwaite woke me out of my sleep at midnight to meet the Gaba Tepe deputation was but a heightened, tightened sensation thirteen hours later.

No doubt the panorama was alarming, but we all of us somehow — we on the *Q.E.* — felt sure that Australia and New Zealand had pulled themselves together and were going to give Enver and his Army a very disagreeable surprise.

The contrast of the actual with the might-have-been is the secret of our confidence. Imagine, had these brave lads entrusted to us by the Commonwealth and Dominion now been crowding on the beaches — crowding into their boats — whilst some desperate rearguard was trying to hold off the onrush of the triumphant Turks. Never would any of us have got over so shocking a disaster; now they are about to win their spurs (D.V.).

Here come the Turks! First a shower of shells dropping all along the lower ridges and out over the surface of the Bay. Very pretty the shells — at half a mile! Prince of Wales's feathers springing suddenly out of the blue to a loud hammer stroke; high explosives: or else the shrapnel; pure white, twisting a moment and pirouetting as children in their nightgowns pirouette, then gliding off the field two or three together, an aerial ladies' chain. Next our projectiles, Thursby's from the *Queen*, *Triumph*, *Majestic*, *Bacchante*, *London*, and *Prince of Wales*; over the sea they flew; over the heads of our fighters; covered the higher hillsides and skyline with smudges of black, yellow and green. Smoky fellows these — with a fiery spark at their core, and wherever they touch the earth, rocks leap upwards in columns of dust to the sky. Under so many savage blows, the labouring mountains brought forth Turks. Here and there advancing lines; dots moving over green patches; dots following one another across a broad red scar on the flank of Sari Bair: others following — and yet others — and others — and others, closing in, disappearing, reappearing in close waves converging on the central and highest part of our position. The tic tac of the machine guns and the rattle of the rifles accompanied the roar of the big guns as hail, pouring down on a greenhouse, plays fast and loose amidst the peals of God's artillery: we have got some guns right up the precipitous cliff: the noise doubled; redoubled; quadrupled, expanded into one immense tiger-like growl — a solid mass of the enemy showed itself crossing the green patch — and then the good *Queen Lizzie* picked up her targets — crash!!! Stop your ears with wax.

The fire slackened. The attack had ebbed away; our fellows were holding their ground. A few, very few, little dots had run back over that green patch — the others had passed down into the world of darkness.

A signaller was flag-wagging from a peak about the left centre of our line: "The boys will never forget the *Queen Elizabeth's* help" was what he said.

Jack Churchill was right. At 1.50 a wireless came in to say that the Irish and Hants from the *River Clyde* had forced their way through Sedd-el-Bahr village and had driven the enemy clean out of all his trenches and castles. Ah, well; *that* load is off our minds: every one smiling.

Passed on the news to Birdwood: I doubt the Turks coming on again — but, in case, the 29th Division's feat of arms will be a tonic.

I was wrong. At 3 p.m. the enemy made another effort, this time on the left of our line. We shook them badly and were rewarded by seeing a New Zealand charge. Two Battalions racing due North along the coast and foothills with levelled bayonets. Then again the tumult died away.

At 4.30 we left Gaba Tepe and sailed for Helles. At 4.50 we were opposite Krithia passing "Y" Beach. The whole of the troops, plus wounded, plus gear, have vanished. Only the petrol tins they took for water right and left of their pathway up the cliff; huge diamonds in the evening sun. The enemy let us slip off without shot fired. The last boat-load got aboard the *Goliath* at 4 p.m., but they had forgotten some of their kit, so the Bluejackets rowed ashore as they might to Southsea pier and brought it off for them — and again no shot fired!

Hove to off Cape Helles at quarter past five. Joyous confirmation of Sedd-el-Bahr capture and our lines run straight across from "X" to Morto Bay, but a very sad postscript now to that message: Doughty Wylie has been killed leading the sally from the beach.

The death of a hero strips victory of her wings. Alas, for Doughty Wylie! Alas, for that faithful disciple of Charles Gordon;

protector of the poor and of the helpless; noblest of those knights ever ready to lay down their lives to uphold the fair fame of England. Braver soldier never drew sword. He had no hatred of the enemy. His spirit did not need that ugly stimulant. Tenderness and pity filled his heart and yet he had the overflowing enthusiasm and contempt of death which alone can give troops the volition to attack when they have been crouching so long under a pitiless fire. Doughty Wylie was no flash-in-the-pan V.C. winner. He was a steadfast hero. Years ago, at Aleppo, the mingled chivalry and daring with which he placed his own body as a shield between the Turkish soldiery and their victims during a time of massacre made him admired even by the Moslems. Now; as he would have wished to die, so has he died.

For myself, in the secret mind that lies beneath the conscious, I think I had given up hope that the covering detachment at "V" would work out their own salvation. My thought was to keep pushing in troops from "W" Beach until the enemy had fallen back to save themselves from being cut off. The Hampshires, Dublins and Munsters have turned their own tight corner, but I hope these fine Regiments will never forget what they owe to one Doughty Wylie, the Mr. Greatheart of our war.

The Admiral and Braithwaite have been at me again to urge that the French should hang on another day at Kum Kale. They point out that the crisis seems over for the time being both at Helles and Gaba Tepe and argue that this puts a different aspect on the whole question. That is so, and on the whole, I think "yes" and have asked d'Amade to comply.

At 6.20 p.m. started back intending to see all snug at Gaba Tepe, but, picking up some Turkish guns as targets in Krithia and on the slopes of Achi Baba, we hove to off Cape Tekke and opened fire. We soon silenced these guns, though others, unseen, kept popping. At 6.50 we ceased fire. At 7, Admiral Guépratte came on board and tells us splendid news about Kum Kale. At 2 o'clock the artillery fire from shore and ships became too hot for the Turks entrenched in the cemetery and they put up the white flag and came in as prisoners, 500 of them. A hundred more had been taken during the night fighting, but there was treachery and some of those were killed. Kum Kale has been a brilliant bit of work,

The Landing

though I fear we have lost nearly a quarter of our effectives. Guépratte agrees we would do well to hold on for another 24 hours. At a quarter past seven he took his leave and we let drop our anchor where we were, off Cape Tekke.

So now we stand on Turkish *terra firma*. The price has been paid for the first step and that is the step that counts. Blood, sweat, fire; with these we have forged our master key and forced it into the lock of the Hellespont, rusty and dusty with centuries of disuse. Grant us, O Lord, tenacity to turn it; determination to turn it, till through that open door *Queen Elizabeth* of England sails East for the Golden Horn! When in far off ages men discuss over vintages ripened in Mars the black superstitions and bloody mindedness of the Georgian savages, still they will have to drain a glass to the memory of the soldiers and sailormen who fought here.

Chapter VI – Making Good

27th April, 1915. Getting on for midnight. H.M.S. "Queen Elizabeth." All sorts of questions and answers. At 2 a.m. got a signal from Admiral Guépratte, "Situation at Kum Kale excellent, but d'Amade gave orders to re-embark. It has begun. Much regret it is not in my power to stop it."

Well, so do I regret it. With just one more Brigade at our backs we would have taken Yeni Shahr and kept our grip on Kum Kale; helping along the Fleet; countering the big guns from Asia. But, there it is; as things are I was right, and beggars can't be choosers. The French are now free to land direct at Sedd-el-Bahr, or "V," instead of round by "W."

During the small hours I wrote a second cable to K. telling him Hunter-Weston could not attack Achi Baba yesterday as his troops were worn out and some of his Battalions had lost a quarter of their effectives: also that we were already short of ammunition. Also that "Sedd-el-Bahr was a dreadful place to carry by open assault, being a labyrinth of rocks, galleries, ruins and entanglements." "With all the devoted help of the Navy, it has taken us a day's hard fighting to make good our footing. Achi Baba Hill, only a cannon shot distant, will be attacked to-morrow, the 28th."

Making Good 125

After shipping ammunition for her big guns the *Q.E.* sailed at 7 a.m. for Gaba Tepe where we found Birdwood's base, the beach, being very severely shelled. The fire seemed to drop from half the points of the compass towards that one small strip of sand, so marvellously well defiladed by nature that nine-tenths of the shot fell harmlessly into the sea. The Turkish gunners had to chance hitting something by lobbing shrapnel over the main cliff or one of the two arm-like promontories which embraced the little cove — and usually they didn't! Yet even so the beach was hardly a seaside health resort and it was a comfort to see squads of these young soldiers marching to and fro and handling packing cases with no more sign of emotion than railway porters collecting luggage at Margate.

At 7.55 we presented the Turks with some remarkable specimens of sea shells to recompense them for their trouble in so narrowly searching our beaches. They accepted our 6 inchers with a very good grace. Often one of our H.E. hundred pounders seemed to burst just where a field gun had been spotted: and before our triumphant smiles had time to disentangle themselves from our faces, the beggars would open again. But the 15-inch shrapnel, with its 10,000 bullets, was a much more serious projectile. The Turks were not taking more than they could help. Several times we silenced a whole battery by one of these monsters. No doubt these very batteries are now getting back into concealed positions where our ships' guns will not be able to find them. Still, even so, to-day and to-morrow are the two most ticklish days; after that, let the storm come — our troops will have rooted themselves firmly into the soil.

Have been speaking to the sailors about getting man-killing H.E. shell for the Mediterranean Squadron instead of the present armour piercers which break into only two or three pieces and are, therefore, in the open field, more alarming than deadly. They don't seem to think there would be much good gained by begging for special favours through routine channels. Officialdom at the Admiralty is none too keen on our show. If we can get at Winston himself, then we can rely on his kicking red tape into the waste-paper basket; otherwise we won't be met half way. As for me, I am helpless. I cannot write Winston — not on military business; least of all on Naval business. I am fixed, I won't write to any public personage re my wants and troubles excepting only K. Braithwaite agrees that, especially in war time, no man can serve two masters. There has been so much stiletto work about this war, and I have so often blamed others for their backstairs politics, that I must chance hurt feelings and shall not write letters although several of the Powers that Be have told me to keep them fully posted. The worst loss is that of Winston's ear; high principles won't obtain high explosives. As to writing to the Army Council — apart from K., the War Office is an oubliette.

The foregoing sage reflections were jotted down between 10 and 10.30 a.m., when I was clapped into solitary confinement under armour. An aeroplane had reported that the *Goeben* had come into the Narrows, presumably to fire over the Peninsula with her big guns. There was no use arguing with the sailors; they treat me as if I were a mascot. So I was duly shut up out of harm's way and out of their way whilst they made ready to take on the ship, which is just as much the cause of our Iliad as was Helen that of Homer's. Up went our captive balloon; in ten minutes it was ready to spot and at 10.15 we got off the first shot which missed the *Goeben* by just a few feet to the right. The enemy then quickly took cover behind the high cliffs and I was let out of my prison. Some Turkish transports remained, landing troops. Off flew the shell, seven miles it flew; over the Turkish Army from one sea into another. A miss! Again she let fly. This time from the balloon came down that magic formula "O.K." (plumb centre). We danced for joy though hardly able really to credit ourselves with so magnificent a shot: but it was so: in two minutes came another message saying the transport was sinking by the stern! O.K. for us; U.P. with the Turks. Simple letters to describe a pretty ghastly affair. Fancy that enormous shell dropping suddenly out of the blue on to a ship's deck swarming with troops!

A wireless from Wemyss to say that the whole of Hunter-Weston's force has advanced two miles on a broad front and that the enemy made no resistance.

At 6 p.m. a heavy squall came down from the North and the Aegean was no place for flyers whether heavier or lighter than air. All the Turkish guns we could spot from the ship had been knocked out or silenced, so Birdwood and his men were able to get along with their digging. We cast anchor off Cape Helles at about 6.30 p.m.

At 7 Hunter-Weston came on board and dined. He is full of confidence and good cheer. *He never gave any order to evacuate "Y"; he never was consulted; he does not know who gave the order.* He does well to be proud of his men and of the way they played up to-day when he called upon them to press back the enemy. He has had no losses to speak of and we are now on a fairly broad three-mile front right across the toe of the Peninsula; about two miles from the tip at Helles. Had our men not been so deadly weary, there was no reason we should not have taken Achi Baba from the Turks, who put up hardly any fight at all. But we have not got our mules or horses ashore yet in any numbers, and the digging, and carriage of stores, water and munitions to the firing line had to go on all night, so the men are still as tired as they were on the 26th, or more so. The Intelligence hear that enemy reinforcements are crossing the Narrows. So it is a pity we could not make more ground whilst we were about it, but we had no fresh men to put in and the used Battalions were simply done to a turn.

We did not talk much about the past at dinner, except — ah me, how bitterly we regretted our 10 per cent. margin to replace casualties, — a margin allowed by regulation and afforded to the B.E.F. Just think of it. To-day each Battalion of the 29th Division would have been joined by two keen Officers and one hundred keen men — fresh — all of them fresh! The fillip given would have been far, far greater than that which the mere numbers (1,200 for the Division) would seem to imply. Hunter-Weston says that he would sooner have a pick-me-up in that form than two fresh Battalions, and I think, in saying so, he says too little.

Tired or not tired, we attack again to-morrow. We must make more — much more — elbow room before the Turks get help from Asia or Constantinople.

Are we to strike before or after daylight? Hunter-Weston is clear for day and we have made it so. The hour is to be 8 a.m.

Showed H.W. the cable we got at tea time from K., quoting some message de Robeck has apparently sent home and saying, "Maxwell will give you any support from the garrison of Egypt you may require."

I am puzzled how to act on this. Maxwell won't give me "any support" I "may require"; otherwise, naturally, I'd have had the Gurkhas with me now: he has his own show to run: I have my own show to run: it is for K. to split the differences. K. gave me fair warning before I started I must not embroil him with French, France, or British politicians by squeezing him for more troops. It was up to me to take the job on those terms or leave it — and I took it on. I did think Egypt might be held to be outside this tacit covenant, but when I asked first, directly, for the Indian Brigade; secondly, for the Brigade or even for one Gurkha Battalion, I only got that chilliest of refusals — silence. Since then, there has been some change in his attitude. I do wish K. would take me more into his confidence. Never a word to me about the Indian Brigade, yet now it is on its way! Also, here comes this offer of more troops. Hunter-Weston's reading of the riddle is that troops ear-marked for the Western front are still taboo but that K. finds himself, since our successful landing, in a more favourable political atmosphere and is willing, therefore, to let us draw on Egypt. He thinks, in a word, that as far as Egypt goes, we should try and get what we can get.

Said good-night with mutual good wishes, and have worked till now (1 a.m.) answering wireless and interviewing Winter and Woodward, who had come across from the *Arcadian* to do urgent administrative work. Each seems satisfied with the way his own branch is getting on: Winter is the quicker worker. Wrote out also a second long cable to K. (the first was operations) formally asking leave to call upon Maxwell to send me the East Lancs. Division and showing that Maxwell can have my second Mounted Division in exchange.

Have thought it fair to cable Maxwell also, asking him to hold the East Lancs. handy. K.'s cable covers me so far. No Commander enjoys parting with his troops and Maxwell may play on one of the tenderest spots in K.'s adamantine heart by telling him his darling Egypt will beendangered; still it is only right to give him fair warning.

Lord Hindlip, King's Messenger, has brought us our mails.
28th April, 1915. H.M.S. "Queen Elizabeth." Off Gallipoli. At 9 a.m. General d'Amade came aboard and gave me the full account of the Kum Kale landing, a brilliant piece of work which will add

lustre even to the illustrious deeds of France. I hope the French Government will recognize this dashing stroke of d'Amade's by something more solid than a thank you.

At 9.40 General Paris and the Staff of the Naval Division also came aboard, and were telling me their doings and their plans when the noise of the battle cut short the pow-wow. The fire along the three miles front is like the rumble of an express train running over fog signals. Clearly we are not going to gain ground so cheaply as yesterday.

At 10 o'clock the *Q.E.* was steaming slowly Northwards and had reached a point close to the old "Y" landing place (well marked out by the glittering kerosine tins). Suddenly, inland, a large mass of men, perhaps two thousand, were seen doubling down a depression of the ground heading towards the coast. We had two 15-inch guns loaded with 10,000 shrapnel bullets each, but there was an agony as to whether these were our fellows falling back or Turks advancing. The Admiral and Keyes asked me. The Flag Captain was with us. The thing hung on a hair but the horror of wiping out one of my own Brigades was too much for me: 20 to 1 they were Turkish reinforcements which had just passed through Krithia — 50 to 1 they were Turks — and then — the ground seemed to swallow them from view. Ten minutes later, they broke cover half a mile lower down the Peninsula and left us no doubt as to what they were, advancing as they did in a most determined manner against some of our men who had their left flank on the cliffs above the sea.

The Turks were no longer in mass but extended in several lines, less than a pace between each man. Before this resolute attack our men, who were much weaker, began to fall back. One Turkish Company, about a hundred strong, was making an ugly push within rifle shot of our ship. Its flank rested on the very edge of the cliff, and the men worked forward like German Infantry in a regular line, making a rush of about fifty yards with sloped arms and lying down and firing. They all had their bayonets fixed. Through a glass every move, every signal, could be seen. From where we were our guns exactly enfiladed them. Again they rose and at a heavy sling trot came on with their rifles at the slope; their bayonets glittering and their Officer ten yards ahead of them waving his sword. Some one said they were cheering. Crash! and the *Q.E.* let fly a shrapnel; range 1,200 yards; a lovely shot; we followed it through the air with our eyes. Range and fuse — perfect. The huge projectile exploded fifty yards from the right of the Turkish line, and vomited its contents of 10,000 bullets clean across the stretch whereon the Turkish Company was making its last effort. When the smoke and dust cleared away nothing stirred on the whole of that piece of ground. We looked for a long time, nothing stirred.

One hundred to the right barrel — nothing left for the second barrel! The tailor of the fairy tale with his "seven at a blow" is not in it with the gunnery Lieutenant of a battleship. Our beloved *Queen* had drawn the teeth of the Turkish counter-attack on our extreme left. The enemy no longer dared show themselves over the open downs by the sea, but worked over broken ground some hundreds of yards inland where we were unable to see them. The *Q.E.* hung about here shelling the enemy and trying to help our fellows on for the whole day.

As was signalled to us from the shore by an Officer of the Border Regiment, the Turks were in great strength somewhere not easy to spot a few hundred yards inland from "Y" Beach. Some were in a redoubt, others working down a ravine. A party of our men had actually got into the trench dug by the "Y" Beach covering party on the day of the landing, but had been knocked out again, a few minutes before the *Queen Elizabeth* came to the rescue, and, in falling back, had been (so the Officer signaller told us) "badly cut up." Asked again who were being badly cut up, he replied, "All of us!"

No doubt the *Q.E.* turned up in the very nick of time, at a moment when we were being forced to retire too rapidly. A certain number of stragglers were slipping quietly back towards Cape Helles along the narrow sandy strip at the foot of the high cliffs, so, as it was flat calm, I sent Aspinall off in a small boat with orders to rally them. He rowed to the South so as to head them off and as the dinghy drew in to the shore we saw one of them strip and swim out to sea to meet it half way. By the time the young fellow reached the boat the cool salt water had given him back his presence of mind and he explained, as if it was the most natural thing in the world, that he had swum off to get help for the wounded! After landing, a show of force was needed to pull the fugitives up but once they did pull up they were splendid, and volunteered to a man to follow Aspinall back into the firing line. Many of them were wounded and the worst of these were put into a picket boat which had just that moment come along. One of the men seemed pretty bad, being hit in the head and in the body. He wanted to join in but, naturally, was forbidden to do so. Aspinall then led his little party back and climbed the cliff. When he got to the top and looked round he found this severely wounded man had not only disobeyed orders and followed him, but had found strength to lug up a box of ammunition with him.

"I ordered you not to come," said Aspinall.

"I can still pull a trigger, Sir," replied the man.[*]

To-day's experiences have been of the strangest. As armies have grown and as the range of firearms has increased, the Commander-in-Chief of any considerable force has been withdrawn further and further from the fighting. To-day I have stood in the main battery which has fired a shot establishing, in its way, a record in the annals of destruction.

On our left we had gained three miles and had been driven back a mile or rather more after doing so, apparently by fresh enemy forces. What would have been a promenade if our original covering party had stuck to "Y" Beach, had become too difficult for that wearied and greatly weakened Brigade. On the British right the 88th Brigade pushed back the Turks easily enough at first, but afterwards they too came up against stiffer resistance from what seemed to be fresh enemy formations until at last, i.e., about midday, they were held up. The Reserve were then ordered to pass through and attack. Small parties are reported to have got into Krithia and one complete Battalion gained a position commanding Krithia — so Wemyss has been credibly informed; but things went wrong; they seem to have been *just* too weak.

---

[*] I wanted very much to get this brave fellow a decoration but we were never able to trace him. — *Ian H., 1920.*

Hunter-Weston is confident as ever and says once his men have dug themselves in, even a few inches, they will hold what they have gained against any number of Turks.

We have been handicapped by the trouble that is bred in the bone of any landing on enemy soil. The General wants to strike quick and hard from the outset. To do so he must rush his men ashore and by very careful plans he may succeed; but even then, unless he can lay hands upon wharves, cranes, and all the mechanical appliances to be found in an up-to-date harbour, he cannot keep up the supply of ammunition, stores, food, water, on a like scale. He cannot do this because, just in proportion as he is successful in getting a large number of men on shore and in quickly pushing them forward some distance inland, so will it become too much for his small craft and his beach frontage to cope with the mule transport and carts. Hence, shortage of ammunition and shortage of water, which last was the worse felt to-day. But the heavy fighting at the landings was what delayed us most.

An enemy aeroplane (a Taube) has been dropping bombs on and about the *River Clyde*.

There is little of the "joy of the contest" in fighting battles with worn-out troops. Even when the men respond by doing wonders, the Commander is bound to feel his heart torn in two by their trials, in addition to having his brain tortured on anxiety's rack as to the result. The number of Officers we have lost is terrible.

Seen from the Flagship, the sun set exactly behind the purple island of Imbros, and as it disappeared sent out long flame-coloured streamers into the sky. The effect was that of a bird of Paradise bringing balm to our overwrought nerves.

Have published the following order:

> I rely on all Officers and men to stand firm and steadfast to resist the attempt of the enemy to drive us back from our present position which has been so gallantly won.
>
> The enemy is evidently trying to obtain a local success before reinforcements can reach us; but the first portion of these arrive to-morrow and will be followed by a fresh Division from Egypt.
>
> It behoves us all, French and British, to stand fast, hold what we have gained, wear down the enemy and thus be prepared for a decisive victory.

Our comrades in Flanders have had the same experience of fatigue after hard won fights. We shall, I know, emulate their steadfastness and achieve a result which will confer added laurels to French and British arms.

IAN HAMILTON,
General.

Two cables from K.:

The first repeats a cable he has sent Maxwell. He begins by saying, "In a cable just in from the Dardanelles French Admiral, I see he thinks reinforcements are needed for the troops landed on Gallipoli. Hamilton has not made any mention of this to me. All the same yesterday I cabled him as follows: "

(Here he quotes the cable already entered in by me yesterday.)

K. goes on, "I hope all your troops are being kept ready to embark, and I would suggest you should send the Territorial Division if Hamilton wants them. Peyton's transports, etc., etc., etc."

The second cable quotes mine of last night wherein I ask leave to call for the East Lancs. and says, "I feel sure you had better have the Territorial Division, and I have instructed Maxwell to embark them. My No. 4239 addressed to Maxwell and repeated to you was sent before receiving your telegram under reply. You had better tell him to send off the Division to you. I am very glad the troops have done so well. Give them a message of hearty congratulations on their successful achievement to buck them up."

Bravo K.! but kind as is your message the best buck up for the Army will be the news that the lads from Manchester are on their way to help us.

The cable people have pinned a minute to these two messages saying that the two hours' pull we have over Greenwich time ought to have let K. get my message *before* he wired to Maxwell. He may think Maxwell will take it better that way.

Before going to bed, I sent him (K.) two cables:

(1) "Last night the Turks attacked the Australians and New Zealanders in great force, charging right up to the trenches, bugles blowing and shouting 'Allah Hu!' They

were bayoneted. The French are landing to lend a hand to the 29th Division. Birdwood's men are very weary and I am supporting them with the Naval Division." These, I may say, are my very last reserves.

(2) Telling K. how "I shall now be able to cheer up my troops by the prospect of speedy reinforcements, whilst informing them of your congratulations, and appealing to them to continue as they have commenced," I go on to say that we have used up the French and the Naval Division "so that at present I have no reserve except Cox when he arrives and the remainder of the French." I also say, simply, and without any reference to the War Office previous denial that there *was* any second French Division, "D'Amade informs me that the other French Division is ready to embark if required, so I hope you will urge that it be despatched." As to the delay in letting me have the Indian Brigade; a delay which has to-day, so say the 29th Division, cost us Krithia and Achi Baba, I say "Unluckily Cox's Brigade is a day late, but I still trust it will arrive to-morrow during the day."

Bis dat qui cito dat.* O truest proverb! One fresh man on Gallipoli to-day was worth five afloat on the Mediterranean or fifty loafing around London in the Central Force. At home they are carefully totting up figures — I know them — and explaining to the P.M. and the Senior Wranglers with some complacency that the sixty thousand effective bayonets left me are enough — seeing they are British — to overthrow the Turkish Empire. So they would be if I had that number, or anything like it, for my line of battle. But what are the facts? Exactly one half of my "bayonets" spend the whole night carrying water, ammunition and supplies between the beach and the firing line. The other half of my "bayonets," those left in the firing line, are up the whole night armed mostly with spades digging desperately into the earth. Now and then there is a hell of a fight, but that is incidental and a relief.

---

* "He who gives quickly gives twice"

A single Division of my old "Central Force," so easily to be spared, so wasted where they are, could take this pick and spade work off the fighters. But the civilians think, I am certain, we are in France, with a service of trains and motor transport at our backs so that our "bayonets" are really free to devote their best energies to fighting. My troops are becoming thoroughly worn out. And when I think of the three huge armies of the Central Force I commanded a few weeks ago in England!

29th April, 1915. H.M.S. "Q.E." Off the Peninsula. A biggish sea running, subsiding as the day went on — and my mind grew calmer with the waves. For we are living hand-to-mouth now in every sense. Two days' storm would go very near starving us. Until we work up some weeks' reserve of water, food and cartridges, I shan't sleep sound. Have lent Birdwood four Battalions of the Royal Naval Division and two more Battalions are landing at Helles to form my own reserve. Two weak Battalions; that is the exact measure of my executive power to shape the course of events; all the power I have to help either d'Amade or Hunter-Weston.

Water is a worry; weather is a worry; the shelling from Asia is a thorn in my side. The sailors had hoped they would be able to shield the Southern point of the Peninsula by interposing their ships but they can't. Their gunnery won't run to it — was never meant to run to it — and with five going aeroplanes we can't do the spotting. Our Regiments, too, will not be their superb selves again — won't be anything like themselves — not until they get their terrible losses made good. There is no other way but fresh blood for it is sheer human nature to feel flat after an effort. Any violent struggle for life always lowers the will to fight even of the most cut-and-come-again: don't I remember well when Sir George asked me if the Elandslaagte Brigade had it in them to storm Pepworth? I had to tell him they were still the same Brigade but not the same men. No use smashing in the impregnable sea front if we don't get a fresh dose of energy to help us to push into the, as yet, very pregnable hinterland. Since yesterday morning, when I saw our men scatter right and left before an enemy they would have gone for with a cheer on the 25th or 26th, — ever since then I have cursed with special bitterness the lack of vision which leaves us without that 10 per cent. margin above strength which we could, and should, have had with us. The most fatal heresy in war, and, with us, the most rank, is the heresy that battles can be won without heavy loss — I don't care whether it is in men or in ships. The next most fatal heresy is to think that, having won the battle, decimated troops can go on defeating fresh enemies without getting their 10 per cent. renewed.

At 9 o'clock I boarded H.M.S. *Kennett*, a destroyer, and went ashore. Commodore Roger Keyes came along with me, and we set foot on Turkishsoil for the first time at 9.45 a.m. at "W" Beach. What a scene! An ants' nest in revolution. Five hundred of our fighting men are running to and fro between cliffs and sea carrying stones wherewith to improve our pier. On to this pier, picket boats, launches, dinghies, barges, all converge through the heavy swell with shouts and curses, bumps and hair's-breadth escapes. Other swarms of half-naked soldiers are sweating, hauling, unloading, loading, road-making; dragging mules up the cliff, pushing mules down the cliff: hundreds more are bathing, and through this pandemonium pass the quiet stretchers bearing pale, blood-stained, smiling burdens. First we spent some time speaking to groups of Officers and men and hearing what the Beachmasters and Engineers had to say; next we saw as many of the wounded as we could and then I walked across to the Headquarters of the 29th Division (half a mile) to see Hunter-Weston. A strange abode for a Boss; some holes burrowed into a hillock. In South Africa, this feature which looks like, and actually is, a good observing post, would have been thoroughly searched by fire. The Turks seem, so far, to have left it pretty well alone.

After a long talk during which we fixed up a good many moot points, went on to see General d'Amade. Unluckily he had just left to go on to the Flagship to see me. I did not like to visit the French front in his absence, so took notes of the Turkish defences on "V" and had a second and a more thorough inspection of the beach, transport and storage arrangements on "W."

Roper, Phillimore (R.N.) and Fuller stood by and showed me round.

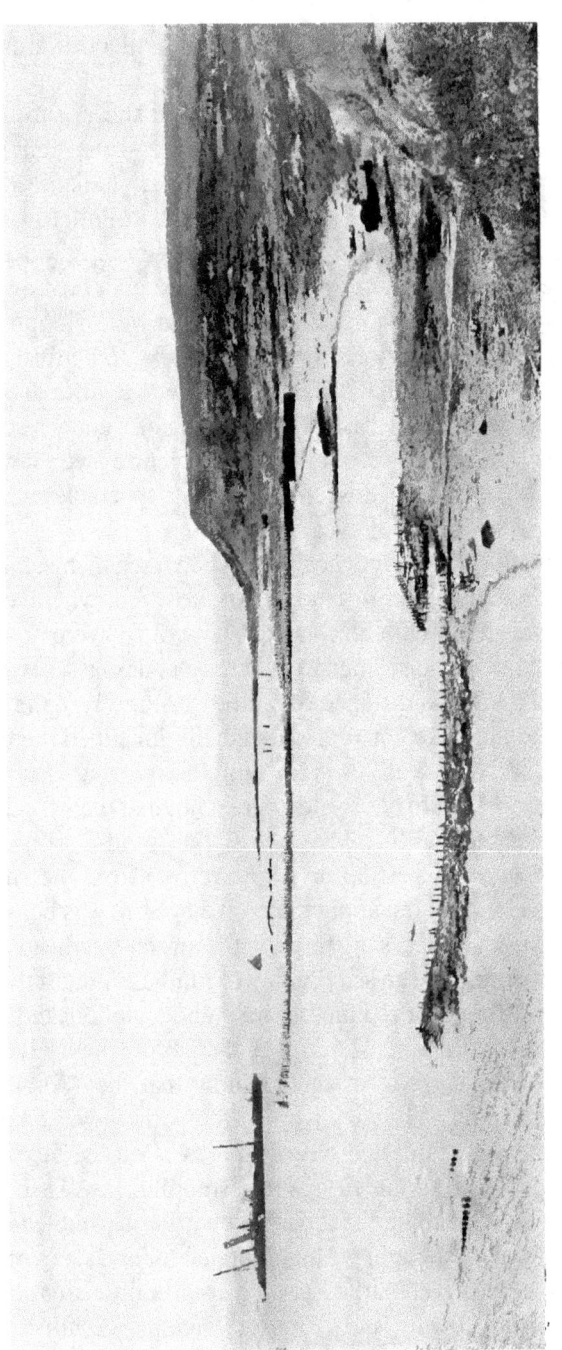

'W' Beach

At 1.30 p.m. re-embarked on the *Q.E.* and sailed towards Gaba Tepe.

After watching our big guns shooting at the enemy's field pieces for some time I could stand it no longer — the sight seeing I mean — and boarded the destroyer *Colne* which took me towards the beach. Commodore Keyes came along, also Pollen, Dawnay and Jack Churchill. Our destroyer got within a hundred yards or so of the shore when we had to tranship into a picquet boat owing to the shallow water. Quite a good lot of bullets were plopping into the water, so the Commodore ordered the *Colne* to lie further out. At this distance from the beach, withdrawn a little from the combat, (there was a hottish scrimmage going on), and yet so close that friends could be recognised, the picture we saw was astonishing. No one has ever seen so strange a spectacle and I very much doubt if any one will ever see it again.

The Australians and New Zealanders had fixed themselves into the crests of a series of high sandy cliffs, covered, wherever they were not quite sheer, with box scrub. These cliffs were not in the least like what they had seemed to be through our glasses when we reconnoitred them at a distance of a mile or more from the shore. Still less were they like what I had originally imagined them to be from the map. Their features were tumbled, twisted, scarred — unclimbable, one would have said, were it not that their faces were now pock-marked with caves like large sand-martin holes, whereinthe men were resting or taking refuge from the sniping. From the trenches that ran along the crest a hot fire was being kept up, and swarms of bullets sang through the air, far overhead for the most part, to drop into the sea that lay around us. Yet all the time there were full five hundred men fooling about stark naked on the water's edge or swimming, shouting and enjoying themselves as it might be at Margate. Not a sign to show that they possess the things called nerves. While we were looking, there was an alarm, and long, lean figures darted out of the caves on the face of the cliffs and scooted into the firing line, stooping low as they ran along the crest. The clatter of the musketry was redoubled by the echoing cliffs, and I thought we had dropped in for a scrap of some dimensions as we disembarked upon a fragile little floating pier and were met by Birdie and Admiral Thursby. A full General landing to inspect overseas is entitled to a salute of 17 guns — well, I got my dues.

But there is no crisis; things are quieter than they have been since the landing, Birdie says, and the Turks for the time being have been beat. He tells me several men have already been shot whilst bathing but there is no use trying to stop it: they take the off chance. So together we made our way up a steep spur, and in two hours had traversed the first line trenches and taken in the lie of the land. Half way we met Generals Bridges and Godley, and had a talk with them, my first, with Bridges, since Duntroon days in Australia. From the heights we could look down on to the strip of sand running Northwards from Ari Burnu towards Suvla Bay. There were machine guns here which wiped out the landing parties whenever they tried to get ashore North of the present line. The New Zealanders took these with the bayonet, and we held five or six hundred yards more coast line until we were forced back by Turkish counter-attacks in the afternoon and evening of the 25th. The whole stretch is now dominated by Turkish fire from the ridges, and along it lie the bodies of those killed at the first onset, and afterwards in the New Zealand bayonet charge. Several boats are stranded along this no man's land; so far all attempts to get out at night and bury the dead have only led to fresh losses. No one ever landed out of these boats — so they say.

Towards evening we re-embarked on the *Colne* and at the very moment of transhipment from the picquet boat the enemy opened a real hot shrapnel fire, plastering with impartiality and liberality our trenches, our beaches and the sea. The *Colne* was in strangely troubled water, but, although the shot fell all about her, neither she nor the picquet boat was touched. Five minutes later we should have caught it properly! The Turkish guns are very well hidden now, and the *Q.E.* can do nothing against them without the balloon to spot; we can't often spare one of our five aeroplanes for Gaba Tepe. Going back we had some long range shots with the 15-inch guns at batteries in rear of Achi Baba.

Anchored off Cape Helles at dark. A reply in from Maxwell about the East Lancs. They are coming!

The worst enemy a Chief has to face in war is an alarmist. The Turks are indeed stout and terrifying fellows when seen, not in a poetry book but in a long line running at you in a heavy jogtrot way with fixed bayonets gleaming. But they don't frighten me as much as one or two of my own friends. No matter. We are here to stay; in so far as my fixed determination can make it so; alive or dead, we stay.

30th April, 1915. H.M.S. Queen Elizabeth. From dawn to breakfast time all hands busy slinging shells — modern war sinews — piles of them — aboard. The Turks are making hay while the sun shines and are letting "V" Beach have it from their 6-inch howitzers on the plains of Troy. So, once upon a time, did Paris shoot forth his arrows over that selfsame ground and plug proud Achilles in the heel — and never surely was any fabulous tendon more vulnerable than are our Southern beaches from Asia. The audacious Commander Samson cheers us up. He came aboard at 9.15 a.m. and stakes his repute as an airman that his fellows will duly spot these guns and that once they do so the ships will knock them out. I was so pleased to hear him say so that I took him ashore with me to "W" Beach, where he was going to fix up a flight over the Asiatic shore, as well as select a flat piece of ground near the tip of the Peninsula's toe to alight upon.

Saw Hunter-Weston: he is quite happy. Touched on "Y" Beach; concluded least said soonest mended. The issues of the day before yesterday's battle seem certainly to have hung on a hair. Apart from "Y" beach might-have-beens, it seems that, further inland, detachments of our men got into a position dominating Krithia; a position from which — could they have held it — Turkish troops in or South of Krithia could have been cut off from their supplies. These men saw the Turks clear out of Krithia taking machine guns with them. But after half an hour, as we did not come on, they began to come back. We were too weak and only one Battalion was left of our reserves — otherwise the day was ours. Street, the G.S.O.I. of the Division, was in the thick of the battle — too far in for his rank, I am told, and he is most emphatic that with one more Brigade Achi Baba would now be in our hands. He said this to me in presence of his own Chief and I believe him, although I had rather disbelieve. To my mind "a miss is as good as a mile" should run a "miss is far worse than a mile." He is a sober-spoken, most gallant Officer. But it can't be helped. This is not the first time in history when the lack of a ha'porth of tar has spoilt the ship of State. I would bear my ills without a groan were it not that from the very moment when I set eyes on the Narrows I was sent to prize open, I had set my heart upon just this very identical ha'porth of tar — *videlicet*,* the Indian Brigade.

Our men are now busy digging themselves into the ground they gained on the 28th. The Turks have done a good lot of gunnery but no real counter-attack. Hunter-Weston's states show that during the past twenty-four hours well over half of his total strength are getting their artillery ashore, building piers, making roads, or bringing up food, water and ammunition into the trenches. This does not take into account men locally struck off fighting duty as cooks, orderlies, sentries over water, etc., etc. Altogether, it seems that not more than one-third of our fast diminishing total are available for actual fighting purposes. Had we even a Brigade of those backward Territorial reserve Battalions with whom the South of England is congested, they would be worth I don't know what, for they would release their equivalent of first-class fighting men to attend to their own business — the fighting.

There are quite a little budget of knotty points to settle between Hunter-Weston and d'Amade, so I made a careful note of them and went along to French Headquarters. By bad luck d'Amade was away, up in the front trenches, and I could not well deliver myself to des Coigns. So I said I would come again sometime to-morrow and once more wended my way along the busy beaches, and in doing so revisited the Turkish defences of "V" and "W." The more I look, the more do I marvel at the invincible spirit of the British soldier. Nothing is impossible to him; no General knows what he can do till he tries. Therefore, he, the British General, must always try! must never listen to the rule-of-thumb advisers who seek to chain down adventure to precedent. But our wounds make us weaker and weaker. Oh that we could fill up the gaps in the thinned ranks of those famous Regiments....!

---

* "Namely."

Had ten minutes' talk with the French Captain commanding the battery of 75's now dug in close to the old Fort, where General d'Amade sleeps, or rather, is supposed to sleep. Here is the noisiest spot on God's earth. Not only do the 75's blaze away merrily from morn till dewy eve, and again from dewy eve till morn, to a tune that turns our gunners green with envy, but the enemy are not slow in replying, and although they have not yet exactly found the little beggars (most cunningly concealed with green boughs and brushwood), yet they go precious near them with big shell and small shell, shrapnel and H.E. As I was standing here I was greeted by an old Manchurian friend, le capitaine Reginald Kahn. He fought with the Boers against us and has taken his immense bulk into one campaign after another. A very clever writer, he has been entrusted by the French Government with the compilation of their official history of these operations.

On my way back to the *Arcadian* (we are leaving the *Queen Elizabeth* for a time) — I met a big batch of wounded, knocked out, all of them, in the battle of the 28th. I spoke to as many of them as I could, and although some were terribly mutilated and disfigured, and although a few others were clearly dying, one and all kept a stiff upper lip — one and all were, or managed to appear — more than content — happy! This scene brought tears into my eyes. The courage of our soldiers goes far beyond belief. Were it not so war would be unbearable. How strongly God keeps the balance even. In fullest splendour the soul shines out amidst the dark shadows of adversity; as a fire goes out when the sunlight strikes it, so the burning, essential quality in men is stifled by prosperity and success.

Later. Our battleships have been bombarding Chunuk — chucking shells into it from the Aegean side of the Peninsula — and a huge column of smoke is rising up into the evening sky. A proper bonfire on the very altar of Mars.

1st May, 1915. H.M.S. "Arcadian." Went ashore first thing. Odd shells on the wing. Visited French Headquarters. Again d'Amade was away. Had a long talk with des Coigns, the Chief of Staff, and told him I had just heard from Lord K. that the 1st Brigade of the new French Division would sail for the Dardanelles on the 3rd inst. Des Coigns is overjoyed but a tiny bit hurt, too, that French Headquarters should get the news first from me and not from their own War Ministry. He insists on my going round the French trenches and sent a capitaine de la Fontaine along with me. Until to-day I had quite failed to grasp the extent of the ground we had gained. But we want a lot more before we can begin to feel safe. The French trenches are not as good as ours by a long chalk, and bullets keep coming through the joints of the badly built sandbag revetment. But they say, "*Un peu de repos, après, vous verrez, mon général.*"*

During my peregrinations I struck the Headquarters of the Mediterranean Brigade under General Vandenberg, who came round his own men with me. A sturdy, thickset fair man with lots of go and very cheery. He is of Dutch descent. Later on I came to the Colonial Brigade Headquarters and made the acquaintance of Colonel Ruef, a fine man — every inch a soldier. The French have suffered severely but are in fine fighting form. They are enchanted to hear about their second Division. For some reason or another they have made up their minds that France is not so keen as we are to make a present of Constantinople to Russia. Their intelligence on European questions seems much better than ours and they depress me by expressing doubts as to whether the Grand Duke Nicholas has munitions enough to make further headway against the Turks in the Caucasus: also, as to whether he has even stuff enough to equip Istomine and my rather visionary Army Corps.

By the time we had passed along the whole of the French second line and part of their front line trenches, I had had about enough. So took leave of these valiant Frenchmen and cheery Senegalese and pushed on to the advanced observation post of the Artillery where I met General Stockdale, commanding the 15th Brigade, R.F.A., and not only saw how the land lay but heard some interesting opinions. Also, some ominous comments on what armies spend and what Governments scrimp: that is ammunition.

At 3 p.m., got back having had a real good sweat. Must have

---

* "A little rest afterwards, you'll see, my General."

walked at least a dozen miles. Soon afterwards Cox, commanding the 29th Indian Brigade, came on board to make his salaam. Better late than never is all I could say to him: he and his Brigade are sick at not having been on the spot to give the staggering Turks a knock-out on the 28th, but he's going to lose no more chances; his men are landing now and he hopes to get them all ashore in the course of the day.

The Intelligence have just translated an order for the 25th April found upon the dead body of a Turkish Staff Officer. "Be sure," so it runs, "that no matter how many troops the enemy may try to land, or how heavy the fire of his artillery, it is absolutely impossible for him to make good his footing. Supposing he does succeed in landing at one spot, no time should be left him to co-ordinate and concentrate his forces, but our own troops must instantly press in to the attack and with the help of our reserves in rear he will forthwith be flung back into the sea."

2nd May, 1915. H.M.S. "Arcadian." Had a sleepless night and strain was too great to write or do anything but stand on bridge and listen to the firing or go down to the General Staff and see if any messages had come to hand.

About 10 p.m. I was on the bridge thinking how dark it was and how preternaturally still; I felt all alone in the world; nothing stirred; even the French 75's had ceased their nerve-racking bark, and then, suddenly, in one instant, hell was let loose upon earth. Like a hundred peals of thunder the Turkish artillery from both Continents let fly their salvoes right, left and centre, and the French and ourselves did not lose many seconds in reply. The shells came from Asia and Achi Baba: in a fiery shower, they fell upon the lines of our front trenches. Half an hour the bombardment and counter-bombardment, and then there arose the deadly crepitation of small arms — no messages — ten times I went back and forward to the signal room — no messages — until a new and dreadful sound was carried on the night wind out to sea — the sound of the shock of whole regiments — the Turkish Allah Din! — our answering loud Hurrahs. The moments to me were moments of unrelieved agony. I tried to think of some possible source of help I had overlooked and could not. To hear the battle cries of the fighting men and be tied to this *Arcadian* — what torture!

Soon, amidst the dazzling yellow flashes of the bursting shells and star bombs, there rose in beautiful parabolas all along our front coloured balls of fire, green, red or white; signals to their own artillery from the pistols of the Officers of the enemy. An ugly feature, these lights so beautiful, because, presumably, in response to their appeal, the Turkish shell were falling further down the Peninsula than at first, as if they had lengthened their range and fuse, i.e., as if we were falling back.

By now several disquietening messages had come in, especially from the right, and although bad news was better than no news, or seemed so in that darkness and confusion, yet my anxious mind was stretched on the rack by inability to get contact with the Headquarters of the 29th Division and the French. Bullets or shell had cut some of the wires, and the telephone only worked intermittently. At 2 in the morning I had to send a battalion of my reserve from the Royal Naval Division to strengthen the French right. At 3 a.m. we heard — not from the British — that the British had been broken and were falling back upon the beaches. At 4 we heard from Hunter-Weston that, although the enemy had pierced our line at one or two points, they had now been bloodily repulsed. Thereupon, I gave the word for a general counter-attack and our line began to advance. The whole country-side was covered with retreating Turks and, as soon as it was light enough to see, our shrapnel mowed them down by the score. We gained quite a lot of ground at first, but afterwards came under enfilade fire from machine guns cunningly hidden in folds of the ground. There was no forcing of these by any *coup de main* especially with worn out troops and guns which had to husband their shell, and so we had to fall back on our starting point. We have made several hundreds prisoners, and have killed a multitude of the enemy.

I took Braithwaite and others of the G.S. with me and went ashore. At the pier at "W" were several big lighters filled with wounded who were about to be towed out to Hospital ships. Spent the best part of an hour on the lighters. The cheeriness of the gallant lads is amazing — superhuman!

Went on to see Hunter-Weston at his Headquarters, — a queer

Headquarters it would seem to our brethren in France! Braithwaite, Street, Hunter-Weston and myself.

Some of our units are shaken, no doubt, by loss of Officers (complete); by heavy losses of men (not replaced, or replaceable, under a month) and by sheer physical exertion. Small wonder then that one weak spot in our barrier gave way before the solid mass of the attacking Turks, who came on with the bayonet like true Ghazis. The first part of the rifle fire last night was entirely from our own men. The break by one battalion gave a grand chance to the only Territorial unit in the 29th Division, the 5th Royal Scots, who have a first-class commanding Officer and are inspired not only by the indomitable spirit of their regular comrades, but by the special fighting traditions of Auld Reekie. They formed to a flank as if on a peace parade and fell on to the triumphant Turkish stormers with the cold steel, completely restoring the fortunes of the night. It would have melted a heart of stone, Hunter-Weston said, to see how tired our men looked in the grey of morning when my order came to hand urging them to counter-attack and pursue. Not the spirit but the flesh failed them. With a fresh Division on the ground nothing would have prevented us from making several thousand prisoners; whether they would have been able to rush the machine guns and so gain a great victory was more problematical. Anyway, our advance at dawn was half heroic, half lamentable. The men were so beat that if they tripped and fell, they lay like dead things. The enemy were almost in worse plight and so we took prisoners, but as soon as we came up against nerveless, tireless machine guns we had to stagger back to our trenches. 191]

As I write dead quiet reigns on the Peninsula, literally dead quiet. Not a shot from gun or rifle and the enemy are out in swarms over the plain! but they carry no arms; only stretchers and red crescent flags, for they are bearing away their wounded and are burying their piles of dead. It is by my order that the Turks are being left a free hand to carry out this pious duty.

The stretcher-bearers carry their burdens over a carpet of flowers. Life is here around us in its most exquisite forms. Those flowers! Poppies, cornflowers, lilies, tulips whose colours are those of the rainbow. The coast line curving down and far away to meet the extravagant blueness of the Aegean where the battleships lie silent — still — smoke rising up lazily — and behind them, through the sea haze, dim outlines of Imbros and Samothrace. Going back, found that the lighter loads of wounded already taken off have by no means cleared the beach. More wounded and yet more. Here, too, are a big drove of Turkish prisoners; fine-looking men; well clothed; well nourished; more of them coming in every minute and mixing up in the strangest and friendliest way with our wounded with whom they talk in some dumb-crambo lingo. The Turks are doing yeoman service for Germany. If only India were pulling her weight for us on the same scale, we should by now be before the gates of Vienna.

In the afternoon d'Amade paid me a long visit. He was at first rather chilly and I soon found out it was on account of my having gone round his lines during his absence. He is quite right, and I was quite wrong, and I told him so frankly which made "all's well" in a moment. My only excuse, namely, that I had been invited — nay pressed — to do so by his own Chief of Staff, I thought it wiser to keep to myself. Yesterday evening he got a cable from his own War Ministry confirming K.'s cable to me about the new French Division; Numbered the 156th, it is to be commanded by Bailloud, a distinguished General who has held high office in Africa — seventy years old, but sharp as a needle. D'Amade is most grateful for the battalion of the Naval Division; most complimentary about the Officers and men and is dying to have another which is, *évidemment*,* a real compliment. He promises if I will do so to ration them on the best of French conserves and wine. The fact is, that the proportion of white men in the French Division is low; there are too many Senegalese. The battalion from the Naval Division gives, therefore, greater value to the whole force by being placed on the French right than by any other use I can put it to although it does seem strange to separate a small British unit by the entire French front from its own comrades.

When d'Amade had done, de Robeck came along. No one on the *Q.E.* slept much last night: to them, as to us, the dark hours had passed like one nightmare after another. Were we miles back from

---

* "Of course."

the trenches as in France, and frankly dependent on our telephones, the strain would be softened by distance. Here we see the flashes; we hear the shots; we stand in our main battery and are yet quite cut off from sharing the efforts of our comrades. Too near for reflection; too far for intervention: on tenter hooks, in fact; a sort of mental crucifixion.

Cox is not going to take his Punjabi Mahommedans into the fighting area but will leave them on "W" Beach. He says if we were sweeping on victoriously he would take them on but that, as things are, it would not be fair to them to do so. That is exactly why I asked K. and Fitz for a Brigade of Gurkhas; not a mixed Brigade.

3rd May, 1915. H.M.T. "Arcadian." At 9 p.m. last night there was another furious outburst of fire; mainly from the French. 75's and rifles vied against one another in making the most infernal *fracas*. I thought we were in for an *encore* performance, but gradually the uproar died away, and by midnight all was quiet. The Turks had made another effort against our right, but they could not penetrate the rampart of living fire built up against them and none got within charging distance of our trenches, so d'Amade 'phones. He also says that a mass of Turkish reserves were suddenly picked up by the French searchlights and the 75's were into them like a knife, slicing and slashing the serried ranks to pieces before they had time to scatter.

Birdie boarded us at 9 a.m. and told us his troubles. He has straightened out his line on the left; after a fierce fight which has cost him no less than 700 fresh casualties. But he feels safer now and is pretty happy! he is sure he can hold his own against anything except thirst. His *band-o-bast* for taking water up to the higher trenches is not working well, and the springs he has struck along the beach and in the lower gullies are brakish. We are going to try and fix this up for him.

At 10 o'clock went ashore with Braithwaite and paid visits to Hunter-Weston and to d'Amade. We had a conference with each of them, Generals and Staff who could be spared from the fighting being present. The feeling is hopeful if only we had more men and especially drafts to fill up our weakened battalions. The shell question is serious although, in this respect, thank Heavens, the French are quite well found. When we got back to the ship, heard a Taube had just been over and dropped a bomb, which fell exactly between the *Arcadian* and the ammunition ship, anchored only about 60 or 70 yards off us!

4th May, 1915. H.M.T. "Arcadian." Last night again there was all sorts of firing and fighting going on, throughout those hours peaceful citizens ear-mark for sleep. I had one or two absolutely hair-raising messages. Not only were the French troops broken but the 29th Division were falling back into the sea. Though frightened to death, I refused to part with my reserve and made ready to go and take command of it at break of dawn. In the end the French and Hunter-Weston beat off the enemy by themselves. But there is no doubt that some of the French, and two Battalions of our own, are badly shaken, — no wonder! Both Hunter-Weston and d'Amade came on board in the forenoon, Hunter-Weston quite fixed that *his* men are strained to breaking point and d'Amade emphatic that *his* men will not carry on through another night unless they get relief. To me fell the unenviable duty of reconciling two contrary persuasions. Much argument as to where the enemy was making his main push; as to the numbers of our own rifles (French and English) and the yards of trenches each (French and English) have to hold. I decided after anxious searching of heart to help the French by taking over some portion of their line with the Naval Brigade. There was no help for it. Hunter-Weston agreed in the end with a very good grace.

In writing K. I try to convey the truth in terms which will neither give him needless anxiety or undue confidence. The facts have been stated very simply, plus one brief general comment. I tell him that the Turks would be playing our game by these assaults were it not that in the French section they break through the Senegalese and penetrate into the position. I add a word of special praise for the Naval Division, they have done so well, but I know there are people in the War Office who won't like to hear it. I say, "I hope the new French Division will not steam at economic, but full, speed"; and I sum up by the sentence, "The times are anxious, but I believe the enemy's cohesion should suffer more than ours by these repeated night attacks."

Chapter VII – Shells

To-day, the 4th, shells were falling from Asia on both "V" and "W" Beaches. We have landed aeroplanes on the Peninsula. The Taube has been bothering us again, but wound up its manœuvres very decently by killing some fish for our dinner. Approved an out-spoken cable from my Ordnance to the War Office. Heaven knows we have been close-fisted with our meagre stocks, but when the Turks are coming right on to the assault it is not possible to prevent a spurt of rapid fire from men who feel the knife at their throat. "Ammunition is becoming a very serious matter, owing to the ceaseless fighting since April 25th. The *Junia* has not turned up and has but a small supply when she does. 18 pr. shell is vital necessity."

5th May, 1915. H.M.T. "Arcadian." A wearing, nerve-racking, night-long fire by the Turks and the French 75's. They, at least, both of them, seem to have a good supply of shell. To the Jews, God showed Himself once as a pillar of fire by night; to the French soldier whose God is the 75 He reveals Himself in just the same way, safeguarding his flimsy trenches from the impact of the infidel horde. The curse of the method is its noise — let alone its cost. But last night it came off: no Turks got through anywhere on the French front and the men had not to stand to their arms or use their rifles. We British, worse luck, can't dream of these orgies of explosives. Our batteries last night did not fire a shot and the men had to drive back the enemy by rifle fire. They did it easily enough but the process is wearing.

An answer has come to my prayer for 18 pr. stuff: not the answer that turns away wrath, but the answer that provokes a plaster saint.

"We have under consideration your telegram of yesterday. The ammunition supply for your force, however, was never calculated on the basis of a prolonged occupation of the Gallipoli Peninsula, we will have to reconsider the position if, after the arrival of the reinforcements now on their way out to you, the enemy cannot be driven back and, in conjunction with the Fleet, the Forts barring the passage of the Dardanelles cannot be reduced. It is important to push on."

Now von Donop is a kindly man despite that overbearing "von": yet, he speaks to us like this! The survivors of our half dead force are to "push on"; for, "it is important to push on" although Whitehall seems to have time and to spare to "consider" my cable and to "reconsider the position." Death first, diagnosis afterwards. Wherever is the use of reconsidering the position now? The position has taken charge. When a man has jumped off Westminster Bridge to save a drowning Russian his position has got beyond reconsideration: there is only one thing to do — as quickly as you can, as much help as you can — and if it comes to a choice between the *quick* and the *much*: hark to your swimmer and hear him cry "Quick! Quick!! Quick!!!"

The War Office urge me to throw my brave troops yet once more against machine guns in redoubts; to do it on the cheap; to do it without asking for the shell that gives the attack a sporting chance. I don't say they are wrong in so saying; there may be no other way out of it; but I do say the War Office stand convicted of having gone hopelessly wrong in their estimates and preparations. For we must have been held up somewhere, surely; we must have fought *somewhere*. I suppose, even if we had forced the Straits — even if we had taken Constantinople without firing a shot, we must have fought somewhere! Otherwise, a child's box of tin soldiers sent by post would have been just the thing for the Dardanelles landing! No; it's not the advice that riles me: it's the fact that people who have made a mistake, and should be sorry, slur over my appeal for the stuff advances are made of and yet continue to urge us on as if we were hanging back.

A strong wind blows and Helles is smothered in dust. Hunter-Weston spent an hour with me this morning and an hour with the G.S. putting the final touches to the plan of attack discussed by us yesterday. The Lancashire Brigade of the 42nd Division has landed.

Hunter-Bunter stayed to lunch.

Later. In the afternoon went ashore and inspected the Lancashire Brigade of the East Lancs. Division just landed; and a very fine lot of Officers and men they are. They are keen and ready for tomorrow. Yes, to-morrow we attack again: I have men enough now but very, very little shell. The Turks have given us three bad nights and they ought to be worn out. With our sea power we can shift a couple of Brigades from Gaba Tepe to Helles or vice versa quicker than the Turks can march from the one theatre to the other. So the first question has been whether to reinforce Gaba Tepe from Helles or vice versa. For reasons too long to write here I have decided to attack in the South especially as I had a cable from K. himself yesterday in which he makes the suggestion:

"I hope," he says, "the 5th" (that's to-day) "will see you strong enough to press on to Achi Baba anyway, as delay will allow the Turks to bring up more reinforcements and to make unpleasant preparations for your reception. The Australians and New Zealanders will have had reinforcements from Egypt by then, and, if they hold on to their trenches with the help of the Naval Division, could spare you a good many men for the advance."

Old K. is as right as rain here but a little bit after the shower. Had he and Maxwell tumbled to the real situation when I first saw with my own eyes the lie of the land instead of the lies on their maps; and had they let me have the Brigade of Gurkhas I asked for by my letters and by my cable of 24th March, and by word of mouth and telephone up to the last moment of my leaving Egypt, these homilies about the urgency of seizing Achi Baba would be beside the mark, seeing we should be sitting on the top of it.

In the matter of giving K. is built on the model of Pharaoh: nothing less than the firstborn of the nation will make him suffer his subjects to depart from Egypt; and Maxwell sees eye to eye with him — that is natural. No word of the bombs and trench mortars I asked for six weeks ago, but the "bayonets" are coming in liberally now.

Two of Birdwood's Brigades sail down to-night and join up with a Brigade from the Naval Division, thus making a new composite Division for the Southern theatre. The 29th, who have lost so very heavily, are being strengthened by the new Lancashire Fusilier Brigade, and Cox's Indian Brigade. By no manner the same thing, this, as getting drafts to fill up the ranks of the 29th. Always in war there is three times better value in filling up an old formation than in making up the total by bringing in a new formation. I have given the French the Naval Brigade; the new, Naval-Australian Division is to form my general reserve.

So there! To-morrow morning. We have men enough, and good men too, but we are short of pebbles for Goliath of Achi Baba. These three nights have made a big hole in our stocks. Hunter-Weston feels that all is in our favour but the artillery. In Flanders, he says, they would never attack with empty limbers behind them; they would wait till they were full up. But the West is not in its essence a time problem; there, they can wait — next week — next month. If we wait one week the Turks will have become twice as strong in their numbers, and twice as deep in their trenches, as they are to-day. Hunter-Weston and d'Amade see that perfectly. I hold the idea myself that it would be good tactics, seeing shell shortage is our weakness, to make use of the half hour before dawn to close with the enemy and then fight it out on their ground. To cross the danger zone, in fact, by night and overthrow the enemy in the grey dawn. But Hunter-Weston says that so many regimental officers have been lost he fears for the Company leading at night: for that, most searching of military tests, nothing but the best will do.

Hard up as we are for shell he thinks it best to blaze it away freely before closing and to trust our bayonets when we get in. He and d'Amade have both of them their Western experience to guide them. I have agreed, subject only to the condition that we must keep some munitions in reserve until we hear for certain that more is on its way.

The enemy had trusted to their shore defences. There was no second line behind them — not this side of Achi Baba, at least. Now, i.e., ever since the failure of their grand attempt on the night of the 2nd-3rd May, they have been hard at work. Already their lines cover quite half the ground between the Aegean and the Straits; whilst, in rear again, we can see wired patches which we guess to be enfilading machine gun redoubts. We must resolutely and at all cost make progress and smash up these new spiders' webs of steel before they connect into elastic but unbreakable patterns.

9th May, 1915. H.M.T. "Arcadian." Three days on the rack! Since the morning of the 6th not a word have I written barring one or two letters and one or two hasty scraps of cables. Now, D.V., there is the best part of a day at my disposal and it is worth an effort to put that story down.

First I had better fix the sequence of the munition cables, for upon them the whole attack has hung — or rather, hung fire.

On the 6th, the evening of the opening day, we received a postscript to the refusal already chronicled:

> Until you can submit a return of the amount you have in hand to enable us to work out the rates of expenditure, it is difficult to decide about further supplies of ammunition.

When I read this I fell on my knees and prayed God to grant me patience. Am I to check the number of rounds in the limbers; on the beaches and in transit during a battle? Two days after my S.O.S. the War Office begin to think about tables of averages!

I directed my answer to Lord K. himself:

With reference to your No. 4432 of 5th inst., please turn to my letter to you of 30th March,* wherein I have laid stress on the essential difference in the matter of ammunition supply between the Dardanelles and France. In France, where the factories are within 24 hours' distance from the firing line, it may be feasible to consider and reconsider situations, including ammunition supply. Here we are distant a fortnight. I consider that 4.5 inch, 18 pr. and other ammunition, especially Mark VII rifle ammunition, should instantly be despatched here *via* Marseilles.

Battle in progress. Advance being held up by stubborn opposition.

Within a few hours K.'s reply came in; he says:

It is difficult for me to judge the situation unless you can send me your expenditure of ammunition for which we have repeatedly asked. The question is not affected by the other considerations you mention.

If space and time have no bearing on strategy and tactics, then K. is right. If ships sail over the sea as fast as railways run across the land; if Helles is nearer Woolwich than Calais; then he is right. I use the capital K. here impersonally, for I am sure the great man did not indite the message himself even though it may be headed from him to me.

Late that night came another cable from the Master General of the Ordnance saying he was sending out "in the next relief ship 10,000 rounds of 18 pr. shrapnel, and 1,000 rounds of 4.5 inch high explosive."

But why the next relief ship? It won't get here for another three weeks and by that time we should be, by all the laws of nature and of war, in Davy Jones's locker. True, we don't mean to be, whatever the Ordnance may do or leave undone but, so far as I can see, that won't be their fault. Neither I nor my Staff can make head or tail of these cables. They seem so unlike K.; so unlike all the people. Here we are: The Turks in front of us — too close: the deep sea behind us — too close. We beg them "instantly" to send

---

* Quoted on p. 56.

us 4.5 inch and other ammunition; "instantly, *via* Marseilles": they tell us in reply that they will send 1,000 rounds of the vital stuff, the 4.5 high explosive, "*in the next relief ship*"! Why, even in the South African War, before the siege of Ladysmith, one battery would fire five hundred rounds in a day. And this 1,000 rounds in the next relief ship (*via* Alexandria) will take three weeks to get to us whereas stress was laid by me upon the Marseilles route.

Now, to-day, (the 9th), I have at last been able to send the Ordnance a statement (made under extreme difficulty) of our ammunition expenditure; up to the 5th May; i.e., before the three days' battle began. We were then nine million small arm still to the good having spent eleven million. We had shot away 23,000 shrapnel, 18 pr., and had 48,000 in hand. We had fired off 5,000 of that (most vital) 4.5 howitzer and had 1,800 remaining. A.P.S. has been added saying the amounts shown had been greatly reduced by the last two days' battle. Actually, they have fallen to less than half and, as I have said, we had, on the evening of the 7th, only 17,000 rounds of 18 pr. on hand for the whole Peninsula. Out of this we have fought the battle of the 8th and I believe we have run down now to under 10,000, some fear as low as 5,000.

Very well. Now for my last night's cable which, in the opinion of my Officers, summarises general result of lack of shell:

> For the past three days we have fought our hardest for Achi Baba winding up with a bayonet charge by the whole force along the entire front, from sea to sea. Faced by a heavy artillery, machine gun and rifle fire our troops, French and British alike, made a fine effort; the French especially got well into the Turks with the bayonet, and all along, excepting on our extreme left, our line gained ground. I might represent the battle as a victory, as the enemy's advanced positions were driven in, but essentially the result has been failure, as the main object remains unachieved. The fortifications and their machine guns were too scientific and too strongly held to be rushed, although I had every available man in to-day. Our troops have done all that flesh and blood can do against semi-permanent works, and they are not able to carry them. More and more munitions will be needed to do so. I fear this is a very unpalatable conclusion, but I see no way out of it.

I estimate that the Turks had about 40,000 opposed to our 25,000 rifles. There are 20,000 more in front of Australian-New Zealand Army Corps' 12,000 rifles at Gaba Tepe. By bringing men over from the Asiatic side and from Adrianople the Turks seem to be able to keep up their strength. I have only one more brigade of the Lancashire Territorial Division to come; not enough to make any real effect upon the situation as regards breaking through.

Hard must be the heart that is not wrung to think of all these brave boys making their effort; giving their lives; all that they had; it is too much; almost more than can be borne.

Now to go back and make my notes, day by day, of the battle:

On the 6th instant we began at 11.30 after half an hour's bombardment, — we dared not run to more. A strong wind was blowing and it was hard to land or come aboard. Till 2 p.m. I remained glued to the telephone on board and then went ashore and saw both Hunter-Weston and d'Amade in their posts of command. The live long day there were furious semi-detached fights by Battalions and Brigades, and we butted back the enemy for some 200 or 300 yards. So far so good. But we did not capture any of the main Turkish trenches. I still think we might have done as well at much less cost by creeping up these 200 or 300 yards by night.

However!

At 4.30 we dropped our high-vaulting Achi Baba aspirations and took to our spades.

The Hood Battalion of the Royal Naval Division had been roughly handled. In the hospital clearing tent by the beach I saw and spoke to (amongst many others) young Asquith, shot through the knee, and Commander Wedgwood, who had been horribly hurt by shrapnel. Each in his own way was a calm hero; wrapped in the mantle bequeathed to English soldiers by Sir Philip Sidney. Coming back in the evening to the ship we watched the Manchester Brigade disembarking. I have never seen a better looking lot. The 6th Battalion would serve very well as picked specimens of our race; not so much in height or physique, but in the impression they gave of purity of race and distinction. Here are the best the old country can produce; the hope of the progress of the British ideal in the world; and half of them are going to swap lives with Turks whose relative value to the well-being of humanity is to theirs as is a locust to a honey-bee.

That night Bailloud, Commander of the new French Division, came to make his salaam. He is small, alert, brimful of jokes and of years; seventy they say, but he neither looks it nor acts it.

The 7th was stormy and the sea dangerously rough. At 10 a.m. the Lancashire Fusilier Brigade were to lead off on our left. They could not get a move on, it seemed, although we had hoped that the shelling from the ships would have swept a clear lane for them.

The thought that "Y" Beach, which was holding up this brigade, was once in our hands, adds its sting to other reports coming from that part of the field. In France these reports would have been impersonal messages arriving from afar. In Asia or Africa I would have been letting off the steam by galloping to d'Amade or Hunter-Weston. Here I was neither one thing nor the other: neither a new fangled Commander sitting cool and semi-detached in an office; nor an old fashioned Commander taking personal direction of the show. During so long drawn out a suspense I tried to ease the tension by dictation. From the carbons I select these two paragraphs: they occur in a letter fired off to Colonel Clive Wigram at "11.25 a.m., 7th May, 1915."

> I broke off there because I got a telephone message in from Hunter-Weston to say his centre was advancing, and that by a pretty piece of co-operation between Infantry and Artillery, he had driven the Turks out of one very troublesome trench. He cannot see what is on his left, or get any message from them. On his left are the Lancashire Fusiliers (Territorials). They are faced by a horrid redoubt held by machine guns, and they are to rush it with the bayonet.* It is a high thing to ask of Territorials but against an enemy who is fighting for his life, and for the existence of his country, we have to call upon every one for efforts which, under any other conditions, might be considered beyond their strength.
>
> Were we still faced by the Divisions which originally held the Gallipoli Peninsula we would by now, I firmly believe, be in possession of the Kilid Bahr plateau. But every day a regiment or two dribble into Gallipoli, either from Asia or from Constantinople, and

---

* Captured by the Gurkhas five days later — by surprise. — *Ian H., 1920.*

in the last two days an entire fresh Division has (we have heard) arrived from Adrianople, and is fighting against us this morning. The smallest demonstration on the part of Bulgaria would, I presume, have prevented this big reinforcement of fresh troops reaching the enemy, but it seems beyond the resources of diplomacy to get anyone to create a diversion.

At 4.30 I ordered a general assault; the 88th Brigade to be thrown in on the top of the 87th; the New Zealand Brigade in support; the French to conform. Our gunners had put more than they could afford into the bombardment and had very little wherewithal to pave the way.

By the 4th instant I had seen danger-point drawing near and now it was on us. Five hundred more rounds of howitzer 4.5 and aeroplanes to spot whilst we wiped out the machine guns; that was the burden of my prayer. Still, we did what we could and for a quarter of an hour the whole of the Turkish front was wreathed in smoke, but these were naval shells or 18 pr shrapnel; we have no 18 pr high explosive and neither naval shells nor shrapnel are very much good once the targets have got underground. On our left no move forward.* Elsewhere our wonderful Infantry fought like fresh formations. In face of a tempest of shot and shell and of a desperate resistance by the Turks, who stuck it out very bravely to the last, they carried and held the first line enemy trenches. At night several counter-attacks were delivered, in every case repulsed with heavy loss.

We are now on our last legs. The beautiful Battalions of the 25th April are wasted skeletons now; shadows of what they had been. The thought of the river of blood, against which I painfully made my way when I met these multitudes of wounded coming down to the shore, was unnerving. But every soldier has to fight down these pitiful sensations: the enemy may be harder hit than he: if we do not push them further back the beaches will become untenable. To overdrive the willingest troops any General ever had under his command is a sin — but we must go on fighting to-

---

* This was by General Hunter-Weston's order: the machine guns of the enemy had too good a field of fire. — *Ian. H., 1920.*

morrow! On Saturday, the 8th, I went ashore and by 9.30 had taken up my quarters in a little gully between "W" and "X" Beaches within 60 yards of the Headquarters of the Royal Naval Division. There I was in direct telephonic touch with both Hunter-Weston and d'Amade. The storm had abated and the day was fine. Our troops had now been fighting for two days and two nights but there were messages in from the front telling us they were keen as ever to get something solid for their efforts. The Lancashire Fusiliers Brigade had been withdrawn into reserve, and under my orders the New Zealand Brigade was to advance through the line taken up during the night by the 88th Brigade and attack Krithia. The 87th Brigade were to try and gain ground over that wicked piece of moorland to the West of the great ravine which — since the days when it was in the hands of the troops who landed at "Y" — has hopelessly held up our left. Every gun-shot fired gives me a pain in my heart and adds to the deadly anxiety I feel about our ammunition. We have only one thousand rounds of 4.5 H.E. left and we dare not use any more. The 18 pr shrapnel is running down, down, down to its terminus, for we *must* try and keep 10,000 rounds in hand for defence. The French have still got enough to cover their own attacks. The ships began to fire at 10.15 and after a quarter of an hour the flower of New Zealand advanced in open order to the attack. After the most desperate hand to hand fighting, often by sections or sometimes by groups of half a dozen men, we gained slowly, very slowly, perhaps a couple of hundred yards. There was an opinion in some quarters that we had done all we could, but I resolved firmly to make one more attempt. At 4 o'clock I issued orders that the whole line, reinforced by the Australians, should on the stroke of 5.30 fix bayonets and storm Krithia and Achi Baba. At 5.15 the men-of-war went at it hot and strong with their big guns and fifteen minutes later the hour glass of eternity dropped a tiny grain labelled 5.30 p.m. 8.5.1915 into the lap of time.

As that moment befell, the wide plain before us became alive. Bayonets sparkled all over the wide plain. Under our glasses this vague movement took form and human shape: men rose, fell, ran, rushed on in waves, broke, recoiled, crumbled away and disappeared.

At the speed of the minute hand of a watch the left of our line crept forward.

On the right, at first nothing. Then suddenly, in the twinkling of an eye, the whole of the Northern slopes of the Kereves Dere Ravine was covered by bright coloured irregular surging crowds, moving in quite another way to the khaki-clad figures on their left: one moment pouring over the debatable ground like a torrent, anon twisted and turning and flying like multitudes of dead leaves before the pestilent breath of the howitzers. No living man has ever seen so strange a vision as this: in its disarray; in its rushing to and fro; in the martial music, shouts and evolutions!

My glasses shook as I looked, though I *believe* I seemed very calm. It seemed; it truly seemed as if the tide of blue, grey, scarlet specks was submerging the enemy's strongholds. A thousand of them converged and rushed the redoubt at the head of the Kereves Dere. A few seconds later into it — one! two!! three!!! fell from the clouds the Turkish six inchers. Where the redoubt had been a huge column of smoke arose as from the crater of a volcano. Then fast and furious the enemy guns opened on us. For the first time they showed their full force of fire. Again, the big howitzers led the infernal orchestra pitting the face of no man's land with jet black blotches. The puppet figures we watched began to waver; the Senegalese were torn and scattered. Once more these huge explosions unloading their cargoes of midnight on to the evening gloom. All along the Zouaves and Senegalese gave way. Another surge forward and bayonets crossed with the Turks: yet a few moments of tension and back they fell to their trenches followed by salvo upon salvo of shell bursts. Night slid down into the smoke. The last thing — against the skyline — a little column of French soldiers of the line charging back upwards towards the lost redoubt. After that — darkness!

The battle is over. Both sides have fought with every atom of energy they possessed. The heat is oppressive. A heavy mail from England. On shore all quiet. A young wounded Officer of the 29th Division said it was worth ten years of tennis to see the Australians and New Zealanders go in. Began writing at daylight and now it is midnight. No word yet of the naval offer to go through.

Issued a special order to the troops. They deserve everything that anyone can give them in this world and the next.

GENERAL HEADQUARTERS,
9th May, 1915.

Sir Ian Hamilton wishes the troops of the Mediterranean Expeditionary Force to be informed that in all his past experiences, which include the hard struggles of the Russo-Japanese campaign, he has never seen more devoted gallantry displayed than that which has characterised their efforts during the past three days. He has informed Lord Kitchener by cable of the bravery and endurance displayed by all ranks here and has asked that the necessary reinforcements be forthwith dispatched. Meanwhile, the remainder of the East Lancashire Division is disembarking and will henceforth be available to help us to make good and improve upon the positions we have so hardly won.

10th May, 1915. H.M.T. "Arcadian." Fell asleep last night thinking of Admirals, Commodores and men-o'-war and of how they *might*, within the next forty-eight hours, put another complexion upon our prospects. So it seemed quite natural when, the first thing in the morning, a cable came in with the tea asking me whether I have been consulting de Robeck as to "the future operations that will be necessary." K. adds, "I hope you and the Admiral will be able to devise some means of clearing a passage."

Have just cabled back "Every day I have consultations with the Admiral": I cannot say more than this as I am not supposed to know anything about de Robeck's cable as to the "means of clearing a passage" which went, I believe, yesterday. No doubt it lay before K. when he wired me. I have not been shown the cable; I have not been consulted about it, nor, I believe, has Braithwaite, but I do happen to be aware of its drift.

Without embarking on another endless yarn let me note the fact that there are two schools amongst our brethren afloat. Roger Keyes and those of the younger school who sport the executive curl upon their sleeves are convinced that now, when we have replaced the ramshackle old trawlers of 18th March by an unprecedented mine-sweeping service of 20-knot destroyers under disciplined crews, the forcing of the Straits has become as easy ... well; anyway; easier than what we soldiers tried to do on Saturday. Upon these fire-eaters de Robeck has hitherto thrown cold water. He thought, as we thought, that the Army would save his ships. But our last battle has shown him that the Army would only open 215]the Straits at a cost greater than the loss of ships, and that the time has come to strike home with the tremendous mechanism of the Fleet. On that basis he quickly came to terms with the views of his thrusting lieutenants.

On two reservations, he still insisted:

(1) he was not going to deprive me of the close tactical support of his battleships if there was the least apprehension we might be "done in" in his absence.
(2) He was not going to risk his ships amongst the mines unless we were sure, if he did get through, we could follow on after him by land.

On both issues there was, to my thinking, no question:

(1) Although we cannot push through "under present conditions without more and more ammunition," *vide* my cable of yesterday, all the Turks in Asia will not shift us from where we stand even if we have not one battleship to back us.
(2) If the ships force the Straits, beyond doubt, we can starve out the Turks; scupper the Forts and hold the Bulair lines.

We know enough now about the communications and reserves of food and munitions of the Turks to be positively certain they cannot stick it on the Peninsula if they are cut off from sea communication with Asia and with Constantinople. Within a fortnight they will begin to run short; we are all agreed there.

So now, (i.e., yesterday) the Admiral has cabled offering to go through, and "now" is the moment of all others to let Lord K. clearly face the alternative to that proposal. So I have said (in the same cable in which I answer his question about consultations with the Admiral) "If you could only spare me two fresh Divisions organized as a Corps I could push on with great hopes of success both from Helles and Gaba Tepe; otherwise I am afraid we shall degenerate into trench warfare with its resultant slowness."

Birdie ran down from Anzac and breakfasted. He brings news of an A.1 affair. Two of his Battalions, the 15th and 16th Australians, stormed three rows of Turkish trenches with the bayonet, and then sat down in them. At dawn to-day the enemy counter-attacked in overwhelming strength. The healthy part of the story lies herein, that our field guns were standing by in action, and as the enemy came on they let them have it hot with shrapnel over a space of 300 yards. Terrible as this fire was, it failed to beat off the Turks. They retook the trenches, but they have paid far more than their price, for Birdwood assures me that their corpses lie piled up so thick one on top of the other that our snipers can take cover behind them.

A curious incident: during the night a Fleet-sweeper tied up alongside, full of wounded, chiefly Australians. They had been sent off from the beach; had been hawked about from ship to ship and every ship they hailed had the same reply — "full up" — until, in the end, they received orders to return to the shore and disembark their wounded to wait there until next day. The Officers, amongst them an Australian Brigadier of my acquaintance, protested; and so, the Fleet-sweeper crew, not knowing what to do, came and lashed on to us.* No one told me anything of this last night, but the ship's Captain and his Officers and my own Staff Officers have been up on watches serving out soup, etc., and tending these wounded to the best of their power. As soon as I heard what had happened I first signalled the hospital ship *Guildford Castle* to prepare to take the men in (she had just cast anchor); then I went on board the Fleet-sweeper myself and told the wounded how sorry I was for the delay in getting them to bed. They declared one and all they had been very well done but "the boys" never complain; my A.G. is the responsible official; I have

---

* Long afterwards I heard that a responsible naval officer, being determined that this instance of lack of method should be brought to my personal notice, had hit upon the plan of ordering the Fleet-sweeper crew to do what they did. — *Ian H., 1920.*

told him the *band-o-bast* has been bad; also that a Court of Enquiry must be called to adjudicate on the whole matter.

Were an example to be sought of the almighty influence of "Time" none better could be found than in the fact that, to-day, I have almost forgotten to chronicle a passage in K.'s cable aforesaid that might well have been worth the world and the glories thereof only forty-eight short hours ago. K. says, "More ammunition is being pushed out to you *via* Marseilles." I am glad. I am deeply grateful. Our anxieties will be lessened, but *that same message, had it only reached us on Saturday morning, would have enabled us to fire 5,000 more shrapnel and 500 more 4.5 howitzer H.E. to cover our last assault!*

Chapter VIII – Two Corps or an Ally?

11th May, 1915. H.M.T. "Arcadian." Day dull and overcast. Vice-Admiral came over to see me in the morning. Neither of us has had a reply to his cable; instead, he has been told two enemy submarines are on their way to pay us a visit. The approach of these mechanical monsters opens up vistas thronged with shadowy forebodings. De Robeck begs me to set his mind at ease by landing with my Staff forthwith. Have sent Officers to survey the ground between Helles and Sedd-el-Bahr and to see if they can find room for us. We would all rather be on shore than board ship, but Helles and "V" Beaches are already overcrowded, and we should be squeezed in cheek by jowl, within a few hundred yards of the two Divisional Headquarters Staffs.

12th May, 1915. H.M.T. "Arcadian." Raining hard. Busy all morning. A cable from Lord K. to say he is sending out the Lowland Division. We are all as pleased as Punch! especially (so Braithwaite tells me) Roger Keyes who looks on this as a good omen for the naval attack proposals. Had he not meant the Fleet to shove in K. must have made some reference to the second Division, surely. Have cabled back at once to K. giving him warmest thanks and begging him to look, personally, into the question of the command of the coming Division. Have begged him to take Leslie Rundle's opinion on the point and have pressed it by saying, "Imperturbable calm in the Commander is essential above all things in these operations." Most of the troop transports have left their anchorage and gone back to Mudros for fear of submarines.

Went ashore at 3 o'clock. Saw Hunter-Weston and then inspected the 29th Division just in from the firing line. The ground was heavy and sloppy after the rain. I walked as far as the trenches of the 86th Brigade and saw amongst other Corps the Essex, Hants, Lancashire Fusiliers and 5th Royal Scots. Spent over an hour chatting to groups of Officers and men who looked like earth to earth, caked as they were with mud, haggard with lack of sleep, pale as the dead, many of them slightly wounded and bandaged, hand or head, their clothes blood-stained, their eyes blood-shot. Who could have believed that only a fortnight ago these same figures were clean as new pins; smart and well-liking! Two-thirds of each Battalion were sound asleep in pools of mud and water — like corpses half buried! This sounds horrible but the hearty welcome extended to us by all ranks and the pride they took in their achievements was a sublime triumph of mind over matter. Our voluntary service regulars are the last descendants of those rulers of the ancient world, the Roman Legionaries. Oh that their ranks could be kept filled and that a mould so unique was being used to its fullest in forming new regulars.

On my way back to the beach I saw the Plymouth Battalion as it marched in from the front line. They were quite different excepting only in the fact that they also had done marvels of fighting and endurance. They were done: they had come to the end of their tether. Not only physical exhaustion but moral exhaustion. They could not raise a smile in the whole battalion. The faces of Officers and men had a crushed, utterly finished expression: some of the younger Officers especially had that true funeral set about their lips which spreads the contagion of gloom through the hearts of the bravest soldiers. As each company front formed the knees of the rank and file seemed to give way. Down they fell and motionless remained. An hour or two of rest, their Colonel says, will make all the difference in what the French call their *allure*, but not quite so soon I think. These are the New Armies. They are not specialised types like the Old Army. They have nerves, the defects of their good qualities. They are more susceptible to the horrors and discomforts of what they were never brought up to undergo. The philosophy of the battlefield is not part of their panoply. No one fights better than they do — for a spell — and a good long spell too. But they have not the invincible carelessness or temperamental springiness of the old lot — and how should they?

In the evening I received General d'Amade who had come over to pay his farewell visit. He is permitted to let me see his order of recall. "Important modifications having come about in the general political situation" his Government have urgent need for his services on a "military mission." D'Amade is a most charming, chivalrous and loyal soldier. He has lost his son fighting in France and he has had his headquarters right down in the middle of his 75's where the infernal din night and day must indeed murder sleep. He is a delightful person and, in the combat, too brave. We all wish him luck. For Kum Kale and for what he has done, suffered and lost he deserves great Kudos in his country.

By order of the Vice-Admiral this ship is to anchor at Tenedos. My informal confab with the heroes of the 29th Division, and their utter unconsciousness of their own glorious conduct have moved me to write these few words in their honour:

GENERAL HEADQUARTERS,
12th May, 1915.

For the first time for 18 days and nights it has been found possible to withdraw the 29th Division from the fire fight. During the whole of that long period of unprecedented strain the Division has held ground or gained it, against the bullets and bayonets of the constantly renewed forces of the foe. During the whole of that long period they have been illuminating the pages of military history with their blood. The losses have been terrible, but mingling with the deep sorrow for fallen comrades arises a feeling of pride in the invincible spirit which has enabled the survivors to triumph where ordinary troops must inevitably have failed. I tender to Major-General Hunter-Weston and to his Division at the same time my profoundest sympathy with their losses and my warmest congratulations on their achievement.

IAN HAMILTON,
General.

Also I have penned a farewell line to d'Amade:

GENERAL HEADQUARTERS,
MEDN. EXPED. FORCE,
12th May, 1915.

MON GÉNÉRAL,

With deep personal sadness I learn that your country has urgent need of your great experience elsewhere.

From the very first you and your brave troops have done all, and more than all, that mortal man could do to further the cause we have at heart. By day and by night, for many days and nights in succession, you and your gallant troops have ceaselessly struggled against the enemy's fresh reinforcements and have won from him ground at the bayonet point.

The military records of France are most glorious, but you, Mon Général, have added fresh brilliancy, if I may say so, even to those dazzling records.

The losses have been cruel: such losses are almost unprecedented, but it may be some consolation hereafter to think that only by so fierce a trial could thus have been fully disclosed the flame of patriotism which burns in the hearts of yourself and your men.

With sincere regrets at your coming departure but with the full assurance that in your new sphere of activity, you will continue to render the same valuable service you have already given to France.

I remain,
Mon Général,
Your sincere friend,
IAN HAMILTON,
General.

13th May, 1915. H.M.T. "Arcadian." Hot and bright. Dead calm sea. Last night a dense fog during which a Turkish Torpedo boat sneaked down the Straits and torpedoed the *Goliath*. David and his

GENERAL D'AMADE

sling on the grand scale. No details yet to hand. The enemy deserve decorations — confound them!

Got hold of a Fleet-sweeper and went off to Cape Helles. Again visited Headquarters 29th Division, and afterwards walked through the trenches of the 87th Brigade. Saw that fine soldier, Brigadier-General Marshall, in command. Chatted to no end of his men — Inniskillings, Dublin Fusiliers, etc. They have recovered their exhaustion; have cleaned up, and look full of themselves, twice the size in fact. As I stepped on to the little pier at Cape Helles an enemy's six-incher burst about 50 yards back, a lump of metal just clearing my right shoulder strap and shooting into the sea with an ugly hiss. Not a big fragment but enough!

The Staff have made up their minds that we should be very much in the wrong box if we dossed down on the toe of the Peninsula. First, — unless we get between the Divisional Generals and the enemy, there is literally no room! Secondly, — I should be further, in point of time, from Birdwood and his men than if I was still on board ship. Thirdly, — the several Headquarters of Divisions, whether French or British, would all equally hate to have Braithwaite and myself sitting in their pockets from morning to night. Have sent out another party, therefore, to explore Tenedos and see if we can find a place there which will serve us till we can make more elbow room on Gallipoli.

The Gurkhas have stalked the Bluff Redoubt and have carried it with a rush! They are absolutely the boys for this class of country and for this class of enemy.

Cabled Lord K. about the weakness of the 29th Division. At the very moment when we are hoping so much from a fresh push made in conjunction with a naval attack, the Division, the backbone of my force, are short by over 11,000 men and 400 Officers! As a fighting unit they are on their last legs and when they will be set upon their feet again Lord K. knows. Were we in France we'd get the men to-morrow. If I had my own depots in Egypt still I could see my way, but, as things are, there seems no chance of getting a move on for another fortnight. Have cabled K. saying, "I hope the 29th Division is soon to be made up to strength. I had no idea when I left England that the customary 10 per cent. reinforcement was not being taken with it by the Division although it was to operate at so great a distance from its base." If K. gets into a bad temper over the opening of my cable, its tail end should lift him out again. For the enemy's extremely tenacious right has been shifted at last. Under cover of a hooroosh by the Manchesters, the Gurkhas have rushed a bluff 600 yards ahead of our line and are sticking to their winnings.

14th May, 1915. H.M.T. "Arcadian." Hot day, smooth sea. Disembarking to bivouac on shore. What a contrast we must present to the Headquarters in France! There the stately *Château*; sheets, table-cloths and motor cars. Here the red tab patricians have to haul their own kits over the sand.

In the afternoon d'Amade came back with General Gouraud, his successor, the new Chief of the French. A resolute, solid looking *gaillard* is Gouraud. He brings a great reputation with him from the Western Front.

Quite late the Admiral came over to see me. He brings bad news. Roger Keyes and the forwards will be cut to the heart. The Admiralty have turned down the proposal to force the Straits simultaneously by land and sea. We are to go on attacking; the warships are to go on supporting.

From the earliest days great commanders have rubbed in the maxim, "If you attack, attack with all your force." Our people know better; we are to go on attacking with half our force. First we attack with the naval half and are held up — next we attack with the army half and are held up.

The Admiral has changed his mind about our landing and thinks it would be best not to fix G.H.Q. at Tenedos; first, because there might be delay in getting quickly to Anzac; secondly, because Tenedos is so close to Asia that we might all be scuppered in our beds by a cutting-out party of Besika Bay ruffians, unless we had a guard. But we can't run to the pomp and circumstance of a Commander-in-Chief's guard here.

15th May, 1915. H.M.T. "Arcadian." Till 3 p.m. the perspiring Staff were re-embarking their gear. Sailed then for Helles when I saw Hunter-Weston who gave me a full account of the attacks made on the newly gained bluff upon our left. Shells busy bursting on "W" Beach. Some French aeroplanes have arrived — God be praised! Shocked to hear Birdie has been hit, but another message to say nothing serious, came close on the heels of the first. Anchored at Imbros when I got a cable asking me what forces I shall need to carry right through to a finish. A crucial question, very much affected by what the Admiral told me last night. Nothing easier than to ask for 150,000 men and then, if I fail say I didn't get what I wanted, but the boldest leaders, Bobs, White, Gordon, K., have always "asked for more" with a most queasy conscience. On the face of it I need many more men if the Fleet is not to attack, and yet I am not even supposed to have knowledge, much less an opinion, as to what passes between the Fleet and the Admiralty!

16th May, 1915. H.M.T. "Arcadian." De Robeck came off the *Lord Nelson*, his new Flagship, in the morning. The submarines are shadowing him already, and there seems little doubt they are on their way.

Bridges has been badly wounded. The news upset me so got hold of H.M.S. *Rattlesnake* (Commander Wedgwood), and started off for Anzac. Went ashore and saw Birdie. Doing so, I received a different sort of salute from that to which a Commander-in-Chief landing on duty is entitled by regulation. Quite a shower of shell fell all about us, the Turks having spotted there was some sort of "bloke" on the *Rattlesnake*. We went round a bit of the line, and found all well, the men in great heart and, amidst a constant crackle of musketry, looking as if they liked it. Birdie himself is still a little shaken by his wound of yesterday. He had a close shave indeed. A bullet came through the chinks of a sandbag and scalped him. He fell to the ground senseless and pouring with blood, but when he had been picked up and washed he wanted to finish his round of the trenches.

Embarked again under brisk shell fire and proceeded to the hospital ship *Gascon* where I saw General Bridges. He looked languid and pale. But his spirit was high as ever and he smiled at a little joke I managed to make about the way someone had taken the shelling we had just gone through. The doctors, alas, give a bad, if not desperate, account of him. Were he a young man, they could save him by cutting off his leg high up, but as it is he would not stand the shock. On the other hand, his feet are so cold from the artery being severed that they anticipate mortification. I should have thought better have a try at cutting off the leg, but they are not for it. Bridges will be a real loss. He was a single-minded, upright, politics-despising soldier. With all her magnificent rank and file, Australia cannot afford to lose Bridges. But perhaps I am too previous. May it be so!

Spent a good long time talking to wounded men — Australians, New Zealanders and native Indians. Both the former like to meet someone who knows their native country, and the natives brighten up when they are greeted in Hindustani. On returning to Imbros, got good news about the Lancashire Territorials who have gained 180 yards of ground without incurring any loss to speak of. They are real good chaps. They suffer only from the regular soldiers' fault; there are too few of them here.

17th May, 1915. H.M.T. "Arcadian." 10 p.m. Too much work to move. In the evening the Admiral came to see me and read my rough draft for an answer to Lord K.'s cable. We show the Navy all our important operations cables; they have their own ways of doing things and don't open out so freely. On the face of it, we are invited to say what we want. Well, to steer a middle course between my duty to my force and my loyalty to K. is not so simple as it might seem. That middle course is (if I can only hit it) my duty to my country. The chief puzzle of the problem is that nothing turns out as we were told it would turn out. The landing has been made but the Balkans fold their arms, the Italians show no interest, the Russians do not move an inch to get across the Black Sea (the Grand Duke Nicholas has no munitions, we hear); our submarines have got through but they can only annoy, they cannot cut the sea communications, and so the Turks have not fled to Bulair. Instead, enemy submarines are actually about to get at us and our ships are being warned they may have to make themselves scarce: last — in point of time — but not least, not by a long way, the central idea of the original plan, an attack by the Fleet on the Forts appears to have been entirely shelved.

At first the Fleet was to force its way through; we were to look on; next, the Fleet and the Army were to go for the Straits side by side; to-day, the whole problem may fairly be restated on a clean sheet of paper, so different is it from the problem originally put to me by K. when it was understood I would put him in an impossible position if I pressed for reinforcements. We should be on velvet if we asked for so many troops that we must win if we got them; whereas, if we did not get them we could say victory was impossible. But we are not the only fighters for the Empire. The Admiral, Braithwaite, Roger Keyes agree with me that the fair and square thing under the circumstances is to ask for *what is right*; not a man more than we, in our consciences, believe we will really need, — not a man less.

Actually, after much heart searching and head scratching, my mind has made itself up and has gone home by cable to-day. The statement is entirely frank and covers all the ground except as regards the Fleet, a pidgin which flies out of range:

(M.F. 234).
"Your No. 4644 cipher, of the 14th instant. The following is my appreciation of the situation:

On the one hand, there are at present on the Peninsula as many troops as the available space and water supply can accommodate.

On the other hand, to break through the strong opposition on my front will require more troops. I am, therefore, in a quandary, because although more troops are wanted there is, at present, no room for them.* Moreover, the difficulty in answering your question is accentuated by the fact that my answer must depend on whether Turkey will continue to be left undisturbed in other parts and therefore free to make good the undoubtedly heavy losses incurred

---

* I learnt afterwards that great play had been made with this third paragraph of my cable by the opponents of the Dardanelles idea; in doing so they slurred over the words "at present," also the fifth paragraph of the same cable, overleaf. — *Ian H., 1920.*

Two Corps or an Ally? 177

here by sending troops from Adrianople, Keshan, Constantinople and Asia; we now have direct evidence that the latter has been the case. If the present condition of affairs in this respect were changed by the entry into the struggle of Bulgaria or Greece or by the landing of the Russians, my present force, kept up to strength by the necessary drafts, plus the Army Corps asked for in my No. M.F. 216 of the 10th May, would probably suffice to finish my task. If, however, the present situation remains unchanged and the Turks are still able to devote so much exclusive attention to us, I shall want an additional army corps, that is, two army corps additional in all.

I could not land these reinforcements on the Peninsula until I can advance another 1,000 yards and so free the beaches from the shelling to which they are subjected from the Western side and gain more space; but I could land them on the adjacent islands of Tenedos, Imbros and Lemnos and take them over later to the Peninsula for battle. This plan would surmount the difficulties of water and space on the Peninsula and would, perhaps, enable me to effect a surprise with the fresh divisions.

I believe I could advance with half the loss of life that is now being reckoned upon, if I had a liberal supply of gun ammunition, especially of high explosive.

Only bitterest experience has forced me to insert the two stipulations which should go without saving, (1) that my force is kept up to strength, (2) that I have a decent allowance of gun ammunition, especially of high explosives.

Will Lord K. meet us half way, I wonder? He is the idol of England, and take him all in all, the biggest figure in the world. He believes, he has an instinct, that here is the heel of the German Colossus, otherwise immune to our arrows. Let him but put his foot down, and who dare say him nay?

The most vital of my demands is that my formations should be kept full. An extra 50,000 men in the shape of a new army corps is one thing. An extra 50,000 men to feed war-trained units already in the field is another, and very different, and very much better thing. The value of keeping the veteran corps up to strength and the value of the same number of rifles organized into raw battalions commanded by inexperienced leaders is as the value of the sun to the moon. But K. and I have never seen eye to eye here, and never will. The spirit of man is like a precious stone: the greater it is the more room in it for a flaw. Who in the world but K. would have swept up all the odds and ends of detachments from about twenty different regiments of mine sent from Pretoria to Elandsfontein to bring up remounts and clothing to their units; who but K. could have conceived the idea of forming them into a new corps and expecting them to fight as well as ever — instead of legging it like the wind as they did at the first whistle of a bullet? On the other hand, who but K., at that time, could have run the war at all?

The 29th Division have managed to snatch another 150 yards from the enemy, greatly strengthening the bluff upon which the Gurkhas dug themselves in.

18th May, 1915. H.M.T. "Arcadian." Villiers Stuart, Birdie's Staff Officer, has been killed on Anzac by a shell. The submarine E.14 sailed into harbour after a series of hair-raising adventures in the Sea of Marmora. She is none the worse, bar the loss of one periscope from a Turkish lucky shot. Her Commander, Boyle, comes only after Nasmith as a pet of Roger Keyes! She got a tremendous ovation from the Fleet. The exploits of the submarine give a flat knock-out to Norman Angell's contention that excitement and romance have now gone out of war.

Have asked that the Maoris may be sent from Malta to join the New Zealanders at Anzac. I hope and believe that they will do well. Their white comrades from the Northern Island are very keen to have them.

19th May, 1915. H.M.T. "Arcadian". Compton Mackenzie has come on board. He is to be attached to the Intelligence. General Gouraud and his Chief of Staff, Girodon, lunched. I do not know many French Officers, but Girodon happens to be an old acquaintance. I met him six years ago on the Austrian manœuvres. He is a delightful personality; a very sound soldier and a plucky one also. I reminded him how, in 1906, he had told me that the Germans would end by binding together all the other peoples of Europe against the common danger of their dominance. This was at Teschen on the borderland between Austrian and Prussian

Two Corps or an Ally?   179

Silesia during the Austrian Manœuvres. He remembered the occasion and the remark. Well, he has proved a true prophet!

A cable from K. in answer to mine giving two more Army Corps as my minimum unless some neutral or Allied Power is going to help us against the Turks. I knew he would be greatly upset:

(4726, cipher).
Private and personal. With reference to your telegram No. M.F. 234, I am quite certain that you fully realize what a serious disappointment it has been to me to discover that my preconceived views as to the conquest of positions necessary to dominate the forts on the Straits, with naval artillery to support our troops on land, and with the active help of naval bombardment, were miscalculated.

A serious situation is created by the present check, and the calls for large reinforcements and an additional amount of ammunition that we can ill spare from France.

From the stand-point of an early solution of our difficulties, your views, as stated, are not encouraging. The question whether we can long support two fields of operation draining on our resources requires grave consideration. I know that I can rely upon you to do your utmost to bring the present unfortunate state of affairs in the Dardanelles to as early a conclusion as possible, so that any consideration of a withdrawal, with all its dangers in the East, may be prevented from entering the field of possible solutions.

When all the above is taken into consideration, I am somewhat surprised to see that the 4,500 which Maxwell can send you are apparently not required by you. With the aid of these I had hoped that you would have been in a position to press forward.

The Lowland Division is leaving for you.

This is a queer cable. Seems as if K. was beginning to come up against those political forces which have ever been a British Commander's bane. The words in which he begs me to try and prevent "a withdrawal with all its dangers in the East...from entering the field of possible solutions," sounds uncommonly like a cry for help. He means that I should help him by remembering, and by making smaller calls upon him. But the only way I can *really* help him is by winning a battle: to pretend I could win that battle without drafts, munitions and the Army Corps asked for would be a very short-lived bluff both for him and for me. We have had it from other sources that this strange notion of running away from the Turk, after singeing his beard, has arisen in London and in France. So now that the murder has peeped out, I am glad to know where we are and to feel that K. stands solid and sound behind us. He need have no fear; all that man can do I will do by pressing on here and by asking for not one man or round more than is absolutely essential for the job.

As to that passage about the 4,500 Australians, a refusal of Australians would indeed be good cause for surprise — only — it has never taken place, and never will take place. I can only surmise that my request made to Maxwell that these 4,500 men should come to me as drafts for my skeleton units, instead of as a raw brigade, has twisted itself, going down some office corridor, into a story that I don't want the men! K. tells me Egypt is mine and the fatness thereof; yet, no sooner do I make the most modest suggestion concerning anything or anyone Egyptian than K. is got at and I find he is the Barmecide and I Schac'abac. "How do you like your lentil soup?" says K. "Excellently well," say I, "but devil a drop is in the plate!" I have got to enter into the joke; that's the long and the short of it. But it is being pushed just a trifle too far when I am told I *apparently do not require* 4,500 Australians!

The whole of K.'s cable calls for close thinking. How to try and help him to pump courage into faint-hearted fellows? How to do so without toning down my demands for reinforcements? — for evidently these demands are what are making them shake in their shoes. Here is my draft for an answer: I can't change my estimate: it was the least I could safely ask for: but I can make it clear I do not want to ask for more than he can give:

(M.F. 243).

With reference to your No. 4726, cipher. Private and personal. You need not be despondent at anything in the situation. Remember that you asked me to answer on the assumption that you had adequate forces at your disposal, and I did so.

Maxwell must have misinformed you. I want the Australian reinforcements to fill existing cadres. Maxwell, possibly not to disappoint senior officers, has sent them as weak brigades, which complicates command and organization exceedingly.

We gain ground surely if slowly every day, and now at 11 p.m. the French and Naval Divisions are fighting their way forward.

Tidings of great joy from Anzac. The whole of the enemy's freshly-arrived contingent have made a grand assault and have been shattered in the attempt. Samson dropped bombs on them as they were standing on the shore after their disembarkation. Next, they were moved up into the fight where a tremendous fire action was in progress. Last, they stormed forward in the densest masses yet seen on the Peninsula. Then, they were mown down and driven back headlong. So they have had a dreadnought reception. This has not been a local trench attack but a real battle and a fiery one. I have lost no time in cabling the glorious news to K. The cloud of these coming enemy reinforcements has cast its shadow over us for awhile and now the sun shines again.

20th May, 1919. H.M.T. "Arcadian." Aubrey Herbert saw me before dinner. He brings a message from Birdie to say that there has been some sort of parley with the enemy who wish to fix up an armistice for the burial of their dead. Herbert is keen on meeting the Turks half way and I am quite with him, *provided* Birdie clearly understands that no Corps Commander can fix up an armistice off his own bat, and *provided* it is clear we do not ask for the armistice but grant it to them — the suppliants. Herbert brings amazing fine detail about the night and day battle on the high ridges. Birdie has fairly taken the fighting edge off Liman von Sanders' two new Divisions: he has knocked them to bits. A few more shells and they would have been swept off the face of the earth. As it is we have slaughtered a multitude. Since the 18th we are down to two rounds per gun per diem, but the Turks who have been short of stuff since the 8th instant are now once more well found. Admiral Thursby tells me he himself counted 240 shells falling on one of Birdwood's trenches in the space of ten minutes. I asked him if that amounted to one shell per yard and he said the whole length of the trench was less than 100 yards. On the 18th fifty heavy shells, including 12-inch and 14-inch, dropped out of the blue vault of heaven on to the Anzacs. Everyone sorry to say good-bye to Thursby who goes to Italy.

Rumours that Winston is leaving the Admiralty. This would be an awful blow to us out here, would be a sign that Providence had some grudge against the Dardanelles. Private feelings do not count in war, but alas, how grievous is this set-back to one who has it in him to revive the part of Pitt, had he but Pitt's place. Haldane, too. Are the benefits of his organization of our army to be discounted because they had a German origin? *Fas est et ab hoste doceri.** Half the guns on the Peninsula would have been scrap-iron had it not been for Haldane! But if this turns out true about Winston, there will be a colder spirit (let them appoint whom they will) at the back of our battleships here.

21st May, 1915. H.M.T. "Arcadian." Imbros. De Robeck came on board with Lieutenant-Commander Boyle of E. 4 fame. I was proud indeed to meet the young and modest hero. He gets the V.C.; his other two officers the D.S.O.; his crew the D.C.M.

Also he brought with him the Reuter giving us the Cabinet changes and the resignations of Fisher and Winston and this, in its interest, has eclipsed even V.C.s for the moment. De Robeck reminded me that Lord K.'s cable (begging me to help him to combat any idea of withdrawal) must have been written that very day. A significant straw disclosing the veering of the winds of high politics! Evidently K. felt ill at ease; evidently he must now be sitting at a round table surrounded by masked figures. Have just finished writing him to sympathize; to say he is not to worry about me as "I know that as long as you remain at the War Office no one will be allowed to harm us out here." Nor could they if he were the K. of old; the K. who downed Milner and Chamberlain by making a peace by agreement with the Boers and then swallowed a Viceroy and his Military Member of Council as an appetiser to his more serious digest of India. But is he? Where are the instruments? — gone to France or gone to glory. Callwell is the exception.

I would give a great deal for one good talk with K. — I would indeed. But this is not France. Time and space forbid my quitting

---

* "One should learn even from one's enemies."

the helm and so I must try and induce the mountain to come to Mahomet. My letter goes on to say, "Could you not take a run out here and see us? If once you realize with your own eyes what the troops are doing I would never need to praise them again. Travelling in the *Phaeton* you would be here in three days; you would see some wonderful things and the men would be tremendously bucked up. The spirit of all ranks rises above trials and losses and is confident of the present and cheery about the future."

Quite apart from any high politics, or from my coming to a fresh, clear, close understanding with K. on subjects neither of us understood when last we spoke together, I wish, on the grounds of ordinary tactics, he could make up his mind to come out. The man who has *seen* gains self-confidence and the prestige of his subject when he encounters others who have only *heard* and *read*. K. might snap his fingers at the new hands in the Cabinet once he had been out and got the real Gallipoli at their tips.

I can't keep my thoughts from dwelling on the fate of Winston. How will he feel now he realizes he is shorn of his direct power to help us through these dark and dreadful Straits? Since I started nothing has handicapped me more than the embargo which a double loyalty to K. and to de Robeck has imposed upon my communications to Winston. What a tragedy that his nerve and military vision have been side-tracked: his eclipse projects a black shadow over the Dardanelles.

Very likely the next great war will have begun before we realize that the three days' delay in the fall of Antwerp saved Calais. No more brilliant effort of unaided genius in history than that recorded in the scene when Winston burst into the Council Chamber and bucked up the Burgomeisters to hold on a little bit longer. Any comfort our people may enjoy from being out of cannon shot of the Germans — they owe it to the imagination, bluff and persuasiveness of Winston and to this gallant Naval Division now destined to be starved to death!

Sent my first despatch home to-day by King's Messenger. Never has story been penned amidst so infernal a racket.

Chapter IX – Submarines

22nd May, 1915. H.M.T. "Arcadian." News in to say that yesterday, whilst Herbert was here to take orders about an armistice, some sort of an informal parley actually took place. Both sides suddenly got panic stricken, thinking the others were treacherous, and fire was opened, some stretcher bearers being killed. Nothing else was to be expected when things are done in this casual and unauthorized way. I felt very much annoyed, but Aubrey Herbert was still on board and I saw him before breakfast and told him Walker seemed to have taken too much upon himself parleying with the Turks and that Birdwood must now make this clear to everyone for future guidance. Although Aubrey Herbert is excessively unorthodox he quite sees that confabs with enemies must be carried out according to Cocker.

After breakfast landed at Cape Helles. Inspected the detachment of the Works Department of the Egyptian Army as it was on its way to the French Headquarters. Colonel Micklem was in charge. At Sedd-el-Bahr lunched with Gouraud and his Staff. General Bailloud rode up just as I was about to enter the porch of the old Fort. He was in two minds whether or not to embrace me, being in very high feather, his men having this morning carried the Haricot redoubt overlooking the Kereves Dere. At lunch he was the greatest possible fun, bubbling over with jokes and witty sallies. Just as we were finishing, news came through the telephone that Bailloud's Brigade had been driven in by a big Turkish counter-attack, with a loss of 400 men and some first class officers. Most of us showed signs, I will not say of being rattled, but of having stumbled against a rattlesnake. Gouraud remained unaffectedly in possession of himself as host of a lunch party. He said, "We will not take the trenches by not taking the coffee. Let us drink it first, and then we will consider." So we drank our coffee; lit our smokes, and afterwards Gouraud, through Girodon, issued his orders in the most calm and matter-of-fact way. He declares the redoubt will be in our hands again to-morrow.

Our lunch was to furnish us with yet another landmark for bad luck. As we were leaving, a message came in to say that an enemy submarine had been sighted off Gaba Tepe. The fresh imprint of a tiger's paw upon the pathway gives the same sort of feel to the Indian herdsman. Tall stories from neighbouring villages have been going the round for weeks, only half-believed, but here is the very mark of the beast; the horror has suddenly taken shape. He mutters the name of God, wondering what eyes may even now be watching his every movement; he wonders whose turn will come first — and when — and where. This was the sort of effect of the wireless and in a twinkling every transport round the coast was steering full steam to Imbros. In less than no time we saw a regatta of skedaddling ships. So dies the invasion of England bogey which, from first to last, has wrought us an infinity of harm. Born and bred of mistrust of our own magnificent Navy, it has led soldiers into heresy after fallacy and fallacy after heresy until now it is the cause of my Divisions here being hardly larger than Brigades, whilst the men who might have filled them are "busy" guarding London! If one rumoured submarine can put the fear of the Lord into British transports how are German or any other transports going to face up to a hundred British submarines? The theory of the War Office has struggled with the theory of the Admiralty for the past five years: now there is nothing left of the War Office theory; no more than is left of a soap bubble when you strike it with a battleaxe. Some other stimulus to our Territorial recruiting than the fear of invasion will have to be invented in future.

After lunch went to the Headquarters of the 29th Division where all the British Divisional Generals had assembled together to meet me. The same story everywhere — lack of men, meaning extra work — which again means sickness and still greater lack of men. On my return found a letter from the Turkish Commander-in-Chief giving his "full consent" to the armistice he himself had asked me for! A save-face document, no doubt: the wounded are all Turks as our men did not leave their trenches on the 19th; the dead, also, I am glad to say, almost entirely Turks; but anyway, one need not be too punctilious where it is a matter of giving decent burial to so many men.

GRAND QUARTIER GÉNÉRAL DE LA 5ᴹᴱ ARMÉE
OTTOMANE.
le 22 mai 1915.

EXCELLENCE!

J'ai l'honneur d'informer Votre Excellence que les propositions concernant la conclusion d'un armistice pour enterrer les morts et secourir les blessés des deux parties adverses, ont trouvé mon plein consentement — et que seule nos sentiments d'humanité nous y ont déterminés.

J'ai investi le lieutenant-colonel Fahreddin du pouvoir de signer en mon nom.

J'ai l'honneur d'être avec l'assurance de ma plus haute considération.

(*Sd.*) "LIMAN VON SANDERS,"
Commandant en chef de la 5ᵐᵉ
Armée Ottomane."

Commandant en chef des Forces Britanniques,
Sir John Hamilton, Excellence.*

---

* Grand Headquarters of the 5th Ottomann Army.
May 22, 1915.

Your Excellency!

I have the honor to inform Your Excellency that the proposals concerning the conclusion of an armistice to bury the dead and rescue the wounded of both

23rd May, 1915. H.M.T. "Arcadian." Blazing hot. Wrote all day. Had an hour and a half's talk with de Robeck — high politics as well as our own rather anxious affairs. No one knows how the new First Lord will play up, but Asquith, for sure, chucks away his mainspring if he parts with Winston: as to Fisher, he too has energy but none of it came our way so he will have no tears from us, though he has friends here too. The submarine scare is full on; the beastly things have frightened us more than all the Turks and all their German guns.

24th May, 1915. H.M.T. "Arcadian." Vice-Admiral Nicol, French Naval Commander-in-Chief, came aboard to pay me a visit. Armistice from 9.30 a.m. to 4.30 p.m. for burial of Turkish dead. All went off quite smoothly.... This moment, 12.40 p.m. the Captain has rushed in to say that H.M.S. *Triumph* is sinking! He caught the bad news on his wireless as it flew. Beyond doubt the German submarine. What exactly is about to happen, God knows. The fleet cannot see itself wiped out by degrees; and yet, without the fleet, how are we soldiers to exist? One more awful conundrum set to us, but the Navy will solve it, for sure.

25th May, 1915. H.M.T. "Arcadian." Bad news confirmed. The Admiral came aboard and between us we tried to size up the new situation and to readjust ourselves thereto. Our nicely worked out system for supplying the troops has in a moment been tangled up

---

opposing parties, have found my full consent - and that our feelings of humanity alone have made us so determined.
    I have invested Lieutenant-Colonel Fahreddin with the power to sign on my behalf.
    I have the honor to convey the assurances of my highest consideration.
                    (Sd.) "Liman von Sanders,"
               Commander-in-Chief of the 5th
                    Ottoman Army."

Commander-in-Chief of the British Forces,
    Sir John Hamilton, Excellency.

into a hundred knotty problems. Instead of our small craft working to and fro in half mile runs, henceforth they will have to cover 60 miles per trip. Until now the big ocean going ships have anchored close up to Helles or Anzac; in future Mudros will be the only possible harbour for these priceless floating depots. Imbros, here, lies quite open to submarine attacks, and in a northerly gale, becomes a mere roadstead. The Admiral, who regards soldiers as wayward water babes, has insisted on lashing a merchantman to each side of the *Arcadian* to serve as torpedo buffers. There are, it seems, at least two German submarines prowling about at the present moment between Gaba Tepe and Cape Helles. After torpedoing the *Triumph* the same submarine fired at and missed the *Vengeance*. The *Lord Nelson* with the Admiral, as well as three French battleships, zig-zagged out of harbour and made tracks for Mudros in the afternoon. We are left all alone in our glory with our two captive merchantmen. The attitude is heroic but not, I think, so dangerous as it is uncomfortable. The big ocean liners lashed to port and starboard cut us off from air as well as light and one of them is loaded with Cheddar. When Mr. Jorrocks awoke James Pigg and asked him to open the window and see what sort of a hunting morning it was, it will be remembered that the huntsman opened the cupboard by mistake and made the reply, "Hellish dark and smells of cheese." Well, that immortal remark hits us off to a T. Never mind. Light will be vouchsafed. Amen.

The burial of 3,000 Turks by armistice at Anzac seems to have been carried out without a hitch. All these 3,000 Turks were killed between the 18th and 20th instant. By the usual averages this figure implies over 12,000 wounded so the Lord has vouchsafed us a signal victory indeed. Birdwood's men were all out and his reserves, or rather the lack of them, would not permit him to counter-attack the moment the enemy's assault was repulsed. When we read of battles in histories we feel, we see, so clearly the value of counter-attack and the folly of passive defence; but, in the field, the struggle has sometimes been so close that the victorious defence are left gasping. The enemy were very polite during the armistice, and by way of being highly solemn and correct, but they could not refrain from bursting into laughter when the Australians held up cigarettes and called out "baksheesh."

Last night the French and the Naval Brigade made a good advance with slight loss. The East Lancs also pushed on a little bit.

26th May, 1915. H.M.T. "Arcadian." Entertained a small party of Australian officers as my private guests for 48 hours, my idea being to give them a bit of a rest. Colonel Monash, commanding 4th Australian Infantry Brigade, was the senior. He is a very competent officer. I have a clear memory of him standing under a gum tree at Lilydale, near Melbourne, holding a conference after a manœuvre, when it had been even hotter than it is here now. I was prepared for intelligent criticisms but I thought they would be so wrapped up in the cotton wool of politeness that no one would be very much impressed. On the contrary, he stated his opinions in the most direct, blunt, telling way. The fact was noted in my report and now his conduct out here has been fully up to sample.

A horrid mishap. Landing some New Zealand Mounted Rifles at Anzac, the destroyer anchored within range of the Turkish guns instead of slowly steaming about out of range until the picket boats came off to bring the men ashore. The Turks were watching and, as soon as she let go her anchor, opened fire from their guns by the olive, and before the destroyer could get under weigh six of these fine New Zealand lads were killed and forty-five wounded. A hundred fair fighting casualties would affect me less. To be knocked out before having taken part in a battle, or even having set foot upon the Promised Land — nothing could be more cruel.

A special order to the troops:

GENERAL HEADQUARTERS,
25th May, 1915.

1. Now that a clear month has passed since the Mediterranean Expeditionary Force began its night and day fighting with the enemy, the General Commanding desires me to explain to officers, non-commissioned officers and men the real significance of the calls made upon them to risk their lives apparently for nothing better than to gain a few yards of uncultivated land.

2. A comparatively small body of the finest troops in the world,

French and British, have effected a lodgment close to the heart of a great continental empire, still formidable even in its decadence. Here they stand firm, or slowly advance, and in the efforts made by successive Turkish armies to dislodge them the rotten Government at Constantinople is gradually wearing itself out. The facts and figures upon which this conclusion is based have been checked and verified from a variety of sources. Agents of neutral powers possessing good sources of information have placed both the numbers and the losses of the enemy much higher than they are set forth here, but the General Commanding prefers to be on the safe side and to give his troops a strictly conservative estimate.

Before operations began the strength of the defenders of the Dardanelles was:

Gallipoli Peninsula . . . . 34,000 and about 100 guns.

Asiatic side of Straits. 41,000

All the troops on the Gallipoli Peninsula and fifty per cent. of the troops on the Asiatic side were Nizam, that is to say, regular first line troops. They were transferable, and were actually transferred to this side upon which the invaders disembarked. Our Expeditionary Force effected its landing it will be seen, in the face of an enemy superior, not only to the covering parties which got ashore the first day, but superior actually to the total strength at our disposal. By the 12th May, the Turkish Army of occupation had been defeated in several engagements, and would have been at the end of their resources had they not meanwhile received reinforcements of 20,000 infantry and 21 batteries of Field Artillery.

Still the Expeditionary Force held its own, and more than its own, inflicting fresh bloody defeats upon the newcomers and again the Turks must certainly have given way had not a second reinforcement reached the Peninsula from Constantinople and Smyrna amounting at the lowest estimate to 24,000 men.

3. From what has been said it will be understood that the Mediterranean Expeditionary Force, supported by its gallant comrades the Fleet, but with constantly diminishing effectives, has held in check or wrested ground from some 120,000 Turkish troops elaborately entrenched and supported by a powerful artillery.

The enemy has now few more Nizam troops at his disposal and

not many Redif or second class troops. Up to date his casualties are 55,000, and again, in giving this figure, the General Commanding has preferred to err on the side of low estimates.

Daily we make progress, and whenever the reinforcements close at hand begin to put in an appearance, the Mediterranean Expeditionary Force will press forward with a fresh impulse to accomplish the greatest Imperial task ever entrusted to an army.

27th May, 1915. H.M.T. "Arcadian." The *Majestic* has been torpedoed and has sunk off Cape Helles. Got the news at mid-day. Fuller, my Artillery Commander, and Ashmead-Bartlett, the correspondent, were both on board, and both were saved — minus kit! About 40 men have gone under. Bad luck. A Naval Officer who has seen her says she is lying in shallow water — 6 fathoms — bottom upwards looking like a stranded whale. He says the German submarine made a most lovely shot at her through a crowd of cargo ships and transports. Like picking a royal stag out of his harem of does. To my Staff, they tell me, he delivered himself further but, as I said to the Officer who repeated these criticisms to me, "judge not that ye be not judged."

28th May, 1915. H.M.T. "Arcadian." Went for a walk with the Admiral. He refuses any longer to accept the responsibility of keeping us afloat. As Helles, Anzac and Tenedos have each been ruled out, we are going to doss down on this sandbank opposite us. One thing, it will be central to both my theatres of work.

29th May, 1915. H.M.T. "Arcadian." The Commodore, Roger Keyes, arrived mid-day and invited me to come over to Helles with him on a destroyer, H.M.S. *Scorpion*. He was crossing in hopes — *in hopes,* if you please — of hitting off the submarine. The idea that it might hit him had not seemed to occur to him. On the way we were greatly excited to see the bladder of an indicator net smoking. So we rushed about the place and bombs were got ready to drop. But the net remained motionless and, as the water was too deep for the submarine to be lying at the bottom, it seemed (although no one dared to say so) that a porpoise had been poking fun at the Commodore.

View of "V" Beach, Taken from S.S. "River Clyde" "*Central News*" *phot.*

Landing at Helles inspected the various roads, which were in the making. Next saw Hunter-Weston. Canvassed plans with him and felt myself refreshed. Then went on to Gouraud's Headquarters, taking the Commodore with me. My Commanders are an asset which cancels many a debit. Gouraud is in excellent form and gave us tea. Walked down to "V" Beach at 6 p.m.

When we got on to the pier, which ends in the *River Clyde*, we found another destroyer, the *Wolverine*, under Lieutenant-Commander Keyes, the brother of the Commodore. She was to take us across, and (of all places in the world to select for a berth!) she had run herself alongside the *River Clyde* which was, at that moment, busy playing target to the heavy guns of Asia. I imagined that taking aboard a boss like the Commander-in-Chief, as well as that much bigger boss (in naval estimates) his own big brother, the Commodore, our Lieutenant-Commander would nip away presto. Not a bit of it! No sooner had he got us aboard than he came out boldly and very, very slowly, stern first, from the lee of the *River Clyde* and began a duel against Asia with 4-inch lyddite from the

Wolverine's after gun. The fight seems quite funny to me now but, at the time, serio-comic would have better described my impressions. Shells ashore are part of the common lot; they come in the day's work: on the water; in a cockleshell — well, you can't go to ground, anyway!

Heavy fighting at Anzac. The Turks fired a mine under Quinn's Post and then rushed a section of the defence isolated by the explosion. At 6 in the morning the crater was, Birdie says, most gallantly retaken with the bayonet. There are excursions and alarms; attacks and counter-attacks; bomb-showers to which the bayonet charge is our only retort — but we hold fast the crater!

When I tell them at home that if they will give me munitions enough to let me advance two miles I will give them Constantinople, that is the truth. On paper, the Turks no doubt might assert with equal force that if they got forces enough together to drive the Australians back a short two hundred yards they could give the Sultan the resounding prestige of a Peninsula freed from the Giaour. But that would require more Turks than the Turks could feed, whereas we know we could do it now, as we are — given the wherewithal — trench mortars, hand grenades and bombs, for example.

A message from Hanbury Williams, who is with the Grand Duke Nicholas, to say that all idea of sending me a Russian Army Corps to land at the Bosphorus has been abandoned!!!

30th May, 1915. H.M.T. "Arcadian." Went to Anzac in a destroyer. The Cove was being heavily shelled, and the troops near the beach together with the fatigue parties handling stores and ammunition, had dashed into their dugouts like marmots at the shadow of an eagle. Birdwood came out to meet me on this very unhealthy spot; indeed, in spite of my waving him back, he walked right on to the end of the deserted pier. Just as we were getting near his quarters, a couple of shrapnel burst at an angle and height which, by the laws of gravity, momentum and velocity ought to have put a fullstop to this chronicle. Actually, we walked on — through the "Valley of Death" — past the spot where the brave Bridges bit the dust, to the Headquarters of the 4th Australian

Infantry Brigade. Thence I could see the enemy trenches in front of Quinn's Post, and also a very brisk bomb combat in full flame where the New Zealand Mounted Rifles were making good the Turkish communicating post they had seized earlier in the day.

Nothing more strange than this inspection. Along the path at the bottom of the valley warning notices were stuck up. The wayfarer has to be as punctilious about each footstep as Christian in the "Pilgrim's Progress." Should he disregard the placards directing him to keep to the right or to the left of the track, he is almost certainly shot. Half of the pathway may be as safe as Piccadilly, whilst he who treads the other had far better be up yonder at hand grips with the Turks. Presumably some feature of the ground defilades one part, for the enemy cannot see into the valley, although, were they only 20 yards nearer the edge of the cliff, they would command its whole extent. The spirit of the men is invincible. Only lately have we been able to give them blankets: as to square meals and soft sleeps, these are dreams of the past, they belonged to another state of being. Yet I never struck a more jovial crew. Men staggering under huge sides of frozen beef; men struggling up cliffs with kerosine tins full of water; men digging; men cooking; men card-playing in small dens scooped out from the banks of yellow clay — everyone wore a Bank Holiday air; — evidently the ranklings and worry of mankind — miseries and concerns of the spirit — had fled the precincts of this valley. The Boss — the bill — the girl — envy, malice, hunger, hatred — had scooted far away to the Antipodes.

All the time, overhead, the shell and rifle bullets groaned and whined, touching just the same note of violent energy as was in evidence everywhere else. To understand that awful din, raise the eyes 25 degrees to the top of the cliff which closes in the tail end of the valley and you can see the Turkish hand grenades bursting along the crest, just where an occasional bayonet flashes and figures hardly distinguishable from Mother earth crouch in an irregular line. Or else they rise to fire and are silhouetted a moment against the sky and then you recognize the naked athletes from the Antipodes and your heart goes into your mouth as a whole bunch of them dart forward suddenly, and as suddenly disappear. And the bomb shower stops dead — for the moment; but, all the time, from that fiery crest line which is Quinn's, there comes a slow constant trickle of wounded — some dragging themselves painfully along; others being carried along on stretchers. Bomb wounds all; a ceaseless, silent stream of bandages and blood. Yet three out of four of "the boys" have grit left for a gay smile or a cheery little nod to their comrades waiting for their turn as they pass, pass, pass, down on their way to the sea.

There are poets and writers who see naught in war but carrion, filth, savagery and horror. The heroism of the rank and file makes no appeal. They refuse war the credit of being the only exercise in devotion on the large scale existing in this world. The superb moral victory over death leaves them cold. Each one to his taste. To me this is no valley of death — it is a valley brim full of life at its highest power. Men live through more in five minutes on that crest than they do in five years of Bendigo or Ballarat. Ask the brothers of these very fighters — Calgoorlie or Coolgardie miners — to do one quarter the work and to run one hundredth the risk on a wages basis — instanter there would be a riot. But here, — not a murmur, not a question; only a radiant force of camaraderie in action.

The Turks have heaps of cartridges and more shells, anyway, than we have. They have as many grenades as they can throw; we have — a dozen per Company. There is a very bitter feeling amongst all the troops, but especially the Australians, at this lack of elementary weapons like grenades. Our overseas men are very intelligent. They are prepared to make allowances for lack of shell; lack of guns; lack of high explosives. But they know there must be something wrong when the Turks carry ten good bombs to our one bad one; and they think, some of them, that this must be my fault. Far from it. *Directly* after the naval battle of the 18th March — i.e., over two months ago, I wrote out a cable asking for bombs. I sent this on my own happy thought, and I had hoped for a million by the date of landing five weeks later. But I got, practically, none; nor any promise for the future. In default of help from home, we have tried to manufacture these primitive but very effective projectiles for ourselves with jam pots, meat tins and any old rubbish we can scrape together. De Lothbinière has shown ingenuity in thus making bricks without straw. The Fleet, too, has played up and de Robeck has guaranteed me two thousand to be made by the artificers on the battleships. Maxwell in Egypt has been improvising a few; Methuen at Malta says they can't make them there. But what a shame that the sons of a manufacturing country like Great Britain should be in straits for engines so simple.

Yesterday and to-day we have fired, for us, a terrible lot of shells (1,800 shrapnel) but never was shot better spent. We reckon the enemy's casualties between 1,000 and 2,000 mainly caused by our guns playing on the columns which came up trying to improve upon their lodgment in Quinn's Post. Add this to the 3,000 killed, and, say, 12,000 wounded on the 18th instant, and it is clear no troops in the world can stand it very long. But we are literally at the end of our shrapnel; and as to high explosive, according to the standards of the gunners, we have never had any!

Left on a picket boat with Birdie to board my destroyer to an accompaniment of various denominations of projectiles. One or two shells burst hard by just as we were scrambling up her side.

Vice-Admiral Nicholls called after my return. Courtauld Thomson, the Red Cross man, dined; very helpful; very well stocked with comforts and everyone likes him, even the R.A.M.C.

31st May, 1915. H.M.T. "Arcadian." Worked in the forenoon. Gouraud, Girodon and Hunter-Weston lunched and we spent the afternoon at the scheme for our next fight. Each of us agreed that Fortune had not been over kind. By one month's hard, close hammering we had at last made the tough *moral* of the Turks more pliant, when lo and behold, in broad daylight, thousands of their common soldiery see with their own eyes two great battleships sink beneath the waves and all the others make an exit more dramatic than dignified. Most of the Armada of store ships had already cleared out and now the last of the battleships has offed it over the offing; a move which the whole of the German Grand Fleet could not have forced them to make! What better pick-me-up could Providence have provided for the badly-shaken Turks? No more inquisitive cruisers ready to let fly a salvo at anything that stirs. No more searchlights by night; no more big explosives flying from the Aegean into the Dardanelles!

Submarines

1st June, 1915. Imbros. Came ashore and stuck up my 80-lb. tent in the middle of a sandbank whereon some sanguine Greek agriculturalist has been trying to plant wheat.

We shall live the simple life; the same life, in fact, as the men, but are glad to be off the ship and able to stretch our legs.

Hard fighting in the North zone and the South. Both outposts captured by us on the 29th May at Anzac and on the French right at Helles heavily attacked. In the North we had to give ground, but not before we had made the enemy pay ten times its value in killed and wounded. Had we only had a few spare rounds of shrapnel we need never have gone back. The War Office have called for a return of my 4.5 howitzer ammunition during the past fortnight, and I find that, since the 14th May, we have expended 477 shell altogether at Anzac and Helles combined. In the South the enemy twice recaptured the redoubt taken by the French on the 29th, but Gouraud, having a nice little parcel of high explosive on hand, was able to drive them out definitely and to keep them out.

2nd June, 1915. Imbros. Working all day in camp. Blazing hot, tempered by a cool breeze towards evening. De Robeck came ashore and we had an hour together in the afternoon. Everything is fixed up for our big attack on the 4th. From aeroplane photographs it would appear that the front line Turkish trenches are meant more as traps for rash forlorn hopes than as strongholds. In fact, the true tug only begins when we try to carry the second line and the flanking machine guns. Gouraud has generously lent us two groups of 75s with H.E. shell, and I am cabling the fact to the War Office as it means a great deal to us. When I say they are lent to us, I do not mean that they put the guns at our disposal. They are only ours for defensive purposes; that is to say, they remain in their own gun positions in the French lines and are to help by thickening the barrage in front of the Naval Division.

De Robeck and Keyes are quite as much at sea as Braithwaite and myself about this original scheme of the British Government for treating a tearing, raging crisis; i.e., by taking no notice of it. I guess that never before in the history of war has a Commander asked urgently that his force might be doubled and then got no orders; no answer of any sort or kind!

When I sent K. my M.F. 234 of the 17th May asking for two Corps, or for Allies, one or the other, I got a reply by return expressing his disappointment; since then, nothing. During that fortnight of silence the whole of the Turkish Empire has been moving — closing in — on the Dardanelles. Then, by a side-wind I happen to hear of the abstraction of a Russian Army Corps from my supposed command; an Army Corps, who by the mere fact of "being," held off a large force of Turks from Gallipoli.

So I have put down a few hard truths. Unpalatable they may be but some day they've got to be faced and the sooner the better. Time has slipped away, but to-day is still better than to-morrow.

What a change since the War Office sent us packing with a bagful of hallucinations. Naval guns sweeping the Turks off the Peninsula; the Ottoman Army legging it from a British submarine waving the Union Jack; Russian help in hand; Greek help on the *tapis*. Now it is our Fleet which has to leg it from the German submarine; there is no ammunition for the guns; no drafts to keep my Divisions up to strength; my Russians have gone to Galicia and the Greeks are lying lower than ever.

No. M.F. 288. From General Sir Ian Hamilton to Earl Kitchener. With reference to my telegrams No. M.F. 274 of 29th May, and No. M.F. 234 of 17th May. If the information sent by Hanbury-Williams, to which I referred in my No. M.F. 274, is correct it is advisable that I should send you a fresh appreciation of the situation.

I assumed in my No. M.F. 234 that you had adequate forces at your disposal, but on the other hand I assumed that some 100,000 Turks would be kept occupied by the Russians. By the defection of Russia, 100,000 Turks are set free in the Caucasus and European Turkey. After deduction of casualties there are at least 80,000 Turks now against us in the Peninsula. There are 20,000 Turks on the Bulgarian frontier which, assuming that Bulgaria remains neutral, are able to reinforce Gallipoli; some, in fact, have already arrived showing the restoration of Turkish confidence in King Ferdinand. Close by on the Asiatic side there remain 10,000 Turks, making a total of 210,000, to which must be added 65,000 who are under training in Europe.

The movement of the Turkish troops has already begun. There

are practically no troops left in Smyrna district, and there are already in the field numbers of troops from European garrisons, while recently it was reported that more are coming.

The movement of a quarter of a million men against us seems to be well under way, and although many of these are ill-trained still with well-run supply and ammunition columns and in trenches designed by Germans the Turk is always formidable.

As regards ammunition, the enemy appears to have an unlimited supply of small-arm ammunition and as many hand-grenades as they can fling. Though there is some indication that gun ammunition is being husbanded, it was reported as late as 27th May, that supplies of shells were being received *via* Roumania, and yesterday it was suggested that artillery ammunition can be manufactured at Constantinople where it is reported that over two hundred engineers have arrived from Krupp's.

At the same time, the temporary withdrawal of our battleships owing to enemy submarines has altered the position to our disadvantage; while not of the highest importance materially this factor carries considerable moral weight.

Taking all these factors into consideration, it would seem that for an early success some equivalent to the suspended Russian co-operation is vitally necessary. The ground gained and the positions which we hold are not such as to enable me to envisage with soldierly equanimity the probability of the large forces adumbrated above being massed against my troops without let or hindrance from elsewhere. Fresh light may be shed on the matter by the battle now imminent, but I am cabling on reasoned existing facts. Time is an object, but if Greece came in, preferably *via* Enos, the problem would be simplified. It is broadly my view that we must obtain the support of a fresh ally in this theatre, or else there should be got ready British reinforcements to the full extent mentioned in my No. M.F. 234, though as stated above the disappearance of Russian co-operation was not contemplated in my estimate.

3rd June, 1915. Imbros. Meant to go to Anzac; sea too rough; in the afternoon saw de Robeck and Roger Keyes. Braithwaite came over and we went through my cable of yesterday. The sailors would just as soon I had left out that remark about the enemy being bucked up by the retreat of our battleships. But the passage implied also that their mere visible presence was shown to be most valuable. Both of them agree that I am well within the mark in saying what I did about the loss of my Russian Army Corps. Roger Keyes next launched a dry land criticism. He rightly thinks that the weakness of our *present* units is *the* real weakness: he thinks we are far more in need of drafts than of fresh units; he suggests that a rider be sent now to insist that the estimates in yesterday's cable were only made on the assumption that my present force is kept up to strength. I did press that very point in my first cable of 17th May, which is referred to in the opening of this cable; further, we keep on saying it every week in our War Office cable giving strengths. After all, K. is 65. He still believes "A man's a man and a rifle's a rifle"; I still believe that half the value of every human being depends upon his environment: we are not going to convert one another now.

As we were actually talking, Williams brought over an answer:

No. 5104, cipher. From Earl Kitchener to General Sir Ian Hamilton. With reference to your No. M.F. 288. Owing to the restricted nature of the ground you occupy and the experience we have had in Flanders of increased forces acting in trench positions, I own I have some doubts of an early decisive result being obtained by at once increasing the forces at your disposal, but I should like your views as soon as you can — to-day if possible. Are you convinced that with immediate reinforcements to the extent you mention you could force the Kilid Bahr position and thus finish the Dardanelles operations?

You mentioned in a previous telegram that you intended to keep reinforcements on islands, is this your intention with regard to the Lowland Division, now on its way to you, and the other troops when sent?

K.'s brief cable is *intensely* characteristic. I have taken down hundreds of his wires. We are face to face here with his very self at *first hand*. How curiously it reveals the man's instinct, or genius — call it what you will.

K. sees in a flash what the rest of the world does not seem to see so clearly; viz., that the piling up of increased forces opposite entrenched positions is a spendthrift, unscientific proceeding. He wishes to know if I mean to do this. To draw me out he assumes if I get the troops, I *would* at once commit them to trench warfare by crowding them in behind the lines of Helles or Anzac. Actually I intend to keep the bulk of them on the islands, so as to throw them unexpectedly against some key position which is *not* prepared for defence. But I have to be very careful what I say, seeing that the Turks got wind of the date of our first landing from London *via* Vienna. Least said to a Cabinet, least leakage.

That is not all. Curt as is the cable it has yet scope to show up a little more of our great K.'s outfit. His infernal hurry. "To-day": I am to reply, to-day! He has taken some two and a half weeks to answer my request for two Army Corps and I am to answer a far more obscure question in two and a half minutes. Why, since my appeal of 17th May the situation has not stood still. A Commander in the field is like a cannon ball. If he stops going ahead, he falls dead. You can't stop moving for a fortnight and then expect to carry on where you left off; I think the Duke of Wellington said this; if he didn't he should have. To err is to be human and the troops, if sent at once, may or may not, fulfil our hopes. All we here can say is this:

(1) If the Army Corps had been sent at once (i.e., two weeks ago) the results should have been decisive.
(2) If the Army Corps are not sent at once, there can be no early decision.

Braithwaite, De Robeck and Keyes agree to (1) and (2) but the cabled answer will not be so simple and, in spite of K.'s sudden impatience, I must sleep over it first.

Written whilst Williams waits:

No. M.F. 292. From General Sir Ian Hamilton to Earl Kitchener. Secret. To-morrow, 4th June, I am fighting a general action. Therefore I feel sure that you will wish me to defer my answer to your telegram No. 5104, cipher, until I see the result.

These lofty strategical questions must not make me forget an equally vital munitions message just to hand. I have cabled K. twice in the past day or two about shells. On the 1st instant I had said:

I still await the information promised in your x. 4773, A. 5, of 19th instant. In my opinion the supply of gun ammunition can hardly be considered adequate or safe until the following conditions can be filled:

(1) That the amounts with units and on the Lines of Communication should be made up to the number of rounds per gun which is allowed in War Establishment figures of 29th Division.
(2) That these full amounts should be maintained and despatched automatically without any further application from us, beyond a weekly statement of the expenditure which will be cabled to you every Saturday.
(3) In view of the number and the extent of the entrenchments to be dealt with it is necessary that a high proportion of high explosive shell for 18 pounder and howitzers be included in accordance with the report of my military advisers.

We now have his reply:

No. 5088, cipher. From Earl Kitchener to Sir Ian Hamilton. With reference to your telegrams No. M.F. 281 and No. M.F.G.T. 967. We cannot supply ammunition to maintain a 1,000 rounds a gun owing to the demands from France, but consignments are being sent which amount to 17 rounds per gun per day for the 18 pounder and 4.5.-inch howitzer; this is considered by General Joffre and Sir John French as necessary. As much as possible of other natures will be sent. As regards quantities, you will be informed as early as possible. As available, H.E. shells will be sent for 18 pounder guns and howitzers.

If we get 17 rounds per gun per day for the 18 pounders and 4.5 howitzers we shall indeed be on velvet. To be given what satisfies Joffre and French — that sounds too good to be true. So ran my thoughts and Braithwaite's on a first reading. Then came the C.R.A. who puts another light on the proposal and points out that the implied comparison with France is fallacious. We are undergunned here as compared with France in the proportion of 1 to 3. I mean to say that, in proportion to "bayonets" we have rather less than one third of the "guns." *Therefore*, if we were really to have munitions on the scale "considered necessary by General Joffre and Sir John French," we ought to have three times 17 rounds per day per gun; i.e. 51 rounds per day per gun. But never mind. *If we do get* the 17 rounds we shall be infinitely better off than we have been: "and so say all of us!" Putting this cable together with yesterday's we all of us feel that the home folk are beginning to yawn and rub their eyes and that ere long they may really be awake.

4th June, 1915. Imbros. Left camp after breakfast and boarded the redoubtable *Wolverine* under that desperado Lieutenant-Commander Keyes. The General Staff came alongside and we made our way to Cape Helles through a blinding dust storm — at least, the dust came right out to sea, but it was on shore that it became literally blinding.

On the pier I met Gouraud who walked up with me. Gouraud was very grave but confident. My post of command had been "dug out" for me well forward on the left flank by Hunter-Weston. In that hole two enormous tarantulas and I passed a day that seems to me ten years. The torture of suspense; the extremes of exaltation and of depression; the Red Indian necessity of showing no sign: all this varied only by the vicious scream of shell sailing some 30 feet over our heads on their way towards the 60 pounders near the point. A Commander feels desperately lonely at such moments. On him, and on him alone, falls the crushing onus of responsibility: to be a Corps Commander is child's play in *that* comparison. The Staff are gnawed with anxiety too — are saying their prayers as fast as they can, no doubt, as they follow the ebb and flow of the long khaki line through their glasses. Yes, I have done that myself in the old days from Charasia onwards. Yet how faintly is my anguish reflected in the mere anxiety of their minds.

Chapters could be written about this furious battle fought in a whirlwind of dust and smoke; some day I hope somebody may write them. After the first short spell of shelling our men fixed bayonets and lifted them high above the parapet. The Turks thinking we were going to make the assault, rushed troops into their trenches, until then lightly held. No sooner were our targets fully manned than we shelled them in earnest and went on at it until — on the stroke of mid-day — out dashed our fellows into the open. For the best part of an hour it seemed that we had won a decisive victory. On the left all the front line Turkish trenches were taken. On the right the French rushed the *"Haricot"* — so long a thorn in their flesh; next to them the Anson lads stormed another big Turkish redoubt in a slap-dash style reminding me of the best workof the old Regular Army; but the boldest and most brilliant exploit of the lot was the charge made by the Manchester Brigade* in the centre who wrested two lines of trenches from the Turks; and then, carrying right on; on to the lower slopes of Achi Baba, had *nothing* between them and its summit but the clear, unentrenched hillside. They lay there — the line of our brave lads, plainly visible to a pair of good glasses — there they actually lay! We wanted, so it seemed, but a reserve to advance in their support and carry them right up to the top. We said — and yet could hardly believe our own words — "We are through!"

Alas, too previous that remark. Everything began to go wrong. First the French were shelled and bombed out of the *"Haricot"*; next the right of the Naval Division became uncovered and they had to give way, losing many times more men in the yielding than in the capture of their ground. Then came the turn of the Manchesters, left in the lurch, with their right flank hanging in the air. By all the laws of war they ought to have tumbled back anyhow, but by the laws of the Manchesters they hung on and declared they could do so for ever. How to help? Men! Men, not so much now to sustain the Manchesters as to force back the Turks who were enfilading them from the *"Haricot"* and from that redoubt held for awhile by the R.N.D. on their right.

I implored Gouraud to try and make a push and promised that the Naval Division would retake their redoubt if he could retake the *"Haricot"*. Gouraud said he would go in at 3 p.m. The hour came; nothing happened. He then said he could not call upon his men again till 4 o'clock, and at 4 o'clock he said definitely that he would not be able to make another assault. The moment that last message came in I first telephoned and then, to make doubly sure,

---

* The Fifth Lancs Fusiliers were also working with this Brigade and behaved with great bravery. — *Ian H., 1920.*

ran myself to Hunter-Weston's Headquarters so as not to let another moment be lost in pulling out the Manchester Brigade. I had 500 yards to go, and, rising the knoll, I would have been astonished, had I had any faculty of astonishment left in me, to meet Beetleheim, the Turk, who was with French in South Africa. I suppose he is here as an interpreter, or something, but I didn't ask. Seeing me alone for the moment he came along. He had quite a grip of the battle and seemed to hope I might let the Manchesters try and stick it out through the night, as he thought the Turks were too much done to do much more.

But it was not good enough. To fall back was agony; not to do it would have been folly. Hunter-Weston felt the same. When Fate has first granted just a sip of the wine of success the slip between the cup and lip comes hardest. The upshot of the whole affair is that the enemy still hold a strong line of trenches between us and Achi Baba. Our four hundred prisoners, almost all made by the Manchester Brigade, amongst whom a good number of officers, do not console me. Having to make the Manchesters yield up their hard won gains is what breaks my heart. Had I known the result of our fight before the event, I should have been happy enough. Three or four hundred yards of ground plus four hundred prisoners are distances and numbers which may mean little in Russia or France, but here, where we only have a mile or two to go, land has a value all its own. Yes, I should have been happy enough. But, to have to yield up the best half — the vital half — of our gains — to have had our losses trebled on the top of a cheaply won victory — these are the reverse side of our medal for the 4th June.

Going back we fell in with a blood-stained crowd from the Hood, Howe and Anson Battalions. Down the little gully to the beach we could only walk very slowly. At my elbow was Colonel Crauford Stuart, commanding the Hood Battalion. He had had his jaw smashed but I have seen men pull longer faces at breaking a collar stud. He told me that the losses of the Naval Division has been very heavy, the bulk of them during their retreat. From the moment the Turks drove the French out of the *"Haricot"* the enfilade fire became murderous.

On the beach was General de Lisle, fresh from France. He is taking over the 29th Division from Hunter-Weston who ascends to the command of the newly formed 8th Army Corps. De Lisle seemed in very good form although it must have been rather an eye-opener landing in the thick of this huge stream of wounded. How well I remember seeing him galloping at the head of his Mounted Infantry straight for Pretoria; and my rage when, under orders from Headquarters, I had to send swift messengers to tell him he must rein back for some reason never made clear.

5th June, 1915. Imbros. Best part of the day occupied in a hundred and one sequels of the battle. The enemy have been quiet; they have had a belly-full. De Robeck came off to see me at 5.30, to have a final talk (amongst other things) as to the Enos and Bulair ideas before I send my final answer to K. If we dare not advertise the detail of our proposed tactics, we may take the lesser risk of saying what we are *not* going to attempt. The Admiral is perfectly clear against Bulair. There is no protection there for the ships against submarines except Enos harbour and Enos is only one fathom deep. After all, the main thing they want is that I should commit myself to a statement that if I get the drafts and troops asked for in my various cables, I will make good. That, I find quite reasonable.

6th June, 1915. Imbros. A very hot and dusty day. Still sweeping up the *débris* of the battle. Besides my big cable have been studying strengths with my A.G. The Battalions are dwindling to Companies and the Divisions to Brigades.

The cable is being ciphered: not a very luminous document: how could it be? The great men at home seem to forget that they cannot draw wise counsels from their servants unless they confide in them and give them *all* the factors of the problem. If a client goes to a lawyer for advice the first thing the lawyer asks him to do is to make a clean breast of it. Before K. asks me to specify what I can do if he sends me these unknown and — in Great Britain — most variable quantities, Territorial or New Army Divisions, he ought to make a clean breast of it by telling me:

(1) What he has.

(2) What Sir John French wants.
(3) Whether Italy will move — or Greece.
(4) What is happening in the Balkans, — in the Caucasus, — in Mesopotamia.

After all, the Armies of the Caucasus and of Mesopotamia are not campaigning in the moon. They are two Allied Armies working with me (or supposed to be working with me) against a common enemy.

The first part of my cable I discuss the cause which led to the disappointing end to the battle of the 4th already described and then go on to say:

> I am convinced by this action that with my present force my progress will be very slow, but in the absence of any further important alteration in the situation such as a definite understanding between Turkey and Bulgaria, I believe the reinforcements asked for in my No. 234 will eventually enable me to take Kilid Bahr and will assuredly expedite the decision. I entirely agree that the restricted nature of the ground I occupy militates against me in success, however much I am reinforced; that was why in my Nos. M.F. 214 and M.F. 234 I emphasized the desirability of securing co-operation of new Allied Forces acting on a second line of operations. I have been very closely considering the possibility of opening a new line of operations myself, *via* Enos, if sufficient reinforcements should be available. The Vice-Admiral, however, is at present strongly averse to the selection of Enos owing to the open and unprotected nature of anchorage and to the presence of enemy submarines. Otherwise Enos offers very favourable prospects, both strategically and tactically, and is so direct a threat to Constantinople as to necessitate withdrawal of Turkish troops from the Peninsula to meet it. Smyrna or even Adramyti which are not open to the same objections are too far from me, but the effect of entry of a fresh Ally at either place would inevitably make itself felt before very long in preventing further massing of the Turkish army against me, and perhaps even in drawing off troops; a considerable moral and political effect might also be produced, and all information points to those districts being denuded of troops.
>
> With regard to the employment of the reinforcements asked for in my No. M.F. 234, General Birdwood estimates that four Brigades

are necessary to clear and extend his front sufficiently to prepare a serious move towards Maidos. I should therefore allocate a corps to the Australian-New Zealand Army Corps as the other two brigades would be required to give weight to his advance. The French Force as at present constituted, and the Naval Division which has been roughly handled, would be replaced in front of the line by the other corps. This reinforcement to be exclusive of any help we may receive from Allied troops operating on a second line of operations so distant as Smyrna.

With reference to your last paragraph I have no alternative, until Achi Baba is in my possession, but to keep reinforcements on islands or elsewhere handy. I have made arrangements at present, however, for one Infantry Brigade and Engineers of the Lowland Division on the Peninsula, one Infantry Brigade at Imbros and the remaining Infantry Brigade at Alexandria to be ready to start at 12 hours' notice whenever I telegraph for it. Besides all the reasons given above, no troops in existence can continue fighting night and day without respite.

Three weeks have passed now since I asked for two British Corps or for Allies and still no reply or notice of any sort except that message of the 3rd instant expressing doubts as to whether any good purpose will be served by sending us help "at once." Well; there hasn't been much "at once" about it but I have not played the Sybilline book trick or doubled my demand with each delay as I ought perhaps to have done. Now I think we are bound to hear something but I can't make out what has come over K. of K. In the old days his prime force lay in his faculty of focusing every iota of his energy upon the pivotal project, regardless (so it used to appear) of the other planks of the platform. A "side show" to him meant the non-vital part of the business, *at that moment*: it was not a question of troops or of ranks of Generals. For the time being the interests of an enterprise of five thousand would obliterate those of fifty. No man ever went the whole hog better. He would turn the whole current of his energy to help the man of the hour. The rest were bled white to help him. If they howled they found that K. and his Staff were deaf, and for the same reason, as the crew of Ulysses to the Sirens. Several times in South Africa K., so doing, carried the Imperial Standard to victory through a series of hair's breadth escapes. But to-day, though he sees, the power of believing in his own vision and of hanging on to it like a bulldog, seems paralysed. He hesitates. Ten short years ago, if K.'s heart had been set on Constantinople, why, to Constantinople he would have gone. Paris might have screamed; he would not have swerved a hair's breadth till he had gripped the Golden Horn.

7th June, 1915. Imbros. Left camp early and went to Cape Helles on a destroyer. On our little sandbag pier, built by Egyptians and Turkish prisoners, I met General Wallace and his A.D.C. (a son of Walter Long's). Wallace has come here to take up his duty as Inspector-General of Communications. About ten days ago he was forced upon us. He is reputed a good executive Brigadier of the Indian Army, but we want him, not to train Sepoys but to create one of the biggest organizing and administrative jobs in the world. His work will comprise the whole of the transhipment of stores from the ships to small craft; their dispatch over 60 miles of sea to the Peninsula, and the maintenance of all the necessary machinery in good running order. The task is tremendous, and here is a simple soldier, without any experience of naval men or matters, or the British soldier, or of Administration on a large scale, or even of superior Staff duties, sent me for the purpose.

We want a competent business man at Mudros, ready to grapple with millions of public money; ready to cable on his own for goods or gear by the ten thousand pounds worth. We want a man of tried business courage; a man who can tackle contractors. We are sent an Indian Brigadier who has never, so far as I can make out, in his longish life had undivided responsibility for one hundred pounds of public belongings. I cabled to K. my objection as strongly as seemed suitable, but he tells me to carry on. He tells me to carry on and, in doing so, throws an amusing sidelight upon himself. Into his cable he sticks the words, "Ellison cannot be spared." K. believes that my protest *re* Wallace has, at the back of it, a wish to put in the Staff Officer he took from me when I started. He doesn't believe in my zeal for efficiency at Mudros; he thinks my little plan is to work General Ellison into the billet. Certainly, I'd like an organizer of Ellison's calibre, but he had not, it so happens, entered my mind till K. put him there!

Landing at "W" Beach, I walked over to the 9th Division and met Generals Hunter-Weston, de Lisle and Doran. As we were having our confab, the Turkish guns from Asia were steadily pounding the ridge just South of Headquarters. One or two big fellows fell within 100 yards of the Mess. After an A.1 lunch (for which much glory to Carter, A.D.C.) visited Gouraud at French 281] Headquarters. Going along the coast we were treated to an exciting spectacle. The Turkish guns in Asia stopped firing at Headquarters and turned on to a solitary French transport containing forage, which had braved the submarines and instead of transhipping (as is now the order) at Mudros, had anchored close to "V" Beach. After several overs and unders they hit her three times running and set her on fire. Destroyers and trawlers rushed to her help. Bluejackets boarded her; got her fire under control; got her under steam and moved out. The amazing part of the affair lay in the conduct of the Turks. Having made their three hits, then was the moment to sink the bally ship. But no; they switched back once more onto the Peninsula, and left their helpless prize to make a leisurely and unmolested escape. Anyone but a Turk would have opened rapid fire on seeking his target smoking like a factory chimney, ringed round by a crowd of small craft. But these old Turks are real freaks. Their fierce courage on the defensive is the only cert about them. On all other points it becomes a fair war risk to presume upon their happy-go-lucky behaviour. If this crippled ship had been full of troops instead of hay they would equally have let her slip through their fingers.

I stayed the best part of an hour with Gouraud. He can throw no light from the French side upon the reason for the strange hesitations of our Governments. As he says, after reporting an entirely unexpected and unprepared for situation and asking for the wherewithal to cope withit, a Commander should get fresh orders. Either: we cannot give you what you ask, so fall back onto the defensive; or, go ahead, we will give you the means. Taking leave we came back again by the 29th Headquarters where I saw Douglas, commanding the 42nd Division. Got home latish. As I was on my way to our destroyer took in a wireless saying that submarine E.11 had returned safely after three fruitful weeks in the Marmora.

A most singular message is in:

(No. 5199).
From Earl Kitchener to General Sir Ian Hamilton.

 With reference to your telegram No. M.F. 301, instead of sending such telegrams reporting operations, privately to Earl Kitchener, will you please send them to the Secretary of State. A separate telegram might have been sent dealing with the latter part about Doran.

 May the devil fly away with me if I know what that means! Braithwaite is as much at a loss as myself. No one knows better than we do how much store K. sets on having all these messages addressed to him personally. There's more in this than meets the common or garden optic!

 Very heavy firing on the Peninsula at 8 o'clock; a ceaseless tremor of the air which — faint here — denotes tremendous musketry there.

Chapter X – A Decision and the Plan

8th June, 1915. Imbros. We are getting "three Divisions of the New Army"! The Cabinet "are determined to support" us! And why wouldn't they be? Thus runs the cable:

> (No. 5217, cipher). Your difficulties are fully recognized by the Cabinet who are determined to support you. We are sending you three divisions of the New Army. The first of these will leave about the end of this week, and the other two will be sent as transport is available.
>
> The last of the three divisions ought to reach you not later than the first fortnight in July. By that time the Fleet will have been reinforced by a good many units which are much less vulnerable to submarine attack than those now at the Dardanelles, and you can then count on the Fleet to give you continuous support.
>
> While steadily pressing the enemy, there seems no reason for running any premature risks in the meantime.

In face of K.'s hang-fire cable of the 3rd, and in face of this long three weeks of stupefaction, thank God our rulers have got out of the right side of their beds and are not going to run away.

The first thing to be done was to signal to the Admiral to come over. At 2 p.m. he and Roger Keyes turned up. The great news was read out and yet, such is the contrariness of human nature that neither the hornpipe nor the Highland Fling was danced. Three weeks ago — two weeks ago — we should have been beside ourselves, but irritation now takes the fine edge off our rejoicings. Why not three weeks ago? That was the tone of the meeting. At first: but why be captious in the very embrace of Fortune? So we set to and worked off the broad general scheme in the course of an hour and a half.

Just as the Admiral was going, Ward (of the Intelligence) crossed over with a nasty little damper. The Turks keep just one lap ahead of us. Two new Divisions have arrived and have been launched straightway at our trenches. At the moment we get promises that troops asked for in the middle of May will arrive by the middle of July the Turks get their divisions in the flesh: so much so that they have gained a footing in the lines of the East Lanes: but there is no danger; they will be driven out. We have taken some prisoners.

Dined on board the *Triad*. Sat up later than usual. Not only had we news from home and the news from the Peninsula to thresh out, but there was much to say and hear about E.11 and that apple of Roger Keyes' eye, the gallant Nasmith. Their adventures in the sea of Marmora take the shine out of those of the Argonauts.

Coming back along the well-beaten sandy track, my heart sank to see our mess tent still lit up at midnight. It might be good news but also it might not. Fortunately, it was pleasant news; i.e., Colonel Chauvel, commanding 1st Australian Light Horse Brigade, waiting to see me. I had known him well in Melbourne where he helped me more than anyone else to get the hang of the Australian system. He stays the night.

9th June, 1915. Imbros. A cable saying the new Divisions will form the 9th Corps and asking me my opinion of Mahon as Corps Commander. I shall reply at once he is good up to a point and brave, but not up to running a Corps out here.

Have been sent a gas-mask and a mosquito-net. Quite likely the mask is good bizz and may prolong my poor life a little bit, but this is problematical whereas there's no blooming error about the net.

This morning instead of being awakened at 4.30 a.m. by a cluster of house-flies having a garden party on my nose I just opened one eye and looked at them running about outside my entrenchments, then closed it and fell asleep again for an hour.

10th June, 1915. Imbros. Nothing doing but sheer hard work. The sailors the same. Sent one pretty stiff cable as we all agreed that we must make ourselves quite clear upon the question of guns and shell. After all, any outsider would think it a plain sailing matter enough — a demand, that is to say, from Simpson-Baikie at Helles that he should be gunned and shell supplied on the same scale as the formations he quitted on the Western Front only a few weeks ago. Simpson-Baikie has been specially sent to us by Lord K., who has a high opinion of his merits. A deep-thinking, studious and scientific officer. Well, Baikie says that to put him on anything like the Western Front footing he wants another forty-eight 18-pounders; eight 5-inch hows.; eight 4.5. hows.; eight 6-inch; four 9.2 hows.; four anti-aircraft guns and a thousand rounds a month per field gun; these "wants" he puts down as an absolute minimum. He also wishes me at once to cable for an aeroplane squadron of three flights of four machines each, one flight for patrol work; the other two for spotting.

There is no use enraging people for nothing and "nothing" I am sure would be the result of this demand were it shot in quite nakedly. But I have pressed Baikie's vital points home all the same, *vide* attached:

(No. M.F. 316).

Your No. 5088. After a further consideration of the ammunition question in light of the expenditure on the 4th and 5th June, I would like to point out that I have only the normal artillery complement of two divisions, although actually I have five divisions here. Consequently, each of my guns has to do the work which two and 287] a half guns are doing in Flanders. Any comparison based on expenditure per gun must therefore be misleading. Also a comparison based on numbers of troops would prove to be beside the point, for conditions cannot be identical. Therefore, as I know you will do your best for me and thus leave me contented with the decision you arrive

A Decision and the Plan 215

at, I prefer to state frankly what amount I consider necessary. This amount is at least 30 rounds a day for 18-pr. and 4.5 howitzer already ashore, and I hope that a supply on this scale may be possible. The number of guns already ashore is beginning to prove insufficient for their task, for the enemy have apparently no lack of ammunition and their artillery is constantly increasing. Therefore I hope that the new divisions may be sent out with the full complement of artillery, but, if this is done, the ammunition supply for the artillery of the fresh divisions need only be on the normal scale.

Since the above was written, I have received a report that the enemy has been reinforced by 1,300 Germans for fortress artillery; perhaps their recent shooting is accounted for by this fact.

As to our Air Service, the way this feud between Admiralty and War Office has worked itself out in the field is simply heart-breaking. The War Office wash their hands of the air entirely (at the Dardanelles). I cannot put my own case to the Admiralty although the machines are wanted for overland tactics — a fatal blind alley. All I could do I did this afternoon when the Admiral came to tea and took me for a good stiff walk afterwards.

11th June, 1915. Imbros. Sailed over to Anzac with Braithwaite. Took Birdwood's views upon the outline of our plan (which originated between him and Skeen) for entering the New Army against the Turks. To do his share, *durch und durch** (God forgive me), he wants three new Brigades; with them he engages to go through from bottom to top of Sari Bair. Well, I will give him four; perhaps five! Our whole scheme hinges on these crests of Sari Bair which dominate Anzac and Maidos; the Dardanelles and the Aegean. The destroyers next took us to Cape Helles where I held a pow wow at Army Headquarters, Generals Hunter-Weston and Gouraud being present as well as Birdwood and Braithwaite. Everyone keen and sanguine. Many minor suggestions; warm approval of the broad lines of the scheme. Afterwards I brought Birdie back to Anzac and then returned to Imbros. A good day's

---

* "Through and through."

work. Half the battle to find that my Corps Commanders are so keen. They are all sworn to the closest secrecy; have been told that our lives depend upon their discretion. I have shown them my M.F. 300 of the 7th June so as to let them understand they are being trusted with a plan which is too much under the seal to be sent over the cables even to the highest.

Every General I met to-day spoke of the shortage of bombs and grenades. The Anzacs are very much depressed to hear they are to get no more bombs for their six Japanese trench mortars. We told the Ordnance some days ago to put this very strongly to the War Office. After all, bombs and grenades are easy things to make if the tails of the manufacturers are well twisted.

12th June, 1915. Imbros. Stayed in camp where de Robeck came to see me. I wonder what K. is likely to do about Mahon and about ammunition. When he told me Joffre and French thought 17 rounds per gun per day good enough, and that he was going to give me as much, there were several qualifications to our pleasure, but we *were* pleased, because apart from all invidious comparisons, we were anyway going to get more stuff. But we have not yet tasted this new French ration of 17 rounds per gun.

Are we too insistent? I think not. One dozen small field howitzer shells, of 4.5. calibre, save one British life by taking two Turkish lives. And although the 4.5. are what we want the old 5-inch are none so bad. Where would we be now, I wonder, had not Haldane against Press, Public and four soldiers out of five stuck to his guns and insisted on creating those 145 batteries of Territorial Field Artillery?

A depressing wire in from the War Office expressing doubt as to whether they will be able to meet our wishes by embarking units complete and ready for landing; gear, supplies, munitions all in due proportion, in the transports coming out here from England. Should we be forced to redistribute men and material on arrival, we are in for another spell of delay.

Altogether I have been very busy on cables to-day. The War Office having jogged my elbow again about the Bulair scheme, I have once more been through the whole series of pros and cons

A Decision and the Plan 217

with the Admiral who has agreed in the reply I have sent: clear negative. Three quarters of the objections are naval; either directly — want of harbours, etc.; or indirectly — as involving three lines of small craft to supply three separate military forces. The number of small craft required are not in existence.

13th June, 1915. Imbros. The War Office forget every now and then other things about the coastline above the Narrows. I have replied:

"Your first question as to the fortification of the coast towards Gallipoli can be satisfactorily answered only by the Navy as naval aeroplane observation is the only means by which I can find out about the coast fortifications. From time to time it has been reported that torpedo tubes have been placed at the mouth of Soghan Dere and at Nagara Point. These are matters on which I presume Admiral has reported to Admiralty, but I am telegraphing to him to make sure as he is away to-day at Mudros. I will ask him to have aeroplane reconnaissance made regarding the coast fortifications you mention, to see if it can be ascertained whether your informant's report is correct, but there are but few aeroplanes and the few we have are constantly required for spotting for artillery, photographing trenches, and for reconnaissances of the troops immediately engaged with us."

I am being forced by War Office questions to say rather more than I had intended about plans. The following cable took me the best part of the morning. I hope it is too technical to effect a lodgment in the memories of the gossips:

(No. M.F. 328). From General Sir Ian Hamilton to War Office. With reference to your No. 5441, cipher. From the outset I have fully realized that the question of cutting off forces defending the Peninsula lay at the heart of my problem. See my No. M.F. 173, last paragraph, and paragraphs 2 and 7 of my instructions to General Officer Commanding Australian and New Zealand Army Corps, of 13th April, before landing. I still consider, as indicated therein, that the best and most practicable method of stopping enemy's communications is to push forward to the south-east from Australian and New Zealand Army Corps.

"The attempt to stop Bulair communications further North than the Australian and New Zealand Army Corps position would give the Turks too much room to pass our guns. An advance of little more than two miles in a south-eastern direction would enable us to command the land communications between Bulair and Kilid Bahr. This, in turn, would render Ak Bashi Liman useless to the enemy as a port of disembarkation for either Chanak or Constantinople. It would enable us, moreover, to co-operate effectively with the Navy in stopping communication with the Asiatic shore, since Kilia Liman and Maidos would be under fire from our land guns.

It was these considerations which decided me originally to land at Australian and New Zealand Army Corps position, and in spite of the difficulties of advancing thence, I see no reason to expect that a new point of departure would make the task any easier. I have recently been obliged by circumstances to concentrate my main efforts on pushing forward towards Achi Baba so as to clear my main port of disembarkation of shell fire. I only await the promised reinforcements, however, to enable me to take the next step in the prosecution of my main plan from the Australian and New Zealand Army Corps.

I cannot extend the present Australian position until they arrive. See my No. M.F. 300, as to estimate of troops required, and my No. 304, 7th June, as to state of siege at Australian and New Zealand Army Corps. If I succeed the enemy's communications *via* Bulair and, with the Navy's help, *via* Asiatic coast should both be closed, as far as possible, by the one operation. If, in addition, submarines can stop sea communications with Constantinople the problem will be solved.

With regard to supplies and ammunition which can be obtained by the enemy across the Dardanelles, since Panderma and Karabingha are normally important centres of collection of food supplies, both cereals and meat, and since the Panderma-Chanak road is adequate, it would be possible to provision the peninsula from a great supply depot at Chanak where there are steam mills, steam bakeries and ample shallow draught craft. If land communications were blocked near Bulair, ammunition could only be brought by sea to Panderma, and thence by road to Chanak or by sea direct to Kilid Bahr.

Either for supplies or ammunition, however, the difficulty of effectively stopping supply by sea may be increased by the large number of shallow craft available at Rodosto, Chanak, Constantinople and Panderma. But as soon as I can make good advance south-east from Australian and New Zealand Army Corps, my guns, plus the submarines, should be able to make all traffic from the Asiatic shore very difficult for the enemy.

It is vitally important that future developments should be kept absolutely secret. I mention this because, although the date of our original landing was known to hardly anyone here before the ships sailed, yet the date was cabled to the Turks from Vienna.

The message took some doing and could not, therefore, get clear of camp till 11 o'clock when I boarded the destroyer *Grampus*, and sailed for Helles. Lunched with Hunter-Weston at his Headquarters, and then walked out along the new road being built under the cliffs from "W" Beach to Gurkha Gully. On the way I stopped at the 29th Divisional Headquarters where I met de Lisle. Thence along the coast where the 88th Brigade were bathing. In the beautiful hot afternoon weather the men were happy as sandboys. Their own mothers would hardly know them — burnt black with the sun, in rags or else stark naked, with pipes in their mouths. But they like it! After passing the time of day to a lot of these boys, I climbed the cliff and came back along the crests, stopping to inspect some of the East Lancashire Division in their rest trenches.

Got back to Hunter-Weston's about 6 and had a cup of tea. There Cox of the Indian Brigade joined me, and I took him with me to Imbros where he is going to stay a day or two with Braithwaite.

14th June, 1915. Imbros. K. sends me this brisk little pick-me-up:

> Report here states that your position could be made untenable by Turkish guns from the Asiatic shore. Please report on this.

No doubt — no doubt! Yet I was once his own Chief of Staff into whose hands he unreservedly placed the conduct of one of the most crucial, as it was the last, of the old South African enterprises: I was once the man into whose hands he placed the defence of his heavily criticized action at the Battle of Paardeburg. There it is: he used to have great faith in me, and now he makes me much the sort of remark which might be made by a young lady to a Marine. The answer, as K. well knows, depends upon too many imponderabilia to be worth the cost of a cable. The size and number of the Turkish guns; their supplies of shell; the power of our submarines to restrict those supplies; the worth of our own ship and shore guns; the depth of our trenches; the *moral* of our men, and so on *ad infinitum*. The point of the whole matter is this: the Turks haven't got the guns — and we know it: if ever they do get the guns it will take them weeks, months, before they can get them mounted and shells in proportion amassed.

MEN BATHING AT HELLES

K. should know better than any other man in England — Lord Bobs, alas, is gone — that if there was any real fear of guns from Asia being able to make us loosen our grip on the Peninsula, I would cable him quickly. Then why does he ask? Well — and why shouldn't he ask? I must not be so captious. Much better turn the tables on him by asking him to enable us to knock out the danger he fears:

> (No. M.F. 331). From General Sir Ian Hamilton to Earl Kitchener. With reference to your telegram No. 5460. As already reported in my telegram, fire from the Asiatic shore is at times troublesome, but I am taking steps to deal with it. Of course another battery of 6-inch howitzers would greatly help in this.

A Decision and the Plan

By coincidence a letter has come in to me this very night, on the very subject; a letter written by a famous soldier — Gouraud — the lion of the Ardennes, who is, it so happens, much better posted as to the Asiatic guns than the Jeremiah who has made K. anxious. The French bear the brunt of this fire and Gouraud's cool decision to ignore it in favour of bigger issues marks the contrast between the fighter who makes little of the enemy and the writer who makes much of him. I look upon Gouraud more as a coadjutor than as a subordinate, so it is worth anything to me to find that we see eye to eye at present. For, there is much more in the letter than his feelings about the guns of Asia: there is an outline sketch, drawn with slight but masterly touches, covering the past, present and future of our show:

Corps Expéditionnaire d'Orient.
   CABINE DU GÉNÉRAL.
       N. Cab.
       SECRET.

Q.G. le 13 juin 1915.

Le Général de Division Gouraud, Commandant le Corps Expéditionnaire d'Orient, à Sir Ian Hamilton, G.C.B., D.S.O., Commandant le Corps Expéditionnaire Méditerranéen.
Quartier Général.

MON GÉNÉRAL,
   Vous avez bien voulu me communiquer une dépêche de Lord Kitchener faisant connaître que le Gouvernement anglais allait envoyer incessamment aux Dardanelles trois nouvelles divisions et des vaisseaux moins vulnérables aux sous-marins. D'après les renseignements qui m'ont été donnés, on annonce 14 de ces monitors; 4 seraient armés de pièces de 35 à 38 m/ 4 de pièces de 24, les autres de 15.
   C'est donc sur terre et sur mer un important renfort.
   J'ai l'honneur de vous soumettre ci-dessous mes idées sur son emploi.
   Jetons d'abord un coup d'oeil sur la situation. Il s'en dégage, ce me semble, deux faits.
   D'une part, le combat du 4 juin, qui, malgré une préparation sérieuse n'a pas donné de résultat en balance avec le vigoureux et

couteux effort fourni par les troupes alliées, a montré que, guidés par les Allemands, les Turcs ont donné à leur ligne une très grande force. La presqu'île est barrée devant notre front de plusieurs lignes de tranchées fortement établies, précédées en plusieurs points de fil de fer barbelés, flanquées de mitrailleuses, communiquant avec l'arrière par des boyaux, formant un système de fortification comparable à celui du grand Front.

Dans ces tranchées les Turcs se montrent bons soldats, braves, tenaces. Leur artillerie a constamment et très sensiblement augmenté en nombres et en puissance depuis trois semaines.

Dans ces conditions, et étant donné que les Turcs ont toute liberté d'amener sur ce front étroite toute leur armée, on ne peut se dissimuler que les progrès seront lents et que chaque progrès sera couteux.

Les Allemands appliqueront certainement dans les montagnes et les ravins de la presqu'île le système qui leur a réussi jusqu'ici en France.

D'autre part l'ennemi parait avoir changé de tactique. Il a voulu au début nous rejeter à la mer; après les pertes énormes qu'il a subi dans les combats d'avril et de mai, il semble y avoir renoncé du moins pour le moment.

Son plan actuel consiste à chercher à nous bloquer de front, pour nous maintenir sur l'étroit terrain que nous avons conquis, et à nous y rendre la vie intenable en bombardant les camps et surtout les plages de débarquement. C'est ainsi que les quatre batteries de grosses pièces récemment installées entre Erenkeui et Yenishahr ont apporté au ravitaillement des troupes une gêne qu'on peut dire dangereuse, puisque la consommation dans dernières journées a légèrement dépassé le ravitaillement.

Au résumé nous sommes bloqués de front et pris par derrière. Et cette situation ira en empirant du fait des maladies, résultant du climat, de la chaleur, du bivouac continuel, peut être des épidémies, et du fait que la mer rendra très difficile tout débarquement dès la mauvaise saison, fin août.

Ceci posé, comment employer les gros renforts attendus. Plusieurs solutions se présentent à l'esprit.

Primo, en Asie.

C'est la première idée qui se présente; étant donné l'intérêt de se rendre maître de la région Yenishahr-Erenkeui, qui prend nos plages de débarquement à revers.

Mais c'est là une mesure d'un intérêt défensif, qui ne fera pas faire un pas en avant. Il est permis d'autre part de penser que les

A Decision and the Plan 223

canons des monitors anglais, qui sont sans doute destinés à détruire les défenses du détroit, commenceront par nous débarrasser des batteries de l'entrée. Enfin nous disposerons d'ici peu d'un front de mer Seddul-Bahr Eski Hissarlick, dont les pièces puissantes contrebattront efficacement les canons d'Asie.

Secundo, vers Gaba-Tépé.

Au Sud de Gaba Tépé s'étend une plaine que les cartes disent accessible au débarquement. Des troupes débarquées là se trouvent à 8 kilomètres environ de Maidos, c'est à dire au point où la presqu'île est la plus étroite.

Sans nul doute, trouveront elles devant elles les mêmes difficultés qu'ici et il sera nécessaire notemment de se rendre maître des montagnes qui dominent la plaine au Nord. Mais alors que la prise d'Achi Baba ne sera qu'un grand succès militaire, qui nous mettra le lendemain devant les escarpements de Kilid-Bahr, l'occupation de la région Gaba Tépé-Maidos nous placerait au delà des détroits, nous permettrait d'y constituer une base où les sous-marins de la mer de Marmara pourraient indéfiniment s'approvisionner.

Si le barrage des Dardanelles n'était pas brisé, il serait tourné.

Tertio, vers Boulair.

Cette solution apparait comme le plus radical, celui qui déjouerait le plan de l'ennemi. Constantinople serait directement menacé par ce coup retentissant.

Toute la question est de savoir si, avec leurs moyens nouveaux, les monitors, les Amiraux sont en mesure de protéger un débarquement, qui comme celui du 25 avril nécessiterait de nombreux bateaux.

En résumé, j'ai l'honneur d'émettre l'avis de poser nettement aux Amiraux la question du débarquement à Boulair, d'y faire reconnaître l'état actuel des défenses par bateaux, avions et si possible agents, sans faire d'acte de guerre pour ne pas donner l'éveil.

Au cas où le débarquement serait jugé impossible, j'émet l'avis d'employer les renforts dans la région Gaba-Tépé, où les Australiens ont déjà implanté un solide jalon.

Concurremment, je pense qu'il serait du plus vif intérêt pour hâter la décision, de créer au Gouvernement Turc des inquiétudes dans d'autres parties de l'Empire, pour l'empêcher d'amener ici toutes ses forces.

Dans cet ordre d'idées on peut envisager deux moyens. L'un, le plus efficace, est l'action russe ou bulgare. La Grèce est mal placée géographiquement pour exercer une action sur la guerre. Seule la

Bulgarie, par sa position géographique, prend les Turcs à revers. Sans doute, à voir la façon dont les Turcs amènent devant nous les troupes et les canons d'Adrianople, ont ils un accord avec la Bulgarie, mais la guerre des Balkans prouve que la Bulgarie n'est pas embarrassée d'un accord si elle voit ailleurs son intérêt. La question est donc d'offrir un prix fort à la Bulgarie.

L'autre est de provoquer des agitations dans différentes parties de l'Empire, d'y faire opérer des destructions par des bandes, d'obliger les Turcs à y envoyer du monde. Cela encore vaut la peine d'y mettre le prix.

Je suis, avec un profond respect, mon Général,
Votre très dévoué,
(Sd.) GOURAUD.

H.Q. June 13, 1915.

Eastern Expeditionary Corps.
General's cabin.
N. Cab.
Secret.

Major General Gouraud, Commandant of the Eastern Expeditionary Corps, to Sir Ian Hamilton, G.C.B., D.S.O., Commandant of the Mediterranean Expeditionary Corps.

Dear Sir,

You have kindly communicated to me a dispatch from Lord Kitchener informing me that the British Government will shortly be sending to the Dardanelles three new divisions and vessels less vulnerable to U-boats. According to the information I have been given, 14 of these monitors have been announced, 4 of which will be armed with 35 to 38 m guns, 4 with 24 m guns and the others with 15 m guns.

This represents a major reinforcement on land and at sea.

I have the honor of submitting to you below my ideas on its use.

First, let's take a look at the situation. It seems to me that two facts stand out.

On the one hand, the battle of June 4, which, despite serious preparation, did not produce results that weighed up against the vigorous and costly effort made by the Allied troops, showed that, guided by the Germans, the Turks had given their line a very great deal of strength. In front of our front line, the peninsula is blocked by several lines of well-established trenches, preceded at several points

A Decision and the Plan 225

by barbed wire, flanked by machine guns, communicating with the rear by gutters, forming a fortification system comparable to that of the Grand Front.

In these trenches, the Turks proved to be good soldiers, brave and tenacious. Their artillery has steadily and significantly increased in numbers and power over the last three weeks.

Under these conditions, and given that the Turks are free to bring their entire army to this narrow front, it is clear that progress will be slow and that each advance will be costly.

In the mountains and ravines of the peninsula, the Germans will undoubtedly apply the system that has succeeded so far in France.

On the other hand, the enemy seems to have changed tactics. At first, he wanted to drive us back into the sea; but after the enormous losses he suffered in the fighting of April and May, he seems to have given up on this, at least for the moment.

His current plan is to try to block us from the front, to keep us on the narrow ground we have conquered, and to make life unbearable for us there by bombarding the camps and especially the landing beaches. The four batteries of large artillery recently installed between Erenkeui and Yenishahr have caused a dangerous hindrance to the supply of troops, since consumption in recent days has slightly exceeded supply.

In short, we're blocked from the front and caught from behind. And this situation is set to worsen as a result of the illnesses caused by the climate, the heat, the constant bivouac, perhaps even epidemics, and the fact that the sea will make it very difficult to land at the end of August.

Now that we've got that out of the way, how are we going to use the large reinforcements we're expecting? Several solutions come to mind.

First, in Asia.

This is the first idea that comes to mind, given the importance of gaining control of the Yenishahr-Erenkeui region, which takes our landing beaches by surprise.

But this is a defensive measure, which will not take us a step forward. On the other hand, it's safe to assume that the guns of the English monitors, which are no doubt intended to destroy the defenses of the strait, will start by ridding us of the batteries at the entrance. Finally, we will soon have a Seddul-Bahr Eski Hissarlick waterfront, whose powerful guns will effectively counter the Asian guns.

Secondly, towards Gaba-Tépé.

To the south of Gaba-Tépé lies a plain that the maps say is

accessible for landing. Troops disembarking there would find themselves some 8 kilometers from Maidos, i.e. at the point where the peninsula is narrowest.

Undoubtedly, they will face the same difficulties as here, and it will be necessary to take control of the mountains that dominate the plain to the north. But while the capture of Achi Baba will only be a great military success, which will put us the next day in front of the Kilid-Bahr escarpments, the occupation of the Gaba Tépé-Maidos region would place us beyond the straits, allowing us to set up a base where the submarines of the Sea of Marmara could be supplied indefinitely.

If the Dardanelles barrier wasn't broken, it would be opened.

Thirdly, to Boulair.

This solution appeared to be the most drastic, the one that would thwart the enemy's plan. Constantinople would be directly threatened by this resounding blow.

The question is whether, with their new means, the monitors, the Admirals are in a position to protect a landing which, like that of April 25, would require numerous ships.

To sum up, I have the honor of advising the Admirals to put the question of a landing at Boulair squarely before them, and to have the current state of the defenses there surveyed by boats, planes and, if possible, agents, without making an aggressive move so as not to create an alarm.

In the event of landing being deemed impossible, I recommend using reinforcements in the Gaba-Tépé region, where the Australians have already established a solid foothold.

At the same time, I think it would be of the greatest benefit to hasten the decision, to create concern for the Turkish Government in other parts of the Empire, to prevent it from bringing all its forces here.

There are two possible ways of doing this. The first, and most effective, is Russian or Bulgarian action. Greece is poorly placed geographically to influence the war. Only Bulgaria, by virtue of its geographical position, can take the Turks by the scruff of the neck. No doubt, judging by the way the Turks are bringing their troops and cannons from Adrianople before us, they have an agreement with Bulgaria, but the Balkan war proves that Bulgaria is not troubled by an agreement if it sees its interests elsewhere. So the trick is to offer Bulgaria a high price.

The other is to provoke unrest in various parts of the Empire, to have armed bands destroy it, to force the Turks to send people there.

This too is worth the price.
I am, with deepest respect, my General,
Yours very truly,
(Sd.) Gouraud.

Boarded a destroyer at 11.15 a.m. and sailed straight for Gully Beach. Then into dinghy and paddled to shore where I lunched with de Lisle at the 29th Divisional Headquarters. Hunter-Weston had come up to meet me from Corps Headquarters.

With both Generals I rode a couple of miles up the Gully seeing the 87th Brigade as we went. When we got to the mouth of the communication trench leading to the front of the Indian Brigade, Bruce of the Gurkhas was waiting for us, and led me along through endless sunken ways until we reached his firing line.

Every hundred yards or so I had a close peep at the ground in front through de Lisle's periscope. The enemy trenches were sometimes not more than 7 yards away and the rifles of the Turks moving showed there was a man behind the loophole. Many corpses, almost all Turks, lay between the two lines of trenches. There was no shelling at the moment, but rifle bullets kept flopping into the parapet especially when the periscope was moved.

At the end of the Gurkha line I was met by Colonel Wolley Dod, who took me round the fire trenches of the 86th Brigade. The Dublin Fusiliers looked particularly fit and jolly.

Getting back to the head of the Gully I rode with Hunter-Weston to his Corps Headquarters where I had tea before sailing.

When I got to Imbros the Fleet were firing at a Taube. She was only having a look; flying around the shipping and Headquarters camp at a great height, but dropping no bombs. After a bit she scooted off to the South-east. Cox dined.

15th June, 1915. Imbros. Yesterday I learned some detail about the conduct of affairs the other day — enough to make me very anxious indeed that no tired or nervy leaders should be sent out with the new troops. So I have sent K. a cable!:

(No. M.F. 334). From General Sir Ian Hamilton to Earl Kitchener.
  With reference to the last paragraph of your telegram No. 5250, cipher, and my No. M.F. 313. I should like to submit for your consideration the following views of the qualities necessary in an Army Corps Commander on the Gallipoli Peninsula. In that position only men of good stiff constitution and nerve will be able to do any good. Everything is at such close quarters that many men would be useless in the somewhat exposed headquarters they would have to occupy on this limited terrain, though they would do quite good work if moderately comfortable and away from constant shell fire. I can think of two men, Byng and Rawlinson. Both possess the requisite qualities and seniority; the latter does not seem very happy where he is, and the former would have more scope than a cavalry Corps can give him in France.

Left camp the moment I got this weight off my chest; boarded the *Savage*, or rather jumped on her ladder like a chamois and scrambled on deck like a monkey. It was blowing big guns and our launch was very nearly swamped. Crossing to Helles big seas were making a clean sweep of the decks. Jolly to look at from the bridge.

After a dusty walk round piers and beaches lunched with Hunter-Weston before inspecting the 155th and 156th Brigades. On our road we were met by Brigadier-Generals Erskine and Scott-Moncrieff. Walked the trenches where I chatted with the regimental officers and men, and found my compatriots in very good form.

Went on to the Royal Naval Division Headquarters where Paris met me. Together we went round the 3rd Marine Brigade Section under Brigadier-General Trotman. These old comrades of the first landing gave me the kindliest greetings.

Got back to 8th Corps Headquarters intending to enjoy a cup of tea *al fresco*, but we were reckoning without our host (the Turkish one) who threw so many big shell from Asia all about the mound that, (only to save the tea cups), we retired with dignified slowness into our dugouts. Whilst sitting in these funk-holes, as we used to call them at Ladysmith, General Gouraud ran the gauntlet and made also a slow and dignified entry. He was coming back with me to Imbros. As it was getting late we hardened our hearts to walk across the open country between Headquarters and the beach, where every twenty seconds or so a big fellow was raising Cain. Fortune favouring we both reached the sea with our heads upon our shoulders.

An answer is in to our plea for a Western scale of ammunition, guns and howitzers. They cable sympathetically but say simply they can't. Soft answers, etc., but it would be well if they could make up their minds whether they wish to score the next trick in the East or in the West. If they can't do that they will be doubly done.

A purely passive defence is not possible for us; it implies losing ground by degrees — and we have not a yard to lose. If we are to remain we must keep on attacking here and there to maintain ourselves! But; to expect us to attack without giving us our fair share — on Western standards — of high explosive and howitzers shows lack of military imagination. A man's a man for a' that whether at Helles or Ypres. Let me bring my lads face to face with Turks in the open field, we *must* beat them every time because British volunteer soldiers are superior individuals to Anatolians, Syrians or Arabs and are animated with a superior ideal and an equal joy in battle. Wire and machine guns prevent this hand to hand, or rifle to rifle, style of contest. Well, then the decent thing to do is to give us shells enough to clear a fair field. To attempt to solve the problem by letting a single dirty Turk at the Maxim kill ten — twenty — fifty — of our fellows on the barbed wire, — ten — twenty — fifty — *each of whom is worth several dozen Turks*, is a sin of the Holy Ghost category unless it can be justified by dire necessity. But there is no necessity. The supreme command has only to decide categorically that the Allies stand on the defensive on the West for a few weeks and then Von Donop can find us enough to bring us through. Joffre and French, as a matter of fact, would hardly feel the difference. If the supreme command can't do that; and can't even send us trench mortars as substitutes, let them harden their hearts and wind up this great enterprise for which they simply haven't got the nerve.

If only K. would come and see for himself! Failing that — if only it were possible for me to run home and put my own case.

16th June, 1915. Imbros. Gouraud, a sympathetic guest, left for French Headquarters in one of our destroyers at 3.30 p.m. He is a real Sahib; a tower of strength. The Asiatic guns have upset his men a good deal. He hopes soon to clap on an extinguisher to their fire by planting down two fine big fellows of his own Morto Bay way: we mean to add a couple of old naval six-inchers to this battery. During his stay we have very thoroughly threshed out our hopes and fears and went into the plan which Gouraud thinks offers chances of a record-breaking victory. If the character of the new Commanders and the spirit of their troops are of the calibre of those on his left flank at Helles he feels pretty confident.

Talking of Commanders, my appeal for a young Corps Commander of a "good stiff constitution" has drawn a startling reply:

> (No. 5501, cipher). From Earl Kitchener to Sir Ian Hamilton. Your No. M.F. 334. I am afraid that Sir John French would not spare the services of the two Generals you mention, and they are, moreover, both junior to Mahon, who commands the 10th Division which is going out to you. Ewart, who is very fit and well, would I think do. I am going to see him the day after to-morrow.
>
> Mahon raised the 10th Division and has produced an excellent unit. He is quite fit and well, and I do not think that he could now be left behind.

So the field of selection for the new Corps is to be restricted to some Lieutenant-General senior to Mahon — himself the only man of his rank commanding a Division and almost at the top of the Lieutenant-Generals! Oh God, if I could have a Corps Commander like Gouraud! But this block by "Mahon" makes a record for the seniority fetish. I have just been studying the Army List with Pollen. Excluding Indians, Marines and employed men like Douglas Haig and Maxwell, there *are* only about one dozen British service Lieutenant-Generals senior to Mahon, and, of that dozen only two are *possible* — Ewart and Stopford! There *are* no others. Ewart is a fine fellow, with a character which commands respect and affection. He is also a Cameron Highlander whose father commanded the Gordons. As a presence nothing could be better; as a man no one in the Army would be more welcome. But he

A Decision and the Plan

would not, with his build and constitutional habit, last out here for one fortnight. Despite his soldier heart and his wise brain we can't risk it. We are unanimous on that point. Stopford remains. I have cabled expressing my deep disappointment that Mahon should be the factor which restricts all choice and saying,

> However, my No. M.F. 334[*] gave you what I considered to be the qualities necessary in a Commander, so I will do my best with what you send me.
> With regard to Ewart. I greatly admire his character, but he positively could not have made his way along the fire trenches I inspected yesterday. He has never approached troops for fifteen years although I have often implored him, as a friend, to do so. Would not Stopford be preferable to Ewart, even though he does not possess the latter's calm?

I begin to think I shall be recalled for my importunity. But, in for a penny in for a pound, and I have fired off the following protest to a really disastrous cable from the War Office saying that the New Army is to bring *no* 4.5-inch howitzers with it; no howitzers at all, indeed, except sixteen of the old, inaccurate 5-inch Territorial howitzers, some of which "came out" at Omdurman and were afterwards — the whole category — found so much fault with in South Africa. Unless they are going to have an August push in France they might at least have lent us forty-eight 4.5 hows. from France to see the New Army through their first encounter with the enemy. They could all be run back in a fast cruiser and would only be loaned to us for three weeks or a month. If the G.S. at Whitehall can't do those things, they have handed over the running of a world war to one section of the Army. I attach my ultimatum: I cannot make it more emphatic; instead of death or victory we moderns say howitzers or defeat:

> (No. 5489, cipher, M.G.O.) From War Office to General Officer Commanding-in-Chief, Mediterranean Expeditionary Force. Your No. M.F. 316. It is impossible to send more ammunition than we are

---

[*] See page 228.

sending you. 528 rounds per 18-pr will be brought out by each Division. Instead of 4.5-inch howitzers we are sending 16 5-inch howitzers with the 13th Division, as there is more 5-inch ammunition available. By the time that the last of the three Divisions arrive we hope to have supplied a good percentage of high explosive shells, but you should try to save as much as you can in the meantime. Until more ammunition is available for them, we cannot send you any 4.5-inch howitzers with the other two Divisions, and even if more 5-inch were sent the fortnightly supply of ammunition for them would be very small.

(No. M.F. 337). From General Sir Ian Hamilton to War Office. With reference to your No. 5489, cipher. I am very sorry that you cannot send the proper howitzers, and still more sorry for the reason, that of ammunition. The Turkish trenches are deep and narrow, and only effective weapon for dealing with them is the howitzer. I realize your difficulties, and I am sure that you will supply me with both howitzers and ammunition as soon as you are able to do so. I shall be glad in the meantime of as many more trench mortars and bombs as you can possibly spare. We realize for our part that in the matter of guns and ammunition it is no good crying for the moon, and for your part you must recognize that until howitzers and ammunition arrive it is no good crying for the Crescent.

The Admiral and Godley paid me a visit; discussed tea and sea transport, then a walk.

There is quite a break in the weather. Very cold and windy with a little rain in the forenoon.

17th June, 1915. Imbros. Smoother sea, but rough weather in office. A cable from the Master General of the Ordnance in reply to my petition for another battery of 6-inch howitzers:

(No. 5537, cipher, M.G.O.) From War Office to the General Officer Commanding-in-Chief, Mediterranean Expeditionary Force. Your telegram No. M.F. 331. We can send out another battery of 6-inch howitzers, but cannot send ammunition with it. Moreover, we cannot increase the present periodical supply, so that if we send the additional howitzers you must not complain of the small number of rounds per gun sent to you, as experience has shown is sometimes

A Decision and the Plan   233

done in similar cases. It is possible that the Navy may help you with 6-inch ammunition. Please say after consideration of the above if you want the howitzers sent.

My mind plays agreeably with the idea of chaining the M.G.O. on to a rock on the Peninsula whilst the Asiatic batteries are pounding it. That would learn him to be an M.G.O.; singing us Departmental ditties whilst we are trying to hold our Asiatic wolf by the ears. I feel very depressed; we are too far away; so far away that we lie beyond the grasp of an M.G.O.'s imagination. That's the whole truth. Were the Army in France to receive such a message, within 24 hours the Commander-in-Chief, or at the least his Chief of the Staff, would walk into the M.G.O.'s office and then proceed to walk into the M.G.O. I can't do that; a bad tempered cable is useless; I have no weapon at my disposal but very mild sarcasm:

(No. M.F. 343). From General Sir Ian Hamilton to War Office. Your No. 5537, cipher, M.G.O. Please send the battery of 6-inch howitzers. Your admonition will be borne in mind. Extra howitzers will be most useful to replace pieces damaged by enemy batteries on the Asiatic side of the Dardanelles. No doubt in time the ammunition question will improve. Only yesterday prisoners reported that 14 more Turkish heavy guns were coming to the Peninsula.

Have written another screed to French. As it gives a sort of summing up of the state of affairs to-day I spatchcock (as Buller used to say) the carbon:

GENERAL HEADQUARTERS,
MEDITERRANEAN EXPEDITIONARY FORCE,
17th June, 1915.

MY DEAR FRENCH,
　　It must be fully a month since I wrote you but no one understands better than you must do, how time flies under the constant strain of these night and day excursions and alarms. Between the two letters there has been a desperate lot of fighting, mostly bomb and bayonet work, and, except for a good many Turks gone to glory, there is only a few hundred yards of ground to show for it all at Anzac, and about

a mile perhaps in the southern part of the Peninsula. But taking a wider point of view, I hope our losses and efforts have gained a good deal for our cause although they may not be so measurable in yards. First, the Turks are defending themselves instead of attacking Egypt and over-running Basra; secondly, we are told on high authority, that the action of the Italians in coming in was precipitated by our entry into this part of the theatre; thirdly, if we can only hold on and continue to enfeeble the Turks, I think myself it will not be very long before some of the Balkan States take the bloody plunge.

However all that may be, we must be prepared at the worst to win through by ourselves, and it is, I assure you, a tough proposition. In a manœuvre battle of old style our fellows here would beat twice their number of Turks in less than no time, but, actually, the restricted Peninsula suits the Turkish tactics to a 'T.' They have always been good at trench work where their stupid men have only simple, straightforward duties to perform, namely, in sticking on and shooting anything that comes up to them. They do this to perfection; I never saw braver soldiers, in fact, than some of the best of them. When we advance, no matter the shelling we give them, they stand right up firing coolly and straight over their parapets. Also they have unlimited supplies of bombs, each soldier carrying them, and they are not half bad at throwing them. Meanwhile they are piling up a lot of heavy artillery of very long range on the Asiatic shore, and shell us like the devil with 4.5, 6-inch, 8, 9.2 and 10-inch guns — not pleasant. This necessitates a very tough type of man for senior billets. X — Y — , for instance, did not last 24 hours. Everyone here is under fire, and really and truly the front trenches are safer, or at least fully as safe, as the Corps Commander's dugout. For, if the former are nearer the Infantry, the latter is nearer the big guns firing into our rear.

Another reason why we advance so slowly and lose so much is that the enemy get constant reinforcements. We have overcome three successive armies of Turks, and a new lot of 20,000 from Syria are arriving here now, with 14 more heavy guns, so prisoners say, but I hope not.

I have fine Corps Commanders in Birdwood, Hunter-Weston and Gouraud. This is very fortunate. Who is to be Commander of the new corps I cannot say, but we have one or two terrifying suggestions from home.

Last night a brisk attack headed by a senior Turkish Officer and a German Officer was made on the 86th Brigade. Both these Officers were killed and 20 or 30 of their men, the attack being repulsed. Against the South Wales Borderers a much heavier attack was launched. Our fellows were bombed clean out of their trenches, but only fell back 30 yards and dug in. This morning early we got maxims on to each end of the place they had stormed, and then the Dublins retook it with the bayonet. Two hundred of their dead were left in the trench, and we only had 50 casualties — not so bad! A little later on in the day a d———d submarine appeared and had some shots at our transports and store ships. Luckily she missed, but all our landing operations of supplies were suspended. These are the sort of daily anxieties. All one can do is to carry on with determination and trust in providence.

I hope you are feeling fit and that things are going on well generally. Give my salaams to the great Robertson, also to Barry. Otherwise please treat this letter as private. With all kind remembrance.

      Believe me,
        Yours very sincerely,
        (*Sd.*) IAN HAMILTON.

Chapter XI – Bombs and Journalists

Our beautiful East Lancs. Division is in a very bad way. One more month of neglect and it will be ruined: if quickly filled up with fresh drafts it will be better than ever. Have cabled:

> (M.F.A. 871). From General Sir Ian Hamilton to War Office. The following is the shortage of officers and rank and file in each Brigade of the XLIInd East Lancashire Division including the reinforcements reported as arriving:
>
> 125th Brigade . . . . 50 Officers, 1,852 rank and file.
>
> 126th Brigade . . . . 31 Officers, 1,714 rank and file.
>
> 127th Brigade . . . . 50 Officers, 2,297 rank and file.
>
> A stage of wastage has now been reached in this Division, especially in the 127th Manchester Brigade, when filling up with drafts will make it as good or better than ever. If, however, they have to go on fighting in their present condition and suffer further losses, the remnants will not offer sufficiently wide foundation for reconstituting cadres.

Lord Kitchener might also like to know this, that a satisfactory proportion of the officers recently sent out to fill casualties are shaping very well indeed.

An amalgam of veterans and fresh keen recruits, cemented by a common county feeling as well as by war tradition, makes the best fighting formation in the world. The veterans give experience and steadiness; — when the battle is joined the old hands feel bound to make good their camp-fire boastings to the recruits. The recruits bring freshness and the spirit of competition; — they are determined to show that they are as brave as the old fighters. But, if the East Lancs. go on dwindling, the cadre will not retain strength enough to absorb and shape the recruits who will, we must suppose, some day be poured into it. A perishing formation loses moral force in more rapid progression than the mere loss of members would seem to warrant. When a battalion which entered upon a campaign a thousand strong, — all keen and hopeful, — gets down to five hundred, comrades begin to look round at one another and wonder if any will be left. When it falls to three hundred, or less, the unit, in my experience, is better drawn out of the line. The bravest men lose heart when, on parade, they see with their own eyes that their Company — the finest Company in the Army — has become a platoon, — and the famous battalion a Company. A mould for shaping young enthusiasms into heroisms has been scrapped and it takes a desperate long time to recreate it.

I want to be sure K. himself takes notice and that is why I refer to him at the tail end of the cable. We have also cabled saying that the idea of sending so many rounds per gun per day was excellent, but that "we have received no notice of any despatch later than the S.S. *Arabian*, which consignment" (whenever it might arrive?) "was only due to last until the day before yesterday"! So this is what our famous agreement to have munitions on the scale deemed necessary by Joffre and French pans out at in practice. Two-fifths of their amount and that not delivered!

Dined with the Admiral on board the *Triad*. A glorious dinner. The sailormen have a real pull over us soldiers in all matters of messing. Linen, plate, glass, bread, meat, wine; of the best, are on the spot, always: even after the enemy is sighted, if they happen to feel a sense of emptiness they have only to go to the cold sideboard.

Coming back found mess tent brilliantly lit up and my staff entertaining their friends. So I put on my life-saving waistcoat and blew it out; clapped my new gas-mask on my head and entered. They were really startled, thinking the devil had come for them before their time.

Just got a telegram saying that M. Venezelos has gained a big majority in the Greek Election. Also, that the King of Greece is dying, and that, therefore, the Greek Army can't join us until he has come round or gone under.

18th June, 1915. Imbros. Went over to Kephalos Camp to inspect Rochdale's 127th (Manchester) Brigade. The Howe Battalion of the 2nd Naval Brigade were there (Lieutenant-Colonel Collins), also, the 3rd Field Ambulance R.N.D. All these were enjoying an easy out of the trenches and, though only at about half strength, had already quite forgotten the tragic struggles they had passed through. In fattest peace times, I never saw a keener, happier looking lot. I drew courage from the ranks. Surely these are the faces of men turned to victory!

Some twenty unattached officers fresh from England were there: a likely looking lot. One of the brightest a Socialist M.P.

The inspection took me all forenoon so I had to sweat double shifts after lunch. Hunter-Weston came over from Helles at 7.15 p.m. and we dined off crayfish. He was in great form.

The War Office can get no more bombs for our Japanese trench mortars! A catastrophe this! Putting the French on one side, we here, in this great force, possess only half a dozen good trench mortars — the Japanese. These six are worth their weight in gold to Anzac. Often those fellows have said to me that if they had twenty-five of them, with lots of bombs, they could render the Turkish trenches untenable. Twice, whilst their six precious mortars have been firing, I have stood for half an hour with Birdie, watching and drinking in encouragement. About one bomb a minute was the rate of fire and as it buzzed over our own trenches like a monstrous humming bird all the naked Anzacs laughed.

Then, *such* an explosion and a sort of long drawn out ei-ei-ei-ei cry of horror from the Turks. It was fine, — a real corpse-reviving performance and now the W.O. have let the stock run out, because some ass has forgotten to order them in advance. Have cabled a very elementary question: "Could not the Japanese bombs be copied in England?"

Being the Centenary of Waterloo, the thoughts and converse of Hunter-Weston and myself turned naturally towards the lives of the heroes of a hundred years ago whose monument had given us our education, and from that topic, equally naturally, to the boys of the coming generation. Then wrote out greetings to be sent by wire on my own behalf and on behalf of all Wellingtonians serving under my command here: this to the accompaniment of unusually heavy shell fire on the Peninsula.

Later. Have just heard that after a heavy bombardment the Turks made an attack and that fighting is going on now.

19th June, 1915. Imbros. The Turks expended last night some 500 H.E. shells; 250 heavy stuff from Asia and some thousands of shrapnel. They then attacked; we counter-attacked and there was some confused in-and-out Infantry fighting. We hear that the South Wales Borderers, the Worcesters, the 5th Royal Scots and the Naval Division all won distinction. Wiring home I say, "If Lord Kitchener could tell the Lord Provost of Edinburgh how well the 5th Bn. Royal Scots have done, the whole of this force would be pleased." The Turks have left 1,000 dead behind them. Prisoners say they thought so much high explosive would knock a hole in our line: the bombardment was all concentrated on the South Wales Borderers' trench.

Writing most of the day. Lord K. has asked the French Government to send out extra quantities of H.E. shell to their force here; also, he has begged them to order Gouraud to lend me his guns. In so far as the French may get more H.E. this is A.1. But if K. thinks the British will *directly* benefit — I fear he is out of his reckoning: it would be fatal to my relations with Gouraud, now so happy, were he even to suspect that I had any sort of lien on his guns. Unless I want to stir up jealous feelings, now entirely quiescent, I cannot use this cable as a lever to get French guns across into our area. Gouraud's plans for his big attack are now quite complete. A million pities we cannot attack simultaneously. That we should attack one week and the French another week is rotten tactically; but, practically, we have no option. We British want to go in side by side with the French — are burning to do so — but we cannot think of it until we can borrow shell from Gouraud; and, naturally, he wants every round he has for his own great push on the 21st. Walked down in the evening to see what progress was being made with the new pier. Colonel Skeen, Birdwood's Chief of Staff, dined and seems clever, as well as a very pleasant fellow.

20th June, 1915. Imbros. Rose early. Did a lot of business. The King's Messenger's bag closed at 8 a.m. Told K. about the arrival of fresh Turkish troops and our fighting on the 18th. The trenches remain as before, but the Turks, having failed, are worse off.

I have also written him about war correspondents. He had doubted whether my experiences would encourage me to increase the number to two or three. But, after trial, I prefer that the public should have a multitude of councillors. "When a single individual," I say, "has the whole of the London Press at his back he becomes an unduly important personage. When, in addition to this, it so happens, that he is inclined to see the black side of every proposition, then it becomes difficult to prevent him from encouraging the enemy, and from discouraging all our own people, as well as the Balkan States. If I have several others to counterbalance, then I do not care so much."

Fired off a second barrel through Fitz from whom I have just heard that my Despatch cannot be published as it stands but must be bowdlerized first, all the names of battalions being cut out. Instead of saying, "The landing at 'W' had been entrusted to the 1st Bn. Lancashire Fusiliers (Major Bishop) and it was to the complete lack of the sense of danger or of fear of this daring battalion that we owed our astonishing success," I am to say, "The landing, etc., had been entrusted to a certain battalion."

The whole of this press correspondence; press censorship; despatch writing and operations cables hang together and will end by hanging the Government.

My operations cables are written primarily for K., it is true, but they are meant also to let our own people know what their brothers and sons are up against and how they are bearing up under unheard of trials. There is not a word in those cables which would help or encourage the enemy. I am best judge of that and I see to it myself.

What is the result of my efforts to throw light upon our proceedings? A War Office extinguisher from under which only a few evil-smelling phrases escape. As I say to Fitz:

"You seem to see nothing beyond the mischief that may happen if the enemy gets to know too much about us; you do not see that this danger can be kept within bounds and is of small consequence when compared with the keenness or dullness of our own Nation."

The news that the War Office were going to send us no more Japanese bombs spread so great a consternation at Anzac that I have followed up my first remonstrance with a second and a stronger cable:

(No. M.F. 348). From General Sir Ian Hamilton to War Office. Your No. 5272, A.2.[*] I particularly request that you may reconsider your proposal not to order more Japanese bombs. These bombs are most effective and in high favour with our troops whose locally-made weapons, on which they have frequently to rely, are far inferior to the bombs used by the Turks. Our great difficulty in holding captured trenches is that the Turks always counter-attack with a large number of powerful bombs. Apparently their supply of these is limitless. Unless the delay in arrival is likely to extend over several months, therefore, I would suggest that a large order be sent to Japan. We cannot have too many of these weapons, and this should not cancel my No. M.F.Q.T. 1321, which should be treated as additional.

---

[*] Stated no more Japanese bombs could be supplied.

Drafted also a long cable discussing a diversion on the Asiatic shore of the Dardanelles. So some work had been done by the time we left camp at 9.15 a.m., and got on board the *Triad*. After a jolly sail reached Mudros at 2 p.m., landing on the Australian pier at 3 p.m. Mudros is a dusty hole; *ein trauriges Nest*,[*] as our German friends would say.

Worked like a nigger going right through Nos. 15 and 16 Stationary Hospitals. Colonel Maher, P.M.O., came round, also Colonel Jones, R.A.M.C., and Captain Stanley, R.A.M.C. Talked with hundreds of men: these are the true philosophers.

21st June, 1915. Mudros. Went at it again and overhauled No. 2 Stationary Hospital under Lieutenant-Colonel White, as well as No. 1 Stationary Hospital commanded by Lieutenant-Colonel Bryant. The doctors praised me for inventing something new to say to each man. But all the time in my mind was the thought of Gouraud. I have wanted him to do it absolutely on his own, and I could not emphasize this better than by coming right away to Mudros. Back to the *Triad* by 1 p.m. No news. Weighed anchor at once, steaming for Imbros, where we cast anchor at about 6 p.m. Freddie Maitland has arrived here, like a breath of air from home, to be once more my A.D.C.; his features wreathed in the well-known, friendly smile. The French duly attacked at dawn and the 2nd Division have carried a series of redoubts and trenches. The 1st Division did equally well but have been driven back again by counter-attacks. Fighting is still going on.

While I have been away Braithwaite has cabled home in my name asking which of the new Divisions is the best, as we shall have to use them before we can get to know them.

22nd June, 1915. Imbros. An anxious night. Gouraud has done splendidly; so have his troops. This has been a serious defeat for the Turks; a real bad defeat, showing, as it does, that given a

---

[*] "A sad place."

modicum of ammunition we can seize the strongest entrenchments of the enemy and stick to them.

(No. M.F. 357). From General Sir Ian Hamilton to Secretary of State for War. After 24 hours' heavy and continuous fighting a substantial success has been achieved. As already reported, the battle of 4th-5th June resulted in a good advance of my centre to which neither my right nor my left were able to conform, the reason being that the Turkish positions in front of the flanks are naturally strong and exceedingly well fortified. At 4.30 a.m. yesterday, General Gouraud began an attack upon the line of formidable works which run along the Kereves Dere. By noon the second French Division had stormed and captured all the Turkish first and second line trenches opposite their front, including the famous Haricot Redoubt, with its subsidiary maze of entanglements and communication trenches. On their right, the first French Division, after fierce fighting, also took the Turkish trenches opposite their front, but were counter-attacked so heavily that they were forced to fall back. Again, this Division attacked, again it stormed the position, and again it was driven out. General Gouraud then, at 2.55 p.m., issued the following order:

'From Colonel Viont's report it is evident that the preparation for the attack at 2.15 p.m. was not sufficient.

'It is indispensable that the Turkish first line of trenches in front of you should be taken, otherwise the gains of the 2nd Division may be rendered useless. You have five hours of daylight, take your time, let me know your orders and time fixed for preparation, and arrange for Infantry assault to be simultaneous after preparation.'

As a result of this order, the bombardment of the Turkish left was resumed, the British guns and howitzers lending their aid to the French Artillery as in the previous attacks. At about 6 p.m., a fine attack was launched, 600 yards of Turkish first line trenches were taken, and despite heavy counter-attacks during the night, especially at 3.20 a.m., all captured positions are still in our hands. Am afraid casualties are considerable, but details are lacking. The enemy lost very heavily. One Turkish battalion coming up to reinforce, was spotted by an aeroplane, and was practically wiped out by the seventy-fives before they could scatter.

Type of fighting did not lend itself to taking prisoners, and only some 50, including one officer, are in our hands. The elan and contempt of danger shown by the young French drafts of the last contingent, averaging, perhaps, 20 years of age, was much admired by all. During the fighting, the French battleship *St. Louis* did excellent service against the Asiatic batteries. All here especially regret that Colonel Girodon, one of the best staff officers existing, has been severely wounded whilst temporarily commanding a brigade. Colonel Nogués, also an officer of conspicuous courage, already twice wounded, at Kum Kale, has again been badly hit.

Girodon is one in ten thousand; serious, brave and far sighted. The bullet went through his lung. We are said to have suffered nearly 3,000 casualties.

They say that the uproar of battle was tremendous, especially between midnight and 4 a.m. Some of our newly arrived troops stood to their arms all night thinking the end of the world had come.

At 6 p.m. de Robeck, Keyes, Ormsby Johnson and Godfrey came over from the flagship to see me.

Have got an answer about the Japanese trench mortars and bombs. In two months' time a thousand bombs will be ready at the Japanese Arsenal, and five hundred the following month. The trench mortars — bomb guns they call them — will be ready in Japan in two and a half months' time. Two and a half months, plus half a month for delay, plus another month for sea transit, makes four months! There are some things speak for themselves. Blood, they say, cries out to Heaven. Well, let it cry now. Over three months ago I asked — *my first request* — for these primitive engines and as for the bombs, had Birmingham been put to it, Birmingham could have turned them out as quick as shelling peas.

Am doing what I can to fend for myself. This Dardanelles war is a war, if ever there was one, of the ingenuity and improvised efforts of man against nature plus machinery. We are in the desert and have to begin very often at the beginning of things. The Navy *now* assure me that their Dockyard Superintendent at Malta could make us a fine lot of hand grenades in his workshops if Lord Methuen will give him the order.

So I have directed a full technical specification of the Turkish hand grenades being used against us with effects so terrible, to be sent on to Methuen telling him it is simple, effective, that I hope he can make them and will be glad to take all he can turn out.

23rd June, 1915. Imbros. Another day in camp. De Robeck and Keyes came over from the *Triad* to unravel knotty points.

Am enraged to recognize in Reuter one of my own cables which has been garbled in Egypt. The press censorship is a negative evil in London; in Cairo there is no doubt it is positive. After following my wording pretty closely, a phrase has been dovetailed in to say that the Turks have day and night to submit to the capture of trenches. These cables are repeated to London and when they get back here what will my own men think me? If, as most of us profess to believe, it is a mistake to tell lies, what a specially fatal description of falsehood to issue short-dated bulletins of victory with only one month to run. I have fired off a remonstrance as follows:

> (No M.F. 359). From General Sir Ian Hamilton to War Office. A Reuter telegram dated London, 16th June, has just been brought to my notice in which it is stated that the Press Bureau issues despatch in which the following sentence occurs: 'Day and night they (the Turks) have to submit to capture of trenches.' This information is incorrect, and as far as we are aware, has not been sent from here. This false news puts me in a false position with my troops, who know it to be untrue, and I should be glad if you would trace whence it emanates.
> Repeated to General Officer Commanding, Egypt.

24th June, 1915. Imbros. Three days ago we asked the War Office to let us know the merits of the three new Divisions. The War Office replied placing them in the order XIth; XIIth; Xth, and reminding me that the personality of the Commander would be the chief factor for deciding which were to be employed in any particular operation. K. now supplements this by a cable in which he sizes up the Commanders. Hammersley gets a good *chit* but the phrase, "he will have to be watched to see that the strain of trench warfare is not too much for him" is ominous. I knew him in

October, '99, and thought him a fine soldier. Mahon, "without being methodical," is praised. Shaw gets a moderate eulogy, but we out here are glad to have him for we know him. On these two War Office cables Hammersley and the 11th Division should be for it.

After clearing my table, embarked with Braithwaite and Mitchell aboard the *Basilisk* (Lieutenant Fallowfield) and made her stand in as close as we dared at Suvla Bay and the coast to the North of it. We have kept a destroyer on patrol along that line, and we were careful to follow the usual track and time, so as to rouse no suspicions.

To spy out the land with a naval telescope over a mile of sea means taking a lot on trust as we learned to our cost on April 25th. We can't even be sure if the Salt Lake *is* a lake, or whether the glister we see there is just dry sand. We shall have to pretend to do some gun practice, and drop a shell on to its surface to find out. No sign of life anywhere, not even a trickle of smoke. The whole of the Suvla Bay area looks peaceful and deserted. God grant that it may remain so until we come along and make it the other thing.

On my return the Admiral came to hear what I thought about it all. Our plan is bold, but there never was a state of affairs less suited to half and half, keep-in-the-middle-of-the-road tactics than that with which the Empire is faced to-day. If we get through here, now, the war will, must be, over next year. My Manchurian Campaign and two Russian Manœuvres have taught me that, from Grand Duke to Moujiks, our Allies need just that precise spice of initiative which we, only we in the world, can lend them. Advice, cash, munitions aren't enough; our palpable presence is the point. The arrival of Birdwood, Hunter-Weston and Gouraud at Odessa would electrify the whole of the Russian Army.

As to the plan, I have had the G.S. working hard upon it for over a fortnight (ever since the Cabinet decided to support us). Secrecy is so ultra-vital that we are bound to keep the thing within a tiny circle. I am not the originator. Though I have entirely fathered it, the idea was born at Anzac. We have not yet got 330] down to precise dates, units or commanders but, in those matters, the two cables already entered this morning should help. The plan is based upon Birdwood's confidence that, if only he can be strengthened by another Division, he can seize and hold the high

THE NARROWS FROM CHUNUK BAIR

crest line which dominates his own left, and in my own concurrence in that confidence. Sari Bair is the "keep" to the Narrows; Chunuk Bair and Hill 305 are its keys: i.e., from those points the Turkish trenches opposite Birdwood can be enfiladed: the land *and* sea communications of the enemy holding Maidos, Kilid Bahr and Krithia can be seen and shelled and, in fact, any strong force of Turks guarding the European side of the Narrows can then be starved out, whilst a weak force will not long resist Gouraud and Hunter-Weston. As to our tactical scheme for producing these strategical results, it is simple in outline though infernally complicated in its amphibious and supply aspects. The French and British at Helles will attack so as to draw the attention of the Turks southwards. To add to this effect, we are thinking of asking the Anzacs to exert a preliminary pressure on the Gaba Tepe alarum to the southwards. We shall then give Birdwood what he wants, an extra division, and it will be a problem how to do so without letting the enemy smell a rat. Birdwood's Intelligence are certain that no trenches have been dug by the enemy along the high ridge from Chunuk Bair to Hill 305. He is sure that with one more Division under his direct command, plus the help of a push from Helles to ease his southern flank, he can make good these dominating heights.

But, here comes the second half of the plan: the balance of the reinforcements from home are also to be thrown into the scale so as at the same time to give further support to Birdwood on his *northern* flank and to occupy a good harbour (Suvla Bay) whence we can run a light railway line and more effectively feed the troops holding Sari Bair than they could be fed from the bad, cramped beaches of Anzac Cove. This will be the more necessary as the process of starving out the Turks to the south must take time. Suvla Bay should be an easy base to seize as it is weakly held and unentrenched whilst, tactically, any troops landed there will, by a very short advance, be able to make Birdwood's mind easy about his left. Altogether, the plan seems to me simple in outline, and sound in principle. The ground between Anzac and the Sari Bair crestline is worse than the Khyber Pass but both Birdwood and Godley say that their troops can tackle it. There are one or two in the know who think me "venturesome" but, after all, is not "nothing venture nothing win" an unanswerable retort?

De Robeck is excited over some new anti-submarine nets. They are so strong and he can run them out so swiftly that they open, he seems to think, new possibilities of making landings, — not on open coasts like the North of the Aegean but at places like Yukeri Bay, where the nets could be spread from the North and South ends of Tenedos to shoals connecting with Asia so as to make a torpedo proof basin for transports. The Navy, in fact, suddenly seem rather bitten with the idea of landing opposite Tenedos. But whereas, this very afternoon, our own eyes confirmed the aeroplane reports that Suvla Bay is unentrenched, weakly held and quiescent, only yesterday a division of the enemy were reputed to be busy along the whole of the coastline to the South of Besika Bay.

I have raised a hornet's nest by my objection to faked cables; but I will not have it done. They may suppress but they shall not invent.

(No. M.F. 366). From General Sir Ian Hamilton to War Office. Your No. 12431. I do not object to General Officer Commanding, Egypt, publishing any telegram I send him, as I write them for that purpose. But I do object to the addition of news which is untrue, and which can surely be seen through by any reading public. If we can take trenches at our will, why are we still on this side of Achi Baba?

In compliance with Lord Kitchener's instructions I send a telegram to the Secretary of State for War and repeat it to Egypt; also to Australia and New Zealand if it affect these Dominions. Please see your No. 10,475, code, and my No. M.F. 285, instructing me to do this. These telegrams are practically identical when they leave here, and are intended to be used as a communique and to be published. Instead of this I find a mutilated and misleading Cairo telegram reproduced in London Press in place of the true version I sent to the Secretary of State for War.

General Paris crossed from Helles to dine and stay the night. After dinner, Commodore Backhouse came over to make his salaams to his Divisional Chief.

Gouraud has sent me his reply to Lord K.'s congratulations on his victory of the 21st. He says,

Vous prie exprimer à Lord Kitchener mes respectueux remerciements nous n'avons, eu qu'à prendre exemple sur les héroïques régiments anglais qui ont débarqué dans les fils de fer sur la plage de Seddulbahr.*

25th June, 1915. *Imbros.* At 8 a.m. walked down with Paris to see him off. Worked till 11 a.m. and then crossed over to "K" Beach where Backhouse, commanding the 2nd Naval Brigade, met me. Inspected the Hood, Howe and Anson Battalions into which had been incorporated the Collingwood and Benbow units — too weak now to carry on as independent units. The Hood, Howe and Anson are suffering from an acute attack of indigestion, and Collingwoods and Benbows are sick at having been swallowed. But I had to do it seeing there is no word of the cruel losses of the battle of the 4th being made good by the Admiralty. The Howe, Hood and Anson attacked on our extreme right, next the French. They did most gloriously — most gloriously! As to the Collingwoods, they were simply cut to pieces, losing 25 officers out of 28 in a few minutes. Down at the roots of this unhappiness lie the neglect to give us our fair share of howitzers and trench mortars — in fact stupidity! The rank and file all round looked much better for their short rest, and seemed to like the few halting words of praise I was able to say to them. Lunched with Backhouse in a delicious garden under a spreading fig tree; then rode back.

At 5 p.m. Ashmead-Bartlett had an appointment, K. himself took trouble to send me several cables about him a little time ago. Referring in one of them to the dangers of letting Jeremiah loose in London, K. said, "Ashmead-Bartlett has promised verbally to speak to no one but his Editor, who can be trusted." Verbally, or in writing, my astonishment at K.'s confidence can only find expression in verse:

---

* "Please express my respectful thanks to Lord Kitchener, we just had to follow the example of the heroic English regiments who landed in the iron wire on Seddulbahr beach."

> Oft expectation fails, and most oft there
>   Where most it promises;

He, Ashmead-Bartlett, came to-day to beg me to deliver him out of the hands of the Censor. He wants certain changes made and I have agreed. Next, he fully explained to me the importance of the Bulair Lines and urged me to throw the new Divisions against them. He seems to think he is mooting to me a spick and span new idea — that he has invented something. Finally, he suggests ten shillings and a free pardon be offered to every Turk who deserts to our lines with his rifle and kit: he believes we should thus get rid of the whole of the enemy army very quickly.

This makes one wonder what would Ashmead-Bartlett himself do if he were offered ten shillings and a good supper by a Mahommedan when he was feeling a bit hungry and hard up amongst the Christians. Anyway, there is no type of soldier man fighting in the war who is more faithful to his salt than the Osmanli Turk. Were we to offer fifty pounds per head, instead of ten shillings, the bid would rebound in shame upon ourselves.

Colonel Sir Mark Sykes was my next visitor. He is fulfilling the promise of his 'teens when he was the shining light of the Militia; was as keen a Galloper as I have had on a list which includes Winston and F.E., and, generally, gained much glory, martial, equestrian, histrionic, terpsichorean at our Militia Training Camp on Salisbury Plain in '99. Now he has mysteriously made himself (heaven knows how) into our premier authority on the Middle East and is travelling on some ultra-mysterious mission, very likely, *en passant*,[*] as a critic of our doings: never mind, he is thrice welcome as a large-hearted and generous person.

Dined with de Robeck on board the *Triad*. He is *most* hospitable and kind. I have not here the wherewithal to give back cutlet for cutlet, worse luck.

---

[*] "By the way."

26th June, 1915. Worked till past 11 o'clock, then started for Anzac with Braithwaite per destroyer *Pincher* (Lieutenant-Commander Wyld). After going a short way was shifted to the *Mosquito*(Lieutenant-Commander Clarke). We had biscuits in our pockets, but the hospitable Navy stood us lunch.

When the Turks saw a destroyer come bustling up at an unusual hour they said to themselves, "fee faw fum!" and began to raise pillars of water here and there over the surface of the cove. As we got within a few yards of the pier a shell hit it, knocking off some splinters. I jumped on to it — had to — then jumped off it nippier still and, turning to the right, began to walk towards Birdie's dugout. As I did so a big fellow pitched plunk into the soft shingle between land and water about five or six yards behind me and five or six yards in front of Freddie. The slush fairly smothered or blanketed the shell but I was wetted through and was stung up properly with small gravel. The hardened devils of Anzacs, who had taken cover betwixt the shell-proofs built of piles of stores, roared with laughter. Very funny — to look at!

As the old Turks kept plugging it in fairly hot, I sat quiet in Birdwood's dugout for a quarter of an hour. Then they calmed down and we went the rounds of the right trenches. In those held by the Light Horse Brigade under Colonel G. de L. Ryrie, encountered Lieutenant Elliot, last seen a year ago at Duntroon.

Next, met Colonel Sinclair Maclagan commanding 3rd (Australian) Infantry Brigade. After that saw the lines of Colonel Smith's Brigade, where Major Browne, R.A., showed me a fearful sort of bomb he had just patented.

At last, rather tired by my long day, made my way back, stopping at Birdie's dugout en route. Boarded the *Mosquito*; sailed for and reached camp without further adventure. General Douglas of the East Lancs Division is here. He has dined and is staying the night. A melancholy man before whose eyes stands constantly the tragic melting away without replacement of the most beautiful of the Divisions of Northern England.

27th June, 1915. Imbros. Blazing hot; wound up my mail letters; fought files, flies and irritability; tackled a lot of stuff from Q.M.G.

and A.G.; won a clear table by tea time. In the evening hung about waiting for de Robeck who had signalled over to say he wanted to talk business. At the last he couldn't come.

The sequel to the letter telling me I'd have to cut the names of battalions out of my Despatch has come in the shape of a War Office cable telling me that, if I agree, it is proposed "to have the despatch reviewed and a slightly different version prepared for publication." I hope my reply to Fitz may arrive in time to prevent too much titivation.

An imaginative War Office (were such a thing imaginable) would try first of all to rouse public enthusiasm by letting them follow quite closely the brave doings of their own boys' units whatever these might be. Next, they would try and use the Press to teach the public that there are three kinds of war, (*a*) military war, (*b*) economic war and (*c*) social war. Lastly, they would explain to the Cabinet that this war of ours is a mixture of (*a*) and (*b*) with more of (*b*) than (*a*) in it.

How can economic victory be won? (1) by enlisting the sympathy of America; (2) by taking Constantinople.

The idea that we can hustle the Kaiser back over the Rhine and march on to Berlin at the double emanates from a school of thought who have devoted much study to the French Army, not so much to that of the Germans. But we *can* (no one denies it) hustle the Turks out of Constantinople if we will make an effort, big, no doubt, in itself but not very big compared to that entailed by a few miles' advance in the West. Let us do that and, forthwith, we enlist economics on our side.

None of these things can be carried through without the help of the Press. Second only to enthusiasm of our own folk comes the sweetening of the temper of the neutral. Hard to say at present whether our Censorship has done most harm in the U.K. or the U.S.A. Before leaving for the Dardanelles I begged hard for Hare and Frederick Palmer, the Americans, knowing they would help us with the Yanks just as much as aeroplanes would help us with the Turks, but I was turned down on the plea that the London Press would be jealous.

These are the feelings which have prompted my pen to-day. Writing one of the few great men I know I put the matter like this::

From my individual point of view a hideous mistake has been made on the correspondence side of the whole of this Dardanelles business. Had we had a dozen good newspaper correspondents here, the vital life-giving interest of these stupendous proceedings would have been brought right into the hearths and homes of the humblest people in Britain....

As for information to the enemy, this is too puerile altogether. The things these fellows produce are all read and checked by competent General Staff Officers. To think that it matters to the Turks whether a certain trench was taken by the 7th Royal Scots or the 3rd Warwicks is just really like children playing at secrets. The Censors who are by way of keeping everyone in England in darkness allow extremely accurate outline panoramas of the Australian position from the back; trenches, communication tracks, etc., all to scale; a true military sketch, to appear in the *Illustrated London News* of 5th June. The wildest indiscretions in words could not equal this.

Again I say the Press must win. On no subject is there more hypocrisy amongst big men in England. They pretend they do not care for the Press and *sub rosa** they try all they are worth to work it. How well I remember my Chief of the General Staff coming up to me at a big conference on Salisbury Plain where I had spent five very useful minutes explaining the inwardness of things to old Bennett Burleigh, the War Correspondent. He (the C.G.S.) begged me to see Burleigh privately, afterwards, as it would "create a bad impression" were I seen by everyone to be on friendly terms with the old man! He meant it very kindly: from his point of view he was quite right. I lay no claim to be more candid than the rest of them: quite the contrary. Only, over that particular line of country, I am more candid. Whenever anyone ostentatiously washes his hands of the Press in my hearing I chuckle over the memory of the administrator who was admonishing me as to the unsuitability of a public servant having a journalistic acquaintance when, suddenly, the door opened; the parlour-maid entered and said, "Lord Northcliffe is on the 'phone."

Have told Lord K. in my letter we have just enough shell for one more attack. After that, we fold our hands and wait the arrival

---

* "In secret."

of the new troops and the new outfit of ammunition: not "wait and see" but "wait and suffer." A month is a desperate long halt to have in a battle. A month, at least, to let weariness and sickness spread whilst new armies of enemies replace those whose hearts we have broken, — at a cost of how many broken hearts, I wonder, in Australasia and England?

This enforced pause in our operations is a desperate bad business: for to-day there is a feeling in the air — thrilling through the ranks — that *at last* the upper hand is ours. Now is the moment to fall on with might and main, — to press unrelentingly and without break or pause until we wrest victory from Fortune. Morally, we are confidentbut, — materially? Alas, to-morrow, for our last "dart" before reinforcements arrive a month hence, my shell only runs to a forty minutes' bombardment of some half a mile of the enemy's trenches. We simply have not shell wherewith to cover more or keep it up any longer.

A General laying down the law to a Field Marshal is as obnoxious to military "form" as a vacuum was once supposed to be to the sentiments of nature. The child, who teaches its grandmother to suck eggs, commits a venial fault in comparison. So I have had to convey my precepts insensibly to Milord K. — to convey them in homeopathic doses of parable. The brilliant French success of the 21st-22nd, I explain to him, was due to the showers of shell wherewith they deluged the Turkish lines until their defenders were sitting dazed with their dugouts in ruins about them. Also, in the same epistle, I have tried to explain Anzac.

In the domain of tactics our landing at Helles speaks for itself. Since gunpowder was invented nothing finer than the 29th Division has been achieved. But it will be a long time yet before people grasp that the landing at Anzac is just as remarkable in the imaginative domain of strategy. The military student of the future will, I hope and believe, realize the significance of the stroke whereby we are hourly forcing a great Empire to commit *hari kiri* upon these barren, worthless cliffs — whereby we keep pressing a dagger exactly over the black heart of the Ottoman Raj. Only skin deep — so far; only through the skin. Yet already how freely bleeds the wound. Daily the effort to escape this doom; to push away the threat of that painful point will increase. Even if we were never to make another yard's advance, — here — in the cove of Anzac — is the cup into which the life blood of the Caliphat shall be pressed. And on the whole Gallipoli Peninsula this little cove is the one and only spot whereon a base could have been established, which is sheltered (to a bearable extent) from the force of the enemy's fire. Dead ground; defiladed from inland batteries; deep water right close to the shore!

Enver dares not leave Anzac alone. We are too near his neck; the Narrows!! So on this most precarious, God-forsaken spot he must maintain an Army of his best troops, mostly supplied by sea, — by sea whereon our submarines swallow 25 per cent. of their drafts, munitions and food, just as a pike takes down the duckling before the eyes of their mother on a pond. Hold fast's the word. We have only to keep our grip firm and fast; Turkey will die of exhaustion trying to do what she can't do; drive us into the sea!

Braithwaite and Amery dined. Great fun seeing Amery again. *What* memories of his concealment in the Autocrat's "Special" going to the Vereeniging Conference; of our efforts to create a strategical training ground for British troops in South Africa; of our battles against one another over the great Voluntary Service issue.

Chapter XII – A Victory and After

28th June, 1915. Imbros. The fateful day.

Left camp with Braithwaite, Dawnay and Ward. Embarked on the destroyer *Colne* (Commander Seymour) and sailed for Helles. The fire fight was raging. From the bridge we got a fine view as our guns were being focused on and about the north-west coast. The cliff line and half a mile inland is shrouded in a pall of yellow dust which, as it twirls, twists and eddies, blots out Achi Baba himself. Through this curtain appear, dozens at a time, little balls of white, — the shrapnel searching out the communication trenches and cutting the wire entanglements. At other times spouts of green or black vapour rise, mix and lose themselves in the yellow cloud. The noise is like the rumbling of an express train — continuous; no break at all. The Turks sitting there in their trenches — our men 100 yards away sitting in *their* trenches! What a wonderful change in the art, — no not the art, in the mechanism — of war. Fifteen years ago armies would have stood aghast at our display of explosive energy; to-day we know that our shortage is pitiable and that we are very short of stuff; perilously short. — (Written in the cabin of the *Colne*.)

Jimmy Watson met me on the pier. He is Commandant Advance Base. Deedes also met me and the whole band of us made our way inland to my battle dugout. This is probably our last onslaught before the new troops and new supplies of shell come to hand in about a month from now. We have just enough stuff to deal with one narrow strip by the coast. Had it not been for some help from the French, we could not have entered upon this engagement at all, but must have continued to sit still and be shot at — rather an expensive way of fighting if John Bull could only be told the truth. Now, although the area is limited the battle is a big one, fairly entitled to be called a general action. As I said, the French are helping Simpson-Baikie in his bombardment; the Fleet are helping us with the fire of the *Scorpion*, *Talbot* and *Wolverine*, and Birdwood has been asked to try and help us from Anzac by making a push there to hold the enemy and prevent him sending reinforcements south. On their side the Turks are making a very feeble reply. Looks as if we had caught them with their ammunition parks empty.

I went into the dugout indescribably slack; hardly energy to struggle against the heat and the myriads of flies. I came out of it radiant. The Turks are beat. Five lines of their best trenches carried (or, at least, four regular lines plus a bit extra); the Boomerang Redoubt rushed, and in two successive attacks we have advanced 1,000 yards. Our losses are said to be moderate. The dreaded Boomerang collapsed and was stormed with hardly a casualty. This was owing partly to the two trench mortars lent us by the French and partly to the extraordinary fine shooting of our own battery of 4.5 howitzers. The whole show went like clockwork — like a Field Day. First the 87th Brigade took three lines of trenches; then our guns lengthened their range and fuses and the 86th Brigade, with the gallant Royal Fusiliers at their head, scrambled over the trenches already taken by the 87th, and took the last two lines in splendid style. We could have gone right on but we had nothing to go on with. How I wish the whole world and his wife could have been here to see our lines advancing under fire quite steadily with intervals and dressing as on parade. A wonderful show!

As the 87th Brigade left the trenches at 11 a.m., the enemy opened a hot shrapnel fire on them but although some men fell,

A Victory and After

none faltered as we could see very well owing to the following device. The 29th attackers had sewn on to their backs triangles cut out of kerosine tins. The idea was to let these bright bits of metal flash in the sunlight and act as helios. Thus our guns would be able to keep an eye on them. The spectacle was extraordinary. From my post I could follow the movements of every man. One moment after 11 a.m. the smoke pall lifted and moved slowly on with a thousand sparkles of light in its wake: as if someone had quite suddenly flung a big handful of diamonds on to the landscape.

At 11.30 the 86th Brigade likewise advanced; passed through the 87th and took two more lines of trenches.

At mid-day I signalled, "Well done 29th Division and 156th Brigade. Am watching your splendid attack with admiration. Stick to it and your names will become famous in your homes."

At 1.50 I got a reply, "Thanks from all ranks 29th. We are here to stay."

At 3.15 I ran across and warmly congratulated Hunter-Weston, staying with him reading the messages until about 4 p.m. when I went on to see Gouraud. Hunter-Weston, Gouraud and Braithwaite agree that: *had we only shell to repeat our bombardment of this morning, now, we could go on another 1,000 yards before dark, — result, Achi Baba to-morrow, or, at the latest, the day after; Achi Baba* and fifty guns perhaps with, say, 10,000 prisoners.

At 5 p.m. Gouraud and I walked back to Hunter-Weston's G.H.Q. A load was off our minds — we were wonderfully happy.

At 5.30 a message from Birdie to say the Queenslanders had thrust out towards Gaba Tepe and had "drawn" the Turkish reserves who had been badly hammered by our guns. With this crowning mercy in my pocket, walked down and boarded the destroyer *Scourge* (Lieutenant Tupper) and got back to camp before seven. What a day! May our glorious Infantry gain everlasting *Kudos* — and the Gunners, too, may the good use they made of their shell ration create a legend.

The French official photographer has fixed a moment by snapping Gouraud and myself overlooking the Hellespont from the old battlements.

"Central News" phot.

GENERAL GOURAUD

Midnight. — When I lay down in my little tent two hours ago the canvas seemed to make a sort of sounding board. No sooner did I try to sleep than I heard the musketry rolling up and dying away; then rolling up again in volume until I could stick it no longer and simply had to get up and pick a path, through the brush and over sandhills, across to the sea on the East coast of our island. There I could hear nothing. Was the firing then an hallucination — a sort of sequel to the battle in my brain? Not so; far away I could see faint corruscations of sparks; star shells; coloured fire balls from pistols; searchlights playing up and down the coast. Our fellows were being hard beset to hold on to what they had won; there, where the horizon stood out with spectral luminosity. What a contrast; the direct fear, joy, and excitement of the fighting men out there in the searchlights and the dull anguish of waiting here in the darkness; imagining horrors; praying the Almighty our men may be vouchsafed valour to stick it through the night; wondering, waiting until the wire brings its colourless message!

One thought I have which is in the end a sure sleep-getter — the advancing death. Whether by hours or by years, by inches or by leagues, by bullets or bacilli, we struggle-for-lifers will very soon struggle no more. My last salaams are well-nigh due to my audience and to the stage. That rare and curious being called I is more fragile than any porcelain jar. How on earth it has preserved itself so long, heaven only knows. One pellet of lead, it falls in a heap of dust; the Peninsuladisappears; the fighting men fall asleep; the world and its glories become a blank — not even a dream — nothing!

29th June, 1915. Imbros. Sunlight has scattered the spectres of the night, — they have fled, leaving behind them only the matter-of-fact residuum of heavy Turkish counter-attacks against our fresh-won ground. The fighting took place along the coastline, and the stillness of the night seems to have helped the sounds of musketry across the twelve miles of sea. The attack was most determined: repulsed by bombs and with the bayonet: at daylight the enemy came under a cross-fire of machine guns and rifles and were shot to pieces.

Very early approved the revise of my long cable (for the Cabinet) outlining my hopes and fears:

(No. M.F. 381). From General Sir Ian Hamilton to Earl Kitchener. With reference to your telegram No. 5770, cipher. As the Cabinet are anxious to consider my situation in all its bearings, it is necessary I should open to you all my mind. In my No. M.F. 328 of 13th June, I gave you an outline of my plan, based on the news that I was to be given new divisions, and I told you what I should do with a possible fourth division in my No. M.F. 364 of 23rd June. I am now asked whether I consider a fifth division advisable and necessary.

I have taken time to answer this question, as the addition of each new division necessitates, in such a theatre of war as this, a reconsideration of the whole strategical and tactical situation as well as of the power of the Fleet to work up to the increased demands that would be placed upon it. The scheme which might tempt me (Naval considerations permitting) of landing the 4th and 5th Divisions together with the three divisions and one or two divisions from Cape Helles and Anzac on flank of shore of Gulf of Saros to march on Rodosto and Constantinople I reject because the 4th and 5th Divisions cannot reach me simultaneously with all their transport.

But assuming that reinforcements can only reach me in echelon of divisions I have decided that the best policy would be to adhere to my original plan of endeavouring to turn the enemy's right at Anzac with the first three divisions and to gain a position from Gaba Tepe to Maidos. I should then use the 4th and 5th Divisions, in case of non-success at first to reinforce this wing, and in case of success possibly to effect a landing on the southern shore of the Dardanelles; and since the enemy's forces south of the Straits would probably have been reduced to a minimum in order to oppose my reinforced strength on the Peninsula I should in the latter case count upon these two divisions doing more than hold a bridge-head (see my M.F. 349 of 19th June), and should expect them, reinforced from the northern wing if necessary, to press forward to Chanak and thus to cut off this enemy's sole remaining line of supply.* By these means I should hope

---

* All this was based, be it remembered, upon a complete misconception of the state these two divisions, formerly good, afterwards destined to become splendid, had been allowed to fall into. No one at the Dardanelles, least of all myself, had an inkling that since I had inspected them late in 1914 and found them good, they had

A Victory and After

to compel the surrender of the whole Gallipoli Army. Meanwhile, with my force on the Asiatic side I would be enabled to establish in Morto Bay a base safe from the bad weather which must be expected later on.

With regard to ammunition, the more we can get the more easy will our task be, but I hope we may be able to achieve success at the end of July with the amount available. As we are so far from home, however, we cannot afford to run things too fine, and we shall always be obliged to keep up a large reserve until the arrival of further supply. I should, therefore, like as much as you can spare, particularly high explosive. So far as this question affects sending a 4th and 5th Division I would not refuse them on the score of ammunition alone, because with the Artillery of three new divisions complete I think we shall have as many guns as the terrain will allow us to use in the operations towards Maidos, and also sufficient to compete with any Artillery which the enemy could bring against the detachment operating on the Asiatic shore.

To summarize — I think I have reasonable prospects of eventual success with three divisions, with four the risks of miscalculation would be minimized, and with five, even if the fifth division had little or no gun ammunition, I think it would be a much simpler matter to clear the Asiatic shore subsequently of big guns, etc., Kilid Bahr would be captured at an earlier date and success would be generally assured.

Next, I boiled down yesterday's battle into telegraphic dispatch form:

(No. M.F. 383). From General Sir Ian Hamilton to Secretary of State for War. In continuation of my Nos. M.F. 379 and 382. Plan of operations yesterday was to throw forward left of my line south-east of Krithia, pivoting on point about one mile from the sea, and after advancing extreme left for about half a mile, to establish new line facing east on ground thus gained. This plan entailed the capture in succession of two lines of the Turkish trenches east of the Saghir Dere and five lines of trenches west of it. Australian Corps was ordered to

---

passed into a squeezed-lemon stage of existence and had ceased to be able "to press forward to Chanak." The fact that they were at half strength and that the best of their officers and men had been picked out for the Western theatre was unknown to us at the Dardanelles. — *Ian H., 1920.*

co-operate by making vigorous demonstration. The action opened at 9 a.m. with bombardment by heavy artillery of the trenches to be captured.

Assistance rendered by French in this bombardment was most valuable. At 10.20 our field artillery opened fire to cut wire in front of Turkish trenches and this was effectively done. Great effect on enemy's trench near sea and in keeping down his artillery fire from that quarter was produced by very accurate fire of H.M.S. *Talbot*, *Scorpion*, and *Wolverine*. At 10.45 a small Turkish advanced work in the Saghir Dere, known as the Boomerang Redoubt, was assaulted. This little fort was very strongly sited, protected by extra strong wire entanglements and has long been a source of trouble. After special bombardment by trench mortars and while bombardment of surrounding trenches was at its height part of Border Regiment, at the exact moment prescribed, leapt from their trenches like a pack of hounds pouring out of cover, raced across and took the work most brilliantly.

Artillery bombardment increased in intensity till 11 a.m. when range was lengthened and infantry advanced. Infantry attack was carried out with great dash along whole line. West of Saghir Dere 87th Brigade captured three lines of trenches with little opposition. Trenches full of dead Turks, many buried by bombardment, and 100 prisoners were taken in them. East of Ravine two battalions Royal Scots made fine attack, capturing the two lines of trenches assigned as their objective, but remainder of 156th Brigade on their right met severe opposition and were unable to get forward. At 11.30, 86th Brigade led by 2nd Bn. Royal Fusiliers started second phase of attack West of Ravine. They advanced with great steadiness and resolution through trenches already captured and on across the open, and taking two more lines of trenches reached objective allotted to them, Lancashire Fusiliers inclining half right and forming line to connect with our new position East of Ravine.

The northernmost objective I had set out to reach had now been attained, but the Gurkhas pressing on under the cliffs captured an important knoll still further forward, actually due west of Krithia. This they fortified and held during the night, making our total gain on the left precisely 1,000 yards. During afternoon 88th Brigade attacked trenches, small portion of which remained uncaptured on right, but enemy held on stubbornly, supported by machine guns and artillery, and attacks did not succeed. During night enemy counter-attacked furthest trenches gained but was repulsed with heavy loss. Party of Turks who penetrated from flank between two lines of captured trenches, subjected to machine-gun fire at daybreak, suffered very heavily and survivors surrendered.

Except for small portion of trench already mentioned which is still held by enemy, all, and more than we hoped for, from operations has been gained. On extreme left, line has been pushed forward to specially strong point well beyond limit of advance originally contemplated. Our casualties about 2,000, the greater proportion of which are slight cases of which 250 at Anzac, in the useful demonstration made simultaneously there. All engaged did well, but certainly the chief factor in the success was the splendid attack carried out by XXIXth Division, whose conduct in this as on previous occasions was beyond praise.

Lastly, I wrote out a special Force Order thanking the incomparable 29th.

Winter brought me over a letter just received from Wallace. He is quarrelling with Elliot. For that I don't blame him. At the end of his letter Wallace says, "I feel that the organization of the Lines of Communication and making it work is such a task that I sometimes doubt myself whether I am equal to it." Wallace is a good fellow and a sensible man placed, by British methods, out of his element and out of his depth. Have told Winter to tell him I sympathize and will help him and support him all I know; that if it turns out his strong points lie in another direction than administering a huge business machine, I will try and find a handsome way out for him.

Had been writing, writing, writing since cockcrow so when I heard a trawler was going over with two of the General Staff at mid-day, I could not resist the chance of another visit to the scene of yesterday's victorious advance. Went to see Hunter-Weston but he was up at the front where I had no time to follow him. His Chief of Staff says all goes well, but they have just had cables from my own Headquarters to tell them that heavy columns of Turks are massing behind Achi Baba for a fresh counter-attack. Thought, therefore, the wisest thing was to get back quickly. Reached camp again about 7 p.m., and found more news in office than I got on the spot. Last night's firing on the Peninsula meant close and desperate fighting. Several heavy columns of Turks attacked with bomb and bayonet, and in places some of their braves broke through into our new trenches where the defence had not yet been put on a stable footing. When daylight came we got them enfiladed by machine guns and every single mother's son of them was either killed or captured. So we still hold every yard we had gained.

The attack by a part of the Lowland Division seems to have been mishandled. A Brigade made the assault East of the Ravine; the men advanced gallantly but there was lack of effective preparation. Two battalions of the Royal Scots carried a couple of the enemy's trenches in fine style and stuck to them, but the rest of the Brigade lost a number of good men to no useful purpose in their push against H.12. One thing is clear. If the bombardment was ineffective, from whatever cause, then the men should not have been allowed to break cover.*

30th June, 1915. Imbros. Writing in camp.

More good news. It never rains but it pours. The French have made a fine push and got the Quadrilateral by 8 a.m. with but little loss. The Turks seemed discouraged, they say, and did not offer their usual firm resistance.

At 10.30 a.m. wired Gouraud: "Warm congratulations on this morning's work which will compensate for the loss of your 2,000 quarts of wine. Your Government should now replace it with vintage claret. Please send me quickly a sketch of the ground you have gained."

Gouraud now replies: "Best thanks for congratulations. Sketch being made. If our Government is pleased to send a finer brand of wine to replace what was wasted by the guns of Asia, we Frenchmen will drink it to the very good health of our British comrades in arms."

How lucky I signalled de Robeck 8 p.m. yesterday to let us keep the *Wolverine* and *Scorpion* "in case of a night attack!" Sure enough there was another onslaught made against our northernmost post. Two Turkish Regiments were discovered in mass creeping along the top of the cliffs by the searchlights of the *Scorpion*. They

---

* See Appendix I for the exact facts which were not known to me until long afterwards. — *Ian H., 1920.*

were so punished by her guns that they were completely broken up and the Infantry at daylight had not much to do except pick up the fragments. 300 Turks lay dead upon the ground. Also, hiding in furze, have gleaned 180 prisoners belonging to the 13th, 16th and 33rd Regiments. A Circassian prisoner carried in a wounded Royal Scot on his back under a heavy fire.

Three wires from Helles; the first early this morning; the last just to hand (11 p.m.) saying that the lack of hand grenades is endangering all our gains. The Turks are much better armed in this respect. De Lisle says that where we have hand grenades we can advance still further; where we have not, we lose ground. At midday, we wired our reply saying we had no more hand grenades we feared but that we would do our best to scrape up a few; also that several trench mortars had just arrived from home and that they would be sent over forthwith.

Have returned some interesting minutes on the Dardanelles, sent me from home, with this remark: "Looking back I see now clearly that the one fallacy which crept into your plans was non-recognition of the pride and military *moral* of the Turk. There was never any question of the Turk being demoralized or even flustered by ships sailing past him or by troops landing in his rear. *At last, I believe,* this *moral* is beginning to crack up a little (not much) but nothing less than murderous losses would have done it. In their diaries their officers speak of this Peninsula as the Slaughterhouse."

Brigadier-General de Lothbinière and Major Ruthven lunched and young Brodrick and I dined together on board the *Triad* with the hospitable Vice-Admiral. We were all very cheery at the happy turn of our fortunes; outwardly, that is to say, for there was a skeleton at the feast who kept tap, tap, tapping on the mahogany with his bony knuckles; tap, tap, tap; the gunfire at Helles was insistent, warning us that the Turks had not yet "taken their licking." But when I get back, although there is nothing in from Hunter-Weston there is an officer from Anzac who has just given me the complete story of Birdwood's demonstration on the 28th. The tide of war is indeed racing full flood in our favour.

When we were working out our scheme for the attack of the 29th Division and 156th Brigade the day before yesterday, as well as Gouraud's attack of yesterday, we had reckoned that the Turkish High Command would get to realize by about 11 a.m. on the 28th that an uncommon stiff fight had been set afoot to the sou'-west of Krithia. L. von S. would then, it might be surmised, draw upon his reserves at Maidos and upon his forces opposite Anzac: they would get their orders about mid-day: they would be starting about 1 p.m.: they would reach Krithia about dusk: they would use their "pull" in the matter of hand grenades to counter-attack by moonlight. So we asked Birdie to make one of his most engaging gestures just to delay these reinforcements a little bit; and now it turns out that the Australians and New Zealanders in their handsome, antipodean style went some 50 per cent. better than their bargain:

(1) At 1 p.m. on the 28th the Queensland giants darted out of their caves and went for the low ridge covering Gaba Tepe, that tenderest spot of the Turks. They got on to the foot of it and, by their dashing onslaught, drew the fire of all the enemy guns; but, what was still better, heavy Turkish columns, on the march, evidently, from Maidos to the help of Krithia, turned back northwards and closed in for the defence of Gaba Tepe. As they drew near they came under fire of our destroyers and of the Anzac guns and were badly knocked about and broken up. So both Krithia and the French Quadrilateral have had to do without the help of these reinforcements from the reserves of Liman von Sanders. One of the neatest of strokes and the credit of it lies with the Queenslanders who were not content to flourish their fists in the enemy's face but ran out and attacked him at close quarters.

(2) Now comes the sequel! Birdie has just sent in word of the best business done at Anzac since May 19th!! The success of his demonstration towards Gaba Tepe had given the Turks a bad attack of the jumps, followed by a thirst for vengeance. Yesterday, they got *very* nervy during a dust storm and for two hours the whole of their Army kept up high pressure fire from every rifle and machine gun they could bring to bear. They simply poured out bullets by the

A Victory and After 269

million into the blinding dust. Things then gradually quieted down till 1.30 this morning when a very serious assault — very serious for the enemy — was suddenly launched against the Anzac left, the brunt of it falling on Russell's New Zealand Mounted Rifles and Chauvel's Australian Light Horse; a bad choice too! Our victory complete; bloodless for us. Their defeat complete; very bloody. Nine fresh enemy battalions smashed to bits: fighting went on until dawn: five hundred Turks laid out and counted: no more detail but that is good enough to go to sleep upon.

1st July, 1915. Imbros. Good news from Helles continues. In the early hours of last night an attack was made on the Gurkhas in J trenches. When they ran out of bombs the Turks bombed them out. Headed by Bruce their Colonel, whom they adore, they retook the trench and, for the first time, got into the enemy with their *kukris* and sliced off a number of their heads. At dawn half a battalion of Turks tried to make the attack along the top of the cliff and were entirely wiped out.

Against this I must set down cruel bad news about Gouraud. An accursed misadventure. He has been severely wounded by a shell. Directly I heard I got the Navy to run me over. He was already in the Hospital ship; I saw him there. A pure toss up whether he pulls round or not; luckily he has a frame of iron. I was allowed to speak to him for half a minute and he is full of pluck. The shell, an 8-incher from Asia, landed only some half a dozen yards away from him as he was visiting his wounded and sick down by "V" Beach. By some miracle none of the metal fragments touched him, but the sheer force of the explosion shot him up into the air and over a wall said to be seven feet high. His thigh, ankle and arm are all badly smashed, simply by the fall. We could more easily spare a Brigade. His loss is irreparable. By personal magnetism he has raised the ardour of his troops to the highest power. Have cabled to Lord K. expressing my profound sorrow and assuring him that "the grave loss suffered by the French, and indirectly by my whole force," is really most serious, as I know, I say, "the French War Minister cannot send us another General Gouraud."

2nd July, 1915. Imbros. Worked all day in camp. Birdie, with Onslow, his A.D.C — *such* a nice boy — came over from Anzac in the morning and stayed with me the day, during which we worked together at our plan. At night we all went over together to H.M.S. *Triad* to dine with the Vice-Admiral.

Birdwood is quite confident that with a fresh Division and a decent supply of shell he can get hold of the heights of Sari Bair, whereby he will enfilade the whole network of Turkish trenches, now hedging him round. The only thing he bargains for is that G.H.Q. so work the whole affair from orders down to movements, that the enemy get no inkling of our intentions. The Turks so far suspect nothing, and Koja Chemen Tepe and Chunuk Bair, with all the intervening ridge, are still unentrenched and open to capture by a *coup-de-main*. Even if the naval objections to Bulair could be overcome, Sari Bair remains the better move of the two. With the high ridges of Sari Bair in our hands we could put a stop to the Turkish sea transport from Chanak which we could neither see nor touch from Bulair. The tugs with their strings of lighters could not run by day, and as soon as we could get searchlights fixed up, they would find it very awkward to show themselves in the Straits by night. As to the enemy land communications, as soon as we can haul up our big guns we should command, and be able to search, all the ground between the Aegean and the Dardanelles. Now is the moment. Birdwood says that he and his men have exactly the same feeling that we have down at Helles — the feeling, namely, that now at last, we have got a right moral pull over the Turks. All we want is enough material to turn that faith into a mile or two of mountains.

Making full use of their advantage in hand grenades, the Turks again won their trench back from the Gurkhas last night; a trench which was the key to a whole system of earthworks. Bruce had been wounded and they had no officers left to lead them, so de Lisle had to call once more on the 29th Division and the bold Inniskilling Fusiliers retook that trench at a cost of all their officers save two.

A Victory and After   271

There are some feats of arms best left to speak for themselves and this is one of them.
Wrote Lord K. as follows:

Dictated.

GENERAL HEADQUARTERS,
MEDTN. EXPEDITIONARY FORCE.
2nd July, 1915.

MY DEAR LORD KITCHENER,
There seems to be a lull in this tooth-and-nail struggle which has kept me on tenterhooks during the past four days and nights. But we have on our maps little blue arrows showing the movements of at least a Division of troops in various little columns from above Kereves Dere, from Soghon Dere river, from Kilid Bahr and even from within gun-shot of Achi Baba, all converging on a point a mile or two northwest of Krithia. So it looks as if they were going to have one more desperate go at the Gurkha knoll due west of Krithia, and at the line of trench we call J.13 immediately behind it which was also held by the Gurkhas.

Last night they bombed the Gurkhas out of the eastern half of J.13 and the Inniskilling Fusiliers had to take it again at the point of the bayonet just as day broke.

You can have small idea of what the troops are going through. The same old battalions being called on again and again to do the forlorn hope sort of business. However, each day that passes, these captured positions get better dug in, and make the Turks' counter-attack more costly.

The cause of the attack made the night before last on Anzac has been made quite clear to us by a highly intelligent Armenian prisoner we have taken. The strictest orders had been issued by His Excellency Commanding-in-Chief on the Peninsula that no further attacks against our works were to be made unless, of course, we took any ground from them when we must be vigorously countered. But it was explained to the men that the losses in attack had proved too heavy, whereas, if they had patience and waited a week or ten days in their trenches, then at last we would come out and try to attack them when they would kill us in great quantities. However, Enver Pasha appeared in person amongst the troops at Anzac, and ordered three regiments to attack whilst the whole of the rest of the line supported them by demonstrations and by fire. It was objected this was against the command of their local chief. He brushed this objection aside, and told them never to look him in the face again if they failed to drive the Australians into the sea. So off they went and they certainly did not drive the Australians into the sea (although they got into their support trenches at one time) and certainly most of them never looked Enver in the face again, or anyone else for that matter.

The old battle tactics have clean vanished. I have only quite lately realized the new conditions. Whether your entrenchments are on the top of a hill or at the bottom of a valley matters precious 364] little: whether you are outflanked matters precious little — you may hold one half of a straight trench and the enemy may hold the other half, and this situation may endure for weeks. The only thing is by cunning or surprise, or skill, or tremendous expenditure of high explosives, or great expenditure of good troops, to win some small tactical position which the enemy may be bound, perhaps for military or perhaps for political reasons, to attack. Then you can begin to kill them pretty fast.

3rd July, 1915. Imbros. Very hot; very limp with the prevalent disease but greatly cheered up by the news of yesterday evening's battle at Helles. The Turks must have got hold of a lot of fresh shell for, at 5.30 p.m., they began as heavy a bombardment as any yet seen at Helles, concentrating on our extreme left. We could only send a feeble reply. At 6 o'clock the enemy advanced in swarms, but before they had covered more than 100 yards they were driven back again into the Ravine some 800 yards to our front. H.M.S. *Scorpion* and our machine guns played the chief hand. At 7 p.m. the Turkish guns began again, blazing away as if shells were a drug in the market, whilst, under cover of this very intense fire, another two of their battalions had the nerve to emerge from the Ravine to the north-east of our forward trenches and to move in regular lines — shoulder to shoulder — right across the open. Hardly had they shown themselves when the 10th Battery R.F.A. sprayed them beautifully with shrapnel. The Gurkha supports were rushed up, and as there was no room for them in the fire trenches they crept into shell craters and any sort of hole they could find from which to rake the Turks as they made their advance. The enemy's officers greatly distinguished themselves, waving their swords and running well out into the open to get the men forward. The men also had screwed up their courage to the sticking point and made a big push for it, but, in the end, they could not face our fire, and fell back helter-skelter to their mullah. Along the spot where they had stood wavering awhile before they broke and ran, there are still two clearly marked lines of corpses.

Wrote a letter to Sclater saying I cannot understand his request for fuller information about the drafts needed to make my units up to strength. We have regularly cabled strengths; the figures are correct and it is the A.G. himself who has ordered us to furnish the optimistic "ration" strengths instead of the customary "fighting" strengths. The ration strength are for the Q.M.G., but unless the A.G. wishes to go on living in a fool's paradise, why should he be afraid of knowing the numbers we cannot put into the line of battle!

Have also written Cowans protesting once more that we should have business brains to run the most intricate business proposition at present on tap in the world — our communications. During the past month the confusion at Mudros, our advanced base, becomes daily worse confounded. Things meant for Anzac go to Helles, and *vice versa*: or, not infrequently, stores, supplies or luxuries arrive and are sent off on a little tour to Alexandria and Malta before delivery. The system would be perfect for the mellowing of port or madeira, but when it is applied to plum and apple jam or, when 18 pr. shell are sent to howitzers, the system needs overhauling. I know the job is out of the way difficult. There is work here for Lesseps, Goethals and Morgan rolled into one: work that may change the face of the world far, far more than the Suez or Panama Canals and, to do it, they have put in a good fighting soldier, quite out of his setting, and merely because they did not know what to do with him in Egypt! In case Cowans shares K.'s suspicions about my sneaking desire for Ellison, I say, "I assure you; most solemnly I assure you, that the personal equation does not, even in the vaguest fashion, enter into my thoughts. Put the greatest enemy I possess in the world, and the person I most dislike, into that post, and I would thank God for his appointment, on my knees, provided he was a competent business man."

Again:

I am in despair myself over it. Perhaps that is putting it rather strong as I try never to despair, but seriously I worry just as much over things behind me as I do over the enemy in front of me. What I want is a really big man there, and I don't care one D. who he is. A man I mean who, if he saw the real necessity, would wire for a great English contractor and 300 navvies without bothering or referring the matter to anyone.

A cable to say that the editing of my despatch is ended, and that the public will be let into its dreadful secrets in a day or two. But, I am informed there are passages in it whose "secret nature will be scrupulously observed." What passages? I cannot remember any secrets in my despatch.

Have been defending myself desperately against the War Office who want to send out a Naval Doctor to take full charge and responsibility for the wounded (including destination) the moment they quit dry land. But we must have a complete scheme of evacuation *by land and sea*, not two badly jointed schemes. So I have asked, who is to be "Boss"? Who is to see to it that the two halves fit together? The answer is that the War Office are confident "there will be no friction" (bless them!); they say, "nothing could be simpler than this arrangement and no difficulty is anticipated. Neither is boss and the boundary between the different spheres of activity of the two officers might be laid down as the high-water mark." (Bless them again!). Have replied:

> I have struggled with your high-water mark silently for weeks and know something about it. Had I bothered you with all my troubles you would, I respectfully submit, realize that your proposal is not simple but extraordinarily complicated, even pre-supposing seraphic dispositions on either side. If you determine finally that these two officers are to be independent, I foresee that you will greatly widen the scope of dual control which is now only applicable to my great friend the Admiral and myself.
>
> Either Babtie must order up the ships when and where he wants them, or Porter must order the wounded down when he is ready for them. This is my considered opinion.*

---

* The considered opinion proved right. — *Ian H., 1920.*

A Victory and After   275

Have also sent an earnest message to K. — just the old, old story — saying that what I want *first* is drafts, and only *second* fresh divisions. My old Chief has been his kind self again: so very considerate has he been in his recent messages that I feel it almost brutal to press him or to seem to wish to take advantage of his goodness. But we are dealing with lives of men and I *must* try and make myself clear:

I am anxious with regard to the question of reinforcements for units. During the period 28th to 30th June, the Brigades of the XXIXth and Lowland Divisions dropped in strengths approximately as follows: 86th from 71 officers, 2,807 others to 36 and 1,994; 87th from 65 and 2,724 to 48 and 2,075; 88th from 63 and 2,139 to 46 and 1,765; 156th from 102 and 2,839 to 30 and 1,399. All Officers who have arrived from England to date are included in the above figures. Maxwell has agreed to let me have 80 young Officers from Egypt. Of the other ranks I have no appreciable reinforcements to put in. This is the situation after an operation carried out by the XXIXth and two brigades of LIInd Divisions, which was not only successful but even more successful than we anticipated; wherein the initial losses on 28th June were comparatively small, namely 2,000, but as the result of numerous counter-attacks day and night, have since swelled to some 3,500.

The drafts promised in your No. 5793, A.G.2a, would, provided there were no more casualties, bring the units of the XXIXth Division to approximately 75 per cent. of establishment, but would leave none available as further reinforcements.

In view of the operations on a larger scale, with increased forces, I feel I should draw your attention to the risk introduced by the theatre of operations being so far from England. I have no reserves in base depots now, while the operations we are engaged in are such that heavy casualties are to be expected. The want of drafts ready on the spot to fill up units which have suffered heavily might prevent me pressing to full advantage as the result of a local success. At a critical moment I might find myself compelled to suspend operations until the arrival of drafts from England. This might involve a month and in the meantime the enemy would have time to consolidate his position. The difficulty of the drafts question is fully realized, but I think you should know exactly how I am placed and that I should reflect and make clear the essential difference between the Dardanelles and France in so far as the necessity of mobilizing first reinforcements for each unit is concerned. Our real need is a system which will enable me to maintain drafts for the deficiencies in depots on my lines of communications with Egypt.

If K. did not want brief spurts sandwiched between long waits, all he had to do was to tell his A.G. to see to it that the XXIXth Division was kept up to strength. A word and a frown would have done it. But he has not said the word, or scowled, and the troops have by extraordinary efforts and self-sacrifice carried through the work of strong battalions with weak ones — but only to some extent. That is the whole story.

4th July, 1915. Imbros. Church Parade this morning. Made a close inspection of the Surrey Yeomanry under Major Bonsor. Even with as free a hand as the Lord Almighty, it would be hard to invent a better type of fighting man than the British Yeomanry; only, they have never been properly appreciated by the martinets who have ruled our roost, and chances have never been given to them to make the most of themselves as soldiers.

The Escort was made up of men of the 29th Division under Lieutenant Burrell of the South Wales Borderers — that famous battalion which stormed so brilliantly de Tott's battery at the first landing, — also of a detachment of Australians under Lieutenant Edwards and a squad of New Zealanders under Lieutenant Sheppard, fine men all of them, but very different (despite the superficial resemblance imparted by their slouch hats) when thus seen shoulder to shoulder on parade. The Australians have the pull in height and width of chest; the New Zealanders are thicker all through, chests, waists, thighs.

After Church Parade, boarded H.M.S. *Basilisk* (Lieutenant Fallowfield) and steamed to Helles. The Turks, inconsiderate as usual, were shelling Lancashire Landing as we got ashore. Every living soul had gone to ground. Strolled up the deserted road with an air of careless indifference, hopped casually over a huge splosh of fresh blood, and crossed to Hunter-Weston's Headquarters. Had I only been my simple self, I would have out-stripped the hare for swiftness, as it was, I, as C.-in-C., had to play up to the dugouts. As

A Victory and After

Hunter-Weston and I were starting lunch, an orderly rushed in to say that a ship in harbour had been torpedoed. So we rushed out with our glasses and watched. She was a French transport, the *Carthage*, and she took exactly four minutes to sink. The destroyers and picket boats were round her as smart as flies settle on a lump of sugar, and there was no loss of life. Sad to see the old ship go down. I knew her well at Malta and Jean once came across in her from Tunis. She used to roll like the devil and was always said, with what justice I do not know, to be the sister ship to the *Waratah* which foundered so mysteriously somewhere off the Natal coast with a very good chap, a M.F.H., Percy Brown, on board.

At 2.30 General Bailloud, now commanding the French, came over to see me. When he had finished his business which he handles in so original a manner as to make it a recreation, I went off with Hunter-Weston and Staffs to see General Egerton of the Lowland Division. Egerton introduced me to Colonel Mudge, A.A.G., Major Maclean, D.A.A.G. (an old friend), Captain Tollemashe, G.S.O.3, and to his A.D.C., Lieutenant Laverton. We then went on and saw the 156th Brigade. Passed the time of day to a lot of the Officers and men. Among those whose names I remember were Colonel Pallin, acting Brigadier; Captain Girdwood, Brigade Major; Captain Law, Staff Captain; Colonel Peebles, 7th Royal Scots; Captain Sinclair, 4th Royal Scots; Lieutenant McClay, 8th Scottish Rifles. The last Officer was one of the very few — I am not sure they did not say the only one — of his Battalion who went into the assault and returned untouched.

The whole Brigade had attacked H. 12 on the 28th ult. and lost a number of good men. The rank and file seemed very nice lads but — there was no mistaking it — they have been given a bad shake and many of them were down on their luck. As we came to each Battalion Headquarters we were told, "These are the remnants of the ——," whatever the unit was. Three times was this remark repeated but the fourth time I had to express my firm opinion that in no case was the use of the word "remnant," as applied to a fighting unit "in being," an expression which authority should employ in the presence of the men.

Re-embarked in H.M.S. *Basilisk* and got back to Imbros fairly late.

A set of Turkish Divisional orders sent by the Turkish General to the Commander of their right zone at Helles has been taken from a wounded Turkish officer. They bear out our views of the blow that the 29th Division have struck at the enemy's *moral* by their brilliant attack on the 28th inst.

> There is nothing that causes us more sorrow, increases the courage of the enemy and encourages him to attack more freely, causing us great losses, than the losing of these trenches. Henceforth, commanders who surrender these trenches from whatever side the attack may come before the last man is killed will be punished in the same way as if they had run away. Especially will the commanders of units told off to guard a certain front be punished if, instead of thinking about their work supporting their units and giving information to the higher command, they only take action after a regrettable incident has taken place.
> I hope that this will not occur again. I give notice that if it does, I shall carry out the punishment. I do not desire to see a blot made on the courage of our men by those who escape from the trenches to avoid the rifle and machine gun fire of the enemy. Henceforth, I shall hold responsible all Officers who do not shoot with their revolvers all the privates who try to escape from the trenches on any pretext. Commander of the 11th Division, Colonel Rifaat.

In sending on this order to his battalions, the Colonel of the 127th Regiment adds:

> To Commander of the 1st Battalion. The contents will be communicated to the Officers and I promise to carry out the orders till the last drop of our blood has been shed.

Then followed the signatures of the company commanders of the Battalion. There is a savage ring about these orders but they are, I am sure, more bracing to the recipients than laments and condolences over their losses.

5th July, 1915. Imbros. Spent a long, hot day hanging at the end of the wire. Heavy firing on the Peninsula last night under cover of which the Turks at dawn made, or tried to make, a grand, concerted attack. Not a soul in England, outside the Ordnance, realizes, I believe, that barring the guns of the 29th Division and the few guns of the Anzacs, our field artillery consists of the old 15-prs., relics of South Africa, and of 5-inch hows., some of them Omdurman veterans. Quite a number of these guns are already unserviceable and, in the 42nd Division, to keep one and a half batteries fully gunned, we have had to use up every piece in the Brigade. The surplus personnel are thus wasted. To take on new Skoda or Krupp guns with these short-range veterans is rough on the gunners. Still, but for the Territorial Force we should have nothing at all, and but for those guns to-day some of the enemy might have got home.

A sort of professional gossip turned up to-day from G.H.Q. France. We do not seem to be so popular as we deserve to be in *la belle France!* But what I would plead were I only able to get at Joffre and French is that we are "such a little one." Were we all to be set down in the West to-morrow with our shattered, torn formations, they'd put us back into reserve for a month's rest and training. As for the guns, they'd scrap the lot. *They* don't want ancient 15-prs. and 5-inch hows. out there. They picture us feasting upon their munitions, but half of what we use they would not touch with a barge pole and, of the good stuff, one Division in France will fire away in one day what would serve to take the Peninsula.

Braithwaite has a letter from the D.M.I. telling him that 5,000 Russians sailed from Vladivostock on the 1st inst. to join us here. One Regiment of four Battalions plus one Sotnia of Cossacks. A reinforcement of 5,000 stout soldiers tumbling out of the skies! Russians placed here are worth twice their number elsewhere, not only because we need rifles so badly, but because of the moral effect their presence should have in the Balkans.

This little vodka pick-me-up has come in the nick of time to hearten me against the tenor of the news of to-day which is splendid indeed in one sense; ominous in another. The Turks are being heavily reinforced. All the enemy troops who made the big attack last night were fresh arrivals from Adrianople. I do not grumble at the attack (on the contrary we like it), but at the reason they had for making it, which is that two fresh Divisions, newly arrived, asked leave to show their muscle by driving us into the sea. Full details are only just in. The biggest bombardment took place at Anzac. A Turkish battleship joined in from the Hellespont, dropping about twenty 11.2-inch shells into our lines. At Helles, all night, the Turks blazed away from their trenches. At 4 a.m. they opened fire on our trenches and beaches with every gun they could bring to bear from Asia or Achi Baba. Their Asiatic Batteries alone fired 1,900 rounds, of which 700 fell on Lancashire Landing. At least 5,000 shell were loosed off on to Helles. A lot of the stuff was 6-inch and over. The bombardment was very wild and seemed almost unaimed. Soon after 4 a.m. very heavy columns of Turks tried to emerge from the Ravine against the left of the 29th Division. "It wanted to be the hell of a great attack," as one of the witnesses, a moderate spoken young gentleman, states. When the Commanders saw what was impending they sent messages to Simpson-Baikie begging him to send some 4.5 H.E. shell into the Ravine which was beginning to overflow. He was adamant. He had only a few rounds of H.E. and he would not spend them, feeling sure his 18 prs. with their shrapnel were masters of the field. At 6 a.m. out came the Turks, not in lines, but just like a swarm of bees. Our fellows never saw the like and began to wonder whenever they were going to stop, and what on earth *could* stop them! Thousands of Turks in a bunch, so the boys say, swarmed out of their trenches and the Gully Ravine. Well, they were stopped *dead*. There they lie, *still*. The guns ate the life out of them.

It was our central group of artillery who did it. As that big oblong crowd of Turks showed their left flank to Baikie's nine batteries they were swept in enfilade by shrapnel. The fall of the shell was corrected by the two young R.A. subalterns at the front, neither of whom would observe in the usual way through his periscope. They looked over the parapet because that method was more sure and quick, and the stress of the battle was great. There is a rumour that both were shot through the head: I pray it may be but a rumour. Out of all these Turks some thirty only reached our parapets. The sudden destruction which befell them was due in the main to the devotion of these two young heroes. At 7.30 a.m. the Turks tried to storm again. Some of them got in amongst the Royal Naval Division, who brought up their own supports and killed 300, driving out the rest. Ninety dead Turks are laid out on their parapet. Another, later, enemy effort against the right of the 29th

Division was clean wiped out. 150 Turks are dead there. But it is on the far crestline they lie thick.

Every one of these attacking Turks were *fresh* — from Adrianople! Full of fight as compared with their thrice beaten brethren. If the Turks are given time to swap troops in the middle of fighting, we can't really tell how we stand. Still; they are not now as fresh as they were. They have lost a terrible lot of men since the 28th. The big Ravine and all the small nullahs are chock-a-block with corpses. Their casualties in these past few days are put at very high figures by both Birdie and H.W. and it is probable that 5,000 are actually lying dead on the ground. I have on my table a statement made by de Lisle; endorsed by Hunter-Weston and dated 4th instant, saying that 1,200 Turkish dead can be counted corpse by corpse from the left front. The actual numbers de Lisle estimates as between 2,000 and 3,000. Now we have to-day's losses to throw in. The Turks are burning their candle fast at the Anzac as well as the Helles end. Ten days of this and they are finished.*

Naturally, my mind dwells happily just now upon our incoming New Army formations. Yet every now and then I feel compelled to look back to regret the lack of systematic flow of drafts and munitions which have turned our fine victory of the 28th into a pyrrhic instead of a fruitful affair. When Pyrrhus gained his battle over the Romans and exclaimed, "One more such victory and I am done in," or words to that effect, he had no organized system of depots behind him from which the bloody gaps in his ranks could be filled. A couple of thousand years have now passed and we are still as unscientific as Pyrrhus. A splendid expeditionary force sails away; invades an Empire, storms the outworks and in doing so knocks itself to bits. Then a second expeditionary force is sent, but that would have been unnecessary had any sort of arrangement been thought out for promptly replacing first wastages in men and in shell.

---

* This period fell between two of my despatches. As most writers have naturally based themselves on those despatches, the full understanding of the blows inflicted on the Turks between June 29th and July 13th has never yet been grasped; nor, it may be added, the effect which would have been produced had the August offensive been undertaken three weeks earlier. — *Ian H., 1920.*

6th July, 1915. From early morning till 5 p.m. stuck as persistently to my desk as the flies stuck persistently to me. After tea went riding with Maitland. Then with Pollen to dine on board H.M.S. *Triad*. The two Territorial Divisions are coming. What with them and the Rooskies we ought to get a move on this time. Discoursed small craft with the Admiral. The French hate the overseas fire — small blame to them — and Bailloud agrees with his predecessor Gouraud in thinking that one man hit in the back from Asia affects the *moral* of his comrades as badly as half a dozen bowled over by the enemy facing them. The Admiral's idea of landing from Tenedos would help us here, but it is admitted on all hands now that the Turks have pushed on with their Asiatic defences, and it is too much to ask of either the New Army or of the Territorials that they should start off with a terrible landing.

7th July, 1915. No escape from the steadily rising flood of letters and files, — none from the swarms of filthy flies. General Bailloud and Colonel Piépape (Chief of Staff) came across with Major Bertier in a French torpedo boat to see me. They stayed about an hour. Bailloud's main object was to get me to put off the attack planned by General Gouraud for to-morrow. Gouraud has worked out everything, and I greatly hoped in the then state of the Turks the French would have done a very good advance on our right. The arrival of these fresh Turkish Divisions from Adrianople does make a difference. Still, I am sorry the attack is not to come off. Girodon is a heavy loss to Bailloud. Piépape has never been a General Staff Officer before; by training, bent of mind and experience he is an administrator. He is very much depressed by the loss of the 2,000 quarts of wine by the Asiatic shell. Since Gouraud and Girodon have left them the French seem to be less confident. When Bailloud entered our Mess he said, in the presence of four or five young Officers, "If the Asiatic side of the Straits is not held by us within fifteen days our whole force is *voué à la destruction*."[*] He meant it as a jest, but when those who

---

[*] "Doomed to destruction."

prophesy destruction are *gros bonnets*; big wigs; it needs no miracle to make them come off — I don't mean the wigs but the prophecies. Fortunately, Bailloud soon made a cheerier class of joke and wound up by inviting me to dine with him in an extra chic restaurant at Constantinople.

Have told K. plainly that the employment of an ordinary executive soldier as Boss of so gigantic a business as Mudros is suicidal — no less. Heaven knows K. himself had his work cut out when he ran the communications during his advance upon Khartoum. Heaven knows I myself had a hard enough job when I became responsible for feeding our troops at Chitral, two hundred miles into the heart of the Himalayas from the base at Nowshera. Breaking bulk at every stage — it was heart-breaking. First the railway, then the bullock cart, the camel, the mules — till, at the Larram Pass we got down to the donkey. But here we have to break bulk from big ships to small craft; to send our stuff not to one but to several landings, to run the show with a mixed staff of Naval and Military Officers. No, give me deserts or precipices, — anything fixed and solid is better than this capricious, ever-changing sea. The problem is a real puzzler, demanding experience, energy, good temper as well as the power of entering into the point of view of sailors as well as soldiers, and of being (mentally) in at least three places at once:

From General Sir Ian Hamilton to Earl Kitchener.
(No. M.F. 424).

Private. I am becoming seriously apprehensive about my Lines of Communication and am forced to let you know the state of affairs.

Much of the time of General Headquarters has been taken up during the last few days considering matters relating to Mudros and Lines of Communication generally. The Inspector-General of Communications must be a man of energy and ideas. The new Divisions will find the Mudros littoral on arrival better prepared for their reception than it was a month ago. The present man is probably excellent in his own line, but he himself in writing doubts his own ability to cope with one of the most complicated situations imaginable. Please do not think for a moment that I am still hankering after Ellison, I only want a man of that type, someone, for instance, like Maxwell or Sir Edward Ward. Unless I can feel confident in the Commandant of my Lines of Communication I shall always be looking behind me. Wallace could remain as Deputy Inspector-General of Communications. Something, however, must be done meanwhile, and I am sending Brigadier-General Hon. H.A. Lawrence, a man of tried business capacity and great character, to Mudros to-day as dry-nurse.

I have followed up this cable in my letter to Lord K. of date, where I say, "I have just seen Bertie Lawrence who I am sending to reinforce Wallace. He is bitterly disappointed at losing his Brigade, but there is no help for it. He is a business man of great competence, and I think he ought to be able to do much to get things on to a ship-shape footing. General Douglas is very sorry too and says that Lawrence was one of the best Brigadiers imaginable."

The last sentence has been written, I confess, with a spice of malice. When, about a month ago, I had hurriedly to lay my hands on a Commander for the 127th Brigade, I bethought me of Bertie Lawrence, then G.S.O. to the Yeomanry in Egypt. The thrust of a Lancer and the circumspection of a Banker do not usually harbour in the same skull, but I believed I knew of one exception. So I put Lawrence in. By return King's Messenger came a rap over the knuckles. To promote a dugout to be a Brigadier of Infantry was risky, but to put in a Cavalry dugout as a Brigadier of Infantry was outrageous! Still, I stuck to Lorenzo, and lo and behold! Douglas, the Commander of the East Lancs. Division, is fighting tooth and nail for his paragon Brigadier!*

Since 19th March we have been asking for bombs — any kind of bombs — and we have not even got answers. Now they offer us some speciality bombs for which France, they say, has no use.

I have replied:

---

* Lawrence never looked back. After his good work at Mudros I put him in to command the 53rd Division, and the War Office made no objection, I suppose because they were beginning to hear about him. As is well known, he went on then from one post to another till he wound up gloriously as Chief of the General Staff on the Western Front. — *Ian H., 1920.*

I shall be most grateful for as many bombs of this and any other kind as you can spare. Anything made of iron and containing high explosive and detonator will be welcome. I should be greatly relieved if a large supply could be sent overland via Marseilles, as the bomb question is growing increasingly urgent. The Turks have an unlimited supply of bombs, and our deficiencies place our troops at a disadvantage both physically and morally and increase our difficulties in holding captured trenches.

Could you arrange for a weekly consignment of 10,000 to be sent to us regularly?

De Lisle came over to dine and stay the night.

8th July, 1915. H.M.S. "Triad." Tenedos. Started off in H.M.S. *Triad* ith Freddie Maitland, Aspinall and our host, the Admiral.

Had a lovely sail to Tenedos where Colonel Nuillion (acting Governor) and Commander Samson, now Commandant of the Flying Camp, came on board. After lunch, rowed ashore. There was some surf on and I jumped short, landing (if such an expression may pass) in the sea. Wet feet rather refreshing than otherwise on so hot a day. Tenedos is lovely. Each of these islands has its own type of coasts, vegetation and colouring: like rubies and diamonds they are connected yet hardly akin. Climbed Tenedos Hill, our ascent ending in a desperate race for the crest. My long legs and light body enabled me to win despite the weight of age. Very hot, though, and the weight of age has got even less now.

From the top we had an hour's close prospecting of the opposite coasts, where the Turks have done too much digging to make landing anything but a very bloody business. Half a mile to the South looks healthier, but they are sure to have a lot of machine guns there now. The landing would be worse than on the 25th April. Anyway, *I am not going to do it.*

On the ground we now have a fair showing of aeroplanes, but mostly of the wingless sort. At this precise moment only two are really fit. K. has stuck to his word and is not going to help us here, and I can't grumble as certainly I was forewarned. Had he only followed Neville Usborne's £10,000,000 suggestion, we might now be bombing the Turks' landing places and store depots, as well as spotting every day for our gunners. But these naval airmen, bold fellows, always on for an adventurous attack, are hardly in their element when carrying out the technical gunnery part of our work.

Re-embarked, and during our sail back saw a trawler firing at a submarine, whilst other trawlers and picket boats were skurrying up from all points of the compass. Nets were run out in a jiffy, but I fear the big fish had already given them the slip. Cast anchor about 7 o'clock.

Colonel Dick and Mr. Graives dined.

9th July, 1915. Spent the morning writing for the King's Messenger. My letter to K. (an answer to that of Fitz to me) tells him:

(1) That we have passed through the most promising week since the first landing. The thousand yards' advance on the left and the rows of dead Turks left by the receding tide of their counter-attack are solid evidences to the results of the 28th ult., and of the six very heavy Turkish assaults which have since broken themselves to pieces against us.

(2) That Gouraud's loss almost wipes out our gains. Bailloud does not attack till next week when he hopes to have more men and more ammunition, but will this help us so much if the Turks also have more men and more ammunition?

(3) That the Asiatic guns are giving us worry, but that I hope to knock them out with our own heavy guns (the French 9.4s and our own 9.2s) just being mounted. When the new Monitors come they ought to help us here.

(4) That "*power of digestion, sleeping and nerve power are what are essential above all things to anyone who would command successfully at the Dardanelles. Compared with these qualifications most others are secondary.*"

(5) That the British and Australians are marvels of endurance, but that I am having to pull the Indian Brigade right out and send them to Imbros. Their Commander, fine soldier though he be, is too old for the post of Brigadier; he ought

A Victory and After

to be commanding a Division; and the men are morally and physically tired and have lost three-fourths of their officers: with rest they will all of them come round.

(6) That Baldwin's Brigade of the 13th Division have been landed on the Peninsula and are now mixed up by platoons with the 29th Division where they are tumbling to their new conditions quite quickly. They have already created a very good impression at Helles.

Godley and his New Zealander A.D.C. (Lieutenant Rhodes), both old friends, came over from H.M.S. *Triad* to lunch. Hunter-Weston crossed from Helles to dine and stay the night.

10th July, 1915. Imbros. These Imbros flies actually drink my fountain pen dry! Hunter-Weston left for Helles in the evening.

Yesterday a cable saying there were no men left in England to fill either the 42nd Division or the 52nd. We have already heard that the Naval Division must fade away. Poor old Territorials! The War Office are behaving like an architect who tries to mend shaky foundations by clapping on another storey to the top of the building. Once upon a time President Lincoln and the Federal States let their matured units starve and thought to balance the account by the dispatch of untried formations. Why go on making these assurances to the B.P. that we have as many men coming in voluntarily as we can use?

Have refused the request made by His Excellency, Weber Pasha, who signs himself Commandant of the Ottoman Forces, to have a five hours' truce for burying their piles of dead. The British Officers who have been out to meet the Turkish parlementaires say that the sight of the Turkish dead lying in thousands just over the crestline where Baikie's guns caught them on the 5th inst. is indeed an astonishing sight. Our Intelligence are clear that the reason the Turks make this request is that they cannot get their men to charge over the corpses of their comrades. Dead Turks are better than barbed wire and so, though on grounds of humanity as well as health, I should like the poor chaps to be decently buried, I find myself forced to say no.

Patrick Shaw Stewart came to see me. I made Peter take his photo. He was on a rat of a pony and sported a long red beard. How his lady friends would laugh!

Chapter XIII – K.'s Advice and the P.M.'s Envoy

11th July, 1915. Worked in my office from early morning till 12.45. The whole scheme for to-morrow's attack is cut and dried, according to our cloth: time tables fixed and every round counted.

Freddy Stopford and his Staff turned up from Mudros. Stopford in very good form. The first thing he did was to deliver himself of a personal message from Lord K. He (Stopford) wrote it down, in the ante-room, the moment he left the presence and I may take it as being as good as verbatim. Here it is:

> Lord Kitchener told me to tell you he had no wish to interfere with the man on the spot, but from closely watching our actions here, as well as those of General French in Flanders, he is certain that the only way to make a real success of an attack is by surprise. Also, that when the surprise ceases to be operative, in so far that the advance is checked and the enemy begin to collect from all sides to oppose the attackers, then, perseverance becomes merely a useless waste of life. In every attack there seems to be a moment when success is in the assailant's grasp. Both the French and ourselves at Arras and Neuve Chapelle lost the opportunity.

BRAITHWAITE, SIR IAN AND FREDDIE MAITLAND   "*Central News*" *phot*

Well said! K. has made Stopford bring me in his pocket the very text for what I wanted to say to him. Only my grumbling thoughts find expression by my pen but I have plenty of others and my heart has its warm corner for K. whenever he cares to come in.

As I told Stopford, K. has not only anticipated my advice but has dived right down into this muddle of twentieth century war and finds lying at the bottom of it only the old original idea of war in the year 1. At our first landing the way was open to us for just so long as the *surprise* to the Turks lasted. That period here, at the Dardanelles, might be taken as being perhaps twice as long as it would be on the Western front which gave us a great pull. The reason was that land communications were bad and our troops on the sea could move thrice as fast as the Turks on their one or two bad roads. Yet, even so, there was no margin for dawdling. Hunter-Weston and d'Amade had tried their best to use their brief *surprise* breathing space in seizing the Key to the opening of the Narrows — Achi Baba, and had failed through lack of small craft, lack of water, lack of means of bringing up supplies, lack of our 10 per cent. reserves to fill casualties. At that crucial moment when we had beaten the local enemy troops and the enemy reinforcements had not yetcome up, we could not get the men or the stuff quick enough to shore. Still, we had gained three or four miles and there were spots on the Peninsula where, to-day, three or four miles would be enough. Also, supposing he had to run a landing, his (Stopford's) action would take place under much easier conditions than Hunter-Weston's on April 25th. First and foremost, in our "beetles" or barges, conveying 500 men under their own engines, we had an instrument which reduced the physical effort three quarters. This meant half the battle. When we made our original landing at Anzac we could only put 1,500 men ashore, per trip, at a speed of 2½ miles per hour, in open cutters. Were a Commander to repeat that landing now, he would be able to run 5,000 men ashore, per trip, at a speed of five miles per hour with no trouble about oars, tows, etc., and with protection against shrapnel and rifle bullets. As to the actual landing on the beach, that could be done — we had proved it — in less than one quarter of the time. Each beetle had a "brow" fixed on to her bows; a thing to be let down like a drawbridge over which the men could pour ashore by fours; the same with mules, guns, supplies, they could all be rushed on land as fast as they could be handled on the beaches. Secondly, we had already been for some time at work to fix up the wherewithal to meet our chronic nightmare, the water trouble. Thirdly, the system of bringing up food and ammunition from the beaches to the firing line had now been practically worked out into a science at Helles and Anzac where Stopford would be given a chance of studying it at first hand.

As to place, date, command, and distribution of forces, these were still being considered; still undetermined; and I could say no more at present. Braithwaite was away at Helles but, if he would go over to the General Staff, he would find Aspinall, my G.S. (1), and the Q. Staff who would give him the hang of our methods and post him in matters which would be applicable to any date or place.

There was more in this message as taken down by Stopford. After going into some details of trench warfare, K.'s message went on:

> It is not the wish of the Cabinet that Sir Ian Hamilton should make partial attacks. They (the Cabinet) consider it preferable that he should await the arrival of his reinforcements to make one great effort, which, if successful, will give them the ridge commanding the

Narrows. It is not intended, however, that Sir Ian should do nothing in the meantime and if he gets a really good opportunity he is to seize it.

There is something in this reminds me of Kuropatkin's orders to Stakelberg, yet I am glad to find that our spontaneously generated scheme jumps with the views of the Cabinet, for, there is only one "ridge commanding the Narrows" (Kilid Bahr is a plateau), and it is that ridge we mean to try for by "one great effort."

In my reply I shall merely acknowledge. Sari Bair is my secret; my Open Sesame to the cave where the forty thieves of the Committee of Union and Progress have their Headquarters. It makes me uneasy to think the Cabinet are talking about Sari Bair.

A battle is a swirl of "ifs" and "ands." The Commander who enters upon it possessed by some just and clear principle is like a sailing ship entering a typhoon on the right tack. After that he lives from hand to mouth. How far will wise saws cut ice? How much nearer do you get to shooting a snipe by being *told* how not to take your aim? Well thought out plans and preparations deserve to win; order and punctuality on the part of subordinates tend to make the reality correspond to the General Staff conception; surprise, if the Commander can bring it off, is worth all K. can say of it; the energy and rapidity of the chosen troops will exploit that surprise for its full value — bar, always, Luck — the Joker; and Wish to Fight and Will to Win are the surest victory getters in the pack. The more these factors are examined, the more sure it is that everything must in the last resort depend upon the *executive* Commander; and here, of course, I am referring to an *enterprise*, not to a huge, mechanically organized dead-lock like the western front.

Stopford was away in G.H.Q. Staff tents all afternoon; afterwards both he and Adderley, his A.D.C., dined. Stopford likes Reed who is, indeed, a very pleasant fellow to work with. Still, I stick to what I wrote Wolfe Murray: the *combination* of Stopford and Reed is not good; not for this sort of job.

MAJ.-GEN. SIR G. F. ELLISON, K.C.M.G.

F. A. Swaine phot.

12th July, 1915. Imbros. Had meant to start for Helles an hour before daylight to witness the opening of the attack by the French Corps and the Lowland Division. But am too bad with the universal complaint to venture many yards from camp.

Stopford and Staff breakfasted. He has fallen in love with our ideas. After lunch he and his party left for Mudros. Am forcing myself to write so as to ease the strain of waiting: the battle is going on: backwards and forwards — backwards and forwards — I travel between my tent; the signal station, and the G.S. map tent.

A delightful message from K., thanking me for my letters: patting me on the back; telling me that Altham is coming out to run the communications, and Ellison to serve on my Staff.

Thank heavens we are at last to have a business man at the head of our business! As to Ellison, K.'s conscience has for long been smiting him for not having let me take my own C.G.S. with me in the first instance. But Braithwaite has won his spurs now in many a hair-raising crisis, so K. may let his mind rest at ease.

Freddie Maitland and I dined with the Vice-Admiral who kept a signaller on special watch for my messages from the shore — but nothing came in. He, the Admiral, wants to take all the 600 stokers serving in the Royal Naval Division back to the ships. This will be the last straw to the Division. We had the treat of being taken off the *Triad* in the Admiral's racing motor boat and when we got ashore found good news which I have just cabled home:

> In the southern section we attacked at daylight to-day with our right and right centre. After heavy fighting lasting all day the troops engaged, namely, the French Corps and the LIInd Lowland Division, have succeeded in carrying the two strongly held and fortified lines of Turkish trenches opposite to them. The ground covered by the advance varies in depth from 200 to 400 yards, and if we can maintain our gains against to-night's counter-attacks the effect of the action will be not only to advance but greatly to strengthen our line. Full details to-morrow.

13th July, 1915. Imbros. Still feeling very slack. Nothing clear from Helles. My cable best explains:

> Troops have been continuously engaged since my last cable, but situation is still too confused to admit of definition, especially as telephone wires all cut by shell or rifle fire.
>
> So far as can be gathered the sum total of the engagements taking place in a labyrinth of trenches is satisfactory up to the hour of

K.'s Advice and the P.M.'s Envoy 295

cabling and we have taken some 200 prisoners. I hope I shall be able to send definite news to-morrow morning.

Oh, energy, to what distant clime have you flown? I used to be energetic; not perhaps according to Evelyn Wood's standards — but still — energetic! Yet, see me to-day, when a poor cousin to the cholera — this cursed enteritis — lays me by the heels; fills me with desperate longing to lie down and do nothing but rest. More than half my Staff and troops are in the same state of indescribable slackness and this, I think, must be the reason the Greeks were ten long years taking Troy.

Some newspaper correspondents have arrived. I have told them they may do whatever they d——d well please. Ashmead-Bartlett is vexed at his monopoly being spoiled. Charlie Burn, who came with the King's bag, lunched. The Vice-Admiral, Roger Keyes, and Flag-Lieutenant Bowlby dined; very good of them to leave their own perfectly appointed table for our rough and ready fare. The A.D.C.s between them managed to get some partridges, opulent birds which lent quite a Ritzian tone to our banquet.

As was expected, the Turks counter-attacked heavily last night but were unable to drive us out except in one small section on our right. To-day, fighting is still going on and the Naval Division are in it now. We have made a good gain and taken over 400 prisoners and a machine gun. We are still on the rack, though, as there are a lot of Turks not yet cleared out from holes and corners of our new holding, and ammunition is running very short. If our ammunition does not run out altogether and we can hold what we have, our total gain will be 500 yards depth.

Since June 4th, when we had to whang off the whole of our priceless 600 rounds of H.E., we have had *none* for 18-prs. on the Peninsula — not one solitary demnition round; nor do we seem in the least likely to get one solitary demnition round. Hunter-Weston and his C.R.A. explain forcibly, not to say explosively, that on the 28th June the right attack would have scored a success equally brilliant to that achieved by the 29th Division on our left, had we been able to allot as many shell to the Turkish trenches assaulted by the 156th Brigade — Lowland Division — as we did to the sector by the sea. But we could not, because, once we had given a fair quota to the left, there was not enough stuff in our lockers for the right. Such is war! No use splitting the difference and trying to win everywhere like high brows halting between Flanders and Gallipoli. But I *am* sick at heart, I must say, to think my brother Scots should have had to catch hold of the hot end of the poker. Also to think that, with another couple of hundred rounds, we should have got and held H. 12. H. 12 which dominates — so prisoners say — the wells whence the enemy draws water for the whole of his right wing.

To-day the old trouble is a-foot once again. Hunter-Weston tells us the Turkish counter-attacks are being pressed with utmost fury and are beginning to look ugly, as we can give our infantry no support from our guns although the enemy offer excellent artillery targets. When K. is extra accommodating it is doubly hard to be importunate, but it's got to be done::

General Sir Ian Hamilton to Earl Kitchener.

With reference to my telegrams No. M.F. 328 of 13th June and No. M.F. 381 of 28th June. Each successive fight shows more clearly than the last how much may hang on an ample supply of ammunition, more especially high explosive howitzer ammunition. In my telegram No. M.F. 381 I said that I hoped we might be able to achieve success with the ammunition already promised, and I adhere to that opinion; but every additional 100 rounds means some reduction of risks and greater assurance of success. I raise this question again because I gather from what I hear that matters in the other theatre of operations may possibly be at a standstill without much prospect of any vital alteration before the autumn fairly sets in. If this should be the case it is for you to consider whether a larger and more regular supply of ammunition should be sent to me in order to give this force the utmost chance of gaining an early success. Judging from the increased effect of the bombardments before the last two attacks on facilitating the Infantry advance I am led to hope that this success would not be long delayed under the cumulative effect of unremitting bombardment. If, therefore, any change in the general situation should make it possible to allow me temporary preferential claim to all the ammunition I should like, I would ask for the following amounts to be here by 1st August, in addition to those accompanying the troops and already promised, namely, 4.5-inch howitzer, 3,000 rounds; 5-inch howitzer,

7,000 rounds; 6-inch howitzer, 5,000, and 9.3-inch howitzer, 500 rounds, all high explosive. I should also ask for a monthly supply on the following scale, first consignment to arrive before 15th August:

18-pr.	300,000
4.5-inch howitzer	30,000
5-inch howitzer	30,000
6-inch howitzer	24,000
60-pr.	15,000
9.2-inch howitzer	6,000

The howitzer ammunition to be all high explosive, the 60-pr. to be one-third shrapnel and two-thirds high explosive, and the 18-pr. to be half of each.

The above monthly scale includes ammunition for the following additional ordnance which I should like to get, namely, two batteries of 4.5-inch howitzers for each of the Xth and XIth Divisions (since 5-inch howitzers are found to be too inaccurate to bombard the enemy trenches even in close proximity to our own), one battery of 6-inch howitzers and four 9.2-inch howitzers.

On the assumption already made it might be possible for you to arrange to forward to Ordnance Stores, Marseilles, the ammunition asked for to be here by 1st August. Time would thus be gained to accumulate the supply required, and I could arrange with the Vice-Admiral to send a fast steamer of 1,000 tons hold capacity to bring the consignment of high explosives from Marseilles. To get the steamer coaled, to arrive at Marseilles, coal again and be ready to receive the ammunition, would take seven days.

Please understand that this suggestion is only prompted for the following reasons: (1) My growing belief that ample artillery might, within a limited period, lead to quite a considerable success in this theatre, and (2) because the reports which reach me seem to indicate that an offensive is not likely to be undertaken elsewhere at present (and I have mainly asked for offensive ammunition).

The monthly supply above detailed I should not expect would be required for more than two months.

If our Government really — whole-heartedly — *will* that there should be a complete success in the East, they must, equally, with whole hearts and braced-up *will*, resist (for a while) the idea of any offensive in the West. In saying this I speak of the A.B.C. of war. The main theatre is where the amphibious power wishes to make it so. This cable of mine sent to a man like Lord K. is a very strong order. But now is the time to speak up and let him realize that he must let the fields of France lie fallow for the summer if he wishes to plough the Black Sea waves in autumn.

14th July, 1915. Imbros. Wrote letters in the morning, and in the evening went for a ride to the Salt Lake and there inspected the new aeroplane camp on the far side of the water.

Last night more counter-attacks, all driven off. The French right is now actually on the mouth of the Kereves Dere where it runs into the sea. We have made about 500 prisoners and have captured a machine gun. Hunter-Weston had to transfer the command of the 52nd Division, temporarily, to Shaw, the new Commander of the 13th Division.

Baikie is crying out to us for shells as if *we* were bottling them up! There are none.

15th July, 1915. Imbros. The answer has come in from the War Office: the answer, I mean, to mine of the day before yesterday in which it is suggested that *if* our rich brethren were off their feed for the moment, some crumbs of high explosive might be spared:

> We have great difficulty in sending you the amounts of ammunition mentioned in our No. 5770, cipher, and even now the proportion of 18-pr. high explosive will be less than stated therein. In response, however, to your No. M.F. 444, we are adding 1,000 rounds 4.5-inch, 500 — 5-inch, 500 — 6-inch and 75 — 9.2-inch. It will be quite impossible to continue to send you ammunition at this rate, as we have reduced the supply to France in order to send what we have to you, and the amounts asked for in the second part of your telegram could not be spared without stopping all operations in France. This, of course, is out of the question.

"This, of course, is out of the question." "Stopping all operations in France" is the very kernel of the question. If half the things we hear about the Bosche forces and our own are half true, we have no prospect of dealing any decisive blow in the West till next spring. And an indecisive blow is worse than no blow. But we can *hold on* there till all's blue. Now H.E. is offensive and shrapnel is defensive. I ought to attack at once; French mustn't. Therefore, we should be given, *now*, dollops of H.E.

This talk does not come through my hat. Some of the best brains on the Western field are in touch with those of some of my following here. The winning post stares us in the face; my old Chief gallops off the course; how can I resist calling out? And then I get this "of course" cable (not written by K. I feel sure) which shows, if it shows anything, that "of course" we ought never to have come here at all! Simple, is it not? In war all is simple — that's why it's so complex. Never mind; my cable has not been wasted. We reckon the 1,100 extra rounds it has produced may save us 100 British casualties.

Rode over to "K" Beach and inspected the 25th Casualty Clearing Station, Commandant Lieutenant-Colonel Mackenzie. Walked through the different hospital wards talking to some twenty officers and two hundred men; mostly medical cases. Did not think things at all up to the mark. Made special note of the lack of mosquito nets, beds, pyjamas and other comforts. For weeks past Jean has been toiling to get mosquito nets bought and made up, which was simple, and to get them out to us, which seems impossible. Too bad when so much money is being spent to see men lying on the ground in their thick cord breeches in this sweltering heat, a prey to flies and mosquitoes.

Discussing the landing of the New Divisions in Suvla Bay and the diversion to be made by Legge on the right by storming Lone Pine, Birdwood makes it clear in a letter just to hand, that he has told his two Divisional Generals everything. I had not yet gone into some of these details with Hunter-Weston, Stopford or Bailloud, all Corps Commanders, for I am afraid of the news filtering down to the juniors and from them, in the mysterious way news does pass, to the rank and file of both services. Thence to the Turks is but a step. Were the Turks to get wind of our plan, there would be nothing for it but to change the whole thing, even now, at the eleventh hour.

Lieutenant-Colonel F. G. Fuller, my late G.S.O. (1) in the Central Force, came over to lunch. He is now G.S.O. (2) of the 9th Corps.

At 5.30 p.m. rode over to "K" Beach for the second time and inspected the Indian Brigade under Brigadier-General Cox. They had to be pulled out some time ago and given a rest. On parade were the 5th, 6th and 10th Gurkha Battalions with the 14th Sikhs. Walked down both lines and chatted with the British and Indian Officers. The men looked cheerful and much recovered. In the evening Charlie Burn, King's Messenger, and Captain Glyn came to dinner. Glyn has been sent out as a sort of emissary, but whether by K. or by the Intelligence or by the Admiralty neither Braithwaite nor I are quite able to understand.

Cabled the War Office *insisting* that the lack of ammunition is "disturbing." Also, that "half my anxieties would vanish" if only the Master-General of Ordnance would see to it himself that the fortnightly allowance could be despatched regularly. I could hardly put it stronger.

Midnight. — Just back from G.S. tent with the latest. So far, so good. Bailloud and Hunter-Weston have carried two lines of Turkish trenches, an advance of two to four hundred yards. But the ammunition question has reached a crisis, and has become dangerous — very dangerous. On the whole Southern theatre of operations, counting shell in limbers and shell loaded in guns, we have 5,000 rounds of shrapnel. No high explosive — and fighting is still going on!

Hi jaculis illi certant defendere saxis.[*]

To whomsoever of my ancestors bequeathed me my power of detachment deep salaams! How many much better men than myself would not close their eyes to-night with a battle on the balance and 5,000 rounds wherewith to fight it? But I shall sleep — D.V.; I

---

[*] "These darts compete to defend the rocks."

can't create shell by taking thought any more than Gouraud could retake the *Haricot* by not drinking his coffee.

16th July, 1915. Imbros. Forcing myself to work though I feel unspeakably slack; wrangling with the War Office about doctors, nurses, orderlies and ships for our August battles. A few days ago I sent the following cable and they want to cut us down:

> It seems likely that during the first week of August we may have 80,000 rifles in the firing line striving for a decisive result, and therefore certain that we shall then need more medical assistance. Quite impossible to foresee casualties, but suppose, for example, we suffered a loss of 20,000 men; though the figure seems alarming when put down in cold blood, it is not an extravagant proportion when calculated on basis of Dardanelles fighting up to date. If this figure is translated into terms of requirements such a battle would involve conversion of, say, 30 transports into temporary hospital ships, and necessitate something like 200 extra medical officers, with Royal Army Medical Corps rank and file and nurses in proportion. If my prognosis is concurred in, these should reach Mudros on or about 1st August. Some would D.V., prove superfluous, and could be sent back at once, and in any case they could return as soon as possible after operations, say, 1st September. Medical and surgical equipment, drugs, mattresses in due proportion. In a separate message I will deal with the deficiencies in ordinary establishment, but I think it best to keep this cable as to specified and exceptional demands distinct.

17th July, 1915. Imbros. After lunch felt so sick of scribble, scribble, scribble whilst adventure sat seductive upon my doorstep that I fluttered forth. At 2 o'clock boarded H.M.S. *Savage*(Lieutenant-Commander Homer) and, with Aspinall and Freddie, steered for Gully Beach. We didn't cast anchor but got into a cockleshell of a small dinghy and rowed ashore under the cliffs, where we were met by de Lisle. Along the beach men were either bathing or basking mother-naked on the hot sand — enjoying themselves thoroughly. I walked on the edge of the sea, as far as the point which hides the gully's mouth from the Turkish gunners, and was specially struck by the physique and class of the 6th East

Lancashires under Colonel Cole Hamilton. Then mounted and rode to the Headquarters of General Shaw, commanding the 13th (new) Division. Shaw was feeling his wounds; he had already been once round his lines; so I would not let him come again. But Colonel Gillivan, G.S.O.1, Major Hillyard, G.S.O.2, Captain Jackson, G.S.O.3, Colonel Burton, A.A. and Q.M.G., joined us. First we went to the Headquarters of the 39th Brigade commanded by Brigadier-General Cayley (the Brigade Major is Captain Simpson). Then I went and looked at the trenches J.11-12-13, where I met Colonel Palmer of the 9th Warwicks, Colonel Jordan, D.S.O., of the 7th Gloucesters, Colonel Nunn of the 9th Worcesters, Colonel Andrews of the 7th North Staffordshires. We tramped through miles of trenches. The men were very fit and cheery. It was the day when they were relieving one another by companies from the reserve and there was a big crowd in the Ravine. De Lisle told me that one week had made the most astonishing difference to the savvy of these first arrivals of the New Army. At first there was confusion, loss of energy and time; by the end of the week they had picked up the wrinkles of the veterans. There was a good lot of shelling from the Turks but, humanly speaking, we were all quite snug and safe in the big gully or moving down the deep communication trenches. No one, not even the new 13th Division, paid the smallest deference to the projectiles.

Now began one of these semi-comic, semi-serious adventures which seem to dog my footsteps. Just as I got into the little dinghy, two bluejackets pulling and a Petty Officer steering, the Turks began to shell H.M.S. *Savage* as she lay about a hundred yards out. She did not like it, and, instead of waiting to let us get aboard, Commander Homer thought it wiser to sheer off about half a mile. When she quitted the Turks turned their guns on to our cockleshell, and although none of the shot came near us they still came quite near enough to interest the whole gallery of some thousands of bathing Tommies who, themselves safe in the dead ground under the cliff, were hugely amused to see their C.-in-C. having a hot time of it. After ten minutes hard rowing we got close to the destroyer and she, making a big circle at fairly high speed, came along fast as if she was going to run us down, with the idea of baffling the aim of the enemy. Not a bad notion as far as the destroyer was concerned but one demanding acrobatic qualities of a very high order on the part of the Commander-in-Chief. Anyway just as she was drawing abreast and I was standing up to make my spring a shell hit her plump and burst in one of her coal bunkers, sending up a big cloud of mixed smoke and black coal dust. The Commander was beside himself. He waved us off furiously; cracked on full steam and again left us in the lurch. We laughed till the tears ran down our cheeks. Soon, we had reason to be more serious, not to say pensive. The *Savage* showed a pair of clean heels this time and ran right away to Helles. So there we were, marooned, half a mile out to sea, in a tiny dinghy on which the Turks again switched their blarsted guns. The two bluejackets pulled themselves purple. They were both of them fat reservists and the mingling of anxiety and exertion, emotion and motion, made the sweat pour in torrents down their cheeks. Each time a shell plunked into the water we brightened up; then, gradually, until the next one splashed, our faces grew longer and longer. At last we got so far away that the Turks gave us up in disgust. How much I should like to see that battery commander's diary. Altogether, by the time we had boarded the *Savage*, we had been in that cursed little dinghy for just exactly one hour, of which I should think we were being gently shelled for three quarters of an hour. On board the destroyer no harm to speak of: only one man wounded.

Cast anchor at Imbros at 9 p.m. General Legge and Captain H. Lloyd came over to stay the night. Mail from England.

Have cabled again to stir them up about the hospital ships.

18th July, 1915. Church Parade. Inspected troops. Wrote in camp all the afternoon. Walked out to the lighthouse in the evening and watched the shells bursting over Gully Beach where we were yesterday. How often have I felt anxious seeing these shrapnel through the telescope. On the spot, as I know from yesterday's experience, their bark is worse than their bite. Colonel Ward of the Intelligence came to dinner and Captain Doughtie, commanding H.M.S. *Abercrombie*, paid me a visit.

19th July, 1915. Too much office work. Mr. Schuler, an Australian journalist and war correspondent, turned up. Seems a highly intelligent young fellow. He had met me on tour in Australia. Gave him leave to go anywhere and see everything. The Staff shake their heads, but the future is locked away in our heads, and the more the past is known the better for us.

Braithwaite has heard from the War Office that the Brigade of Russians which had started from Vladivostock to join us here has been counter-ordered. The War Office seem rather pleased than otherwise that this reinforcement has fallen through. Why, I can't imagine. As they are sending us a big fresh force of Britishers, they probably persuade themselves that 5,000 Russians would be more trouble than they are worth, but they forget the many thousands of shortage in my present formations. Since they fixed up to send me the new Divisions I must have lost ten thousand rifles, but as all my old Divisions remain at the Dardanelles *in name*, they are being regarded at home, we strongly suspect, as a sort of widow's cruse, kept full by miracles instead of men and still, therefore — Divisions!

In the evening the Vice-Admiral came over and we rode together down to the Naval Seaplane Camp. The King's Messenger left at 5 p.m.

20th July, 1915. Imbros. Wrote double quick, then galloped over to Kephalos to see the New Army, *sub rosa*. The men we struck were A.1. They belong to the 32nd and 34th Brigades of the 11th Division. The 33rd has gone to Helles to get salted.

Hunter-Weston is still staying with the Admiral. He has had a hard time and a heavy responsibility and is quite worn out. I devoutly trust he may be on his legs again ere long. Have put in Stopford to act for him at Helles. This should teach the young idea how to shoot. With every aspect of the command and administration of the Southern theatre of operations thus under his immediate orders he has a rare chance of learning how to do it and how not to do it.

F. A. *Swaine phot.*
LIEUT.-GEN. SIR A. HUNTER-WESTON, K.C.B., D.S.O.

21st July, 1915. — Just signed a letter to the Chief of the Imperial General Staff and as it gives the run of my thoughts at the moment I spatchcock the opening and final paras:

> My dear Wolfe Murray,
>
> How do you manage to find time to write these charming letters of yours with your own hand? They come like a gift from some oriental potentate and carry with them the same moral obligations; i.e., that they ought to be returned in kind. But to-day the time limit interposes, and I know you will pardon me for once if I dictate.
>
> I am immensely interested in what you say with reference to the 29th Division being below strength, namely, that we are getting short of men. Well, — though one of the keenest voluntary service people existing, I have always envisaged the fact that during a war we might be driven to compulsion. Also in writing out fully my views on this subject (views which I was not permitted by late Chiefs of the General Staff to publish) I have always, for that reason, pressed for National Registration. It does no one any harm, and rubs into the mind of the young man that, under certain conditions, the State has first pull on his pocket, labour, life and everything else. But, of course, if your own wish that the 29th Division should take out 10 per cent. extra for drafts (like the regiments do in France), had been carried into effect, they would never have fallen as low as they actually did.
>
> Freddy Stopford and Reed have been staying with me for 24 hours, and the former is now in command of the 8th Corps on the Peninsula, Hunter-Weston having gone sick. He asked to stay with the Admiral for a couple of days' rest, and the very moment he got safe on board ship the overstrain of the past month told on him and he went down with a sharp go of fever. I earnestly pray he will get right again quickly for there are not many Commanders of his calibre. Freddy Stopford will now have a good chance of getting the hang of this sort of fighting generally, surrounded as he will be by Hunter-Weston's experienced Staff. After sending my last letter I rather repented of one or two harsh things I said about Reed. There is some truth in them, but I need not have said them. I hope he will do very well out here.

Now since that letter was written (yesterday) in comes a cable from K. saying Winston can't leave England but that Hankey starts in his place.

K. says he is sure I will give him every facility.

K.'s Advice and the P.M.'s Envoy

A pretty stuffy cable in from the War Office on the Hospital ships and medical personnel and material wrangle which is still going on. I, personally, have checked every item of my estimate with closest personal attention, although it took me hours in the midst of other very pressing duties. This is not Braithwaite's pidgin but Woodward's and there was no help for it. Our first landing found out a number of chinks in our arrangements, and now, my Director of Medical Services is (quite naturally) inclined to open his mouth as wide as if ships were drugs in the market. So I have tried very hard, without too much help, to hit the mean between extravagance and sufficiency. Now the War Office, who would be the first to round on me if anything went wrong with my wounded, query my demands as if we had just splashed off a cable asking for the first things that came into our heads!

I am all for thrift in ships, but thrift in the lives of my wounded comes first; my conscience is clear and I have answered sticking to my point, — firmly! They say the thing is impossible; I have retaliated by saying it is imperative.

Chapter XIV – The Force — Real and Imaginary

22nd July, 1915. Imbros. Had a jolly outing to-day. Left for Cape Helles by trawler just before 10 o'clock. Aspinall, Bertier and young Brodrick came with me. Lunched at 8th Army Corps Headquarters with Stopford and handed him a first outline scheme of the impending operations. We read it through together and he seems to take all the points and to be in general agreement. Left Aspinall behind to explain any questions of detail which might not seem clear, whilst I went a tour of inspection through the Eski Lines of trenches held by the 6th and 7th Manchesters of the 42nd Division. These Eski Lines were first held about the 7th or 8th May and have since been worked up, mainly by the energy of de Lisle, into fortifications, humanly speaking, impregnable. General Douglas, Commander of the Division, came round with me. He reminds me greatly of his brother, the late Chief of the Imperial General Staff; excellent at detail; a conscientious, very hard worker. When I had seen my Manchester friends I passed on into the Royal Naval Division Lines. There General Paris convoyed me through his section as far as Zimmerman's Farm, where I was joined by Bailloud with his Chief of Staff and Chief of Operations.

Together we made our way round the whole of the French trenches winding up at de Tott's Battery.

After this whopping walk, we left by pinnace from below de Tott's wondering whether the Asiatic Batteries would think us game worth their powder and shot. They did not and so we safely boarded our trawler at Cape Helles. Didn't get back to Imbros Harbour till 9 p.m. Being so late, boarded the ever hospitable *Triad* on chance and struck, as usual — hospitality. Hunter-Weston is really quite ill with fever. He did not want to see anyone. As we were sitting at dinner I saw him through the half open door staggering along on his way to get into a launch to go aboard a Hospital ship. He is suffering very much from his head. The doctors prophesy that he will pull round in about a week. I hope so indeed, but I have my doubts. Aspinall reports that Stopford is entirely in accord with our project and keen.

23rd July, 1915. Imbros. Spent day in camp trying to straighten things out: (1) the personal, (2) the strategical and (3) the administrative arrangements.

- (1) Hunter-Weston has to go home and I have begged for Bruce Hamilton in his place, and have told them I would have a great champion in him. He and Smith-Dorrien were my best Brigadiers in South Africa. They stood on my right hand and on my left all the way between Bloemfontein and Pretoria, and I never quite made up my mind as to which was the better. Bruce is a fighting man with an iron frame, and, in Gallipoli, his chief crab, his deafness, will be rather a gain to him.
- (2) Bailloud, with his own War Minister in the background, is doing all he knows to get 20,000 of my new troops allotted to a side show, not for strategy's sake, but for the tactical relief of his troops from the shelling. I quite sympathize with his reason as, after all, he is responsible for his own troops and not for the larger issue. But, to take one objection only, the Navy could not land a force at Besika Bay and at the same time carry out landings at Suvla and

Anzac. Again, since Bailloud urged these views, the guns fixed up at de Tott's Battery have already begun to gain mastery over the fire from the site of Troy. When we have one of the new 14-inch gunned monitors moored off Rabbit Island we shall get cross fire observations and give the Turkish Asiatic guns the clean knock out. Amphibious operations are ticklish things: allied operations are ticklish things: but the two together are like skating on thin ice arm in arm with two friends who each want to cut a figure of his own.

(3) Slovenly bills of lading. Bertie Lawrence, who was sent to Mudros in June when things were growing desperate, was here yesterday and has made a report on the present business situation which, though less chaotic, is still serious. There are not launches enough to enable people to get about. There are not lighters enough to work the daily transhipment of 300 tons. But the worst trouble lies in the bills of lading. Sometimes they arrive a week after their ships. Usually cargo shipped at Malta or Alexandria is omitted. Half the time we can't lay hands on vital plant, tackle, supplies, munitions, because we have no means of knowing what is, or is not, on board some ship in the harbour. The trouble is of old date but has reached its climax owing to our shortage of rounds for our 18-pounders.

We were notified a new fuse key would be required for the new shells on the 12th June. The shells arrived but the keys were not despatched till the 15th July! The vouchers are all wrong, and there, in idleness, lies the stuff that spells success. A soldier is not a conjurer that he should be handed over a fully laden ship and told to ferret out a fuse key.

24th July, 1915. Last night the Turkish Commander drove his troops into their tenth attack upon our extreme left where they were beaten off as usual with a loss of several hundreds — this time we only suffered about a dozen casualties. Together with Braithwaite,

I rode over to "K" Beach at 11 a.m. to inspect part of the 11th Division there encamped. General Hammersley, Divisional Commander, met me. Also Colonel Malcolm, his General Staff Officer and Major Duncan. The first Brigade I looked at was Sitwell's — the 34th. A fine looking lot of men:

8th Northumberland Fusiliers,
5th Dorsets,
9th Lancashire Fusiliers,
1 Coy. 11th Manchester Fusilers.

Next I passed on to Haggard's Brigade — the 32nd. On parade were:

9th West Yorkshires,
6th Yorkshires,
8th West Riding Regiment,
6th York and Lancashires.

Lastly I inspected the 67th and 68th Companies R.E. of the 134th Fortress Company, as well as the Field Ambulance. Officers and men looked splendid. I was glad indeed to be able to congratulate Hammersley on his command. The doctors tell me, that, short as has been their stay, a large number of the men are already infected by the prevalent disease. Well, they don't look like that, — and it won't kill them that's certain, for I have had it on me strong for the best part of two months. But it knocks out the starch from its victims, and if fair play existed in moonlit lands, every white man here should be credited with 25 per cent. extra kudos for everything that he does with his brains or his body under the shadow of this pestilence.

Have got a reply from the War Office (Q.M.G.2) making light of my shipping troubles and saying the War Office has always cabled full advices. What can I say to that? As the lamb thought to himself when the wolf began to growl.

25th July, 1915. Spent most of the day in camp. Church Parade at 9 a.m. Charles Lister came over from "K" Beach to lunch. He is a fascinating creature and has made a name for himself with the Naval Division, where standards are high, as being the keenest of the keen and the bravest of the brave. Hammersley, Malcolm and Aitkin called in the evening, but I had gone for a stroll and missed them.

The great Turkish attack timed by all our spies for the 23rd has never come off but, as showing the fine spirit which animates the Anzacs, it is worth noting that on that day not one soul reported sick. They would not go near the doctors for fear they might be made to miss a battle.

Last night the French took a small trench, and though the Turks had a dash at it in the morning, they were easily beaten off. Twice out of three times we gain something when we fight and the third time we lose no ground.

Given, therefore, the factors of the problem, men, munitions and the distance to be covered (two to three miles), the result pans out like a proposition by Euclid. No question of breaking through is involved as in any other theatre, but merely a question of pushing back a very clearly limited number of yards. The men have in their hearts a reservoir of patience which will never run dry so long as they are sure of the Will to Win at their backs. They need have no qualms about G.H.Q. here, but politicians are more — shall we say, mercurial? And the experts from France are throwing cold water on our cause by day and night. Therefore, as the Fleet is not going to have a dash, it is just as well we are about to try the one great effort and get it done quickly. We will gain a lot of ground; so much is certain, and it's as sure as anything can be in war that somewhere we shall make good a key to the position.

26th July, 1915. Stifling. Am sticking out about the lack of proper advices of shipments. Ammunition *makes* itself scarce enough without being *made* scarce. Rare and curious articles are worth careful booking; that's the text of my cable.

27th July, 1915. Imbros. Hard at it. Altham came in to see me and spent an hour and a half. A man of business! Mahon arrived at mid-day. Very cheery but he feels that he is the only Lieutenant-General executively employed with troops who has so small a command as a Division. He says that either he should be given a Corps, or that his Lieutenant-General's rank should be reverted to that of Major-General. I quite agreed. I feel as strongly as he does that, as a Lieutenant-General, he is clean out of his setting in a Major-General's appointment and has blocked the way to a go-ahead young Corps Commander, because that Corps Commander must, by K.'s decision, be his senior. Still, there didn't seem to be anything to be done, so after my telling him how things stood here, and hearing with great pleasure the fine account he gave me of his Irish Division, we adjourned to lunch. Colonel King, his G.S.O. (1), also lunched and seemed to be a very nice fellow. After lunch they both went off to the G.S. to be posted.

Admiral Wemyss came over from Mudros and saw me. He is senior to de Robeck but has waived that accident of rank seeing we are at war. An interesting man and a Keyesite; i.e., he'd go right through the Straits to-morrow, — or go under. He is one of those men, none too common in the Services, whose mind has gained breadth in the great world without losing its keenness. These rival tenets are straining the fabric of the Fleet, but, as I constantly tell our General Staff, my course is as clear to me as a pikestaff. I back the policy of the *de facto* Naval Commander-in-Chief — my own coadjutor. There is a temptation to do wrong, but I resist it. What would it not be to me were the whole Fleet to attack as we land at Suvla! But obviously I cannot go out of my own element to urge the Fleet to actions, the perils of which I am professionally incompetent to gauge.

At 5.30 p.m. I went off riding with de Robeck, Ormsby Johnson and Freddie Maitland. We cantered over to Seaplane Camp; passed the time of day to the men there and over-hauled some of the machines. Coming back, we passed through part of the 11th Division Camp; all very ship-shape and clean. Freddie Maitland and I dined on board the *Beryl* with Sir Douglas Gamble. He seems highly pleased with everyone and everything; I wouldn't go quite so far! There we met de Robeck, Keyes, Altham, Ellison and Captain Stephens. Got back at 11.

28th July, 1915. A cable from K. about Hunter-Weston's breakdown, telling me the Prime Minister thinks that Bruce Hamilton is too old for active work and heavy strain. Instead I am to have Davies. I know Joey Davies — everyone does. But I also know Bruce Hamilton. There is no tougher man or more resolute fighter in the Army. In my letter to K. I said, "The only man I can think of who would really inspire me with full confidence in these emergencies, excursions and alarms, would be Bruce Hamilton. Bruce Hamilton is a real fighting man, and his deafness here would be a great asset as he would be able to sleep through the shell and rifle fire at night."

The older Officers will be sorry indeed to hear Bruce Hamilton is barred. Shaw, the new Commander of the 13th Division, will be especially disappointed.

Admiral Gamble came off to see me and afterwards dined. I was very careful as I don't want to be quoted about the Sister Service. Gamble sings praise of our outfit, but I can't help wondering how, when and where he has got it into his head that we have small craft in abundance!

29th July, 1915. Imbros. Stuck to camp, and lucky I did so, for the cipher of a queer cable from S. of S. for War came in and called for as much thought as is compatible with prompt handling. The message begins with a ripe sugar plum:

"At this stage of the operations which you have conducted with so much ability and in which your troops have so greatly distinguished themselves, we" (this "we" is a new expression; the S. of S. always says "I") "consider it advisable to summarize what we are placing at your disposal for the effort which we hope will bring your operations to a successful termination.

"We have sent you out" and then the cable launches out into an inventory of the forces entrusted to me which, though very detailed, is yet largely based on what we call the widow's cruse principle. As to the demnition total, "we" tells "me," categorically, (as the Lawyers say when they describe the whiteness of soot) that I have "a total of about 205,000 men for the forthcoming operations." The A.G. who brought me the cable could make nothing of it. Braithwaite then came over and he could make nothing of it. We can none of us see the point of pretending to *us* that my force has been kept up to the strength all the time, or of adding bayonets to the French or of assuming to *us* that *we* possess troops which Maxwell has told me time and again he requires for Egyptian defence. Were these figures going to the enemy Chief they might intimidate him — coming here they alarm me. There is a "We" at the other end of the cable which knows so little that it tells me, who know every gun, rifle and round of ammunition I have at my disposal, that I have double that number to handle. We won't defeat the enemy by paper strengths. As far as sentiments go, the cable is by chalks the heartiest handshake we poor relations to the West have had since we started. From the outset we've been kicked by phrases such as, if you don't hurry up we will have to "reconsider the position," etc., etc. Now, the "Wees" wind up with a really wonderful paragraph::

> We should like to hear from you after considering your plans whether there is anything further in the way of personnel, guns or ammunition we can send you, as we are most anxious to give you everything you can possibly require and use. You will realize that as regards ammunition we have had to stop supplying France to give you the full output, which will be continued as long as possible; in the short time available before the bad weather intervenes the Dardanelles operations are now of the highest importance.

The position seems now, to me, extraordinarily delicate. Are we to let the mistakes in this flattering cable slide, and build upon its promises, or, are we to pull whoever believes these figures out of their fool's paradise? Well, I feel we must have it out and although deeply grateful for the nice words and for the splendid effort actually being made, we *cannot* let it be assumed by *anyone* that our vanishing Naval and Territorial Divisions are complete and up to strength. As to ammunition, I asked plainly over a fortnight ago, for what I thought was necessary to rapid success. I was told in so many words that France would not spare it; though it would have been a small affair to them. Now; as if these cables had no existence, they ask if there is "anything in the way of *personnel, guns or ammunition you can possibly require and use.*" The truth is, I don't like this cable; in spite of its flowery opening I don't like it at all. As to personnel, I ask for young and energetic commanders, Byng and Rawlinson, and am turned down. Next I ask for an old and experienced Commander, Bruce Hamilton, and am turned down. Next I say that Reed, who would be a good staff officer to some Generals, is not well suited to Stopford; I am turned down. I try to get a business man to run Mudros and have been turned down till just the other day. In all these points the War Office are supreme and are acting well within their rights. But they show some want of consistency in talking to me all of a sudden, as if it was a matter of course I should be met half way in my wishes.

So there and then we roughed out this reply:

> Your Nos. 6583 and 6588. Your appreciation of our efforts will afford intense gratification and encouragement to everyone.
>
> In regard to what we should like if it is available in the shape of guns and ammunition, please see my No. M.F. 444, of 13th July, which still holds good. As to the final paragraph of your No. 6583, I did not realize that you were stopping supplies to France in order to give us full output, since a fortnight ago your No. 6234 stated that it was then impossible for you to send the ammunition I asked for, and that it would be impossible to continue supplies even on a much lower scale, since it would involve the reduction of supplies to France. Naturally, I have always realized that you, and not I, must judge of the comparative importance of the demands from the Dardanelles and from France.
>
> With regard to numbers, the grand total you mention does not take into account non-effectives or casualties; it includes reinforcements such as LIVth and part of the LIIIrd Divisions, etc., which cannot be here in time for my operation, and it also includes Yeomanry and Indian troops which, until this morning, I was unaware were at my unreserved disposal. For the coming operation, the number of rifles available is about half the figure you quote, viz., 120,000. I am only anxious, in emphasizing this point, to place the statement regarding my strength on the correct basis, and one which gives a true view of the position.

The Force — Real and Imaginary 317

What I want in a hurry is as much additional high explosive shell as you can send me up to amounts asked for in my No. M.F. 444, and as many of the 4.5-inch and 6-inch howitzers asked for in that telegram as there is ammunition for. I am despatching a ship immediately, and its time of arrival at Marseilles will be telegraphed later.

With regard to sending the IInd Mounted Division unmounted, I am at once telegraphing Maxwell to obtain his views.

The Mail bag went out this morning.

Hankey is now busy going over the Peninsula. I have not seen much of him. A G.S. Officer has been told off to help him along and to see that he does not get into trouble. I am not going to dry nurse him. He showed me of his own free will a copy of a personal cable he had sent to Lord Kitchener in which he says, speaking of his first visit to Anzac, "Australians are superbly confident and spoiling for a fight." This is exactly true and I feel it is good that one who has the ear of the insiders should say it. I wrote Wolfe Murray a week ago that he was a successor to those Commissioners who were sent out by the French Republic in its early days. Actually, I am very glad to have him. Lies are on the wing, and he, armed with the truth, will be able to knock some of them out hereafter when he meets them in high places.

I have been bothered as to how to answer a letter from a statesman for whom I cherish great respect, who has always been very kind to me and whom I like very much. He writes:

> It may interest you to know the Cabinet has entrusted the superintendence of the Dardanelles business to a comparatively small and really strong committee drawn equally from the two parties. We most thoroughly understand the extreme difficulty of your task and the special conditions of the problem in front of you and the Admiral. All we ask from you is complete confidence and the exact truth. We are not babes and we can digest strong meat. Do not think that we ever want anything unpleasant concealed from us, nor do we want you ever to swerve one hair's breadth from your own exact judgment in putting the case before us, certainly never on the pleasant side; if you ever swerve pray do so on the unpleasant side.... If you want more ammunition say so....

"Could you eat a bun, my boy?" said the old gentleman to the little boy looking in at the shop window. "Could I eat ten thousand b ... buns and the baker who baked them?" So the dear little fellow answered. If I want more ammunition indeed? If ...? I fear the "comparatively small and really strong committee." They fairly frighten me. There they sit, all wishing us well, all evidently completely bamboozled. "If you want more ammunition, say so!" Anyway, my friend means me well but my path is perfectly clear; I have only one Chief — K. — and I correspond with no one but him, or his Staff, whether on the subject of ammunition or anything else....

As to the letter, I know it is entirely kind, genuine and inspired by the one idea of helping me. But I've got to say no thank you in some unmistakable manner. So I have replied:

> I am grateful for your reassuring remarks about your Committee having confidence in my humble self. For my part I have confidence in the *moral* of my troops and in the devotion of the Navy which are the two great and splendid assets amidst this shifting kaleidoscope of the factors and possibilities of war.
>
> I am not quite sure that I clearly understand your meaning about cabling home the exact truth. Is there any occasion on which I have failed to do so? I should be very sorry indeed to think I had consciously or unconsciously misled anyone by my cables. There is always, of course, the broad spirit of a cable which depends on the temperament of the sender. It is either tinged with hope or it has been dictated by one who fears the worst. If you mean that you would prefer a pessimistic tone given to my appreciations, then I am afraid you will have to get another General.

30th July, 1915. Gascoigne of "Q" branch lunched. On getting news of the decisive victory on the Euphrates I caused a *feu de joie* to be fired precisely at 5 p.m. by all the troops on the Peninsula. At the appointed hour I walked up the cliff's edge whence I clearly heard the roll of fire. The question of whether musketry sounds will carry so far is settled. Evidently the Turks have taken up the challenge for it was quite a long time before the distant rumbling died away. In the cool of the evening took a walk. Commandant

Bertier and la Borde dined.

Stopford, now commanding at Helles, has endorsed a report from the Commander of the 42nd East Lancs Division saying that out of a draft of 45 recruits just come from home three have been cast as totally unfit and nine as permanently unfit through blindness. Stopford says that he can't understand this, as the second line Battalion, from which these poor fellows were selected, contained good soldiers and tall fellows quite lately when they were under his command in England. Have cabled the facts home; also the following, showing the result of the Admiralty's attitude towards their own Naval Division now Winston has departed:

> (No. M.F. 505). From General Sir Ian Hamilton to War Office. The effective strength of the Marine Brigade is now reduced to 50 officers and 1,890 rank and file. In addition, only five battalions, Royal Naval Volunteer Reserve Battalions, are now remaining in the Division, as the Anson Battalion has been withdrawn for special work in connection with the forthcoming operations. Moreover, 300 men, stokers, from this division have been handed over to the Navy for work in auxiliary vessels, see my telegram No. M.F.A. 1377, of 11th July. I have consequently decided to reduce the division to eight battalions and to reorganize it into two brigades as a temporary measure. Can you give me any idea when the reinforcements for this division are likely to be despatched and when they may be expected here? I should like to see the division again at its strength of 12 battalions, and do not want to lose it, as it contains a very valuable war-trained nucleus, but unless it is brought under army administration, it does not appear likely that it can be maintained.

31st July, 1915. Imbros. Quiet day spent in trying to clear my table before sailing for Mitylene to see the new Irish Division. The grand army with which some War Office genius credited us appear to have served their purpose. At our challenge they have now taken to their heels like Falstaff's eleven rogues in buckram suits. The S. of S. (cabling this time as "I" and not as "We,") says, "it is not worth while trying to reconcile numbers by cable and it is difficult to make up accurate states."

Do not let me forget, though, that a slice of solid stuff is sandwiched into this cable — we are to get some 4.5 shell *via* Marseilles; H.E. we hope: also, two batteries of 4.5 howitzers: also that the A.G. has been trying hard to feed the 29th Division. The Territorials are the people who are being allowed to go to pot — not a word of hope even, and before the eyes of everyone.

1st August, 1915. Imbros. The usual rush before leaving. No time to write. Sent two cables, copies attached. The first to the War Office, in answer to one from the A.G. wherein he plumes himself upon the completeness of the 29th Division. That completeness, alas, is only so relatively; i.e., in comparison with the sinking condition of the Territorial Divisions:

> We are deeply grateful to you for the drafts you have despatched for the XXIXth Division as the fighting existence of that fine formation has been prolonged by their timely arrival, but I fear that you are very wide of the mark in your assumption that these drafts have completed the Division.
>
> As I have ventured to point out incessantly since my arrival here, constant large numbers of casualties must occur between the demands for and the arrival of drafts owing to the length of the sea voyage. It was for this very plain reason that it was doubly necessary to have here the 10 per cent. margin granted in the case of battalions going to France. We must always be considerably under establishment in the absence of some such margin.
>
> I fully realize, in saying this, that it may be quite impossible to meet such demands as I suggest, but I feel bound to let you know the only possible terms on which any unit in this force can ever be up to establishment.
>
> At the present moment, excluding 1,700 drafts coming on *Simla* and *Themistocles*, the actual infantry strength of the XXIXth Division is 219 officers and 8,424 other ranks.

The second cable is to K. The War Office Army has melted into thin air and it only remains to express my heartfelt thanks for the real Army:

With reference to your No. 6645. Very many thanks. You have done everything for us that man can do. The ship will probably not reach me in time but since I know that the ammunition is actually *en route* for me, and that it will (D.V.) arrive, I need not husband what we have, but can fire freely if I see great results thus obtainable. The Turk, at any rate, where he knows that he is fighting for Constantinople, is a stubborn fighter, and the difficulty is not so much in the taking of positions as in the maintaining of them.

Hence the extra ammunition you are sending me will come in the nick of time. The ship will arrive at Marseilles 7 p.m. 4th August, as I telegraphed to the Quartermaster-General yesterday. Many thanks for the two batteries of 4.5-inch howitzers, they are worth their weight in gold to us.

At 5 p.m. embarked on H.M.S. *Chatham* (Captain Drury Lowe) with George Lloyd of the General Staff and young Brodrick. At 6 p.m. sailed for Mitylene.

2nd August, 1915. H.M.S. "Chatham," Mitylene. We opened Mitylene Harbour at 5.30 a.m. So narrow was the entrance, and so hidden, that at first it looked as if the *Chatham* was charging the cliffs; next as if her long guns must entangle themselves in the flowering bushes on either side of the channel; then, as we sailed out over a bay like a big turquoise, I felt as though we were at peace with all men, making a pilgrimage to the home of Sappho, and that we had left far behind us these giant wars. But only for a moment!

After early breakfast, where I met Captain Grant of H.M.S. *Canopus*, left in a steam pinnace to inspect the 30th Brigade under Brigadier-General Hill.

Inspected:

H.M.T. *Alaudia*, 9.30 a.m.
    6th Royal Dublin Fusiliers,
    7th Royal Dublin Fusiliers,
        Col G. Downing, 7th R.D.F., in command.

H.M.T. *Andania*, 10.30 a.m.
  6th R. Inniskilling Fusiliers,
  5th Royal Irish Fusiliers,
    Lt.-Col. M. Pike, 5th R.I.F., in command.

H.M.T. *Canada*, 11.30 a.m.
  6th Royal Irish Fusiliers,
    Lt.-Col. F. A. Greer in command.

H.M.T. *Novian*, 12 p.m.
  5th Royal Inniskilling Fusiliers,
    Lt.-Col. H. Vanrennan in command.

The Royal Irish Fusiliers and Royal Inniskilling Fusiliers had not got back on board ship by the time I was ready for them, so I hurried off by motor launch to a landing in another part of the Bay and, walking through a village, caught them resting by their piled arms after a route march. All of these men looked very well and cheery. The villagers were most friendly and had turned out in numbers, bringing presents of flowers and fruit. Not more than 60 per cent. of the men are Irish, the rest being either North of England miners or from Somerset.

In the evening, crossed the glassy bay and motored to pay a double-barrelled visit to the Military and Civil Governors. Topping the watershed, yet another pleasure shock. Through the sea haze Mitylene shines out like an iridescent bubble of light. Never had I seen anything so vivid in its colour and setting as this very ancient, very small, very brilliant city of Mitylene. Rio de Janeiro, Sydney, the Golden Horn are sprawling daubs to flawless Mitylene.

Hesketh Smith and Compton Mackenzie were with us. The Governors very polite. The soldier man is a Cretan and seemed a good sort. We took tea at the Hotel and then made our way back to the *Chatham*. Found messages from G.H.Q. to say all's well and stuff being smuggled in without hitch at Anzac. At 7 p.m. we sailed for Imbros; a breeze from the West whipping up little waves into cover for enemy periscopes. So the moment we left the harbour we took on a corkscrew course, dodging and twisting like snipe in an Irish bog, to avoid winding up our trip in the dark belly of a

German submarine. Soon emerged from the sea a huge piled up white cloud, white and clear cut at first as the breast of a swan upon a blue lake, slowly turning to deep rose colour flecked here and there with gold. As it swallowed up the last lingering colours of the sunset, the world grew grey, then black, and we were, humanly speaking, safe.

3rd August, 1915. Imbros. Anchored at Imbros roadstead 5.30 a.m. Braithwaite not up yet so Altham got first innings about transport and supply.

Next the G.S. All our preliminaries are working on quite smoothly towards the climax and, so far, it seems likely the Turks have no notion of the scheme.

Girodon steamed over from Helles to see me and went back again in the evening. He is the mirror of French chivalry, modesty and good form, besides being an extraordinary fine soldier.

The 33rd Brigade, sent by me to gain wisdom at Helles, have now been brought here so that the whole 11th Division can start off together.

Just as the peculiar foggy air of Lancashire is essential to the weaving of the finer sorts of tissues, so an atmosphere of misunderstandings would really seem to suit the War Office.

In the cable telling me I would have 205,000 troops for my push, the S. of S. had informed me categorically that the 8,500 Yeomanry and mounted troops in Egypt, as well as 11,500 Indian troops and the Artillery stationed there *were mine*.

As the present garrison of Egypt numbers over 70,000 and as the old peace garrison of Egypt was 5,000 and as, further, there is no question of serious attack on Egypt from outside, it seemed to us there might be men in this part of the message. Leaving the Indian troops out of the account, for the moment, I therefore wired to Maxwell and asked him if he thought he would be able to organize a *portion* of the 8,500 mounted men, in order that, at a pinch, they might be able to come and reinforce us here. So the matter stood when I got another cable from the S. of S. telling me 5,000 drafts are "*en route* or under orders" to join the 29th Division and that the War Office are "unable to carry out your views about additional marginal drafts." S. of S. then goes on:

> Maxwell wires that you are taking 300 officers and 5,000 men of his mounted troops. I do not quite understand why you require Egyptian Garrison troops while you have the LIIIrd Division at Alexandria, and the LIVth, the last six battalions of which are arriving in five or six days, on the *Aquitania*.
>
> When I placed the Egyptian Garrison at your disposal to reinforce at the Dardanelles in case of necessity, Maxwell pointed out that Egypt would be left very short, and I replied that you would only require them in case of emergency for a short time, and that the risk must be run. I did not contemplate, however, that you would take troops from the Egyptian Garrison until those sent specially for you were exhausted. How long will you require Maxwell's troops, and where do you intend to sendthem? They should only be removed from Egypt for actual operations and for the shortest possible time.

We may read this cable wrong but it seems to us to embody a topsy-turvy tactic! To wait till one part of your forces are killed off (for that is the plain English of "exhausted") before you bring up the other part of your forces.

It is not easy to know what to do. The very best we can do, it sometimes seems to me, is to keep quiet rather than add one iota to the anxieties of people staggering under a load of responsibilities and cares. In the good old days the Gordons fought in two decisive battles in two Continents within a few months and no one worried the War Office about drafts! The 92nd carried on — had to carry on; they fell to quarter strength — still they were the Gordons and they carried on, just as if they counted a thousand rifles in their ranks. Now, I am quite prepared to do that to-day — *if that is the policy*. If that *were* the policy; not one grouse or grumble should ever cross my lips. But that is *not* the policy. Press and People believe a Division is a unit made up in scientific proportions of different branches and numbering a certain number of rifles. They are told so; the War Office keep telling them so; they believe it, and, in fact, it is an absolute necessity of this modern trench war that it should be so. Although the Gordons got no *drafts* between the battle of Kandahar and the battle of Majuba Hill, they got six months' *rest*; which was even better. In those days, apart from sieges, a battle was an event, here it is the rest or respite that is an event. Even British soldiers can't stick day and night fighting for ever. The attack spirit begins to ebb *unless* it is fed with fresh blood. Whether K.'s mind, big with broad views, grasps this new factor with which he has never himself come into personal contact, God knows. But for his sake, every bit as much as for my own, it is up to me to keep hammering, hammering, hammering at drafts, drafts, drafts.

Dined with the ever hospitable and kind hearted de Robeck on *Triad*. The Navy are still divided. Some there are who would wish me to urge the Admiral to play first fiddle in the coming attack. This *I will not do*. I have neither the data nor the technical knowledge which would justify me to my conscience in doing so.

4th August, 1915. Imbros. Have been out seeing the New Army at work. Some of the XIth Division were practising boat work in the evening and afterwards a Brigade started upon a night march into the mountains. The men are fit, although just beginning to be infected with the Eastern Mediterranean stomach trouble; i.e., the so-called cholera, which saved Constantinople from the Bulgarians in the last war.

5th August, 1915. Imbros. The day so longed for is very near now. O that it had come at the period of our victories! But there is time enough still, and the first moves of the plan are working smooth as oiled machinery. For the past few nights there has been steady flow into Anzac of troops, including a Division of the New Army. This has taken place, without any kind of hitch, under the very noses of the Turkish Army who have no inkling of the manœuvre — as yet! The Navy are helping us admirably here with their organization and good sea discipline. Also, from what they tell me, Shaw and the 13th Division of the New Army are playing up with the clockwork regularity of veterans. All this marks us up many points to the good, before even the flag drops. For, given the fine troops we have, the prime factors of the whole conception; the factors by which it stands or falls; are:

(1) Our success in hoodwinking the Turks; i.e., surprise.
(2) Our success in getting the 13th Division and the Indian Brigade unnoticed into Anzac.
(3) Our success in landing the Divisions from Imbros, Lemnos and Mitylene, at moments fixed beforehand, upon an unknown, unsurveyed, uncharted shore of Suvla. Of these three factors (1) and (2) may already be entered to our credit; (3) is on the knees of the Navy.

The day before the start is the worst day for a Commander. The operation overhangs him as the thought of another sort of operation troubles the minds of sick men in hospitals. There is nothing to distract him; he has made his last will and testament; his affairs are quite in order; he has said *au revoir** to his friends with what cheeriness he can muster. Looking back, it seems to me that during two months every conceivable contingency has been anticipated and weighed and that the means of dealing with it as it may arise is now either: embodied in our instructions to Corps Commanders, or else, set aside as pertaining to my own jurisdiction and responsibility. To my thinking, in fact, these instructions of ours illustrate the domain of G.H.Q. on the one hand and the province of the Corps Commander on the other very typically. The General Staff are proud of their work. Nothing; not a nosebag nor a bicycle has been left to chance.†

Davies and Diggle, his A.D.C., lunched and the Admiral came to haul me out for a walk about 6 p.m.

Have written K. by this evening's Mail bag about the sickness of the Australians, and indeed of all the troops here, excepting only the native Indian troops, and also about our Medical *band-o-bast* for the battle. No question about it, the Dardanelles was the theatre of all others for our Indian troops.

Have now seen all the New Army units except six Battalions

---

* "Goodbye."

† See Appendix III containing actual instructions, together with a brief explanatory heading. — *Ian H., 1920.*

of the 10th Division.
French has written me a very delightful letter.

Chapter XV – Sari Bair and Suvla

6th August, 1915. Imbros. O! God of Bethel, by whose hand thy people still are fed, — I am wishing the very rare wish, — that it was the day after to-morrow. Men or mice we will be by then, but I'd like to know which. K.'s New Army, too! How will they do? What do they think? They speak — and with justice — of the spirit of the Commander colouring the *moral* of his men, but I have hardly seen them, much less taken their measure. One more week and we would have known something at first hand. Now, except that the 13th Division and the 33rd Brigade gained good opinions at Helles, all is guess work.

Went down to "K" Beach to see the 11th Division go off. Young Brodrick, who was with us, proved himself much all there on the crowded pier and foreshore; very observant; telling me who or what I had not noticed, etc. First the destroyers were filling up and then the lighters. The young Naval Officers in charge of the lighters were very keen to show me how they had fixed up their reserves of ammunition and water. Spent quite a time at this and talking to Hammersley and Malcolm, his G.S.O. (1); also to Coleridge, G.S.O. (2), and to no end of Regimental Officers and

Suvla from Chunuk Bair

men. Hammersley has been working too hard; at least he looked it; also, for the occasion, rather glum. Quite natural; but I always remember Wolseley's remark about the moral stimulus exerted by the gay staff officer and his large cigar. The occasion! Yes, each man to his own temperament. Some pray before battle; others dance and drink. The memory of Cromwell prevails over that of Prince Rupert with most Englishmen but Prince Rupert, *per se*, usually prevailed over Cromwell. To your adventurous soldier; to our heroes, Bobs, Sir Evelyn, Garnet Wolseley, Charles Gordon (great psalm-singer though he was) an occasion like to-night's holds the same intoxicating mixture of danger and desire as fills the glass of the boy bridegroom when he raises it to the health of his enigma in a veil. But I don't know how it is; I used to feel like that; now I too am terribly anxious. Disappointed not to see Stopford nor Reed. They were to have been there. Besides the men on the beetles there are men packed like herrings upon the decks of the destroyers. I had half a mind to cruise round in the motor launch and say a few words to them Elandslaagte fashion, but was held back by feeling that the rank and file don't know me and that there was too long an interval before the entry into the danger zone.

The sea was like glass — melted; blue green with a dull red glow in it: the air seemed to have been boiled. Officers and men gave me the "feel" of being "for it" though over serious for British soldiers who always, in my previous experience, have been extraordinarily animated and gay when they are advancing "on a Koppje day." These new men seem subdued when I recall the blaze of enthusiasm in which the old lot started out of Mudros harbour on that April afternoon.

The *moral* of troops about to enter into battle supplies a splendid field of research for students of the human soul, for then the blind wall set in everyday intercourse between Commander and commanded seems to become brittle as crystal and as transparent. Only for a few moments — last moments for so many? But, during those moments, the gesture of the General means so much — it strikes the attitude of his troops. It is up to Stopford and Hammersley to make those gestures. Stopford was not there, and is not the type; Hammersley is not that type either. How true it is that age, experience, wisdom count for less than youth, magnetism and love of danger when inexperience has to be heartened for the struggle.

Strolled back slowly along the beach, and, at 8.30, in the gathering dusk, saw the whole flotilla glide away and disappear ghostlike to the Northwards. The empty harbour frightens me. Nothing in legend stranger or more terrible than the silent departure of this silent Army, K.'s new Corps, every mother's son of them, face to face with their fate.

But it will never do to begin the night's vigil in this low key. Capital news from the aeroplanes. Samson has sent in photographs taken yesterday, showing the Suvla Bay area. Not more than 100 to 150 yards of trenches in all; half a dozen gun emplacements and, the attached report adds, no Turks anywhere on the move.

7th August, 1915. Imbros. Sitting in my hut after a night in the G.S. tent. One A.D.C. remains over there. As the cables come in he runs across with them. Freddie Maitland runs fast. I am watching to see his helmet top the ridge of sand that lies between. The 9th Corps has got ashore; some scrapping along the beaches but no wire or hold-up like there was at Sedd-el-Bahr: that in itself is worth fifty million golden sovereigns. The surprise has come off!

I'd sooner storm a hundred bloody trenches than dangle at the end of this wire. But now, thank God, the deadliest of the perils is past. The New Army are fairly ashore. That worst horror of searchlights and of the new troops being machine gunned in their boats has lifted its dark shadow.

At Anzac, the most formidable entrenchment of the Turks, "Lone Pine," was stormed yesterday evening by the Australian 1st Brigade; a desperate fine feat. At midnight Birdie cabled, "All going on well on right where men confident of repelling counter-attack now evidently being prepared: on left have taken Old No. 3 Post and first ridge of Walden Point, capturing machine gun: progress satisfactory, though appallingly difficult: casualties uncertain but on right about 100 killed; 400 wounded."

At Helles a temporary success was scored, but, during the early part of the night, counter-attacks have brought us back to "as you were." Fighting is going on and we ought to be pinning the enemy to the South which is the main thing.

From Suvla we have no direct news since the "All landings successful" cable but we have the repetition of a wireless from G.H.Q. IXth Corps to the Vice-Admiral at 7.58 a.m. saying, "Prisoners captured state no fresh troops have arrived recently and forces opposed to us appear to be as estimated by G.H.Q. Apparently one Regiment only was opposed to our advance on left."

I have caused this cable to be sent to Stopford:

> 4.20 p.m. G.H.Q. to 9th Corps. Have only received one telegram from you. Chief glad to hear enemy opposition weakening and knows you will take advantage of this to push on rapidly. Prisoners state landing a surprise so take every advantage before you are forestalled.

8th August, 1915. Imbros. Another night on tenter hooks: great news: a wireless from a warship to tell us the Suvla troops are up on the foothills: two cables from Stopford: many messages from Anzac and Helles.

> 2.12 a.m. IXth Corps to G.H.Q. As far as can be ascertained 33rd Brigade hold line the sea about 91.I.9 to Suvla East corner[*] of Salt Lake to Lala Baba inclusive. North of Salt Lake 31st and 32nd Brigade extended East of Asmak 117.U. preparatory. 34th Brigade advancing having followed retreating enemy towards line diagonally across 117.X. and 117.D. One battalion latter Brigade occupy high ground about square 135.X.

> 5.10 a.m. IXth Corps to G.H.Q. Yilghin Burnu is in our hands. No further information.

Awful work at Lone Pine. Desperate counter-attacks by enemy, but now Birdie thinks we are there to stay. Bulk of Turkish reserves engaged there whilst Godley's New Zealanders and the

---

[*] Must have meant south-east? — *Ian H., 1920.*

Sari Bair and Suvla

new 13th Division under Shaw are well up the heights and have carried Chunuk Bair. Koja Chemen Tepe not yet; but Chunuk Bair will do: with that, we win!

At Helles we have pushed out again and the East Lancs Division have gallantly stormed the Vineyard which they hold. The Turks are making mighty counter-attacks but their columns have been cut to pieces by the thin lines of the Lancashire Fusiliers. Neither from Helles nor from the Southern area of Anzac are the enemy likely to spare men to reinforce Sari Bair or Suvla.

At 11.30 I ordered the *Arno* for mid-day sharp. Then happened one of those aquatic incidents which lend an atmosphere all their own to amphibious war. Rear-Admiral Nicholson, in local naval command here, had ordered the *Arno* to fill up her boilers. Some hitch arose, some d——d amphibious hitch. Thereupon, without telling me, he ordered the Commander of the *Arno* to draw fires, so that, when my signal was sent, a reply came from the Rear-Admiral saying he was sorry I should be inconvenienced, but he thought it best to order the fires to be drawn; otherwise the boilers might have suffered. When, at a crisis, a boiler walks into the middle of his calculations, a soldier is simply — boiled! I could not altogether master my irritation, and I wrote out a reply saying this was not a question of convenience or inconvenience but one of preventing a Commander-in-Chief from exercising his functions during battle. I sent the signal down to the signal tent and about an hour later Braithwaite came over and said he had taken it upon himself to tone it down.* Just as well, perhaps, but here I was, marooned upon an island!

No other ship could be signalled. As a rule there was a destroyer on patrol about Helles which could be called up by

---

* Long afterwards — long after the Dardanelles Commission had finished their Report — I had the curiosity to get permission to look at the log of the *Exmouth* (Rear-Admiral Nicholson) to see how my cable had been translated. Here it is, very much Bowdlerized: "Sent 11.45, received 11.59. Sir I. Hamilton to Rear-Admiral 3. Urgent. 'Understand *Arno* drawing fires. Can this be stopped and *Arno* sent (to) *Mercedes* to water at once? *Arno* specially put at my disposal by Vice-Admiral and I may require her at any moment.'" The *Mercedes* was the ship with our military drinking water.

wireless, but to-day there was no getting hold of it. I began to be afraid we should not get away till dark when, at about 3.30 p.m. Nicholson signalled that the *Triad* was sailing for Suvla at 4.15 p.m., and would I care to go in her, the *Arno* following after she had watered. We were off like a shot, young Brodrick, Captain Anstey and myself for Suvla. Braithwaite remained to carry on with Anzac and Helles. The moment I quit my post I drop out and he takes up the reins. His hands are capable — fortunately! To-day's cables before I left were right from Helles; splendid from Anzac and nothing further from Suvla[*]

---

[*] There is a hiatus in my diary here which I must try and bridge over by a footnote especially as my story seems to run off the rails when I say that "nothing further" had come in from Suvla. At 10.50 a.m. a further cable did come in from Suvla:

> Approximate position of troops under General Hammersley this morning. Two battalions 33rd Brigade sea to S.E. corner of Salt Lake: will be moved forward shortly to connect if possible with Anzac troops. Two battalions 33rd holding Yilghin Burnu. Position on Hill 500 yards East Yilghin Burnu not yet certain. From Yilghin Burnu 31st Brigade holds line through Baka Baba crossroads, thence North to about 118 0 2. 32nd and 34th Brigades ordered forward from Hill 10 (117 R) where they spent night to line 118 M.R.W. to fill gap with Tenth Division. Detailed information of Tenth Division not yet definite: will report later. Consider Major-General Hammersley and troops under him deserve great credit for result attained against strenuous opposition and great difficulty.

Manifestly, the data in this cable were not enough to enable me to form any opinion of my own as to the credit due to anyone; but every soldier will understand that it was up to me to respond:

> To G.O.C. 8th Corps.
> From General Sir Ian Hamilton.
>   You and your troops have indeed done splendidly. Please tell Hammersley how much we hope from his able and rapid advance.

I made no written note of this 10.50 a.m. cable (or of my reply to it) at the time and, eighteen months later, no mental note of it remained, probably because it had only added some detail to the news received during the night. But I had reason to regret this afterwards when I came to read the final Report of the Dardanelles Commission, paragraph 89. There I see it stated that "with regard to this message" (my pat on the back for Hammersley) "Sir Frederick Stopford informed us that the result of the operations on the night of the 6th and day of the

As we sailed in, that bay, always till now so preternaturally deserted and silent, was alive and bustling with ships and small craft. A launch came along from the *Chatham* and I jumped in whilst we were still going pretty fast and shot off to see de Robeck. He seemed to think things naval were going pretty well and that Rear-Admiral Christian had been coping quite well with his share, but suggested that, as he was under a severe strain, I had better leave him alone. As to the soldiers' show, he said what Turks were on the ground, and there weren't many, had been well beaten — but — but — *but*; and all I could get him to say was that although he was well aware the fighting at Helles and Anzac demanded my closest attention; still, that was in practised hands and he had felt bound to wireless to beg me to come up to Suvla and see things for myself.

Roger Keyes said then that the landings had come off, on the whole, A.1. Our G.H.Q. idea, which the Navy had shared, that the whole of the troops should be landed South of Lala Baba had been sound. The 33rd Brigade had landed there without shot fired; the 32nd had been sharply, but notvery seriously opposed; the Brigade (the 34th) which we, to meet the wish of the Corps, had tried to land for them opposite Hill 10 inside the Bay, instead of with the others as we had originally arranged, had only been able to find depth at the mouth of the Salt Lake; had suffered loss from rifle fire and had been thrown into disorder by the grounding of some lighters. The long wade through the water and mud had upset the cohesion of the Brigade.

Aspinall now turned up. He was in a fever; said our chances were being thrown away with both hands and that he had already cabled me strongly to that effect. Neither the Admiral's message

---

7th was not as satisfactory as he would have liked but he gathered from Sir Ian Hamilton's congratulations that his dispositions and orders had met with the latter's approval"

As to my actual feelings that forenoon, I do remember them well. At sunrise victory seemed assured. As morning melted into mid-day my mind became more and more uneasy at the scant news about the Irish Division and at the lack of news of a further advance of the 11th Division. This growing anxiety drove me to quit my headquarters and to take ship for Suvla.

nor Aspinall's had reached me.*

Not another moment was to be lost, so Keyes took us both in his motor boat to H.M.S. *Jonquil* to see Stopford. He (Stopford) seemed happy and said that everything was quite all right and going well. Mahon with some of his troops was pressing back the Turks along Kiretch Tepe Sirt. There had been a very stiff fight in the darkness at Lala Baba and next morning the Turks had fought so hard on a little mound called Hill 10 that he (Stopford) had been afraid we were not going to be able to take it at all. However, it had been taken, but there was great confusion and hours of delay in deploying for the attack of the foothills. They were easily carried in the end but by that time the men were so thirsty and tired that they did not follow up the beaten enemy.

"And where are they now?" I asked.

"There," he replied, "along the foot of the hills," and he pointed out the line, north to south.

"But they held that line, more or less, yesterday," I said.

"Yes," said Stopford, and he went on to explain that the Brigadiers had been called upon to gain what ground they could without serious fighting but that, actually, they had not yet occupied any dominating tactical point. The men had been very tired; he had not been able to get water up to them or land his guns as quickly as he had hoped. Therefore, he had decided to postpone the occupation of the ridge (which might lead to a regular battle) until next morning.

"A regular battle is just exactly what we are here for" was what I was inclined to say, but what I did say was that most of this was

---

* The Admiral's wireless had said, so I was told: "It is important we should meet — shall I come to Kephalos or are you coming to Suvla?" As stated in text I did not get this cable at the time nor did I ever get it. Four years later the signal logs of the only ships through which the message could have passed; viz., *Triad*, *Exmouth*, *Chatham*, were searched and there is no trace of it. So I think it must have been drafted and overlooked. — *Ian H., 1920.*

Aspinall's cable: "Just been ashore where I found all quiet AAA. No rifle fire, no artillery fire and apparently no Turks AAA. IXth Corps resting AAA. Feel confident that golden opportunities are being lost and look upon the situation as serious." I received this next morning from Braithwaite. — *Ian H., 1920.*

news to me; that he should have instantly informed me of his decision that he could not obey my cabled order of yesterday afternoon to "push on rapidly." Stopford replied that he had only made up his mind within the past hour or so; that he had just got back from the shore and was going to send me a full message when I arrived.

Now, what was to be done? The Turks were so quiet it seemed to me certain they must have taken the knock-out. All along the beaches, and inland too, no end of our men were on the move, offering fine targets. The artillery which had so long annoyed Anzac used to fire from behind Ismail Oglu Tepe; i.e., within point blank range of where our men were now strolling about in crowds. Yet not a single shell was being fired. Either, the enemy's guns had been run back over the main ridge to save them; or, the garrison of Ismail Oglu Tepe was so weak and shaken that they were avoiding any move which might precipitate a conflict.

I said to Stopford, "We must occupy the heights at once. It is imperative we get Ismail Oglu Tepe and Tekke Tepe *now*!"

To this he raised objections. He doubted whether the troops had got their water yet; he and Reed were agreed we ought to get more guns ashore; the combination of naval and military artillery was being worked out for the morning; orders would all have to be re-written. He added that, whilst agreeing with me on principle as to the necessity for pushing on, there were many tactical reasons against it, especially the attitude of his Generals who had told him their men were too tired. I thought to myself of the many, many times Lord Bobs, French, every leader of note has had to fight that same *non possumus*; of the old days when half the victory lay in the moral effort which could impel men half dead with hunger, thirst and sleeplessness to push along. A cruel, pitiless business, but so is war itself. Was it not the greatest of soldiers who said his Marshals could always find ten good reasons for putting off an attack till next day!

So I said I would like to see the G.O.C. Division and the Brigadiers personally so as to get a better grip of things than we could on board ship in harbour. Stopford agreed; nothing, he said, would please him more than if I could succeed where he had failed, but would I excuse him from accompanying me; he had not been very fit; he had just returned from a visit to the shore and he wanted to give his leg a chance. He pointed out Hammersley's Headquarters about 400 yards off and said he, Hammersley, would be able to direct me to the Brigades.

So I nipped down the *Jonquil's* ladder; tumbled into Roger Keyes' racing motor boat and with him and Aspinall we simply shot across the water to Lala Baba. Every moment was priceless. I had not been five minutes on the *Jonquil* and in another two I was with Hammersley.

Under the low cliffs by the sea was a small half-moon of beach about 100 by 40 yards. At the North end of the half-moon was Hammersley. Asked to give me an idea of the situation he gave me much the same story as Stopford. The 9th West Yorks and 6th Yorks had done A.1 storming Lala Baba in the dark. There had been marching and counter-marching in the move on Hill 10. The Brigadier had not been able to get a grip of his Battalions to throw them at it in proper unison and form. A delay of precious hours had been caused in the attack on Yilghin Burnu by a Brigadier who wanted to go forward finding himself at cross purposes with a Brigadier who thought it better to hold back. At present all was peaceful and he expected a Staff Officer at any moment with a sketch showing the exact disposition of his troops. He could not, he feared, point me out the Brigade Headquarters on the ground. The general line held followed the under features of the hills.

Malcolm, G.S.O.1, was then called and came up from the far end of the little beach. He was in the act of fixing up orders for next morning's attack. I told both Officers that there had never been a greater crisis in any battle than the one taking place as we spoke. They were naturally pleased at having got ashore and to have defeated the Turks on the shore, but they must not fly away with the idea that with time and patience everything would pan out very nicely. On the contrary, it was imperative, absolutely imperative, we should occupy the heights before the enemy brought back the guns they had carried off and before they received the reinforcements which were marching at that very moment to their aid. This was no guess: it *was* so: our aeroplanes had spotted Turks marching upon us from the North. We might be too late now; anyway our margin was of the narrowest.

Hammersley assured me that sheer thirst, and the exhaustion of the troops owing to thirst, had been the only reason why he had not walked on to Ismail Oglu Tepe last night. After Yilghin Burnu had been carried, there was nothing to prevent the occupation of the heights as the Turks had been beat, but no one could fight against thirst.

I asked him how the water question stood. He said it had been solved by the landing of more mules; there was no longer any serious supply trouble. All the troops were now watered, fed and rested. They had been told they should gain as much ground as they could without committing themselves to a general action, but they had not, in fact, made much progress. Thereupon, I pressed again my view that the Division should get on to the ridge forthwith. Let the Brigade-Majors, I said, pick out a few of their freshest companies and get on to the crest right now. Hammersley still clung to the view that he could not get any of his troops under weigh before daylight next morning. The units were scattered; no reconnaissance had been made of the ground to their front; that ground was jungly and blind; it would be impossible to get orders round the whole Division in time to let the junior ranks study them. Hammersley's points were made in a proper and soldierly manner. Every General of experience would be with him in each of them, but there was one huge danger rapidly approaching us; already casting its shadow upon us, which, to me as Commander-in-Chief, outweighed every secondary objection. We might have the hills at the cost of walking up them to-day; the Lord only knew what would be the price of them to-morrow. Helles and Anzac were both holding the Turks to their own front, but from Asia and Bulair the enemy were on the march. Once our troops dug themselves in on the crest no number of Turks would be able to shift them. But; if the Turks got there first? If, as Colonel Malcolm said, it was impossible to get orders round the Division in time, — a surprising statement — was there no body of troops — no Divisional reserve — no nothing — which could be used for the purpose of marching a couple of miles? Seemingly, there was no reserve! Never, in all my long soldiering had I been faced with ideas like these. I have seen attack orders dictated to a Division from the saddle in less than five minutes. Here was a victorious Division, rested and watered, said to be unable to bestir itself, even feebly, with less than twelve hours' notice! This was what I felt and although I did not say it probably I looked it, for Malcolm now qualified the original *non possumus* by saying that although the Irish and the 33rd and 34th Brigades could not be set in motion before daylight, the 32nd Brigade, which was concentrated round about Sulajik, would be ready to move at short notice.

The moment had now come for making up my mind. I did so, and told Hammersley in the most distinct terms that I wished this Brigade to advance *at once and dig themselves in on the crestline.*[*] If the Brigade could fix themselves upon the heights overlooking Anafarta Sagir they would make the morning advance easy for their comrades and would be able to interfere with and delay the Turkish reinforcements which might try and debouch between the two Anafartas during the night or march down upon Suvla from the North. Viewed from the sea or studied in a map there might be some question of this hill, or that hill, but, on the ground it was clear to half an eye that Tekke Tepe was the key to the whole Suvla Bay area. If by dawn, I said, even one Company of ours was well entrenched on the Tekke Tepe height we should have the whip hand of the enemy in the opening moves next morning.

Hammersley said he understood my order and that the advance should be put in hand at once. Malcolm hurried off; I left a little before 6.30 and went, *via* the *Chatham*, back to the *Triad*. The *Arno* had by now come in, but de Robeck has kindly asked me not to shift quarters if Anzac and Helles troubles will permit me to stay the night at Suvla.

All was dead quiet ashore till 11 p.m. I was on the bridge until then and, seeing and hearing nothing, felt sure the Brigade had made good Tekke Tepe and were now digging themselves in.

Captain Brody dined. The scraps of news picked up from the sailormen, mainly by young Brodrick, confirm what the soldiers

---

[*] Looking to the distance of Sulajik, the Brigade might have been expected to move in about an hour and a half. But, as I did not know at the time, or indeed till two years later, this Brigade was *not* concentrated. Only two battalions were at Sulajik; the other two, the 6th East Yorks and the 9th West Yorks, were in possession of Hill 70, *vide* map. — *Ian H., 1920.*

had told us about the landing inside Suvla Bay along the narrow strip of land West of the Salt Lake. The attacks on Hill 10 went to pieces, not against the Turks, but by mishap. The first assault made by one or two Companies succeeded, but the assailants were taken for Turks and were attacked in turn and driven off by others of our men. A most distressing affair.

If there was hesitation and mix-up in the general handling, the Regimental folk atoned and there were many incidents of initiative and daring on the part of battalions and companies.

Mahon with some of his Irish and a Manchester Battalion are fighting well and clearing Kiretch Tepe Sirt. Until this morning bullets from that ridge were falling on "A" Beach; now the working parties are not in any way disturbed.

9th August, 1915. Imbros. With the first streak of dawn I was up on the bridge with my glasses. The hills are so covered with scrub that it was hard to see what was going on in that uncertain light, but the heavyish shrapnel fire was a bad sign and the fact that the enemy's guns were firing from a knoll a few hundred yards East of Anafarta Sagir was proof that our troops were not holding Tekke Tepe. But the Officer of the Watch said that the small hours passed quietly; no firing ashore during the hours of darkness. Could not make head or tail of it!

As the light grew stronger some of ours could be seen pushing up the western slopes of the long spur running out South-west from Anafarta. The scrub was so thick that they had to climb together and follow-my-leader along what appeared to be cattle tracks up the hill. On our right all seemed going very well. Looking through naval telescopes we thought — we all thought — Ismail Oglu Tepe height was won. Very soon the shrapnel got on to those bunches of men on our left and there was something like a stampede from North to South. Looking closer we could see the enemy advancing behind their own bursting shrapnel and rolling up our line from the left on to the centre. Oh for the good "Queen Bess," her high command, and her 15-inch shrapnel! One broadside and these Turks would go scampering down to Gehenna. The enemy counter-attack was coming from the direction of Tekke Tepe and moving over the foothills and plain on Sulajik. Our centre made a convulsive effort (so it seemed) to throw back the steadily advancing Turks; three or four companies (they looked like) moved out from the brush about Sulajik and tried to deploy. But the shrapnel got on to these fellows also and I lost sight of them.

Then about 6 a.m., the whole lot seemed suddenly to collapse: including the right! Not only did they give ground but they came back — some of them — half-way to the sea. But others made a stand. The musketry fire got very heavy. The enemy were making a supreme effort. The Turkish shell fire grew hotter and hotter. The enemy's guns seemed now to be firing not only from round about Anafarta Sagir, but also from somewhere between 113 and 101, 2,500 yards or so South-west of Anafarta. Still these fellows of ours; not more than a quarter of those on the ground at the outset — stuck it out. My heart has grown tough amidst the struggles of the Peninsula but the misery of this scene well nigh broke it. What kept me going was the sight of Sari Bair — I could not keep my eyes off the Sari Bair ridge. Guns from all sides, sea and land, Turks and British, were turned on to it and enormous explosions were sending slices off the top of the high mountain to mix with the clouds in the sky. Under that canopy our men were fighting for dear life far above us!

Between 7.30 and 8.0 the Turkish reinforcements at Suvla seemed to have got enough. They did not appear to be in any great strength: here and there they fell back: no more came up in support: evidently, they were being held: failure, not disaster, was the upshot: few things so bad they might not be worse. By 8.0 the musketry and the shelling began to slacken down although there was a good deal of desultory shooting. We were holding our own; the Welsh Division are coming in this morning; but we have not sweated blood only to hold our own; our occupation of the open key positions has been just too late! The element of surprise — wasted! The prime factor set aside for the sake of other factors! Words are no use.

Looked at from the bridge of the *Triad* — not a bad observation station — the tendency of our men to get into little groups was very noticeable: as if they had not been trained in working under fire in the open. As to the general form of our attack against the hills on our right, it seemed to be what our French Allies call *décousu*.* After a whole day's rest and preparing, there might have been more form and shape about the movement. Yet it was for the sake of this form and shape that the Turkish reinforcements have been given time to get on to the heights. Our stratagems worked well, but there is a time limit set to all make-believes; the hour glass of fate was set at forty-eight hours, and now the sands have run out.

Before going over to Anzac I had to get hold of Stopford so as to hear what news had come in from Hammersley and from Mahon. If only Mahon is pushing forward to Ejelmer Bay and can occupy the high range to the East of it that would make amends for much. After breakfast, therefore, at 8.30 got into a launch and landed at Ghazi Baba with young Brodrick as my only companion. Our boat took us into a deep, narrow creek cut by nature into the sheer rock just by Ghazi Baba — a name only; there is nothing to distinguish that spot from any other. Along the beach feverish activity; stores, water, ammunition, all the wants of an army being landed. Walking up the lower slope of Kiretch Tepe Sirt, we found Stopford, about four or five hundred yards East of Ghazi Baba, busy with part of a Field Company of Engineers supervising the building of some splinter-proof Headquarters huts for himself and Staff. He was absorbed in the work, and he said that it would be well to make a thorough good job of the dug-outs as we should probably be here for a very long time. I retorted, "Devil a bit; within a day or two you will be picking the best of the Anafarta houses for your billet."

From the spot he had selected the whole of Suvla Bay and the Salt Lake lay open; also the Anafartas and Yilghin Burnu. But, being on a lower spur of Kiretch Tepe Sirt, his post was "dead" to the fighting taking place along the crest of Kiretch Tepe Sirt itself. I remarked on this and asked what news of the Irish, saying that now we were certainly forestalled at Yilghin Burnu and, apparently, on Tekke Tepe also, it was doubly essential Mahon should make a clean sweep of the ridge. Stopford said he was

---

* "Disjointed."

confident he would be able to do so, aided as he would be by the fire from the ships in the harbour — a fire which enfiladed the whole length of this feature.

As to this morning's hold up, Stopford took it philosophically, which was well so far as it went, but he seemed hardly to realize that the Turks have rushed their guns and reinforcements here from a very long way off whilst he has been creeping along at the rate of a mile a day. Stopford expected Hammersley would be in to report progress in person; he will keep me well posted in his news and he understands that the Welsh Division will be at his disposal to help the 11th Division.

As Stopford could give me no recent news from Mahon I suggested I should go and find out from him personally how matters then stood. Stopford said it was a good idea but that he himself thought it better not to leave his Headquarters where messages kept coming in. I agreed and started with George Brodrick to scale the hill.

About half a mile up we struck a crowd of the Irish Pioneer Regiment (Granard's) filling their water bottles at a well marked on the map as Charak Cheshme. In their company we now made our way Northwards along a path through fairly thick scrub as high as a man's waist. We were moving parallel to, and about 300 yards below, the crestline of the ridge. When we had gone another mile a spattering of "overs" began to fall around like the first heavy drops of a thunderstorm. So wrapped in cotton wool is a now-a-days Commander-in-Chief that this was the first musketry fire I could claim to have come under since the beginning of the war. To sit in a trench and hear flights of bullets flop into the sandbag parapet, or pass harmlessly overhead, is hardly to be under fire. An irregular stream of Irishmen were walking up the path along with us; one of them was hit just ahead of me. He caught it in the thigh and stretcher men whipped him off in a jiffy. At last we got to a spot some 2½ miles from Suvla and had not yet been able to find Mahon. So I sat down behind a stone, somewhere about the letter "K" of Kiretch Tepe Sirt, and sent young Brodrick to espy the land. He found that we had pulled up within a couple of hundred yards of the Brigade Headquarters, where portions of the 30th, 31st and 34th Brigades (sounds very formidable but only five

Battalions) were holding a spur and preparing to make an attack. General Mahon was actually in the Brigade Headquarters (a tiny ditch which only held four or five people) and came back to where I was sitting. He is angry, and small wonder, at the chaos introduced somehow into the Corps. He is commanding some of Hammersley's men and Hammersley has the bulk of his at the far extremity of the line of battle. He besought me to do my utmost to get Hill and his troops back to their own command.

I told him G.H.Q. had always understood Stopford would land his, Mahon's, two Brigades intact at A Beach. When the naval people could not find a beach at A, they, presumably with Stopford's concurrence, had most unluckily dumped them ashore several miles South at C Beach. This was the cause of the mix-up of his Division which Stopford, no doubt, would take in hand as soon as he could. Mahon seemed in fighting form. He said he could clear the whole of Kiretch Tepe Sirt, but that he did not want to lose men in making frontal attacks, so he was trying to work round South through the thick scrub so as to shift the enemy that way. He had reckoned five or six hundred men were against him — gendarmes. But there were more than there had been at daylight. My talk with Mahon made me happier. Here, at least, was someone who had an idea of what he was doing. The main thing was to attack before more Turks came down the coast. My own idea would certainly have been to knock the Turks out by a bayonet charge — right there. So far they had not had time to dig a regular trench, only a few shallow scrapings along a natural fold of the ground. If Mahon wished to make a turning movement, then, I think, he would have been well advised to take it by the North where the ground over which he must advance was not only unentrenched and clear of brush, but also laid quite open to the supporting fire of the Fleet. But I kept these views to myself until I could see Stopford; said good-bye to Mahon and wished him luck; found Brodrick had wandered off on his own to see the fun at close quarters; legged it, all alone, down the open southern slope of the Kiretch Tepe Sirt and got down into ground less open to snipers' fire from the scrub-covered plain.*

Then, still quite alone, I made my way back South-west towards Ghazi Baba on Suvla Bay. After a little I was joined by two young Irish soldiers. I don't know who or what they took me for; certainly not for the Generalissimo. They came along with me and discussed identical adventures from diametrically different standpoints. One, in fact, was an optimist; the other a pessimist. One found fault with the war for not giving him enough hardship and adventure; the other was entirely fed up with adventures and hardships. This seems a trivial incident to jot down amidst issues so tremendous, but life is life, and my chat with these youngsters put some new life into me. Nearing the shore, I again struck Stopford's Headquarters, now beginning to look habitable. Braithwaite, and one or two others of my Staff turned up from Imbros at that moment. He shoved some cables into my hand and

---

* My Aide-de-Camp, George Brodrick, has permitted me to use the following extract from a letter of his written to his father, Lord Midleton, at the time.

> I went to Suvla with Sir Ian in the afternoon of August 8th, and we arrived to find 'Nothing doing.' The beaches and hillsides covered with our men almost like a Bank Holiday evening at Hampstead Heath. Vague shelling by one of our monitors was the only thing which broke the peace of a most perfect evening — a glorious sunset.
>
> We went over to the Destroyer where General Stopford had his Headquarters, and I fancy words of exhortation were spoken to him. We slept on the Triad, Admiral de Robeck's Yacht. I had a camp bed on the Bridge, so as to hear any happenings during the night. About dawn our Monitors started to shell the heights behind Anafarta and a sort of assault was made; the Turkish battery opened with shrapnel, and our fellows did not seem to get very far.
>
> We went ashore on 'A' beach about 8 a.m. and walked up to Stopford's Headquarters, as he had gone ashore the night before. They all seemed a very lifeless crew, with but little knowledge of the general situation and no spirit in them. We made our way on across some rocky scrubby country towards Brigade Headquarters; fairly heavy rifle fire was going on, and after about two miles bullets began to ping unpleasantly all round us. I persuaded Sir Ian to lie down behind a rock, much against his will, and went on myself another 150 yards to where the Brigade Staff were sitting in a dip behind a stone wall. They told me that about 800 Turks were in front of them with no machine guns. We had 3 Battalions in the firing line and two in reserve and yet could not get on.

hastened off to interview Reed. Helles and Anzac have been duly warned we are both here for a few hours; all the component parts of my machine, its cranks, levers, pulleys, are assembled at Imbros, and G.H.Q. simply cannot be left under a junior much longer. Meanwhile I told Stopford about Mahon and the gendarmes. When I said that the sooner the Kiretch Tepe nettle was grasped the less it would sting, he informed me he had issued an order that Commanderswere not to lose men by making frontal attacks on trenches but were to turn them.

So here is a theory which South African practice proved to be more often wrong than right being treated as an axiom at Gallipoli!

We next went into the question of digging a defensive line of trenches half-way between Corps Headquarters and Mahon's force. Here we were in accord. No man knows his luck and the tide may turn any moment. Both at Liao-Yang and the Shaho the Japanese began to dig deep trenches directly they captured a position.

Young Brodrick rejoined me here; rather anxious at having lost me. He had found Mahon with the Brigade Staff. He had been shown the exact positions on a rough sketch map made by one of the Officers. We had three Battalions in the firing line and two in reserve. The gendarmerie had been reinforced and were now estimated at 700 without machine guns or artillery. We had a mountain battery shelling the gendarmes and a monitor occasionally gave them a big fellow. The Brigade Staff had said nothing to him about a battalion working round to the South. I repeated this to Stopford and begged him to make a push for it here.

By now Braithwaite had finished with Reed, so we hurriedly discussed his budget of news. Hammersley is expected but he has not turned up yet. Indeed the situation is still by no means free from anxiety although the arrival of the Welsh Division gives confidence. A battalion of the 32nd Brigade did get up on to Tekke Tepe last night, it seems, but were knocked off this morning before they had time to entrench.* Seeing they should have had several hours time to dig in, that seems strange. Braithwaite handed me a

---

* Only one Company we hear now. — *Ian H., 15.8.15.*

bunch of signals and wires; also the news of what I had known at the back of my mind since morning, — the fact that we had not got Sari Bair! Then we started back to see de Robeck and Keyes. For the first time in this expedition Roger Keyes seemed down on his luck: we had often before seen him raging, never dejected. These awful delays: delay in landing the Irish; delay in attacking on the 7th; delay all night of the 7th; delay during the day of the 8th and night of the 8th, have simply deprived him of the power of speech, — to soldiers, that is to say, though, to shipmates, no doubt...!

Now for Anzac. Since dawn a fever about Anzac had held me. Shades of Staff College Professors, from you no forgiveness to a Chief who runs about the mountain quitting his central post. But the luminous shade of Napoleon would better understand my desperation. Some Generals are just accumulators of the will of the C.-in-C. When that is the case, and when they run down, there is only one man who can hope to pump in energy.

Exact at noon Roger Keyes and I pushed off in the racing motor boat. On our way we stopped at "C" beach and picked up Commander Worsley. Next to Anzac, but at the Cove, found that Birdwood had left word he would meet me at the ex-Turkish Post No. 2, — so, as the water was shoal in spots, we rowed down there in a dinghy, along the shore where our lives would not have been worth half a minute's purchase just three days ago.

After scrambling awhile over the new trenches, Birdwood, Godley and I sat down on a high spur above Godley's Headquarters which gave us a grand outlook over the whole Suvla area, and across to Chunuk Bair. Here we ate our rations and held an impromptu council of war; Shaw, commanding the new 13th Division, joining in with us. All three Generals were in high spirits and refused to allow themselves to be damped down by the repulse of the morning's attack on the high ridge. They put down that check to the lethargy of Suvla. Had Stopford taken up any point on the watershed yesterday when it was unoccupied except by some fugitives, the whole Turkish position on the Peninsula would have become so critical that they could not have spared the numbers they have now brought up to defend "Q" and Koja Chemen Tepe. The Anzac Generals allowed that they themselves had got into arrears in their time tables, but they had been swift compared to Suvla.

Elliott and Fry phot.
GENERAL SIR W. R. BIRDWOOD, G.C.M.G., K.C.B.

Even as Godley was holding forth, messages came to hand to say that the Turks were passing from the defensive to the offensive and urging fresh attacks on the New Zealanders holding Chunuk Bair. Godley is certain the Turks will never make us quit hold. Shaw, who also has some of his men up there, is equally confident. Birdwood thinks Chunuk Bair should be safe, though not so safe as it would have been had we held on to that ridge at "Q" where Baldwin's delay from causes not yet known, lost us the crestline this morning. Birdie said he could have cried, and is not quite sure he didn't cry, when the bombardment stopped dead and minute after minute passed away, from one minute to twenty, without a sign of Baldwin and his column who had been booked to spurt for the top on the heels of the last shell. Unaided, the 6th Gurkhas got well astride the ridge, but had to fall back owing to the lack of his support. None the less, these Anzac Generals are in great form. They are sure they will have the whip hand of the Narrows by tomorrow.

Birdie was offered my last reserves, the 54th Essex Territorials under Inglefield. But he can't water them. The effort to carry food, water and cartridges to the firing lines is already overtaxing the Corps. If Inglefield's men were also pushed in they simply could not be kept going. When communication trenches have been dug and brushwood and rocks flattened out, it will be easier. Till then, the Generals agreed they would rather the extra pressure was applied from Suvla. Birdwood and Godley were keen, in fact, that the Essex Division should go to Stopford so that he might at once occupy Kavak Tepe and, if he could, Tekke Tepe. All that the Anzacs have seen for themselves, or heard from their own extreme left or from aeroplanes, leads them to believe that the Turkish reinforcements to the Suvla theatre came over the high shoulder of Tekke Tepe or through Anafarta Sagir about dawn this morning and that the enemy are in some strength now along the ridge between Anafarta Sagir and Ismail Oglu Tepe with a few hundred on Kiretch Tepe Sirt: the Turkish centre was a gift to us yesterday; certainly yesterday forenoon; now it can only be won by hard fighting. But the Turks have not yet had time to work round on to the high ridges east of Suvla Bay and although a few Turks did pass over Kavak Tepe, it seems to be now clear of any enemy.

There is no sign of life on the bare Eastern slope of that mountain. Probably one half of the great crescent of hills which encircles the Suvla plain and, in places, should overlook the Narrows, still lies open to an advance.

So together we composed a message to Stopford and Godley sent it off by telephone — now rigged up between the two Corps Headquarters: the form was filled in by Godley; hence his counter signature:

TO: G.O.C., IXth Corps.		
Sender's number. N.Z.G. 103	*Day of month.* 9	*In reply to number* AAA
After speaking to Birdwood and Godley think most important use fresh troops could be put to if not urgently required to reinforce would be the occupation as early as possible of the commanding position running through square 137-119 AAA Ismail Oglu Tepe are less vital to security of base. SIR IAN HAMILTON.		
From *Place* Fisherman's Hut. *Date* 2 p.m. 9th August, 1915.		
A. J. GODLEY, Maj. Gen.		

  Took leave of the Anzacs and the Anzac Generals about 4.30 p.m. The whole crowd were in tip-top spirits and immensely pleased with the freedom and largeness of their newly conquered kingdom. We of the G.H.Q. were bitten by this same spirit; Suvla took second place in our minds and when we got on board the *Arno* the ugly events of the early morning had been shaken, for the moment, out of our minds. But, on the sail home, we were able to look at the Peninsula as a whole. Because the Anzacs, plus the 13th

Elliott and Fry phot.
LIEUT.-GEN SIR A. J. GODLEY, K C.B., K.C.M.G.

Division of the New Army, had carried through a brilliant stroke of arms was a reason, not for shutting our eyes to the slowness of the Suvla Generals, but for spurring them on to do likewise. There is nothing open to them now — not without efforts for which they are, for the time being, unfit — but Kavak Tepe and the Aja Liman Anafarta ridge. So, on arrival at 6 p.m., wrote out the following message from myself to General Stopford:

> I am in complete sympathy with you in the matter of all your Officers and men being new to this style of warfare and without any leaven of experienced troops on which to form themselves. Still I should be wrong if I did not express my concern at the want of energy and push displayed by the 11th Division. It cannot all be want of experience as 13th have shown dash and self-confidence. Turks were almost negligible yesterday once you got ashore. To-day there was nothing to stop determined commanders leading such fine men as yours. Tell me what is wrong with the 11th Division. Is it the Divisional Generals or Brigadiers or both?I have a first-rate Major General I can send at once and can also supply two competent Brigadiers. You must get a move on or the whole plan of operations is in danger of failing, for if you don't secure the AJA LIMAN ANAFARTA ridge without delay the enemy will. You must use your personal influence to insist on vigorous and sustained action against the weak forces of the Turks in your front, and while agreeing to the capture of W Hills and spur mentioned in C.G.S. letter to you of to-day, it is of vital importance to the whole operation that you thereafter promptly take steps to secure the ridge without possession of which SUVLA BAY is not safe. You must face casualties and strike while the opportunity offers and remember the AJA LIMAN ANAFARTA ridge is your principal and dominant objective and it must be captured. Every day's delay in its capture will enormously multiply your casualties. I want the name of the Brigadier who sent the message to say his left was retiring owing to a strong attack and then subsequently reported that the attack in question has never developed. Keep Birdwood informed as he may be able to help you on your right flank.

This message seemed so important that it was sent by hand of Hore-Ruthven and another Officer by special destroyer. Braithwaite tells me that, when he was at 9th Corps Headquarters to-day he showed General Stopford the last two paragraphs of this memo which I had written when toning down the wording of a General Staff draft::

C.G.S.
(1) I do not think much good rubbing it into these fellows, there are very few Turks opposed to them. We have done it, and that was right, but we must not overdo it.
(2) But the men ought to be made to understand that really the whole result of this campaign may depend on their quickly getting a footing on the hills right and left of Anafarta. Officers and rank and file must be made to grasp this.
(3) If Lindley and his new men were kept intact and thrown in on the Anzac flank, surely they ought to be able to make a lodgment.

(*Initialled*), "IAN H."

Chapter XVI – Kavak Tepe Attack Collapses

10th August, 1915. Imbros. Had to remain at G.H.Q. all day — the worst of all days. My visit to Anzac yesterday had infected me with the hopes of Godley and Birdwood and made me feel that we would recover what we had missed at Suvla, and more, if, working from the pivot of Chunuk Bair, we got hold of the rest of Sari Bair.

They believed they would bring this off and then the victory would have been definite. Now — Chunuk Bair has gone!

The New Zealand and New Army troops holding the knoll were relieved by two New Army Battalions and, at daylight this morning, the Turks simply ran amok among them with a Division in mass formation. Trenches badly sited, they say, and Turks able to form close by in dead ground. Many reasons no doubt and lack of swift pressure from Suvla. The Turks have lost their fear of Stopford and concentrated full force against the Anzacs. By Birdie's message, it looks as if the heavy fighting was at an end — an end which leaves us with a fine gain of ground though minus the vital crests. Next time we will get them. We are close up to the summit instead of having five or six hundred feet to climb.

News from Suvla still rotten. Here is the result of Hammersley's visit to Stopford after I left:

August 9. 5.35. Suvla Bay.

Dear Braithwaite,
   I have had a talk with Hammersley and he tells me that his troops are much exhausted, have had very heavy fighting, severe losses and have felt the want of water very much. He does not consider that they are fit to make a fresh attack to-morrow.
   I have decided after consultation with him to make an attempt on the ridge about Abrikja with three fresh Territorial Battalions and six which have been used to-day. I am afraid from what I hear that the Naval guns do not have much effect on account of difficulty of accurate observation but I will arrange a programme, to be carefully timed, with Brigadier-General Smith, my Brigadier R.A., and of course all the field guns will also help. I *must* see Smith so please ask the V. Admiral to place a boat at Smith's disposal to bring him here to see me and then to see Generals Hammersley and Lindley. General Lindley will be in immediate command of the operations as all troops engaged in the attack will be Territorials.
   I trust the attack will succeed though to-day's did not, but in view of the urgency of the matter I feel the attempt ought to be made.
   It is absolutely necessary that I should see Smith.

Yours sincerely,
(*Sd*.) "Fred W. Stopford.

At mid-day, got a cable from the 9th Corps saying that Lindley's Division had duly gone at Hill 70, a key feature on the ridge, about 1,500 yards North-east of Yilghin Burnu — and had failed!

In giving me this news, Stopford proposes to make a second attack this afternoon with the same Division. Have caused Braithwaite to cable:

> Hear you propose attacking again. Chief doubts advisability with tired troops after morning's failure; if you agree consolidate where you are and rest and reorganize.

In a letter from Stopford in answer to my signal of yesterday from Fisherman's Hut, he says:

Kavak Tepe Attack Collapses

No. 1. Date, Aug. 9. Time, 4 p.m.
                      Place, Suvla Bay.
To:

DEAR SIR IAN,

I have received your message from Fisherman's Hut. Hammersley has not been able to advance to-day, but the Turks have been counter-attacking all day and he has had to put in one of the Territorial Brigades to prevent being driven back. I quite realize the importance of holding the high ground East of Suvla Bay, but as the Turks advance through the gap between the two Anafartas where all the roads are, it is absolutely necessary to keep sufficient troops between Anafarta Sagir and Ismail Oglu Tepe, as otherwise if I were to seize the high ground between Anafarta Sagir and Ejelmer Bay without securing this gap, I might find myself holding the heights and the Turks pouring down to the harbour behind me. I will bear what you say in mind, and if I get an opportunity with fresh troops of taking the heights whilst holding on tight to my right flank I will do so. I understand that one reason why it was necessary to go for Ismail Oglu Tepe was that if I did not hold the Turks there they would fire into the rear of Birdwood's troops attacking Hill 305.

I am, Sir,
Yours sincerely,

(*Sd*.) "FRED W. STOPFORD.

For myself I wish the Turks would try to pour down over that flat, open country by the Salt Lake to seize the beaches under the guns of the warships.

Well, we had Chunuk Bair in our hands the best part of two days and two nights. So far the Turks have never retaken trenches once we had fairly taken hold. Have they done so now? I hope not. Birdie and Godley are at work upon a scheme for its recapture. The Turks are well commanded: that I admit. Their Generals knew they were done unless they could quickly knock us off our Chunuk Bair. So they have done it. Never mind: never say die. Meanwhile we have the East Anglian Division available to-morrow, and I have been over in the G.S. marquee working out ways and means of taking Kavak Tepe which may also give us an outlook, more distant, but yet an outlook, on to the Dardanelles.

11th August, 1915. Imbros. Did not dare to break away from the wire ends. A see-saw of cardinal events between Suvla and Anzac.

A workable scheme of attack has now been put into such shape as to let Stopford dovetail his Corps orders into it, and first thing sent him this cable:

> G.H.Q. to IXth Corps. General Commanding wishes 54th Division Infantry to attack line Kavak Tepe peak 1195.5. at dawn to-morrow after night march to foothills; G.S.O. proceeding with detailed instructions. See Inglefield, make arrangements and give all assistance possible by landing 53rd Signal Company, water gear and tools. 53rd Division becomes general reserve.

At 4.30 p.m., a letter from Stopford anent the failure of the 53rd Division, — depressing in itself but still more so in its inferences as to the 54th Division. He says these troops showed "no attacking spirit at all. They did not come under heavy shell fire nor was the rifle fire very severe, but they not only showed no dash in attack but went back at slight provocation and went back a long way. Lots of the men lay down behind cover, etc. They went on when called upon to do so by Staff and other Officers but they seemed lost and under no leadership — in fact, they showed that they are not fit to put in the field without the help of Regulars. I really believe that if we had had one Brigade of Regulars here to set an example both the New Army and Territorials would have played up well with them but they have no standard to go by."

Worse follows, for Stopford takes back his assurance given me after my cable of the 9th when he said, "given water, guns and ammunition, I have no doubt about our being able to secure the hills." He tells me straight and without any beating about the bush, "I am sure they" (the Territorials) "would not secure the hills with any amount of guns, water and ammunition assuming ordinary opposition, as the attacking spirit was absent; chiefly owing to the want of leadership by the Officers."

Ignoring our Kavak Tepe scheme, he goes on then to ask me in so many words, not to try any attack with the 54th Division but to stick them into trenches.

This letter has driven me very nearly to my wits' ends. Things can't be so bad! None of us have any complaint at all of the New Army troops; only of their Old Army Generals. Stopford says the 13th Division were not reliable when they were at Helles, whereas now, under Godley at Anzac they have fought like lions.

Rushed off in this, the good tub *Imogene* (Lieutenant-Commander Potts). There the rushing ceased as she steamed along so slowly that we didn't get to Suvla till 7 p.m. Walked up with Braithwaite and Freddie to the 9th Corps Headquarters. Saw Stopford. Wrestled with him for over an hour; Braithwaite doing ditto with Reed.

Stopford urged that these last two Territorial formations sent out to us were sucked oranges, the good in them having been drafted away into France and replaced by rejections. He says he would have walked on to the watershed the first day had we only stiffened his force with the 29th Division. There happened to be some pretty decisive objections but there was no use entering into them then. So I merely told him that the 9th Corps and the Territorials being now well ashore we may be able to bring up the 29th. No doubt — had we a couple of Regular Divisions here — British or Indian — at full strength — no doubt we could astonish the world. Having the 53rd and the 54th Divisions, half-trained and at half strength, I tried to make Stopford see we must cut our coats with the stuff issued to us. The 54th were good last winter, and, even if the best have been picked out of them, the residue should do well under sound leadership: Inglefield was a practised old warrior, and would not let him down.

There was nothing solid to go upon in crying down the credit of the 54th beyond hearsay and the self-evident fact that they are half their nominal strength. To assume they won't put up a fight is a certain way of making the best troops gun-shy. We are standing up to our necks in a time problem, and the tide is on the rise. There is not a moment to spare. The Turks have reinforced and they have brought back their guns; that is true. Now they will begin to dig trenches — indeed they are already digging — and more and more enemy troops will be placed in reserve behind the Anafartas and to the East of the Tekke Tepe — Ejelmer Bay range. On the 10th the Helles people reported that, in spite of their efforts to hold the Turks, they had detached reinforcements to the North. These extra reinforcements may arrive to-morrow at Anzac or on the Anafartas; but, for at least another twenty four hours, they will not be able to get round to the high ridge between Anafarta and Ejelmer Bay. So far as can be seen by aeroplane scouting, this ridge is still unoccupied; certainly it is unentrenched.

Stopford who, at first, was dead set on digging agreed to have a dart at Kavak Tepe. He will throw the 54th at it. He will turn out the 9th Corps and, if chance offers, they will attack along their own front. His chief remaining ghost inhabits the jungly bit of country between Anafarta Ova and the foothills. In that belt he fears the Turkish snipers may harass our line of supply so that, when the heights are held, we may find it hard to feed and water our garrison. The New Armies and Territorials have no trained counter-snipers and are much at the mercy of the skilled Anatolian shikarris who haunt the close country.

So I suggested blockhouses on the South African system to protect our line where it passed through the three quarters of a mile or so of close country. The enemy artillery would not spot them amongst the trees. I promised him also one hundred picked Australian bushmen, New Zealand Maoris and Gurkhas to act as scouts and counter-snipers.

Stopford took to this idea very kindly; has fixed up a Conference of 9th Corps and Territorial Generals early to-morrow morning to discuss the whole plan, and will make every effort to occupy Kavak Tepe to-morrow night. Stopford seemed in much better form to-night; I think he is more fit: there has been 24 hours' delay but by waiting that time Inglefield and the Essex will have the help of a body of first-class scouts — quite a luminous notion. Stopford, himself, presides at to-morrow's Conference. Inglefield is a good, straight fellow, not so young as we were in South Africa, but quite all right.

Boarded the *Imogene*. Dropped anchor at 11 p.m. at Imbros.

12th August, 1915. Imbros. Last thing last night Stopford promised to let me know the result of the conference to be held at his Headquarters, and upon the plans for the lines of supply. Sent him a reminder:

Kavak Tepe Attack Collapses

G.H.Q. to IXth Corps. Have you arranged practical system for supplying troops in the event of Tekke Tepe ridge being secured?

A cable from K.:

I am sorry about the Xth and XIth Divisions in which I had great confidence. Could you not ginger them up? The utmost energy and dashare required for these operations or they will again revert to trench warfare.

K.'s disappointment makes me feel *sick*! I know the great hopes he has built on these magnificent Divisions and I know equally well that he is not capable of understanding how he has cut his own throat, the men's throats and mine, by not sending young and up-to-date Generals to run them. K. in this, and this alone, is with Tolstoi. The men are everything; the man nothing. Have cabled back saying, "I am acting absolutely as you indicate by 'ginger'; I only got back at 11 last night from a further application of that commodity. As a result a fresh attack will be made tomorrow morning by the IXth Corps and the LIVth Division."

As to the New Army I point out to K. that "they are fighting under conditions quite foreign to their training and moreover they have no regulars to set them a standard": also, (and pray Heaven it is truth) "Everyone is fully alive to the necessity for dash, so I trust the attack of to-morrow will be much better done than were the two previous attempts."

Hardly had my cable to K. been despatched when Stopford gives us a sample specimen of "dash" by his answer to my reminder. He wires:

IXth Corps to G.H.Q. I foresee very great difficulty. The only system possible at first probably will be convoy under escort.

Twelve hours ago, more or less, Stopford had agreed that there was a difficulty which it was up to him to solve and that, at first, (i.e., till blockhouses had been built) the system would be convoy under escort. We ask him what he had done, expecting to get the particulars worked out by his Staff after the conference of Generals, and this is the reply!

Five minutes later, in came another wire giving the general situation at Suvla; saying the 53rd Division had failed to clear ground from which the right of the advance of the 54th Division might be threatened, and that Stopford wished to postpone his night march another four and twenty hours.

So this is the result of our "ginger," and Braithwaite or I must rush over to Suvla at once. Meanwhile, tactics and Kavak Tepe must wait.

Wired back:

> In the circumstances the operation for to-morrow is postponed. Chief sending C.G.S. over now to see you.

Braithwaite went: is back now: has seen both Stopford and Reed: has agreed (with a sad heart) on my behalf to the night march being put off another twenty four hours.

Have had, therefore, to cable K. again, shouldering the heavy blame of this further delay:

> (No. M.F. 545). From General Sir Ian Hamilton to Earl Kitchener. After anxiously weighing the pros and cons, I have decided that it is wiser to wait another 24 hours before carrying out the general attack mentioned in my No. M.F. 543. Braithwaite has just returned from the IXth Corps, and he found that the spirit and general organization were improving rapidly. A small attack by a Brigade, which promised well, was in progress. This morning the Xth Division captured a trench.

The story of the Suvla Council of War: At first the Generals were for fighting. Inglefield, of the LIVth, who is told off for the attack, was keen. All he asked was, a clean start from Anafarta Ova. If his Division could jump off, intact and fresh, from that well-watered half-way house, Kavak Tepe was his. The LIIIrd Division for their part agreed to make good Anafarta Ova; to clear out the snipers and to hold the place as a base for the LIVth.

So at 10 a.m. Stopford issued orders saying the LIVth must march off at 4 p.m. moving East of Anafarta Ova. Then, — when at last all seemed settled, in came a message from the G.O.C. LIIIrd Division, saying he could not undertake to clear Anafarta

Ova of snipers and to hold it as a cover to the advance of the LIVth.

Stopford thereupon cancelled his first order, and, at 1.15 p.m., issued fresh orders directing the LIVth Division *to send in one of their own Brigades* as an advance guard to clear the ground up to a point East of Anafarta Ova. Braithwaite stayed at Corps Headquarters at Suvla until this Brigade, the 163rd, was moving on Anafarta Ova driving the snipers before them. Mahon, too, after sitting for three days where I left him on the morning of the 9th, has got tired of looking at the gendarmesand has carried their trenches by the forbidden frontal bayonet charge without much trouble or loss although, naturally, these trenches have been strengthened during the interval.

Amidst these tactical miss-fires entered Hankey. He has had a cable from his brother Secretary, Bonham Carter, saying the Prime Minister wishes him to stay on longer and that Lord K. would like to know if he can do anything to give an impetus to the operations. Hankey showed me this cable; also his answer:

> Reference your 6910. I am glad to stay as desired. The chief thing you could send to help the present operations would be more ammunition. For supplies already sent everyone is most grateful. It is also important that units should be kept up to strength.
>
> As General Officer Commanding has already apprised you fully of the situation I have nothing to add.

In the Gordons' Mess "a Marine" used to stand as synonym for emptiness. Asquith's "Marine"[*] is the reverse. Into two sentences totalling 27 words he boils down the drift of hundreds of cables and letters.

13th August, 1915. Imbros. Well, I must put it down. Worked till lunch. In the afternoon, left in H.M.S. *Arno* and sailed over to Suvla to have a last look over the *band-o-bast* for to-morrow's twice to-morrowed effort. First, saw the Admiral and Commodore

---

[*] Hankey belonged to the Royal Marine Artillery. — *Ian H., 1920.*

who are simply dancing with impatience. No wonder. Whether or no Kavak Tepe summit gives a useful outlook on to the back of Sari Bair and the Dardanelles, at least it will give us the whip hand of the guns on the Anafarta ridge and save our ships from the annoying attentions they are beginning to receive. The sailors think too they have worked out an extra good scheme for ship and shore guns.

Stopford then came aboard; in the mood he was in aboard the *Jonquil* on the 8th, — only more so! The Divisional Generals are without hope, that is the text of his sermon. Hopeless about to-night, or to-morrow, that is to say; for there are rosy visions and to spare for next week, or the week after, or any other time, so long as it is not too near us. There is something in this beats me. We are alive — we are quite all right — the Brigade of the LIVth sent on to Kuchuk Anafarta Ova made good its point. True, one battalion got separated from its comrades in the forest and was badly cut up by Turkish snipers just as was Braddock's force by the Redskins, but this, though tragic, is but a tiny incident of a great modern battle and the rest of the 163rd Brigade have not suffered and hold the spot whence, it was settled, the attack on Kavak Tepe should jump off. Nothing practical or tactical seems to have occurred to force us to drop our plan.

But no; Stopford and Reed count the LIIIrd Division as finished: the LIVth incapable of attack; the rest of the IXth Corps immovable.

If I accept; we have lost this battle. We are not beaten now — the men are not — but if I accept, we are held up.

There is no way out. Whether there is any good looking back even for one moment, God knows; I doubt it! But I feel so acutely, I seem to see so clearly, where our push for Constantinople first began to quit the rails, that I must put it down right here. The moment was when I asked for Rawlinson or Byng, and when, in reply, the keen, the young, the fit, the up-to-date Commanders were all barred, simply and solely that Mahon should not be disturbed in his Divisional Command. I resisted it very strongly: I went so far as to remind K. in my cable of his own sad disappointment at Bloemfontein when he (K.) had offered him a Cavalry Brigade and he returned instead to his appointment in the Sudan. The question that keeps troubling me is, ought I to have fought it further; ought I to have resigned sooner than allow generals old and yet inexperienced to be foisted on to me?

These stories about the troops? I do not accept them. The troops have lost heavily but they are right if there were leaders.

I know quite well both Territorial Divisions. I knew them in England that is to say. Since then, they have had their eyes picked out. They have been through the strainer and the best officers and men and the best battalions have been serving for months past in France. The three show battalions in the 54th (Essex) Division are in France and their places have been taken by the 10th and 11th London and by the 8th Hants. Essex is good; London is good and Hants is good; but the trinity is not Territorial. The same with the Welshmen.

Yet even so; taking these Territorials as they are; a scratch lot; half strength; no artillery; not a patch upon the original Divisions as I inspected them in England six months ago; even so, they'd fight right enough and keen enough if they were set fair and square at their fence.

In the fight of the 10th the Welshmen were not given a chance. Sent in on a narrow front — jammed into a pocket; — as they began to climb the spur they caught it from the guns, rifles and machine guns on both flanks.

We might still do something with a change of commanders. But I have been long enough Military Secretary both in India and at home to realize that ruthlessness here is apt to be a two-edged sword. You can't clap a new head on to old shoulders without upsetting circulation and equilibrium. Still, I would harden my heart to it now — to-night — were not my hands tied by Mahon's seniority. Mahon is the next senior — in the whole force he stands next to myself. Had not Bruce Hamilton been barred by the P.M. when I wanted to put him in vice Hunter-Weston at Helles, the problem would be simple enough. Even if I had not, at the outset, given that well-tried, thrusting old fighter the conduct of the Suvla enterprise, at least I would have brought him in on the morning of the 9th instant quite easily and without causing any upset to anyone or anything. He ranks both Stopford and Mahon and nothing would have been simpler than to let him bring up a contingent of troops from Helles, when, automatically, he would have taken command in the Suvla area. What it would have meant to have had a man imbued with the attack spirit at the head of this IXth Corps would have been just — victory!

Anchored at 9 p.m. and, before going to bed, sent following cable:

> From General Sir Ian Hamilton to Secretary of State for War.
>
> The result of my visit to the IXth Corps, from which I am just back, has bitterly disappointed me. There is nothing for it but to allow them time to rest and reorganize, unless I force Stopford and his Divisional Generals to undertake a general action for which, in their present frame of mind, they have no heart. In fact, these generals are unfit for it. With exceeding reluctance I am obliged to give them time to rest and reorganize their troops.
>
> Though we were to repeat our landing operations a hundred times, we would never dare hope to reproduce conditions so favourable as to put one division ashore under cover of dark and, as the day broke, have the next division sailing in to its support. No advantage was taken of these favourable conditions and, for reasons which I can only explain by letter, the swift advance was not delivered, — therefore, the mischief is done. Until we are ready to advance again, reorganized and complete, we must go slow.

14th August, 1915. Imbros. Before breakfast, Braithwaite brought me a statement of our interview of last night with Stopford. He dictated it, directly he got back last night; i.e., about three hours after the event. I agree with every word:

> Notes of an interview which took place on board H.M.S. *Triad* between 6 and 7 p.m. on the 13th August, 1915, between the General Commanding and Sir Frederick Stopford, commanding 9th Corps.
>
> *Present*:
>
> General Sir Ian Hamilton, G.C.B., D.S.O., A.D.C.,
> Lieut.-General Hon. Sir Frederick Stopford, K.C.M.G., etc.,
> Major-General Braithwaite, C.B.

Kavak Tepe Attack Collapses

Sir Frederick represented that the 9th Corps were not fit to undertake an advance at the present moment. Questioned why, he replied that the losses had been considerable, that the disorganization of units was very great, and that the length of the line he had to hold was all too thinly held as it was. He stated that his Divisional Generals were entirely of the same opinion as himself; in fact, he gave us completely the impression that they were 'not for it,' but he only specifically mentioned Hammersley and Lindley. He said water was no difficulty. He implied that the troops were getting better every day, and given time to rest and reorganize, he thought they would be able in time to make an advance. But he was very emphatic on the point that at present such a thing as an attack had practically no chance of success. He told us that the opposition in the centre about Anafarta Ova could no longer be classed as sniping, but that it was regular opposition. But as he also told us that his landing was an opposed landing, I think perhaps that during the short time he has been on active service in this country he has not quite realized what opposition really means. But the salient fact remains that none of his Divisional Generals who would be employed in the attack thought that that attack would have any chance of success whatever. Indeed, he saw every difficulty, and though he kept saying that he was an optimist, he foresaw every bad thing that could possibly happen and none of the bright spots. It was a most depressing interview, but it left no doubt in the minds of the hearers that it would be quite useless to order an attack to be undertaken by a Commander and Divisional Generals whose hearts were confessedly not in it, who saw a Turk behind every bush, a battalion behind every hill, and a Brigade behind every mountain.

At lunch time Lord K. answered my last night's cable:

If you should deem it necessary to replace Stopford, Mahon and Hammersley, have you any competent Generals to take their place? From your report I think Stopford should come home.

This is a young man's war, and we must have commanding officers that will take full advantage of opportunities which occur but seldom. If, therefore, any Generals fail, do not hesitate to act promptly.

Any Generals I have available I will send you.

Close on the top of this tardy appreciation of youth, comes

another cable from him saying he has asked French to let me have Byng, Horne and Kavanagh. "I hope," he says, "Stopford has been relieved by you already."

Have cabled back thanking him with all my heart; saying I shall be glad of the Generals he mentions as "Byng, Kavanagh and Horne are all flyers."

Between them, these two messages have cleared the air. Mahon's seniority has been at the root of this evil. K.'s conscience tells him so and, therefore, he pricks his name now upon the fatal list. But he did not know, when he cabled, that Mahon had done well. I shall replace Stopford forthwith by de Lisle and chance Mahon's seniority.

De Robeck came over for an hour in the evening.

Lord and Lady Brassey arrived in the *Sunbeam*, together with two young friends. They have both of them shown great enterprise in getting here. The dear old man gave me a warm greeting, but also something of a shock by talking about our terrible defeat: by condoling and by saying I had been asked to do the impossible. I have *not* been asked to do anything impossible in taking Constantinople. The feat is perfectly feasible. For the third time since we began it trembled in the balance a week ago. Nor is the capture of Suvla Bay and the linking up thereof with Anzac a defeat: a cruel disappointment, no doubt, but not a defeat; for, two more such defeats, measured in mere acreage, will give us the Narrows. A doctor at Kephalos, it seems, infected them with this poison of despondency. In their *Sunbeam* they will make first class carriers.

15th August, 1915. Imbros. De Lisle has come over to relieve Stopford. He has got his first instructions[*] and is in close communication with myself and General Staff on the preparations for the next move which will be supported by the Yeomanry from Egypt and by some more artillery. I had meant to make time to run across to Suvla to-day but Stopford may wish to see me on his way to Mudros so I shall sit tight in case he does.

---

[*] See Appendix IV containing actual letter of instructions. — *Ian H., 1920.*

Kavak Tepe Attack Collapses 369

Cables to and from K. about our new Generals. Byng, Maude and Fanshawe are coming. A brilliant trio. All of the three Fanshawe brothers are good; this one worked under me on Salisbury Plain. Maude is splendid! Byng will make every one happy; he never spares himself. K. has agreed to let de Lisle hold the command of the 9th Corps until Byng turns up. He wants Birdie to take over the control of the whole of the Northern theatre, i.e., Anzac and Suvla. I must think over this. Meanwhile, have cabled back, "I am enchanted to hear Byng, Maude and Fanshawe are coming — I could wish for no better men."

Sent also following which explains itself:

When I appointed de Lisle to command temporarily the IXth Corps I sent the following telegram to Mahon:

'Although de Lisle is junior to you, Sir Ian hopes that you will waive your seniority and continue in command of the Xth Division, at any rate during the present phase of operations.'

To this Mahon sent the following reply:

'I respectfully decline to waive my seniority and to serve under the officer you name. Please let me know to whom I am to hand over the command of the Division.'

Consequently, I have appointed Brigadier-General F. F. Hill to command temporarily the Division and have ordered Mahon to go to Mudros to await orders. Will you please send orders as to his disposal. As Peyton is not due from Egypt till 18th August, he was not in any case available.

Also:

Personal. You will like to know that the XIIIth Division is said to have fought very well and with great tenacity of spirit. In many instances poor company leading is said to have been responsible for undue losses.

16th August, 1915. Imbros. A great press of business. Amongst other work, have written a long cable home giving them the whole story up to date. Lots of petty troubles. Stopford goes to Mudros direct. De Lisle makes a thorough overhaul at Suvla.

Glyn and Hankey both looked in upon me. It is a relief to have an outsider of Hankey's calibre on the spot. He said, "Thank God!" when he heard of K.'s cable, and urged Birdie should be told off to take Suvla in hand, in his stead. I suppose the G.S. have let him get wind of K.'s identical suggestion. As I told Hankey, I have not yet made up my mind. But it would be an awkward job for Birdie with all the Anzacs to run, and no nearer Suvla really — in point of time — than we are. Nor is he staffed for so big a business. Hankey has been too long away from executive work to realize that difficulty. But the decisive factor is this; that having been closely associated with him and with his work for a good many years, I know as Hankey cannot know, how much of his strength lies in his personal touch and presence: spread his powers too wide he loses that touch. Felt the better for my talk with Hankey. He can grasp the bigness of what we are up against and can yet keep his head and see that the game is worth the candle and that it is in our hands the moment we make up our minds to pay the price of the illuminant.

Have written to the Chief of the Imperial General Staff saying:

> I have just been through a horrible mental crisis quite different from the ordinary anxiety of the battlefield, where I usually see what I think to be my way and chance it. I refer to Freddy Stopford. Here is a man who has committed no fault; whose life-long conscientious study of his profession has borne the best fruits in letting him see the right thing to do and how it should be done. And yet he fails when many a man possessing not one quarter of his military qualifications carries on with flying colours. For there is no use beating about the bush now and, simply, he was not big enough in character to face up to the situation. It overwhelmed him.

[...]

> A month ago we had the Turks down, undoubtedly and, whenever we could get a little ammunition together, we were confident we could take a line of trenches. As for their attacks, it was

obvious their men were not for it. Now their four new Divisions of fine fighting material seem to have animated the whole of the rest of the force with their spirit, and the Turks have never fought so boldly as they are doing to-day. They are tough to crack, but D.V., we will be the tougher of the two.

17th August, 1915. Imbros. From his cable of the 14th, K. seems prepared to see me relieve Mahon of his command. But Mahon is a fighter and if I give him time to think over things a bit at Mudros, he'll be sure to think better. I am sure the wisest course to take, is to take time. A Lieutenant-General in the British Army chucking up his command whilst his Division is actually under fire — is a very unhappy affair. Lord Bobs used to say that a soldier asked, for the good of the cause, to serve as a drummer boy under his worst enemy should do so not only with alacrity but with joy. Braithwaite agrees with me that we must just take the responsibility of doing nothing at all and of leaving him quietly to cool down at Mudros. Hill, who carries on, was the General in command at Mitylene when I inspected there; he is a good fellow; he was anxious to push on upon that fatal 7th August at Suvla and everyone says he is a stout fellow.

Have got the name of the doctor who upset the Brasseys with his yarns. He declares he only retailed the tales of the wounded youngsters whom he tended. No more to be said. He has studied microbes extensively but one genus has clearly escaped his notice: he has never studied or grasped the fell methods of the microbes of rumour or panic. Am I sure that I myself have not crabbed my own show a bit in telling the full story of our fight to K. this afternoon? No, I am by no means sure.

(No. M.F. 562.) From General Sir Ian Hamilton to Earl Kitchener. Have thought it best to lay the truth fully before you, and am now able to give a complete *résumé* of the past week's operations, and an appreciation of the situation confronting me.

In broad outline, my plan was to hold the Turks in the Southern zone by constant activity of French and VIIIth Corps, and to throw all the reinforcements into the Northern zone with the object of defeating the enemy opposite Anzac, seizing a new base at Suvla, and gaining a position astride the narrow part of the peninsula. With this object, I reinforced General Birdwood with the XIIIth Division, 29th Brigade, Xth Division, and 29th Indian Brigade, all of which were secretly dribbled ashore at Anzac Cove on the three nights preceding commencement of operations. This was done without arousing the suspicions of the enemy. Arrangements were made for the XIth Division to land at Suvla Bay on the same night as General Birdwood commenced his attack. Meanwhile, the Turks were deceived by ill-concealed preparations for landings on Asiatic coast near Mitylene, at Enos, South of Gaba Tepe.

Following is detailed plan of operations:

On the afternoon of 6th August the VIIIth Corps were to attack Krithia trenches, and simultaneously General Birdwood was to attack Lone Pine trenches on his right front, as though attempting to break out in this direction. In this way it was hoped to draw the Turkish reinforcements towards Krithia and Gaba Tepe and away from Anzac's left and Suvla Bay. At 10 p.m. General Birdwood's main attack was to develop on his left flank, the Turkish outposts were to be rushed and an advance made in several columns up the precipitous ravines leading to Chunuk Bair and the summit of Hill 305, which it was hoped might be captured before daybreak.

As soon as the high ridge was in our hands an advance was to be made down the Hill 305 to take in the rear the trenches on Baby 700 (see enlarged map of Anzac positions) and at the same time the troops in the original Anzac position were to attack all along the line in an endeavour to break out and hurl the enemy off the Sari Bair. Mean while the XIth Division was to commence landing 10.30 p.m. on 6th August, one brigade inside Suvla Bay, two brigades on shore to South were to seize and hold all hills covering Bay and especially Yilghin Burnu and Ismail Oglu Tepe on which enemy were believed to have guns which could bring fire to bear either on back of General Birdwood's advance on Hill 305, or on Suvla Bay. The ridge from Anafarta Sagir to Aja Liman was also to be lightly held. The Xth Division, less one brigade, was to follow XIth Division at daybreak and LIIIrd Division was held in general reserve. The LIVth Division had not arrived and could not be employed in the first instance.

The moment Stopford had fulfilled the above tasks, which, owing to the small number of the enemy in this neighbourhood and the absence of any organized system of trenches, were considered comparatively easy, he was to advance South-west through Biyuk Anafarta with the object of assisting Birdwood in the event of his attack being held up.

Reliable information indicated the strength of the enemy about Suvla Bay to be one regiment, one squadron and some Gendarmerie with at most twelve guns, and events have shown that this estimate was correct. It was also believed that the enemy had 36,000 in the Southern zone, 27,000 against Anzac, and 37,000 in reserve. Also 45,000 near Keshan who could not arrive for three days and 10,000 on Asiatic shore.

The attack by the VIIIth Corps opposite Krithia took place as arranged, but was met by determined opposition. Some enemy trenches were captured, but the Turks were found in great strength and full of fight. They counter-attacked repeatedly on the night of 6th/7th, and eventually regained the ground we had taken. Prisoners captured stated that the Turks had planned to attack us that night in any case which accounts for their strength.

In the Northern zone General Birdwood's afternoon attack was successful and Lone Pine trenches were captured by a most gallant Australian assault. Throughout the day, and for three successive days the enemy made repeated attempts to recapture the position, but each time were repulsed with severe loss. At 10 p.m. the main advance on the left flank by the New Zealanders, XIIIth Division, 29th Brigade and Cox's Brigade began, and in spite of stupendous difficulties, moving by night in most difficult country, all enemy's posts in foot of hills were rushed and captured up to and including Damakjelik Bair. The enemy was partly surprised, but his reinforcements were all called up, and this, coupled with the extreme difficulty of the country, made it impossible to reach the crest of the hill that day or the following. The position immediately below the crest, however, was reached, and on the morning of the 8th, after severe fighting, two battalions of the XIIIth Division and Gurkhas reached the top of Kurt Ketchede, and two battalions of New Zealanders established themselves on the crest of the ridge at Chunuk Bair.

Unfortunately, the troops on Kurt Ketchede were shelled off the ridge by our own gun fire, and were unable to recapture it; and 48 hours later two battalions of the XIIIth Division, who had relieved tired New Zealanders on Chunuk Bair, were driven back by determined daybreak assault, carried by the Turks in many successive lines, shoulder to shoulder. Our troops were too weary, and much too disorganized to make a counter-attack at that time, and could only maintain positions below crest. Water supply, which had always been an anxiety, began to fail, and grave difficulties arose which prevented the possibility of reinforcing Birdwood, and almost necessitated our giving up our gains. All this, however, has now been put right.

Meanwhile, Stopford's Corps at Suvla had landed most successfully, but, owing to lack of energy and determination on the part of leaders, and, perhaps, partly to the inexperience of the troops, had failed to take advantage of the opportunities as already reported.

The result is that my coup has so far failed. It was soon realized that it was necessary to give impetus to the IXth Corps, and the LIIIrd Division was put in on 8th-9th. By this time the LIVth Division was available as general reserve. Unfortunately, the LIIIrd Division broke in my hand, leaving me like a fencer with rapier broken, and by the time the LIVth Division arrived the remaining troops of the Corps were too tired and disorganized for further immediate effort.

The IXth Corps holds the position from Kiretch Tepe Sirt, bench mark 2; Sulajik; Yilghin Burnu, with right flank thrown south to connect with Birdwood at Kazlar Chair. Godley has picket between Kazlar Chair and Damakjelik Bair, whence his line runs South-east to the spur South of Abdel Rahman Bair, thence South-west to square 80 D, South-east again to within 300 yards of Point 161 on Chunuk Bair, and thence back to the left of the Anzac position.

De Lisle has at his disposal the Xth Division, less one brigade, the XIth, LIIIrd and LIVth Divisions; total rifles, owing to casualties, under 30,000. The Suvla losses have been too severe considering extent and nature of the fighting that has taken place, and can only be attributed to the inexperience of the troops and their leaders, and the daring way in which the enemy skirmishers presumed upon it in the broken and wooded country. Birdwood has lost about 13,000 since the action began, and has now available some 25,000 rifles. The VIIIth Corps has 23,000 rifles, and the French 17,000 rifles.

The Turks have continued to be most active in the South, no doubt with the object of preventing us moving troops, but apparently they have now no more than 35,000 in this zone. The majority of the enemy Commander's troops are against Anzac and in reserve in the valley between Hills 305 and 261, his strategic flank.

In the Northern zone, in the fighting line at Suvla and Anzac and in reserve he may now have in all 75,000, and can either reinforce Hill 305 or issue through the gap between the two Anafartas to oppose any attack on Ismail Oglu Tepe or on the ridge running thence to Anafarta Sagir. He has guns on Hill 305, on Ismail Oglu Tepe, and on the ridge North of Anafarta Sagir from which he can shell landing places at Suvla Bay, but is not holding the latter ridge in strength, nor do I think he has enough troops to enable him to do so.

The position regarding the Turkish reinforcements from Keshan

Kavak Tepe Attack Collapses   375

is not clear. Only small parties have been located by aeroplanes marching South, and it appears that either this information was incorrect or that the enemy's forces had already got as far as the peninsula before fighting began.

I consider it urgently necessary to seize Ismail Oglu Tepe and Anafarta Sagir at the earliest possible moment, and I have ordered de Lisle to make the attempt at the earliest opportunity. I have also ordered Birdwood to make a fresh attack on Hill 305 as soon as troops are reorganized and the difficulties of water supply solved, but for this he will require drafts and fresh troops. I have great hopes that these attacks may yet be successful, but it is impossible to disguise the fact that owing to the failure of the IXth Corps to take advantage of opportunities and the fact that surprise may now be absent, and that the enemy is prepared and in much greater strength, my difficulties are enormously increased. In any case my cadres will be so depleted as a result of action that I shall need large reinforcements to enable me to bring the operations to a happy conclusion.

The Turkish losses have been heavier than ours, and the total number of prisoners taken is 702, but I estimate that they have now in the peninsula at least 110,000 rifles to my 95,000 and they have all the advantage of position. They have, apparently, all the ammunition they need and obtain reinforcements as they are wanted. In particular, we have had no news of the arrival of the 45,000 troops reported to be at Keshan, and only one of the Asiatic Divisions has as yet come over. I had hoped that their reinforcements would be of poor quality and not a match for ours but this is not the case, and unfortunately the Turks have temporarily gained the moral ascendency over some of our new troops. If, therefore, this campaign is to be brought to an early and successful conclusion large reinforcements will have to be sent to me — drafts for the formations already here, and new formations with considerably reduced proportion of artillery. It has become a question of who can slog longest and hardest.

Owing to the difficulty of carrying on a winter campaign, and the lateness of the season, these troops should be sent immediately. My British Divisions are at present 45,000 under establishment, exclusive of about 9,000 promised or on the way. If this deficit were made up, and new formations totalling 50,000 rifles sent out as well, these, with the 60,000 rifles which I estimate I shall have at the time of their arrival, should give me the necessary superiority, unless the absence of other enemies allows the Turks to bring up large additional reinforcements.

I hope you will realize how nearly this operation was a success complete beyond anticipation. The surprise was complete, and the army was thrown ashore in record time, practically without loss, and a little more push on the part of the IXth Corps would have relieved the pressure on Anzac, facilitated the retention of Chunuk Bair, secured Suvla Bay as a port, and threatened the enemy's right in a way that should have enabled Anzac to turn a success into a great victory.

We are up against the Turkish Army which is well commanded and fighting bravely.

After all's said and done the troops at Helles and Anzac are still perfectly game and we have got nearer our goal. We started forth to:

(1) Seize Suvla Bay;
(2) Break out of Anzac and join on to Suvla;
(3) Seize Sari Bair crestline;
(4) Hold enough of the hinterland of Suvla Bay to make it a comfortable harbour.

(1) and (2) we have carried through handsomely. We have trebled our holding at Anzac and we have put Suvla Bay in our pocket. (3) we have not done; we are short of it by a couple of hundred yards; (4) we have not done; it is a practicable harbour but subject certainly to annoyance. In honest, gambler's language, we have won a good stake but we have not broke the Ottoman Bank.

De Lisle reports confusion throughout Suvla Bay area. He *must* have three or four days to pull the troops together before he organizes a fresh offensive. The IXth Corps has been *un corps sans tête*.

Chapter XVII – The Last Battle

18th August, 1915. Imbros. Freddie and I left in the *Arno* this morning; Braithwaite and his boy Val came with us. We sailed for Suvla *via* Anzac and held a meeting which was nearer a Council of War than anything up to date. Dawnay, Deedes and Beadon stood by; so did Generals Skeen, Hammersley and Peyton. Reed, C.G.S., IXth Corps, was also present. The discussion of the steps to be taken within the next two or three days lasted an hour and a half. Every one who spoke had studied the data and the ground and there was no divergence of view, which was a comfort. Our attack will have as its objective the seizure of a foothold on the high ground. Anzacs will co-operate. As I explained to the Generals, we hardly dare hope to make a clean break through till drafts and fresh munitions arrive as the Turks now have had too long to dig in. But if we can seize and keep a point upon the watershed (however small) from which we can observe the drop of our shell, we can knock out the landing places of the Turks. At the end, I told them I had asked for 95,000 fresh rifles, 50,000 in new formations, 45,000 to bring my skeleton units up to strength, adding, that if I was refused that help then I felt Government had better get someone cleverer than myself to put their Fleet into the Marmora.

The Generals seemed satisfied with my demands and sympathetic towards my personal attitude.

As to the coming attack, the tone of the Conference was hopeful. They agreed that the nut was hard for our enfeebled forces to crack, but they seemed to think that if we were once to get the enemy on the run, with the old 29th Division and the new, keen Yeomanry on their heels, we might yet go further than we expected. One Brigade of the 29th Division has been brought round from Helles to put shape and form into the 53rd Division. Peyton's men are to be attached to the Irish Division. There is a new spirit of energy and hope in the higher ranks but the men have meanwhile been aimlessly marched and counter-marched, muddled, and knocked about so that their spirit has suffered in consequence.

No end of Yeomen on the beaches; the cream of agricultural England. Many of them recognized me from my various home inspections. Would like very much to have had a war inspection, but the enemy gunners are too inquisitive.

De Lisle tells me he has now been round every corner of Suvla and that the want of grip throughout the higher command has been worse than he dared to put on paper. To reorganize will take several weeks; but we have to try and act within two or three days.

Skeen told us that when the Turks stuck up a placard saying Warsaw had fallen, the Australians gave three hearty cheers.

The chief trouble in making plans for the coming attack lies in the want of cover on, and for a mile inland of, the Suvla Bay beaches. The whole stretch of the flat land immediately East and South of the Bay lies open to the Turkish gunners. This is no longer a serious drawback if the men are holding lines of trenches. But when the trench system is not yet in working order, and they want to deploy, then it is so awkward a factor that I would have been prepared to turn the whole battle into a night attack. The others were not for it. They thought that the troops were not highly enough trained and had lost too many officers to be able to find their way over this country in the darkness. They are in immediate touch with the men: I am not.

Lindley asked if he might walk with me to the Beach, and on the way down he told me frankly his Division had gone to pieces and that he did not feel it in himself to pull it together again. Very fine of him to make a clean breast of it, I thought, and said so: also advised him to put what he had told me into writing to de Lisle, when we will relieve him and I promised for my part, to try and fit him with some honourable but less onerous job.

On Hammersley's report, Sitwell, Brigadier of the 34th Brigade, 11th Division, has just been relieved of his command.

19th August, 1915. Imbros. Sat sweating here, literally and metaphorically, from morn till dewy eve. King's Messenger left in the evening. Altham came over from Mudros. He stays to-night and we will work together to-morrow when the mails are off my mind.

Hankey dined and left with the King's Messenger by the *Imogene*. He has been a real help. The Staff has never quite cottoned to the chief among us takin' notes, but that is, I think, from a notion that it is not loyal to Lord K. to press the P.M.'s P.S. too closely to their bosom. From my personal standpoint, it will be worth anything to us if, amidst the flood of false gossip pouring out by this very mail to our Dardanelles Committee, to the Press, to Egypt and to London Drawing Rooms, we have sticking up out of it, even one little rock in the shape of an eye-witness.

A shocking aeroplane smash up within a few yards of us. A brilliant young Officer (Captain Collet of the R.F.C.) killed outright and three men badly hurt.

20th August, 1915. Stayed in my tent keeping an eye on to-morrow. Put through a lot with Altham. Am pressing him to hurry up with his canteens at Helles, Anzac and Suvla. In May I cabled the Q.M.G. begging him either to let me run a canteen on the lines of the South African Field Force Canteen, myself; or, to run it from home, himself; or, to put the business into the hands of some private firm like the Mess and Canteen Company, or Lipton's, or Harrods or anything he liked. In South Africa we could often buy something. In France our troops can buy anything. Here, had they each the purse of Fortunatus, they could buy nothing. A matter this, I won't say of life and death, but of sickness and health. Now, after three months without change of diet, the first canteen ship is about due. A mere flea bite of £10,000 worth. I am sending the whole of it to the Anzacs to whom it will hardly be more use than a bun is to a she bear. Only yesterday a letter came in from Birdie telling me that the doctors all say that the sameness of the food is making the men sick. The rations are A.1., but his men now loathe the very look of them after having had nothing else for three months. Birdie says, "If we could only get this wretched canteen ship along, and if, when she comes she contains anything like condiments to let them buy freely from her, I believe it would make all the difference in the world. But the fact remains that at present we cannot count on anything like a big effort from the men who have been here all these months."

De Robeck came over at 4 p.m., by formal appointment, to talk business, and deadly serious business at that! He has heard, by cable I suppose, that the people at home will see him through if he sees his way to strike a blow with the Fleet. He takes this as a pretty strong hint to push through, or, to make some sort of a battleship attack to support us. De Robeck knows that when the Fleet goes in our fighting strength goes up. But he can gauge, as I cannot, the dangers the Fleet will thereby incur. Every personal motive urges me to urge him on. But I have no right to shove my oar in — no right at all — until I can say that we are done unless the Fleet do make an attack. Can I say so? No; if we get the drafts and munitions we can still open the Straits on our own and without calling on the sister Service for further sacrifice. So I fell back on first principles and said he must attack if he thought it right from the naval point of view but that we soldiers did not call for succour or ask him to do anything desperate: "You know how we stand," I said; "do what is right from the naval point of view and as to what *is* right from that point of view, I am no judge."

The Admiral went away: I have been no help to him but I can't help it.

Hardly had he gone when Braithwaite (who had heard what was in the wind by a side wind) came and besought me to try and induce the Admiral to slip his battleships at the Straits. All the younger men of war are dying to have a dash, he said. That's as it may be but my mind is clear. If a sailor on land is a fish out of water, a soldier at sea is like a game cock in a duckpond. When de Robeck said on March 22nd he wanted the help of the whole Army that was quite in order. He would not have been in order — at least, I don't think so — had he said in what manner he wanted the Army to act after it had got ashore. We are being helped now by the Navy; daily, hourly: we could not exist without the Fleet; but it is not for me to say I think the battleships should or should not take chances of mines and torpedoes.

Brodrick is quite seedy. We are all afraid he won't be able to stick it out much longer although he is making the most heroic efforts. In the morning I attended the funeral of young Collet, killed yesterday so tragically. A long, slow march through heavy sand all along the beach to Kephalos; then up through some small rocky gullies, frightfully hot, until, at last, we reached a graveyard. The congregation numbered many of the poor boy's comrades who seemed much cut up about his untimely end.

The P.M. has answered my cable to Lord K. asking for 45,000 rifles to fill up and for 50,000 fresh rifles. K. is in France, he says, and I will have my answer when he gets back. The 5th Royal Scots are down to 289 rank and file. I have just cabled about them. Something must be done. Certainly it must be "out" for that particular unit if they don't very soon get some men. The War Office still refer to them as a Battalion!

21st August, 1915. Sailed for Suvla about 1 o'clock with Braithwaite, Aspinall, Dawnay, Deedes, Ellison, Pollen and Maitland. The first time I have set forth with such a Staff. Not wishing to worry de Lisle, I climbed up to the Karakol Dagh, whence I got something like a bird's eye view of the arena which was wrapt from head to foot in a mantle of pearly mist. Assuredly the Ancients would have ascribed this phenomenon to the intervention of an Immortal. Nothing like it had ever been seen by us until that day and the cloud — mist — call it what you will — must have had an unfortunate bearing on the battle. On any other afternoon the enemy's trenches would have been sharply and clearly lit up, whilst the enemy's gunners would have been dazzled by the setting sun. But under this strange shadow the tables were completely turned; the outline of the Turkish trenches were blurred and indistinct, whereas troops advancing from the Ægean against the Anafartas stood out in relief against a pale, luminous background.

As a result of our instructions; of conferences and of the war council we had got our plan perfectly clear and ship-shape. Everyone understood it. The 10th Division was Corps reserve and was lying down in mass about the old Hill 10 in the scrub. We had to trust to luck here as they were under the enemy's fire if they were spotted. But very strict orders as to keeping low and motionless had been issued and we had just to hope for the best. The Yeomanry were also Corps reserve at Lala Baba where they were safe. But when they advanced, supposing they had to, they would have to cross a perfectly open plain under shell fire. This was the special blot on the scheme but there was no getting away from it. There was no room for them in the front line trenches and communication trenches to the front had not yet been dug.

As to the attack: on the extreme right the Anzacs and Indian Brigade were to push out from Damakjelik Bair towards Hill 60. Next to them in the right centre the 11th Division was to push for the trenches at Hetman Chair. On the left centre the 29th Division were to storm the now heavily entrenched Hill 70. Holding that and Ismail Oglu Tepe we should command the plateau between the two Anafartas; knock out the enemy's guns and observation posts commanding Suvla Bay, and should easily be able thence to work ourselves into a position whence we will enfilade the rear of the Sari Bair Ridge and begin to get a strangle grip over the Turkish communications to the Southwards. From the extreme left on Kiretch Tepe Sirt by the sea, to Sulajik where they joined the 29th Division the 53rd and 54th Divisions were simply holding the line.

Only the broad outline of the fighting was visible through the dim twilight atmosphere and I have not yet got any details. Our bombardment began at 2.30 and lasted till 3 p.m., very inadequate in duration but the most our munitions would run to. Then, to the accompaniment of quick battery salvoes of shrapnel from the enemy and a heavy rattle of musketry, the whole line from about a mile due East of the Easternmost point of the Salt Lake down to Damakjelik Bair, nearly two miles, began to stir and move

Eastwards. We had the joy of seeing the Turks begin to clear out of the trenches on Hill 70, and by 3.30 p.m. it seemed as if distinct progress was being made: about that time it was I saw the Yeomen marching in extended order over the open ground to the South of the Salt Lake in the direction of Hetman Chair. The enemy turned a baddish shrapnel fire on to them, and although they bore it most unflinchingly, old experience told me that their nervous fighting energy was being used up all the time. If only these men could have been brought within charging distance, fresh and unbroken by any ordeal! But here was just one of the drawbacks of the battlefield and no getting over it.

After a bit, I went down to de Lisle and found him sitting on a little spur about fifty yards from his own Headquarters with one of his Staff Officers. He was smoking a pipe — quite calm. There is usually nothing to be said or to be done once our war dogs have been slipped. A soldier might as well try to correct the aim of his bullet after he has pulled the trigger! Whilst I was there we heard — probably about 4.30 — that the 11th Division had captured the Turkish first line trenches which run North and South of Hetman Chair. Real good news this. We were considerably bucked up. Climbed back to Karakol Dagh but, from that time onwards, could make out nothing of the course of the battle save that Ismail Oglu Tepe was not yet taken. As to Knoll 70, it was completely shrouded in dust and smoke. Sometimes it seemed as if the Turkish guns were firing against it; sometimes we thought they were our own. Far away by Kaiajik Aghala things looked well as many enemy shrapnel were bursting there or thereabouts showing our men must have got home. By 6.30 it had become too dark to see anything. The dust mingling with the strange mist, and also with the smoke of shrapnel and of the hugest and most awful blazing bush fire formed an impenetrable curtain.

As the light faded the rifles and guns grew silent. So I clambered down off my perch and went again to de Lisle's post of command where I found him still sitting. He had seen no more than I had seen. The bulk of our reserves had been thrown in. No more news had come to hand. All was quiet now. Our *rôle*, in fact, was finished, and Marshall, the man on the spot, by now held our destinies in his hands. Firm hands too. The telephone was working all right and I told de Lisle to try and get a message through to him quickly saying that I hoped he would be able to dig in and hold fast to whatever he had gained. I have no fears about de Lisle's nerve; nor of Marshall's.

Went on board and sailed for Headquarters, through darkness made visible by the fires blazing on the battlefield. No shooting. Got on the wires and found no news from Anzac nor more from de Lisle. Crossed backwards and forwards the best part of the night between my tent and the G.S. tent, but de Lisle had heard nothing definite enough to report. Brodrick still has fever. Ruthven has been wounded.

22nd August, 1915. Suvla gone wrong again; Anzac right. Left G.H.Q. at 11 o'clock with Braithwaite, Commodore Keyes, Captain Phillimore, Aspinall, Beadon, Freddy and Val in the *Arno* and went direct to Anzac. There I picked up Birdie and heard the Anzac part of the battle. The Indian Brigade have seized the well at Kabak Kuyu, and that fine soldier, Russell, fixed himself into Kaiajik Aghala and is holding on there tooth and nail. There was fighting going on there at the moment but Russell is confident. How delightful it is to have to deal with men who are confident!

This success of old Cox's is worth anything. The well alone, I suppose, might be valued at twenty or thirty thousand a year seeing it gives us beautiful spring water in free gift from Mother Earth instead of very dubious fluid conveyed at God only knows what cost from the Nile to Anzac Cove. If we can only hold on to Kaiajik Aghala, then the road between Anzac and Suvla will be freed from the sniper's bullet.

Went on to Suvla and landed with all my posse, remaining in consultation with Corps Headquarters till 3.30.

Our attack on Hill 70 and Ismail Oglu Tepe has failed. The enemy has dug himself well in by now and, therefore, we depended far more on our gun fire than we did on the 7th, 8th, 9th and 10th. Unfortunately, the bombardment seems to have been pretty near futile — not the fault of the gunners, but simply because, on the one hand, the mist interfered with the accuracy of their aim, on the other, shortage of shell prevented them from making up for inaccuracy by quantity. Then the bush fires seem to have come along in the most terrible fashion and interposed between our brave 29th and the Turks. The ancient Gods fought against us yesterday: mist and fire, still hold their own against the inventions of man. Last but not least, all are agreed the fine edge of the 11th Division has been at last blunted — and small wonder: there is no use attacking any more with the New Army until it has been well rested and refreshed with new drafts.

So far de Lisle has no clear or connected story of the battle. The 29th Division say they were shouldered off their true line of attack by the 11th Division, then driven in by the fire; the 11th Division, on their side, say that the Yeomen barged into them and threw them off their line. Had we been able to dig in we would have made good a lot of ground. But Marshall, not showy or brilliant but one of my most sound and reliable soldiers, decided, although he knew my wishes and hopes, that the troops had got themselves so mixed up and disorganized that it would be imprudent. So orders were issued by him, on the battlefield, to fall back to the original line. There was neither use nor time to refer back to de Lisle and he had to come to the decision himself. I am quite confident he will be able to give good reasons for his act. Many of the men did not get the order and were still out at daylight this morning when they were heavily attacked by the Turks and fell back then of themselves into their old trenches. Another case of "as you were." We have lost a lot of men and can only hope that the Turks have lost as many. I don't think for a moment they did, not at least in the Suvla Bay sphere, but Cox and Russell claim to have accounted for a very great number of them in their first retreat and in their counter-attacks in the Southern sector of the battle.

23rd August, 1915. Imbros. Not one moment, till to-day, to weigh bearing of K.'s message of the 20th instant, — the message sent me in reply to my appeal for 50,000 fresh troops and 45,000 drafts. In it K. tells me that a big push is going to take place in the Western theatre, and that I "must understand that no reinforcements of importance can be diverted from the main theatre of operations in France." Certain named transports are carrying, he says, more troops to Egypt, and he hopes Maxwell will be able to spare me some. If we can't get through with these we must hang on as best we may.

To-day it has been up to us to try and bring home to the Higher Direction the possible effects of trying to do two things at once; i.e., break through in France and break through here. We are to stand aside for a month or so just when we have made a big gain of ground but not the decisive watershed gain; when the Turks, despite their losses in life, shell, trenches and terrain, are shaken only; not yet shattered.

K. sees all the Allied cards — we don't. But we do know our own hand. We know that our Navy have now come clean down on the Ægean side of the fence, and have determined once for all to make no attack on their own. We have the *feel* of the situation in our bones and it was up to us — I *think* it was — to rub it in that although the British War Direction may decree that the Dardanelles are to hang on without further help, indefinitely, yet sickness is not yet under their high command, nor are the Turks.

So Dawnay, who is making a name for himself as a master of plain business diction, was told off to draft me an answer to the War Office which should remove as many beams as possible out of their optics. He overdid it: the whole tone of it indeed was despondent, so much so that, as I told Braithwaite, a S. of S. for War getting so dark a presentment of our prospects would be bound to begin to think it might be better to recall the whole expedition. So I rewrote the whole thing myself:

> (No. M.F. 578). From General Sir Ian Hamilton to Secretary of State for War. We will endeavour to do the best possible with forces at our disposal; we quite understand reason for your inability to send us reinforcements necessary to bring operations to a successful conclusion, and thank you for putting it so plainly. After the failure of the IXth Corps to take prompt action after landing I took immediate steps to persevere with plan in spite of absence of surprise and reinforced northern wing with 2nd Mounted Division from Egypt and XXIXth Division from Cape Helles. These movements and the necessary reorganization of the IXth Corps formations which had become very mixed took time, so that I was not able to renew the attack until 21st August.

By then enemy positions in Ratilva Valley had been immeasurably strengthened and I was confronted with the difficulty that if I could not drive the Turks back between Anafarta Sagir and Biyuk Anafarta my new line from right of old Anzac position to sea coast North-east of Suvla Bay would be more than I could hold with the troops at my disposal. It would thus be a case of giving up either Anzac Cove or Suvla Bay. Therefore, as a preliminary step to my fresh offensive I determined to mass every man available against Ismail Oglu Tepe which position it was necessary for me to capture whether as a first step towards clearing the valley, or, if this proved impossible and I was thrown on the defensive, to secure comparative immunity from shell fire either for Suvla Bay or Anzac Cove.

De Lisle planned the attack well. The LIIIrd and the LIVth Divisions were to hold enemy from Sulajik to Kiretch Tepe Sirt, and XXIXth Division and XIth Division were to attack Ismail Oglu Tepe with two Brigades of Xth Division and the IInd Mounted Division (5,000 rifles) in corps reserve. I arranged that General Birdwood should co-operate by swinging his left flank to Susak Kuyu and Kaiajik Aghala.

The troops attacked with great dash and stormed the lower slopes of the hill in spite of strong entrenchments, but I regret to say they were not able to attain their objective nor even to consolidate the position gained and yesterday found the whole line back in their original trenches except the left of the Australians where one battalion of Gurkhas and new Australian Battalion continue to hold Susak Kuyu. Casualties not yet to hand, but I fear they amounted to some 6,000 in all. This renewed failure combined with the heavy total casualties since 6th August, and the fact that sickness has been greatly on the increase during the last fortnight has profoundly modified my position, and as you cannot now give me further reinforcements it is only possible for me to remain on the defensive. Naturally, I shall keep on trying to harry the Turks by local attacks and thus keep alive the offensive spirit but it must be stated plainly that no decisive success is to be looked for until such time as reinforcements can be sent.

The total casualties including sick since 6th August amount to 40,000, and my total force is now only 85,000, of which the fighting strength is 68,000. The French fighting strength is about 15,000. Sick casualties are becoming abnormal chiefly owing to troops other than late arrivals being worn out with hardship and incessant shell fire, from which even when in reserve they are never free. Where Anzac evacuated 100 a day they are now evacuating 500, where Royal Naval

Division evacuated 10 they are now evacuating 60. The result is that I have only some 50,000 men in the North to hold a line from the right of Anzac to the sea North-east of Suvla, a distance of 23,000 yards.

When there is no serious engagement, but only daily trench fighting, the average net wastage from sickness and war is 24 per cent. of fighting strength per month. The Anzac Corps, the XXIXth Division and the XLIInd Division are very tired and need a rest badly. Keeping these conditions in view, it appears inevitable that within the next fortnight I shall be compelled to relinquish either Suvla Bay or Anzac Cove, and must also envisage the possibility of a still further reduction of my front in the near future. Taking the first question of abandoning Anzac Cove and closing to the North, Suvla Bay is now netted and comparatively secure from torpedo attack. Further, it offers certain facilities for disembarkation in winter gales. It has, therefore, some decided advantages but though I should be able to hold it safely at present, it would present no facilities for further contraction of my line to meet the future wastage of my force. On the other hand, by retiring South of Suvla I could first hold a line Lala Baba — Yilghin Burnu — Kaiajik Aghala, and then, when normal wastage diminished my strength below this limit I could, if necessary, withdraw into the original Anzac position. For these reasons it must probably be Suvla and not Anzac which must be given up, though on account of its advantages as indicated above, and on account of the moral effect of retiring, you may rely on my not relinquishing it a single day before I am compelled.

I do not wish to paint a gloomy picture. It is a simple problem of arithmetic and measurement. On the basis of normal wastage and the present scale of drafts my total fighting strength by the middle of December, including the French, will be only, say, 60,000. Of this force, a certain percentage must of necessity be resting off the peninsula, and the remainder will only suffice to hold Cape Helles and the original Anzac line unless, of course, the enemy collapses. Until now, however, the Turks replace casualties promptly, although frequently by untrained men. Also our other foe, sickness, may abate, but seeing how tired are the bulk of my force, I doubt if it would be wise to reckon on this.

At 11.15, red hot from France, there arrived in camp Byng (to command the 9th Corps), Maude and Fanshawe (to command Divisions); also Tyrrell and Byng's A.D.C., Sir B. Brooke, nephew of my old friend, Harry Brooke. All three Generals remained for lunch and then the two Divisionals made off respectively to the 11th and 13th Divisions. Byng and Brooke stayed and dined. These fellows seem pretty cheery. Maude especially full of ardour which will, I hope, catch on.

24th August, 1915. Imbros. Been resolving yesterday's long cable. How often it happens that a draft letter, if only it is well put, fixes the mind into its grooves. My words were brighter than Dawnay's but the backbone was not really me. No one knows better than myself that a great deal more than arithmetic or measurement will be needed to make me give ground at Suvla. The truth is, it is infinitely difficult to spur these high folk on without frightening them; and then, if you frighten them, you may frighten them too much. That's why cables are no substitutes for converse.

To a Commander standing in my shoes, the forces of the infidels are not one half of the battle. The wobblers sit like nightmares on my chest. "Tell them the plain truth" cries conscience. What is the plain truth? Where is it? Is it in Dawnay's draft, or is it in my message, or does it lie stillborn in some cable unwritten? God knows — I don't! But one thing at least is true: to steer a course between an optimism that deprives us of support and a pessimism that may wreck the whole enterprise, there indeed is a Scylla and Charybdis problem, a two-horned dilemma, or whatever words may best convey the notion of the devil.

The blessed cable is now lying on the well-known desk where K. will frown at it through his enormous spectacles. Then he calls the Adjutant-General and tells him Hamilton must be mad as all his formations are full to overflowing and yet he says he is 45,000 short. Next enters the Master-General of the Ordnance with a polite bow and K. tells him Hamilton must be delirious as he keeps on raving for shell, bombs, grenades although as he, Von Donop, knows well, he has been sent more guns and explosives than any man has ever enjoyed in war. Impossible to be so disrespectful to the Field Marshal or so inconsiderate to their department as to reject the soft impeachment. How easily do the great ones of this world kid themselves back into a comfortable frame of mind! Then

K. stalks off to the Dardanelles Committee.

Turns out that Cox and Russell did even better than Birdwood had thought in the fighting on the 21st and the morning of the 22nd. They have killed more Turks and the line held runs well out to the North-east and quite a good long way to the North of Kaiajik Aghala.

Byng left to take over his command. Davies came over from Helles and stayed for dinner.

The *Imogene* sailed in with Mails. News by wireless of German Naval defeat in the Baltic and Italian declaration of war against Turkey. Well, that part at least of K.'s aspirations has come off; we have dragged in Italy. Now — will she send us a contingent?

Davies dined. With his ideas still framed on Western standards he puts it forcibly, not to say ferociously, that we must, must, *must* be given our fair share of trench mortars, bombs and gun ammunition. Fresh from France he watched the artillery preparation at Helles and (although we had thought it rather grand) says we simply don't know what the word bombardment means. Instead of seeing, as in the Western theatre, an unbroken wall of flame and smoke rising above the enemy trenches about to be stormed, here he saw a sprinkling of shells bursting at intervals of 20 yards or so — a totally different effect. And yet the Turks are as tough as the Germans and take as much hammering!

When I read the British Press, starved and yet muzzled, I feel as if I could render my country no better service than to kill my friend the Censor and write them one or two articles.

By surprise either Army can bulge in a sector of the opposing lines but, until one Army loses its *moral*, neither Army can break through. An engine will be found to restore marches and manœuvres but, at this historic moment, our tactics are at that stage. To break through, Armies must advance some six or seven miles; otherwise they can't bag the enemy's big guns. But, the backbone of their attack, their own guns, can't support them when they get beyond five or six miles. The enemy reserves come in; they come at last to a stop. A three or four mile advance *should* be easy enough, but, in the West, that would mean just three or four miles of land; nothing more. But *here*, those three or four miles —

nay, two or three miles — (so ineffective in France) are an objective in themselves; they give us the strategical hub of the universe — Constantinople!

Suppose even that by paying the cost in lives we did succeed in driving the Germans over the Rhine, still we stand to gain less than by taking this one little peninsula! A quarter of the energy they are about to develop for the sake of getting back a few miles of *la belle France* could give us Asia; Africa; the Balkans; the Black Sea; the mouths of the Danube: it would enable us to swap rifles for wheat with the Russians; more vital still, it would tune up the hearts of the Russian soldiery to the Anglo-Saxon pitch.

Victory by killing Germans is a barbarous notion and a savage method. A thrust with small forces at a weak spot to bring the enemy to their knees by loss of provinces, resources and prestige is an artistic idea and a scientific stroke: the one stands for a cudgel blow, the other for rapier play.

We take it for granted that we have to "push" in France and Flanders; that we *have* to exhaust ourselves in forcing the invaders back over their own frontiers. Whereas, content to "hold" there, we might push wherever else we wished.

I can well understand that a Frenchman should say, "Let the world go hang provided I get back my *Patrie*,[*] whole; undivided and at once." Indeed, only the other day, one of the best French Generals here, after speaking of the decisive, world-embracing consequences of a victory at the Dardanelles, went on to say, "But we ought to be in France." Seeing my surprise he added, "Yes, I am quite illogical, I admit, but until our nine *departements*[†] are freed from the Boche, world strategy and tactics may go to the devil for me."

Have been writing my weekly budget. Part of my letter to K. harks back to the first Suvla landing, and tries to give him a better notion of the failure to profit by the enemy's surprise. Not that I have yet got any very clear conception of the detail myself. No

---

[*] "Homeland."

[†] "Departments."

coherent narrative does, in fact, exist. New troops, new Staff, new Generals, heavy losses, have resulted in the confusions, gaps and contradictions still obscuring the story of those first few days.

Now that I am getting more precise news about what fighting there was, it seems clear that this great mass of young, inexperienced troops failed simply because their leaders failed to grasp the urgency of the time problem when they got upon the ground, although, as far as orders and pen and ink could go, it had been made perfectly clear. But, in face of the Turk, things wore another and more formidable shape. Had Lord Bobs been Commander of the 9th Corps; yes, just think of it! How far my memory carries me back. Every item needed for the rapid advance: water, ammunition, supplies and mules closely and personally checked and counter-checked. Once the troops landed a close grip kept on the advance. At the first sign of a check nothing keeps him from the spot. The troops see him. In an hour they are up upon the crest.

So far, so good. We had not another Lord Bobs and it would not have been reasonable of us to expect him. But when I come to the failure of the 21st, where I have a seasoning of Regulars — as well as a commander of energy — still we do not succeed. This time, no doubt, the enemy were on the scene in force and had done ten days' digging; the non-success, in fact, may be traced to the loss of the element of surprise; energy, in fact, was met by preparation. The battle had to be fought like a manœuvre battle and yet the enemy were ready for us, more or less, and already fairly well entrenched. Since the morning of the 7th the chances had been rising steadily against us. Still, even so, the lack of precise detail baffles me almost as much as in the case of the first Suvla landing.

393

Chapter XVIII – Misunderstandings

25th August, 1915. Imbros. Davies left for Helles at mid-day. Was to have gone with him but heard that Bailloud with Captain Lapruin would like to see me, so stayed to receive them.

Have got K.'s answer to my cable pointing out the probable results of his declared intention of sending us no "reinforcements of importance" during an indeterminate period.

(No. 7315, cipher). From Earl Kitchener to General Sir Ian Hamilton. Your No. 578. You will, I hope, fully discuss the situation described by you with Birdwood and the Generals who have just joined you, and, when a thorough examination on the ground of the whole state of affairs has been made, give me the opinion at which you arrive.

It has been a sad disappointment to me that the troops have not been able to do better, and that the drafts and reinforcements sent out to you and Egypt, excluding any you have drawn from Egypt, amounting from 6th August to 47,000, have not proved sufficient to enable you to contemplate holding your positions.

Braithwaite and I have been electrified by this reference to 47,000 drafts and reinforcements: it is so much Greek to us here:

had there been any question of reinforcements coming to us on that scale, my 578 of 23rd August would never have been sent.
On the heels of this has followed another:

(No. 7319, cipher). From Earl Kitchener to General Sir Ian Hamilton. My No. 7315. I hope that the result of your deliberations will reach me by Friday morning, as the decision to be taken is one of considerable importance.

I have replied off the reel:

(No. M.F. 588). From General Sir Ian Hamilton to Earl Kitchener. With reference to your telegrams Nos. 7315 and 7319. I feel sure you cannot think I would be capable of sending a telegram of such import as my No. M.F. 578 without the deepest consideration and sense of my personal responsibility which remains unaffected by any amount of conferences with my subordinate commanders. I was careful in this instance, however, to discuss the situation on the spot with both Corps Commanders concerned and I then cabled you my considered opinion. I constantly visit both Suvla and Anzac and have personally thoroughly examined the state of affairs. In view of your telegram No. 7172, cipher, I do not understand your allusion to 47,000 drafts and reinforcements from 6th August as we have not been advised of any such number as 47,000. I felt bound to lay the case plainly before you as to what might have to be undertaken, though I do not contemplate giving up any position one hour before I need. If the present wastage from sickness continues, however, and if my cadres are allowed to fall below their present attenuated strength I may be compelled to undertake such a step as I have indicated.

Bailloud arrived at tea time. Away from Piépape he is another person. At dinner, he cracked jokes even about serious things like the guns of Asia.

Brodrick was carried off to the Hospital ship. The doctors think there should be no real danger. We shall all miss him very much; as an aide he has been A.1.; sympathetic and thoughtful.

Braithwaite dined to meet Bailloud.

GENERAL BAILLOUD

"*Exclusive News*" *phot.*

26th August, 1915. After clearing my table and taking early lunch, started off in the *Arno* with C.G.S., Pollen, Freddie and Val. Sailed for Suvla and went up straight to see Byng, brought by the whirl of Fortune's wheel from a French chateau to a dugout. During the two days he has been here, he has been working very hard. I hope he may not too regretfully look back towards *la belle France*. Our old "A" Beach was being briskly shelled as we walked down to our boats. Between Hill 10 and the sea there were salvoes of shrapnel falling and about every thirty seconds a big fellow, probably a six incher, made a terrible hullaballoo. The men working at piling up stores "carried on."

When we got back to G.H.Q. there was a heavy thunderstorm in progress. Mail bag closed 9.30.

During our inspection at Suvla this "Personal" from K. to myself has been deciphered:

(No. 7337, cipher). From Earl Kitchener to General Sir Ian Hamilton. Personal. I considered it advisable, that as the decision the Government may have to come to on your No. 578 is one of grave importance, the Generals out there should previously fully consider the situation on the Gallipoli Peninsula; hence my No. 7315. It was intended to obviate any possibility of overlooking points and in such cases two or more heads sometimes elucidate matters that might otherwise be missed or not given due weight to. It was in no way intended thereby to detract from the importance of your views on the subject or to minimise your personal responsibility for them.

I have no idea of the French Generals' views on the matter, and you were apparently not fully considering the drafts and reinforcements that were being sent out.

A detailed telegram is being sent you from the office of the 47,000 men mentioned in my No. 7315.

I hope that the return of Younghusband's Brigade from Aden to Egypt will still further increase these in a day or two (less one battalion).

But you should look on the forces in Egypt and your own as a whole, allowing, of course, for the proper defence of Egypt, when you take the general situation at the Dardanelles into consideration.

Do you think the Navy could do anything more than they are already doing to help the situation? I hear it is thought that they could land heavy naval 6-inch guns on positions such as those in square 92 M and other points, and might threaten from Aja Liman the main road of Turkish supplies between Karna Bili and Solvili (by gunfire from ships) and also bring a heavy and effective shell fire on the Turkish positions at and behind Anafarta. There is a cabinet to-morrow.

I would much like to sleep over this cable — so plain seemingly; really so obscure. At face value, how splendidly it simplifies the Dardanelles problem! Had I been, all along, as this cable seems to make me, the C.-in-C. of the Eastern Mediterranean with Maxwell administering my Egyptian Base, then, humanly speaking, this entry would have been dated from Constantinople. But am I? I can't believe it even now, with the words before me. Anyway, whether by my own fault or those of others, one thing is certain, namely, that up to date there has been misunderstanding. Now, the Cabinet of to-morrow forces me to send a momentous wire without too much time to think it over. To clear my brain let me set down the sequence of facts as they have so far appeared to me:

Less than a week ago — 20th inst. — K. cables me he is sending certain units to Egypt and certain other units to the Dardanelles. The units and their ships are named. He says there is going to be a big push in France and that I must look to these troops, earmarked for the Dardanelles, plus any I "can obtain from Egypt" to carry on. He winds up by saying, "It is hoped the troops going to Egypt will enable Maxwell to send you more fighting men on your demand."

This same assumption that the G.O.C., Egypt, and myself are two equals each having equal command over his own troops, is fully borne out by another cable of the 21st August. My cable of 23rd August is based on these messages; i.e. on the idea that we must carry on here for a good long time to come with very little to help us. Then comes K.'s of the 25th telling me he is sorry 47,000 drafts and reinforcements he has sent to Maxwell and myself since 6th August are not going to be enough to enable me to hold on. But no one can make head or tail of these 47,000 drafts and reinforcements; no one can run them to ground. He has notified me the units and the ships, but the total coming to Maxwell *and* myself don't tot up to that figure, much less the portion of them detailed for the Dardanelles.* Now comes to-day's cable in which Egypt is spoken of as being mine, and the fatness thereof. Taking this message *per se*, any one might imagine I could draw any troops I

---

* As will be seen further on the 47,000 actually panned out at 29,000, of whom two battalions were at once diverted to Egypt, whilst two other battalions turned out to be non-fighting formations. — *Ian H., 1920.*

liked from that country provided that *I* thought *I* was leaving enough to defend the Suez Canal: and, apparently, the 47,000 men are about to make an effort to materialize inasmuch as we are told that details are being wired us. Finally, Younghusband's Brigade sails to help us!

27th August, 1915. Imbros. As there is a Cabinet to-day I had to get off my answer last night. In it I have made a desperate effort to straighten out the tangle:

> (No. M.F. 589). From General Sir Ian Hamilton to Earl Kitchener. On returning from Suvla I have just found your No. 7337, cipher. I hope there may be no misunderstanding as to meaning or intention of my No. M.F. 578. I asked in my No. M.F. 562 for such drafts and reinforcements as I considered necessary for the campaign to be brought to a conclusion before the winter began. You told me in your No. 7172 that you could spare no more reinforcements beyond those mentioned therein, and that if I could not achieve success with these I must remain on the defensive for some considerable time. I explained situation in my No. M.F. 578, and said that the question was one of arithmetic and measurement. I was anxious to hold all I had got and to gain more, but I required all my available force at the present time merely to hold what I had got. I pointed out that meanwhile a large proportion of my troops were urgently in need of rest, and sickness was so great that unless reinforcements were sent out my force would soon be too small for the number of yards of front to be held. In that case, i.e., if reinforcements could not be spared, but in that case only, it would be necessary to contract my line. This welcome news of 47,000 reinforcements, however, alters the whole situation. Such a number will do much to complete my diminished cadres, and should materially lessen sick rate by giving more chance of taking tired troops out of the trenches. Byng can certainly remain where he is at present, and will even be able to rest some of the tired XXIXth Division, while the arrival of the Australian Brigade will give General Birdwood a similar chance of resting some of his troops.
>
> General Birdwood meanwhile is to make a further advance to-morrow on the left flank, to gain possession of important tactical feature, which will eventually help an advance when the time arrives. Byng is getting everything in order and has infected all around him with his own energy and cheeriness and has quickly grasped the

Misunderstandings

whole situation.

In communication with Maxwell I find I can have seven Territorial Force units and the Scottish Horse, and now I have your welcome news of Younghusband's Brigade. Please believe I am the last man in the world to give up anything we have gained except under direct necessity, which I trust may now never arise. The Navy is supporting me to its full capacity. The guns of the four ships in Suvla Bay take on the Turkish positions you mention almost as well as and certainly more safely than if they were landed and placed where you suggest. Moreover, Navy cannot lend those guns unless I supply the detachments to work them from the Naval Division, and the latter is fully employed at present and cannot spare the men. We are constantly sending ships round to Aja Liman to fire at enemy positions from there, but I know you realize that one must not rely too much upon effective fire on land targets from ships which are not moored, as is the case in Suvla Bay.

I have not consulted the French General about the situation in the North as he is at the Southern end and on the right of the line there. He thinks more of Asia than of these operations in which he has no troops engaged, but I discussed the matter with him only last night. Before I sent my No. M.F. 578 I discussed every point closely for two hours with the Corps Commanders.

In the evening my A.G. brought me the promised details of the 47,000 drafts and reinforcements. He has gone into the detail in proper A.G. spirit, namely, as an arithmetician rather than a tactician. The result has given us a shock! 10,000 men of the 54th Division and 4,000 drafts are shown in the War Office cable as being still due to come to me as reinforcements whereas they had actually landed on the Peninsula; had, indeed, been shown in my total fighting strength of 68,000 in my original cable, M.F. 578 of 23rd August, and are, too many of them, alas already *hors de combat*. Here is the passage sent four days ago: "The total casualties including sick since 6th August amount to 40,000, and my total force is now only 85,000 of which the fighting strength is 68,000." In this 68,000 were included 14,000 of the men shown in *subsequent* War Office cables as being drafts and reinforcements on their way to the Dardanelles!

So my A.G. has become a bit suspicious about the balance of the 47,000. On paper, he says, it looks as if I might expect to draw from Egypt and England 30,000 reinforcements, but — he remarks sententiously — "we know by now that paper is one thing and men are different." As to Younghusband's Brigade, it turns out they cannot be employed here: too many Mahomedans. Have sent the following reply:

> (No. M.F. 595). From General Sir Ian Hamilton to Secretary of State for War. With reference to your telegram No. 7337, cipher. Have now received details of the 47,000 drafts and reinforcements in your No. 7354 cipher, and I find that this figure includes nearly 10,000 men of the LIVth Division and 4,234 drafts, all of whom had been landed on the peninsula when I wrote my No. M.F. 578, and were reckoned in the total fighting strength of 68,000 mentioned in that telegram. The statement, however, shows that I can expect from England and Egypt during the next six weeks a total of some 29,000 reinforcements, including new formations and two battalions of non-fighting lines of communication troops.
>
> This is a better situation than I was led by your 7172, cipher, to expect, and you may rely on me to do the best I can with this addition to my present very depleted strength. I hope, however, you realize that whereas my British Divisions are now more than 55,000 rifles below their establishment only 17,000 of these 29,000 are drafts, and before the last of the drafts can arrive these divisions will have lost another 25 per cent. of their remaining number by normal wastage.
>
> In regard to Younghusband's Brigade, I learn that the three battalions are practically half Mahomedans, and I am advised that it is better if it can be avoided not to use Mahomedans so near the heart of Islam. Would it not be possible to exchange these for some Hindu regiments in France?

These cables give us an uncomfortable feeling that the people at home wish to regard us as stronger than we are — a different thing from wishing to add to our strength.

On the other hand, another sort of message has come in which sheds a ray of hope across our path so darkened at many other points:

> (No 7372, cipher). From Earl Kitchener to General Sir Ian Hamilton. Although it is understood that we do not at present see our way to change the recent decision not to send any fresh complete divisional

Misunderstandings

units, we wish to have all the material possible on which to form a judgment from time to time. Therefore, will you please telegraph me your opinion, from the point of view of the military and strategical situation now existing on the peninsula, as to the prospects there are, after the experience you have recently had, of our achieving the main objective of turning the Turks out and what force you would consider would be required to do this.

Taylor of the G.S. lunched. A big parcel mail came in. Brodrick is to be sent to Alexandria.

28th August, 1915. Imbros. Braithwaite and I both feel we must take time to think over last night's last cable and I have wired to say so.

Cox's attack on Knoll 60 to the North-east of Kaiajik Aghala came off well. The New Zealanders under Russell and the Connaught Rangers did brilliantly. Fighting is still going on.

A reply from the War Office to mine of last week wherein I pointed out that the once splendid 5th Battalion Royal Scots had fallen from a strength of 1,000 down to 289. They have had no one since the campaign began. To-day the Battalion is just over 250 — a Company! Now I am officially told that "no reinforcements can be found for the 1/5th Battalion of Royal Scots." This is the Battalion which did so well about 11 o'clock on the dreadful night of the 2nd May. I shall cable the Lord Provost of Edinburgh. If we could get into touch with the human beings of Edinburgh they would help us to keep a battalion like the Royal Scots on their legs even if they had to break up half a dozen new formations for the purpose.

Freddie and I dined with de Robeck on board H.M.S. *Triad.* The V.A. was well pleased with my cable of the 26th.

29th August, 1915. Imbros. Last night two cables:

(No. 7414, cipher. C.I.G.S.). From War Office to General Headquarters, Mediterranean Expeditionary Force. Reference your No. M.F.Q.T. 2737. The two Territorial Force battalions originally detailed — *see* my No. 7172 of 20th August — to sail in the *Orsova* will be taken by the *Ceramic*. Of these, the 2/5th Devons is only about 700 strong and contains a large percentage of recruits, while the 1/6th Royal Scots contains about 40 per cent. partially trained men and a new Commanding Officer who has only just been appointed. Until it has had further training neither battalion is fit for anything more than garrison duty. I suggest that under these circumstances the *Ceramic* should proceed direct to Egypt.

(No. 7401, cipher, 554/A.3.). From War Office to Inspector-General of Communications, Mediterranean Expeditionary Force. We are receiving from Malta and Alexandria very large demands for materials and explosives for making grenades. The supply of these seriously interferes with our manufacture of grenades. At present we are hoping to send you 30 to 40,000 grenades weekly and this figure will be increased. When the materials already sent out to Malta and Alexandria have been used up, can the manufacture of grenades at those places cease? Please reply at once; the matter is urgent.

Do what I will my pen carries me away and I find myself writing like an ill-conditioned "grouser." As an old War Office "hand" I ought to know — and I do know — the frightful time of stress under which Whitehall labours. But, just look at these two cables, you innocent and peaceful citizen of a thousand years hence! The residue of the famous 47,000 rifles sent me by the Adjutant-General are now being valued by the official valuer, the Chief of the Imperial General Staff. In all our calculations the 2/5th Devons has hitherto masqueraded as an efficient battalion at full strength. Figures are sometimes more eloquent than words!

As to the second cable, that deals us a worse blow. Seeing clearly, at last, we should extract no hand grenades from the War Office, we turned to Maxwell and Methuen, who have interested themselves in our plight and have been making us so many that, with what we ourselves can add to their manufacture, we are at last beginning to make things hum in the Turkish trenches. Then in comes this War Office cable to crush our nascent industry and give us in exchange some pious aspirations.

There is no good making any trouble about the hand grenades. As to the two raw battalions, I am asking they be sent, raw and weak as they are, as I can train them in the trenches much better and more quickly than they could be trained in Egypt or England.

Church Parade; office work; sailed over to "K" Beach; inspected Clearing Stations and walked up to site for new camp. Then back to G.H.Q., to meet the V.A. and Roger Keyes. They remain the best of friends always.

This evening we were all in good form owing to the news from Anzac. Knoll 60, now ours throughout, commands the Biyuk Anafarta valley with view and fire — a big tactical scoop.

30th August, 1915. Imbros. Still good news from Anzac. Seeing that the stunt was on a small scale, we seem to have got into the Turks with a vengeance. In falling back as well as in counter-attacking after we had taken Hill 60, the enemy were exposed to the fire from our trenches along the Kaiajik Dere. Birdie declares that they have lost 5,000. We have taken several machine guns and trench mortars as well as some fifty prisoners. Have sent grateful message to all on the spot.

At 10.30 four Russian Officers made their salaams. They are to report how things are going, and they seem to have the usual quick Slav faculty for grasping essential points combined, no doubt, with the usual Slav slackness which lets them go again. I told them everything I knew. They told us that our landing had saved the whole Army of the Caucasus; that the Grand Duke knew it and that His Imperial Highness bitterly regretted that, first of all, sheer lack of supplies; afterwards the struggles in Galicia and Poland, had prevented Istomine and his Army Corps from standing by to help.

At 1.30 the C.G.S., Deedes, Val., Freddy and I crossed to Helles in the *Arno*. Had a hard afternoon's walking, going first to 8th Corps Headquarters; next to the Royal Naval Division and last to the 52nd Divisional Headquarters. Returned to the 8th Corps Headquarters and there met Bailloud. He is now full of good cheer. Got back to Headquarters without adventure or misadventure.

Have cabled home a suggestion made to me by Mahon, that the 16th Irish Division at home might be used to fill up the gaps in the units of the 10th Division out here.

31st August, 1915. After early lunch, left in the *Arno* for Suvla. With me were Braithwaite, Manifold, Freddy and Val. Walked up to the 9th Corps Headquarters and saw Byng. I am very anxious indeed he should work his men up into the mood for making a push. He charms everyone and he is fast pulling his force together. Maude, Fanshawe, and de Lisle seem to be keen to do something, but Byng, though he also is keen, has the French standards for ammunition in his head. He does not think we have enough to warrant us in making an attack. Also, he does not realize yet that if he is going to wait until we are fitted out on that scale he will have to wait till doomsday.

Walked to de Lisle's Headquarters and saw him, and on to the 11th Divisional Headquarters where I met Fanshawe and Malcolm. With them I climbed back on to Karakol Dagh and sat me down on the identical same stone whereon I sweated blood during that confused and indecisive battle of the 21st August. From the Karakol Dagh I got a very fair idea of our whole trench system. On either flank we hold the hills; elsewhere we are on the flat. The 11th Division have recovered and only need drafts to be as good a formation as any General could wish to command. In the evening I left in the *Arno* carrying off with me de Lisle and Captain Hardress Lloyd to dine and stay the night. Quentin Agnew also dined.

My first feeble little attempt to act on K.'s assumption that Egypt and its army are mine has fallen a bit flat. The War Office promptly agreed to my taking these two weak, half-trained battalions, the 1/6th Royal Scots and 2/5th Devons, to be trained in my trenches. That was yesterday. But the Senoussi must have heard of it at once, for Maxwell forthwith cables, "The attitude of the Senoussi is distinctly dangerous and his people have been latterly executing night manœuvres round our post at Sollum." To me, the night manœuvres of these riff-raff seem ridiculous. But distance, perhaps, has lent its enchantment to my view.

The quibble that the troops in Egypt are mine has been broken to pieces by my first touch! I have renounced the two battalions with apologies and now I daresay the Senoussi will retire from his night manœuvres round Sollum and resume his old strategic position up Maxwell's sleeve.

1st September, 1915. Imbros. Remained at Headquarters working. Wrote, amongst other things, to K. as follows:

> I have just finished two days' hard physical exercise going round visiting Egerton and Paris with Davies, and Fanshawe and de Lisle with Byng. At Helles everything is quite right although they have only troops enough there for the defensive. They are getting a lot of stores in, and the really only anxious feature of the situation is the health of the men who are very, very tired right through, having had no sort of relief for months, and who go sick in large numbers.
>
> [...]
>
> Fanshawe is first class. Full of go and plans, he will, if the Lord spares him, be a real treasure. Maude and Mahon I am going to see after Mail-day, and then I shall hope to inspect our new captured position on the left of Anzac.
>
> I do not know if they showed you the cable saying Hammersley has gone home very ill with a clot of blood in his leg. He has to lie perfectly prostrate and still, so I am told, as the least movement might set it loose and it would then kill him. Evidently he was not really fit to have been sent out on service. And this was the man, remember, on whom, under Stopford, everything depended for making a push.
>
> This Suvla Bay country, a jungle ringed round by high mountains, is essentially a country for Boers or for Indian troops. De Lisle and others who have watched them closely in India, say that a native soldier on the Peninsula (although there, too, he goes to pieces if he loses his Officers and under too prolonged a strain) is worth at least two Indian soldiers in France. The climate suits him better, but, most of all, the type of enemy is more or less the sort of type they are accustomed to encounter. Not *Sahibs* and *Ghora Log* in helmets but *Mussalman Log* in turbans. As to the South Africans there can be no two opinions, I think, that they would stand these conditions better than those of Northern Europe. Indeed, we have one or two Boers serving now with the Australians, and they have done extremely well.

Some of K.'s questions take my breath away. I wish very much indeed he could come and spend a week with me. Otherwise I feel hopeless of making him grasp the realities of the trenches. On the 30th of August he cables, "If required, I could send you a fresh consignment of junior Officers. Or have you sufficient supernumerary Officers to fill all casualties?" I have replied to him that, in my four regular Divisions, I am short of 900 effective Officers in the Infantry alone. To meet my total shortage of 1,450 Officers I have twenty-five young gentlemen who have lately been sent out here to complete their training!

De Lisle and Hardress Lloyd sailed back to Suvla in the evening.

Chapter XIX – The French Plan

2nd September, 1915. Imbros. An ugly dream came to me last night. My tent was at Imbros right enough, and I was lying in my little camp bed, and yet I was being drowned, held violently under the Hellespont.

The grip of a hand was still on my throat; the waters were closing over my head as I broke away and found myself wide awake. I was trembling and carried back with me into the realms of consciousness an idea that some uncanny visitor had entered my tent. Already the vision was fading. I could visualize the form of the presence, but the face remained hidden in shadow. Never had I suffered from so fearful a dream. For hours afterwards I was haunted by the thought that the Dardanelles were fatal; that something sinister was a-foot; that we, all of us, were pre-doomed.

Dreams go by contraries. Strange that so black a night should be followed by a noon so brilliant — so brilliant beyond compare.

K. cables the French are going to send three or four Divisions to work with us along the Asiatic mainland. From bankrupt to millionaire in 24 hours. The enormous spin of fortune's wheel makes me giddy!

These French Divisions will be real Divisions: *must* be; they have no others.

O, Hallelujah!

The sending of a force of three or four Divisions to operate on the Asiatic mainland, independent as regards command, but in close relation with the British forces on the Peninsula, is being considered by the French Government. They will require an exclusively French military base at Mitylene, and us to help with transport and fleet.

So far I have not discussed any details with the French, and have simply told them we shall be delighted to have the help, which would be given by such an expedition, towards the solution of the Dardanelles problem.

Presumably they would require their two divisions now at Cape Helles. What forces would you require to relieve them? I have asked Sir John French if the XXVIIth and XXVIIIth Divisions could be spared for this purpose.

Wire me any points that you think I had better settle with the French authorities.

*Deo volente** we are saved; Constantinople is doomed. How clearly stand forth the mosques and minarets of the Golden Horn.

Mr. Murdoch, an Australian journalist, paid me a visit to thank me for having stretched a point in his favour by letting him see the Peninsula. Seemed a sensible man.

Glyn and Holdich dined: both clever fellows in different ways. Dawnay and Glyn after dinner left for England. Dawnay goes to explain matters first hand to K. Next to my going home myself, or to K. himself coming out here, this is the best I can do. Dawnay is one of the soundest young officers we have, but he is run down physically (like most of us) and jaded. He should benefit by the trip and so should the rumour-mongers at home.

3rd September, 1915. Imbros. Two cables: one to say that the news about the French Divisions must be kept dark; the other, in reply to a question by me, refusing to let me consult de Robeck on the

---

* "God willing."

matter. So Braithwaite and I had to make out our cable expressing our delight and thankfulness, and advising how the troops might best be used entirely on our own. The cable took some doing but got it off my chest by mid-day and then sailed with Ellison, Braithwaite and Val by the *Arno* to Suvla. We landed this time on Lala Baba instead of at our usual Ghazi Baba. Every five minutes the Turks plumped one six-incher on to the beach. But nobody now seems to mind. A lot of Generals present; Byng, Mahon, Marshall, Maude and Peyton. Mahon took me up to the top of Lala Baba and showed me the disposition of his division. He kindly asked us all to tea at his Headquarters but as someone added that Ashmead-Bartlett was going to take a cinema photo of the scene I thought I would not be thus immortalized. The Scottish Horse were bivouacking on the beach; they have just landed but already they have lost a member or two of their Mess from shell fire. No wonder they looked a little bewildered, but soon they will shake down. When we got back to the *Arno* we found she had been hit by shrapnel, but no damage.

Things at Suvla are pulling together. No one gave me more confidence than Maude. His mind travels beyond the needs of the moment. He is firmly convinced that no very out-of-the-way effort by the Allies is needed to score a big point in the War Game and that our hold-up here is not a reality but only a hold-up or petrefaction of the brains of the French and of our Dardanelles Committee. I longed to tell him he was doing them both, especially the French, an injustice, and that four splendid divisions were as good as on their way, but I had to content myself with saying to him and to all the Generals that I was overjoyed at a piece of news received yesterday.

4th September, 1915. Imbros. Life would be as ditchwater were it not stirred to its depths by K.'s secret cable. Sailed over with Freddie at 11.30 to "K" Beach and inspected the 88th Brigade. Had given orders to the *Arno* to stand by and to take me over to Anzac in the afternoon, but the weather was so bad that I could not get off to her in the motor boat.

At 7.15 p.m. the V.A. sent his picket boat for me and Freddie and I went on board the *Triad*. At 10 p.m. she started for Mudros.

5th September, 1915. H.M.S. "Triad." Mudros. Anchored at Mudros at 6 a.m. Breakfast over, was met by Altham, Colonel McMunn and Captain Stephens who took me ashore. There I met Lindley, now commanding the troops on the island; also General Legge (commanding the 2nd Australian Division); Lord Dudley and Colonel Forster. Lindley seems pleased at having been given this command; says he feels like a man out hunting who has a bad fall but alights on his feet, and Altham tells me he is doing the work very well. Dudley, too, seemed full of business and contented with his lot.

The moment I got through the reception stunt I set myself to work like a nigger at the Red Cross stunt: that's how people talk now-a-days. Saw the 15th Stationary Hospital; the 110th Indian Field Ambulance; "C" Section of No. 24 British Indian Hospital; ate a hearty lunch; inspected 1st Australian Stationary Hospital. Walking round a Hospital and seeing whether things are clean and bright is a treat but trying to cheer people up and give a fillip to all good works — that implies an expenditure of something vital and leaves a man, after a few hours, feeling the worse for wear.

By 4.45 the day's task was well over so refreshed myself by some right soldier business reviewing the 4th Gurkhas under Major Tillard — a superb battalion — 1,000 strong!!! Had forgotten what a full battalion looks like. At 5.45 wound up by inspecting a huge Convalescent Depot under Colonel Forde and got back to the *Triad* just in time for dinner. Wemyss dined also.

6th September, 1915. H.M.S. "Triad." Mudros. After breakfast sailed over to Mudros West; Lindley met me, also a host of doctors. Walked to No. 3 Australian Hospital with an old acquaintance whose Italian name slips my memory at the moment; then to No. 2 Australian Stationary Hospital; then to Convalescent Depot of Lowland Division. At 12.30 ran down to my launch and was swiftly conveyed to lunch on board the *Europa* with Admiral Wemyss. Such a lunch as a lost voyager may dream of in the desert. Like roses blooming in a snowdrift, so puffs and pies and kickshaws of all rarest sorts appeared upon a dazzling white tablecloth, and then — disappeared. We too had to disappear and sail back to Mudros West again. Horses were waiting and I rode to No. 18 Stationary Hospital and made a thorough overhaul of it from end to end; then tea with the Officers of No. 1. In No. 3 Australian General were eighty nurses; in No. 3 Canadian Stationary seven nurses; in No. 1 Canadian Stationary twenty-four nurses. Since Lady Brassey descended in some miraculous manner upon Imbros, they were the first white women I had seen for six months. Their pretty faces were a refreshing sight: a capable crowd too: all these Hospitals were in good order, but the sick and wounded in charge of the girls looked the happiest — and no wonder. The Canadian Medicos are fresh from France and discoursed about *moral*. Never a day passed, so they said, in France, but some patient would, with tears in his eyes, entreat to be sent home. Here at Mudros there had never been one single instance. The patients, if they said anything at all, have showed impatience to get back to their comrades in the fighting line. We discussed this mystery at tea and no one could make head or tail of it. In France the men got a change; are pulled out of the trenches; can go to cafes; meet young ladies; get drinks and generally have a good time. On the Peninsula they are never safe for one moment (whether they are supposed to be resting or are in the firing line) from having their heads knocked off by a shell.

Returned to the *Triad* in time for dinner.

Admiral vexed as his motor boat has gone ashore. Bowlby is with it trying to get it off.

The French Admiral commanding the Mediterranean Fleet has just sailed in.

7th September, 1915. Imbros. At 9.30 left the *Triad* to call on Admiral de la Perriera on board the *Gaulois*. Thence to *H.M.S. Racoon*(Lieutenant-Commander Hardy) and started back for Imbros, where we arrived in time for tea.

8th September, 1915. Imbros. Trying to clear a table blocked with papers as a result of my two days' trip. Have written to K. as the Mail bag goes to-morrow. Have told him I have had a nice letter from Mahon, thanking me for allowing him to rejoin his Division and saying he hopes he may stay with them till the end. Have given him all my Mudros news and have sent him a memo. submitted to me by Birdwood showing how much of the sickness on the Peninsula seems due to the War Office having hung up my first request for a Field Force Canteen.

FISH FROM THE ENEMY

"*Central News*" *phot.*

Here is one of the enclosures to Birdwood's memo.:

N. Z. and A. Division.

I desire to draw attention to the remarkable drop in the sick evacuations from this Brigade as shown by the following figures:

    August 28 — 59.
        "   29 — 64.
        "   30 — 58.
        "   31 — 17.
    Sept. 1 — 2.
        "   2 — 6.

I am convinced that this amelioration, and the observable improvement in the condition of the men are largely to be attributed to the distribution, on August 30 and 31 of Canteen Stores, providing a welcome change of dietary.

I strongly recommend that every effort be made to maintain such Canteen supplies.

(Sd.), MONASH.

9th September, 1915. Imbros. At 9.30 Admiral de la Perriera returned my call. At 11.50 Braithwaite, Freddy and I went aboard the *Gaulois*.

A five course lunch and I had to make a speech in French.

When I got back I found that General Marshall, commanding the 53rd Division, had come over from Suvla to stay with me. Lancelot Lowther dined; he told us all the important things he was doing.

10th September, 1915. Imbros. Lancelot Lowther left with the Mails at 7 a.m., glad, I suspect, to shake from his feet the sand of these barbaric Headquarters.

Not easy to get Marshall to loosen his tongue about the battle of the 21st, and he would not, or could not, add much to my knowledge. The strength of Marshall depends not on what he seems but upon what his officers and men know. He has got his chance amidst the realities of war. In peace, except by a miracle, he would never have risen above the command of a Battalion. The main reason I cannot draw him about the battle of the 21st is, beyond doubt, that he does not want to throw blame on others.

Marshall is a matter-of-fact, unemotional sort of chap, yet he told the sad tale of young O'Sullivan's death in a way which touched our hearts. O'Sullivan was no novice where V.C.s were the stake and the forfeit sudden death.

11th September, 1915. Imbros. Ran across in the motor boat to see the 86th Brigade under Brigadier-General Percival. Went, man by man, down the lines of the four battalions — no very long walk either! These were the Royal Fusiliers (Major Guyon), Dublin

Fusiliers (Colonel O'Dowda), Munster Fusiliers (Major Geddes), Lancashire Fusiliers (Major Pearson).

Shade of Napoleon — say, which would you rather not have, a skeleton Brigade or a Brigade of skeletons? This famous 86th Brigade is a combination. Were I a fat man I could not bear it, but I am as unsubstantial as they themselves. A life insurance office wouldn't touch us; and yet — they kept on smiling!

12th September, 1915. Imbros. The C.O.'s, Geddes, Pearson, Guyon and O'Dowda, lunched: an ideal lot; young, ardent, on the spot. Marshall left by the Suvla trawler. Windy day, but calmer in the evening and at night rained a little.

13th September, 1915. Imbros. Crossed again with Freddie Maitland and inspected the 87th Field Ambulance (Highland Territorials from Aberdeen) under Colonel Fraser. Became so interested the dinner hour was forgotten — a bad mark for a General. Much pleased with the whole show: up to date, and complete in all respects. Got back lateish. Altham dined. Sat up at business till midnight.

Dictated a long letter to Callwell, Director of Military Operations at the War Office, on the suicidal behaviour of the Military Censor. In South Africa, my Chief of the Staff's latchkey let many a clandestine tit-bit slip through to keep interest alive in England. K. regularly, when the mails came back to roost, went for me, but the messages had got home and done their duty as good little tit-bits should. The B.P. cannot work up the full steam of their war energy when the furnaces of their enthusiasms are systematically damped down; shut off from any breath from outside. Your sealed pattern censor sees nothing beyond the mischief that may happen if the enemy gets to know too much about us; he does not see that this danger is negligible when compared with the keenness or dullness of the nation.

The French Plan

General Headquarters,
Medtn. Expeditionary Force,
13th September, 1915.

Dear Callwell,

I am about to commit an atrocity by writing to an overworked man on a subject which may seem to him of secondary importance. Still, to the soldiers out here, the said subject means encouragement or discouragement coming to them through the medium of their home letters, — so vital a factor in victory or failure that the thought emboldens me to proceed.

Our misfire of last month came within only a fine hair's breadth of the grand coup and caused us proportionately bitter disappointment at the moment. Yet, looking back over the whole affair in a more calm and philosophical spirit, any General, I think, would now be bound to admit that in some respects at least fortune had not been too unkind.

The Australians and New Zealanders have been extricated from what by all the laws and traditions of war, was, in theory, an untenable position; their borders have been enlarged; the heights they hold have become more elevated and commanding; they have been entirely released from shelling on the one flank and, on the other, the shelling has dwindled away to next door to nothing. North of them again we have captured a more or less practicable winter harbour, and have extended our grip on the coastline. From the extreme South point of Anzacs to their extreme North was formerly 2¾ miles. From the extreme South point of Anzacs to our extreme North point (along which there is inter-communication) is now 13 miles. Thus we force the enemy to maintain a much larger number of troops on the Peninsula (where he is already slowly bleeding to death under the stress of his supply and transport difficulties) or else dangerously to weaken parts of his line.

As to the fighting by which this has been accomplished, there is nothing from beginning to end that any army need be ashamed of. Every word I sent home in my Proemial cables might have been published without raising a blush to the cheek of the most ardent Imperialist. In saying this I do not, of course, assume that raw troops could tackle a totally strange and uncomfortable proposition with the swift directness and savvy of veterans. The feat performed by the Australians and New Zealanders was of the class of the storming of the heights of Abraham, only it was infinitely, infinitely more difficult in every respect.

On the other side, still assuming the philosophical mantle, consider what might have happened. Had the Australians and New

Zealanders been average troops, they would perhaps have burst through the first series of wire entanglements and trenches, but they would not have stormed the second, still less the third, fourth, fifth or sixth lines. Again, had the Turks got the smallest inkling of our intention, the landing at Suvla Bay would have failed altogether, and the New Armies would have been virtually smashed to pieces without being able to show any *quid pro quo*.

We soldiers out here have then it seems to me, much for which to thank God on our bended knees. That, at least, is my personal attitude.

How is it then that our letters from home are filled with lamentations and that, having just gained a proportionately very large accretion of territory, we see headlines in the papers such as 'The Gallipoli standstill,' whereas it does not seem to occur to anyone to speak about 'The French standstill'?

Well, I will tell you. The system upon which the Press Bureau approaches the eagerly attentive ear of the British Public is the reason.

Why I begged the War Office to change the method by which I sent copies of my Proemial cables to Maxwell was that I found he (animated, of course, by the best intentions) was improving the successes and minimising the failures. The finishing touch was given when, one day, he inserted the phrase 'The enemy is demoralized and has to submit by day and by night to our taking his trenches.' Obviously, even the most stupid fellaheen after reading such a sentence must, in the course of time, begin to ask himself how, if trenches are being easily taken by day and by night, we still remain on the wrong side of Achi Baba!

Turning now to the Press Bureau and our landing, there was nothing in that landing, as I have just said, which need have caused sorrow to a soul in the British Isles excepting, of course, the deplorable heavy casualties which are inseparable now from making any attack. But, on the 23rd of August a correspondent cables to an American paper a sensational story of a decisive victory, which the Press Bureau must have known to be a tissue of lies. Had the lies taken the shape of disasters to the British there would not, from the point of view of us soldiers, have been the smallest objection to publishing them. Suppose Mr. X, for instance, had said that the landing did not succeed, and had been driven off with immense slaughter? Apart from the fact that such a cable would have made many poor women in England unhappy for a few hours, the fabrication would have done us positive good: when the truth was known the relief would have been enormous, we would have gained handsome recognition of what had actually been done, and German inspired lies would have been discounted in future.

But there is no *moral* in the world that can stand against a carefully engineered disappointment. When you know perfectly well that the spirits of the people are bound to be dashed down to the depths within a few days, it is unsound statesmanship surely so to engineer the Press that you raise those selfsame spirits sky high in the meantime. To climb up and up is a funny way to prepare for a fall! If you know that your balloon must burst in five minutes you use that time in letting out gas, not in throwing away ballast. If you want to spoil a man's legacy of £500 tell him the previous evening he has been left £50,000!

As I began by saying, do please forgive me, my dear Callwell, for taking up your most precious time. But you are more in touch with this particular business than anyone else at the War Office and, from your large mindedness, I feel sure you will be able to spare me some sympathy, and perhaps even get some recognition for the general principle I herewith put forward:

(1). Do not too curiously censor false alarmist reports put about by the enemy. Let the papers publish them with a query and then smash them as soon as this can be done with positive certainty.
(2). Mercilessly censor any report which you think is, even in the smallest degree, overstating your own case.

The system needs courage but, with the British Public, it would pay!
      Yours sincerely,
       (*Sd*.), "IAN HAMILTON.

As suspense had, by now, become unbearable, cabled home asking S. of S. to "let me know, as soon as you can safely do so," when the new divisions may be expected. I tell him I have "informal" news from the French but dare not take action on that.

14th September, 1915. Imbros. Mails in with Ward as King's Messenger. Captain Vitali (Italian liaison officer) and Captain Williams dined. Vitali is worried about his status. He was told in the first instance he was to be liaison officer between General

Cadorna and myself. On this understanding we agreed to his coming to our Headquarters. Once he was here the Italian Government (not Cadorna he is careful to explain) said he must be permanently attached to us. Vitali feels himself in a false position as he thinks that, — had we known, we might not have let him come. Personally, I am quite glad to have him; but we did not have much talk as, immediately after dinner, Braithwaite brought me the decipher of Lord K.'s answer to my reminder to him. This has greatly saddened me and takes up the whole of my thoughts.

(No. 7843, cipher). From Earl Kitchener to General Sir Ian Hamilton. Reference your No. M.F. 630. I have just returned from France where I went to settle up the questions asked in that telegram which were in a very indefinite state owing apparently to a decision having been arrived at by the French Government without reference to their military advisers. The outcome of my meeting with Millerand, Joffre and Sarrail was that the French force of four Divisions proposed to be sent to the Dardanelles cannot leave until the result of the approaching offensive in France is determined. If it be as successful as hoped for your position in the Dardanelles would naturally be affected favourably. It is hoped that the issue will be clear in the first few days of October, and if indecisive, that by 10th October two of our Divisions may be at Marseilles for embarkation to be followed closely by the four French Divisions. The embarkation and transport of so large a force would, it is thought, take about a month, but this has still to be worked out in detail, so that by about the middle of November would be the time when all would be ready.

In the meantime, as transport is available, I shall continue to send you reinforcements and drafts of which you are fully informed, up to 20th instant, and on which you should alone calculate.

Sarrail, backed by General Bailloud, is greatly in favour of the French expedition being employed independently on the Asiatic shore.

Joffre greatly doubts the wisdom of this course, and Millerand requested me to ask you to state fully and confidentially, for his personal information, your opinion on this matter.

Joffre's objections appear to be that a landing in Asia opens up a very wide field if the force be not immediately successful, and that in that case more troops, munitions and drafts would be eventually required than he could spare with due regard to the safety of France.

Secondly, he is not very confident of Sarrail's leadership,

particularly as the plans Sarrail has made seem to be worthless. Joffre is having careful plans worked out by his Staff for the expedition on the Asiatic shore which, he says, though unfinished, do not look promising. The same objection on his part would not, I gather, be felt if the French troops were given a definite area and objective on the Gallipoli Peninsula, where the scope of their activities, and consequently the support required from France, could be limited.

Where's the use of M. Millerand's consulting me over what lies on the far side of a dead wall? Had he asked me to show why action here should have priority over action in France, then I might have been of some use. But that is settled: the four French Divisions earmarked for the East will not now be sent until *after* "the results of the coming offensive in France have been determined." "If the success of this push equals expectations you will reap the benefit." If indecisive then, "by the 10th October," two British Divisions and four French Divisions will be at Marseilles ready to sail out here: "about the middle of November would be the time when everything would be ready." There are altogether too many ifs and ands and pots and pans about Millerand's question. When a man starts going West who can foretell how long it will take him to arrive at the East?

(1) If the push in the West is victorious we will score, says K. That is so. Far as the Western battlefield lies from the scene of our struggle, the report of a German defeat in France would reverberate Eastwards and would lend us a brave moral impetus. But the point I would raise is this: did K., as representing a huge Eastern Empire, press firmly upon Millerand and Joffre the alternative, — *if the push in the East is victorious the West will score*?

What express strategical gain do they expect from pushing back the Germans? A blow which merely destroys a proportion of men and material without paralysing the resources of the enemy is a blow in the air. War cannot be waged by tactics alone. That is a barbaric method. To bend back the German lines in the West, or to push the first line back on to the second or third, or twentieth, has of itself but slight strategical or economic import.

Here, on the other hand, we have literally in our grasp a clear cut gift offered us by the Gods. The impossible part, the landing, is done. All that remains is so many fresh men and so many thousand shell. The result is not problematical, but mathematical. Napoleon is the only man who has waged a world war in the world as we know it to-day. Napoleon said, I think it was on the famous raft, "Who holds Constantinople is master of the world." And there it lies at the mercy of the Briton — could he only convince Joffre that the shortest cut to freeing his country from the Germans lies through the Dardanelles.

The principles which should underlie Entente strategy will be clear to military historians although obscured to-day by jealousies and amateurishness: just the usual one, two, three they are, in this order:

(a) Hold the sea.
(b) Hold the West.
(c) Smash the Turk.

A couple of miles won by us here gives England wheat and Russia rifles; gives us the whip hand in the Balkans plus security in a couple of Continents. A couple of miles lost by us here leaves the German with a strengthened grip upon all the real world objectives for which he went to war: it leaves us with a ruined prestige in Asia. But what is all that to Joffre to whom, as a good Frenchman, the Balkans; the bracing up of the Russian Army; all the Odessa corn; Asia and Africa thrown in, do not count against one *departement* of *la Patrie*.

(2) If the push in the West is indecisive then our push is only to be postponed. Postponed! The word is like a knell. To write it gives me a feeling of sick despair. Only postponed! As well cable at once, *only* ruined!!

(3) But there is a third eventuality not mentioned by Lord K. How if our attack upon the main strength of the entrenched Germans is beaten off? To Joffre France comes first and the rest nowhere — every time: that is natural. But our Higher Direction are not Frenchmen — not yet! Armageddon is actually being fought *here*, at the Dardanelles, and the British outlook is focused

"*Exclusive News*" *phot.*

MARSHAL LIMAN VON SANDERS

on France. We are to sit here and rot away with cholera, and see the winter gales approach, until the big push has been made in the West where men can afford to wait — where they are healthy — where time is all on their side. And this push in the West is against the whole German Empire linked to all its own vast resources by a few miles of the best railways in the world. We *can* attack here with more men and more munitions than the enemy the very moment we care to accept the principle that, *at this moment*, Constantinople and the heartening up of Russia and ascendency amongst the Balkan States are not only the true positive objectives of our strategy, but are the sole strategical stunts upon the board. We can do so because of our sea power. We can borrow enough howitzers, aeroplanes, munitions and drafts from the West; apply them here and then, if necessary, return them. We are not exploiting our own special characteristics, mobility and sea power!

Easy to preach patience to a nation in agony? Yes, for the whole agony of the whole world is more important even than the agonies of France. We've got to win the war and win it quick. There's only one way to do that. The resources of the Entente are not equal to carrying on two offensives at the same moment. If our Army in the West will just sit tight awhile, we here will beat the Turks, and snip the last economic lien binding the Central Powers to the outside world.

Once more, our game is to *defend* in the West until the *attack* in the East has borne economic fruit in the shape of ships and corn: political fruit in the sentiment of the Balkans: military fruit in the fillip given to the whole force of the Entente by actual tactical contact between the British soldiers and the rank and file of the Ruskies. The collapse of the Central Powers, — eclipsed in full view of all Asia and Africa by the smoke from the funnels of the British Fleet at anchor in the Golden Horn is what we are after here. Even if French and Joffre do drive the German main hordes back to the Rhine the scope of their scoop would be far less than ours, for we by getting to Constantinople can starve those main armies stiff.

How few of our people know anything of the Russians. At least, I have been attached for eight months to the Armies which fought against them in the field; have visited Russia and Siberia and have done two peace manœuvres as their guest. To send superior officers to Russia only produces jealousy; to send supplies only breeds dishonesty. But with 50,000 British soldiers as yeast we could leaven 5,000,000 Muscovites; we could fire their inert masses with our ardour; this is the best of all uses to which 50,000 British soldiers could at present be put.

From the early days when he told me the New Army should go to Salonika, K. had an intuition at the back of his big mind that victory would dawn in the East. But he is no longer the K. of K., the old K. of Khartoum and Pretoria. He still has his moments of God-sent intuition. First, he had *absolute* knowledge that the Germans would come through Belgium: I repeat this. The assumption was not uncommon perhaps, but he *knew the fact*! Secondly, when everyone else spoke of a six weeks' war; when every other soldier I can think of except Douglas Haig believed he'd be back before the grouse shooting was over; K. went nap on a three years' war. Pray heaven he was wrong; but, right or wrong, he has already proved himself to have been nearer the mark than anyone else. Thirdly, he had a call (by heavenly telepathy, I suppose) that his New Armies must go out to the East. There is no more question about this than there is about Belgium and the three years' duration. He has told me so; time and again.

Why then does he not act accordingly if he's in the Almighty know? Because he can't. With the one exception of the Battle of Paardeberg, he never in his palmiest days pretended to be a man of action. But now he has lost his faculty of forcing others to act. He makes a spurt but he can't stay the distance. He has met Millerand, French and Joffre in Council and allowed the searchlights of his genius to be snuffed out! That is what surprises me: He, who once could deflect Joe Chamberlain and Milner from their orbits; who twisted stiff-necked Boers round his little finger; who bore down Asquith, Winston, Prince Louis and Beatty in Valetta Harbour — East *versus* West — Mediterranean *versus* North Sea — who, from 8 p.m. to 2 a.m., withstood, wrestled with and overthrew Haldane's arguments in favour of his taking up the succession to the Duke of Connaught, and that although he had one arm tied to his side by having taken the King's shilling. What a marvel he was and now —

Ichabod!

There is something so tragical in what home letters let us guess that the pity of it almost makes me forget our own stillborn projects.

15th September, 1915. Imbros. Altham and Major Hood left G.H.Q. for L. of C. Headquarters. Had another hour with Altham before he got aboard his destroyer. Gave an interview to Buchanan, A.M.S. After lunch, Braithwaite, Val, Wells, Deedes, Freddie and myself went off to Suvla aboard H.M.S. *Scourge* (Lieutenant-Commander Tupper). On landing, Braithwaite branched off to see the G.S. Byng has a keen sense of humour; is energetic and by his looks and manner attracts all ranks. No one could wish a better corps commander and I have never in all my experience known anyone take greater and more minute trouble with his field days and manœuvres than he did in Egypt the year before the war. But his sojourn on the Western front has given him inflated standards as to the number of guns and stocks of H.E. shell which are essential to success; especially with troops who have suffered heavy losses. Perhaps he is right. This para. from a letter written to the great man to-night explains more generally what I feel:

> Maude is burning to get on and do something and I heard him myself ask Byng when he was going to let him have a dash. As to Byng, I think myself he is not quite sure yet about the spirit of his men. I have been trying to spur him on for the last day or so, although only by very gentle hints, as I think, with a man of Byng's great reputation, one must leave him to himself for as long as possible. I daresay he may be quite right and very wise. Still, these reinforcements have brought the Suvla Bay troops up to no less than 37,000 men, and I am most anxious they should do something soon a little more rapid than sapping out slowly towards the enemy's lines — which they are doing.

After my talk with Byng, we went on to meet Fanshawe and de Lisle. Maude came along with me as far as the crestline. I asked him about his Division. He replied: "Sir Ian, may I be frank with you about the Division?"

At these ominous words I shivered. They positively gave me the shivers. So I braced myself up when I answered, "But of course!"

Maude then said, "If you give the order now, and will arrange for a little artillery support, my Division will storm and hold on to any thousand yards of Turkish trench you like to point out; tomorrow."

I could have embraced him, but I had to go steady and explain to him that a Corps Commander must judge all his Divisions and that, taking the situation as a whole, Byng did not think it fair on the men to let them have a dart yet — not, at least, till they had more munitions at their back. Byng has had wide experiences in the West and he looks on it as trying the men unfairly to ask them to attack without a preliminary bombardment on a scale which we cannot at present afford.

"Yes," said Maude, "that is all very well but after all you must remember the Turks have neither the artillery nor the munitions the Germans have at their command on the Western front."

"Well," I replied, "you put your points to Byng and you know I am a man who never yet in my life refused a good brave offer like yours." He has a great admiration for Byng and so, though sadly, he went away.

Fanshawe met me at the South end of the Division trenches, as bright and keen as a new nail. His men, too, seem full of go. Fanshawe hopes to carry the whole ridge whenever he gets the order. The 11th Division promise to be as fine a unit as any in the Army once they get their gaps filled in.

16th September, 1915. Imbros. We had quite a lively morning here. At 7.30 an enemy's biplane dropped four bombs on our Headquarters camp and got away with hardly a shot fired at it. At 7.50 an enemy's Taube came over and dropped bombs near my Signal Tent, also a little summer shower of small steel darts: five men were wounded. At 8.10 a.m. yet another enemy biplane circled round but was kept at a respectful distance by the ship's guns.

Gave an interview to Colonel Stewart, Armoured Car Squadron.

Vice-Admiral Foumet and Staff called on me in the forenoon. He replaces Admiral Nicol gone sick. Mails went out this evening. Freddie and I gave tone to our debilitated constitutions by dining with the ever hospitable V.A. on the *Triad*.

A cable from Dawnay saying Lord K. "would not regard unfavourably" a withdrawal from Suvla Bay.

Dawnay left under the cloud of the 21st August. He it was who rough-drafted the cable (in very much stronger terms than my final version) suggesting that we might have to draw in our horns if we were not kept up to strength. Since then our skies have cleared; the spirit of the men has risen to set fair and we have got drafts enough, not for a big push but certainly to enable us to be delighted should the Turks attempt any sort of an attack, either at Suvla or anywhere else. The Turks, in fact, are strictly on the defensive both actually and in their spirit.

17th September, 1915. Imbros. Had been going to Anzac to inspect and then to bring Birdie back to stay with me. But the weather was too bad. He got here all right as the wind is from the North and he was able to climb aboard under the lee of Nibrunesi Point. Just as well, perhaps, we did not go, for one way or another a good deal of extra work had to be got through. One thing; two cables from Maxwell to the War Office have been repeated to us here; inadvertently we think; divertingly for sure. The story is this:

A few days ago we were offered the 51st and 53rd Sikhs who, despite their titles, are half Mahomedan. After consulting Cox, Birdie and other Indian Army Officers I cabled back saying we would gladly have them "as soon as transport can be arranged," unless French is willing to exchange them for two purely non-Mahomedan units. Here are the collateral cables from Maxwell to the War Office:

> Both the 51st and 53rd Sikhs have already been disembarked. They had better remain off ship as long as possible, I think, since they are reported to be feverish. The troopship can wait at Port Said. The men on the canal, I should like to point out, barely get two nights in bed per week.

I have been asked by Hamilton to send him a double Company of Patiala Sikhs to reinforce the 14th Sikhs. I can do this, and if you concur I think it is a better arrangement than to send him the 51st and 53rd Sikhs.

The Sikhs meant for Gallipoli are gone; we shall never see them more; they mount guard by night against the ghosts of the Suez Canal.

Another thing; a Correspondent writes in and tells us that for the honour of his profession he feels bound to let us know that Mr. Ashmead-Bartlett has secretly sent home an uncensored despatch *per*, of all people in the world, Mr. Murdoch!

I had begun to wonder what had come over Mr. Murdoch and now it seems he has come over me!

The next paper on the table was my draft cable of advice for M. Millerand. Joffre wants his four Divisions to land on the Peninsula; Sarrail wishes them to work along the Asiatic side. No doubt the views of the French Generals are being coloured by their wish to stand as clear as they can of British command. So I have been careful to sweep away *that* obstacle by offering to stand down. Now they can fix up the problem on its merits:

> Closest consideration has been given to your No. 7843, cipher. Until now I have consistently opposed a landing on the Asiatic side of the Straits with less than 6 divisions — see my telegram No. M.F. 349 of 19th June. On Gallipoli Peninsula area and difficulties of supply limited liabilities of the opposing forces whereas mainland of Asia gave scope for the deployment of large forces by the enemy. Now, however, the situation is clearing up and there has been a great change in the conditions.
>
> The Turks had formerly 10,000 to 12,000 men on Asiatic shore with large reserves on the Peninsula available to cross over there if necessary. Now Anatolia and Syria have been drained of troops to oppose us on the Peninsula where the Turks have far longer front to hold, namely, 9½ miles instead of 2½, whilst our position and strength at Suvla and Anzac are more threatening to their communications than was our position at Anzac in June. If, therefore, we can be strong enough to maintain pressure on whole Turkish line on the Peninsula it is unlikely that Turks could detach troops to

oppose French landing on Asiatic shore. Assuming even that the Turks were enabled to release every soldier from Thrace by a definite understanding being arrived at with Bulgaria, I calculate they might gather a total of five divisions but of these probably only one or at most two would be on Asiatic side at beginning of the operations and would probably be scattered so that opposition in strength to surprise landing is improbable. Moreover, only one of the divisions is composed of good Nizam troops, others believed to be not up to establishment. The Asiatic coast down to Yukeri Bay is now heavily trenched but I do not think much has been done below that point. Supposing, therefore, French bring good divisions at war strength and succeed in keeping their destination secret, they appear to have a good chance of obtaining good covering positions without much loss and of thence advancing on Chanak defeating any Turkish forces sent against them. Degree of their success would depend on whether the entrenched positions which have been prepared on the Kum Kale — Ehren Keui road could be turned by the good road which leads from Yukeri through Ezine and Ishiklar to Chanak, as it is unlikely that Turks would be able to quickly organize new defensive positions with entirely new line of supply. The distance of landing place from objective is a secondary consideration. It is easier to march and fight 100 miles than to take three lines of trenches. In the one case there is room for manœuvre at which Turks are bad while in the other case siege warfare results at which the Turks stand supreme. Once Ehren Keui reached, the Turks between that place and Kum Kale would be forced to retire and Kum Kale would become our base, thereby greatly shortening line of supply. Supposing Turks endeavoured to make bridgehead on Chanak promontory, the country is so big that large forces would be necessary and once the Turks were cut off from North their supply difficulties would be most serious. French possession of Chanak should be equivalent to victory, but as Turks are stubborn fellows it is better to confine anticipations to commencement of results which I consider would be as follows: Cutting off of Turkish supply line Chanak to Akbashi Liman. Narrows would be useless to Turks. Nagara communications could be cut. Our 15-inch howitzer could be used to batter Kilid Bahr forts. Allied Fleets should be able to enter Marmora without loss.

Turning to alternatives. If French were held up and unable to reach Chanak, at least the last Turkish reserves would have been used up and I think happy termination of operations though postponed would begin to come clearly into view. Supposing the worst happened and that the French were compelled to fall back after landing. In that case a clear road for retirement to a bridgehead would be open. Positions covering landing could be taken up and there they would continue to draw towards them considerable Turkish forces which would otherwise be available for use on Peninsula.

Finally, greater difficulties beset all other schemes. The notorious military disadvantages of independent command would be less harmful if the respective armies were separated by the Straits than if they were mixed up together on Peninsula. As Achi Baba is now one of the strongest fortresses in Europe, it would be unpopular to palm off the Cape Helles end upon the French. Moreover, all the French here are, and always have been, dead set on Asia. If the French were employed at Suvla they would have to fight side by side with the British, a situation which, with co-equal commanders, would be a military absurdity. Were that course decided upon, I would ask the Allied Governments to make up their minds which General had the most daring, brains and experience, and if it were the Frenchman I would serve under him loyally.

As to making the attempt to the North of the Gulf of Xeros: a landing there is certain to be opposed, and the Turkish reinforcements which are always held ready in the neighbourhood of Uzunkiupru and Keshan could arrive in strength very quickly and imperil the whole project. A further objection lies in the distance of the French intermediate base and great strain it would throw on Allied Fleets. Finally, it is all-important that absolute secrecy should be maintained. I suggest that it should be allowed to leak out that the destination of the French is Enos, this would probably have the effect of tricking Turkish troops in Thrace, as Enos is a destination which would gain most credence.

Birdie has at last worn off the fine edge of his keenness; he looks a little tired: General Russell, the New Zealander, dined also and was in great form.

18th September, 1915. Imbros. A cable to say that the French Government are anxious to form two bases each capable of supplying three Divisions: one to be at Mudros, the other at Mitylene. Is it business? In spite of delay, in spite of lost chances, is it business?

Chapter XX – Loos and Salonika

Left G.H.Q. at noon to-day, 18th, sailed to Helles; lunched with Davies; went up to inspect the East Lancs Division. The trenches are in apple-pie order and the men are in good heart, but the stomach has always been held to be the mainstay of the fighting man, and theirs are in the grip of enteritis. Stopped at 5th Corps Headquarters on my way back.

De Putron and la Borde came back with me. Struck an interesting scientist called Lawes whilst I was in the Lancashire trenches. As we were entering the harbour at Kephalos an enemy Taube tried to drop a bomb aboard. No harm.

Dined with the V.A. together with Birdie, Lord Anglesey and Freddie.

When we got back found this from War Office. Rather amusing to be in the know of the counter moves and to see their outcome:

> The exchange of battalions mentioned in No. 7873, cipher, of 14th September cannot be effected, so that at present the 51st and 53rd Sikhs will not proceed to France. From the General Officer Commanding, Egypt's, telegram No. 1854. E. of 15th September, it

is understood that he can send you another double company of Patiala Sikhs to reinforce the 14th Sikhs. Possibly this will suffice for your requirements in the meantime, and the 51st and 53rd Sikhs will be left at the disposal of General Officer Commanding, Egypt. If so, will you please make arrangements with him accordingly?:
Repeated to General Officer Commanding, Egypt.

Our defeat is a foregone conclusion: the Senoussi is too strong for us. All the same I am determined to press the matter to an issue, if only to have a clean cut precedent as to whether we do have a first call on troops in Egypt or whether it is the other way about. We want these men so badly. They don't get sick here; are worth four European Battalions at present, and Birdie has become most anxious to get them, especially the 53rd. So I am cabling to Maxwell just to send us our troops (for they are ours) forthwith and have cabled to the War Office:

> With reference to your telegram No. 8012, cipher. In accordance with your telegram No. 8711, of 11th September, I am asking General Officer Commanding, Egypt, to send here, at once, the 51st and 53rd Sikhs, as I cannot do without them. I shall be very glad to receive the Patiala Sikhs as well, as the 14th Sikhs are badly in need of a reinforcement.

Imagine had we been sent Indian Divisions for Suvla and if the New Army, Territorials and Yeomen had been sent instead to France! Each category would have given (let me put it mildly) double value. The heat, the thirst, the scrub, the snipers, all so disconcerting to our fresh contingents would have been commonplaces of frontier warfare to our Indian troops. See what the handful with us here have achieved. Yet in vain do I write and cable my personal entreaties to Beauchamp Duff, the all-powerful Commander-in-Chief in India, and a very old friend, for two hundred Sikhs: first he offers me a couple of hundred Brahmins wherewith to fill the ranks of the famous 14th Sikhs and then, when I hesitate before a proposal which appears monstrous, withdraws even that offer. Again, I beg for 200 recruits for the 14th, saying I will train them myself; I am refused — very politely and at great length — refused, because it would be "politically inexpedient" to send them. In vain do we try to get our own two battalions through the Egyptian morass; they are going to stick and do sentry go over nothing. Why; were there any real trouble in Egypt I could land a whole Division there within four and a half days!

As for the New Army and Territorials, gradually entered with their veteran comrades in the trenches of France and Flanders, they too would have had more familiar surroundings and fairer play — as everyone here now recognizes, too late!

The crystals of history take shape while we fight. As in a glass darkly the outlines begin to appear to anyone who has a moment wherein to peer beyond the end of the war. Everything has gone by the contrary. Our people have done as well as their neighbours, and better, with their imaginations, whether in diplomacy, strategy or tactics. Where the Gibbon or Plutarch who survives the War Office Censor is going to damn their reputations into heaps is over their failure in business commonsense. Under their noses, parts of their system, were two great live organisms; the Indian Army and the Territorial Force. From the moment the mobilization flag was dropped it was up to them to work tooth and nail to treble or quadruple these sound, vigorous existing entities. What have they done? After a year of war, the Indian Army and the Territorial Army are staggering on their last legs instead of being the best part of our forces. Compare the East Lanes Division, who had the good fortune to escape from War Office clutches by getting right out to Egypt at the outbreak of the war, with Territorial Divisions which have remained since then under the eyes and in the hands of the War Office!

The Turks are still withdrawing troops from the Caucasus front to ours. Good for the Russians. Whilst I was at Helles, the enemy guns started a heavy bombardment along the whole of our nine mile front from the right of Anzac to the left of Suvla; a heavy musketry fire also along the Turkish trenches. An attempt was then made to launch infantry assaults against our lines, but these fizzled out, the rank and file having no heart for the job. There is no doubt the Turks have had enough of it. They can still hold on, but that's about all.

19th September, 1915. Imbros. News in to say that the Turkish rank and file at Suvla are not equal to any attack. At the end of the bombardment yesterday a few officers jumped on to the parapet and waved their swords; the men shouted from the safety of the trenches — that was all. Alec McGrigor arrived from Alexandria as A.D.C. *vice* Brodrick. At 9 p.m. an enemy aeroplane dropped a couple of bombs. Very jolly having Birdie here. He says that his latest returns show a daily sick list of ten per battalion of British or Australian troops and of one per battalion of Indian troops.

20th September, 1915. Imbros. Nothing doing. There is still scope for action at Suvla but we can't get them to take up any little schemes we may suggest. Shell shortage is the invariable answer. At 5 p.m. Birdie and Anglesey went back to Anzac.

21st September, 1915. Imbros. Further development of the Sikh comedy: Maxwell cables, "No. 1883 E. Your No. M.F. 648. I have received no orders to send these regiments. According to my last information from the War Office they were to remain here, as I require them, but that I should send you a double company of Patiala Sikhs to reinforce the 14th Sikhs."

I have cabled this on to the War Office, saying, "As I understand it, your No. 8012 of 18th September does not mean that the War Office havewithdrawn the offer of these two regiments, which are urgently required here. I therefore hope that you will give early authority to General Officer Commanding, Egypt, to send them on to Mediterranean Expeditionary Force."

The battalions were thrown at my head when that grand statement was made as to the grand army I commanded; now where are they?

Started off with Taylor, Freddie and Colonel Napier (British Military Attaché to Bulgaria) for Anzac. No shelling. Went round the whole left centre and left of Birdie's position to right and left of Cheshire Point, and saw the new Australian Division — very fine fellows. Bullets were on the whistle and "the boys" were as keen and happy as any real schoolboys. Memories of the Khyber,

Chitral and Tirah can hardly yield samples of a country so tangled and broken. Where the Turks begin and where we end is a puzzler, and if you do happen to take a wrong turning it leads to Paradise. Met various Australian friends — a full-blown Lord Mayor — many other leading citizens both of Melbourne and of Sydney.

At 5 p.m. re-embarked. Napier gave birth to a happy thought on our way back. His idea is that we should transfer the troops on the Gallipoli Peninsula to Salonika so as to hearten up the Serbians and Greeks and dishearten our enemies at Sofia. He has pressed his view, he said, on the Foreign Office. I asked him if his Chief, the Minister at Sofia, stood behind him. He said he could not vouch for his Minister's views, but that he, Napier, had power in his capacity as Military Attaché to correspond with the British Government direct.

K. himself did at one time toy with the thought of sending his New Army to Serbia either under Rundle or myself, and was only restrained by the outbreak of typhus in that country. But, keen as I was for the warpath, a very little study of the terrain and supply question was enough to cool my ardour.

Salonika is ruled out by history. In all the campaigns waged of old in these very regions the part played by Salonika has been naval, not military. There must have been some reason for this: there was; it still exists — geography! You could not, and cannot, carry out anything big *via* a couple of narrow cracks through a trackless labyrinth of mountains. The problem is a repetition of the Afghanistan dilemma. A big army would starve at Nisch and along the Danube; a small army would be swallowed up by the enemy. Unless they are going to trust to Bulgaria and Roumania for supplies, one British Army Corps is about as much as can manage to live and fight in Serbia. If they want to make Serbia safe their only possible chance is to push through to Constantinople! There is no other way. I said all this to Napier and a lot more besides and left him keener on Salonika than ever.

He actually thinks that from Salonika we could do what could be done by us at any time at the Dardanelles! Salonika is no alternative to the Dardanelles. I wish the War Office could hear Gouraud; Gouraud, that big sane man with local knowledge. How strong he used to be on the point that Greece lay altogether outside the sphere of any military action by the Entente. We can't feed Russia with munitions through Salonika, nor can we bring back Russian wheat *via* Salonika, — not much, seeing we would not be able to feed ourselves were we fifty miles into the mountains. Salonika is a military mare's nest.

Scatters Wilson and Captain Cheape dined and stayed the night. The King's Messenger arrived with the Mails.

Three cables:

(No. M.F. 654). From General Sir Ian Hamilton to War Office. Only two machine guns per battalion are being brought by the City of London battalions, the balance, by order of General Officer Commanding, Egypt, being handed over to Chief Ordnance Officer, Egypt. The former telegraphs that this has been done by your order. There is nothing that is more important to my force than an ample supply of these guns. I would therefore request that early authority should be given to General Officer Commanding, Egypt, to send on these guns.

(No. I.D. 116). From General Headquarters, Mediterranean Expeditionary Force, to War Office. My No. I.D. 110. Please inform me whether Murdoch has arrived, and whether my information was correct as regards his carrying a despatch for Sir Harry Lawson from Ashmead-Bartlett.

(No. 8108, cipher). From War Office to General Headquarters, Mediterranean Expeditionary Force. Your No. I.D. 116. A despatch answering the description has been taken from Murdoch at Marseilles. You should delay action, however, until we have seen it and you hear from us further.

The despatch should have been censored here and ought, therefore, to be sent back here for censoring. The War Office, I suppose, want to have first look in!

22nd September, 1915. Scatters and Cheape sailed back for Suvla at 6.45 a.m. — just in good time to avoid a raid on our Headquarters carried out by three Taubes between 7.50 and 8 a.m. A dozen bombs dropped; no serious harm done.

Heseltine, King's Messenger, came to dinner.

Bad news from Bulgaria. She is mobilizing, not, we may be sure, for the sake of helping those who do not help themselves. Well do I remember Ferdinand, as long ago as 1909, turning to me and saying as he pointed to a picture of himself in the robes of a Byzantine Emperor, *"Quand vous arrivez au Bosphore, pensez à moi."** Well, there is one good side to working over a narrow Peninsula, under the guns of your own Fleet, all the Bulgars in the Balkans cannot add a rifle to the number of enemy troops on Gallipoli, who already, can only be munitioned, watered and fed with the greatest difficulty. The more targets the enemy cram on to their present narrow front the merrier for our gunners; the better the chance for our submarines starving the lot of them. So long as our Fleet holds the Ægean, we may snap our fingers at the Bulgarians, whereas they, were they fools enough to come here, would live on tenter hooks lest haply some fine morning our Fleet should sail into the Marmora.

Yes, two or three battleships in the Marmora! Think of it! The sea communications, Constantinople-Gallipoli and Asia-Gallipoli, would cease, *ipso facto*, to exist. The railways between Europe and Constantinople and Asia and Constantinople must shut down. In a fortnight the Turks on the Peninsula begin to pack up; in a month the Turks in Constantinople move bag and baggage from Europe to Asia. Ferdinand watching the cat's jump, prepares to turn those 400,000 bayonets of his against the Kaiser. So wags my world in the might-be; very much "might-be" for the Navy are turning down the "to be" for the third time of asking. Three times the Sibyl makes her prodigious offer: May — August — September a new world for old battleships: two — four — six!

23rd September, 1915. Stormy weather: the *Imogene* could hardly crawl out. Have written K. to tell him how day succeeds day, never without incident, but never with achievement; how we are burnt up with longing to get on and how we know that he is as anxious. Yet,

---

* "When you reach the Bosphorus, think of me."

as I tell him, *we* "can't force the pace." How can we? We have not the wherewithal — the stuff. "Byng would like to have four days' successive bombardment for an hour, and then attack, and speaks of one H.E. shell per yard as pat as if they were shells we could pick up on the seashore. I have assured him it is no earthly use; that he shall have his share of what I have got, but that stuff for bombardment is simply not in existence, — not here, at least."

24th September, 1915. Imbros. Fought against exasperation all day. As I thought:

> (No. 8193, cipher). From Earl Kitchener to General Sir Ian Hamilton. In the existing situation, the two battalions referred to in your No. M.F. 655 of 21st September, should remain for the present in Egypt. I have informed Maxwell to this effect.

K. has re-opened the idea of giving up Suvla, saying, "it might become necessary in certain eventualities to abandon that area."

In my reply I have said, "I hope there will be no question now of the abandonment of Suvla.... In the Northern zone I have now more troops than at the time of my telegram, my line is stronger, the old troops are resting, the new troops are improving, and preparations are being made for a local advance. At this stage withdrawal will be a great moral victory for the Turks. Moreover, it would release a large number of enemy divisions to oppose the Russians in Asia, or for other enterprises."

Another cable also sent dealing with the ever present, ever pressing, ever ghastlier shortage upon the Peninsula generally:

> My present shortages, 21st September, of infantry rank and file are 2,645 in the XXIXth Division, 17,166 in the three New Army Divisions, and 23,986 in the four Territorial Divisions, totalling 43,797; out of respective establishments of 11,652, 37,869 and 44,824, total, 97,345.

Were the Royal Naval Division included the percentage would be worse.

Peter Pollen and I dined with the Admiral. After dinner, we

discussed Fox-Ferdinand's little tricks. The Admiral had heard a lot about his flirtations with the Duke of Mecklenburg lately sent from Berlin on some sort of an ambassadorial mission to the Balkans. I told him of my visit to Sofia during the interval which took place between Prince Ferdinand proclaiming himself Tsar, and the tardy and unenthusiastic recognition of his new rank by Great Britain. Ferdinand's Court Chamberlain asked me to dine. I wanted to refuse as I had meant to go on to Constantinople, but Sir George Buchanan, our Minister, begged me to accept. Diplomatic relations were broken off; he had not seen Ferdinand for a month: he wanted to know what that Prince would say to me: "*but*," he added, "you must on no account go in uniform. Seeing you are on the Army Council it would almost amount to a recognition of his Kingship if you went there in uniform."

I thought this a little far-fetched; however, I wrote back and said that I had the honour to accept, but that, as I was travelling, I had only my *kleine Uniform*;[*] i.e., undress kit, handy. I proposed, therefore, with permission to take the liberty of presenting myself in evening dress, wearing miniature medals and decorations and the ribbon of the Grand Cross of the Bath.

By return messenger an answer came back, "His Majesty particularly wished once more to see the admirable British uniform:" would I come in *kleine Uniform*; meanwhile, to put me quite at my ease, H.M. had commanded the Court also to wear undress. I showed this to Sir George, who laughed and said, "He is too sharp; he has done us; you must go now — there is no help for it." So I went in my grubby blue serge and found Ferdinand and the whole of his Court blazing with orders in the fullest of full dress!

25th September, 1915. To Anzac in the *Arno*. Birdie met me and we walked along the lower part of the left of the Australian trenches until we reached the New Zealanders and were joined by Godley. Lunched with General Inglefield; then plodded through the trenches held by his Division (the 54th; nice-looking boys) and by

---

[*] "Little uniform."

the Indian Brigade. On the left of the Indian Brigade I was met by Peyton who did pilot to me through the Scottish Horse section. The Bard joined us here and was in great form, full of administrative good works as in South Africa. The Scottish Horse are as keen as schoolboys out for their first shoot. They were very proud of themselves and of the effect their rifles with telescopic sights had produced when put into the hands of gillies and deer stalkers, and at every twenty yards or so there was a Scottish Horseman looking along his sights, finger on trigger, and by his side a spotter whose periscope was fixed on the opposite loophole. The moment a Turkish shadow darkened the loophole the word was given, the bullet sped. Not a very big mark a loophole at over 100 yards but they got it, they said, one try out of three.

At the end of the Scottish Horse we came to the Worcester Yeomanry trench. But time was up[*] and I had to make tracks for Anzac where we had tea with Birdie, who had stuck to us throughout the tour. Imbros by dinner-time. The quietest day, bar none, we have had on the Peninsula since we first landed. Not a shot was fired anywhere except by our own snipers.

26th September, 1915. Imbros. Last night, after dinner, Braithwaite came across with a black piece of news in his pocket:

> (No. 8229, cipher). From Earl Kitchener to General Sir Ian Hamilton. On account of the mobilization of the Bulgarian Army Greece has asked the Allies to send a force to Salonika in order to enable her to support Serbia should the latter be attacked by Bulgaria, as well as by German forces from the North. No doubt you realize that if by such action Bulgaria joins hands with the Central Powers they will have a clear road to Constantinople and Gallipoli, and be able to send large quantities of ammunition or troops, rendering your position very hazardous.
>
> Both France and ourselves have promised to send between us the troops asked for, viz., 150,000 men, and urgency is essential. It is

---

[*] We had to get into Kephalos Harbour before dark; otherwise the submarine indicator nets were damaged. — *Ian H.*

evident that under these circumstances some troops will have to be taken from the Dardanelles to go to Salonika, but it must be clearly understood that there is no intention of withdrawing from the Peninsula or of giving up the Dardanelles operations until the Turks are defeated. Your staff officer has suggested to me that you saw no difficulty in reducing the length of your line and concentrating your forces by withdrawing from the position now held around Suvla Bay to the neighbourhood of the Kaiajik Aghala position whence a line might be drawn to the sea.

Before the situation was changed by the Bulgarians' action we considered that, owing to the marshy nature of the country now occupied at Suvla and the approaching winter, this reduction of front would be strategically advantageous. Hence my telegram No. 8162 to which your No. M.F. 664 replies.

An offensive along practically the whole line in France has now commenced. The infantry are attacking to-day. Far-reaching results are anticipated which, if secured, should greatly affect your situation.

The projected dispatch of reinforcements of French and British divisions for Asiatic operations must be in abeyance until a decision in the Western theatre can be reached. The troops now at the Dardanelles which are required for Salonika would be two divisions, preferably the Xth and XIth. The French would also have to withdraw either a brigade or a division from their force at Helles for the same purpose. The Yeomanry now *en route* to you would also have to be diverted to Salonika and we should have to arrange to mount them from Egypt after their arrival.

Cable me at once your ideas as to meeting these requirements. The Dardanelles Committee consider a withdrawal from Suvla to be advisable under the circumstances, but they had not seen your telegram No. 664. We have been asked to send the 15-inch howitzer, now on board ship at Mudros, to Belgrade as soon as possible.

Amen — so be it! Our mighty stroke at the vitals of the enemy is to break itself to pieces against the Balkans. God save the King! May the Devil fly away with the whole of the Dardanelles Committee!!

What arguments — what pressure — I wonder can have moved K. to swap horse in mid-Dardanelles? In December K. as good as told me I was "for it" if the day should come along for his New Army to help the Serbians. G.H.Q. in France had belittled his effort to create it; they had tried to throw cold water on it (the New

Army) and now we should see how they liked it going to Salonika! The reason why K., at that time, turned the project down was his view that one Army Corps was too small a force to launch into those regions of great armies and that, if the Germans turned seriously in that direction, it would be gobbled up. But two Army Corps would starve, seeing we had no pack transport and that the railway would only feed 40,000 men. Nor had we any mountain guns. In February he resurrected the question but that time he was put off by the typhus. "Whatever destroys my New Army," he said, "it shall not be the Serbian lice."

Now he cables as if he was being quite consistent and sensible, *now*, when in every aspect, the odds have turned against the undertaking. As to the Bulgarians having "a clear road to Constantinople and Gallipoli" my memorable dinner with Ferdinand, and his insistence on his "pivotal" position, makes me perfectly certain that the bones of no Bulgarian grenadier will fertilize the Peninsula — whatever happens. And if the inconceivable were conceivable and Ferdinand were to work for anything but his own immediate gain — there is no room for them here! That fact is cast iron. The Turkish Empire is *here* in full force. Enver can't feed more! These numbers cause us no alarm. Since the last abortive effort of the Turkish Command to get their men to attack every soldier in the trenches knows well that the enemy are afraid of us. They dare not attack, they will not attack, and they cannot attack. We know that quite well. If K. would only come out here he would realize that the Turk has lost his sting. I don't mean to say he is not still a formidable fellow to turn out of his trench, but he can't attack any more: and that is just the moment we have chosen to sit down and do nothing; now, when the enemy has been brought to a standstill!

During my absence Bailloud has wired saying he had received orders from his own Minister of War to arrange for sending away one Division of the C.E.O. and Braithwaite has cabled the startling news to our S. of S. for War.

Well, well. If the Greeks and ourselves are going to push through the mountains to help the Serbs to hold Belgrade and the line of the Danube, why then, no doubt, we are embarking upon something that would be fine were it feasible — something more hopeful than sitting at Salonika and in its salubrious suburbs, the "political" advantages of which were preached to us by Napier.

But let no man hereafter talk of Dardanelles adventures. *Mon Dieu!**

Once again see the dupes of maps preparing to dash out their brains, or rather the brains of others, against the rocks. If only Joffre and K. had looked at Belgrade over the guns of an Austrian Battery in Semlin, as I did in 1909! The line of the Danube is untenable except by a very large force against the very large forces that can, and will, be brought against it and there is no Fleet there to feed a large force. Also, the communications of such a defending force will not only be mechanically rotten but will also be strategically at the tender mercy of the most cunning Prince in Europe. We may think we have squared Ferdinand. But it is easier to square the circle than square a fox.

On the Danube, the Central Powers can put *and keep* six men to our one, *unless* we control the river from its mouth to Belgrade. This we can only do by forcing the Dardanelles.

After outlining an answer for Braithwaite to draft, I started off at 10.45 for Anzac and Suvla. With me were Taylor, Gascoigne, Lieutenant Moore and Freddie. From Anzac I walked along the old communication trench for a couple of miles, and then went round General Taylor's Brigade along the front by Green Hill and the Chocolate Hills. The heat was very exhausting.

Yesterday's calm has proved to be the prelude to an attempted storm. At 5 a.m. there was a big bombardment of the front line trenches, and the Turks made a gesture of defiance. The gesture did not go beyond fixing bayonets and shouting "Allah!" and the only result has been to render Suvla more convinced than ever that the Turks are absolutely fed up.

After invigorating myself with a good draught of regimental spirit, set forth to walk back to Anzac. Half way I halted at the Indian Brigade Headquarters, and, on the invitation of the hospitable Colonel Palin, had a square meal. Met Allanson, the brave commander of the 6th Gurkhas; Allanson who scaled the heights of Sari Bair and entered for a few hectic hours into the

---

* "My God!"

Loos and Salonika 443

promised land. Oh, what a wonderful adventure his has been! To have seen the Dardanelles and their defences lying flat at his feet! To feel — as he says he did — that he held the whole Turkish Army by the throat!

To-day's inspection has once more brought me into personal touch with the perfect confidence felt both at Anzac and Suvla in the demoralization of the Turks. This has nerved me to cable agreeing to spare the 10th and 53rd Divisions from Suvla as well as a Brigade of French from Helles and four and a half Brigades of British Field Artillery:

(No. M.F. 675). From General Sir Ian Hamilton to Secretary of State for War. Reference your No. 8229. Let me begin by saying that I quite realize that, to you, playing for your large stakes, the Dardanelles operation may temporarily become of a secondary nature. In spite of the Salonika scheme I am, however, particular to note that it is not intended to withdraw from the Gallipoli Peninsula, nor to give up here until the Turks are beaten. Bearing this in mind it becomes my duty to point out the objection to the abandonment of Suvla Bay, the consequences of which at this stage would, I consider, be so grave that I am warranted in running much risk to get you your two divisions by other means. The situation has greatly changed since I first suggested the possibility of abandoning the Bay, and its abandonment at this stage would, I feel convinced, enormously accentuate the difficulties of any subsequent attempt to capture the Narrows; unless, as a result of our landing troops at Salonika, Bulgaria were induced to side with us and not against us. Even when I told you in my No. M.F. 578 of 23rd August that the diminution of my forces might compel me to contract my line, I could not view the project without misgiving, in spite of the fact that, at that time, I had landed few reinforcements and little artillery in the new zone, and my views are not rightly interpreted when it is said that I saw no great difficulty in the enterprise. After I had received the reassuring news of reinforcements I sent you my No. M.F. 589 of 26th August and I have from that date been pouring in large quantities of reinforcements and supplies in anticipation of winter, and have landed a large additional amount of artillery. Therefore, I could not hurriedly evacuate the Bay without sacrificing the majority of supplies and warlike stores. I might also have very considerable losses, for the Turks, who were previously 700 yards away, are now within bombing distance in places. They have a large number of guns in the northern zone and a retirement could only be effected under heavy fire, which with unseasoned troops would make the retreat a hazardous one. As explained in my No. M.F. 664 evacuation of the Bay would involve with it the *eventual* evacuation of all but the original Anzac position. But even if this last step were not necessary the withdrawal of British soldiers from Suvla would be an overwhelming victory for the Turks. Our position in the Dardanelles would be entirely altered for the worse and even the effect of our landing of troops at Salonika might be discounted in Bulgarian eyes. At the present moment the Turkish commissariat difficulties and tales of starving families which the wounded bring back from Constantinople are having a bad effect on their *moral* and the number of desertions is on the increase. Two Turkish attempts at the offensive have broken down completely during the last week as their troops refused to leave cover. If I give ground the Turkish *moral* will immediately recover and instead of containing over 60,000 Turks in the Northern Zone there would be large numbers set free to go elsewhere. All these arguments seem to prove plainly that to evacuate a yard of Suvla would be a most serious, and might prove a disastrous step. I would therefore prefer to run the risk of holding the line defensively with fewer troops in order to spare two divisions for the new enterprise.

I have at present one division in Corps Reserve at Suvla and the 1st Australian Division resting at Mudros and also one brigade resting at Imbros. By bringing the tired Australians back and making them replace the Mounted Division in the section north of Susak Kuyu I could spare Xth and LIIIrd Divisions or else Xth and XIth. I could also spare one French brigade from Cape Helles without replacing it by troops from Suvla, and a total of 4½ British Field Artillery brigades. This would at any rate enable me to postpone any evacuation at Suvla and if the withdrawal became necessary later on there would be less loss involved in supplies and stores, as I could gradually make necessary preparations for this deplorable contingency.

The 15-inch howitzer is at Alexandria and can be sent whenever you desire on the receipt of instructions. To-morrow I am having a conference here with the Corps Commanders concerned to consider the details. I hope that you realize that though the IXth Corps consists of Xth, XIth and XIIIth Divisions there are attached to it LIIIrd Welsh Division, Mounted Division and XXIXth Division, and I therefore sincerely trust you will not contemplate the withdrawal of the Corps Staff and Corps Commander to accompany the two divisions destined for Salonika, for I have absolutely no one to replace them.

27th September, 1915. After breakfast a dove, the German sort, flew across from Chanak and dropped four bombs on our Headquarters; all wide; no damage. At 11 o'clock Birdwood and Byng came over for a confab on the last upset. Both Generals went word by word through my M.F. 657 of the 26th September, — (1) as to drawing in our horns at Suvla, — (2) as to our power of holding on after we lose the 10th and 53rd Divisions. They concur in my cables and are emphatic as to the futility of making a gift of ground to any enemy who are shaking in their shoes. What the Turks want is a gift, not of ground but of high explosive shell. A few thousand pounds worth of that and Byng would go ahead and settle their hash for good. Birdie stayed to lunch during which meal I got a message from Bailloud telling me flat that he had orders from his Government to get one Division over to Mudros forthwith. As long as I am in command no soldier but myself shall handle the troops entrusted to me. I have sent the following reply: "Sorry that as my orders already telegraphed to you this morning are specific, I cannot permit any movement of troops away from the Peninsula pending further instructions."

Ross and Nevinson (Press Correspondents), who have been away on a jaunt, called on me and had tea. Lord William Percy and Sir Walter Barttelot dined.

28th September, 1915. Office. At midnight an enemy aeroplane let us have a taste of his high explosive — no harm done. At 10.30 this morning another came over and dropped a couple of bombs into the aerodrome close by — two men hit.

Colonel Dorling reported himself to me as Senior Paymaster.

A cable from K. saying he is glad to meet me as to holding on at Suvla. He agrees in fact that to draw in our horns would merely set free six Turkish Divisions to attack us elsewhere. He agrees also with my choice of Divisions for Salonika. K. seems astonished at the behaviour of the French Government in sending tactical orders direct to Bailloud. Most extraordinary, he calls it. He wants Byng to go to Salonika and winds up gloriously by telling me of the great things they are doing in France; that, up to the present, 23,000 prisoners and over 40 guns have been taken, and that he hopes there are more of each to follow. This fine success, he says, should help us along in the East. So it should. I have cabled the good news across and ordered a *feu de joie** to be fired everywhere on the Peninsula in honour of the victory. The ball was opened at Helles at 7 p.m., the Turks replied vigorously with every gun and rifle they could bring to bear, and rarely, I imagine, has a "furious joy" expressed itself more furiously.

Nowhere in the Empire has this fine victory brought more heartfelt relief and joy than at the Dardanelles: to have been brought to a standstill, for the third time of asking, for *nothing*; that was the fear which had haunted us.

29th September, 1915. Work. At 11 a.m. tore myself away from my papers to play principal part in a gay little ceremony. Outside my office a guard of honour of Surrey Yeomanry, Naval Division and Australians formed three sides of a square. Bertier, de la Borde and Pelliot were led in smiling like brides going up to the altar, and, after a tiny speech, I decorated the first with the D.S.O. and the other two with the Military Cross. All three Officers are most popular, and there were loud cheers. De la Borde had tea and Mitchell came in at the same time to say good-bye. We are all distressed at losing Mitchell. He is a very fine specimen of the sailor of the modern school. Efficient, modest, untiring at his work. He has collaborated in the most loyal and devoted manner with the G.S., and I don't know how we should ever have got on without him.

Nevinson, the Correspondent, came again with Maxwell, the Press Censor. Nevinson wants to find out whether it would be worth his while to go to Salonika. I would like to lend him a hand for he is such a nice fellow, but the matter is about as secret as can be, and I don't feel myself free to say much. The Captains of H.M.S. *Cornwall* and *Cornwallis* dined; also Flight Commander Samson and Ward, King's Messenger. The last named starts to-morrow night and carried off with him my letter to K. Amongst other things I write:

---

* "Bonfire."

In the cables which have passed between us, I have found it anything but an easy business to strike the happy mean between executing your wishes promptly and cheerfully on the one hand, and, on the other, giving you a faithful impression of how we should stand here once your orders had been carried out.

If I make too little of the dangers which surround me, then you may be encouraged to weaken me still further, thereby jeopardizing the whole of this enterprise. But if I allow my anxieties to get too much the upper hand, why then I may be ruining some larger enterprise, the bearing of which I have no means of gauging.

I then explain the situation and wind up:

> In the small hours of the morning, before I have had my matutinal cup of tea, the immediate outlook gives me a feeling of cold feet in a more aggravated form than I have hitherto experienced. The whole plan of the French Asiatic subsidiary operation has gone, for the meantime, by the board. England and France between them cannot find men enough, I should think, to send considerable forces to Asia as well as run an entirely new show elsewhere. Indeed, Naval requirements alone would seem entirely to forbid it. But I must not worry you any more with surmises. After all, nothing great in this world was ever easily accomplished. Never has there been such an example of that as in the Dardanelles Expedition. How many times has success seemed to be on the point of crowning our efforts, and yet, on each occasion, just as we are beginning to see light through the tangle of obstacles, preparing for an assault, or whatever it may be, something occurs to upset the apple-cart. None the less we do advance, and we will succeed in the end. I feel I am playing it rather low down inflicting on you the outline of my own trouble at a moment when your own must be infinitely greater.
>
> Reading over this letter which I have not now time to re-write or correct, it strikes me that in concentrating my mind purely on the Dardanelles I may have given a wrong impression of my general attitude towards your latest demand. No one can realize, I believe, more clearly than I do that the Dardanelles operations themselves hinge for their success to a very large extent upon the maintenance of a barrier between the Central Powers and Constantinople. As far as reinforcements of men to the enemy in the field are concerned, such inter-communication would not be so fatal as might perhaps be imagined. The Gallipoli Peninsula is a limited area, and if the

Germans had a million men at Constantinople they could not, under present conditions, add many, if any, to the numbers already opposed to us. But the free transit of coal, flour, ammunition and big guns might well put us all in the cart — the cart being in this instance, the sea.

My A.D.C. has brought me an irritated message from the A.G., War Office:

> Your No. M.F.A. 4003 of the 24th instant. Are you aware that your telegram was really a demand for 60,000 men with a weekly supply in addition. We do not see how to meet such large numbers in view of the present situation in France. Have the numbers at Base, Alexandria, and men returning from hospital, etc., been taken into account? Please state what are your minimum requirements to carry on with.

Am I aware, etc.? Why certainly; *and so is the A.G.* To ignore facts is one thing; to be ignorant of them is another. These facts are, or should be, the daily bread of his Department. I resent this surprise; it is not genuine. If, as the A.G. says, they have not got the men to send, why in God's name do they go on telling the people they *have* got them?

Have drafted out this answer:

> A.G. My telegram No. M.F.A. 4003 told you the number required to bring and keep all formations up to establishment and, as an estimate, the numbers given therein are accurate. There is nothing new in that telegram; it is only the culmination of many demands, the deficiency, which was serious enough before, being aggravated by the prevailing epidemic. I took into account the numbers in Base depots and men returning from hospital. I certainly hope that there may be a decrease in the sick rate and that there will be an increase in the numbers returning from hospital, but that cannot make any difference to my present shortage of establishment though it would affect the strength of monthly drafts required.
>
> I would like further to point out that only 750 of the 20,000 drafts now coming are for the Territorial Force, the remainder being for the Regulars. Hence assuming that wastage will be equally distributed over all the eight divisions, the estimated shortage of 30,490 on 9th

October will be constituted as follows: Four Territorial Force divisions, 26,583; four Regular divisions, 3,907.

When my No. M.F.A. 4003 was sent no question had arisen of denuding my force for a fresh expedition elsewhere. I fully realize that you cannot send what does not exist and I will do the best possible with what you, knowing my situation, are able to send; but I do not consider that it is possible to view my position in winter with any equanimity unless I am to receive substantial drafts and unless a normal flow of reinforcements for all divisions can be arranged so as to counter the difficulties that are inherent in keeping a force operating so far from England up to establishment.

30th September, 1915. Imbros. Peace on the Peninsula; trouble at G.H.Q. The 10th Division is taking its departure from Suvla undisturbed by the enemy. Not a shot is being fired. Some say this denotes extraordinary skill in the conduct of the withdrawal; others, extraordinary delight on the part of the Turks to see them clearing out. I don't believe in either theory. The Turks have been fought to a standstill and there is no attack left in them — not under *any* circumstances or temptation; that is what I believe in my heart, otherwise I would refuse point blank to strip myself of two full divisions under their noses. Still, it is nervous work presuming to this extent upon their fatigue and I will not agree to the 53rd going too, as the loss of three Divisions would leave an actual hole in our line. Meanwhile, it is a relief to hear that the move is going on just like peacetime. As to G.H.Q., all is held up by uncertainty. Our whole enterprise hangs still in the balance. No date for the sailing of our troops for Salonika can yet be fixed, and we may get them back. Am glued to the cable terminus waiting, waiting, waiting. I have agreed to let the 2nd Brigade of the French go!

This cable sent to-day to Lord K. explains itself:

The following has just been received from Bailloud: 'I have the honour to inform you that I have received a telegram from the French Minister of War ordering me (1) to embark one division of the Corps Expéditionnaire immediately for Salonika; (2) to organize this division, which will be placed under my command, into two brigades of Metropolitan Infantry with two groups of 75 mm., one group of mountain artillery, one battery of 125 mm. howitzer and four 120 mm.

guns. I am taking steps to execute this order and to hold the present section of the French line with the force remaining in the Peninsula, which will be placed under General Brulard.'

I said in my telegram No. M.F. 675, that I could only spare one brigade of the French. I desire to place on record that if this order of the French Government is carried out the LIIIrd Division cannot possibly be spared without seriously endangering the safety of this force and the whole future of the Dardanelles enterprise. Even if I were to keep the LIIIrd Division it would not relieve me of intense anxiety. The fact will not escape your notice that the division to go is being re-constructed so that nothing but European troops are included, thus leaving an undue proportion of Senegalese. This constitutes such a grave danger that, if I had the power, I would refuse to allow Bailloud to carry out this order of his Government. It need hardly be pointed out that all your hopes of success in the Balkans would be upset by a disaster at Cape Helles. Even when I said that I could spare one French Infantry Brigade the Commander of the VIIIth Corps, who is one of the last men in the Army to express alarmist views, represented to me, in view of the physical condition of a large proportion of his troops, the gravity of the case in the strongest terms.

A reminder of mine *re* the Ashmead-Bartlett incident has drawn an amusing and highly unexpected answer from the War Office:

> Murdoch was found to be carrying a despatch for the Prime Minister criticizing military operations in Gallipoli. He carried nothing for Lawson.

I could not help laughing heartily at the blue looks of Tyrrell, the Head of our Intelligence. After all, this is Asquith's own affair. I do not for one moment believe Mr. Asquith would employ such agencies and for sure he will turn Murdoch and his wares into the wastepaper basket. I have reassured Tyrrell. Tittle-tattle will effect no lodgment in the Asquithian brain.

Lieutenant Moore from the Military Secretary's office in London dined. He has been useful to us. During the night there was rain and heavy fog. The evacuation of Suvla by the 10th Division goes on without the smallest hitch and is almost finished — all except the guns. Whether the Turks have fallen asleep or only closed an eye is the question of the hour but Birdwood's Intelligence are certain they are stone cold and cannot be dragged to the attack.

1st October, 1915. Imbros. S. of S. cables he will not overlook our wants in the matter of ammunition but that "at the present moment all he can get has to be sent to France." I have thanked him. Not a word from France since we fired the *feu de joie*.

K. believes in the East and sends shell to the West. The reason is that K.'s *beliefs* are only intuitions; he believes in the same sort of way that Elijah knew certain things.

The principle underlying the world war seems to me this: that wherever the new system of trenches, dug-outs, barbed wire, can reach its fullest development, *there* we should prefer the defensive. Wherever this new system cannot be fully developed, there the old ideas hold good and there are the theatres for the offensive. In France and Flanders where both sides are within a few hours' run, on good railways, from their own chief arsenals and depôts the new system attains prodigious power. In the Turkish Empire almost all the conditions; railways, material, factories, etc., are favourable to the old and unfavourable to the new conditions.

To me these views appear as clear as crystal and as unanswerable as Euclid. The tenacity of the new system of defence; the pressure of France; the apathy of a starved military opinion; the fact that all our most powerful soldiers are up to their necks in the West, combine to keep us ramming our heads against the big pile of barbed wire instead of getting through by the gate called strait.

Next Braithwaite with the following electrical bombshell:

> By Bailloud's report I see that he considers that the French line can be held by one division. If, on reconsideration, you agree with this view can you spare the LIIIrd Division?

K. has pounced like a hawk on Bailloud's statement (which I cabled to him yesterday) that he is taking steps for Brulard to hold the French section with one division.

Have answered::

(No. M.F. 703). From General Sir Ian Hamilton to Earl Kitchener. Your No. 8409, cipher. Not one word of my No. M.F. 693 can I take back. The situation at Cape Helles cannot be fully realized. May I remind you that when on 20th August I moved the XXIXth Division to Suvla, I left at Cape Helles only the minimum garrison compatible with safety. Since that date the total British troops there have decreased in strength from 15,300 to 13,300 rifles, and now I am losing a French composite division which is made up of the only troops of the Corps Expéditionnaire on whom I can rely, as well as 44 guns. It is my considered opinion that to leave protection of Cape Helles to one division of Colonial troops, plus 13,300 worn-out British Territorials and Naval Volunteers, is running too serious a risk. To-day, therefore, I am moving one brigade of XXIXth Division back from Suvla to reinforce VIIIth Corps in order to have some regular troops there on whom I can rely. This makes it impossible to spare the LIIIrd Division. The change of opinion on the part of Bailloud, when he gets away from a position which I have found it difficult to persuade him to hold with two divisions, and which he now, as you say, thinks can be held with one division composed largely of blacks, is startling enough to need no comment. If you want to get at his real opinion, suggest that he stays here with one division while Brulard goes to Salonika.

A despatch from Bailloud has *just* reached me on the situation in French section after his own departure with one division. It is as follows::

'One division will then be defending our present line with an effective strength reduced by half, and with Infantry which comprises only Colonial contingents, half European and half native. I feel it to be my duty to expose the situation to you in order that you may be able to decide whether the time has not now arrived to reduce the present section of the C.E.O., making part of it occupied by British troops and holding a solid reserve in rear of the Allies' first line capable of dealing with any situation.'

I believe this indicates Bailloud's real opinion; it is a curious contrast to that quoted in your No. 8409, cipher, dated 30th September.

At 11.30 crossed to "K" and inspected the 87th Brigade of the 29th Division. Lucas, of the Berks Regiment, commanded. Saw the Border Regiment under Colonel Pollard; then the renowned Royal Inniskilling Fusiliers under Major Pierce, the full strength of the Battalion on parade "all present" was 220! Next the K.O.S.B.s; they were under the command of Major Stoney; last the South Wales Borderers under the command of Captain Williams.

The men were in rags and looked very tired. This is the first time in the campaign our rank and file have seemed sorry for themselves. Ten days of rest had been promised them and now they are being hurried back to the trenches before they have had a week. My heart goes out to them entirely. Were I they I would feel mad with me. The breaking of my word to the 29th Division has to be shouldered by me just like all the other results of this new Balkan adventure; the withdrawal of the Irish and the French for Salonika leaves no margin of rest for what's left.

Inspected also the West Riding Field Company of Royal Engineers under Major Bayley, and the West Lancashire Field Ambulance.

A long letter from Maxwell putting his point of view about the 51st and 53rd Sikhs. Were we both sealed-pattern Saints we'd be bound to fall foul of one another working under so perverse a system. He has written me very nicely; nothing could be nicer. I have replied by return:

> Yours of 24th just received. As to the wires about the 51st and 53rd between myself and the War Office, and your remarks thereon, we stand so much on one platform, and are faced so much by the same difficulties, that I think it ought to be fairly easy for us to come to an understanding in most conceivable circumstances, as indeed our co-operation up to date has shown.
>
> If Egypt goes, then I shall not last very long. If I am wiped out, I think it will be the preface to trouble in Egypt.*

---

* The last time this subject was broached between Lord Kitchener and myself was immediately after the evacuation of Helles. Everyone was intensely relieved, especially Lord Kitchener, for he had realized better than our politicians the desperate stakes we had planked down in our gamble with the Clerk of the Weather. Yet in that very moment when the burden of an intolerable anxiety had

As to myself I am 60,000 below strength. I had a cable from the War Office a day or two ago expressing naïve astonishment at this figure. I replied that the figure was accurate and that there was nothing new about it as it only denoted the accumulation of a state of things which had been continuously reported since the very first day when we started off from England minus the ten per cent. margin of excess given to every unit going across to France. This is the essential cause of our repeated failure to make that last little push which just differentiates partial from conclusive success. In every case this has been so. Had I been able to throw in my ten per cent. margin on the third day after landing, there is no doubt in the world we would have got right up on to Achi Baba. Afterwards, each engagement we fought, although our total numbers may have been largely increased, the old formations were always at half strength or something less. However, I won't bother you about this as your time is too precious to enter into 'might-have-beens' and so is mine.

Meantime, my line is very, very thin, and the men are getting entirely worn out. In the midst of this I am called upon to send away two Divisions, the French and the Irish, to —— you know where. I have done so without a murmur, although it puts me into a ticklish position. Reinforcements are now to be diverted elsewhere and my command is not an enviable one. I quite understand the necessity of trying to maintain a barrier between Essen and Constantinople. I quite understand also the danger of doing so at the expense of this attenuated, exhausted force. I have represented the facts home, and it is for them to decide.

Dined with the Admiral.

---

just been lifted from his shoulders he took the occasion to declare to me that he stood by every word he had said. What he "had said," was that any withdrawal from the Dardanelles must react in due course upon Islam, and especially upon Egypt. Cairo, he held to be the centre of the Mahomedan doctrine and the pivotal point of our great Mahomedan Imperium. An evacuation of the Dardanelles would serve as an object lesson to Egypt just as our blunders in the Crimea had served as a motive to the Indian mutineers. Ultimate success was not the point in either case. The point was that the legend of the invincibility of British troops should be shattered in some signal and quite unmistakable fashion. "The East," he said, "moved slowly in the fifties, and it will move slowly now. We've had a wonderful delivery but — depend upon it — the price has yet to be paid!" — *Ian H., 1920.*

2nd October, 1915. The despatch of the Salonika force and their outfit are absorbing all my energies. Our whole Expeditionary Force is being drawn upon to send the 10th Division creditably turned out to the new theatre. The twenty-four hours' delay caused by the political crisis at Athens has been a godsend in enabling me to reclothe and re-equip the detachment from top to toe. The supplies for my own force are now exhausted, but, — on the principle of the starving garrison who threw loaves over the ramparts at the besiegers, we must try and make a good first impression on the Greeks.

The submarine catcher, or the "Silver Baby" as the men call it, has been flying about all day, without luck. Gascoigne and Bertier dined. Blazing hot; quite a setback to August temperatures.

Chapter XXI – The Beginning of the End

3rd October, 1915. Imbros. Church Parade. Inspected escort, men of the Howe and Nelson Battalions and a contingent from the 12th and 26th Australian Infantry. At 12.15 Bailloud, Brulard and Girodon arrived from Mudros for a last conference. Everything is fixed up. We are going to help the derelict division of French in every way we can. Bailloud, for his part, promises to leave them their fair share of guns and trench mortars. Whenever I see him I know he is one of the best fellows in the world. We went down and waved farewells from the pier. He was quite frank. He does not think the Allies have either the vision or the heart to go through with Gallipoli: he begins to suspect that the big push on the Western Front is going to yield no laurels: so Salonika hits his fancy.

Lieutenants Weston and Schemallach of the Australians and Lieutenant Gellibrand of the Naval Division lunched. A Mr. Unsworth came to talk over gifts for the Australian troops. He seems a capital chap; full of go and goodwill to all men.

4th October, 1915. Imbros. Vague warnings have taken shape in an event. A cable from K. telling me to decipher the next message myself. I have not drafted out an average of fifty telegrams a day for Lord K. for six months at a stretch without knowing something of his *modus scribendi*. The Staff were pleasantly excited at the idea that some new move was in the wind. I knew the new move — or thought I did.

Well, not that: not exactly that; not this time. But the enemies of our enterprise have got our range to a nicety and have chucked their first bomb bang into the middle of my camp.

A "flow of unofficial reports from Gallipoli," so K. cables to me, is pouring into the War Office. These "unofficial reports" are "in much the same strain" (perhaps they spring from the same source?). "They adversely criticize the work of the Headquarters Staff and complaints are made that its members are much out of touch with the troops. The War Office also doubt whether their present methods are quite satisfactory." K. therefore suggests "some important changes in your Headquarters Staff; for instance, if you agreed, Kiggell from home to take Braithwaite's place with you. Should you, however, decline and desire to remain as at present, may we assume that we are quite safe in regarding these unofficial reports as not representing the true feelings of the troops?"

So ——! On the face of it this cable seems to suggest that a man widely known as a straight and capable soldier should be given the shortest of shrifts at the instance of "unofficial reports"; i.e., camp gossip. Surely the cable message carries with it some deeper significance!

I am grateful to old K. He is trying to save me. He picked out Braithwaite himself. Not so long ago he cabled me in his eagerness to promote him to Major-General; he would not suggest substituting the industrious Kiggell if he didn't fear for me and for the whole of this enterprise.

K. wants, so he says, "some important change"; that cannot mean, surely, that he wants a sufficiently showy scapegoat to feed the ravenous critics — or does it? Perhaps, he's got to gain time; breathing space wherein to resume the scheme which was sidetracked by the offensive in France and smashed by the diversion to Salonika. Given time, our scheme may yet be resumed. The Turks are in the depths. Sarrail with his six divisions behind him could open the Narrows in no time. I see the plan. K. must have a splendid sacrifice but by the Lord they shan't have the man who stood by me like a rock during those first ghastly ten days.

The new C.R.E., General Williams, and Ellison turned up for lunch. Williams gave us the first authentic news we have had about those Aden excursions and alarms.

An amusing aftermath of the evacuation by the French and Irish Divisions. When the last of Bailloud's troops had embarked the Turks dropped manifestoes from aeroplanes along the lines of the Senegalese calling upon these troops to make terms and come over now that their white comrades had left them to have their throats cut. I have cabled this queer item to the S. of S. Evidently the enemy were quite well aware of our withdrawal. Then *why* didn't they shell the beaches? At French Headquarters they believe that the Turks were so glad to see our backs that they hardly dared breathe (much less fire a shell) lest we should change our minds.

5th October, 1915. First thing another cable from K. saying, "I think it well to let you know" that it is "quite understood by the Dardanelles Committee that you are adopting only a purely defensive attitude at present." Also: "I have no reason to imagine you have any intention of taking the offensive anywhere along the line seeing I have been unable to replace your sick and wounded men." But, if he knows I *can't* take the offensive, why trouble to cable me that the Dardanelles Committee expect me to adopt "only a purely defensive attitude"? I realize where we stand; K., Braithwaite and I, — on the verge. We are getting on for two months now since the August fighting — all that time we have been allowed to do nothing — literally, allowed to do nothing, seeing we have been given no shell. What a fiasco! The Dardanelles is not a sanatorium; Suvla is not Southend. With the men we have lost from sickness in the past six weeks we could have beaten the Turks twice over. Now Government seem to be about to damn everything — themselves included.

But after all, who am I to judge the Government of the British

The Beginning of the End

Empire? What do I know of their difficulties, pledges, and enemies — whether outside or inside the fold?

I have no grouse against Government or War Office — still less against K. — though many hundred times have I groused.*

Freely and gratefully do I admit that the individuals have done their best. Most of all am I indebted — very deeply indebted — to K. for having refrained absolutely from interference with my plan of campaign or with the tactical execution thereof.

But things are happening now which seem beyond belief. That the Dardanelles Committee should complacently send me a message to say we "quite understand that you are adopting only a purely defensive attitude at present" is staggering when put side by side with the carbon of this, the very last cable I have sent them. "I think you should know immediately that the numbers of sick evacuated in the IXth Corps during the first three days of October were 500 men on the 1st instant; 735 men on the 2nd instant and 607 men on the 3rd instant. Were this rate kept up it would come to 45 per cent. of our strength evacuated in one month."

Three quarters of this sickness is due to inaction — and now the Dardanelles Committee "quite understand" I am "adopting only a purely defensive action at present." I have never adopted a defensive attitude. They have forced us to sit idle and go sick because — at the very last moment — they have permitted the French offensive to take precedence of ours, although, on the face of it, there was no violent urgency in France as there is here. Our

---

* I think I hardly knew how often till I came to read through my diary in cold print. But all the time I was conscious, and am still more so now, of K.'s greatness. Still more so now because, when I compare him with his survivors, they seem measurable, he remains immeasurable.

I wish very much I could make people admire Lord K. understandingly. To praise him wrongly is to do him the worst disservice. The theme can hardly be squeezed into a footnote, but one protest must be made all the same. Lord Fisher gives fresh currency to the fable that K. was a great organizer. K. hated organization with all his primitive heart and soul, because it cramped his style.

K. was an individualist. He was a Master of Expedients; the greatest probably the world has ever seen. Whenever he saw any organization his inclination was to smash it, and often — but not always — he was right. This may sound odd in Anglo-Celtic ears. But most British organizations are relics of the past. They are better smashed than patched, and K. loved smashing. — IAN H., 1920.

men in France were remarkably healthy; they were not going sick by thousands. But I feel too sick myself — body and soul — to let my mind dwell on these miseries.

Sealed my resolution (resignation?) by giving my answer about Braithwaite. Though the sins of my General Staff have about as much to do with the real issues as the muddy water had to do with the death of the argumentative lamb, I begin by pointing out to the War Office wolf that "no Headquarters Staff has ever escaped similar criticism."

Grumblings are an old campaigner's *vade mecum*.* Bred by inaction; enterprise and activity smother them. A sickness of the spirit, they are like the flies that fasten on those who stay too long in one place. Was Doughty Wylie "much out of touch with the troops" when he led the Dublins, Munsters and Hampshires up from "V" beach and fell gloriously at their head? Was Williams "out of touch" when he was hit? Was Hore Ruthven? "As to Braithwaite," I say, "my confidence in that Officer is complete. I did not select him; you gave him to me and I have ever since felt most grateful to you for your choice."

Now — I feel better.

The plot thickens. A cable just come in from the S. of S. for War:

> The following statement has been made in letter to Prime Minister, Australia, by Mr. Murdoch: 'The fact is that after the first day at Suvla an order had to be issued to officers to shoot without mercy any soldier who lagged behind or loitered in advance.' Wire me as to the truth or otherwise of this allegation.

Murdoch must be mad. Or, is there some method in this madness?

Mr. Murdoch was not a war correspondent; he is purely a civilian and could hardly have invented this "order" on his own. No soldier could have told him this. Someone not a soldier — someone so interested in discrediting the Dardanelles Campaign

---

* Literally, "Go with me," but here used to refer to a type of small reference book carried in one's pocket.

that he does not scruple to do so even by discrediting our own troops must have put this invention about,*per* Murdoch. Doubtless we strike here upon the source of these "unofficial statements" which have been flowing into the War Office. All I remember of his visit to me here is a sensible, well-spoken man with dark eyes, who said his mind was a blank about soldiers and soldiering, and made me uncomfortable by an elaborate explanation of why his duty to Australia could be better done with a pen than with a rifle. He was one week at the Press Correspondents' camp and spent, so they tell me, a few hours only at Anzac and Suvla, never once crossing to Helles. If then his letter to his Prime Minister is a fair sample of the grounds upon which Braithwaite has been condemned, Heaven help us all!

As a relief to these disagreeable thoughts, a Taube dropped a couple of bombs into camp. She flew so high that she was hard to see until the bursting shrapnel gave us her line. As she made tracks back through the trackless blue, the ships gave her a taste of some big projectiles, 12-inches or 9.2. The aerial commotion up there must have been considerable.

At noon, sailed over to Suvla in H.M.S. *Savage*. We took our lunch on board. As we came into harbour the Turks gave us a shell or two from their field guns, then stopped. Young Titchfield, the Duke of Portland's son, met us at the beach and brought us along to Byng's Headquarters, where I met also de Lisle and Reed. After hearing their news I started off with the whole band to make a tour of the trenches held by the 88th Brigade, under General Cayley. On the way I was taken up to "Gibraltar" observation post to get a bird's-eye view of the line. Besides my old friends of the 29th Division I saw some of the new boys, especially the 1st Newfoundland Battalion under Colonel Burton, and the 2/1st Coy. of the London Regiment. This was the Newfoundlanders' first day in the trenches and they were very pleased with themselves. They could not understand why they were not allowed to sally forth at once and do the Turks in. The presence of these men from our oldest colony adds to the extraordinary mix-up of people now fighting on the Peninsula. All the materials exist here for bringing off the biblical coup of Armageddon excepting only the shell.

In the course of these peregrinations I met Marshall of the 53rd

Division, Beresford, commanding the 86th Brigade, and Colonel Savage, R.E.

After tea with Byng, including the rare treat of a slice of rich cake, we went down to our friend H.M.S. *Savage*. The wind had risen to a fairly stiff gale, and the sea was beginning to get very big. Those field gun shells had caused the *Savage* to lie a desperate long way out to sea; we had a very stiff pull in the teeth of the waves, and every one of us began to think that salt water rather than the bullet was going to end our days. However, we just managed by the skin of our teeth and the usual monkey tricks, to scramble up on board. As I said in my wrath when I first stood on the firm deck, I would sooner have a hundred shells fired at me by the Turks.

Captain Davidson commanding H.M.S. *Cornwallis* dined; everyone liked him very much.

6th October, 1915. Left General Headquarters soon after 11 o'clock for Helles, taking with me Aspinall and Freddie. Lunched with Davies at 8th Corps Headquarters.

Afterwards rode across to Royal Naval Division and saw Paris. Then went with Bertie Lawrence, commanding 52nd Division, to his lines. Our route lay up Achi Baba Nallah and along the trenches to the Horse Shoe; then along Princes Street trench up the Vineyard, and back along the Krithia Nallah to the Headquarters of the 156th Brigade. There we mounted our horses and rode back to Corps Headquarters. I brought Steward back with me to dine and sleep the night. Colonel Tyrrell and Major Hunloke (King's Messenger) also dined.

7th October, 1915. Wasted energy brooding over the addled eggs of the past. Are the High Gods bringing our new Iliad to grief in a spirit of wanton mischief? At whose door will history leave the blame for the helpless, hopeless fix we are left in — rotting with disease and told to take it easy?

That clever fellow Deedes dined; also Rowan Hamilton, son of my old Simla friend the Colonel of that name.

The Beginning of the End 463

8th October, 1915. Imbros. At 11 a.m. Ellison, Taylor, Gascoigne and Freddie sailed with me for Anzac. There we lunched with the ascetic Birdie and Staff off bully beef, biscuits and water. Then, the whole lot of us, together with de Crespigny, Birdie's Staff Officer, hurried five miles an hour down the communication trench to the Headquarters of the Indian Brigade. After greetings we shoved on and saw the 2nd Lovat Scouts under Lieutenant-Colonel Stirling and met, whilst going round their line, Major Morrison Bell and Captain Oppenheim. They seemed in very good fettle, and it would have been hard to find a finer lot of men. Taking leave of the 2nd Lovat Scouts, we worked along the trenches of the Fife and Forfar Yeomanry, under Colonel Mitchell, until we came to the 1st Lovat Scouts under Colonel Bailey. Lovat himself was sick, but Peyton commanding the 2nd Mounted Division turned up just when the inspection was at an end. He had got lost in the trenches, or we had. Next time the way was lost there was no mistake as to who had made the mistake.

Birdie and I were pushing along as fast as we could leg it back towards Anzac. In the maze of trenches we came to a dividing of the ways. Two jolly old Sikhs were sitting at the junction. I asked if the road to the left led to the Headquarters of the Indian Brigade. They said, "Yes," so on we went, I leading, Birdie following. The trench got shallower and shallower until, in a little grove of trees, it petered out entirely. But it seemed to begin again in the other side and so we crossed through the trees. Once there we found that the supposed trench was only a shallow scratching up of the earth, and that we were standing within a hundred yards of the Turkish lines just about half way between them and the Lovat Scouts! I shouted to Birdie and we turned and ran for it — for our lives, I mean. Luckily the Turks were slow at spotting us, all except one who was a rank bad shot: so tumbling back into the trenches from which we had emerged, we saved ourselves by the skin of our teeth. I could not have been smarter about dodging two or three bullets had it been the beginning of our enterprise and had the high minarets of Constantinople glittered before my eyes.

When we got back to where the two old Sikhs were sitting, as placid as idols, Birdie gave them his opinion of their ancestors. On reaching the Australian and New Zealand Division we were done to a turn, but Godley revived us with tea and then we made our way back to our destroyer and to Headquarters. It was dark when we arrived and a bad storm was setting in — wind and rain — which went on till midnight.

Replies have come in to our enquiries as to Mr. Murdoch's statement to the Prime Minister of Australia that British Officers had been ordered to "shoot without mercy any soldier who lagged behind or loitered." As the Secretary of State seems to take this charge seriously, I thought it well, before I sent my answer, just to make sure that no subordinate had said, or done, or written anything which could plausibly be twisted into this lie. The Generals have denied indignantly; are furious, in fact, at the double insult to their men and to themselves.

Have cabled accordingly:

(No. M.F.A.B. 4491). From General Sir Ian Hamilton to Secretary of State for War. With reference to your No. 8554 M.O. 414 of the 5th inst. I have *pro forma* made full enquiries and I find that there is no truth whatever in the allegation made by Murdoch.

9th October, 1915. Had made my *band-o-bast* for running over to Helles, but the Vice-Admiral cabled he wanted to see me if he could at 11.45. Anyway the sea is still a bit rough for the crossing and landing. A lot of damage was done last night to the Anzac piers, two of them being clean washed away. Peter Pollen is off colour. Freddie and I dined on board the *Triad*.

Whilst at dinner got full reports both from Suvla and Anzac as to the effects of the storm. The southerly gale, which not only washed away the piers but sunk the water lighters at Anzac, has done no harm at Suvla except that three motor lighters have been driven ashore. The Admiral is clear that, during southerly gales we shall have to supply both Anzac and Suvla by the new pier just north of Ari Burnu. The promontory is small but last night it gave complete protection to everything in its lea. By sinking an old ship we can turn Ari Burnu into quite a decent little harbour.

10th October, 1915. Made my deferred visit to Helles, going over this morning in the *Arno* with Braithwaite, Val and Alec McGrigor. Looked in at the Clearing Hospital and cast an eye over Lancashire Landing. Then, in company with Jimmy Watson and Colonel Ayres, walked up to Corps Headquarters where we had a fine lunch with Davies, de Rougemont and the melancholy Yarr. Afterwards rode across to the Headquarters of the Royal Naval Division and on to their trenches, some 3½ miles. Generals Mercer and Paris followed us through their trenches. The Hood and Hawke Battalions were in the firing line where we talked to great numbers of old comrades of all ranks. Glad to meet Freyberg again (the man who swam to light the flares at Enos). Kelly of the Hood Battalion too, I saw, and Fairfax of the Hawke, also Commander King of the Drake Battalion and Burrows, a gunner who was running a bombing school with much zeal on a piece of ground specially patronized by the Turks as a target for their own shelling practice. Got back to Helles by the Saghur Dere and the Gulley. Going down the Gulley, nearly lost two of our attendant Generals, a shrapnel bursting between them with a startling loud report caused by the high banks of the Gulley on either side.

In the Gulley we met a swarm of old friends from Kent; Brigadier-General Clifton-Browne, an officer whose command I had inspected both at Potchefstroom and near Canterbury, with a Brigade of West and East Kent and Sussex Yeomen. They made a brave showing, but he tells me some of them have caught this wretched enteritis already. Amongst others, I spoke to Douglas, commanding the East Lancashire Division, Major Edwards of the Sussex Yeomanry, Major Sir S. Scott and Colonel Whitburn of the West Kent Yeomanry, Colonel Lord Guilford, East Kent Yeomanry. A cheerier crowd no one could wish to meet. If these are the type of men who spin black yarns for home wear, I can only say that not the most finished actors could better disguise their despair. General King, R.A., rode part of the way back with us.

After all this hard exercise, got back to the *Arno* in a lather of sweat about 6 o'clock carrying Davies with me. Leslie Wilson, commanding the Hawke Battalion, had gone sick to-day, so sent him a telegram after dinner to the Hospital ship *Somali*, telling him his trenches had been found in apple-pie order.

11th October, 1915. Bad night with this beastly complaint. De Robeck came up at 11 o'clock to see me. He has had a message from the Admiralty asking him what number of extra troops could be maintained on the Peninsula if the units there now were brought up to strength. The Admiral asked me for the figures and the A.G. brought them over. My force as a whole is as near as may be to half strength. Half of that half are sick men. We have 100,000 men on the Peninsula, 50,000 of whom are unfit: if the unfits were up to strength there would be 200,000 men on the Peninsula as well as excitement and movement which would greatly reduce the disease. Bearing in mind that the Anzacs have been well supported by their Governments and that their units are fairly strong, these figures show what wait-and-see-sickness has meant to British Regiments.

The tone of this Admiralty question had seemed cheerful: almost as if the Higher Direction were thinking of putting us on our legs but, in the evening, another cable from K. gave a different and a very ominous complexion to the future:

> From Earl Kitchener to General Sir Ian Hamilton. What is your estimate of the probable losses which would be entailed to your force if the evacuation of the Gallipoli Peninsula was decided on and carried out in the most careful manner?
>
> No decision has been arrived at yet on this question of evacuation, but I feel that I ought to have your views.
>
> In your reply you need not consider the possible future danger to the Empire that might be thus caused.*

If they do this they make the Dardanelles into the bloodiest tragedy of the world! Even if we were to escape without a scratch, they would stamp our enterprise as the bloodiest of all tragedies! K. has always sworn by all his Gods he would have no hand in it.

---

* Lord K.'s reason for putting in this last paragraph may be obscure unless I make it clear. As explained in a previous footnote, Lord K. knew that I knew his strong personal view that the smashing blow to our military reputation which would be caused by an evacuation of the Dardanelles must, in course of time, imperil our hold upon Egypt. Therefore, for the moment, it was necessary to warn me that the problem must be considered in the purely military, tactical, aspect. — I*an* H.*1920.*

I won't touch it, and I think he knew that and calculated on that when he cabled. Anyway, let K., cat or Cabinet leap where they will, I must sleep upon my answer, but that answer will be NO!

Just as I am turning in, a cable from the S. of S. saying, "there is an idea that Sir John Maxwell is not sending you as many troops as he might from Egypt. Have you any complaints on this score?" Rather late in the day this "idea." Certainly, I have never made any "complaints" and I don't mean to do so now. The War Office have only to look up their returns and see how many men are being maintained to defend us from the Senoussi!

Maxwell has never had less than 70,000 troops in Egypt, a country which might have been held with 10,000 rifles — ever since we landed here, that is to say. My troops can sail back to Egypt very much faster than the Turks — or the Senoussi for that matter — can march to the Canal.

In the same cable the S. of S. asks what is the cause of the sick rate and remarks that, "some accounts from the Dardanelles indicate that the men are dispirited." Small wonder if they were! When they see two Divisions taken away from the Peninsula; when their guns can't answer those of the enemy; when each unit finds itself half-strength, and falling — why then, tumbling as they do to the fact that we won't get through till next year, they *ought* to be unhappy. But the funny thing is that the Cabinet, the Secretaries of State, are the people who are "dispirited" and *not* the people out here. If the P.M. could walk round the trenches of the Naval Division at Helles, or if K. could exchange greetings with the rank and file at Anzac and Suvla, they would find a sovereign antidote for the blues and would realize that it was they who were down-hearted and *not* the men at the Dardanelles. There was an old French Colonel, killed at Gravelotte; he had studied the classic world battles and he shows that it was never the front line who gave way first, but always the reserves: they, the reserves, watched bloodshed in cold blood until they could stand it no longer and so took to their heels whilst the fighting men were still focussed upon victory. Not the enemy in front but the friends behind are the men who spread despondency and alarm.

Charley Burn has arrived on the *Imogene* with Dawnay.

Davies went back to Helles after tea. Dawnay says K. was most interested in him and most charming to him all through his stay until his last interview just before he started on his return journey. K.'s manner then, he said, had changed — so much so as to give him an impression that the great man was turning, or was being turned, against all of us out here. K.'s conduct at the first meetings is in full harmony with his message sent to Braithwaite for me by Fitz about a fortnight ago, saying I possessed his fullest confidence. The change of manner was marked and Dawnay is sure he made no mistake about it. But nothing has happened since the date of Dawnay's arrival and departure save a very well engineered withdrawal of the 10th and the French Divisions for which, in point of fact, we have all been rather expecting congratulations. Dawnay thinks some queer things are happening. He could — or would — say nothing more.

12th October, 1915. Imbros. Early in the morning got off my answer to K.'s evacuation cable. The elements, the enemy and ourselves are the three factors of the problem. Were I to measure my problem by the night flitting of the Irish and French Divisions (who lost neither man nor beast in the process), I could guarantee that we would shoot the moon with the balance of the force smoothly, swiftly and silently. That is to say, supposing the Turks and the weather remain constant. But these are two most inconstant things: no one can tell how a Turk will behave under any given conditions; the Turks themselves do not know how they will behave: the weather now is written down by the meteorologists for sudden changes; for storms. Unsettled weather is due and ought to be reckoned upon. Imagine a blow coming up from the South when the evacuation is half way through. That does not seem to be, and is not, any great stretch of imagination. Well then, having so imagined, we get a disaster only equalled in history by that of the Athenians at Syracuse: a disaster from which the British Empire could hardly hope to recover.

Twice backwards and forwards to the General Staff Marquee with the draft of my guesses, my first being that we would probably lose 35 to 45 per cent. But the General Staff have also been consulting their oracle and were clear for 50 per cent. Months of the most anxious calculations will not get a white man one whit forrarder in seeing into the brains of an Asiatic Army or in forecasting Mediterranean weather. Safest to assume that both brains and weather will behave as the German General Staff would wish them to behave rather than as they chanced to behave when the French and Irish went off a few days ago. So have ended by taking the Staff's figure because any figure being, in any case, the wildest of shots, their shot best suits my views on the issue.

> From General Sir Ian Hamilton to Earl Kitchener. Our losses would depend on such uncertain factors, enemy's action or inaction, weather, question whether we could rely on all troops covering embarkation to fight to the last, that impossible to give you straight answer especially until I have permission to consult Admiral. Once discussing this very problem with General Gouraud, we came to the conclusion that at Cape Helles we must sacrifice two divisions out of total of six divisions and Cape Helles easiest of three places to get away from. My opinion now is that it would not be wise to reckon on getting out of Gallipoli with less loss than that of half the total force as well as guns, which must be used to the last, stores, railway plant and horses. Moral of those who got off would fall very low. One quarter would probably get off quite easily, then the trouble would begin. We might be very lucky and lose considerably less than I have estimated. On the other hand, with all these raw troops at Suvla and all these Senegalese at Cape Helles, we might have a veritable catastrophe.

Do the men toying with the idea of bringing off our men not see that thereby the Turks will be let loose somewhere; not nowhere? Do they not see that if they are feeling the economic pinch of keeping their side of the show in being, the Turks, much weaker economically, must be feeling it much more!

It was a relief to get this perilous stuff off my chest, and in a brighter frame of mind, sailed for Anzac on the destroyer *Lewis*. We took biscuits and bully beef with us but the hospitable sailors insisted on regaling us with a hot meal. Sat in cabin all the way as usual writing up my record. Freddie tells me that these studious habits of mine have started the shave that I spend my time composing poetry, especially during our battles!

At Anzac Birdwood took us round the trenches and underground passages about Russell's Top and Turk's Head, held by the 5th Brigade, 2nd Division, under Legge. Half way up to Russell's Top was the 3rd Battery Australian Field Artillery: talked with Major King, the C.O. Next unit was the 20th Infantry Battalion under Major Fitzgerald. Colonel Holmes, commanding the 5th Infantry Brigade, and Wilson, his Brigade Major, took us through their cave dwellings. Ex-westerners say that in France they have nothing to touch these Australian tunnellings. In one place they are boring into a crater only 20 feet from the Turkish trench. There is nothing unusual in the fact, but there is in the great depth they are going down so as to cross the danger zone far below the beaten track of mines and counter-mines. On the steep slope in another place there is a complete underground trench running parallel to, and only a short bomb-throw from, a Turkish trench. We went through it with a lantern. Sandbags, loopholes, etc., all are there, but blind! They are still veiled from view by several feet of clay. To-morrow night the Anzacs are going to chip off the whole upper crust of earth, and when light dawns the Turks will find a well equipped trench, every loophole manned, within bombing range of their own line.

Other notables met with were Major Murphy of the 20th Infantry Battalion, Major Anderson (an old friend) commanding the Australian Field Artillery, and Captain Perry Oakdene, the Engineer Officer on the job. Saw Birdie and returned in the destroyer about 6.30. The day had been so quiet that it would have been almost dull had it not been for the sightseeing — hardly a shot was fired by Turk or Anzac with either gun, trench mortar or rifle.

Bishop Price, the Bishop of North China, and Charlie Burn, King's Messenger, dined. The quietness of the Bishop was remarkable.

Have cabled the S. of S. for War in answer to his enquiries about the causes of the sickness, and as to whether Maxwell is not holding up my share of troops in Egypt, saying: (1) that "constant strain and infection by dust and flies" have caused the sickness but that the men are getting better; (2) that "we have been under the impression that drafts meant for us and due to us have been retained in Egypt; also, that men discharged fit from Hospitals have been held back, but I have represented this last point to Maxwell personally as I always feel I am not the person to gauge Maxwell's needs. On 27th September, I asked him to send up all available Australian — New Zealand Army Corps drafts and reinforcements, and, as you already know, am at present in telegraphic correspondence about these reinforcements coming straight here without being kept in Egypt for training at all."

CREMATING THE ENEMY DEAD   "*Central News*" phot.

At 10.40, after clearing my table, went with Ellison, Taylor, and Freddie on board H.M.S. *Lefroy* (Commander Edwards) and steamed for "V" Beach. Enjoyed a fine luncheon with Brulard and then started off for the trenches. At Morto Bay we were met by Captain de Bourbon, a big handsome man with the characteristic Bourbon cut of countenance. He took us first to the *château* whence we worked down along the trenches to where our extreme right overlooks the Kerevez Dere. General Faukard was here and he thinks that we ought easily to get complete mastery of both sides of the Kerevez Dere as soon as we get the means and the permission to shove ahead again. When we do that the advance will let our Fleet another half mile up the Straits and the "spotting" for the ships' guns will double their value in the Narrows. From the Kerevez Dere we worked along the fire trenches towards the French centre and then, getting to a sheltered strip of country, walked back across the open to the second line. From the second line we made our way, still across the open, to the third line, over a heather covered strip. No one ever moves here by daylight except in double quick time as there is always danger of drawing a shell either from Asia or from Achi Baba and so it was that "Let the dead bury the dead" had been the motto and that we met many corpses and skeletons. Merciful God, what home tragedies may centre in each of these sinister bundles. But it is the common lot — only quicker. Here, too, we found excavations made by the French into a burial ground believed to be of the date 2,500 B.C. The people of that golden age had the sentimental idea of being buried in couples in big jars. A strange notion of our Allies unburying quiet people who had enjoyed dreamless rest for 2,000 years whilst, within a few yards, their own dead still welter in the parching wind.

Had meant to run across and see Davies but time had slipped away and so we made tracks for H.M.S. *Lefroy*, and on back here to G.H.Q., where a letter from Callwell was laying in wait as a refresher after my fatigues.

Callwell begins by saying he encloses a document written by my late visitor, Mr. K. A. Murdoch, although "there are certain statements in this which are palpably false," and although Dawnay has pointed out to him at the War Office "a number of passages in it which are wholly incorrect as matters of actual fact." He says, Lord K., "who has not had time to read it yet," thinks I ought to be given a chance of defending myself.

Callwell goes on to write about the Press Censorship and my plea for publicity and then says he dislikes the Salonika stunt "because I am not quite clear of where we are going to, and the immediate result at the present is to take away from you troops that you can ill spare." Also, because "we may be involving ourselves in operations on a great scale in the heart of the Balkans, the result of which it is very difficult to foresee."

Godley dined. Captain Davidson, R.N., the Senior Naval Officer in harbour now, is a real Godsend. He looks after us as if we were Admirals of the Fleet.

The Beginning of the End

Have now read, marked, learnt and inwardly indigested Callwell's enclosure; viz., the letter written by Mr. K. A. Murdoch to the Prime Minister of Australia. Quite a Guy Fawkes epistle. Braithwaite is "more cordially detested in our forces than Enver Pasha." "You will trust me when I say that the work of the General Staff in Gallipoli is deplorable." "Sedition is talked round every tin of bully beef on the Peninsula." "You would refuse to believe that these men were really British soldiers...the British physique is very much below that of the Turks. Indeed, it is quite obviously so. Our men have found it impossible to form a high opinion of the British K. men and Territorials. They are merely a lot of childlike youths, without strength to endure or brains to improve their conditions." "I shall always remember the stricken face of a young English Lieutenant when I told him he must make up his mind for a winter campaign." "I do not like to dictate this sentence, even for your eyes, but the fact is that after the first day at Suvla an order had to be issued to Officers to shoot without mercy any soldier who lagged behind or loitered in an advance."

Well, Well! I should not worry myself over the out-pourings of our late guest, who has evidently been made a tool of by some unscrupulous person, were it not that Mr. Asquith has clothed the said out-pourings in the title, number, garb and colour of a verified and authentic State paper. He has actually had them printed on the famous duck's egg foolscap of the Committee of Imperial Defence, and under his authority, as President and Prime Minister, they have been circulated round the Government and all the notables of the Empire without any chance having been offered to me (or to K.) of defending the honour of British Officers or the good name of the British Rank and File. K. tells Callwell I should be given the opportunity of making a reply. Not having read it himself he has not yet grasped the fact that he also should have been given the opportunity of making a reply to the aspersions upon his selections. As for me, by the time my answer can get home and can be printed and circulated the slanders will have had over a month's start in England and very likely two months' start in Australia, where all who read them will naturally conclude their statements must have been tested before ever they were published in that impressive form.

Here we see an irresponsible statement by an ignorant man and I instinctively feel as if it were being used as one more weapon to force Asquith's hand and to ruin our last chance. I only hope it may not prove another case of, "Behold, how great a matter a little fire kindleth!"

Certain aspects of this affair trouble my understanding. The covering note (dated 25th September) which encloses the letter to the Prime Minister of Australia (dated 23rd September) is addressed by Mr. Murdoch to Mr. Asquith by name. In that covering note Mr. Murdoch says, "I write with diffidence, and only at Mr. Lloyd George's request." Within three days (so great the urgency or pressure) Mr. Asquith causes — as he, President of the Committee of Imperial Defence, alone can cause — the covering note as well as the seven or eight thousand words of the letter to be printed and circulated round the big wigs of Politics, as well as (to judge by the co-incident hardening of the tone of this mail's papers) some of the Editors. Not one word to me as to Mr. Murdoch's qualifications or as to the truth or falsity of his statements, until these last have been a week in circulation. Then, I receive; first, a cable saying unofficial reports had come in censuring my General Staff and that I had better, therefore, let Braithwaite go; secondly, a cable asking me whether the absurd story of my having ordered my own soldiers to be shot "without mercy " is well-founded; thirdly, a bad last, the libellous letter itself.

Yet Mr. Asquith did know the paper contained *some* falsehoods. He *may* have attached weight to Mr. Murdoch's tale of the feelings of French soldiers at Helles (although he never found time to go there): he *may* have believed Mr. Murdoch when he says that Sir John Maxwell "has a poor brain for his big position"; that "our men feel that their reputation is too sacred to leave in the hands of Maxwell"; that Sir William Birdwood "has not the fighting quality or big brain of a great General"; that General Spens was "a man broken on the Continent" (although he never was broken and never served on the Continent); that "Kitchener has a terrible task in getting pure work from the General Staff of the British Army, whose motives can never be pure, for they are unchangeably selfish"; that "from what I saw of the Turk, I am convinced he is...a better man than those opposed to him" (although, actually, Mr. Murdoch saw nothing of the Turks). The P.M. may have taken these views at their face values: even, he *may* have swallowed Mr. Murdoch's picture of the conscientious Altham "wallowing" in ice whilst wounded were expiring of heat within a few hundred yards; but *Mr. Asquith has seen the K. Army* and, therefore, *he cannot have believed* that these soldiers have suddenly been transformed into "merely a lot of childish youths without strength to endure or brains to improve their conditions."

Once more; these reckless scraps of hearsay would not be worth the paper they are printed on were it not that they are endorsed with the letters C.I.D., the stamp of the ministerial Holy of Holies. Only the Prime Minister himself, personally, can so consign a paper. Lord K. and I were both members of the C.I.D., and members of long standing. For the President to circularize our fellow members behind our backs with unverified accusations is a strange act, foreign to all my ideas of Mr. Asquith. On this point Callwell is quite clear: the Murdoch letter was published to the C.I.D. on the 28th ult. and Callwell writes on the 2nd inst., and says Lord K. "has not had time to read it yet."* But nothing else is clear. In fact, the whole thing is foreign to all my ideas of Mr. Asquith. He does not need to work the C.I.D. oracle in this way. As P.M. he has only to speak the word. He does not work the Press oracle either: not his custom: also he likes K. The whole thing is a mystery, of which I can only say with Hamlet — "miching mallecho; it means mischief."

14th October, 1915. Imbros. Colder than ever. We are told that the winter will kill the flies and that with their death we shall all get hearty and well. Meanwhile, they have turned to winged limpets.

Being Mail day as well as rough, stuck to camp. My friend England sailed into harbour in the *Chelmer* and came up to lunch. In the evening he took Godley back to Anzac. Duncannon came to

---

* Lest anyone should imagine there is any privilege or secrecy attached to this document it may be well to explain that all the best passages came back to me from Melbourne in due course; often with marginal comment. — *IAN H., 1920.*

dinner. I have made him liaison officer with the French in place of de Putron who has gone to Salonika with Bailloud.

As to the Murdoch unpleasantness, I began an *exposé* to be sent to the Governor General of Australia; another to the Secretary of the C.I.D. But Pollen, Braithwaite and Dawnay (the last of whom had been shown the document whilst he was at home, though he had said nothing to me about it) thought this was to make much ado about nothing. They cannot believe Lord K. will trouble himself about the matter any further and they think it best handled in lighter vein. Is K. still the demi-God, that is the question? Anyway, there is simply no time this Mail to deal with so many misstatements, so that has settled it.

General Headquarters,
Medtn. Expeditionary Force,
14th October, 1915.

Dear Callwell,

I have read Mr. Murdoch's letter with care, and I have tried to give it my most impartial consideration and not to allow myself in reply to be influenced in any way by the criticisms he may have felt himself bound to make upon myself personally.

What does this letter amount to? Here we have a man, a journalist by profession, one who is quick to seize every point, and to coin epithets, which throw each fleeting impression into strongest relief. He comes armed with a natural and justifiably enthusiastic admiration for everything connected with the Commonwealth to which he belongs, and ready to retail to his Minister or his public anything that can contribute to show the troops they have sent in an heroic light.

Here he obtains his first sight of war and of the horrors and hardships inseparable from it. He finds men who have just been through some of the hardest fighting imaginable and who have suffered terrible losses; he finds probably that very many of those whom he hoped to see, certainly many of those of whose welfare their motherland would wish to hear, are killed, wounded or laid up with illness, — he finds all this and he becomes very deeply depressed. In such an atmosphere Mr. Murdoch composes his letter, a general analysis of which shows it to be divided, to my mind, into two separate strata.

The Beginning of the End

First an appreciation in burning terms of the spirit, the achievements, the physique and all soldierly qualities of the Australian Forces. Secondly, a condemnation, as sweeping and as unrelieved as his praise in the first instance is unstinted, of the whole of the rest of the force. I myself as C.-in-C., my Generals, my Staff, Lines of Communication, Sir John Maxwell and General Spens at the Base, even the British soldiers collectively and individually, are all embraced in this condemnation which is completed by the inclusion of the entire direction of the Forces at home, both Naval and Military.

Where all are thus tarred with the same brush, I am content to leave it to the impartial reader to decide what reliance can be placed on Mr. Murdoch's judgment. My own feeling certainly is that in his admiration for the Australian Forces, and in his grief at their heavy losses (in both of which feelings I fully share) he has allowed himself to belittle and to criticize us all so that their virtues might be thrown into even bolder relief.

With Mr. Murdoch's detailed points I do not propose to deal, nor do I think you expect me to do so. On every page inaccuracies of fact abound. The breaking of Spens on the Continent, a theatre of war he has never visited; the over-statement of our casualties by more than 40 per cent.; the acceptance as genuine of a wholly mythical order about the shooting of laggards — really the task would be too long. As to the value of Mr. Murdoch's appreciation of the strategical and tactical elements of the situation you can yourself assess them at their true value.

Finally, I do not for one moment believe the general statement put forward to the effect that the troops are disheartened. Neither that statement nor the assertion that they are discontented with the British Officers commanding them has the slightest foundation in fact.

Believe me,
My dear Callwell,
Yours very sincerely,
(Sd.) IAN HAMILTON.

P.S. — I attach correspondence showing how Mr. Murdoch's visit arose. I believe I exceeded my power in giving him permission to come but I was most anxious to oblige the Australian Prime Minister and Senator Pearce. You will see that he promises faithfully to observe any conditions I may impose. The only condition I imposed was that he should sign a declaration identical with that which I attach. He signed and the paper is in my possession.

CORRESPONDENCE.

Dear Sir,
   On the advice of Brigadier-General Legge I beg to request permission to visit Anzac.
   I am proceeding from Melbourne to London to take up the position of managing editor of the Australian news cable service in connection with the *London Times* and at the Commonwealth Government's request am enquiring into mail arrangements, dispositions of wounded, and various matters in Egypt in connection with our Australian Forces. I find it impossible to make a complete report upon changes that have been suggested here until I have a better knowledge of the system pursued at base Y, and on the Mainland, and I beg of you, therefore, to permit me to visit these places.
   I should like to go across in only a semi-official capacity, so that I might record censored impressions in the London and Australian newspapers I represent, but any conditions you impose I should, of course, faithfully observe.
   I beg to enclose (*a*) copy of general letter from the Prime Minister and (*b*) copy of my instructions from the Government. I have a personal letter of introduction to you from Senator Pearce, Minister of Defence.
   May I add that I had the honour of meeting you at the Melbourne Town Hall, and wrote fully of your visit in the Sydney *Sun* and Melbourne *Punch*; also may I say that my anxiety as an Australian to visit the sacred shores of Gallipoli while our army is there is intense.
   Senator Millen asked me to convey his most kindly remembrances to you if I had the luck to see you and in case I have not I take this opportunity of doing so.
   As I have only four weeks in which to complete my work here and get to London a 'collect reply by cable to C/o Colonel Sellheim, Australian Intermediate Base, Cairo, would greatly oblige.
            I have the honour to be,
                Sir,
                    Your obediently,
                        (*Sd.*) KEITH A. MURDOCH.

            C/o Colonel Sellheim, C.B.,
                A.I.F. Intermediate Base,
                    Cairo.
                August 17, 1915."

The Beginning of the End

COMMONWEALTH OF AUSTRALIA,
PRIME MINISTER'S DEPARTMENT,
MELBOURNE.

July 14th, 1915.

This letter will serve to introduce Mr. Keith Arthur Murdoch, a well known journalist, of Melbourne, who is proceeding to Europe to undertake important duties in connection with his profession.

Mr. Murdoch is also undertaking certain inquiries for the Government of the Commonwealth in the Mediterranean Theatre of War. And for any facilities which may be rendered him to enable him the better to carry out these duties I shall be personally obliged.

(*Sd.*) ANDREW FISHER,
Prime Minister.

DEPARTMENT OF DEFENCE,
MELBOURNE,

July 2nd, 1915.

Mr. Keith A. Murdoch,
Alfred Place, Melbourne.

The Minister desires that you furnish a report upon the following matters together with any suggestions for improvements.

1. Arrangements for the receipt and delivery of letters, papers and parcels to and from members of the Australian Imperial Force.
2. Arrangements for the receipt and delivery of cablegrams to and from members of the Australian Imperial Force.
3. Arrangements for notifications to the Department in Australia of the disposition of Australian Wounded in Hospitals.
4. Suggested despatch of special expert corps to Hospitals.
5. Frauds by impersonation at cable offices.

(*Sd.*) T. TRUMBLE,
Acting Secretary for Defence.

When I got this, I hesitated. Evidently the writer was not accredited as a war correspondent and his remark about having written me up in the *Sun* and in *Punch* did not count for much. But

I was anxious then, as ever, that as many journalists as possible should be put into a position for seeing the fine things the troops had done and were doing; I noted the emphasis laid by the writer upon his acceptance of the censorship, and so I took upon myself to exceed my powers and asked Braithwaite to cable to Mr. Murdoch:

> This cable is your authority to come to G.H.Q. at once whence you will be sent to Anzac.
>
> C.G.S., Medforce.

Mr. Murdoch landed on the 2nd instant and on that date signed the following declaration:

> DECLARATION TO BE USED BY WAR CORRESPONDENTS.
>
> I, the undersigned, do hereby solemnly undertake to follow in every particular the rules issued by the Commander-in-Chief through the Chief Field Censor, relative to correspondence concerning the forces in the Field, and bind myself not to attempt to correspond by any other route or by any other means than that officially sanctioned.
>
> Further, in the event of my ceasing to act as correspondent with the British Forces, I will not during the continuance of the War join the forces of any other Power in any capacity, or impart to anyone military information of a confidential nature or of a kind such that its disclosure is likely to prejudice military operations, which may have been acquired by me while with the British Forces in the Field, or publish any writing, plan, map, sketch, photograph or other picture on military subjects, the material for which has been acquired by me in a similar manner, unless first submitted by me to the Chief Field Censor for censorship and passed for publication by him.
>
> (*Signature of Correspondent*)................

15th October, 1915. Imbros. Bitter cold. The whole camp upside down and all the Staff busy with their shift of quarters to the other side of the Bay.

Altham has been at Salonika and came over to report how things were going there. Remembering the accusation of

"wallowing" in ice, I nearly touched him for a Vanilla cream.
As to Salonika, he tells me that, so far, the occupation has been a travesty of any military operation. No plan; no administration; much confusion; troops immobile and likely to sit for weeks upon the beach. The Balkan States Intelligence Officers are on the spot and grasp the inferences. Until the troops landed they were not quite sure whether some serious factor was not about to be sprung upon them: now they are quite sure nothing can happen, big or small, beyond our letting a lot of our bayonets go rusty. Sarrail has been implored by the Serbians to push his troops up into their country, but he has been wise enough to refuse. How can he feed them? On the top of it all, the conduct of the Greeks seems fishy. As to the Bulgarians, they have already thrown off the mask. Although Salonika is going to be our ruin, I can still spare some pity for Sarrail.

Have heard from Birdie who at last gives me leave to see his Lone Pine section. Until now I have never been able to get him to let me go there. Too many bombs, he says, to make it quite healthy for a Commander-in-Chief.

16th October, 1915. Imbros. Had just got into bed last night when I was ferreted out again by a cable "Secret and personal" from K. telling me to decipher the next message myself. The messenger brought a note from the G.S. — most of whom have now gone across to the other side of the Bay — to ask if I would like to be awakened when the second message came in. As I knew the contents as well as if I had written it out myself, I said no, that it was to be brought me with the cipher book at my usual hour for being called in the morning. When I had given this order, my mind dwelt awhile over my sins. Through my tired brain passed thought-pictures of philosophers waiting for cups of hemlock and various other strange and half-forgotten antique images. Then I fell asleep.

Next morning, Peter Pollen came in with the cipher book and the bow-string. I got K.'s message pat in my dreams last night and here it is, to a word, in black and white:

The War Council held last night decided that though the Government fully appreciate your work and the gallant manner in which you personally have struggled to make the enterprise a success in face of the terrible difficulties you have had to contend against, they, all the same, wish to make a change in the command which will give them an opportunity of seeing you.

How far we have travelled, in spirit, since K. sent me his September greetings with spontaneous assurances of complete confidence! Yet, since then, on the ground, I have not travelled at all — have indeed been under the order of the Dardanelles Committee to stand still.

Charles Munro is to relieve me and brings with him a Chief of Staff who will take Braithwaite's place. On my way back I "might visit Salonika and Egypt" so as to be able to give the Cabinet the latest about the hang of things in these places.

When I go, Birdie is to take my place pending Munro's arrival.

De Robeck must give me a cruiser so that we may start for home to-morrow. The offer of a jaunt at Government expense to Salonika and Egypt leaves me cold. They think nothing of spending some hundreds of pounds to put off an awkward moment. What value on earth could my views on Salonika and Egypt possess for people who have no use for my views on my own subject!

After breakfast, read K.'s cable over once more. "A War Council," it seems, decided to make the change. Did the War Council also appoint Munro? K. did not appoint him — anyway. Munro succeeded me at Hythe. In 1897 I was brought home from Tirah to Hythe by Evelyn Wood in order that I might keep an eye on the original ideas which, from India under Lord Roberts, had revolutionized the whole system of British musketry. I left Hythe on the outbreak of the South African War and during that war Munro went there.

He was born with another sort of mind from me. Had he been sent out here in the first instance he would never have touched the Dardanelles, and people who have realized so much may conclude he will now clear out. But it does not follow. Munro's refusal to attempt a landing in the first instance would have served as the

The Beginning of the End

foundation stone for some totally different policy in the Near East. That might perhaps have been a good plan. But to start a campaign with me and try to carry it on with Munro has already been tried and found hardly fair to either of us. The intention of whoever selected Munro is so to use him as to force K. to pull down the blinds. But they may be mistaken in his character.

One thing is sure: whenever I get home I shall do what I can to convince K. that the game is still in his hands if only he will shake himself free from slippery politics; come right out here and run the show himself. Constantinople is the only big big hit lying open on the map at this moment. With the reinforcements and munitions K., as Commander-in-Chief, would have at his command, he can bring off the coup right away. He has only to borrow a suitable number of howitzers and aeroplanes from the Western front and our troops begin to advance. Sarrail has missed the chance of twenty generations by not coming here. Let K. step in. In the whole of the Near East his name alone is still worth an Army Corps. My own chance has gone. That is no reason why my old Chief should not himself make good. I told the War Council we held at Suvla before the battle of the 21st August that if the Government persisted in refusing me drafts and munitions — if they insisted on leaving my units at half-strength — then they would have to get someone cleverer than myself to carry out the job. Well, it has come to that now. K. looms big in the public eye and can insist on not being starved. He must hurry up though! Time enough has been lost, God knows. But even to-day there is time. Howitzers, trench mortars, munitions, men, on a scale France would hardly miss, — the Asiatic side of the Straits would be occupied — and, in one month from to-day, our warships will have Constantinople under their guns. If K. won't listen to me, then, having been officially misinformed that the War Council wish to see me (the last thing they *do* wish), I will take them at their word. I will buttonhole every Minister from McKenna and Lloyd George to Asquith and Bonar Law, — and grovel at their feet if by doing so I can hold them on to this, the biggest scoop that is, or ever has been, open to an Empire.

Rather a sickly lunch. Not so much the news as the Benger's on which we all feasted for our stomach's sake. Birdie came over at 4 p.m. with Ruthven. Both his A.D.C.s are sick. I am going to ask him to take on young Alec McGrigor. Peter and Freddie will come home with Braithwaite and myself. What a true saying, — a friend in need is a friend indeed. Were I handing over to Birdie for good I should feel unalloyed happiness in his well-deserved success.

At tea Ellison, Braithwaite, Bertier, Colonel Sykes and Guest appeared. They looked more depressed than I felt. I had to work like a beaver before I could brighten them up. "I'm not dead yet," I felt inclined to tell them, "no, not by long chalks." What I did say to one or two of them was this: "My credit with Government is exhausted; clearly I can't screw men or munitions out of them. The new Commander will start fresh with a good balance of faith, hope and charity lodged in the Bank of England. He comes with a splendid reputation, and if he is big enough to draw boldly on this deposit, the Army will march; the Fleet will steam ahead; what has been done will bear fruit, and all our past struggles and sacrifices will live."

Dined with Freddie on the *Triad*. De Robeck and Keyes were all that friends can be at such a moment.

17th October, 1915. H.M.S. "Chatham" (At sea). A pretty beastly day within and without. For the within part, all sorts of good-byes to putpain into our hearts; for the without, a cold drizzle chilling us all to the bone.

At 10.30 Brulard and his Staff came over; also Generals Byng and Davies with their Staffs. After bidding them farewell; a function whereat I was grateful to the French for their lightness of touch, I rode over with Braithwaite and the A.D.C.s to the new Headquarters at Kephalos to say good-bye to my own Staff. Although I had meant to live there until we drove the Turks far enough back to let us live on the Peninsula, I had found time to see my little stone hut built by Greek peasants on the side of the hill: deliciously snug. To-day, this very day, I was to have struck my tent and taken up these cosy winter quarters; now I move, right enough, but on the wrong road.

The adieu was a melancholy affair. There was no make-belief, that's a sure thing. Whatever the British Officer may be his forte has never lain in his acting. So, by 2.30, I made my last salute to the last of the old lot and boarded the *Triad*. A baddish wrench parting from de Robeck and Keyes with whom I have been close friends for so long. Up to midnight de Robeck had intended coming home too. Keyes himself is following me in a day or two, to implore the Cabinet to let us at least strike one more blow before we haul down our flag, so there will be two of us at the task.

I wrung their hands. The Bo'sun's whistle sounded. The curtain was falling so I wrung their hands once again and said good-bye; good-bye also to the Benjamin of my personal Staff, young Alec, who stays on with Birdie. A bitter moment and hard to carry through.

Boarded the *Chatham* (Captain Drury-Lowe) and went below to put my cabin straight. The anchor came up, the screws went round. I wondered whether I could stand the strain of seeing Imbros, Kephalos, the camp, fade into the region of dreams, — I was hesitating when a message came from the Captain to say the Admiral begged me to run up on to the quarter deck. So I ran, and found the *Chatham* steering a corkscrew course — threading in and out amongst the warships at anchor. Each as we passed manned ship and sent us on our way with the cheers of brave men ringing in our ears.

FAREWELL ORDER BY GENERAL SIR IAN HAMILTON.

GENERAL HEADQUARTERS,
MEDITERRANEAN EXPEDITIONARY FORCE,
October 17th, 1915.

On handing over the Command of the Mediterranean Expeditionary Force to General Sir C. C. Munro, the Commander-in-Chief wishes to say a few farewell words to the Allied troops, with many of whom he has now for so long been associated. First, he would like them to know his deep sense of the honour it has been to command so fine an Army in one of the most arduous and difficult Campaigns which has ever been undertaken; secondly, he must express to them his admiration at the noble response which they have invariably given to the calls he has made upon them. No risk has been too desperate; no sacrifice too great. Sir Ian Hamilton thanks all ranks, from Generals to private soldiers, for the wonderful way they have seconded his efforts to lead them towards that decisive victory, which, under their new Chief, he has the most implicit confidence they will achieve."

Appendix I – Statement on Artillery
By Brigadier General Sir Hugh Simpson Baikie, ex-commander of the British artillery at Cape Helles

The first landing of British troops at Cape Helles took place on 25th April, 1915. On arriving at that place during the first week in May, I found that heavy fighting had occurred without ceasing from the time of the disembarkation. Having come straight from the Headquarters Staff of the 2nd Army in France, where the question of artillery ammunition was a constant source of anxiety to all the higher commanders, I at once set to work to discover what reserves remained in the hands of G.H.Q. and what the daily expenditure had been since the landing. The greatest difficulty was experienced in obtaining figures of expenditure from the units, so constant had been the fighting, which still continued, and so great the casualties, and consequent confusion in reckoning expenditure. Yet, after some delay, sufficient information was obtained to enable me to demonstrate with certainty that, if such severe fighting continued, the Force would soon be in danger of losing their artillery support.

On the 4th May a cable was sent, I believe, to Lord Kitchener saying that ammunition was becoming a very serious matter owing to the ceaseless fighting; pointing out that 18 pr. shell were a vital necessity and that a supply promised by a certain ship (I believe the S.S. *Funia*) had not turned up. A day or two later, a cable was received by G.H.Q. saying munitions were never calculated on a basis of prolonged occupation of the Peninsula, and that the War Office would have to reconsider the whole position, if more was wanted. If I remember aright, the cable finished by saying, "It is important to push on." A few days later a cable was received saying the War Office would not give us more ammunition until we submitted a return of what was in hand. The compilation of that cut-and-dried return in the midst of a desperate battle was a distracting and never-to-be-forgotten effort, but there was no help for it: no return, no shells; that was the War Office order. The ammunition still in hand lay mostly in the holds of the ships at Mudros, 60 miles away, and did not lend themselves to easy counting; while the actual expenditure was, for reasons already given, an intricate problem indeed.

Continuous cables on the subject of ammunition passed during the next few days between G.H.Q. and the War Office, all of which passed through my hands and some of which I drafted for superior authority. I cannot remember their sequence and not always their purport, but I distinctly remember about the 10th or 11th May a cable being received from Lord Kitchener saying ammunition for Field Artillery was being pushed out*via* Marseilles. I think the figures given were about ten or twenty thousand rounds of 18-pr. and some one thousand rounds of 4.5 howitzer H.E., but I am not sure.

The fact that does remain indelibly impressed on my mind is that I am convinced from the cables that passed through my office that no provision had been made by the War Office to keep up a regular supply of artillery ammunition to the Dardanelles Expedition. The W.O. authority appeared to have given a bonus of ammunition when the Expedition sailed, and to have been somewhat taken aback and annoyed by the fact that a sure and continuous supply should afterwards be demanded.

On 29th May I left G.H.Q. on appointment as Brigadier-General to command all the artillery at Cape Helles, in which capacity I served till September, i.e. through all the big attacks and counter-attacks of June, July and August. In this capacity I was brought face to face with all the deficiencies in artillery *matériel* and ammunition, of which the following were the most important. Although there was only one Battery of 4.5 and one Battery of 6-in. howitzers at Helles there was always an extreme deficiency of howitzer H.E. ammunition. So great was the shortage that immediately on taking up my command I found it necessary to issue a most stringent order that no howitzer on Cape Helles was ever to fire H.E. without my personal authority. When the Turks attacked, 18-prs. and 15-prs. were to support the Infantry with shrapnel; howitzers were only to be used with my personal permission and then were only to fire shrapnel. All howitzer H.E. was to be used exclusively for supporting British attacks by bombarding the Turkish trenches before and during such activities. Throughout the above months, constant appeals were made to me by Infantry Commanders to bombard the Turkish trenches with H.E. in order to retaliate for the loss our men had suffered from the Turkish guns using H.E. Such requests I had invariably to refuse.

There were fifty-six 18-prs. at Helles, when I assumed command on the 29th May, and subsequently they were increased to seventy-two at the end of July. Except for 640 rounds of H.E., which was fired off during the 4th June battle, no more H.E. arrived till the end of July.

Never during my command did the total number of rounds of 18-pr. ammunition at Helles ever reach 25,000. Before one of our attacks, with very careful previous husbanding, the total used perhaps to reach 19,000 to 23,000. The total amount I could therefore allot justifiably for the artillery preparation before an attack of our four British Infantry Divisions never exceeded 12,000 rounds; as from 6,000 to 7,000 must necessarily be kept in reserve to assist in beating off the determined hostile counter-attacks. As I remarked at the beginning of this paper, artillery ammunition was a constant anxiety to the higher commanders on the Western Front also, but never, I believe, had Infantry to attack with so little artillery support as the above. My position in France did not give me any inside knowledge of the details of artillery supply, but in one action at St. Eloi (near Ypres) on 14th or 15th February, in which only 27th Division was concerned, the artillery of this Division (so the C.R.A. informed me) alone fired 10,000 18-pr.

rounds in one night. At a similar action at the same place by the same division about a month later the divisional artillery fired, I believe, a slightly larger amount. Again, at Neuve Chapelle, in February, 1915, each Division had its own divisional artillery and the ammunition expenditure worked out to 150 rounds per 18-pr. gun. These official figures were shown me a few days after the battle by the G.O.C., 2nd Army.

In comparing the ammunition expenditure of France in 1915 and in the Dardanelles, the enormous discrepancy in the number of 18-prs. per Division must be taken into account. Reckoning on the scale of the number of 18-prs. allotted to a British Division in France, we had at Helles little more than sufficient 18-prs. for one Division, yet with this number we had to give artillery support to four Divisions. As to the French artillery at Helles, they could always reckon on being able to expend 40,000 to 45,000 rounds when their two Divisions attacked.

The complete absence of H.E. was severely felt, as shrapnel were of little use for destroying trenches, machine gun emplacements, etc. Therefore, in each and every British attack, success was jeopardized and our infantry exposed to cruel losses, because, firstly, there was not sufficient ammunition to prepare their attack, and, secondly, there was no H.E. (except for howitzers) to destroy the machine guns in their emplacements. The latter, therefore, inflicted great losses on our Infantry in their advance.

Our unfortunate position did not escape the notice of the French, who used at times generously to place under my command some of their field guns and howitzers, but in the latter they were also lamentably deficient, and in ammunition they were, themselves, during May and early June, none too well provided, although towards July their reserves grew more sufficient. The British deficiency in ammunition, however, was so great, and created so much merriment among the French that they christened the British Artillery, "Un coup par pièce"; with which term of endearment I was always personally greeted by the French Artillery General and his Staff, with all of whom I was great friends.

At the battle of 28th June the French were unable to spare us

Appendix I – Statement on Artillery 491

the howitzers or ammunition we begged of them. The failure of the gallant 156th Brigade of the 52nd Division to take the H.12 trenches was essentially due to lack of artillery ammunition, especially of H.E. Allowing for losses that must have been suffered under any condition, I believe that some 700 or 800 Scottish casualties were due to this cause. Before the action the Corps Commander sent for me to say that he did not consider that enough guns and ammunition had been allotted to this portion of the Turkish trenches. I replied that I agreed, but that there were no more available and that to reduce the bombardment of the hostile trenches on the left of our front would gravely prejudice the success of the 29th Division in that quarter and that I understood success there was more vital than on our right flank. After consultation with the G.O.C. 29th Division, the Corps Commander agreed with my allotment of the artillery. We then did our utmost to obtain the loan of more guns, howitzers or ammunition from the French without success and with the result that the attack was beaten off.

So successful had been the attack on our left with its capture of five successive lines of Turkish trenches that we had actually some ammunition to spare. In the afternoon it was agreed that there should be another attack on H.12, preceded by a very short but very intense bombardment from every gun and howitzer we possessed. All artillery arrangements for this were completed before 2.30 p.m., from which hour all the guns waited alert and ready for the Infantry to inform us of the hour they wished us to commence fire. I was in direct telephonic communication with the commander of the 52nd Division, having had a private wire laid on to his Headquarters the previous day. Suddenly, to my horror, I received a telephone message from my Artillery Group Commander, Colonel Stockdale, saying the Infantry were making the assault and that he had no time to do more than fire half a dozen shots!

In the attacks of 12th and 13th July, the French placed some thirty or forty guns and howitzers under British command, and on account of the shortage of British ammunition their guns undertook the whole of the artillery preparation, our artillery confining itself to covering fire during and after the Infantry advance. The counter-attacks were so violent and the calls for artillery support were so incessant that towards the afternoon of the 13th July the British gun ammunition began to get alarmingly low, until finally only about 5,000 rounds of 18-pr. ammunition, including all rounds in Battery charge, remained at Helles. The French were reluctant to supply further artillery support, fearing further attacks on themselves. This was the most anxious night I spent on the Peninsula — all but a limited number of rounds were withdrawn from most Batteries and were placed in horsed ammunition wagons, which perambulated from one side of the British position to the other according to where it seemed most likely the next Turkish attack would take place. These measures were successful and no Battery actually was left without one round at a critical moment, but the position throughout that night was a most dangerous one. Every hour a wire was sent to G.H.Q. giving expression to our crying needs, but there was next to nothing at Mudros, while desperate fighting still went on without a minute's respite. At 11 p.m. that night a trawler did, to the joy of every gunner, reach Helles with 3,000 rounds of 18-pr., but on the arrival of my Staff Officer to unload it, it was found that the fuses were of a new pattern never issued before and that the existing fuse keys would not adjust the fuses. As no new pattern fuse keys had been sent from home the Batteries had to manufacture their own, which was successfully accomplished after two days' delay.

During June two Batteries, and during July two more Batteries of 5-inch howitzers, manned by Territorials, arrived at Helles. During the last week of July the first two Batteries were sent to Anzac. Some of these howitzers were very old and worn by corrosion, and were consequently inaccurate.

The Gun History sheets of some of them showed they had been used at the Battle of Omdurman, seventeen years before, and had been in use ever since. After the big British attacks of 6th and 7th August, their ammunition began to run short. On demand about 500 or 700 rounds were sent up from Mudros — on arrival each shell was found to be of only 40 lb. weight, whereas former shells were of 50 lb. weight. Their fuses were also of new pattern, which existing fuse keys would not fit and, to crown all, no range tables had been sent for this new pattern of shell. In spite of continual

Appendix I – Statement on Artillery 493

letters and telegrams to the War Office, when I left Helles in September no new pattern fuse keys or range tables had ever arrived from England; consequently these shells remained stacked on the Peninsula while the Batteries only fired occasionally for want of ammunition!

On another occasion, when we were in the greatest straits for 15-pr. ammunition, many hundreds of rounds arrived at Helles, which on being landed were discovered by my Staff only to be suitable for the Ehrhardt R.H.A. guns in Egypt, no such guns being in the Dardanelles.

As for heavy artillery, practically speaking, there was none! Only one 6-inch Howitzer Battery (4 howitzers) and one 60-pr. Battery (4 guns) were in action at Helles up to July when four more guns of the latter calibre were landed. Unfortunately, however, the 60-prs. were of little use, as the recoil was too great for the carriages and the latter broke down beyond repair by our limited resources after very few rounds. At the beginning of August only one 60-pr. gun remained in action. Consequently, we had no heavy guns capable of replying to the Turkish heavy guns which enveloped us on three sides, and from whose fire our infantry and artillery suffered severely.

As to spare parts, spare guns and carriages, such luxuries were practically non-existent. No provision appears to have been made by the War Office to replace our guns or their parts, which became unserviceable through use or through damage by the hostile artillery. As the British were holding the lower slopes of the Achi Baba position, and as all our gun positions could be seen into by the Turks with powerful spectacles from their observation posts on the top of Achi Baba, our equipment suffered severely. During June and July one 6-inch howitzer and twenty-five 18-prs. (out of a total of seventy-two) as well as one or two 60-prs., were put out of action by direct hits from the hostile artillery. Such guns were withdrawn to the field workshops on "W" Beach, but as these workshops were exposed to the enemy's artillery fire from three sides, the guns were often further damaged while under repair. Damaged guns had sometimes to wait for days in this workshop until other guns had been damaged in a different place by the hostile artillery. Then possibly one efficient gun could be made up of the undamaged portions of one, two or more guns. Batteries often, therefore, remained for days short of guns on account of the lack of spare parts.

When I assumed command of the artillery at Helles, there were two Batteries of mountain guns (10-prs.) in action, but they were of a prehistoric pattern. In 1899 the Khedive of Egypt possessed in his Army, in which I was then serving, mountain guns which were more up-to-date in every respect. So inaccurate were these 10-prs. that they had to be placed close behind the front trenches lest they should hit our own Infantry, the result being a very heavy casualty list in officers and men amongst their Territorial personnel. Many of these lives could have been saved, had reasonable modern weapons been supplied. These obsolete old guns wore out so quickly that the two Batteries quickly melted into one Battery, and when they finally left Helles for Anzac at the end of July, I believe only 3 guns and their detachments were left in being.

As for anti-aircraft guns, they did not exist at all and the hostile aeroplanes used to fly over and drop bombs *ad lib.* without fear of molestation, the only saving clause being that the enemy appeared to possess almost as few aeroplanes as the British.

In no point of their equipment did the force at Helles suffer so much in comparison with their comrades in France as in the matter of aeroplanes which, at the Dardanelles, were hopelessly deficient not only in the numbers but also in quality. There were not sufficient pilots and there were no observers at all. Brave and efficient as the naval pilots were, they could not be expected to be of any use as artillery spotters unless they had been thoroughly trained for this important duty. This deficiency had to be made good at all costs by drafting young artillery subalterns from their Batteries and sending them to the Air Force, where their lack of training and experience in operation was at first severely felt, although later these lads did magnificent work. Thus Batteries were deprived of their trained subalterns just at the moment when the latter were most required on account of the severe casualties suffered in the landing and during the subsequent early operations. But few of the aeroplanes were fitted with wireless and the receivers on the ground could not take in messages over a distance longer than 5,000 yards. Consequently, each aeroplane had to

Appendix I – Statement on Artillery

return within this radius of the receiver, before its observation could be delivered, thus immensely curtailing the usefulness and efficiency of the aeroplane observation. Owing to the above conditions, aeroplanes could only be used for the counter-batteries firing on hostile artillery.

As regards trench mortars, the supply was hopelessly inadequate. I cannot give the exact figures, but I believe there were not a dozen at Helles during the whole period I was there, and these were of such an indifferent type as to be practically useless, and for this reason no one bothered about them. No provision appears to have been made for the supply of such necessities of trench warfare by the Home Authorities. This appears to be indefensible, as I believe very early in the operations their provision was specially asked for by G.H.Q. The absolute failure to supply such articles of vital necessity eventually led to the French C.-in-C. at Helles lending the British two demizel trench mortars and large quantities of ammunition. These were manned by artillery detachments, and by their magnificent work and the constant demand from the Infantry for their services, it was conclusively proved what an invaluable aid a sufficient supply of these weapons would have been.

From the very first it was apparent to me that the number of British guns at Helles was not sufficient to prepare and support simultaneous Infantry attacks of the whole British Force at this end of the Peninsula. In June I drew up a memorandum to G.H.Q. pointing this out and asking for a big increase of guns, howitzers and ammunition. What happened to this I cannot say. I only know that the guns and ammunition asked for never materialized.

The whole story of the artillery at Helles may be summed up in the following sentences: insufficiency of guns of every nature; insufficiency of ammunition of every nature, especially of H.E.; insufficient provision made by the Home Authorities for spare guns, spare carriages, spare parts, adequate repairing workshops, or for a regular daily, weekly or monthly supply of ammunition; guns provided often of an obsolete pattern and so badly worn by previous use as to be most inaccurate; lack of aeroplanes, trained observers and of all the requisites for air observation; total failure to produce the trench mortars and bombs to which the closeness of the opposing lines at Helles would have lent themselves well — in short, total lack of organization at home to provide even the most rudimentary and indispensable artillery requisites for daily consumption; not to speak of downright carelessness which resulted in wrong shells being sent to the wrong guns, and new types of fuses being sent without fuse keys and new types of howitzer shells without range tables. These serious faults provoked their own penalties in the shape of the heavy losses suffered by our Infantry and artillery, which might have been to a great measure averted if sufficient forethought and attention had been devoted to the "side-show" at the Dardanelles.

After commanding the starved artillery at Helles it was my good fortune to command the artillery of the 21st Army Corps at the third Battle of Gaza, in November, 1917, and also at the great Battle of 19th September, 1918, in which the Turks in Palestine were finally crushed, and I think it may add emphasis to what I have said if I contrast the artillery support of the two campaigns and show the results which ensued. On the night before the third Battle of Gaza, the artillery under my command (to support three Divisions) consisted of the following, viz.: 19½ Batteries (i.e., 78 guns and howitzers) of heavy artillery, comprising 8-inch howitzers, 6-inch guns, 6-inch howitzers and 60-pr. guns — all of the most modern and up-to-date type.

The Field Artillery comprised 108 18-prs. and 36 4.5 howitzers while in addition there were 8 modern mountain howitzers and guns. There was not an artillery weapon in the whole Army Corps that was not efficient and up-to-date, while immediately behind the front line existed perfectly organized workshops capable of executing any repairs. There was ample provision of spare guns, carriages and parts, and an abundance of trench mortars which, though they would have changed the whole face of the Peninsula conflict, could not be used in Palestine owing to the breadth of No Man's Land. Ammunition for every nature of gun and howitzer was pressed upon us in profusion — over a thousand rounds per gun was buried and concealed near every Battery, while immediately behind the fighting line huge reserves were available for immediate use if required. At the advanced railhead, G.H.Q. literally built mountains of ammunition as a further supply; all this

Appendix I – Statement on Artillery 497

in addition to vast quantities stored in depôts in Egypt and on the banks of the Suez Canal. So great was the superabundance of shell, that hundreds of tons were left lying on the ground after the nine days' Battle at Gaza; which it took months to remove. At the battle of the 19th September, 1918, in Palestine conditions were exactly the same. There was an absolute *embarras de richesse* of every artillery requisite. This wealth of artillery material was supported in Palestine by a full complement of artillery, aeroplanes, pilots and observers, the latter being all thoroughly trained and efficient. In addition, by a sufficiency of fighting aeroplanes with most efficient pilots, our artillery were adequately guarded from sunrise to sunset from any hostile aeroplane observation.

In short, our air supremacy was undisputed and absolutely protected our own artillery against damage and molestation from the hostile guns. On the other hand, the enemy's artillery lay at our mercy directly their gun positions were discovered.

The whole science of artillery and aeroplane co-operation had, of course, been vastly extended and perfected since Gallipoli days, but the point I wish to make is this: that in 1917 and 1918 the Palestine Front was fitted out on the same scale, proportionately, as the Western Front; whereas in 1915 this was not the case in the Dardanelles as regards artillery, for instance, only one Division (the 29th) at Helles having 18-pr. guns and the Naval Division having been given no artillery at all!

To put the matter shortly, whereas at Helles I had under my command no more than 88 to 95 guns and howitzers of all natures with scarcely any ammunition or aeroplanes to support four British Divisions; in Palestine at Gaza I had at least 230 guns and howitzers (one-third of which were of heavy calibre) with an abundance of ammunition and a sufficiency of aeroplanes to support the attack of one and a half Divisions, the remaining one and a half Divisions at Gaza being in reserve. At the battle of 19th September, 1918, in Palestine I had, to the best of my recollection, about 360 guns of all calibres to support four Divisions. The terrible casualties suffered by our Infantry at Helles are well known, and my feelings as Artillery Commander unable to give them anything like the support they would have had in France or Flanders may be guessed. But this was made up to me afterwards when I commanded the artillery at Gaza, that strong fortress which was captured by the 21st Army Corps, with certainly under 3,000 casualties and I believe with under 2,000 killed and wounded. At Gaza the Turks were simply crushed by our overwhelming artillery, fed from inexhaustible Ordnance parks and dumps. Before the Infantry attack commenced the position was subjected to a continuous bombardment night and day for six days and six nights from every available gun and howitzer. The Infantry then attacked and took a large portion of the position with a loss of, I believe, under 1,000 men. The Turks counter-attacked, but they melted away under the tremendous artillery barrage and never attempted another during this battle. Next night our Infantry tried to extend their conquest but the Turks had meanwhile brought up an old Gallipoli Division, the 7th, which held them at bay and inflicted upon them serious losses which, I believe, increased their casualties to between two and three thousand. The Corps Commander then decided to let the Infantry stand where they were, to submit the Turks to a further three days' and three nights' bombardment, at the end of which our Infantry advanced again only to find that the Turks were evacuating the whole of the Gaza position. After the Battle of 19th September, 1918, many Infantry commanders of Divisions, Brigades and Battalions have told me the Turks appeared crushed by the terrific artillery bombardment (under cover of which our men advanced) and offered a resistance which, in comparison with our experiences of Gallipoli, can only be called feeble.

The cardinal fact that remains in my mind is that in Palestine the 21st Army Corps always had enough (and more than enough) of every artillery requisite for whatever number of Divisions the Army Corps was composed of; whereas, in Gallipoli, the VIIIth Army Corps at Helles, which was composed of four British Divisions, never had enough Field Artillery or ammunition to support more than one Division, and never possessed sufficient heavy artillery to support more than one Infantry Brigade.

The material part of my statement ends here, and it only remains for me to remind you that all the grievous shortcomings I have exposed were actually made good by the heroism, devotion and sufferings of the Officers and men of the Artillery at Helles,

Appendix I – Statement on Artillery

both Regular, Territorial, Australian and New Zealand. Rest was impossible, as no Battery could ever be withdrawn from the line and all field Batteries were under rifle fire. If placed outside that range, they were destroyed by flanking fire from Turkish guns in Asia. No dug-outs were possible, as dug-outs were understood in France, as there was no timber or roofing for their construction. All ranks were thus exposed night and day to continuous fire, and were sometimes killed as they slept in their valises by stray bullets, thousands of which were fired unaimed every night by the Turks in the hopes of inflicting casualties; water for drinking and washing was almost as precious as guns and shells. The joys of a canteen, as was at that time supplied by the War Office to our Army in France, were unknown; bare rations washed down by a limited allowance of water were our only form of food; everyone suffered more or less from dysentery, spread by the millions of flies which settled on every mouthful we ate and made life almost insupportable by day. No Man's Land was one vast litter of unburied corpses. Yet no man's spirit ever wavered and all ranks remained as bright, as hopeful and as cheerful as on the day of the first great landing. If shells were scarce, complaints were non-existent; all were upheld by the wonderful religion of self-sacrifice. It will ever remain my greatest pride that I had the astonishing good fortune to be associated with such a body of officers and men; to them I owe a debt of gratitude that is beyond redemption, and to them alone is due the credit for any success which the artillery at Helles may have attained in what was one of England's greatest tragedies, but was also one of England's greatest glories.

Appendix II – Dardanelles Expedition Notes

By Lieut.-Colonel Charles Rosenthal,[*] Commanding 3rd Australian Field Artillery Brigade, 1st Australian Division, relating to Artillery at Anzac, from 25th April to 25th August, 1915. (Compiled from personal diary.)

During the early hours of 25th April, 1915, the 3rd Australian Infantry Brigade landed on Gallipoli Peninsula, close to Gaba Tepe, at a point now known as Anzac Beach, followed by other troops of 1st Australian Division and Australian and New Zealand Division.

Arrangements had been made for artillery to land about 10 a.m. on the same morning, but owing to delays in disembarkation of Infantry, and enemy shelling of transports necessitating ships temporarily leaving their allotted anchorage, it was after mid-day before the vessels carrying guns were actually in correct position for disembarkation.

I did not wait for the naval boats to come alongside, but after issuing necessary instructions to Battery Commanders concerning the landing of the guns, I disembarked in a ship's boat manned by a volunteer crew from my Brigade Ammunition Column, accompanied by two officers and sixteen men of my Headquarters' Staff.

---

[*] Now Major-General Sir Charles Rosenthal, K.C.B., C.M.G., D.S.O. — *IAN H. 1920.*

Appendix II – Dardanelles Expedition Notes

Immediately on landing I reported to my C.R.A., and was by him informed that the Divisional Commander had decided no artillery should land during the day. This decision absolutely nonplussed me, and on asking the reason I was informed the position was not considered sufficiently secure to ensure the safety of guns, if emplaced. With this decision I did not agree and urged, without result, that the safety of guns was surely secondary to the proper supporting of the troops already committed.

In view of the above decision instructions were at once sent off to the ships ordering Colonel Johnstone, Commanding 2nd A.F.A. Brigade, and Major Hughes, acting for me in command of 3rd A.F.A. Brigade, to defer disembarkation of guns. Colonel Johnstone, however, by this time had one 18-pr. gun well on the way to the shore. Permission was given for it to be landed and it was brought into action close to the beach against guns at Gaba Tepe, undoubtedly temporarily silencing them.

In the meantime the Indian Mountain Battery attached to 1st Australian Division, which had landed early in the day, was in action doing splendid work though suffering severe casualties.

By the order of Colonel White, G.S.O. (1), 1st Australian Division, I spent the afternoon in collecting Infantry stragglers and getting them forward again to the firing line. At 5 p.m. I reported completion of this task and then proceeded to thoroughly reconnoitre the right flank, overlooking Gaba Tepe, which had seemed to me, from observations made from the ship, to be a suitable area for emplacing of guns.

I returned to Divisional Headquarters just before dark, and informed the C.R.A. and Divisional Commander that I had found suitable places for batteries and could use them effectively.

I had in my reconnaissance conferred with three Battalion Commanders (one of whom was killed a couple of days later), who were delighted to hear that the artillery they were so anxiously waiting for was to come up in support.

After much discussion and persuasion the Divisional Commander agreed to allow me to land two of my three 18-pr. batteries. This approval was shortly afterwards altered to permission to land two guns only, and finally all approval was cancelled, though no information of these decisions officially reached me.

During the night, in anticipation of early arrival of guns, my Headquarters personnel worked untiringly in preparing a track from the beach to the selected sites for guns, and it was not till 5.30 a.m. on 26th that I learned approval to land guns had been cancelled overnight.

During the morning of 26th April one gun of 1st Battery, 1st Brigade, and one gun of 4th Battery, 2nd Brigade, were landed, hauled up the steep hill to their positions, and came into action on the extreme right of ridge overlooking Gaba Tepe.

Later in the day the 7th Battery of my Brigade came into action on the same ridge and the single guns of 1st and 4th Batteries were withdrawn for return to their respective Brigades.

During the afternoon there also came ashore, apparently without order, two guns of 3rd Battery, 1st Brigade, and 8th Battery, 3rd Brigade, but were returned to their respective ships by the C.R.A.

My guns were placed absolutely in the Infantry front trenches, on the sky line, no troops of any kind being in advance of them. It would have been quite useless to take up positions behind the Infantry line in the normal way, owing to the configuration of the ground, for in such cases the lowest range at which the crest could be cleared was 3,000 yards, while our targets were from 500 to 1,000 yards distant. Indeed at night, shrapnel shell with fuse set at zero was frequently used.

Each gun fired during the 26th about 400 rounds, over open sights, and caused very heavy casualties to the enemy.

The whole battery covered a front of 187°, necessitating each gun being personally controlled by an officer and each with its own particular arc of fire.

The supply of ammunition was very difficult. It had to be delivered by hand to the guns over a bullet-swept area, the distance from the beach to the guns being about half a mile, while in this distance the hills rose 400 feet.

By the afternoon of the 3rd May, two guns of 8th Battery, 3rd Brigade, were in action, and 2nd Brigade also had guns in position on the left flank of 1st Australian Divisional Front.

The Australian and New Zealand Division also had 18-prs. in action together with two 4.5-inch Howitzer Batteries, the latter

Appendix II – Dardanelles Expedition Notes

being the only howitzers available up to this time at Anzac.

I was wounded on 5th May, evacuated to Cairo, and did not rejoin my command at Anzac till 26th May. During this interval gun positions, as well as Infantry trenches, had been much improved, and the enemy country in our immediate front which, when I left on 5th May, gave no signs of life, was now well traversed by trenches.

I found in my sector that the guns of my Brigade were now all in action, and the remainder of the artillery of the Division was also emplaced.

About this time 6-inch howitzers were made available and later emplaced, one for left sector, one for the centre, and one for the right, but with very limited quantities of ammunition. Another 6-inch howitzer was landed on 17th June.

I had made continual urgent representations for two 4.7-inch guns for right flank to deal with innumerable targets beyond the range of 18-prs., but it was not till 11th July that one very old and much worn gun arrived, and was placed in position on right flank, firing its first round on 26th July.

On 24th June a Scottish Territorial Howitzer Battery (the 5th Battery, City of Glasgow Lowland Howitzer Brigade) arrived and came under my command.

On 14th July a heavy battery was organized for right flank, consisting of the two 6-inch howitzers and the 4.7-inch gun before mentioned, but ammunition was still very scarce.

On 15th July a 5-inch Howitzer Brigade under Colonel Hope Johnstone commenced to arrive and was complete in position by 18th July.

On 28th July the 4th Battery of Lowland Brigade arrived.

About this time some alterations were made in artillery dispositions and grouping in preparation for impending battle at Suvla Bay and Lone Pine, commencing on 6th August, and on 30th July the artillery of right sector under my command was as follows:

3rd A.F.A. Brigade (18-prs.).
Heavy Battery (two 6-inch howitzers and one 4.7-inch gun).
2 Mountain Guns.
Two 5-inch Howitzer Batteries, Lowland Brigade.
One 5-inch Howitzer Battery, 69th Brigade.

When leaving Australia in 1914 I had urged that a battery of 5-inch howitzers (which I commanded prior to the outbreak of war), together with stocks of ammunition held by Australia, should accompany 1st Australian Division. This was not approved. On arrival at Gallipoli Peninsula, when the need for howitzers was at once apparent, I again re-opened the question, particularly on the 29th May, when the C.R.A. agreed to press for them to be sent forward. The Divisional Commander, on 25th June, cabled Australia definitely asking for this battery, which was at once forwarded, but arrived at the Peninsula too late to be of any service.

Two Australian Field Batteries (together with a Brigade of Infantry) were transferred to Cape Helles on 5th May and did not rejoin the Australian Division at Anzac till 18th August.

With the limited number of guns available it was exceedingly important that transfers might be made very rapidly from one part of our front to another, and on 2nd June I put forward a proposal which was approved immediately to make a road along the entire front just behind the crest on which infantry trenches were sited. This road was completed in about two weeks and was a great boon alike to gunners and Infantry.

Up to 24th August no anti-aircraft guns had been provided, but specially constructed emplacements had been made for 18-prs. to be used against aircraft, and though never successful in bringing down an enemy 'plane they certainly made good enough shooting to cause enemy aviators to treat them with respect. About 20th August three 3-pr. Hotchkiss arrived for anti-aircraft purposes. They were of obsolete pattern and had been manufactured for the Japanese Government many years before. In fact the only range tables provided were printed in Japanese, but thanks to the fact that one of my Sergeants (who was a Master Mariner) spoke Japanese, we succeeded in preparing serviceable range tables.

Two Japanese trench mortars were also used from Infantry trenches with excellent effect, but owing to ammunition supply becoming soon exhausted and no fresh supplies being available they had to be discarded. A good supply of these weapons, together with full supplies of ammunition, would have been invaluable in bombarding enemy front line trenches.

Appendix II – Dardanelles Expedition Notes

The ammunition supply at all times up to the operation of 6th August was a difficult problem. Frequently we had to be rationed to a very small allowance per battery per day, and the guns of the heavy battery were for some time not permitted to fire more than two rounds per day and then only by special permission of the C.R.A.

On 20th June I was first informed that H.E. for 18-pr. was to be supplied, and shortly afterwards a small supply for experiment was landed at Anzac. I think I am right in saying my share was 15 rounds per battery.

On 2nd August our first supply of H.E. arrived, but only 150 rounds per battery.

During the first few months of the campaign, when our stocks of ammunition were desperately low, our guns and gunners had to suffer considerable casualties without being able to effectively reply.

Our batteries were of necessity in many cases under direct observation of the enemy, and only the splendid work of the detachments in building earthworks for their protection made it possible to carry on.

Under the protection of the banks of a small ravine near the beach, our artificers established a workshop, and the extraordinary ingenuity and skill displayed in the repairing and replacing of damaged guns earned for the artificers our most grateful appreciation and thanks.

On 25th August I was evacuated suffering from enteric.

These notes only apply to the right sector, which I commanded.

Appendix III – General Instructions

The Dispatch of a Commander-in-Chief is not a technical document. In it the situation should be set forth, as briefly and clearly as may be, together with a few words indicative of the plan of G.H.Q. for coping with it. After that comes a narrative which ends with thanks to those individuals and units who have earned them. A Dispatch should be so written that civilians can follow the facts stated without trouble: it should not be too technical. But when the Military Colleges and Academies at Camberley, Duntroon, Kingston, West Point and in the European and Japanese capitals set to work in a scientific spirit to apportion praise or blame they are more influenced by the actual instructions and orders issued by the Commander-in-Chief *before and during the battle*, than by any after-the-event stories of what happened. They are glad to know the intentions of the Commander, but his instructions i.e., the actual steps he took to give practical effect to those intentions, are what really interest them.

When I came to write my Dispatch of the 11th December, so much about the actual course of events at Suvla was still obscure, that it had become desirable either to write the narrative in a more technical form than was customary or else to publish my actual instructions simultaneously with the Dispatch. I chose the latter course. The authorities had raised objections to several passages in the Dispatch, and in every case but one, where they had wished me to add something which was not, in my opinion, correct, I had met them. No objection had been raised to the inclusion of my instructions. At 9 p.m. on the night of the 6th January (the Dispatch being due to appear next morning) I received a letter by Special Messenger from the War Office telling me the Press Bureau were wiring to all those to whom the Dispatch had been issued to suppress the instructions!

Whatever the reason of this action may have been, its result was clear enough: my Dispatch was eviscerated at the very moment it was stepping on to the platform. Had I known that these instructions, now given, were to have been cut out, my Dispatch would have been differently written.

IAN H., 1920.

SIR IAN HAMILTON'S INSTRUCTIONS.
To VICE-ADMIRAL, COMMANDING
Eastern Mediterranean Squadron,

17th July, 1915.

SIR, — I have the honour to forward a series of tables drawn up to show in detail the men, animals, vehicles, stores, etc., which it will be required to land in connection with the forthcoming operations. I shall be grateful if you will let me know as early as possible if you consider that any part of the programme indicated presents especially serious difficulties or is likely to require modification.

In informing me of the results of your consideration, I shall be obliged if you will let me know what craft you intend to use in carrying out the disembarkations referred to in tables B, C, D and E, so that detailed arrangements with regard to embarkation and to the allocation of troops, etc., to boats may be prepared.

2. Immediately after the disembarkation of the details referred to in the attached tables it will be necessary, if the operations are

successful, to land 5,000 to 7,000 horses in order to render the force sufficiently mobile to carry the operations to a conclusion. Details as to disembarkation of these horses will be forwarded to you later. In the meantime the horses will be collected at Alexandria, and should subsequently be brought up to Mudros or Imbros, to begin arriving on August 6th.

It will also be necessary to land the remaining portions of the units referred to in the tables (first line transport, etc.), and, further, the remaining units of the formations to which they belong. In this latter category will be included three batteries of heavy artillery with mechanical transport. It will not be required to land any of the above until after August 7th, and details as to numbers, order of disembarkation, etc., will be forwarded to you later.

I have the honour to be, Sir,
Your obedient Servant,

(*Signed*) IAN HAMILTON,
General, Commanding
Mediterranean Expeditionary Force.

Appendix III – General Instructions 509

TABLE A.

TABLE SHOWING UNITS AND DETAILS WHICH IT IS REQUIRED TO LAND GRADUALLY AT ANZAC COVE BEFORE THE MORNING OF THE 3RD OF AUGUST. IT WILL BE NECESSARY TO CARRY OUT THESE DISEMBARKATIONS BY NIGHT, AND THE MOVEMENTS CAN BEGIN AS SOON AS IT IS CONVENIENT TO THE NAVAL TRANSPORT AUTHORITIES.

Unit.	From	To	Personnel.	Vehicles.	Animals.	Stores.	Remarks.
69th Howitzer Bde. R.F.A.	Mudros	Anzac Cove	312	16 guns, 16 wagons, 4 water carts	Nil		
1/3rd City of Glasgow 5" Howitzer Battery	Helles	Anzac Cove	78	4 guns, 4 wagons, 1 water cart	Nil		I.G.C. has already been instructed to arrange for this move.
10th Heavy Battery R.G.A.	On board ship at Mudros	Anzac Cove	11	4 guns, 4 wagons, 1 water cart, 2 G.S. wagons	Nil		
One F.A. Bde. (11th Division, "A" Bde.)	On board ship at Mudros	Anzac Cove	33	16 guns, 32 wagons, telegraph cart, 4 water carts	Nil		I.G.C. has already been instructed to arrange for this move.
Reinforcements for Units of A.N.Z.A.C.	Alexandria	Anzac Cove	7,000 to 8,000	Nil	Nil		
Mule Corps	Helles	Anzac Cove	50	Nil	200		By August 1st.
Ammunition Park	Mudros	Anzac Cove	65	Nil	Nil	S.A. Ammn. 5,500,000 rounds Mk. VII (*a*) (225 tons), 760,000 rounds Mk. VI (30 tons) Gun Ammunition (*b*) 10 pr. 2,700 (19 tons), 18 pr. 5,500 (70 tons), 4.5" How. 1,600 (45 tons), 5" How. 10,000 (330 tons), 6" How. 1,200 (70 tons), 60 pr. 1,000 (30 tons)	

(*a*) If possible, an additional 3,000,000 S.A.A. should be landed, so that half the reserve for the whole Northern Force may be ashore before operations begin (see Table "C" Remarks).
(*b*) If possible, the following additional gun ammunition should also be landed, so that the full reserve for the whole Northern Force may be ashore before operations begin :—

10 pr. .. .. 3,000 rounds }
18 pr. .. .. 10,000 rounds } See Table "C" Remarks.
6" Howitzer .. .. .. 1,000 rounds }

TABLE B.

TABLE SHOWING UNITS AND DETAILS WHICH IT IS REQUIRED TO LAND AT ANZAC COVE ON THE NIGHTS OF AUGUST 3RD/4TH, AUGUST 4TH/5TH AND AUGUST 5TH/6TH.

Unit.	From.	Date.	Personnel.	Vehicles.	Remarks.
6 Battalions (a), 13th Division	Mudros	Night, August 3rd/4th	4,650	Nil	Machine guns and other equipment carried by hand.
Bearer Sub-Division, personnel Anzao	Mudros	Night, August 3rd/4th	100	Nil	
7 Battalions (a), 13th Division	Mudros	Night, August 4th/5th	5,425	Nil	Machine guns and other equipment carried by hand.
Bearer Sub-Division, 1 Field Ambulance, 13th Division	Mudros	Night, August 4th/5th	125	Nil	
4 Battalions, 10th Division..	Mudros	Night, August 5th/6th	3,100	Nil	Machine guns and other equipment carried by hand. Ditto.
29th Indian Brigade and Field Ambulance	Imbros	Night, August 5th/6th	2,000	Nil	
Bearer Sub-Divisions, 2 Field Ambulance, 13th Division	Mudros	Night, August 5th/6th	255	Nil	
3 Field Companies R.E. (a), 13th Division	Mudros	Night, August 5th/6th	525	Nil	Machine guns and other equipment carried by hand. All tools carried by hand.

(a) These units to move from Helles to Mudros as follows:—

1 Brigade } Night, 28th/29th July.
1 Field Company

1 Brigade } Night, 29th/30th July.
1 Field Company

1 Brigade } Night, 30/31st July.
1 Field Company

Appendix III – General Instructions

TABLE C.

Table showing Units and Details which it is required to Land at New Beach during the Night of August 6th/7th, beginning one Hour after Dark (9.30 p.m.). All Troops will come from Imbros, but Horses will come direct except where otherwise stated.

Unit.	Personnel	Horses.	Vehicles.	Remarks.
1 Inf. Bde. and Sig. Sec (*a*)	3,050	36	Nil	Personnel only to be disembarked in the order shown. Animals of Mountain Batteries as soon as there is sufficient light, followed by horses of one 18-pr. Battery (82), and of H.Q. F.A. Brigade (10). Animals of remaining units to follow in the order shown. Supplies and forage for 7 days for these troops and animals to be dumped on the beach as soon as possible, will amount to about 250 tons. S.A.A. 4,000,000 will also have to be landed besides that carried by the troops, say, 150 tons.
1 Bearer Sub-Div.	40	Nil	Nil	
1 Inf. Bde. and Sig. Sec. and 1 W/T Station	3,065	36	Nil	
1 Bearer Sub-Div.	40	Nil	Nil	
Field Co. R.E.	175	16	4 tool carts	
2 Mountain Batts. (*b*)	100	80	Nil	
Div. H.Q. and Sig. Co.	125	28	2 cable wagons, 1 water cart, 2 limbd. R.E. wagons	

1 Inf. Bde. and Pioneer Bn. and Sig. Sec. and 1 W/T Station	3,840	44	Nil	Artillery reserve ammunition will also be required as follows :—
				 To come by trawler from Mudros
				   10 pr. 3,000 rds. (20 tons)
				   18 pr. 10,000 rds. (130 tons)
				   60 pr. 1,000 rds. (30 tons)

7 Bearer Sub-Divs.	300	Nil	Nil	

Appendix III – General Instructions

2 Platoons Div. Cycl. Co.	62	Nil	62 bicycles
2 Field Cos. R.E.	350	32	8 tool carts
1 F.A. Bde. ("L" Bde.) (c)	550	251	16 guns, 44 wagons, 1 telephone wagon, 5 water carts
Ammn. Park Personnel (11 Div.)	65	Nil	Nil
9 Tent Sub.-Divs.	350	84 horses or 144 mules	30 ambulance wagons, 9 water carts, 3 Maltese carts
4 Casualty Clearing Stations	360	Nil	Nil
Bde. Ammn. Col.	60	62	8 ammunition wagons, 1 water cart, 4 S.A.A. wagons
2 Bns. for Beach Parties	1,000	Nil	Nil
Mule Corps	150	300	150 mule carts
Wireless Sec.	18	16	2 two-horse vehicles

Remarks (applies to 1 F.A. Bde.): (See notes to Table A.) If reserve S.A.A. and gun ammunition can be put ashore at Anzac Cove before operations begin this will also be done. But the above-mentioned reserves must also be landed at New Beach in case the congestion on the road from Anzac makes its forwarding a matter of great difficulty.

(a) Helles to Imbros, night July 31st/August 1st.
(b) Helles to Imbros, night August 1st/2nd.
(c) Animals in remarks columns (82 and 10) come from Imbros, remainder from Mudros in horse-ships.

Appendix III – General Instructions

TABLE D.

TABLE SHOWING UNITS AND DETAILS WHICH IT IS REQUIRED TO LAND AT ANZAC COVE BEGINNING AT DAWN AUGUST 7TH. ORDER OF LANDING AS SHOWN. ALL THESE TROOPS WILL COME FROM MUDROS.

Unit.	Personnel.	Horses.	Vehicles.	Remarks.
Medical personnel, tent sub-divisions A. and N.Z.A.C. Field Ambulance	900	Nil	Nil	All spare stretchers to be carried by hand.
Bearer Sub-Divisions of 1 Field Ambulance, 10th Division	125	Nil	Nil	
One 18-pr. Battery and H.Q. F.A. Bde. ("A" Bde.)	120	92	Nil	
10th Heavy Battery R.G.A.	110	70	Nil	
Three 18-pr. Batteries ("A" Brigade)	300	246	Nil	Guns and personnel already ashore. (See Tables A and B.)
Mules of Mule Corps	*	400	Nil	* Sufficient personnel to look after mules.

TABLE E.

TABLE SHOWING UNITS TO BE READY TO LAND IMMEDIATELY AFTER THOSE SHOWN IN TABLES A, B, C AND D. UNITS WILL PROBABLY BE REQUIRED IN THE ORDER SHOWN EITHER AT NEW BEACH OR ANZAC COVE AS CIRCUMSTANCES MAY DICTATE.

Unit.	From	Personnel.	Animals.	Vehicles.	Remarks.
Divl. H.Q. 10th Divn.	Mudros	125	28	2 limbered R.E. wagons, 1 water cart, 2 cable wagons	S.A.A. 2,600,000 rounds besides that carried on the men.
3 Battalions 10th Divn.	Mudros	2,325	40	6 water carts	
6 Battalions 10th Divn.	Port Iero	4,650	76	12 water carts.	
H.Q. Divl. R.E.	Mudros	525	30	12 tool carts, 3 water carts.	
3 Field Cos. R.E. 10th Division Bearer Sub-Divisions of 2 Field Ambulances, 10th Divn.	— Mudros	— 250	— —	— —	
15th Heavy Battery R.G.A.	On board ship—Mudros	121	70	4 guns, 4 wagons, 1 water cart, 2 G.S. wagons.	
Tent Sub-Division of 10th Divn.	Mudros	350	54 horses or 84 mules	15 ambulance wagons, 12 carts.	
Mule Corps	Mudros	150	300	150 carts.	

Appendix III – General Instructions 515

GENERAL OFFICER COMMANDING,
Australian and New Zealand Army Corps.

With reference to your G.288 of 15th July, the Navy is being asked to provide transport for the following ammunition to be landed at Anzac by the 3rd August:

For A. and N.Z.A.C. — Sufficient S.A.A. to bring the amount on shore up to 500 rounds per rifle and 27,500 per machine-gun.
For other Troops. — 300 rounds per rifle and 24,000 rounds per machine-gun (in addition to what the troops will carry on landing).

These will come to 10,000,000 rounds in all, and arrangements are being made to begin landing this ammunition as soon as possible.

2. The following artillery ammunition will also have to be gradually landed and stored, and should all be ashore, if possible, by August 3rd:

10 pr.	5,700	rounds
18 pr. (probably 15 per cent. H.E.)	15,500	”
4.5-in. Howitzer probably half H.E.	1,600	”
5-in. Howitzer majority H.E.	10,000	”
6-in. Howitzer majority H.E.	1,200	”
60 pr. probably two-thirds H.E.	1,000	”

All of this ammunition is not yet arrived, and the proportion of H.E. shell is not yet ascertainable from England. The arrangements suggested in your paragraph 2 (iii.) of your letter are noted, and will be followed as far as possible.

3. With regard to the marking of ammunition-boxes, the necessary arrangements are being prepared. You will be informed of the arrangements and of the system of marking in due course.

    Consignments of Mark VI. and Mark VII. will be sent separately as you suggest.

4. The above figures do not include the periodical replenishment referred to in paragraph 2 (iv.) of your letter. Dispatch of consignments on this account and consignments for the reserve will be notified to you separately.

(*Signed*) W. P. BRAITHWAITE,
Major-General, C.G.S.,
Mediterranean Expeditionary Force.

    Enclosed a copy of tables forwarded to Vice-Admiral, showing troops, animals, stores, etc., which the Navy is being asked to land at Anzac.

22nd July, 1915.

GENERAL OFFICES COMMANDING,
    9th Corps.

The General Commanding wishes me to send you the following outline of his plans for the next general attack, for the exclusive information of yourself, your Divisional Generals, and such Officers of your Corps Headquarters and Divisional Headquarters as you may consider it necessary to take into your confidence. I am to add that it is Sir Ian's wish that as few officers as possible should be made acquainted with it.

2. The general plan is, while holding as many of the enemy as possible in the southern theatre, to throw the weight of our attack on the Turkish forces now opposite the Australian and New Zealand Army Corps. It is hoped, by means of an attack on the front and right flank of these forces, to deal them a crushing blow, and to drive the remnants south towards Kilid Bahr. It will then be

Appendix III – General Instructions 517

the object of the General Commanding to seize a position across the peninsula from Gaba Tepe to Maidos with a protected line of supply from Suvla Bay.

3. The strength of the enemy north of Kilid Bahr at the present time is about 30,000 men. Of these some 12,000 are permanently maintained in the trenches opposite the Anzac position, and the majority of the remainder are held in reserve at Boghali, Kojadere and Eski-Keui. It is believed that there are about three battalions in the Anafarta villages, a battalion at Ismail Oglu Tepe (New map 1/20,000), a battalion near Yilghin Burnu, and small parties of outposts at Lala Baba (Sq. 104.L.) and Ghazi Baba (Sq. 106.N.). The hills due east of Suvla Bay towards Aji Liman are believed to be held only by a few Gendarmerie, but information on this point is at present not precise. The hills near Yilghin Burnu and Ismail Oglu Tepe are known to contain one 4.7-in. gun, one 9.2-in. gun, and three field guns, protected by wire entanglements and infantry trenches, but it is believed that the main defences are against attack from the south or west, and that there is no wire on the northern slopes of the hills; also that the guns can only be fired in a southerly direction.

4. The success of the plan outlined in paragraph 2 will depend on two main factors:

(a) The capture of Hill 305 (Sq. 93.W.).
(b) The capture and retention of Suvla Bay as a base of operations for the northern army.

5. The operations from within the present Anzac position against the enemy on Hill 305 will be carried out by the Australian and New Zealand Corps, temporarily reinforced by the following units of the 9th Army Corps:

13th Division (less 66th, 67th and 68th Brigades, R.F.A.).
29th Infantry Brigade (10th Division).
29th Indian Brigade.
69th Howitzer Brigade, R.F.A.

Appendix III – General Instructions

6. The landing near Suvla will be entrusted to you, and you will have at your disposal:

11th Division.
10th Division (less 29th Brigade).
Highland Mountain Artillery Brigade.
1st/4th Lowland Howitzer Brigade.

The disembarkation of your command, which may be expected to be opposed, though not in great strength, will be after dark at a point immediately south of Lala Baba. The first troops to disembark will be the 11th Division, which will have been concentrated at Imbros previously to the attack, and will be brought across under cover of darkness in destroyers and motor-lighters. It is expected that approximately 4,000 men will be disembarked simultaneously, and that three infantry brigades and the mountain artillery brigade will be ashore before daylight.

Your first objectives will be the high ground at Lala Baba and Ghazi Baba, and the hills near Yilghin Burnu and Ismail Oglu Tepe. It will also be necessary to send a small force to secure a footing on the hills due east of Suvla Bay. It is of first importance that Yilghin Burnu and Ismail Oglu Tepe should be captured by a coup-de-main before daylight in order to prevent the guns which they contain being used against our troops on Hill 305 and to safeguard our hold on Suvla Bay. It is hoped that one division will be sufficient for the attainment of these objectives.

Your subsequent moves will depend on circumstances which cannot at present be gauged, but it is hoped that the remainder of your force will be available on the morning of the 7th August to advance on Biyuk Anafarta with the object of moving up the eastern spurs of Hill 305 so as to assist General Birdwood's attack.

7. The operations from within the present Anzac position will begin during the day immediately preceding your disembarkation (the reinforcements for General Birdwood's force having been dribbled ashore in detachments at Anzac Cove on the three previous nights). The operations will begin with a determined attack on the Turkish left centre, Lonesome Pine and Johnston's Jolly (see enlarged map

of Anzac position), with the object of attracting the enemy's reserves to this portion of the line. The Turks have for long been apprehensive of our landing in the neighbourhood of Gaba Tepe, and it is hoped that an attack in force in this quarter will confirm their apprehensions. At nightfall the Turkish outposts on the extreme right of the enemy's line will be rushed, and a force of 20,000 men will advance in three or more columns up the ravines running down from Chunuk Bair. This advance, which will begin about the same time as your first troops reach the shore, will be so timed as to reach the summit of the main ridge near Chunuk Bair about 2.30 a.m. (soon after moon-rise).

Latest photographs show that the Turkish trenches on this ridge do not extend further north than Chunuk Bair, and it is unlikely that the higher portions of the ridge are held in great strength.

As soon as a lodgement has been effected on this ridge a portion of the attacking force will be left to consolidate the position gained and the remainder will advance south-west against the enemy's trenches near Baby 700, which will be attacked simultaneously by a special detachment from within the Anzac position.

An advance by your force from the east will, as already indicated in paragraph 6, be of great assistance in the event of this attack being checked.

8. The landing of sufficient transport to secure the mobility of your force will be a matter of considerable difficulty. No animals or vehicles of any kind will be able to land in the first instance, and machine-guns, tools and necessary medical and signalling equipment must be carried by hand. All men will land with two iron rations (one day's meat ration only is advised); infantry will carry 200 rounds S.A.A. and machine-gun sections 3,500 rounds in belt boxes. Packs and greatcoats will not be taken ashore. Before dawn it is hoped to land enough horses to secure the mobility of the mountain artillery brigade and one battery R.F.A., and it is hoped that within the first 24 hours the disembarkation of all the personnel, horses and vehicles enumerated in the attached table will be complete.

One brigade R.F.A. 11th Division, 1/4th Lowland 5th Howitzer

Brigade (two batteries) and the 10th Heavy Battery, will be landed at Anzac before the operations commence, and their personnel and horses will disembark on the morning following your disembarkation, and will then be directed along the beach to join your command.

Water is plentiful throughout the Anafarta Valley, but pending the disembarkation of water carts a number of mules with special 8-gallon water bags will be attached to the units of your command.

(Signed) W. P. BRAITHWAITE,
Major-General, C.G.S.,
Mediterranean Expeditionary Force.

P.S. — This letter is never to be out of an officer's possession, and if, as is probable, you require to send it to your Brig.-Gen. G.S., it must be sent to Mudros in charge of an officer.

TABLE.

	Animals.	Vehicles.
11TH DIVISION.		
Divl. H.Q. and Signal Co.	28	1 cart, 2 cable wagons.
3 Infantry Brigades	108	Nil.
Pioneer Battalion	8	Nil.
2 F.A. Brigades	506	32 guns, 88 wagons, 2 telegraph wagons, 10 carts.
1 Heavy Battery R.G.A.	45	4 guns, 4 wagons, 2 G.S. wagons, 1 cart.
3 Field Coys. R.E.	48	12 tool carts.
2 Platoons Divl. Cyclist Co.	Nil	62 bicycles.
3 Field Ambulances	144	30 ambulances, 12 carts.
10TH DIVISION.		
Divl. H.Q. and Signal Co.		
1½ Infantry Brigades		
Pioneer Battalion		
3 Field Cos. R.E.		Transport on approximately the same scale as that for 11th Division.
3 Field Ambulances		
29th Indian Brigade and Indian Field Ambulance.		
2 Mountain Batteries (80 mules).		
2 Battalions (of 500 men each) for Beach parties.		
Mule Corps with 300 mules and 150 carts.		
3 Casualty Clearing Stations.		

Appendix III – General Instructions

Organization Orders for Troops Landing at Anzac.

1. Troops landing at Anzac are to land equipped as follows:

F.S. equipment, including respirator;
Pack and waterproof sheet;
No blanket.
Officers' kit reduced to what they can carry.
No transport of any kind will be available to move baggage or equipment.
Ammunition S.A.A. 200 rounds per rifle or person; 3,500 rounds per machine-gun in belt boxes.
No regimental reserve S.A.A.
Gun, limbers and wagons filled with fused shell.
Water bottles — filled.
Rations — iron rations one day meat and biscuit, two days' groceries.
Sufficient to provide breakfasts.
(Fuel will be issued on shore.)
Tools — infantry. Regimental reserve distributed to individuals and carried on person; Brigade reserve entrenching tools distributed to units, by them to individuals and carried on person.
Engineers — tools for road making and entrenching work — carried on person.
Other arms — usual allotment.
Signal company cable and equipment usually carried in carts to be transferred to barrows.
Ambulances — all available stretchers and equipment of dressing stations only. Tent sub-divisions in readiness to rejoin early.
A.S.C. — Small allowance of distributing equipment, to be brought by advance parties of S. and T. personnel.

Establishments.

2. No horses, attendants or drivers are to land. Brigade Sections of Signal Companies are to land with the brigades they serve.

Appendix III – General Instructions

Tent sub-divisions of field ambulances are not to land.

Equipment carried in technical vehicles is to be transferred to vehicles which can be hand-propelled or else carried on person.

3. Troops should disembark into lighters, etc., in complete units, companies, platoons, and so on, unless much space is sacrificed in so doing.

4. All troops should land wearing two white 6-inch armlets and a white patch on back of right shoulder.

5. No lights or noise are to be permitted while disembarking; troops will move into the lighters or horseboats as quickly as possible.

6. On disembarking troops will be met by staff officers and guides, and will be marched off direct to the ground allotted to them — in no case more than 1,200 yards from the beach. All kit brought must be removed by the troops, and must be taken out of the lighters at the same time as the troops leave.

Special parties to assist with the machine-gun and other loads are to be detailed in the load of each lighter.

7. No lights or talking are permitted on the beach or till the troops reach their allotted area. Fires are not to be lit in any area till 4.15 a.m., and must be extinguished by 8 p.m. Green wood is not to be used; the smoke it causes will draw shell fire.

8. No troops are to leave the area allotted to them between 4 a.m. and 8 p.m. except on special duty with the authority of the Brigade Commander. Piquets will be placed under area arrangements at intervals round the area to prevent men straying independently.

9. Troops may be exposed to desultory shelling during the day or night. This is never aimed, and the best protection against it is to move into the bottom of the gully in which the troops are bivouacked.

10. Troops are not to use any portion of the iron ration with which they land. Issues will be made under brigade arrangements of rations and extras to last the period of their stay.

11. Water is issued on ration at one gallon fresh water per day. This includes water for all purposes. For bathing, the sea is available, but may only be visited after 9 p.m. daily.

12. Latrines for immediate use are dug and marked in each area; additional latrines are to be prepared by units and the strictest orders issued to prevent fouling the ground. Latrines are to be made very deep, as space is much restricted.

13. Casualties of any kind after treatment in the field ambulance affiliated to the brigade will be taken to the casualty clearing station in Anzac Cove for removal to Hospital Ship.
   Urgent cases at any time; others as far as possible between 7.30 and 8.30 p.m. and between 6 and 9 a.m.

14. The following is to be practised by all troops after landing:

   Falling in once during the night in any close formation, and to remain so closed up for a period of at least half an hour, during which passing of commands (messages from front to rear and back again and to the flanks) is to be practised.
   The troops must be accustomed to the starlight, which may be expected during night operations.

15. If aeroplanes pass overhead troops are not to look up, as this will give away the position of bodies of troops and probably draw shell fire.

16. Troops landing should be provided with Maps 1/20,000 of the area in which operations are to take place. These maps to be in bulk, and not issued till after landing.
   Maps 1/10,000 of the Anzac area showing roads and bivouacs will be issued to unit commanders on arrival.

17. Telephone lines will be found laid from Anzac Headquarters to points suitable for Brigade or higher Headquarters. On arrival brigades will join up these points to Anzac.

An officer and two orderlies per brigade will also be detailed to remain at Anzac Headquarters.

Staffs of formations higher than brigades will be located within easy reach of Anzac Headquarters.

G.S.R. Z. 18/2.
Instructions for G.O.C. 9th Army Corps.

Reference Sheet Anafarta Sagir Gallipoli Map 1/20,000.

1. The intentions of the General Commanding for the impending operations, and a rough outline of the task which he has allotted to the troops under your command, were communicated to you in my G.S.R. Z. 18, dated 22nd instant.

2. In addition to the information contained in paragraph 3 of the above quoted letter, small numbers of Turkish mounted troops and Gendarmerie have been reported in the country north of Anzac, and three guns with limbers, each drawn by six oxen, have been seen moving into Anafarta Sagir. An aeroplane photograph has also disclosed the presence of a few trenches on Lala Baba. A sketch of these trenches, which have apparently been constructed for some months, is attached. It is believed that the channel connecting the Salt Lake with Suvla Bay is now dry.

3. Your landing will begin on the night 6th/7th August. Your primary objective will be to secure Suvla Bay as a base for all the forces operating in the northern zone. Owing to the difficult nature of the terrain, it is possible that the attainment of this objective will, in the first instance, require the use of the whole of the troops at your disposal. Should, however, you find it possible to achieve this object with only a portion of your force, your next step will be to give such direct assistance as is in your power to the G.O.C. Anzac in his attack on Hill 305, by an advance on Biyuk Anafarta,

with the object of moving up the eastern spurs of that hill.

4. Subject only to his final approval, the General Commanding gives you an entirely free hand in the selection of your plan of operations.

He, however, directs your special attention to the fact that the hills Yilghin and Ismail Oglu Tepe are known to contain guns which can bring fire to bear on the flank and rear of an attack on Hill 305, and that on this account they assume an even greater importance in the first instance than if they were considered merely part of a position covering Suvla Bay. If, therefore, it is possible, without prejudice to the attainment of your primary objective, to gain possession of these hills at an early period of your attack, it will greatly facilitate the capture and retention of Hill 305. It would also appear almost certain that until these hills are in your possession it will be impossible to land either troops or stores in the neighbourhood of Suvla Bay by day.

5. The troops at your disposal will be:

> 11th Division (less one Brigade R.F.A., at Helles).
> 10th Division (less 29th Infantry Brigade).
> Three squadrons R.N. Armoured Car Division, R.N.A.S. (one squadron motor cycles, six machine guns; one squadron Ford cars, six machine guns; one squadron armoured cars, six machine guns).
> Two Highland Mountain Artillery batteries.

An endeavour will be made to release for your force one or more 5-in. howitzer batteries, now at Anzac, during the day following your initial disembarkation.

6. In order that you may be able to arrange for the disembarkation of your force to agree, so far as Naval exigencies will admit, with the plan of operations on which you decide, the allocation of troops to the ships and boats to be provided by the Navy is left to your decision.

With this object, tables have been drawn up, and are enclosed

Appendix III – General Instructions 527

with these instructions, showing the craft which can be placed at your disposal by the Navy, their capacity, and the points at which the troops can be disembarked. The tables also show what numbers of troops, animals, vehicles, and stores can be landed simultaneously.

The beaches available for your landing on the first night are (1) a frontage of 600 yards in Suvla Bay (sq. 117 Q.V.); (2) a frontage of 1,800 yards S. of Kuchuk Kemikli (sq. 9, 103 z, 104 V; 91 A.B.), called "New Beach" in the tables. It will not be possible in the first instance to land more than one brigade of your force in Suvla Bay, though other vessels can simultaneously be discharging their passengers on New Beach.

7. As regards the time at which the disembarkation may be expected to commence, no craft will be allowed to leave Kephalos Harbour till after dark, and the passage across will take from one and a half to two hours. It is unsafe, therefore, to count on any troops being ashore before 10.30 p.m., and in no case must your approach be disclosed to the enemy till 10 p.m., the hour at which the outposts on the left flank of the Anzac position are to be rushed.

8. No allowance has been made in the tables for the disembarkation of your headquarters, as it is not known at what period of the operations you will wish them to land.

9. Special attention is directed to paragraph 8 of my letter G.S.R. Z. 18, dated 22nd July.

10. The infantry of the 53rd Division will be available as Army Reserve, and will be at the disposal of the General Commanding.

11. Special instructions regarding signal communications will be issued later. In general terms the arrangements will be as follows:
    There is a submarine cable between Imbros and Anzac, and a cable will be laid as soon as practicable from Imbros to Suvla Bay. A submarine cable and a land cable will also be laid between Anzac and Suvla Bay as soon as circumstances permit, probably

before dawn. Pending the completion of this work intercommunication between Anzac and Suvla Bay will be carried out by lamp, and, subject to Naval approval, between Suvla Bay and Imbros by wireless telegraphy.

Two military pack W.T. stations and one R.N. Base W.T. station will be provided at Suvla Bay, four naval ratings will be attached to each station as visual signalling personnel. One of these military pack W.T. stations will be disembarked with the second brigade to land, and will act as a base station pending the arrival of the R.N. Base wireless station. The second military pack W.T. station will be disembarked with the third brigade to land; it will be placed on a flank and used mainly for fire control under the B.G.R.A.*

A wagon wireless station at G.H.Q., Imbros, will be in communication with both these pack W.T. stations.

One officer and 23 other ranks, with two pack animals from the Brigade Signal Section, will be landed with each Infantry Brigade.

These parties will lay their cable by hand and establish telephone and vibrator communication from the beach forward. No vehicles will be landed in the first instance, all necessary stores being man-handled.

Three officers, 74 other ranks, 28 animals and five vehicles will be landed with Divisional Headquarters.

The advance parties will release the brigade sections from the beach and be prepared to lay cable lines by hand.

Two cable wagons will be included in the five vehicles, and should be the first of those vehicles to be disembarked.

As soon as possible after Corps Headquarters go ashore, the personnel of the Divisional Signal Companies will be released from work at the beach.

Arrangements will be made subsequently to disembark an air line detachment and a cable section to provide and pole local lines.

The remainder of the Corps Headquarters Signal Company will be kept in readiness to be forwarded as soon as Corps Headquarters

---

* All W.T. arrangements are subject to alteration, as they have not yet been confirmed by the Vice-Admiral.

Appendix III – General Instructions 529

reports that circumstances admit of its disembarkation.

12. Two Military Landing Officers and their assistant military landing officers will be placed at your disposal from units other than those under your command.

13. In addition to the units mentioned in Tables A-E forwarded to you with my letter G.S.R. Z. 18, dated 23rd July, the following are being dispatched from Alexandria in this order:

> Three Squadrons Armoured Car Division R.N.A.S. (These will be available to land on the morning after your disembarkation begins, if you so desire.)
> (1) H.Q.R.A. 10th Division.
> Two F.A. Brigades 10th Division (modified scale of horses).
> R.A. personnel and ammunition of 10th Divisional Ammunition Park.
> (2) One F.A. Brigade 11th Division (modified scale of horses). One F.A. Brigade 10th Division (modified scale of horses).
> (3) Two F.A. Brigades 13th Division.
> (4) Horses for 11th Division.

and the following will be assembled at Imbros to land when required:

> 11th Divisional Cyclist Company (less two Platoons).
> 10th Divisional Cyclist Company.
> 13th Divisional Cyclist Company.

14. You are requested to submit your proposed plan of operations to G.H.Q. for approval at the earliest possible date.

(Signed) W. P. BRAITHWAITE,
Major-General, C.G.S.,
Mediterranean Expeditionary Force.

29th July, 1915.

Appendix III – General Instructions

Time of Arrival off Coast.	Craft.	Capacity.	Landing Place.	Method of Disembarkation.	Remarks.
In time to disembark all troops, vehicles, horses, stores, etc., by night	10 motor lighters (10 steamboats accompanying)	500 infantry each (and 400,000 rds. S.A.A. if necessary)	7 lighters at New Beach, 3 lighters at Suvla Bay	Land direct on beach	Ammunition if necessary may be left on motor lighters until convenient to land it, according to circumstances.
	10 destroyers	530 infantry each	One attending each motor lighter	Motor lighters take off troops and land them on beach	The disembarkation from the destroyers cannot begin until the 10 motor lighters have landed their complement and returned.
	1 sloop, towing 1 motor lighter and 4 horseboats (1 steamboat accompanying)	600 men 88 horses 8 mtn. guns 30 bicycles	New Beach	Motor lighters and horseboats loaded with guns, horses of mountain and 18-pr. batteries. Sloop loaded with men and bicycles	The sloops and trawler, after casting off their tows, will return to Kephalos. Other horseboats will be there, ready filled with the remainder of the horses required in the first instance for the two Mountain Batteries, the 18-pr. Battery, and the Signal Company. They will pick up these
	1 sloop, towing 4 horseboats (1 steamboat accompanying)	500 men 24 horses 4 18-pr. guns or wagons	New Beach	Horseboats loaded with guns, vehicles, and horses of 18-pr. battery. Sloop loaded with men and bicycles	

Appendix III – General Instructions 531

		New Beach	Horseboats loaded with guns, vehicles, and horses of 18-pr. battery. Trawler available to carry men
1 trawler, towing 4 horseboats (1 steamboat accompanying)	250 men 24 horses 4 18-pr. guns or wagons		
H.M.S. *Endymion*	1,000 men	New Beach or Suvla Bay, as may be convenient	Landed either from outers towed by steamboats, or from motor lighters
H.M.S. *Theseus*	1,000 men		horseboats and tow them over to the beach immediately.

The above would admit of the disembarkation before dawn at and in the neighbourhood of Suvla Bay of :—

Divisional Headquarters.
Signal Co. with 40 horses.
1 W.T. Section and 2 W.T. Stations.
H.Q. F.A. Bde. (18-pr.) with 10 horses.
1 F.A. Battery (18-pr.) with 82 horses.
2 Mountain Batteries with 80 horses.
3 Field Companies R.E.
Bearer Subdivisions of 3 Field Ambulances and part of Casualty Clearing Stations.

3 Infantry Brigades and part of remainder of F.A. Bde. (personnel).
1 Pioneer Battalion.
2 Battalions for Beach parties and part of Ammn. Park personnel.
2 Platoons Divl. Cyclist Co. and part of Tent Subdivisions of Field Ambulances.

The 10 motor lighters will land their complements first, and then the troops from the 10 Destroyers, the two sloops and their tows, and the trawler and her tows, can proceed simultaneously on a front of about 600 yards in Suvla Bay and 1,800 on the beach south of Suvla Bay, directly beach secured. The two landing places are about 2 miles apart. The landing of the troops from H.M.S. *Endymion* and *Theseus* may be able to take place simultaneously, or may have to be deferred until the motor lighters have cleared the destroyers.

Time of Arrival off Coast.	Craft.	Capacity.	Landing Place.	Method of Disembarkation.	Remarks.
At or immediately after dawn	1 horse transport	All horses enumerated in Table C appended to letter G.S.R. Z. 18 of 23rd July, except those already provided for. Water bags and pumps	Suvla Bay	Six of the horseboats from which the 18-pr. and mountain batteries will previously have been landed	Transport comes from Mudros.
	1 mule transport	All mules and mule carts provided for in Tables C and E appended to G.S.R. Z. 18 of 23rd July	Suvla Bay	Six of the horseboats from which the 18-pr. and mountain batteries will previously have been landed	Transport comes from Alexandria.
	6 small transports	5,000 Infantry	Suvla Bay (or New Beach if necessary)	Landed from motor lighters as soon as they have finished clearing the destroyers and (if necessary) H.M.S. Endymion and Theseus	Six battalions 10th Division coming from Port Iero.

Called up from Kephalos as soon as circumstances permit	1 supply ship	7 days' supplies for troops and animals in Tables C and E appended to G.S.R. Z. 18 of 23rd July	Suvla Bay	Landed from motor lighters as soon as the Port Iero troops are cleared	
Called up from Kephalos as soon as circumstances permit	4 small transports	2,700 Infantry	*Suvla Bay* (or *New Beach* if necessary)	Landed from motor lighters as soon as the Port Iero troops are cleared	Three battalions 10th Division from Mudros.
	1 horse transport	All horses and vehicles enumerated in Table E, appended to G.S.R. Z. 18 of 23rd July	Suvla Bay	Landed from horseboats brought up on second trip by the trawler and two sloops, as soon as the horseboats have been emptied	

The above will provide for the disembarkation of the remainder of the troops, etc., enumerated in Tables C and E, appended to letter G.S.R. Z. 18 of 23rd July, that is those not already detailed to be landed before dawn, viz.:—

Remainder of F.A. Brigade (18-pr.).
Remainder of Ammunition Park Personnel.
15th Heavy Battery R.G.A.
Brigade Ammunition Column.
Remainder of Tent Subdivisions of Field Ambulances.

Remainder of Casualty Clearing Stations.
Mule Corps.
Also 4,000,000 rds. S.A.A. Reserve Gun Ammunition (by special trawlers from Mudros) 7 days' supplies for the above troops and animals.

Appendix III – General Instructions

G.S.R. Z. 18/2. July 29th.

GENERAL OFFICER COMMANDING,
   8th Corps.

The General Commanding has decided that his next main attack shall be made in the vicinity of Anzac with the object of placing ourselves astride the Peninsula to the north of Kilid Bahr.

2. The 8th Corps with attached troops is to assist this main operation by offensive action in the south, the scope and form of this action being determined solely with reference to its effects on the main operation.

As the decisive point will be in the neighbourhood of Anzac, all reinforcements will be utilized in that theatre, and it is improbable that any will be available for the southern zone before the middle of August, except such drafts for the 8th Corps and the Corps Exp. Orient as may reach the Peninsula in the next ten days.

3. In order to free sufficient troops to enable the 8th Corps to take the offensive, the French will take over part of the line as defined in Force Order No. 22.

4. In addition to the troops of the 8th Corps and R.N.D. at present at your disposal, the following reinforcements may be expected:

29th Division.	280 due 29th July.
29th Division.	900 due 4th August.
42nd Division	100 due 29th July.
Total	1,280

which, allowing for normal wastage, should give an effective total of 24,780 on 5th August. These numbers, with the shorter line you will be called upon to hold, should leave you with sufficient troops to undertake a limited offensive operation on or about that day.

Appendix III – General Instructions

5. Assuming that you are not attacked in the meanwhile, the total amount of ammunition which should be available at Helles early in August for offensive action, and to maintain a reserve is:

18 pr. 36,000
4.5 inch 2,000
5 inch 4,000   } Plus any amounts saved from normal daily expenditure.
6 inch 545
60 pr. 3,000

but it must be borne in mind that no replacements can be looked for before August 16th.

6. The scope of your offensive action must be based upon these figures, and it is thought that the most suitable objective will be the capture of the Turkish trenches up to the line F. 13, G. 13, H. 13, and H. 12. Plans for this operation should, therefore, be undertaken at once.

7. Pre-supposing that this attack is successful, and that the numbers at your disposal admit of a further advance, the capture of the trenches on the line H. 14 to H. 15, followed perhaps by the capture of Krithia could then be undertaken, and plans for this action should be prepared beforehand. But as the launching of this further attack must be entirely dependent on unknown factors, a definite decision on this point cannot be arrived at beforehand. It is, moreover, essential that the plan of your first attack should not definitely commit your troops to a further advance unless the trend of events should render such a course desirable.

8. As regards the date for launching your first attack, it is thought that the most favourable time would be shortly before the main operations at Anzac begin, and you should therefore arrange for your first attack to take place on the 4th August.

9. Beyond holding the enemy in front of them to their positions and assisting you with artillery fire, the French will not be asked to take

part in your first attack, but, in the event of your reaching Krithia, they will be directed to conform to your movements and to establish themselves on the spurs leading up to Achi Baba.

I will ascertain the amount of artillery support and lean you can expect from the C.E.O., and if the information arrives in time will attach it as an appendix to this letter.

10. The possibility of the southern force being able to capture Achi Baba has not been dealt with in this memorandum, as the attempt should only be made in the event of large reinforcements being available for the southern zone, and these must depend on the course of events in the main theatre.

(*Signed*) W. P. BRAITHWAITE,
Major-General, C.G.S.,
Mediterranean Expeditionary Force.

It will be apparent to you how necessary it is not to allow any suspicion of the reason for the date mentioned in paragraph 8 being told to any person other than your Brigadier-General G.S.

(*Intd.*) W. P. B.

APPENDIX.
French Artillery Support for 8th Corps.

1. One Brigade of 75's will be placed at the disposal of the 8th Corps for the attack on 4th-5th August.
   Of these

   (*a*) One battery will be moved to support closely the attack on Krithia.
   (*b*) One battery will fire up the Nullah E. of Krithia.

2. In addition, six French howitzers will be so disposed as to open fire upon Turkish artillery north of the ridge 150 — Achi Baba peak.

Appendix III – General Instructions 537

INSTRUCTIONS FOR G.O.C. A. AND N.Z. ARMY CORPS.
Reference Map Anafarta Sagir Gallipoli Map 1/20,000.

1. The General Commanding has decided to mass the whole of his reinforcements in and immediately north of the area occupied by the corps under your command, with a view to securing Suvla Bay as a base of operations, driving the enemy off the Sari Bair, and eventually securing a position astride the Gallipoli Peninsula from the neighbourhood of Gaba Tepe to the straits north of Maidos.

2. The general outline for your proposals for the action of the A. and N.Z. Army Corps contained in your G a 89 of 1st July are approved.

3. (*a*) The General Commanding wishes your operations to begin on August 6th with a strong and sustained attack on Hill 125 (Plateau 400), every effort being made to deceive the enemy as to the locality against which our main effort is to be made, and to induce him to believe that it will be directed against his lines opposite the southern portion of your position. In pursuance of this object the Vice-Admiral has arranged that H.M. ships shall in the meantime display increased activity off the coast between Gaba Tepe and Kum Tepe. It has been arranged that soundings shall be taken by night off the coast south of Gaba Tepe; and, on the evening of August 6th, a naval demonstration will be made off this part of the coast, H.M. ships being accompanied by a number of trawlers as if a landing were to be undertaken.

(*b*) The General Commanding further concurs in the subsequent sequence of the operations outlined by you, namely:

- (i) The clearing of the enemy's outposts from the ridges facing Nos. 2 and 3 posts, to be undertaken after nightfall.
- (ii) An attack in as great strength as possible up the Sazli Beit Dere, the Chailak Dere and the Aghyl Dere, against the Chunuk Bair ridge, by night.
- (iii) When the Chunuk Bair ridge is gained, a converging attack from that ridge, and from the north-eastern section

of your present position, against Hill 180 (Baby 700).

4. (*a*) For the above operations the following troops will be at your disposal:

> A. and N.Z. Army Corps.
> 13th Division, less all artillery except 69th F.A. (Howitzer) Brigade.
> 29th Brigade (10th Division).
> 29th Indian Brigade.

(*b*) At the date of commencement of the operations the following troops belonging to or attached to the 9th Army Corps will be at Anzac, but will not, except so far as is stated hereunder, be at your disposal:

> One F.A. Brigade, 11th Division: To rejoin 9th Army Corps as soon as horses are landed.
> 10th Heavy Battery, R.G.A.: Ditto.
> 14th Lowland (Howitzer) Brigade (two Batteries): Arrangements must be made so that these batteries may be free to rejoin the 9th Army Corps before nightfall on August 7th.

5. The operations carried out by the Corps under your command will form part of a general combined offensive undertaken by the whole of the forces of the Gallipoli Peninsula and by the 9th Army Corps, which will be disembarked in the neighbourhood of Suvla Bay, beginning on the night of August 6th-7th.

(*a*) The 8th Army Corps, in conjunction with the Corps Expéditionnaire, will attack the Turkish lines south of Krithia on August 4th and 5th. The attack will be made on a large scale, and will be vigorously pressed, and it is hoped that by its means the enemy will be induced to move part of his central reserves southward into the Cape Helles zone during the 5th and 6th, so that they may not be available in the northern zone on the 6th and 7th.

(*b*) The 9th Army Corps will begin landing in and close to Suvla Bay during the night of August 6th-7th. Three infantry brigades, with one field and two mountain batteries, engineers and medical services, should be ashore before dawn, and will be closely followed by two more infantry brigades and additional artillery and engineers.

The G.O.C. 9th Army Corps has been informed:

(i) That his mission is to secure Suvla Bay as a base of operation for all the forces in the northern zone.
(ii) That the seizure of Yilghin Burnu and Ismail Oglu Tepe ("W" and Chocolate Hills), on account of the presence there of artillery which may interfere with your operations, must be considered as of very special importance.
(iii) That so far as is possible after the fulfilment of his primary mission, he is to render you such direct assistance as may be practicable by moving any available troops via Biyuk Anafarta up the eastern slopes of the Sari Bair.

(c) At the commencement of these operations the infantry of the 53rd Division will be available as Army Reserve and will be at the disposal of the General Commanding.

6. The Vice-Admiral has agreed provisionally to the following allotment of ships affording naval support to the operations:

In Suvla Bay: One 6-in. monitor.
South of Kuchuk: H.M.S. *Endymion*.
Kemliki (Nibrunesi Point): H.M.S. *Edgar*, H.M.S. *Talbot*, one 6-in. monitor, one 9.2-in. monitor.

These ships would be in position at daylight on August 7th, and would mainly be required to support the operations of the 9th Army Corps.

West of Gaba Tepe: H.M.S. *Baccanto*, H.M.S. *Humber*, H.M.S.*Havelock*, one 6-in. monitor.

These ships would be in position at 3 p.m. on August 6th, except H.M.S.*Havelock*, which would be in position at daylight on August

7th. They would be detailed for support of the right flank of the A. and N.Z. Army Corps.

> Off Kum Tepe: One 6-in. monitor.

A separate communication is being sent to you with regard to the final settlement of details as to the support of the operations by naval guns, allocation of targets, etc.

7. Special instructions regarding signal communication will be issued later. In general terms the arrangements will be as follows:

> A submarine cable and a land cable will be laid between Anzac and Suvla Bay as soon as circumstances permit.
> A submarine cable will also be laid as soon as practicable between Imbros and Suvla Bay. Pending the completion of connection between Anzac and Suvla Bay, inter-communication will be carried out by lamp.
> Two military pack W/T stations and a R.N. Base W/T station will be established in the vicinity of Suvla Bay. The W/T station at Anzac will be able to intercept messages from seaplanes, but must not attempt to reply.
> W/T via the ships will be an alternative means of communication between G.H.Q. and the troops ashore in case of interruption of cable communication.
> A system of flares will be arranged for employment on the left flank of your position at dawn on August 7th to indicate to the ships the positions reached by the troops.

8. G.H.Q. will in the first instance be at Imbros.

> (*Signed*) W. P. BRAITHWAITE,
> *Major-General, C.G.S.,*
> *Mediterranean Expeditionary Force.*

G.H.Q., *30th July, 1915.*

Appendix III – General Instructions 541

FORCE ORDER No. 25.
GENERAL HEADQUARTERS,
2nd August, 1915.

1. The total forces of the enemy in the Gallipoli Peninsula are estimated at 100,000.

Of these, 27,000 are in the neighbourhood of Anzac (5th, 19th, 16th Divisions, and 18th and 64th Regiments); 36,000 are in the Southern zone (1st, 4th, 6th Division less one regiment, 7th Division, 11th Division less one regiment, and one regiment each of the 12th, 25th and 3rd Divisions); and 37,000 are in Reserve (9th Division less one regiment, 12th less one regiment, 13th, 14th, and 25th less one regiment, and 10th Divisions). Of this reserve force two Divisions are in the Bulair district and one Division in the Eyerli Tepe zone. There are 12,000 on the Asiatic shore of the Dardanelles (2nd Division and 8th Division less one regiment). There are believed to be five Divisions (45,000 men) in the Keshan area belonging to the 5th and 6th Corps.

All reports tend to show that though the enemy may be expected to fight well in trenches, their *moral* has suffered considerably as a result of their recent heavy casualties, and that their stock of ammunition is low.

2. The General Commanding intends to carry out a combined and simultaneous attack on the enemy in the northern and southern zone commencing on 6th August, in accordance with the special instructions already issued to the Corps Commanders concerned.

During the first phase of these operations the 13th Division (less three 18-pdr. Bdes. R.F.A.), the 29th Infantry Brigade will be attached to the A. and N.Z. Army Corps. Three squadrons R.N. Armoured Car Division and two batteries Highland Mounted Artillery will be attached to 9th Corps. 86th Brigade R.F.A. and 91st Heavy Battery R.G.A. will be attached to 8th Corps.

3. Special instructions regarding embarkation and disembarkation are issued to G.O.C. 9th Corps, G.O.C., A. and N.Z. Corps, and I.G.C., as appended to this order.

542 *Appendix III – General Instructions*

4. The 53rd Division will remain at the disposal of the General Commanding as general reserve.

5. G.H.Q. will remain in the first instance in its present situation.

(*Signed*) W. P. BRAITHWAITE,
Major-General, C.G.S.,
Mediterranean Expeditionary Force.

Issued to: G.O.C. Corps Expéditionnaire; G.O.C. A. and N.Z. Army Corps; G.O.C. 8th Army Corps; G.O.C. 9th Army Corps; G.O.C. 53rd Division; I.G.C.; Vice-Admiral.

APPENDIX TO FORCE ORDER NO. 25.

Embarkations.

1. The embarkation of units of the 9th Corps concentrated at Imbros will be carried out under the orders of G.O.C. 9th Corps, commencing for personnel on 6th August, for vehicles and stores at such earlier date as may be convenient. The necessary ships and boats (lists of which have already been handed to the G.O.C. Corps) will be assembled in the harbour beforehand; and the embarkation programme will be worked out in consultation with Commander Ashby, R.N., who has been detailed by the Vice-Admiral for this purpose, and who will arrange for the various vessels to be in their allotted positions at the hours arranged.

G.O.C. 9th Corps will also be responsible for the allocation to ships or lighters, and for the embarkation of the following units:

> At Imbros: One W.T. Section (Nos. W. 10 and W. 11 Pack Wireless Stations); Two Anson Battalions R.N.D. (for duties on the beach); No. 16 Casualty Clearing Station.
> In transit from Mudros to Imbros: One Casualty Clearing Station.

Units and formations concentrated at Mudros and Mitylene

Appendix III – General Instructions

will be embarked for their various destinations under the orders of I.G.C. in accordance with the programme already issued to that officer.

Military Transport Officers.

2. G.O.C. 9th Corps and I.G.C. respectively will ensure that an officer is appointed Military Transport Officer on every ship for the embarkation of which they are severally responsible (*vide* paragraph 1).

Landing Places.

3. The landings of the 9th Corps will be referred to as "A," "B," and "C" Beaches.

"A" Beach — Square 117.q. and v.
"C" Beach — Square 103.u.z.
"B" Beach — Square 91.b, i, o.
"C" and "B" Beaches are practically contiguous.

Beach Control Personnel.

4. The following naval and military beach control personnel have been appointed for the landing places of the 9th Corps:

Principal Beach Master: Captain H. F. G. Talbot, R.N.
Beach Masters: Commander I. W. Gibson, M.V.O. ("A" Beach), Captain C. P. Metcalfe, R.N. ("B" Beach), Commander C. Tindal-Carril-Worsley ("C" Beach).
Assistant Beach Masters and Beach Lieutenants: Four Lieutenant Commanders, ten Lieutenants, R.N.
Principal Mil. L.O.: Colonel W. G. B. Western, C.B.
Mil. L.O.'s: Major F. W. Pencock, Derbyshire Yeomanry, Major Sir R. Baker, Dorset Yeomanry, Captain Tylsen Wright, A.S.C.
Assistant Mil. L.O.'s: Captain Wade Palmer, Derbyshire

Yeomanry, Captain B. A. Smith, South Notts Hussars, Lieutenant H. V. Browne, Dorset Yeomanry, Lieutenant Krabbe, Berks Yeomanry.

The allocation of the above military officers to the various landing places will be detailed by the P.M.L.O. in consultation with the P.B.M.

Special instructions with regard to beach fatigue parties have already been issued to the G.O.C. 9th Corps.

G.O.C., A. and N.Z. Army Corps will detail such military landing officers, assistant military landing officers, and beach parties for A.N.Z.A.C. as he may consider necessary. The names of officers so appointed will be reported as early as possible to V.A. and to G.H.Q.

The following special service officers are attached to H.Q., A. and N.Z. Army Corps, for such duties in connection with the landing as the G.O.C. may direct:

Major P. R. Bruce, S. Notts Hussars.
Captain C. R. Higgens, County of London Yeomanry.
Captain Sir E. Pauncefort Duncombe, Royal Bucks Hussars.

General Instructions for Landing.

5. All troops will land with two iron rations (one day's meat only in case of troops disembarking at Anzac). Infantry will carry 200 rounds of S.A.A., machine-gun sections 3,500 rounds. Packs will not be worn. A proportion of heavy entrenching tools, signalling and medical gear will be carried by hand. Camp kettles will be handed to the Ordnance Officer of the camp at which units concentrate before embarkation. They will be forwarded and reissued at the first opportunity.

6. Horses will be landed harnessed, and with nosebags filled to their full capacity.

Poles of G.S. wagons will be removed before slinging and made fast to the body of the wagon. Poles of carts, limbers, and limbered wagons will not be removed; these vehicles should be so

Appendix III – General Instructions

placed in the boats that they can be landed pole leading.

Ammunition.

7. The G.O.C. 9th Corps will depute an officer to arrange, in consultation with the P.M.L.O., for the storing of reserve ammunition in convenient localities near the beach. Guards for these stores may be found from the beach fatigue parties.

Water.

8. The strictest economy must be exercised with regard to drinking water. Under arrangements already made by G.H.Q., receptacles filled with water will be landed as early as possible from the ships carrying the mule corps, and will be conveyed to the troops as transport becomes available. Waterproof tanks (2,300 gallon capacity) and lift and force pumps will be available on the *Prah* — R.E. Storeship — in Kephalos Harbour, and will be forwarded by D.Q.M.G., G.H.Q., on request of G.O.C. Corps.

Transport.

9. Transport to supplement that in possession of units will be provided for the 9th Corps and the A.N.Z. Corps by the Indian Mule Corps. The amount of transport for each formation has been calculated to carry rations, water, and S.A.A., making one or two trips a day, according to the anticipated distance of the various units from the beach.

This transport will be handed over, as it is landed, by an officer appointed by the D.S.T., to transport officers of Brigades and divisional troops for allotment as circumstances may require.

Senior transport officers of Divisions will be ordered to report to the following representatives of the D.S.T. immediately on landing:

At Anzac: Lieutenant-Colonel Streidinger, A.D.T.
At "A" Beach: Major Badcock, D.A.D.T.

Appendix III – General Instructions

Supplies.

10. A supply depôt has been formed at Anzac, and it is in charge of Major Izod, A.S.C. A supply depot will be formed by D.S.T. at "A" Beach as soon as supplies can be landed, and will be in charge of Major Huskisson, A.S.C. Senior supply officers of Divisions will be ordered to place themselves in communication with the officer in charge of the nearest supply depôt and to keep him informed of their daily requirements. Supplies will, so far as possible, be handed over to them in bulk at the depôt. Owing to the difficulty in landing sufficient animals in the first instance it is possible that only half rations may be available on the third and fourth days after the operations begin. All units should be specially ordered to husband their rations.

Medical.

11. Arrangements have been made to establish on the beach at Anzac two casualty clearing stations, which will be embarked by I.G.C., and two at "A" Beach, which will be embarked under orders of G.O.C. 9th Corps (*see* paragraph 1). Medical officers will be appointed by G.H.Q. to control these units, and to take charge of the arrangements for evacuation of the wounded from the beach.

(*Signed*) C. F. ASPINALL,
Lieutenant-Colonel,
For Major-General, C.G.S.,
Mediterranean Expeditionary Force.

Appendix IV – Instructions to Major-General H. de Lisle, C.B., D.S.O.

1. The operations of the northern wing of the Army have only been partially successful.

   (*a*) The Australian and New Zealand Army Corps, with the 13th Division and the 29th Brigade of 10th Division attached, has greatly extended the area occupied, and now holds a position under the Chunuk Bair Ridge, which the G.O.C. considers a favourable one from which to launch the final attack on the ridge. The necessity for reorganization after the recent operations, and for establishing a satisfactory system of forwarding water, ammunition and supplies, will involve a delay of some days before the attack on the main ridge can be made.

   (*b*) The 9th Army Corps, less the 13th Division and 29th Brigade, but with the 53rd and 54th Divisions attached, holds the Yilghin Burnu hills, and a line northwards from the easternmost of these two hills roughly straight across the Kuchuk Anafarta Ova to the highest point of the Kiretch Tepe Sirt. Attacks by the 11th Division against the

Ismail Oglu Tepe and the Anafarta spur from the north-west have been made without any success. In the course of the operations the 9th Corps became very much disorganized, and since August 11th the work of reorganization and consolidation has been proceeding.

2. At present the enemy has shown no great strength north of an east and west line through Anafarta Sagir. He has a force operating on and near the Kiretch Tepe Sirt, the strength of which cannot yet be accurately estimated. From present indications this appears to be a detachment which is known to have guarded the coast from Ejelmer Bay to Suvla Bay; it does not appear to have been reinforced to any extent. Across the Kuchuk Anafarta Ova there appear to be no more than snipers. In the region Anafarta Sagir — Ismail Oglu Tepe and the Biyuk Anafarta Valley the enemy has developed considerable strength — his intention being, no doubt, to protect the right of his main force which opposes the Australian and New Zealand Army Corps, and to prevent our advance on the Anafarta gap.

3. The General Commanding has decided to strike as quickly and in as great strength as possible against the enemy's on the line Ismail Oglu Tepe — Anafarta Sagir with the objects, first, of driving in this flank and preparing a further enveloping advance; and, secondly, by clearing the Anafarta spur to deny to the enemy the gun positions and facilities for observation therefrom, which would otherwise endanger Suvla Bay. He considers it imperative to effect this with the least possible delay. In his view the left flank of this advance will require comparatively little protection, at all events in the first instance, in view of the difficulty which the enemy may be expected to find in throwing any considerable force round our left over the high and difficult country north of Anafarta Sagir. It appears that the double purpose of defeating the enemy and securing Suvla Bay as a port for the northern wing of the Army can best be served by an attack on the enemy's right on the Anafarta spur, made with all the strength at our command, while leaving a comparatively small force as left flank guard to clear the enemy's snipers out of the Kuchuk Anafarta Ova and to occupy and press back his detachment in the Ejelmer Bay region.

Appendix IV – Instructions to Major-General de Lisle 549

4. You will have at your disposal the following troops:

11th Division,
10th Division (less 29th Brigade),
53rd Division,
54th Division,

and there is on its way from Egypt to join you the 2nd Mounted Division (5,000 men dismounted), which should be available by August 18th. The 10th, 11th and 53rd Divisions are considerably depleted, and the *moral* of the latter at present leaves much to be desired. There are at present ashore, belonging to the above two F.A. Brigades (three batteries of which are awaiting horses to bring them up from Anzac) and two Heavy Batteries. In addition, two Highland Mountain Batteries, attached to the 9th Corps, are ashore, and the 1/4th Lowland Brigade (two batteries 5-inch howitzers) are at your disposal when they can be brought up from Anzac. It has only been possible to land a bare minimum of horses owing to difficulties in respect of water and the landing of forage.

Three further F.A. Brigades and the 57th Brigade (two batteries) 4.5-inch howitzers are at Mudros ready to be brought up as soon as it is possible to land them. These Brigades will probably have to be landed without any horses in the first instance, and taken into position by the artillery horses already ashore.

5. For the purpose of an early attack in accordance with the plan indicated in paragraph 3, the A. and N.Z. Army Corps will probably not be able to co-operate directly with more than one Infantry Brigade, and it is possible that it may be able to do no more than swing up its left into line with the right of your advance. It is improbable that the 8th Corps and the C.E.O. will be in a position to do more than undertake vigorous demonstrations.

6. With the above in view, you will proceed at once to Suvla Bay and take over command of the 9th Corps. Your immediate and most urgent concern will be to complete the reorganization of the Corps and to prepare as large a force as possible for the offensive against Ismail Oglu Tepe and the Anafarta spur, bearing in mind

that time is of vital importance. You will then consider and report at the earliest moment:

(*a*) What force you consider that you will be able to employ for this purpose.
(*b*) The date on which you will be ready to undertake the offensive.
(c) The method by which you purpose to carry out your task.

(*Signed*) W. P. BRAITHWAITE,
Major-General, C.G.S.,
Mediterranean Expeditionary Force.

Maps

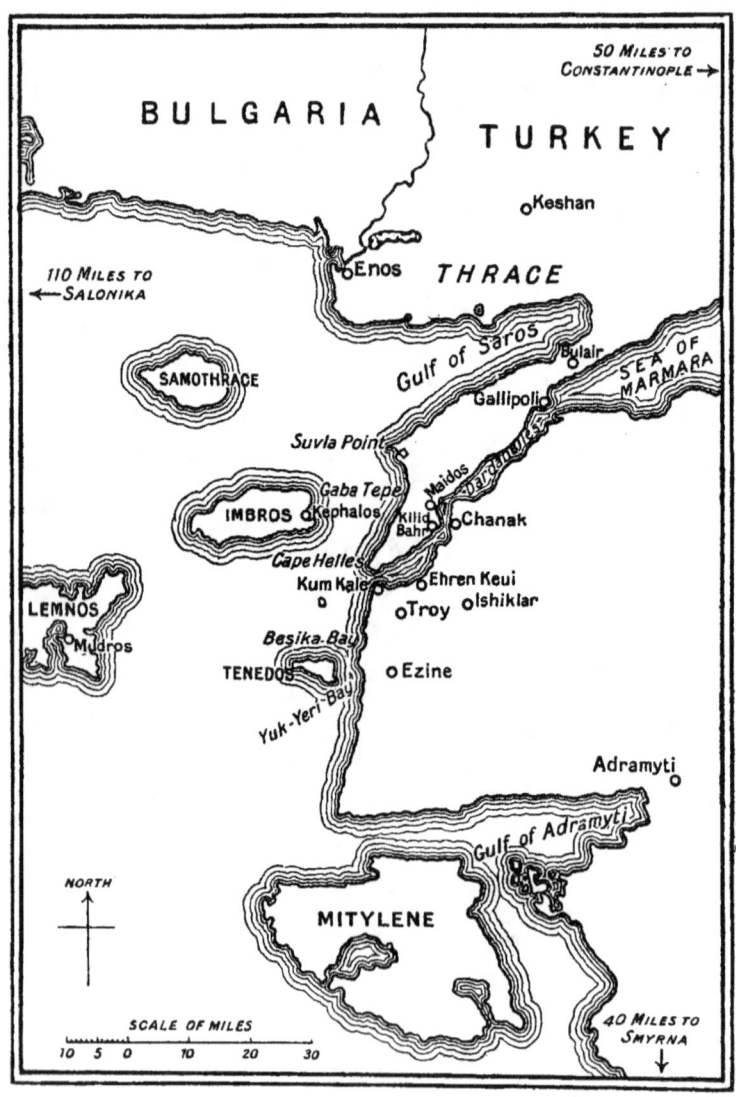

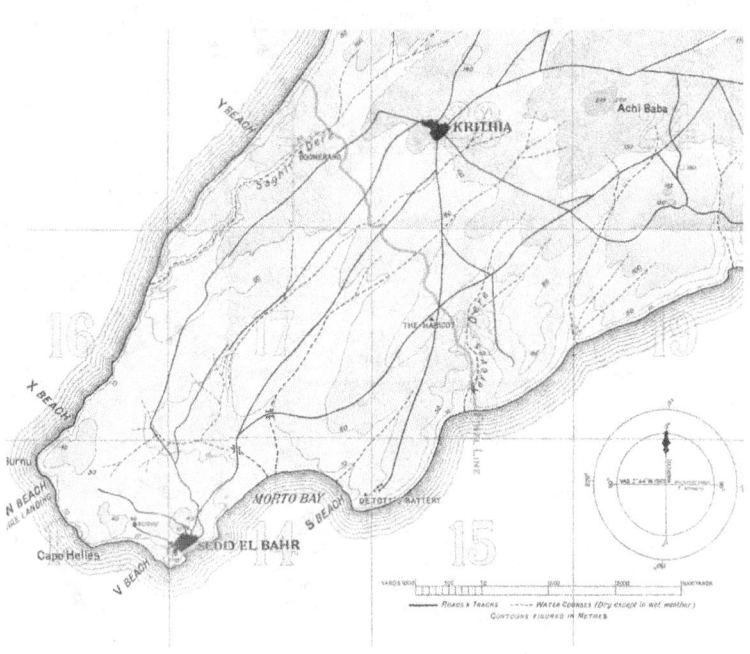

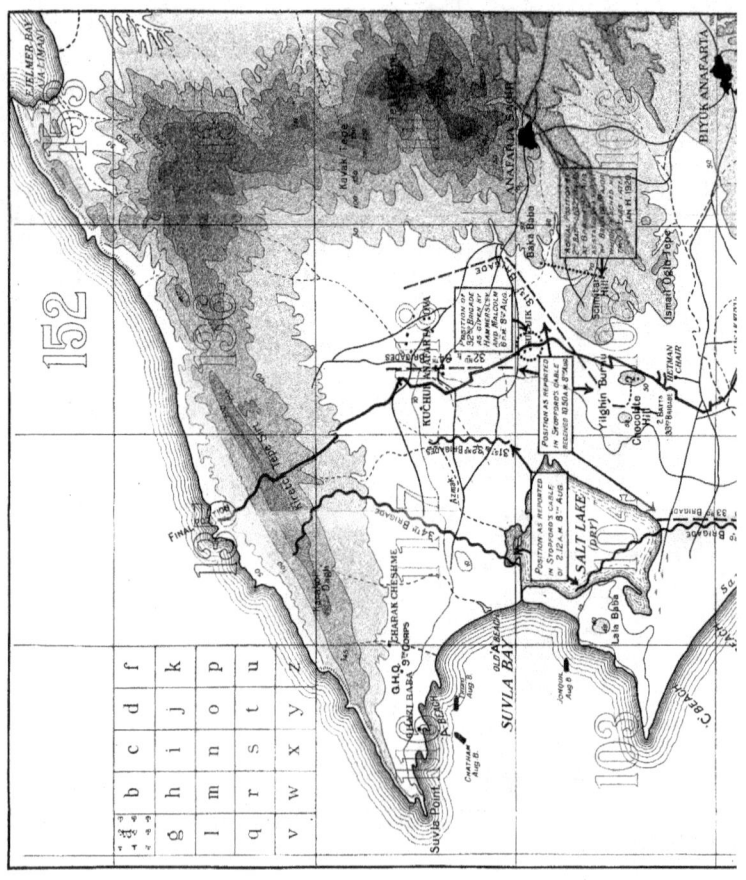

Maps

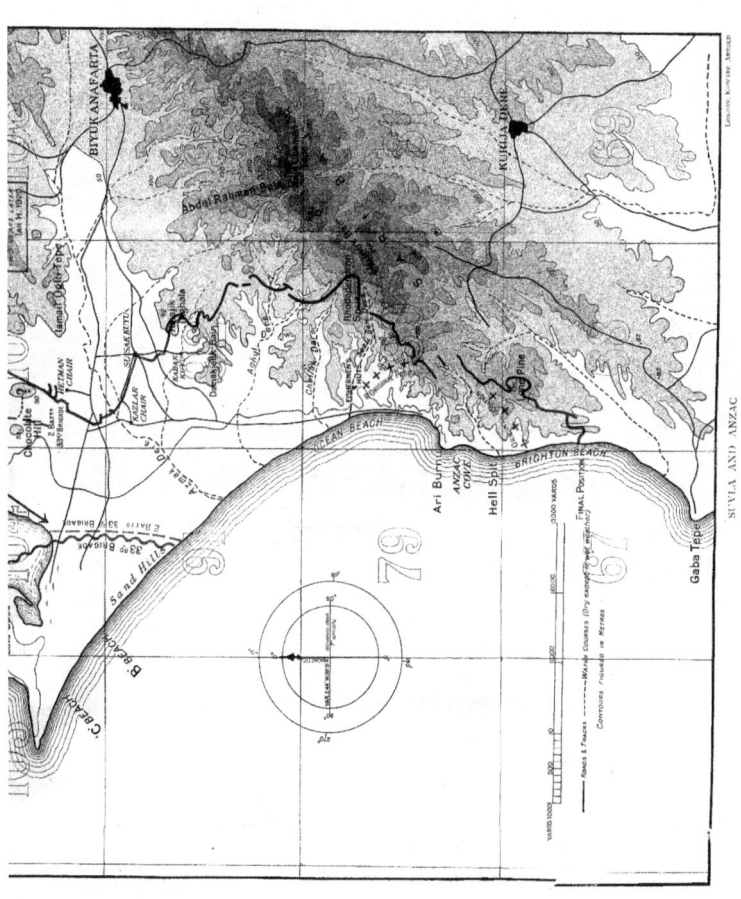

Index

"A" Beach 341, 395, 543, 545, 546
Abdel Rahman Bair 374
Abrikja 356
Achi Baba ... 33, 42, 43, 63, 77, 81, 82, 88, 117, 118, 122, 124, 127, 134, 139, 140, 144, 153-155, 157, 158, 161, 204, 205, 208, 218, 226, 249, 257, 259, 265, 271, 280, 290, 416, 429, 454, 462, 472, 493, 536
Adderley, Lieut.. 292
Adrianople 19, 20, 75, 78, 158, 160, 177, 226, 279, 281, 282
aeroplanes 17, 29, 73, 90, 135, 139, 151, 160, 174, 217, 253, 285, 331, 338, 350, 375, 422, 458, 483, 494, 495, 497, 524
Agnew, Col. Quentin 404

Air Service. 17, 89-91, 215
Aitkin, Capt. 312
Aja Liman 353, 372, 396, 399
Anafarta Ridge. 353, 364
Akbashi Liman 428
Alexandretta 18
Allanson, Col. 442
Altham, Genl. .. 294, 313, 314, 323, 379, 410, 414, 424, 475, 480
Ambulance 238, 311, 410, 414, 453, 524
87th Field 414
Amery, Col. 256
ammunition .. 32, 56, 57, 66, 77, 92, 107, 124, 125, 131, 132, 134, 141, 143, 149, 152, 155-157, 161, 164, 166, 177, 179, 193, 197-199, 202, 214-216, 218, 229, 231-233, 243, 255, 258, 263, 286, 291, 295-298,

Index

300, 312, 315-318, 321, 328, 343, 358, 363, 370, 375, 390, 392, 404, 439, 448, 451, 487-493, 495-498, 500, 502-505, 515, 516, 522, 529, 535, 541, 545, 547
Anafarta... 340-343, 346, 350, 353, 354, 357, 360, 362-364, 367, 372, 374, 375, 387, 396, 403, 517, 518, 520, 525, 537, 539, 547-549
Anafarta Ova... 360, 362-364, 367, 547, 548
Anafarta Sagir.. 340-342, 350, 357, 372, 374, 375, 387, 525, 537, 548
Anatolia.................. 427
Anderson, Maj............. 470
Andrews, Col.............. 302
Anglesey, Lord 430, 433
Anstey, Capt............... 334
Anzac Cove.... 248, 372, 384, 387, 388, 518, 524
Ari Burnu 139, 464
armistice 181, 184, 186-188
Armoured Car Section......... 87
artillery .. 27, 32, 45, 46, 48, 53, 55, 68, 75, 92, 95, 109, 113, 116, 117, 120, 122, 141, 143-145, 154, 157, 159, 179, 190, 191, 199, 214-217, 225, 234, 243, 263, 264, 279, 280, 296, 297, 323, 336, 337, 347, 360, 363, 365, 368, 375, 390, 425, 443, 444, 449, 470, 487-501, 503, 508, 515, 518, 519, 526, 535, 536, 538, 539, 541, 549
Ashmead-Bartlett, Mr....... 87, 191, 250, 251, 295, 409, 427, 435, 450
Aspinall, Lt.-Col..... 119, 130, 131, 285, 291, 301, 308, 309, 335, 338, 381, 384, 462, 546

Asquith, Lieut. Arthur......... 62
Australian ... 30, 64, 66, 87, 92, 95, 112-114, 154, 158, 165, 180, 189, 193, 208, 213, 217, 218, 242, 252, 254, 263, 269, 304, 331, 360, 373, 387, 398, 408, 410, 411, 433, 434, 438, 444, 456, 463, 470, 471, 477-479, 499-502, 504, 515-517, 547, 548
Australian Light Horse ... 213, 269
Australians... 14, 46, 48, 54, 55, 61, 87, 96, 104, 115, 117, 133, 138, 153, 161, 162, 165, 175, 180, 188, 193, 195, 226, 268, 272, 276, 286, 326, 378, 387, 405, 415, 444, 446, 456
26th Bn................ 456
Ayres, Col................. 465
Babtie, Genl................ 274
Baby 700.......... 372, 519, 538
Backhouse, Commodore.. 249, 250
Bailey, Col................. 463
Bailloud, Genl. . 147, 159, 184, 277, 282, 283, 286, 299, 300, 308-310, 393, 394, 403, 418, 441, 445, 449, 450, 452, 456, 476
Baldwin, Genl............... 350
Balkans .. 15, 45, 94, 175, 207, 224, 279, 391, 420, 422, 436, 438, 440, 450, 472
Bard, see Tullibardine........ 439
Barttelot, Sir W. 445
battle .. 7, 14, 23, 33, 34, 36, 37, 39, 40, 51, 62, 81, 85, 100, 102-104, 111, 112, 129, 134, 136, 140, 142, 145, 155-158, 162, 164, 177, 179, 181, 189, 195, 199, 203, 205-207, 216, 219, 224, 229, 234, 237, 243, 244, 250, 255, 258, 261, 263, 272, 273, 280, 281, 291, 292, 294, 300, 301,

558 *Index*

312, 324-326, 330, 333, 336, 338, 345, 364, 377, 378, 381, 383-385, 389, 392, 404, 413, 423, 483, 488-490, 492, 496-498, 503, 506
Bayley 453
Beadon, Lt.-Col. 377, 384
Beetleheim, Capt. 205
Bell, Maj. Morrison.......... 463
Beresford, Genl. 462
Bertier, Maj. 96, 282, 308, 319, 446, 455, 484
Beryl 313
Besika Bay..... 18, 82, 97, 99, 112, 118, 173, 249, 309
Birmingham................ 244
Bishop, Maj. 240, 470
Biyuk Anafarta . 372, 387, 403, 518, 525, 539, 548
blockhouses............. 360, 361
Bluff Redoubt 172
Boers......... 142, 182, 405, 423
bombs 41, 132, 145, 154, 181, 191, 193, 195, 216, 227, 232, 234, 236, 238, 239, 241, 244, 261, 269, 284, 285, 389, 390, 425, 433, 435, 445, 461, 481, 494, 495
Bonsor, Maj................ 276
Boomerang Redoubt 258, 264
Bouvet............... 36, 38, 39
Bowlby, Flag-Lt......... 295, 411
Braithwaite, Capt. V..... 17, 21-26, 28, 29, 40, 46, 47, 49, 51, 53, 60, 69, 70, 80, 91, 93, 96, 104, 106, 109, 112, 116, 118, 119, 122, 126, 145, 146, 148, 163, 167, 172, 176, 197, 199, 201, 211, 215, 219, 242, 246, 252, 256, 257, 259, 279, 291, 294, 300, 304, 310, 315, 323, 333, 334, 336, 346, 347, 353, 356, 359, 362, 363, 366, 371, 377, 380, 381, 384, 386, 393, 394, 401, 404, 409, 413, 418, 424, 439, 441, 442, 451, 457, 458, 460, 461, 465, 468, 473, 474, 476, 480, 484, 516, 520, 529, 536, 540, 542, 550
Brassey 368, 411
Brassey, Lady 368, 411
Bridges, Genl. 31, 53, 95, 139, 174, 175, 193
Brigades. . 50, 71, 85, 129, 153, 154, 158, 180, 185, 206-208, 215, 228, 275, 304, 319, 334, 338, 340, 344, 345, 357, 363, 372, 387, 443, 444, 449, 498, 502, 517, 518, 522, 525, 529, 539, 545, 549
127th 236, 238, 278, 284
1st (Australian) 331
30th 24, 56, 78, 140, 156, 193, 266, 275, 318, 321, 344, 403, 405, 449, 452, 503, 540
32nd. . 304, 311, 332, 334, 335, 340, 347
33rd . . 267, 304, 323, 328, 332, 334, 335, 340
34th . . 304, 311, 332, 334, 335, 340, 344, 379
39th 302
86th ... 71, 168, 227, 234, 258, 259, 264, 275, 413, 414, 462, 541
87th ... 71, 160, 161, 172, 227, 258, 259, 264, 275, 414, 453
88th . . 131, 160, 161, 219, 264, 275, 409, 461
Indian .. 64, 71, 128, 134, 141, 144, 154, 219, 227, 286, 300, 326, 372, 382, 384, 439, 442, 463, 517, 538
Light Horse 213, 252, 269
Manchester 158, 204, 205, 236

Index

Younghusband's ... 396, 398-400
Brodrick, Capt. Hon. G. .. 267, 308, 321, 328, 334, 340, 343-347, 381, 384, 394, 401, 433
Brody, Capt. 340
Brooke, Rupert 62, 98, 100
Brooke, Sir B. 388
Brown, Percy. 277
Browne, Maj. 252, 465, 544
Brulard, Genl. ... 450-452, 456, 471, 484
Bryant, Lt.-Col. 242
Bulair Lines... 19, 29, 75, 104, 164, 251
Bulgaria. ... 94, 160, 177, 198, 207, 226, 428, 433, 434, 436, 439, 443
Bulgarians 325, 436, 441, 481
Burn, Col. C... 18, 19, 97, 295, 300, 467, 470
Burrell 276
Burrows, Capt. 465
Burton, Col. 302, 461
Byng, Genl. 228, 316, 364, 368, 369, 388-390, 395, 398, 404, 405, 409, 424, 425, 445, 462, 484
"C" Beach 348, 543
Cadorna, Genl. 418
Callwell, Genl... 7, 16, 22, 182, 414, 415, 417, 472, 473, 475-477
Camel Corps, Bikaner 64
Cameron, R.N., Capt. .. 18, 33, 230
Campbell, Col. 64
canteen ... 379, 380, 412, 413, 499
Carden, Admiral 24, 25
Casualty Clearing Station, 25th 299, 524, 542
Cayley, Genl. 302, 461
censorship 241, 245, 253, 472, 480
Chanak ... 218, 262, 263, 270, 428, 445
Charak Cheshme 344

Chauvel, Genl. 213
Cheape, Capt. 435
Cheshire Point. 433
Christian, Admiral. 194, 335
Chunuk Bair ... 248, 270, 333, 348, 350, 355, 357, 372-374, 376, 519, 537, 547
Churchill, Rt. Hon. W. ... 22, 23, 36, 42, 52, 60, 89, 91, 125, 182, 183, 187, 251, 306, 319, 423
Clifton-Browne, Genl. 465
Coddan, Capt. 98
Coleridge. 328
Collet, Capt. 379, 381
Collins, Lt.-Col. 238
Colonel Tyrrell 462
Conference .. 40, 42, 45, 46, 48, 78, 148, 189, 254, 256, 360, 361, 378, 444, 456
  17th March 24, 26
  18th April 95
  22nd March 40
  Midnight, 25th April 101, 144, 160, 285, 487, 500
Connaught Rangers 401
Constantinople . 6, 9-11, 16, 17, 19-21, 23, 24, 27, 40, 51, 60, 65, 69, 71, 76, 80, 81, 93, 99, 103, 127, 143, 153, 159, 164, 177, 190, 193, 199, 207, 209, 218, 223, 226, 253, 262, 283, 321, 325, 364, 368, 391, 397, 408, 420, 422, 434, 436, 438, 439, 441, 444, 447, 448, 454, 463, 483
Cowans, Genl. 273
Cox, Genl. 63, 65, 71-73, 134, 144, 148, 219, 227, 300, 385, 390, 426
Damakjelik Bair 373, 374, 382
Danube 20, 391, 434, 441, 442
Davidson, R.N., Capt. 462, 472
Davies, R.N.A.S. Capt. 89
Dawnay, Capt. ... 119, 138, 257, 377, 381, 386, 408, 426, 467,

468, 472, 476
de Bourbon, Capt. 471
de Crespigny, Capt. 463
de la Borde, Lieut. 96, 446
de la Fontaine, Capt. 143
de Lisle, Genl. . . 205, 206, 210, 219,
227, 267, 270, 281, 285,
301, 302, 308, 368-370,
374-376, 378, 379, 381,
383-385, 387, 404-406,
424, 461, 547
de Lothbinière, Genl. 195, 267
de Putron, Maj. 430, 476
de Tott's Battery 107, 276, 309,
310
Deedes, Capt. . . 258, 377, 381, 403,
424, 462
Dent, R.N., Capt. 32, 95, 99
des Coigns, Col. 141-143
Dick, Col. 86, 87, 89, 286
Diggle, Capt. 326
Divisions 16, 20, 32, 42, 48, 85,
89, 159, 164, 172, 177,
181, 185, 198, 206, 212-
215, 221, 224, 232, 242,
245, 251, 252, 262, 263,
275, 279, 282, 283, 297,
299, 304, 315, 316, 320,
326, 359, 361, 365, 371,
374, 375, 382, 387-389,
400, 406-409, 417-419,
425, 427-429, 431, 432,
437, 440, 443-445, 448,
449, 452, 454, 458, 467-
469, 489, 490, 496-498,
522, 523, 541, 545-547,
549
10th . . 230, 327, 382, 403, 449,
450, 455, 517, 518, 526,
529, 538, 547, 549
11th . . 246, 278, 304, 311, 313,
323, 328, 335, 344, 353,
379, 382, 383, 385, 404,
425, 518, 519, 526, 529,
538, 541, 547, 549
13th . . 232, 287, 298, 302, 314,
325, 326, 328, 333, 348,

359, 517, 529, 538, 541,
547
16th (Irish). 403
1st (Australian) 213, 410,
444, 500-502, 504
2nd (Australian). 410
2nd (Mounted). . 386, 463, 549
42nd. . 153, 210, 279, 287, 308,
319, 534
52nd. . 287, 298, 403, 462, 491
53rd . . 284, 358, 359, 362, 378,
382, 413, 426, 427, 430,
431, 443, 445, 449, 453,
461, 527, 539, 542, 547,
549
54th (Essex). . . . 350, 358-360,
362, 365, 382, 399, 438,
547, 549
Irish . . 313, 319, 335, 378, 403
Lowland. . . 167, 179, 200, 208,
266, 275, 277, 293-295,
410, 503, 518, 519, 538,
549
Mounted . . 128, 317, 386, 387,
444, 463, 549
Naval . . . 14, 19, 30, 48, 52, 61,
62, 66, 83, 87, 88, 104,
129, 134, 135, 145, 147,
149, 153, 154, 158, 161,
183, 197, 204, 205, 208,
228, 239, 280, 287, 294,
295, 308, 312, 319, 388,
399, 403, 437, 446, 456,
462, 465, 467, 497
Welsh. 342, 344, 347, 444
Djavad Pasha. 22, 25
Dorling, Col. 445
Dorset Regt., 5th 543, 544
Doughtie, R.N., Capt. 303
Douglas, Genl. 21, 53, 210, 230,
252, 284, 308, 313, 423,
465
Downing, Col. 321
drafts . . 22, 149, 154, 177, 179, 180,
198, 200, 206, 236, 244,
256, 273, 275, 276, 281,
306, 320, 323-325, 375,

Index

377, 380, 385, 388, 393, 394, 396-400, 404, 418, 422, 426, 448, 449, 470, 471, 483, 534
Drake Bn. 63, 465
Drury-Lowe, R.N., Capt. 485
Dublin Fusiliers. 172, 227, 321, 414
Dudley, Lord 410
Duff, Genl. Beauchamp. 431
Duncan, Major. 311
Duncannon, Lord. 475
d'Amade, Genl. 9, 10, 12, 15, 26, 30, 31, 34, 39, 45, 46, 55, 56, 66, 68, 69, 71, 72, 78, 95, 96, 99, 108, 115, 117, 118, 122, 124, 128, 135, 136, 141, 142, 147-149, 154, 155, 158, 159, 161, 169, 170, 173, 290
East Kent Yeomanry 465
East Yorks, 6th 340
Edinburgh, Lord Provost of. ... 239, 401
Edwards, Comr. 471
Edwards, Lieut. 276
Edwards, Maj. 465
Egerton, Genl. 277, 405
Egyptian Gazette 66, 103
Ejelmer Bay. 343, 357, 359, 360, 548
Elliot, Lieut. 252
Ellison, Genl.. .... 17, 209, 273, 284, 294, 314, 381, 409, 458, 463, 471, 484
engineers 41, 45, 55, 136, 199, 208, 343, 453, 522, 539
Enos. 74, 75, 199, 206, 207, 372, 429, 465
Enver Pasha. 21, 271, 473
Erskine, Genl. 228
Eski Lines 308
Essex Regt. 84, 108, 168, 350, 360, 365
Ewart, Genl.. .... 230, 231
Ezine 428
Fairfax, Comr. 465

Fallowfield, R.N., Lieut. ... 246, 276
Fanshawe, Genl. 369, 388, 404, 405, 424, 425
Faukard, Genl. 471
Ferdinand, Tzar 198, 436, 438, 441, 442
Fife and Forfar Yeomanry 463
Fisher, Lord 42, 182, 187, 459, 479
Fitz, see FitzGerald 22, 50, 87, 148, 240, 241, 253, 286, 468
FitzGerald, Col. 470
Fitzgerald, Maj. 470
Fitzmaurice, Mr. 93
Fitzmaurice, R.N., Capt. 92
Forster, Col.. 410
forts .. 16, 17, 34, 36, 37, 39, 45, 47, 54, 60, 61, 75, 152, 164, 176, 179, 428
Foumet, Admiral 426
Fraser, Col. 414
Freddie, see Maitland 242, 252, 285, 294, 301, 313, 331, 359, 377, 395, 401, 409, 414, 424, 426, 430, 433, 442, 462-464, 469, 471, 484
French Corps 293, 294
French Mission 96
French, Sir John 202, 207, 230, 408
Freyberg, Lieut. 465
Fuller, Lieut.-Col. 57, 136, 191, 273, 300
Gamble, Sir D. 313, 314, 453
Gascoigne, Lieut.-Col.. .... 318, 442, 455, 463
Gascon. 174
Gaulois 35, 37, 38, 411, 413
Geddes, Maj. 414
Gellibrand, Lieut. 456
George, Rt. Hon. Lloyd 7, 135, 321, 344, 346, 438, 483
Ghazi Baba 343, 346, 409, 517, 518
Gillivan, Col. 302

Index

Girdwood, Capt. 277
Girodon, Genl. . . 178, 185, 196, 244,
    282, 323, 456
Glyn, Capt. 300, 370, 408
Godfrey, Maj. 109, 119, 244
Godley, Genl. . 53, 55, 95, 139, 232,
    248, 287, 348, 350, 351,
    355, 357, 359, 374, 438,
    464, 472, 475
Goeben 126
Gouraud, Genl. . 173, 178, 184, 185,
    192, 196, 197, 203, 204,
    210, 215, 221, 224, 227,
    228, 230, 234, 239, 240,
    242, 243, 246, 248, 249,
    259, 266, 269, 270, 282,
    301, 434, 469
Graives 286
Grand Duke Nicholas . 89, 143, 175,
    193
Grant, R.N., Capt. . . . 123, 155, 181,
    246, 321
Greece . . 78, 94, 177, 199, 207, 226,
    238, 434, 439
Greeks . . 16, 86, 198, 295, 434, 441,
    455, 481
Green Hill 442
Greer, Lieut.-Col. 322
Guest, Capt. (?) 230, 423, 473,
    484
Guildford Castle 165
Guilford, Col. Lord 465
Gully Ravine 280
Gurkhas . . 41, 48, 50, 53, 54, 64, 65,
    72, 128, 148, 154, 159,
    172, 173, 178, 227, 264,
    269-271, 350, 360, 373,
    387, 410, 442
    4th Bn. 410
    6th Bn. 64, 65, 350, 442
Guyon, Maj. 413, 414
H. 12 . . . . 277, 296, 535
H.I.M.S. Askold 87, 108
H.M.S. Arcadian . . . 61, 72, 86, 100,
    128, 142, 145, 149, 188
H.M.S. Arno . . . 333, 334, 340, 351,
    363, 377, 384, 395, 403,
    404, 409, 438, 465
H.M.S. Basilisk 246, 276, 277
H.M.S. Canopus 321
H.M.S. Chatham 321, 322, 335,
    336, 340, 485
H.M.S. Colne . . . 91, 138, 139, 257
H.M.S. Cornwall 446
H.M.S. Cornwallis . . . 107, 109, 446,
    462
H.M.S. Dublin 89
H.M.S. Goliath . 115, 119, 121, 154,
    170
H.M.S. Jonquil 336
H.M.S. Kennett 136
H.M.S. Lord Nelson 174, 188
H.M.S. Majestic 120, 191
H.M.S. Mosquito 213, 252, 299
H.M.S. Ocean 38
H.M.S. Phaeton 28, 35, 37, 183
H.M.S. Queen 99, 140
H.M.S. Queen Elizabeth 26, 34,
    36, 40, 79, 85-87, 99, 107,
    108, 110, 118, 123, 130,
    140
H.M.S. Racoon 411
H.M.S. Savage . . 301, 302, 461, 462
H.M.S. Scorpion 191, 258, 264,
    266, 272
H.M.S. Scourge 259, 424
H.M.S. Talbot . . 258, 264, 539, 543
H.M.S. Triad . . . 213, 237, 242, 245,
    251, 267, 270, 282, 285,
    287, 294, 309, 325, 334,
    336, 340, 342, 346, 366,
    401, 409-411, 426, 464,
    484, 485
H.M.S. Triumph . . . 47, 92, 99, 120,
    168, 169, 187
H.M.S. Wolverine . . . 192, 203, 258,
    264, 266
H.M.T. Alaudia 321
H.M.T. Andania 322
H.M.T. Canada 322
H.M.T. Novian 322
H.M.T. River Clyde . . 104, 105, 107,
    121, 132, 192
Haig, Sir Douglas 230, 423

Index

Haldane, Lord 182, 216
Hamilton, Col. Cole 302
Hamilton, Genl. Bruce. ... 309, 314, 316, 365
Hamilton, Lieut. Rowan 462
Hammersley. ... 245, 246, 311, 312, 328, 330, 334, 338-340, 343-345, 347, 356, 357, 367, 377, 405
hand grenades 41, 45, 193, 194, 244, 245, 267, 268, 270, 402
Hankey, Col. ... 306, 317, 363, 370, 379
Harding, Col. 64
Hardy, Lieut.-Comr. 411
Hare, Mr. 253, 276
Haricot Redoubt 185, 243
Hawke Bn. 465
Heliopolis 55
Herbert, Aubrey. 181, 184
Heseltine, Capt 436
Hetman Chair 382, 383
Hill 10 .... 334-336, 338, 341, 382, 396
Hill 305 ... 248, 357, 372, 374, 375, 517, 518, 525, 526
Hill 60 .... 382, 403
Hill 70 .... 340, 356, 382-384
Hill, Genl. 321
Hillyard, Maj. 302
Hindlip, Lord. 128
Hogg, Capt. 64
Holdich, Lt.-Col. 408
Holmes, Col. 470
Homer, Lt-Comr. 301, 302
Hood Bn. 158, 205, 465
Hood, Maj. 158, 205, 250, 424, 465
Hope, R.N., Capt. 7, 16, 29, 30, 38, 44, 48, 56, 61, 66, 83, 86, 89, 91, 94, 98, 101, 103, 104, 109, 114, 122, 129, 133, 134, 149, 153, 158, 163, 172, 178, 203, 205, 215, 217, 232, 234, 235, 245, 253, 255, 262, 263, 271, 278, 286, 295, 296, 306, 309, 314, 318, 320, 334, 348, 357, 364, 366, 368, 375, 377, 378, 382, 385, 389, 393-396, 398, 400, 405, 433, 437, 444, 448, 468, 474, 484, 503
Horne, Genl. 368
Horse Shoe 462
hospital ... 145, 158, 165, 174, 242, 269, 299, 301, 303, 307, 309, 394, 410, 411, 448, 465, 524
No. 1 Stationary. 242
No. 16 Stationary. 542
No. 18 Stationary. 411
No. 2 (Australian) Stationary 410
No. 2 Stationary. 242
No. 24 (British-Indian) ... 410
No. 3 (Australian) Stationary 410, 411
No. 3 (Canadian) Stationary 411
hospital ships... 145, 301, 303, 307
Howe Bn.. .... 62, 63, 205, 238, 250, 456
howitzers 24, 27, 45, 56, 66, 74, 76, 77, 92, 95, 117, 140, 162, 202, 220, 229, 231-233, 243, 250, 258, 273, 297, 317, 320, 321, 422, 483, 489-493, 495-497, 503, 504, 536, 549
Hunloke, Maj. 462
Hunter-Weston, Genl. ... 14, 55, 56, 74, 77, 79, 80, 86, 88, 94, 95, 106, 107, 109, 112, 114, 115, 117, 124, 127, 132, 135, 136, 140, 141, 145, 146, 148, 149, 153, 154, 158, 159, 161, 168, 170, 174, 192, 196, 203, 205, 210, 215, 219, 227, 228, 234, 238, 239, 246, 248, 259, 265, 267, 277,

281, 287, 290, 295, 296, 298-300, 304, 306, 309, 365
Imogene... 359, 360, 379, 390, 436, 467
Indian troops 63, 65, 316, 323, 326, 405, 431, 433
Inglefield, Genl....... 350, 358-360, 362, 438
Inniskilling Fusiliers 270, 271, 322, 453
Ishiklar 428
Ismail Oglu Tepe.... 337, 339, 341, 350, 351, 357, 372, 374, 375, 382-384, 387, 517, 518, 526, 539, 548, 549
Istomine, Genl. ... 61, 89, 143, 403
Italy.............. 181, 207, 390
Ivanoff, Capt.................. 87
Jackson, Capt............... 302
Jeanne d'Arc 108
Joffre, Genl...... 16, 202, 216, 229, 237, 279, 418-420, 422, 423, 427, 442
Johnson, R.N., Lieut. Ormsby.. 244, 313
Jones, Col.................. 242
Junia 151
Kabak Kuyu................ 384
Kahn, Capt................. 142
Kaiajik Aghala.. 383, 384, 387, 388, 390, 401, 440
Kaiajik Dere 403
Kantara 63
Karabingha 218
Karakol Dagh 381, 383, 404
Karna Bili 396
Kavanagh, Genl............. 368
Kephalos Camp............. 238
Kereves Dere... 162, 185, 243, 271, 298
Kereves Dere Ravine......... 162
Keshan.... 177, 373-375, 429, 541
Keyes, Commodore...... 138, 384
Keyes, Lt.-Comr......... 192, 203
Kiggell, Genl. 457
Kilid Bahr ... 16, 22, 32, 76, 77, 81, 159, 200, 207, 218, 248, 263, 271, 292, 428, 516, 517, 534
King, Col. 313
King, Comr................. 465
King, Genl. 465
King, Maj.................. 470
Kiretch Tepe Sirt... 336, 341, 343-345, 350, 374, 382, 387, 547, 548
Koja Chemen Tepe .. 270, 333, 348
Krithia. 88, 161, 264, 268, 271, 536
Kum Kale ... 63, 81, 82, 95-97, 99, 108, 109, 112, 117, 118, 122, 124, 128, 169, 244, 428
Kurt Ketchede 373
Lala Baba . 332, 335, 336, 338, 382, 388, 409, 517, 518, 525
Lancashire Division... 53, 163, 219, 236, 465
Lancashire Fusiliers.. 104, 108, 159, 161, 168, 240, 264, 311, 333, 414
9th Bn................. 311
Brigade 154, 159
Lancashire Landing...... 280, 465
landing... 11, 16, 18, 19, 22, 27, 28, 31, 32, 36, 39, 41-44, 47, 50, 60-63, 69, 74, 75, 77-81, 83, 86, 88, 89, 91, 94-99, 101-104, 107, 110, 112, 118, 126, 128-132, 134, 135, 139, 144, 153, 167, 173-175, 177, 189, 190, 192, 195, 201, 206, 210, 216, 217, 219, 225, 226, 228, 235, 240, 242, 249, 255, 262, 267, 276, 280, 282, 285, 286, 290, 291, 299, 307, 322, 326, 332, 339, 341, 348, 358, 366, 367, 372, 374, 377, 386, 391, 392, 403, 416, 418, 419, 424, 427-429, 443, 444, 454, 464, 465, 482,

Index

487, 494, 499-501, 515, 518, 519, 522, 524, 525, 527, 529, 537, 538, 543-546, 549
Lapruin, Capt. 393
Laverton, Lieut. 277
Law, Capt. 277
Law, Rt. Hon. Bonar 483
Lawes, Capt. 430
Lawrence, Genl. 284, 310, 462
Legge, Genl. ... 299, 303, 410, 470, 478
Lemnos .. 30, 36, 41, 74, 79, 85, 86, 89, 91, 93-98, 177, 326
Liman von Sanders, Genl. 80, 82, 187, 268
Lindley, Genl. ... 354, 356, 367, 378, 410
lines of Communication .. 202, 265, 283, 284, 400, 477
Lister, Hon. C. 312
London Regt., 2/1st Coy. 461
11th Bn. 365
Lone Pine . 299, 332, 372, 373, 481, 503
Long .. 5, 20, 21, 29-31, 38, 39, 49, 55, 56, 60, 63, 69, 92, 96, 103, 114, 117, 118, 122, 128, 130, 132, 136, 138-140, 142, 143, 147, 151, 153, 158, 159, 165, 169, 175, 176, 179, 180, 182, 196, 203, 204, 207, 212, 234, 237, 239, 242, 248, 252, 255, 261, 262, 264, 266, 276, 278, 285, 288, 290, 294-296, 304, 312, 315, 318, 321, 324, 330, 333, 335, 337, 339, 341, 343, 344, 358, 364, 365, 370, 377, 381, 389, 390, 397, 413, 414, 419, 424, 426, 436, 445, 453, 457, 460, 462, 475, 477, 484, 485, 519
Lovat, Lord 463
Lowther, Lancelot 413
Lucas, Maj. 453
Mackenzie, Compton. 178, 322
Mackenzie, Lieut.-Col. 299
Maclagan, Col. 252
Maclean, Maj. 277
Maher, Col. 242
Mahon, Genl. ... 213, 216, 230, 231, 246, 313, 336, 341, 343-345, 347, 363-365, 367-369, 371, 403, 405, 409, 412
Maidos. ... 208, 215, 218, 223, 226, 248, 262, 263, 268, 517, 537
Maitland, Capt. F. ... 242, 282, 285, 294, 313, 331, 381, 414
Makalinsky 97
Malcolm, Col. .. 311, 312, 328, 338-340, 404
Manchester Bde. 158, 204, 205, 236
Manchester Regt.
11th Bn. 311
Manifold, Col. 404
Manitou 94, 95
Maoris 178, 360
Marmora ... 17, 19, 37, 40, 77, 178, 210, 213, 377, 428, 436
Marshall, Genl. 172, 383, 385, 409, 413, 414, 461
Matthews, Lt.-Col. 62, 63
Maude, Genl. ... 369, 388, 389, 404, 405, 409, 424, 425
McClay, Lieut. 277
McGrigor, Capt. 433, 465, 484
McKenna, Rt. Hon. R. 483
McMahon, Sir H. 59, 66, 69, 93
McMunn, Col. 410
Mecklenburg, Duke of. 438
Mena Camp 54
Mercer, Genl. 64, 465
Methuen, Lord. .. 63, 196, 244, 245, 402
Mewes, Maj. 62
Micklem, Col. 184
Millen, Senator 478
Millerand, M. .. 418, 419, 423, 427

Index

Mitchell, Col. 463
Mitylene . . 319, 321, 322, 326, 371,
    372, 408, 429, 542
Monash, Col. 189, 413
Moore, Lieut. 442, 450
Mountain Battery, 29th 64, 65,
    347, 501
Mudros . 30, 38, 45, 73, 84, 85, 168,
    188, 209, 210, 217, 242,
    273, 283, 284, 289, 294,
    301, 310, 313, 316, 330,
    368-371, 379, 409-412,
    429, 440, 444, 445, 456,
    488, 492, 508, 520, 542,
    549
Mudros West. 410, 411
Munro, Genl. 482, 483, 485
Munster Fusiliers. 414
Murdoch, Mr. K. A. . 408, 427, 435,
    450, 460, 461, 464, 472-
    476, 478-480
Murphy, Maj. 470
Murray, Genl. Wolfe . . . 17, 24, 292,
    306, 317
Nagara Point 217
Nallah 462
    Achi Baba . . 33, 42, 43, 63, 77,
        81, 82, 88, 117, 118, 122,
        124, 127, 134, 139, 140,
        144, 153-155, 157, 158,
        161, 204, 205, 208, 218,
        226, 249, 257, 259, 265,
        271, 280, 290, 416, 429,
        454, 462, 472, 493, 536
    Krithia 31, 81, 82, 88, 103,
        110, 115, 121, 122, 129,
        131, 134, 140, 161, 248,
        263, 264, 268, 271, 372,
        373, 462, 535, 536, 538
Napier, Col. 93, 433
Napier, Genl. 117
Nasmith, Comr. 178, 213
Nevinson, Mr. 7, 445, 446
New Zealand Mounted Rifles . . 189,
    194, 269
Newfoundland Bn. 461
Nibrunesi Point 426, 539

Nicholas, Grand Duke 89, 143,
    175, 193
Nicholls, Admiral 196
Nicholson, Admiral . . . 21, 333, 334
Nicol, Admiral. 187, 426
Nisch 434
Nogués, Col. 108, 118, 244
Northcliffe, Lord 58, 254
Northumberland Fusiliers 311
Nunn, Col. 302
Oakdene, Capt. Perry. 470
Odessa. 20, 246, 420
Olivant, Lt.-Col. 62
Onslow, Capt. 270
Oppenheim, Capt. 463
Order to the Troops 162, 189
    12th May . . 167, 169, 170, 190
    21st April. 97
    22nd April 97, 98
    25th May 187, 189
    28th April 128, 155, 163
    Farewell. . . . 69, 169, 170, 484,
        485
    Turkish Divisional. 278
Owen, Genl., Cunliffe- 113
O'Dowda, Col. 414
O'Sullivan, V.C. 413
Palin, Col. 64, 442
Pallin, Genl.. 277
Palmer, Col.. 302
Palmer, Maj. 62
Panderma. 218
Paris, Genl. . . . 30, 62, 95, 129, 249,
    308
Paterson, Col. 87
Pearce, Senator 477, 478
Pearson, Maj.. 414
Peebles, Col. 277
Peel, Col. 95
Pelliot, Lieut. 96, 446
Percival, Genl. 413
Percy, Lord William 277, 445
periscopes 7, 41, 45, 322
Perriera, Admiral de la . . . 411, 413
Peter 288, 437, 464, 481, 484
Peyton, Genl. . . . 369, 377, 409, 439,
    463

Index

Phillimore, R.N., Capt. 95, 136, 384
Piépape, Col. 282, 394
Pierce, Admiral 62
Pierce, Maj. 453
Pike, Lt.-Col. 256, 322
plan of attack. 16, 153
    Suvla Landing 391, 392
Plymouth Bn. 62, 103, 168
Pollard, Capt. 453
Pollen, Capt. 26, 40, 138, 230, 282, 381, 395, 437, 464, 476, 481
Porter, Sir James 274
Potts. Lt.-Comr. 359
press . . 3, 4, 24, 58, 59, 87, 93, 103, 104, 108, 127, 144, 153, 179, 191, 200, 216, 240, 241, 245, 249, 253-255, 262, 263, 275, 324, 370, 379, 390, 416, 417, 419, 431, 445, 446, 461, 472, 475, 504, 507, 548
Price, Bishop . . . 123, 165, 226, 227, 339, 370, 454, 470
Princes Street. 462
Punjabis. 64
    69th Bn. 64
    89th Bn. 64
Quadrilateral 266, 268
Queen Victoria's Own Sappers . . 64
Queensland Bn. 268
Quinn's Post 193, 194, 196
Rabbit Island, ... 35
Ratilva Valley 387
Rawlinson, Genl. 228, 316, 364
reconnaissance . . 37, 70, 81, 86, 217, 339, 501
Reed, Genl. 292, 306, 316, 330, 337, 347, 359, 362, 364, 377, 461
Régiment de marche d'Afrique, 175t
    . . . . h68
Régiment, 4th Colonial 68
reinforcements 17, 18, 81, 117, 127, 129, 132-134, 152, 153, 163, 170, 176, 177, 179-181, 190, 191, 199, 200, 207, 208, 218, 225, 226, 234, 236, 248, 255, 258, 262, 268, 275, 290, 291, 316, 319, 338, 340, 342-344, 350, 359, 360, 371-375, 385-387, 393, 394, 396-401, 418, 424, 429, 440, 443, 447, 449, 454, 471, 483, 518, 534, 536, 537
Rhodes, Lieut. 287
Rifaat, Col. 278
Rodosto 75, 218, 262
Roper, Genl. 136
Rosomore, Comr. 33
Ross, Mr. Malcolm 445
Roumania 78, 94, 199, 434
Royal Dublin Fusiliers 321
    6th Bn. 321
    7th Bn. 321
Royal Engineers 453
    134th Fortress Coy. 311
    West Riding Field Coy. . . . 311, 453
Royal Fusiliers. . 108, 258, 264, 413
Royal Inniskilling Fusiliers 322, 453
    5th Bn. 322
Royal Irish Fusiliers 322
    5th Bn. 322
    6th Bn. 322
Royal Scot, wounded. 267
Royal Scots 146, 168, 239, 254, 264, 266, 277, 381, 401, 402, 404
    4th Bn. 277
    5th Bn. 146, 168, 239, 381
    6th Bn. 402, 404
    7th Bn. 254, 277
Ruef, Col. 143
Rundle, Genl. 22, 434
Russell, Genl. . . 384, 385, 390, 401, 429
Russell's Top. 470
Russian officers 403
Ruthven, Maj. Hore- 267, 353,

Ryrie, Col. 384, 460, 484
                           252
S.S. Arabian 237
Saghir Dere 263, 264
Salonika. . . . 14, 423, 430, 434, 435,
       439-446, 449, 452, 453,
       455, 456, 458, 472, 476,
                        480-482
Salt Lake . . 246, 298, 332, 334, 335,
       341, 343, 357, 382, 383,
                             525
Samson, Comr. . . . 89, 90, 140, 181,
                    285, 331, 446
Sari Bair . . 103, 114, 117, 120, 215,
       248, 270, 292, 328, 333,
       342, 348, 355, 364, 372,
       376, 382, 442, 537, 539
Saros 30, 31, 74, 75, 85, 262
Sarrail, Genl. . . . 418, 419, 427, 458,
                         481, 483
Savage, Col. 462
Scatters, see Wilson. 435
Schemallach, Lieut. 456
Schröder 80
Schuler, Mr.. 304
Sclater, Genl. 273
Scott, Maj. Sir S. 228, 465
Scott-Moncrieff, Genl. 228
Scottish Horse 399, 409, 439
Scottish Rifles, 8th Bn. 277
Seaplane Camp 304, 313
Sedd-el-Bahr 62, 63, 79, 81, 82,
       89, 102, 104-111, 115-117,
       119, 121, 124, 167, 184,
                             331
Sellheim, Col. 478
Senegalese. . . . 68, 86, 87, 143, 147,
              149, 162, 450, 458, 469
Serbia 434, 439
Serbians. 434, 440, 481
Seymour, Comr. 257
Shaw, Genl. 246, 288, 298, 302,
              314, 325, 333, 348, 350
Sheppard, Lieut. 276
sickness . . 186, 255, 326, 379, 386-
              388, 394, 398, 412, 458-
                        460, 466, 470

Sikhs . . 64, 300, 426, 427, 430, 431,
                    433, 453, 463
14th Bn. 64, 300, 427, 431,
                             433
53rd Bn. 426, 427, 430, 431,
                             453
Simpson, Capt. . 214, 258, 280, 302,
                             487
Simpson-Baikie, Genl. . . . 214, 258,
                             280
Sinclair, Capt. 252, 277
Sitwell, Genl.. 379
Skeen, Col. 215, 240, 377, 378
Smith, Genl. 356
Smith, Hesketh 322
Smith, R.N., Lieut. 107
Sofia 93, 434, 438
Soghan Dere 217
Solvili 396
Somali 465
South Wales Borderers . . . 107, 109,
              118, 234, 239, 276, 453
2nd Bn. 109
Southland 95
Spens, Genl. 474, 477
St. Louis 244
Stanley, Capt. 242
Stephens, Capt. 314, 410
Stewart, Lieut. Shaw- 288
Stirling, Lt.-Col. 463
Stockdale, Lt.-Col. 143, 491
Stoney, Maj. 453
Stopford, Genl. . 230, 231, 289-293,
       299, 304, 306, 308, 309,
       316, 319, 330, 332, 334,
       336-338, 343-348, 350,
       351, 353, 355-368, 370,
                        372, 405
Street, Col.. . . . 4, 54, 140, 146, 462
Stuart, Lt.-Col. Crauford- 205
Stuart, Maj. Villiers- 178
Sulajik 340, 342, 374, 382, 387
Sultan of Egypt 53, 54, 69, 79,
                             193
Sunbeam 27, 368
Surrey Yeomanry. 276, 446
Susak Kuyu 387, 444

Index

Sussex Yeomanry 465
Suvla Bay . . . 32, 77, 139, 246, 248,
        249, 299, 331, 340, 341,
        343, 346, 350, 353, 356,
        357, 368, 372-374, 376,
        378, 382, 385, 387, 388,
        399, 405, 416, 424, 426,
        440, 443, 503, 517, 518,
        525-528, 537-540, 548,
        549
Sykes, Sir Mark 251, 484
Syria 234, 427
tactics . . 81, 96, 154, 156, 183, 206,
        215, 225, 234, 246, 255,
        272, 362, 390, 391, 419,
        432
Talaat 21
Taube. . 85, 132, 149, 151, 227, 425,
        430, 461
Tekke Tepe 337, 340, 341, 343,
        347, 350, 359, 361
Tenedos . . 26, 29, 30, 34-36, 38, 75,
        85, 89, 101, 115, 118, 169,
        172, 173, 177, 191, 249,
        282, 285
Thomson, Col. Courtauld 196
Thursby, Admiral . 47, 95, 112-114,
        138, 181
Tillard, Maj. 410
Titchfield, Lord 461
Tollemashe, Capt. 277
trench mortars 41, 45, 63, 154,
        193, 216, 229, 232, 238,
        244, 250, 258, 264, 267,
        390, 403, 456, 483, 495,
        496, 504
Trotman, Genl. 228
Tupper, R.N., Lieut. 259, 424
Turk's Head 470
Unsworth, Mr 456
Uzunkiupru 429
"V" Beach 107, 108, 110, 140,
        192, 210, 269, 460, 471
Val, see Braithwaite . 377, 384, 395,
        403, 404, 409, 424, 465
Valley of Death 195
Vandenberg, Genl 143
Vanrennan, Lieut.-Col. 322
Venezelos, M. 78
Vineyard 333, 462
Vitali, Capt. 417, 418
von Donop, Genl. . . . 152, 229, 389
Vyvian, R.N., Capt. 95
"W" Beach 104, 122, 136, 140,
        148, 174, 210, 219, 493
Walden Point 331
Wallace, Genl 209, 265, 284
war correspondents 240, 480
Waratah 277
Ward, Lt.-Col 37, 213, 257, 284,
        303, 417, 446
Wardian Camp 72
Watson, Col. Jimmy 258, 465
Weber Pasha 287
Wedgwood, Comr. . . . 87, 158, 174
Wells, Col. 43, 71, 296, 424
Wemyss, Admiral . . . 26, 38-40, 43,
        44, 80, 83, 84, 94, 95, 99,
        107, 126, 131, 313, 410
West Kent Yeomanry 465
West Yorks Regt., 9th 338, 340
Westminster Dragoons 53
Weston, Lieut. . . . 14, 55, 56, 74, 77,
        79, 80, 86, 88, 94, 95, 106,
        107, 109, 112, 114, 115,
        117, 124, 127, 132, 135,
        136, 140, 141, 145, 146,
        148, 149, 153, 154, 158,
        159, 161, 168, 170, 174,
        192, 196, 203, 205, 210,
        215, 219, 227, 228, 234,
        238, 239, 246, 248, 259,
        265, 267, 277, 281, 287,
        290, 295, 296, 298-300,
        304, 306, 309, 365, 456
Whitburn, Col. 465
White, Lt.-Col. 20, 55, 68, 109,
        111, 120, 122, 145, 147,
        174, 178, 208, 242, 257,
        311, 323, 410, 411, 458,
        469, 481, 501, 523
Wigram, Col. Clive 159
Williams, Capt. 417, 453
Williams, Genl. 458

Williams, Genl. Hanbury...... 193
Winter, Genl... 23, 71, 95, 128, 265, 359, 375, 388, 398, 415, 422, 440, 443, 449, 473, 475, 484
Woodward, Genl. ... 23, 69, 70, 95, 128
Worcester Yeomanry......... 439
Worsley, Comr........... 348, 543
Wyld, Lt.-Comr. 252
Wylie, Col. Doughty- . 48, 121, 122, 460
"X" Beach................. 104
Xeros.................... 429
"Y" Beach..... 104, 115, 117, 119, 121, 130, 131, 140, 159
Yarr, Col 465
Yeni Shahr......... 117, 118, 124
Yeomanry .. 53, 276, 284, 316, 323, 368, 378, 382, 439, 440, 446, 463, 465, 543, 544
Yilghin Burnu .. 332, 334, 338, 339, 343, 356, 372, 374, 388, 517, 518, 539, 547
Yukeri 249, 428
Zimmerman's Farm.......... 308
Zouaves................ 68, 162

About the Author

Sir Ian Hamilton (1853-1947) was a British staff officer, writer and diarist. After serving in multiple campaigns, including the Boer War, he was appointed to lead the British mission to the Japanese Army during the Russo-Japanese War. His military career came to an end in the First World War as a result of the disastrous Gallipoli campaign. After his retirement, he served as the Scottish President of the British Legion.

www.ingramcontent.com/pod-product-compliance
Lightning Source LLC
Chambersburg PA
CBHW051551230426
43668CB00013B/1818